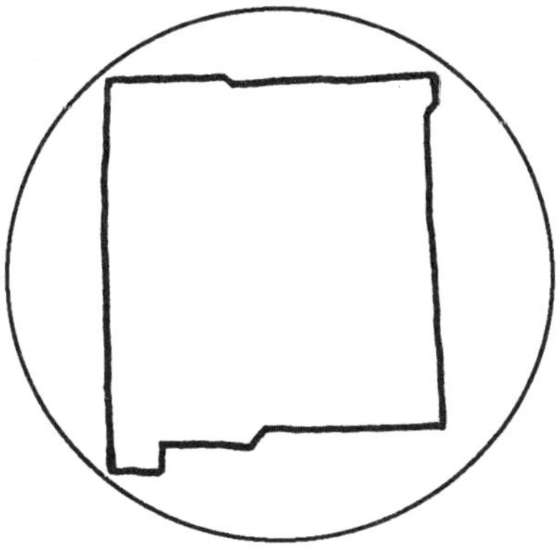

NEW MEXICO

ENVIRONMENTAL LAW HANDBOOK

Third Edition

Rodey, Dickason, Sloan, Akin & Robb, P.A.

Editors

John P. Salazar **James P. Fitzgerald** **Joseph B. Rochelle**

Authors

William C. Schaab
John P. Salazar
Joseph B. Rochelle
Mary P. Keleher
Mark K. Adams
James P. Fitzgerald
Brian H. Lematta
M. Catherine Hayden

Albuquerque

Albuquerque Plaza, Suite 2200
201 3rd Street, N.W., P.O. Box 1888
Albuquerque, New Mexico 87103-1888
(505) 765-5900

Santa Fe

Marcy Plaza, Suite 101
123 East Marcy Street, P.O. Box 1357
Santa Fe, New Mexico 87504-1357
(505) 984-0100

GOVERNMENT INSTITUTES, INC.

Government Institutes, Inc., Rockville, Maryland 20850

Published December 1993.

98 97 96 95 94 93 5 4 3 2 1

ISBN : 0-86587-370-4

Printed in the United States of America.

NEW MEXICO ENVIRONMENTAL LAW HANDBOOK

SUMMARY OF CONTENTS

TABLE OF CONTENTS

CHAPTER II

AIR QUALITY MANAGEMENT

CHAPTER III
WATER QUALITY MANAGEMENT

CHAPTER IV
SOLID WASTE MANAGEMENT

CHAPTER V
HAZARDOUS WASTE MANAGEMENT

CHAPTER VI

UNDERGROUND STORAGE TANK MANAGEMENT

CHAPTER VII
MINING AND OIL AND GAS

CHAPTER VIII
RADIOACTIVE MATERIALS AND WASTE MANAGEMENT

CHAPTER IX

COMMUNITY RIGHT-TO-KNOW AND EMERGENCY PLANNING

CHAPTER X
ADDITIONAL ENVIRONMENTAL LAWS

CHAPTER XI

ENVIRONMENTAL MANAGEMENT BY INDIAN TRIBES AND PUEBLOS

CHAPTER XII
NEW MEXICO ENVIRONMENTAL COMMON LAW

PREFACE

The *New Mexico Environmental Law Handbook* is intended to provide a general guide to a complex series of statutes and regulations that make up New Mexico's environmental laws. We have attempted to include all relevant statutes and regulations adopted prior to October 15, 1993, in this third edition. However, this material is intended only as a brief summary of complex areas of law which are undergoing constant change and evolution. Readers are encouraged to obtain independent legal advice and to consult the appropriate agency and the latest versions of applicable statutes and regulations before dealing with specific situations.

The editors and authors wish to express their gratitude to the staff members of the following State of New Mexico departments, agencies and offices who offered informational and review assistance: New Mexico Environment Department (NMED), Office of General Counsel of NMED, Oil Conservation Division and Mining and Minerals Division of the Department of Energy, Minerals and Natural Resources and Public Safety Department. The NMED contribution to this effort was considerable since many of the authors contacted representatives of one or more bureaus for review and discussion of the various chapters. The NMED Secretary, Deputy Secretary, and Bureau Chiefs were also extremely helpful in their support of the project. We also express our gratitude to numerous staff members at Region 6 of the United States Environmental Protection Agency and to environmental representatives of New Mexico Indian Tribes and Pueblos.

A special note of thanks goes to Linda Alexander, environmental law paralegal, who was of immeasurable assistance in coordinating the effort. Similarly, our thanks are extended to our librarians, Pamela Dempsey and Mary Jebsen, for their considerable assistance in reviewing the accuracy of our references. We also thank Carla Flores, Deborah Martinez-Mullins and Belva Dyer of our computer services staff for their conscientious effort in producing the written product. A special thank you also goes to attorney Ed Ricco of our firm for his extraordinary contribution in the course of reviewing the entire book for us before publication.

Of course, we especially want to thank and acknowledge all of our fellow attorneys at the Rodey Law Firm for their patience, support, understanding and encouragement throughout the course of this undertaking.

ABOUT THE EDITORS AND AUTHORS

The following attorneys are members of the Environment and Natural Resources Department of Rodey, Dickason, Sloan, Akin & Robb, P.A.

William C. Schaab

Mr. Schaab has degrees from Weslayan University, Yale University Law School, and St. John's College (Santa Fe). He is a member of the State Bar of New Mexico and the American Bar Association. His broad professional experience includes corporate and tax law, public utilities law, municipal law, public and corporate finance, Indian law and water rights. His practice concentrates on tax-exempt financing, taxation and securities law. In Indian law, he has been general counsel to Taos Pueblo for 20 years, is special water rights counsel to the Pueblo of Nambe, and for 10 years was Claims Attorney for the Navajo Tribe. He has written articles on international taxation, Indian economic development, and water rights. Mr. Schaab authored the Environmental Management by Indian Tribes and Pueblos Chapter. Mr. Schaab was a member of the faculty for the Government Institutes, Inc. Compliance Course on Fundamentals of New Mexico Environmental Law (1990, 1991, 1992) at which he spoke on environmental management by Indian tribes and Pueblos.

Mark K. Adams

Mr. Adams is a cum laude graduate of Harvard College and Harvard Law School. He is a member of the Albuquerque, New Mexico, Zuni Pueblo and American Bar Associations. Mr. Adams has served as an officer and board member of local professional associations. He practices environmental, corporate, Indian, natural resources and real estate law. He represents natural resources clients in environmental permit applications and hearings before the New Mexico Environment Department, the New Mexico Energy, Minerals and Natural Resources Department, and the Santa Fe County Development Review Committee. He has written a number of articles and spoken at several seminars on mining and other natural resources and Indian law topics. Mr. Adams was a member of the faculty for the Government Institutes, Inc. Compliance Course on Fundamentals of New Mexico Environmental Law (1990, 1991, 1992) at which he spoke on mining and oil and gas. Mr. Adams is a co-author of the Mining and Oil and Gas Chapter.

John P. Salazar

Mr. Salazar, who is the Chairman of the Firm's Environment and Natural Resources Department, is a graduate of the University of New Mexico and Stanford Law School. Mr. Salazar is a member of the Albuquerque, New Mexico and American Bar Associations. He is also a member of the Natural Resources, Energy and Environmental Law Section of the American Bar Association and of the Natural Resources Section of the New Mexico Bar Association. His professional experience and current practice are in the areas of real estate, land use and zoning law, as well as municipal and environmental law. Mr. Salazar has extensive experience in real estate development and deals with environmental law issues in the context of his real estate practice. He is also counsel to a regional solid waste landfill facility located in Valencia County, New Mexico. Mr. Salazar was senior editor and a contributing author to the New Mexico chapter of *State Environmental Law Annual Report* for 1990, 1991 and 1992 (Government Institutes, Inc.). He has spoken on environmental law aspects of land use development and real estate transactions at various professional seminars and has served as program chairman and as a member of the faculty for the Government Institutes, Inc. Compliance Course on Fundamentals of New Mexico Environmental Law (1990, 1991 and 1992) at which he has spoken on the New Mexico environmental protection system and solid waste management. Mr. Salazar, who is senior editor of the *New Mexico Environmental Law Handbook*, authored the New Mexico Environmental Protection System Chapter and the Solid Waste Management Chapter.

James P. Fitzgerald

Mr. Fitzgerald is a graduate of Marist College and received his J.D. from Brooklyn Law School. He is a member of the Albuquerque, New Mexico and American Bar Associations. He is a former assistant city attorney for the City of Albuquerque and practices in the areas of environmental law, municipal law, land use and commercial real estate. Mr. Fitzgerald has lectured on the topic of environmental liability associated with real estate transactions. Mr. Fitzgerald was an editor and a contributing author to the New Mexico chapter of *State Environmental Law Special Report* 1990 and 1991 (Government Institutes, Inc.). He also was a member of the faculty for the Government Institutes, Inc. Compliance Course on Fundamentals of New Mexico Environmental Law (1990, 1991, 1992) at which he spoke on air pollution control. Mr. Fitzgerald, one of the book's editors, authored the Air Quality Management Chapter.

Joseph B. Rochelle

Mr. Rochelle is a summa cum laude graduate of the Springhill College and a graduate of Harvard Law School. Mr. Rochelle is a member of the Albuquerque, New Mexico and American Bar Associations, as well as the Environmental Committee of the American Bar Association Section of Natural Resource, Energy and Environmental Laws. His legal practice includes environmental law, administrative law, and real estate and zoning law. His environmental practice includes advising clients on Superfund, hazardous, mixed, and solid waste laws, and underground storage tank liabilities. He has litigated underground storage tank and toxic tort lawsuits. He has spoken on numerous occasions at seminars on environmental law. His seminar topics have included an overview of state and federal environmental law and regulations, hazardous waste, environmental liabilities associated with real estate and business transactions, lender liability issues, and underground storage tank requirements. Mr. Rochelle was an editor and a contributing author to the New Mexico chapter of *State Environmental Law Special Report* 1990 and 1991 (Government Institutes, Inc.). He also was a member of the faculty for the Government Institutes, Inc. Compliance Course on Fundamentals of New Mexico Environmental Law (1990, 1991, 1992) at which he spoke on hazardous waste management and underground storage tank management.

Mr. Rochelle, one of the book's editors, authored the Hazardous Waste Management and Underground Storage Tank Management Chapters.

Brian H. Lematta

Mr. Lematta is a Phi Beta Kappa graduate of the University of Oregon. He received his J.D. from Columbia University Law School, where he was a Harlan Fiske Stone scholar during his second and third years and served as an associate editor of the *Columbia Journal of Environmental Law*. Mr. Lematta is a member of the New Mexico, Oregon and American Bar Associations. His environmental law practice includes advising and representing mining, financial services, and other clients on matters arising under New Mexico's mining, ground and surface water laws, the federal Clean Water Act and CERCLA. He has lectured extensively on environmental law matters. Mr. Lematta also was a member of the faculty for the Government Institutes, Inc. Compliance Course on Fundamentals on New Mexico Environmental Law (1990, 1991, 1992) at which he spoke on water quality and community right-to-know and emergency planning. He authored the Water Quality Management Chapter and co-authored the Mining and Oil and Gas Chapter.

Mary P. Keleher

Ms. Keleher graduated with honors from the University of Notre Dame, the University of Northern Arizona and was a cum laude graduate of Georgetown University Law School, where she served as articles editor for the Georgetown International Environmental Law Review and authored *Mexican-United States Shared Groundwater*, 1 Geo. Int'l. Envt'l L.R. 113. She is a member of the Albuquerque, New Mexico and American Bar Associations, as well as the New Mexico Bar Association Section of Natural Resources. Prior to attending law school, Ms. Keleher was a technical writer at Sandia National Laboratories, where she specialized in publications related to radioactive waste management. Ms. Keleher practices in the Environment and Natural Resources department with an emphasis on oil and gas and mining law. Ms. Keleher was a member of the faculty for the Government Institutes, Inc. Compliance Course on Fundamentals of New Mexico Environmental Law (1990, 1991, 1992) at which she spoke on radioactive waste management. Ms. Keleher authored the Radioactive Materials and Waste Management Chapter and co-authored the Mining and Oil and Gas Chapter.

M. Catherine Hayden

Ms. Hayden graduated with honors from Barnard College of Columbia University. She also holds degrees from the University of Chicago, the University of Colorado at Boulder, and Kansas State University. She received her law degree from Georgetown University Law Center. Ms. Hayden practices in the Environment and Natural Resources Department of the Rodey Law Firm. She is a member of the Albuquerque, New Mexico and American Bar Associations, as well as the New Mexico Bar Association Section of Natural Resources, Energy and Environmental Law. Ms. Hayden was also a member of the faculty for the Government Institutes, Inc. Compliance course on Fundamentals of New Mexico

Environmental Law (1992) at which she spoke on New Mexico environmental common law. Ms. Hayden authored the Additional Environmental Laws Chapter and the New Mexico Environmental Common Law Chapter.

CHAPTER I
THE NEW MEXICO ENVIRONMENTAL PROTECTION SYSTEM

1.0 THE CONSTITUTIONAL MANDATE

In 1971, the voters of New Mexico amended the state constitution to declare the fundamental importance of the state's environment and to give the New Mexico Legislature direction in protecting the state's natural resources. The language adopted and incorporated into the New Mexico Constitution at Article XX, Section 21 provides:

> The protection of the state's beautiful and healthful environment is hereby declared to be of fundamental importance to the public interest, health, safety and the general welfare. The Legislature shall provide for control of pollution and control of despoilment of the air, water and other natural resources of this state, consistent with the use and development of these resources for the maximum benefit of the people.

The Legislature has taken action in a fashion consistent with the constitutional directive, both before and after its adoption, by enacting substantive environmental legislation and providing the procedural framework within which environmental issues can be addressed.

2.0 THE STATUTORY FRAMEWORK

The Department of Environment Act (DEA)[1] was enacted in 1991 to establish a single department to administer the laws and exercise the functions relating to the environment formerly administered and exercised by the Health and Environment Department.[2] The New Mexico Environment Department (NMED)[3] was the resulting cabinet department established within the executive branch of government.[4]

The administrative head of NMED is the Secretary,[5] who is appointed by the Governor and who serves in the Governor's executive cabinet.[6] It is the Secretary's duty to manage all operations of NMED and to administer and enforce the laws with which the

---

1 N.M. Stat. Ann. §§ 9-7A-1 to -12 (Repl. Pamp. 1991).

2 N.M. Stat. Ann. § 9-7A-3 (Repl. Pamp. 1991).

3 All references in existing law to the Environmental Improvement Agency or the Environmental Improvement Division of the Health and Environment Department are to be construed to mean NMED. N.M. Stat. Ann. § 9-7A-4 (Repl. Pamp. 1991).

4 *Id.*

5 All references in existing law to the Director of the Environmental Improvement Division are to be construed to mean the Secretary. *Id.*

6 N.M. Stat. Ann. § 9-7A-5(A) (Repl. Pamp. 1991).

Secretary or NMED is charged.[7] The Secretary's duties include organizing the department and appointing a director for each division.[8]

NMED is authorized to cooperate with the federal government in the administration of environmental programs in which financial or other participation by the federal government is authorized or mandated under state or federal laws, regulations, rules or orders.[9] The Secretary may enter into agreements with agencies of the federal government to implement environmental programs, subject to availability of appropriate state funds and any provisions of state laws applicable to such agreements or participation by the state.[10]

The Governor or the Secretary may, by appropriate order, designate NMED or any organizational unit of NMED as the single state agency for the administration of any environmental program, when such designation is a condition of federal financial assistance or other participation in the program under applicable federal law, regulation, rule or order.[11] However, whether or not a federal condition exists, the Governor may designate NMED or any organizational unit of NMED as the single state agency for the administration of any environmental program.[12]

Three entities dealing with environmental issues receive staff support from NMED. They are the Environmental Improvement Board (EIB),[13] the Water Quality Control Commission (WQCC),[14] and the Occupational Health and Safety Review Commission (OHSRC).[15] Nevertheless, each of these entities has certain powers, duties and responsibilities which are explicitly exempted from the authority of the Secretary. With regard to EIB, those powers, duties, and responsibilities under the Food Service Sanitation Act, the New Mexico Food Act, the Flour and Bread Act, the Occupational Health and Safety Act, the Environmental Improvement Act, the Air Quality Control Act, the Radiation Protection Act, the Hazardous Waste Act, the Radioactive and Hazardous Materials Act, the Ground Water Protection Act, the Environmental Compliance Act, the Solid Waste Act and its Incineration Provisions, as well as the Rural Infrastructure Act, are exempted from the authority of the Secretary.[16] With regard to WQCC, certain specified provisions of the New

---

7 N.M. Stat. Ann. § 9-7A-6(A) (Repl. Pamp. 1991).

8 N.M. Stat. Ann. § 9-7A-6(B)(3), (9) (Repl. Pamp. 1991).

9 N.M. Stat. Ann. § 9-7A-11(A) (Repl. Pamp. 1991).

10 *Id.*

11 N.M. Stat. Ann. § 9-7A-11(B) (Repl. Pamp. 1991).

12 *Id.*

13 N.M. Stat. Ann. § 9-7A-12 (Repl. Pamp. 1991).

14 N.M. Stat. Ann. § 9-7-14 (Repl. Pamp. 1991).

15 N.M. Stat. Ann. § 9-7-15 (Repl. Pamp. 1991).

16 N.M. Stat. Ann. § 9-7A-12 (Repl. Pamp. 1991).

Mexico Subdivision Act and the Water Quality Act are exempted from the authority of the Secretary.[17] With regard to OHSRC, certain specified provisions of the Occupational Health and Safety Act are exempted from the authority of the Secretary.[18]

3.0 ENVIRONMENTAL IMPROVEMENT BOARD

The Environmental Improvement Board (EIB) consists of five members appointed by the Governor.[19] The members are appointed for overlapping terms, with no term exceeding five years.[20] No more than three members may be appointed from any one political party.[21] At least a majority of the members must be individuals who represent the public interest and who do not derive any significant portion of their income from persons subject to or who appear before EIB on issues related to the federal Clean Air Act or the Air Quality Control Act.[22] EIB elects from its membership a chairman, vice-chairman and secretary and establishes the tenure of these offices.[23] EIB convenes upon the call of the chairman or a majority of its members.[24]

3.1 EIB RESPONSIBILITY

EIB is responsible for environmental management and consumer protection.[25] Specifically, the Board is responsible for promulgating regulations and standards in the following areas: (1) food protection, (2) water supply, (3) liquid waste, (4) air quality management as provided in the Air Quality Control Act, (5) radiation control as provided in the Radiation Protection Act, (6) noise control, (7) nuisance abatement, (8) vector control, (9) occupational health and safety as provided in the Occupational Health and Safety Act, (10) sanitation of public swimming pools and public baths, (11) plumbing, drainage, ventilation and sanitation of public buildings, (12) medical radiation, health and safety certification and standards for radiologic technologists as provided in the Medical Radiation Health and Safety Act, (13) hazardous wastes and underground storage tanks as provided in the Hazardous Waste Act and (14) solid waste as provided in the Solid Waste Act.[26]

---

17 N.M. Stat. Ann. § 9-7-14 (Repl. Pamp. 1991).

18 N.M. Stat. Ann. § 9-7-15 (Repl. Pamp. 1991).

19 N.M. Stat. Ann. § 74-1-4(A) (Repl. Pamp. 1993).

20 *Id.*

21 *Id.*

22 *Id.*

23 N.M. Stat. Ann. § 74-1-4(C) (Repl. Pamp. 1993).

24 *Id.*

25 N.M. Stat. Ann. § 74-1-8(A) (Repl. Pamp. 1993).

26 *Id.*

3.2 INDEPENDENT LEGAL ADVICE

EIB is required to act with independent legal advice.[27] The manner in which such advice must be provided is determined by EIB but it must be provided by one of the following: (1) the office of the Attorney General, (2) independent counsel hired by EIB or (3) another state agency whose function is sufficiently distinct from NMED to assure independent, impartial advice.[28] Nevertheless, attorneys from NMED may act for EIB in lawsuits filed against or on behalf of EIB, and the Attorney General may, at the request of EIB, file and defend lawsuits on behalf of EIB.[29]

3.3 PENALTY FOR VIOLATION OF EIB REGULATION

A person who violates any EIB regulation is guilty of a petty misdemeanor.[30] However, this does not apply to any regulation for which a criminal penalty is otherwise provided by law.[31]

4.0 NEW MEXICO ENVIRONMENT DEPARTMENT

The Environmental Improvement Act (EIA)[32] was enacted to create an agency responsible for environmental management and consumer protection in New Mexico. Specifically, the agency was created to (1) ensure an environment that in the greatest possible measure will confer optimum health, safety, comfort and economic and social well-being on its inhabitants, (2) protect this generation as well as the unborn from health threats posed by the environment and (3) maximize the economic and cultural benefits of a healthy people.[33] Although the EIA speaks in terms of an agency or the Environmental Improvement Agency, the entity to which the EIA now refers is the Department of Environment,[34] which will hereinafter be referred to as the New Mexico Environment Department (NMED).

4.1 NMED RESPONSIBILITY

NMED is responsible for environmental management and consumer protection programs which include maintaining, developing and enforcing regulations and standards in the following areas: (1) food protection, (2) water supply and water pollution as provided in the Water Quality Act, (3) liquid waste, (4) air quality management as provided in the Air Quality Control Act, (5) radiation control as provided in the Radiation Protection Act,

---

27 N.M. Stat. Ann. § 74-1-8.1 (Repl. Pamp. 1993).

28 *Id.*

29 N.M. Stat. Ann. § 74-1-8.1(B) (Repl. Pamp. 1993).

30 N.M. Stat. Ann. § 74-1-10 (Repl. Pamp. 1993).

31 *Id.*

32 N.M. Stat. Ann. §§ 74-1-1 to -10 (Repl. Pamp. 1993).

33 N.M. Stat. Ann. § 74-1-2 (Repl. Pamp. 1993).

34 N.M. Stat. Ann. § 9-7A-4 (Repl. Pamp. 1991).

(6) noise control, (7) nuisance abatement, (8) vector control, (9) occupational health and safety as provided in the Occupational Health and Safety Act, (10) sanitation of public swimming pools and public baths, (11) plumbing, drainage, ventilation and sanitation of public buildings in the interest of public health, (12) medical radiation, health and safety certification and standards for radiologic technologists as provided in the Medical Radiation Health and Safety Act, (13) hazardous wastes and underground storage tanks as provided in the Hazardous Waste Act and (14) solid waste as provided in the Solid Waste Act.[35]

4.2 NMED AUTHORITY

NMED has the power to (1) sue and be sued, (2) make contracts, (3) enter into agreements with environmental and consumer protection agencies of other states and the federal government, (4) serve as agent for New Mexico in matters of environmental management and consumer protection, (5) enforce EIB rules, regulations and orders and environmental management and consumer protection laws for which NMED is responsible, (6) recommend and propose regulations for promulgation by EIB, (7) present data, views or arguments and examine witnesses and otherwise participate at all hearings conducted by EIB or any other administrative agency with responsibility in the areas of environmental management or consumer protection and (8) have such other powers as may be necessary and appropriate for the exercise of the powers and duties delegated to NMED.[36]

5.0 AIR QUALITY MANAGEMENT

The Air Quality Control Act (AQCA)[37] was enacted to establish a mechanism for dealing with health and environmental issues pertaining to air quality.

EIB's jurisdiction over air quality extends to all areas of the state, except within the boundaries of a local authority.[38]

5.1 EIB RESPONSIBILITY AND AUTHORITY

EIB or the local board,[39] if appropriate, is mandated to prevent or abate air pollution[40] and to adopt regulations necessary to achieve this goal, including regulations prescribing air standards within the geographic area of EIB's jurisdiction.[41] Air quality regulations suggested for consideration include regulations to (1) protect visibility in

---

35 N.M. Stat. Ann. § 74-1-7(A) (Repl. Pamp. 1993).

36 N.M. Stat. Ann. § 74-1-6 (Repl. Pamp. 1993).

37 N.M. Stat. Ann. §§ 74-2-1 to -17 (Repl. Pamp. 1993). *See* the Air Quality Management Chapter.

38 *See* Section 5.3 of this Chapter.

39 "Local board" means a municipal county or joint air quality control board created by any local authority. N.M. Stat. Ann. § 74-2-2(K) (Repl. Pamp. 1993).

40 N.M. Stat. Ann. § 74-2-5(A) (Repl. Pamp. 1993).

41 N.M. Stat. Ann. § 74-2-5(B) to (D) (Repl. Pamp. 1993).

mandatory Class I areas,[42] (2) prevent significant deterioration of air quality, (3) achieve national ambient air quality standards in non-attainment areas, (4) prescribe standards of performance for sources, and (5) prescribe emission standards for hazardous air pollutants.[43] These regulations are to be as stringent as, but no more stringent than, federal statutory provisions, regulations and standards.[44]

EIB or the local board may adopt regulations requiring notice to EIB of intent to introduce or permit the introduction of an air contaminant into the air of New Mexico.[45] Similarly, EIB or the local board may, by regulation, require any person emitting an air contaminant to (1) install, use and maintain emission monitoring devices, (2) sample emissions, (3) maintain records of the nature and amount of emissions, (4) submit reports regarding the emissions and the performance of emission control devices and (5) provide other information relating to the emission of air contaminants.[46]

5.2 NMED RESPONSIBILITY AND AUTHORITY

NMED is the state air pollution control agency for all purposes under federal legislation relating to air pollution.[47] In this capacity NMED must (1) take all action necessary to secure for the state and its political subdivisions the benefits of federal legislation, (2) advise, consult, contract with and cooperate with local authorities, other states, the federal government and other interested persons or groups in regard to matters of common interest in the field of air quality control and initiate cooperative action between a local authority and NMED, between one local authority and another or among any combination of local authorities and NMED for control of air pollution in areas having related air pollution problems that overlap the boundaries of political subdivisions, and (3) enter into agreements and compacts with adjoining states and Indian tribes, where appropriate.[48]

---

42 "Mandatory Class I area" means any of the following areas in New Mexico which were in existence on August 7, 1977: (1) national wilderness areas which exceed 5,000 acres in size; and (2) national parks which exceed 6,000 acres in size. N.M. Stat. Ann. § 74-2-2(L) (Repl. Pamp. 1993).

43 N.M. Stat. Ann. §§ 74-2-5(C)(1), (2) (Repl. Pamp. 1993).

44 N.M. Stat. Ann. § 74-2-5(C)(1)(a) (Repl. Pamp. 1993). Note, however, that with regard to solid waste incinerators, EIB is required to establish emission limitations by regulations that are at least as strict as any applicable federal emission limitations and which may be more stringent than those limitations. N.M. Stat. Ann. § 74-2-5(C)(3) (Repl. Pamp. 1993).

45 N.M. Stat. Ann. § 74-2-5(C)(4) (Repl. Pamp. 1993).

46 N.M. Stat. Ann. § 74-2-5(C)(5) (Repl. Pamp. 1993).

47 N.M. Stat. Ann. § 74-2-5.2 (Repl. Pamp. 1993).

48 *Id.*

NMED and the appropriate local agency are also charged with certain additional responsibilities including (1) development of facts, undertaking of investigations and studies and production of information pertaining to emissions, (2) institution of legal proceedings to compel compliance with the AQCA or any EIB regulation, (3) encouragement of voluntary cooperation, (4) consultation with anyone proposing to institute an air contaminant source or device or system for the control thereof, (5) establishment of a small business stationary source technical and environmental compliance assistance program, consistent with Section 507 of the federal act, (6) administration of grants or other funds, (7) classification and recordation of air contaminant sources and (8) development of a plan for the regulation, control, prevention or abatement of air pollution.[49]

5.3 LOCAL AUTHORITY

A "local authority" is any county that was a class A county as of January 1, 1980, or any municipality with a population greater than 100,000 located within a county that was a class A county as of January 1, 1980.[50] A county or municipality meeting these qualifications may assume jurisdiction as a local authority by adopting an ordinance providing for the local administration and enforcement of the AQCA.[51] The ordinance must, among other things, create a local board to perform those functions delegated to the EIB under the AQCA, except for those functions reserved exclusively for the EIB.[52] The ordinance must also create a local agency to administer and enforce the provisions of the AQCA.[53]

5.3.1 Vehicle Emission Inspection and Maintenance Program

Any local authority that is located within a transportation-related pollutant non-attainment area may provide for a vehicle emission inspection and maintenance program.[54]

5.3.2 Joint Powers Agreements

Any local authority that has implemented a vehicle emission inspection and maintenance program may extend the enforcement of that program by entering into joint powers agreements with any contiguous municipality or county within the designated airshed or with NMED.[55]

---

49 N.M. Stat. Ann. § 74-2-5.1 (Repl. Pamp. 1993).

50 N.M. Stat. Ann. § 74-2-2(J) (Repl. Pamp. 1993).

51 N.M. Stat. Ann. § 74-2-4(A) (Repl. Pamp. 1993).

52 N.M. Stat. Ann. § 74-2-4(A)(1) (Repl. Pamp. 1993).

53 N.M. Stat. Ann. § 74-2-4(A)(2) (Repl. Pamp. 1993).

54 N.M. Stat. Ann. § 74-2-4(E) (Repl. Pamp. 1993).

55 N.M. Stat. Ann. § 74-2-4(F) (Repl. Pamp. 1993).

5.3.3 Municipal or County Air Quality Permit Fund

A local authority is required to create, within the municipal or county treasury, a fund to be used for the purpose of paying the reasonable costs of (1) appealing, reviewing and acting upon any applications for a permit, (2) implementing and enforcing the terms and conditions of permits, (3) emissions and ambient monitoring, (4) preparing applicable regulations or guidance, (5) modeling, analysis and demonstrations and (6) preparing inventories and tracking emissions.[56]

5.3.4 EIB Retained Jurisdiction

Notwithstanding local administration and enforcement of the AQCA, EIB and the Secretary retain jurisdiction and control for the administration and enforcement of the AQCA with respect to any act or failure to act, of any municipality or county, that causes or contributes to air pollution.[57]

5.4 LIMITATIONS ON REGULATIONS

The AQCA does not (1) authorize EIB or the local board to make any regulation regarding any condition or quality of the outdoor atmosphere if the condition or air quality level and its effect are confined entirely within the boundaries of the industrial or manufacturing property within which the air contaminants are or may be emitted and public access is restricted within such boundaries, (2) grant EIB or the local board any jurisdiction affecting the relation between employers and employees with respect to or arising out of any condition of air quality or (3) supersede or limit the applicability of any law relating to industrial health, safety or sanitation.[58]

6.0 WATER QUALITY MANAGEMENT

The Water Quality Control Commission (WQCC) is created by the provisions of the Water Quality Act (WQA).[59] WQCC, which is administratively attached to NMED,[60] is the state water pollution control agency for New Mexico for all purposes of the Federal Water Pollution Control Act and the wellhead protection and sole source aquifer programs of the federal Safe Drinking Water Act.[61]

---

56 N.M. Stat. Ann. § 74-2-16 (Repl. Pamp. 1993).

57 N.M. Stat. Ann. § 74-2-4(D) (Repl. Pamp. 1993).

58 N.M. Stat. Ann. § 74-2-11.1 (Repl. Pamp. 1993).

59 N.M. Stat. Ann. §§ 74-6-1 to -16 (Repl. Pamp. 1993). *See* Water Quality Management Chapter.

60 N.M. Stat. Ann. § 74-6-3(F) (Repl. Pamp. 1993).

61 N.M. Stat. Ann. § 74-6-3(E) (Repl. Pamp. 1993).

6.1 WATER QUALITY CONTROL COMMISSION COMPOSITION

WQCC consists of each of the following or a designee: (1) the Secretary of NMED, (2) the Director of the Department of Game and Fish, (3) the State Engineer,[62] (4) the Chairman of the Oil Conservation Commission, (5) the Director of the State Park and Recreation Division of the Energy, Minerals and Natural Resources Department, (6) the Director of the New Mexico Department of Agriculture, (7) the Chairman of the Soil and Water Conservation Commission, (8) the Director of the Bureau of Mines and Mineral Resources at the New Mexico Institute of Mining and Technology and (9) three representatives of the public appointed by the Governor for a term of four years.[63]

6.2 WQCC RESPONSIBILITY AND AUTHORITY

WQCC is empowered to (1) accept and supervise the administration of loans and grants from all public or private sources, (2) adopt a comprehensive water quality program, (3) adopt water quality standards, (4) adopt regulations to prevent or abate water pollution in New Mexico, (5) assign responsibility for administering its regulations to constituent agencies and hear and decide disputes between constituent agencies as to jurisdiction concerning any matters within the purpose of the WQA, (6) enter into agreements with the federal government or other state governments for purposes consistent with the WQA, (7) grant an individual variance from any regulation whenever it is found that compliance will impose an unreasonable burden, (8) adopt regulations requiring the filing of proposed plans and specifications for the construction and operation of new sewer systems, treatment works, or sewage systems and extensions or modifications of, or additions to, new or existing sewer systems, treatment works or sewage systems, (9) adopt regulations requiring notice of intent to introduce or allow the introduction of water contaminants into waters of New Mexico, (10) adopt regulations establishing pretreatment standards and (11) coordinate application procedures and funding cycles for loans and grants with the local government division of the Department of Finance and Administration pursuant to the New Mexico Community Assistance Act (NMCAA).[64] However, WQCC cannot require a permit respecting the use of water in irrigated agriculture, except in the case of a specific practice that documentation or actual case history has shown to be hazardous to public health.[65]

---

[62] The "State Engineer" is a technically qualified registered professional engineer appointed by the Governor who has general supervisory authority of waters of the state and of the measurement, appropriation and distribution thereof and related duties. N.M. Stat. Ann. § 72-2-1 (Repl. Pamp. 1985).

[63] N.M. Stat. Ann. § 74-6-3(A) (Repl. Pamp. 1993).

[64] N.M. Stat. Ann. § 74-6-4 (Repl. Pamp. 1993).

[65] N.M. Stat. Ann. § 74-6-4(K) (Repl. Pamp. 1993).

6.3 CONSTITUENT AGENCIES

The following state agencies are considered constituent agencies of WQCC: (1) NMED, (2) State Engineer and the Interstate Stream Commission, (3) New Mexico Department of Game and Fish, (4) Oil Conservation Commission, (5) State Park and Recreation Division of the Energy, Minerals and Natural Resources Department, (6) New Mexico Department of Agriculture, (7) Soil and Water Conservation Division and (8) New Mexico Bureau of Mines and Mineral Resources at New Mexico Institute of Mining and Technology.[66]

6.4 CONSTITUENT AGENCIES RESPONSIBILITY AND AUTHORITY

Each constituent agency must administer those regulations assigned to it by WQCC.[67] Each constituent agency may (1) receive and expend funds for purposes consistent with the WQA, (2) develop facts and make studies and investigations to carry out its responsibilities, (3) report to WQCC and other constituent agencies water pollution conditions believed to require action, (4) make every reasonable effort to obtain voluntary cooperation in preventing or abating water pollution, (5) enter at reasonable times upon or through any premises in which an effluent source is located or in which are located any records required to be maintained by regulations of WQCC, (6) recommend and propose regulations for promulgation by WQCC and (7) present data, views or arguments and examine witnesses and otherwise participate at all hearings conducted by WQCC or any other administrative agency with responsibility in the areas of environmental management or consumer protection.[68]

6.5 LIMITATIONS AND CLARIFICATION

The Legislature enacted certain provisions to clarify limitations on the application and interpretation of the WQA. For example, the WQA does not: (1) grant WQCC or any other entity the power to take away or modify property rights in water;[69] (2) apply to any activity or condition subject to the authority of EIB pursuant to the HWA, the Ground Water Protection Act or the SWA, except to abate water pollution or to control the disposal or use of septage and sludge;[70] (3) authorize WQCC to adopt any regulation regarding any condition or quality of water if the water pollution and its effects are confined entirely within the boundaries of property within which the water pollution occurs when the water does not combine with other waters;[71] (4) grant WQCC jurisdiction affecting the relation between

---

66 N.M. Stat. Ann. § 74-6-2(J) (Repl. Pamp. 1993).

67 N.M. Stat. Ann. § 74-6-8 (Repl. Pamp. 1993).

68 N.M. Stat. Ann. § 74-6-9 (Repl. Pamp. 1993).

69 N.M. Stat. Ann. § 74-6-12(A) (Repl. Pamp. 1993).

70 N.M. Stat. Ann. § 74-6-12(B) (Repl. Pamp. 1993).

71 N.M. Stat. Ann. § 74-6-12(C) (Repl. Pamp. 1993).

employers and employees with respect to any condition of water quality;[72] (5) supersede or limit the applicability of any law relating to industrial health, safety or sanitation;[73] or (6) permit interference with the exclusive authority of the Oil Conservation Commission over all persons and things necessary to prevent water pollution as a result of oil or gas operations.[74]

Further, except as otherwise required by federal law, reasonable degradation of water quality resulting from beneficial use must be allowed in both the adoption of regulations and water quality standards and in any enforcement action.[75] In either of these situations, degradation of water quality will not result in impairment of water quality to the extent water quality standards are exceeded.[76]

7.0 WQCC RESPONSIBILITY FOR OTHER STATUTES

In addition to its responsibilities pertaining to the WQA, WQCC has additional responsibilities for the administration and enforcement of the Utility Operators Certification Act and the Wastewater Facility Construction Loan Act.

7.1 UTILITY OPERATORS CERTIFICATION ACT

The administration and enforcement of the Utility Operators Certification Act (UOCA)[77] is vested in WQCC , but the WQCC may delegate to NMED the administration and enforcement of any portion of the UOCA except the adoption of regulations and the conducting of hearings on compliance orders.[78] The UOCA makes it unlawful to operate any public water system or public wastewater facility unless the water system or wastewater facility is operated by a certified operator or supervised by a certified supervisor.[79]

7.1.1 WQCC Responsibility and Authority

WQCC is responsible for and given the authority to (1) adopt regulations that classify both water systems and wastewater facilities into categories based on (a) the size and type of the system or facility, (b) the capacity of the system or facility based on the size of the serviced area and the number and size of the users to be served, (c) the type and character of the water or wastewater to be treated and (d) the physical conditions affecting the

---

72 N.M. Stat. Ann. § 74-6-12(D) (Repl. Pamp. 1993).

73 N.M. Stat. Ann. § 74-6-12(E) (Repl. Pamp. 1993).

74 N.M. Stat. Ann. § 74-6-12(G) (Repl. Pamp. 1993).

75 N.M. Stat. Ann. § 74-6-12(F) (Repl. Pamp. 1993).

76 *Id.*

77 N.M. Stat. Ann. §§ 61-33-1 to -10 (Repl. Pamp. 1993).

78 N.M. Stat. Ann. § 61-33-3 (Repl. Pamp. 1993).

79 N.M. Stat. Ann. § 61-33-6 (Repl. Pamp. 1993).

treatment plants, collection systems and distribution systems;[80] (2) adopt regulations providing standards and criteria for the certification of plant operators;[81] (3) approve and accredit schools and training programs;[82] (4) prepare and administer written and practical examinations for certification of applicants;[83] (5) enter into agreements as deemed appropriate;[84] (6) receive and accept financial and technical assistance;[85] (7) appoint a seven-member board from the certified water system operators and wastewater facility operators to function with the WQCC to establish qualifications of operators, classify systems, adopt regulations and advise the administration of the UOCA;[86] and (8) adopt and file rules and regulations under the State Rules Act that are necessary to carry out the provisions of the UOCA.[87]

WQCC must suspend or revoke any certification of an operator who is (1) guilty of fraud or deceit, (2) guilty of gross incompetence, (3) derelict in the performance of a duty, (4) found to have performed in a higher capacity than that in which he or she is certified or (5) convicted of any violation of UOCA certification requirements or any state or federal water quality statutes.[88] WQCC must also establish a variance procedure for water supply system and wastewater facility operating authorities.[89]

7.2 WASTEWATER FACILITY CONSTRUCTION LOAN ACT

The purpose of the Wastewater Facility Construction Loan Act (WFCLA)[90] is to provide local authorities in New Mexico with low-cost financial assistance in the construction of necessary wastewater facilities through the creation of a self-sustaining program in order to improve and protect water quality and public health.[91]

7.2.1 WQCC and NMED Responsibility

WQCC and NMED are given the following responsibilities in order to further the purposes of the WFCLA: WQCC must (1) adopt regulations to govern the application

---

80 N.M. Stat. Ann. § 61-33-4(A) (Repl. Pamp. 1993).

81 N.M. Stat. Ann. § 61-33-4(B) (Repl. Pamp. 1993).

82 N.M. Stat. Ann. § 61-33-4(C) (Repl. Pamp. 1993).

83 N.M. Stat. Ann. § 61-33-4(D) (Repl. Pamp. 1993).

84 N.M. Stat. Ann. § 61-33-4(E) (Repl. Pamp. 1993).

85 N.M. Stat. Ann. § 61-33-4(F) (Repl. Pamp. 1993).

86 N.M. Stat. Ann. § 61-33-4(G) (Repl. Pamp. 1993).

87 N.M. Stat. Ann. § 61-33-4(H) (Repl. Pamp. 1993).

88 N.M. Stat. Ann. § 61-33-7 (Repl. Pamp. 1993).

89 N.M. Stat. Ann. § 61-33-9 (Repl. Pamp. 1993).

90 N.M. Stat. Ann. §§ 74-6A-1 to -15 (Repl. Pamp. 1993) *See* Additional Environmental Laws Chapter.

91 N.M. Stat. Ann. § 74-6A-2 (Repl. Pamp. 1993).

procedure and requirements for providing financial assistance under the WFCLA and must coordinate application procedures and funding cycles with the NMCAA[92] and (2) adopt a system for the ranking of wastewater facility construction projects for financial assistance.[93]

NMED must establish a program to provide financial assistance to local authorities, individually or jointly, for acquisition, construction or modification of wastewater facilities.[94]

8.0 SOLID WASTE MANAGEMENT

The Solid Waste Act (SWA)[95] was enacted to provide for the (1) establishment of a comprehensive solid waste management program, (2) provision of assistance to counties and municipalities for solid waste management, (3) enhancement of the environment, conservation of resources and protection of the public health, safety and welfare, (4) regulation of solid waste, (5) incentives for counties and municipalities to plan for solid waste management at the local level, (6) requirement of permits for the construction, operation, closure and post-closure maintenance of solid waste facilities, (7) promotion of alternatives to disposal by landfill disposal methods and (8) requirement of procurement policies that promote the development of recycling recyclable materials.[96]

8.1 NMED RESPONSIBILITY AND AUTHORITY

NMED has substantial responsibility for the implementation and enforcement of the provisions of the SWA. The following subsections discuss the primary areas of NMED responsibility.

8.1.1 Solid Waste Management Plan

In accordance with the requirements of the SWA, the Secretary submitted a solid waste management plan (Plan) to EIB for approval on December 31, 1992.[97] EIB adopted the Plan on July 9, 1993, and the Plan took effect on August 8, 1993.[98] The Plan includes the following elements: (1) waste characterization, (2) source reduction, (3) recycling, (4) mulching and composting, (5) solid waste facility capacity, (6) education and public information, (7) funding, (8) special waste and household hazardous waste, (9) siting and (10) district recommendations on how to create local solid waste management systems.[99]

---

92 N.M. Stat. Ann. § 74-6A-4(A) (Repl. Pamp. 1993).

93 N.M. Stat. Ann. § 74-6A-7(B) (Repl. Pamp. 1993).

94 N.M. Stat. Ann. § 74-6A-7(A) (Repl. Pamp. 1993).

95 N.M. Stat. Ann. §§ 74-9-1 to -42 (Repl. Pamp. 1993). *See* Solid Waste Management Chapter.

96 N.M. Stat. Ann. § 74-9-2 (Repl. Pamp. 1993).

97 N.M. Stat. Ann. § 74-9-4 (Repl. Pamp. 1993).

98 N.M. Stat. Ann. § 74-9-5 (Repl. Pamp. 1993).

99 N.M. Solid Waste Management Plan §§ 5.1-5.10.

The goal of the Plan is to divert 25% of all solid waste from solid waste disposal facilities by July 1, 1995, and 50% of all solid waste by July 1, 2000.[100]

8.1.2 Solid Waste Management Program

Now that EIB has approved the Plan, it is the responsibility of the Secretary to design a comprehensive state solid waste management program (Program) by December 1, 1993, which must be fully implemented by July 1, 1994.[101] The Program, which is intended to be consistent with the Plan,[102] must be designed to achieve the following objectives: (1) reduction, recycling, collection, transportation, storage, separation, transformation and disposal of solid waste throughout the state, (2) coordinated regional activity for solid waste management within a solid waste district, (3) positive proposals for local action to correct deficiencies in present solid waste management processes, (4) financial, planning and technical assistance to counties and municipalities, state agencies and other persons to achieve cost-effective reduction, recycling, transformation and disposal of solid waste and environmentally safe solid waste management practices, and (5) the education of the general public and the education and training of individuals involved in solid waste management to assure proper solid waste management.[103]

8.1.3 Additional NMED Responsibilities

NMED is responsible for the enforcement and implementation of the solid waste management regulations adopted by EIB.[104] NMED is also required to (1) develop and implement the Program, (2) provide technical assistance on solid waste management matters, (3) promote the planning and application of source reduction, recycling and solid waste facility siting systems, (4) assist in and encourage the development of regional solid waste management, (5) provide the state Economic Development Department with technical assistance to encourage and support the development of certain commercial enterprises, (6) pursue alternative solid waste management methods, (7) pursue market development and expansion for recyclable materials, (8) administer grants for source reduction and recycling programs, (9) promote and assist in the development of a litter control program, (10) advise EIB about devices or measures that may be required as a result of solid waste management operations, (11) increase public education and public awareness, (12) encourage public participation, (13) determine monitoring requirements, (14) contract for implementation of appropriate parts of the Solid Waste Management Program, (15) enter into appropriate and

---

100 N.M. Solid Waste Management Plan § 1.2.

101 N.M. Stat. Ann. § 74-9-12(A) (Repl. Pamp. 1993).

102 *Id.*

103 N.M. Stat. Ann. § 74-9-12(B) (Repl. Pamp. 1993).

104 N.M. Stat. Ann. § 74-9-14 (Repl. Pamp. 1993).

necessary contracts, (16) receive funds and grants for purposes of the SWA and (17) participate in interstate and national initiatives.[105]

8.2 EIB RESPONSIBILITY AND AUTHORITY

In addition to EIB's traditional role of enacting regulations and setting standards, the SWA gives EIB specific implementation responsibility and authority.

8.2.1 Solid Waste Management Regulations

EIB adopted solid waste management regulations on December 31, 1991, that, pursuant to the SWA mandate,[106](1) implement, administer and enforce a program for the cost-effective and environmentally safe siting, construction, operation, maintenance, closure and postclosure care of solid waste facilities, (2) define special waste, (3) establish requirements for the detoxification and disposal of special waste, (4) establish classifications of solid waste facilities and define what types of solid waste may be processed or disposed of in each classification, (5) establish performance standards for the construction and operation of solid waste facilities, (6) establish performance standards for transformation facilities, (7) establish requirements and procedures for the granting or denial of an application to modify a solid waste facility permit, (8) establish requirements and procedures for commercial haulers, (9) establish an applicant fee schedule, (10) establish requirements and procedures for variance applications, (11) establish a list of solid wastes that may not be transferred, disposed of or transformed in a solid waste facility, (12) establish record keeping procedures for solid waste transfer, landfill disposal and transformation facilities and (13) require NMED to establish a solid waste facility operator certification program.[107]

Now that the Plan has been adopted, EIB must (1) review the initial solid waste regulations and make modifications necessary to make the regulations consistent with the Plan,[108] (2) adopt regulations to establish source reduction and recycling programs[109] and (3) adopt regulations to establish solid waste districts.[110]

8.2.2 Financial Responsibility Regulations

EIB is required to adopt regulations establishing financial responsibility requirements for solid waste generators and operators of solid waste facilities designed to assure that there are adequate sources of funds to provide for (1) closure, postclosure inspection and maintenance and environmental monitoring and control, (2) removal and disposal of buildings, fences, roads and other improvements, (3) reclamation of affected or contaminated lands and

---

105 *Id.*

106 N.M. Stat. Ann. § 74-9-8 (Repl. Pamp. 1993).

107 N.M. Solid Waste Management Regulations, EIB/SWMR - 3 (filed Dec. 31, 1991).

108 N.M. Stat. Ann. § 74-9-9 (Repl. Pamp. 1993).

109 N.M. Stat. Ann. § 74-9-10 (Repl. Pamp. 1993).

110 N.M. Stat. Ann. § 74-9-11 (Repl. Pamp. 1993).

waters, (4) construction of any solid waste cover or containment system required as a condition of any solid waste facility permit, (5) stabilization, removal and off-site treatment or disposal of any contaminated material that is being stored or treated, (6) decontamination, dismantling and removal of any solid waste storage treatment or disposal equipment, (7) operation of any environmental monitoring systems or pollution control systems that are required as a condition of any solid waste facility permit or by order of the Secretary and (8) conducting, only for landfill disposal facilities, periodic postclosure inspections of cover systems, surface water diversion structures, monitor wells or systems, pollutant detection and control systems and performing maintenance activities to correct deficiencies that are discovered.[111]

8.2.3 Solid Waste Districts

Because it has approved the Plan, EIB must now establish solid waste districts for the entire state.[112] The boundaries may cross state lines and are not required to be consistent with municipal or county boundaries.[113]

8.2.4 Solid Waste Assessment Fee

EIB is also required to establish the solid waste assessment fee to be imposed upon the disposal of solid waste by a commercial hauler at any solid waste facility if the solid waste was generated outside the solid waste district in which the solid waste facility is located.[114]

8.3 SOLID WASTE AUTHORITY ACT

In 1993, the New Mexico Legislature enacted the Solid Waste Authority Act to allow small towns and municipalities to combine their resources for the creation of a unified solid waste authority.[115] A solid waste authority is considered a state political subdivision that serves the public use by acquiring, improving, maintaining and operating solid waste management-related projects.[116] A separate board of directors governs each solid waste authority.[117]

---

[111] N.M. Stat. Ann. § 74-9-35(A) (Repl. Pamp. 1993).

[112] N.M. Stat. Ann. § 74-9-11(A), (B) (Repl. Pamp. 1993).

[113] N.M. Stat. Ann. § 74-9-11(B), (C) (Repl. Pamp. 1993).

[114] N.M. Stat. Ann. § 74-9-39(A), (B) (Repl. Pamp. 1993).

[115] N.M. Stat. Ann. §§ 74-10-1 to -100 (Repl. Pamp. 1993).

[116] N.M. Stat. Ann. § 74-10-2(B), (C) (Repl. Pamp. 1993).

[117] N.M. Stat. Ann. § 74-10-12 (Repl. Pamp. 1993).

9.0 HAZARDOUS WASTE MANAGEMENT

The Hazardous Waste Act (HWA)[118] was enacted to help ensure the maintenance of the quality of the state's environment, to confer optimum health, safety, comfort and economic and social well-being on its inhabitants and to protect the proper utilization of its lands.[119]

9.1 EIB RESPONSIBILITY AND AUTHORITY

EIB is required to adopt regulations for the management of hazardous waste and underground storage tanks as may be necessary to protect public health and the environment, that are equivalent to, and no more stringent than, federal regulations adopted pursuant to the Resource Conservation and Recovery Act.[120] EIB, however, may adopt regulations for the management of hazardous waste that are more stringent than federal regulations if EIB determines, after notice and a public hearing, that such federal regulations are insufficient to protect health and the environment.[121]

9.1.1 Hazardous Waste Management Regulations

The hazardous waste management regulations deal with each of the following areas pursuant to statutory mandate: (1) identification and listing of hazardous wastes;[122] (2) establishment of standards applicable to generators of hazardous waste, including requirements regarding (a) furnishing of information on the location and description of the generator's facility and on the production or energy recovery activity occurring at that facility, (b) recordkeeping practices, (c) labeling practices, (d) containers, (e) information on the chemical composition of the hazardous waste, (f) programs to reduce the volume and toxicity of hazardous waste generated, (g) reports to NMED and (h) use of a manifest system;[123] (3) establishment of standards applicable to transporters of hazardous waste, including requirements regarding (a) recordkeeping, (b) labeling, (c) manifest system and (d) transportation to the specified treatment, storage or disposal facility;[124] (4) establishment of standards applicable to distributors or marketers of any fuel produced from hazardous waste or any fuel which contains hazardous waste, including information regarding (a) the facility and (b) the production or energy recovery activity;[125]

---

118 N.M. Stat. Ann. §§ 74-4-1 to -14 (Repl. Pamp. 1993). *See* Hazardous Waste Management Chapter.

119 N.M. Stat Ann. § 74-4-2 (Repl. Pamp. 1993).

120 N.M. Stat. Ann. § 74-4-4(A), (C) (Repl. Pamp. 1993).

121 N.M. Stat. Ann. § 74-4-4(D) (Repl. Pamp. 1993).

122 N.M. Stat. Ann. § 74-4-4(A)(1) (Repl. Pamp. 1993).

123 N.M. Stat. Ann. § 74-4-4(A)(2) (Repl. Pamp. 1993).

124 N.M. Stat. Ann. § 74-4-4(A)(3) (Repl. Pamp. 1993).

125 N.M. Stat. Ann. § 74-4-4(A)(4) (Repl. Pamp. 1993).

(5) establishment of performance standards applicable to owners and operators of facilities for the treatment, storage or disposal of hazardous waste, including requirements regarding (a) records, (b) manifest system, (c) treatment, storage or disposal, (d) facilities, (e) contingency plans, (f) maintenance and operation of the facilities, (g) permits, (h) corrective action, and (i) corrective action beyond the boundaries of a facility;[126] (6) requiring each person owning or operating or both owning and operating a facility to have a permit issued pursuant to EIB requirements;[127] (7) establishment of procedures for permits;[128] (8) definition of major and minor modifications;[129] and (9) establishment of procedures for inspection of facilities.[130]

Other regulations to be adopted include regulations dealing with (1) hazardous substance incidents and (2) notification to NMED of any hazardous substance incidents.[131]

9.2 NMED RESPONSIBILITY AND AUTHORITY

NMED has substantial responsibility and authority for enforcing the provisions of the HWA as well as related hazardous waste management regulations.

9.2.1 Entry and Records

The Secretary or authorized representatives in certain instances may enter onto and inspect establishments or other places and obtain information for the purposes of developing or assisting in the development of regulations, conducting any study, taking any corrective action or enforcing the provisions of the HWA.[132]

9.2.2 Hazardous Waste Monitoring

If the Secretary determines that the presence of any hazardous waste at, or the release of any such waste from, a facility or site may present a substantial hazard, the Secretary may issue an order requiring the owner or operator of the facility to monitor, test and analyze the situation in order to ascertain the nature and extent of the hazard at the facility or site.[133]

---

126 N.M. Stat. Ann. § 74-4-4(A)(5) (Repl. Pamp. 1993).

127 N.M. Stat. Ann. § 74-4-4(A)(6) (Repl. Pamp. 1993).

128 N.M. Stat. Ann. § 74-4-4(A)(7) (Repl. Pamp. 1993).

129 N.M. Stat. Ann. § 74-4-4(A)(8) (Repl. Pamp. 1993).

130 N.M. Stat. Ann. § 74-4-4(A)(9) (Repl. Pamp. 1993).

131 N.M. Stat. Ann. § 74-4-4(B) (Repl. Pamp. 1993). *See* Section 9.2.3 of this Chapter.

132 N.M. Stat. Ann. § 74-4-4.3 (Repl. Pamp. 1993).

133 N.M. Stat. Ann. § 74-4-10.1(A) (Repl. Pamp. 1993).

9.2.3 Hazardous Substance Incidents

NMED may (1) take any action necessary or appropriate to protect persons from injury or other harm which might arise from hazardous substance incidents,[134] including but not limited to providing for cleanup and disposal, coordinating the activities of other public officials and taking any other action deemed necessary or appropriate,[135] (2) notify any person who may have incurred or may incur physical injury from a hazardous substance incident that he or she should undergo a medical examination[136] and (3) assess charges against persons responsible for hazardous substance incidents for costs NMED incurs in cleanup of hazardous substance incidents, disposal of hazardous substances and damage to state property.[137]

9.2.4 Imminent Hazards

Whenever the Secretary is in receipt of evidence that any solid waste or hazardous waste or the condition of any underground storage tank may present an imminent and substantial endangerment to health or the environment, the Secretary may bring suit in the appropriate District Court to restrain immediately any person who has contributed or who is contributing to such activity or may take such other action as may be necessary or both.[138]

9.3 LIMITATIONS ON APPLICATION OF THE HWA

Nothing in the HWA applies to any activity or substance subject to the Federal Water Pollution Control Act, as amended, the Safe Drinking Water Act, as amended, or the Atomic Energy Act of 1954, as amended, except to the extent that such application or regulation is not inconsistent with the requirements of such acts.[139] The HWA also does not apply to the treatment, storage or disposal of wastes under a permit issued pursuant to the Surface Mining Act (SMA)[140] or the Federal Surface Mining Control and Reclamation Act of 1977, as amended, or to any farmer disposing of waste pesticides from his or her own use, provided he or she takes certain precautions.[141]

---

134 "Hazardous substance incident" means any emergency incident involving a chemical or chemicals, including but not limited to transportation wrecks, accidental spills or leaks, fires or explosions, which creates the reasonable probability of injury to human health or property. N.M. Stat. Ann. § 74-4-3(H) (Repl. Pamp. 1993).

135 N.M. Stat. Ann. § 74-4-7(A) (Repl. Pamp. 1993).

136 N.M. Stat. Ann. § 74-4-7(B) (Repl. Pamp. 1993).

137 N.M. Stat. Ann. § 74-4-7(C) (Repl. Pamp. 1993).

138 N.M. Stat. Ann. § 74-4-13(A) (Repl. Pamp. 1993).

139 N.M. Stat. Ann. § 74-4-3.1 (Repl. Pamp. 1993).

140 *Id.*

141 *Id.*

9.4 HAZARDOUS WASTE FEASIBILITY STUDY ACT

The Hazardous Waste Feasibility Study Act (HWFSA)[142] requires the Radioactive and Hazardous Materials Committee (RHMC), after consultation with NMED as to the scope of the study, to contract with public or private entities to study the magnitude of the problem of hazardous waste generation and disposal in New Mexico, including current and projected hazardous waste generation rates.[143]

If RHMC determines that generation rates and transportation costs for out-of-state disposal are significant, the study must address the need, location, conceptual design, ownership and estimated cost of a hazardous waste transfer facility to be located within the state.[144] If RHMC determines that there is a need for one or more hazardous waste transfer and waste exchange facilities, it must make appropriate recommendations to the Legislature.[145]

10.0 UNDERGROUND STORAGE TANK MANAGEMENT

Pursuant to the HWA, EIB must adopt regulations concerning underground storage tanks that are equivalent to, and no more stringent than, federal regulations adopted pursuant to the Resource Conservation and Recovery Act and that include standards or requirements for (1) installation, operation and maintenance of underground storage tanks, (2) financial responsibility, (3) inventory control, (4) detection of leaks from and the integrity testing and monitoring of underground storage tanks, (5) the closure and dismantling of underground storage tanks, (6) recordkeeping and (7) the reporting, containment and remediation of all leaks from any underground storage tanks.[146] EIB must also require, by regulation, the owner of an underground storage tank to register the tank with NMED, subject to reasonable conditions.[147]

The Ground Water Protection Act (GWPA)[148] was enacted to deal with the threat to the public health and safety and the environment resulting from the pollution of ground water resources as a result of leaking underground storage tanks.[149] Its purpose is to

---

142 N.M. Stat. Ann. §§ 74-4C-1 to -4 (Repl. Pamp. 1993).

143 N.M. Stat. Ann. § 74-4C-4(A) (Repl. Pamp. 1993).

144 *Id.*

145 N.M. Stat. Ann. § 74-4C-4(B) (Repl. Pamp. 1993).

146 N.M. Stat. Ann. § 74-4-4(C) (Repl. Pamp. 1993).

147 N.M. Stat. Ann. § 74-4-4.4(A) (Repl. Pamp. 1993).

148 N.M. Stat. Ann. §§ 74-6B-1 to -14 (Repl. Pamp. 1993). *See* Underground Storage Tank Management Chapter.

149 N.M. Stat. Ann. § 74-6B-2(A) (Repl. Pamp. 1993).

provide substantive provisions and funding mechanisms that will enable the state to take corrective action[150] at sites contaminated by leakage from underground storage tanks.[151]

10.1 UNDERGROUND STORAGE TANK COMMITTEE

The Underground Storage Tank Committee (USTC) is an advisory committee consisting of seven members including the Secretary of NMED and six members to be appointed by the Governor chosen from the following groups: (1) fire protection districts, (2) elected local government officials, (3) wholesalers of motor fuels, (4) independent retailers of motor fuels, (5) individuals knowledgeable about corrective actions in connection with leaking underground storage tanks and (6) private citizens or interest groups.[152]

USTC's responsibilities are to (1) recommend proposed regulations to EIB or the Secretary, (2) establish procedures, practices and policies for USTC, (3) review all proposed corrective action plans and submit comments to the Secretary and (4) review all proposed payments from the corrective action fund, except those made pursuant to the GWPA payment program, and submit comments to the Secretary .[153]

10.2 UNDERGROUND STORAGE TANK FUND

NMED administers the Underground Storage Tank Fund (USTF), which was created to meet the necessary expenses in the administration and operation of the underground storage tank program.[154]

10.3 CORRECTIVE ACTION FUND

The Corrective Action Fund (CAF) is intended to provide financial assurance coverage required by federal law to allow NMED to (1) take corrective action in response to a release,[155] (2) pay for the costs of a minimum site assessment in excess of $10,000, (3) pay the state's share of federal leaking underground storage tank trust fund cleanup costs and (4) make payments to or on behalf of owners and operators in accordance with the CAF payment program.[156]

---

150 "Corrective action" means an action taken to investigate, minimize, eliminate or clean up a release to protect the public health, safety and welfare or the environment. N.M. Stat. Ann. § 74-6B-3(B) (Repl. Pamp. 1993).

151 N.M. Stat. Ann. § 74-6B-2(C) (Repl. Pamp. 1993).

152 N.M. Stat. Ann. § 74-6B-4(A) (Repl. Pamp. 1993).

153 N.M. Stat. Ann. § 74-6B-4(C) (Repl. Pamp. 1993). The GWPA payment program is set forth in N.M. Stat. Ann. § 74-6B-13 (Repl. Pamp. 1993).

154 N.M. Stat. Ann. § 74-4-4.8(A) (Repl. Pamp. 1993).

155 "Release" means any spilling, leaking, emitting, discharging, escaping, leaching or disposing from an underground storage tank into ground water, surface water or subsurface soils in amounts exceeding 25 gallons. N.M. Stat. Ann. § 74-6B-3(H) (Repl. Pamp. 1993).

156 N.M. Stat. Ann. § 74-6B-7 (Repl. Pamp. 1993).

EIB, after receipt of recommendations from USTC, must adopt regulations establishing priorities for corrective actions at sites contaminated by underground storage tanks.[157] In adopting regulations, EIB is required to follow the procedures of the HWA.[158]

NMED is responsible for expending funds from the CAF in accordance with regulations adopted by EIB or the Secretary for corrective action at sites contaminated by underground storage tanks.[159] NMED must take corrective action at sites in the order of priority on the priority list, except when an emergency threat to public health, safety and welfare or to the environment exists.[160]

10.4 EARLY RESPONSE TEAM

NMED is responsible for creating an early response team that must respond to requests from municipalities or counties for advice and technical assistance regarding alleged releases from underground storage tanks owned or operated by the municipality or county.[161]

11.0 ENERGY, MINERALS AND NATURAL RESOURCES DEPARTMENT

The Energy, Minerals and Natural Resources Department (EMNRD) is established as a cabinet department in the executive branch of government.[162] Among other organizational units it includes (1) the Mining and Minerals Division which deals with mining matters and (2) the Oil Conservation Division which deals with oil, gas and geothermal resources.[163]

11.1 MINING AND MINERALS DIVISION

The Mining and Minerals Division (MMD) enforces and administers laws and regulations relating to mine safety, coal surface mining and abandoned mine lands reclamation.[164]

11.2 NEW MEXICO MINING ACT

The recently enacted (1993) New Mexico Mining Act (NMMA)[165] has among its purposes the promotion of responsible utilization and reclamation of lands affected by

---

157 N.M. Stat. Ann. § 74-6B-7(B) (Repl. Pamp. 1993).

158 N.M. Stat. Ann. § 74-4-5 (Repl. Pamp. 1993).

159 N.M. Stat. Ann. § 74-6B-7(C). (Repl. Pamp. 1993).

160 *Id.*

161 N.M. Stat. Ann. § 74-6B-12(A) (Repl. Pamp. 1993).

162 N.M. Stat. Ann. § 9-5A-3(A) (Repl. Pamp. 1991).

163 *Id.*

164 N.M. Stat. Ann. § 9-5A-4(D) (Repl. Pamp. 1991).

165 N.M. Stat. Ann. §§ 69-36-1 to -20 (Repl. Pamp. 1993).

exploration, mining or the extraction of minerals that are vital to the welfare of New Mexico.[166]

11.2.1 Mining Commission

The NMMA created the Mining Commission which consists of seven voting members, including (1) the Director of the Bureau of Mines and Mineral Resources of the New Mexico Institute of Mining and Technology or an academic from a mining-related field to be appointed for a four-year term by the Governor, (2) the Secretary of Environment or a designee, (3) the State Engineer or a designee, (4) the Commissioner of Public Lands or a designee, (5) the Director of the Department of Game and Fish or a designee, and (6) two members of the public and an alternate for each, to be appointed by the Governor.[167] The public members must be chosen to represent and to balance environmental and mining interests while minimizing conflicts of interest.[168]

11.2.2 Mining Commission Responsibilities

The Commission must, within one year of the effective date of the NMMA, adopt and file reasonable regulations, consistent with the purposes and intent of the NMMA, necessary to implement the NMMA.[169]

11.3 SURFACE MINING ACT

The Surface Mining Act (SMA)[170], which has been on the books since 1979, has among its purposes (1) to establish a program to protect society and the environment from the adverse effects of surface coal mining operations[171] and (2) to assure that surface coal mining operations are conducted in a manner that will protect the environment.[172]

11.3.1 Coal Surface Mining Commission

The Coal Surface Mining Commission (CSMC) was created by the SMA.[173] CSMC consists of each of the following, or a designee: (1) the director of the Bureau of Mines and Mineral Resources, (2) the director of the Department of Game and Fish, (3) the Secretary of NMED, (4) the chairman of the Soil and Water Conservation Commission, (5) the director of the Agricultural Experiment Station of New Mexico State University, (6) the State Engineer, (7) the Commissioner of Public Lands and (8) two public members who are

---

166 N.M. Stat. Ann. § 69-36-2 (Repl. Pamp. 1993).

167 N.M. Stat. Ann. § 69-36-6(A) (Repl. Pamp. 1993).

168 *Id.*

169 N.M. Stat. Ann. § 69-36-7 (Repl. Pamp. 1993).

170 N.M. Stat. Ann. §§ 69-25A-1 to -36 (Repl. Pamp. 1979 & Supp. 1993).

171 N.M. Stat. Ann. § 69-25A-2(A) (Repl. Pamp. 1979).

172 N.M. Stat. Ann. § 69-25A-2(D) (Repl. Pamp. 1979).

173 N.M. Stat. Ann. § 69-25A-4(A) (Repl. Pamp. 1979 & Supp. 1993).

appointed by the Governor with the advice and consent of the Senate.[174] The public members must have, by education, training or experience, expertise related to mining or mine reclamation.[175]

11.3.2 CSMC Responsibilities

CSMC is responsible for performing those duties specified in the SMA relating to the promulgation of regulations and to appeals from the decisions of the director of MMD.[176]

11.4 OIL CONSERVATION DIVISION

The Oil Conservation Division (OCD) administers the laws and regulations relating to oil, gas and geothermal resources, except those laws specifically administered by another authority.[177] The Director of OCD is known as the State Petroleum Engineer.[178]

11.4.1 OCD Responsibility and Authority

OCD has jurisdiction and authority over all matters relating to the conservation of oil and gas and the prevention of waste of potash as a result of oil or gas operations in New Mexico.[179] It has jurisdiction, authority and control of and over all persons, matters or things necessary or proper to enforce effectively the provisions of the Oil and Gas Act (OGA)[180] or any other law of New Mexico relating to the conservation of oil or gas and the prevention of waste of potash as a result of oil or gas operations.[181]

11.4.2 OCD Regulatory Authority

Apart from any other authority, OCD is authorized to make rules, regulations and orders for the following purposes, together with others not enumerated herein: (1) to regulate the disposition of water produced or used in connection with the drilling for or production of oil or gas or both and to direct surface or subsurface disposal of the water in a manner that will afford reasonable protection against contamination of fresh water supplies designated by the State Engineer;[182] (2) to regulate the disposition of non-domestic wastes resulting from the exploration, development, production or storage of crude oil or natural gas to protect public health and the environment;[183] and (3) to regulate the disposition of non-domestic

---

174 *Id.*

175 *Id.*

176 N.M. Stat. Ann. § 69-25A-4(E) (Repl. Pamp. 1979 & Supp. 1993).

177 N.M. Stat. Ann. § 9-5A-4(E) (Repl. Pamp. 1991).

178 N.M. Stat. Ann. § 70-2-5(A) (Repl. Pamp. 1987).

179 N.M. Stat. Ann. § 70-2-6(A) (Repl. Pamp. 1987).

180 N.M. Stat. Ann. §§ 70-2-1 to -38 (Repl. Pamp. 1987 & Supp. 1993).

181 N.M. Stat. Ann. § 70-2-6(A) (Repl. Pamp. 1987).

182 N.M. Stat. Ann. § 70-2-12(B)(15) (Repl. Pamp. 1987 & Supp. 1993).

183 N.M. Stat. Ann. § 70-2-12(B)(21) (Supp. 1993).

wastes resulting from the oil field service industry, the transportation of crude oil or natural gas, the treatment of natural gas or the refinement of crude oil to protect public health and the environment, including administering the WQA.[184]

11.5 OIL CONSERVATION COMMISSION

The Oil Conservation Commission (OCC) is created by the Oil and Gas Act (OGA)[185] and consists of a designee of the Commissioner of Public Lands, a designee of the Secretary of EMNRD and the Director of OCD.[186] The designees of the Commissioner of Public Lands and of the Secretary of EMNRD are to be persons who have expertise in the regulation of petroleum production by virtue of education or training.[187]

11.5.1 OCC Responsibility and Authority

OCC has concurrent jurisdiction and authority with OCD to the extent necessary for OCC to perform its duties as required by law.[188] In addition, any hearing on any matter may be held before OCC if the OCD Director, in his or her discretion, determines that OCC must hear the matter.[189]

12.0 RADIOACTIVE MATERIALS AND WASTE MANAGEMENT

The Radioactive and Hazardous Materials Act (RHMA)[190] created both a joint interim legislative committee known as the Radioactive and Hazardous Materials Committee (RHMC)[191] and the Radioactive Waste Consultation Task Force (RWCTF).[192]

The purpose of the RHMA is to provide a vehicle to address certain specified legislative findings and concerns by centralizing and coordinating information on those concerns and developing recommendations for action.[193] The findings leading to implementation of the RHMA revealed public and state concerns in the area of public health and safety over (1) the proposed Waste Isolation Pilot Plant (WIPP) for defense-related radioactive waste, (2) the safe treatment and disposal of hazardous wastes and the regulation of hazardous waste generators, (3) the effective provision of regulation and information regarding hazardous chemicals in the community and the work place, (4) the effective control

---

184 N.M. Stat. Ann. § 70-2-12(B)(22) (Supp. 1993).

185 N.M. Stat. Ann. §§ 70-2-1 to -38 (Repl. Pamp. 1987 & Cum Supp. 1993).

186 N.M. Stat. Ann. § 70-2-4 (Repl. Pamp. 1987).

187 *Id.*

188 N.M. Stat. Ann. § 70-2-6(B) (Repl. Pamp. 1987).

189 *Id.*

190 N.M. Stat. Ann. §§ 74-4A-2 to -14 (Repl. Pamp. 1993). *See* Radioactive Materials and Waste Management Chapter.

191 N.M. Stat. Ann. § 74-4A-9 (Repl. Pamp. 1993).

192 N.M. Stat. Ann. § 74-4A-6 (Repl. Pamp. 1993).

193 N.M. Stat. Ann. § 74-4A-3(B) (Repl. Pamp. 1993).

of contamination from underground storage tanks, (5) the transportation of radioactive and hazardous materials on New Mexico highways and streets, (6) the disposition of uranium mine and mill tailings and (7) the need to provide efficient and timely emergency response to accidents or natural disasters involving the disposal, storage or transportation of radioactive and hazardous materials.[194]

12.1 RHMC RESPONSIBILITY

RHMC, which consists of six members from the House of Representatives and six members from the Senate,[195] is responsible for examining all matters relevant to the purpose of the RHMA and for submitting recommended legislation to the Legislature.[196] RHMC, in making recommendations, is required to review and monitor the following areas: (1) the generation, treatment, storage, transportation or disposal of radioactive or hazardous materials and wastes, (2) the control and handling of mixed waste[197] transported to the Waste Isolation Pilot Plant site for disposal, (3) the progress and effectiveness of remedial actions at sites contaminated by radioactive or hazardous materials, (4) compliance with the Environmental Protection Agency and the Council on Environmental Quality of the Office of Surface Mining regulations and standards pursuant to federal environmental statutes, (5) the provision of activities and investigations and the dissemination of information by the Environmental Evaluation Group, (6) the disposition of uranium mine and mill tailings, (7) the means through which disposition of low-level wastes may be accomplished, (8) the state emergency response capability, (9) the Ground Water Protection Act regarding the use or management of underground storage tanks and releases, (10) the Hazardous Chemicals Information Act and (11) such matters assigned by the Legislature and resulting from consultations and negotiations with the federal government and other state governments.[198]

12.2 RWCTF RESPONSIBILITY

RWCTF, which consists of the Secretaries of EMNRD, Taxation and Revenue, NMED, Public Safety, and Highway and Transportation, or their designees,[199] is responsible for negotiating with the federal government on behalf of the state in all areas relating to siting, licensing and operating new federal disposal facilities, including research, development and demonstration, for high-level radioactive waste, transuranic radioactive wastes and low-

---

194 N.M. Stat. Ann. § 74-4A-3(A) (Repl. Pamp. 1993).

195 N.M. Stat. Ann. § 74-4A-10 (Repl. Pamp. 1993).

196 N.M. Stat. Ann. § 74-4A-11 (Repl. Pamp. 1993).

197 "Mixed waste" means any mixture of hazardous waste regulated under the Hazardous Waste Act and radioactive waste regulated under the federal Atomic Energy Act of 1954. N.M. Stat. Ann. § 74-4A-4(G) (Repl. Pamp. 1993).

198 N.M. Stat. Ann. § 74-4A-11 (Repl. Pamp. 1993).

199 N.M. Stat. Ann. § 74-4A-6 (Repl. Pamp. 1993).

level radioactive waste.[200] RWCTF is also to identify impacts of new federal disposal facilities[201] and to coordinate the investigation and studies undertaken by all state agencies.[202] RWCTF may recommend legislation[203] and is required to meet regularly with RHMC in order to keep RHMC apprised of its work.[204]

12.3 RWCTF AUTHORITY

RWCTF may make procedural rules deemed necessary to carry out its responsibilities.[205] It may solicit and accept grants[206] and make such contracts as it deems necessary.[207] It may also appoint a representative to any federal or state task force or working group.[208] It may perform such other acts as are necessary in order to perform its responsibilities and must cooperate fully with RHMC.[209]

12.4 RADIOACTIVE MATERIAL TRANSPORT

EIB has exclusive authority to promulgate regulations prescribing the conditions for transport of radioactive material on the highways.[210] However, except as specifically preempted by federal law, the State Highway Commission has the exclusive authority within New Mexico to designate routes for the transport of radioactive material.[211]

13.0 RADIATION PROTECTION ACT

The Radiation Protection Act (RPA)[212] was enacted to establish a mechanism for dealing with the health and environmental aspects of radioactive material and radiation equipment.

EIB is the radiation protection consultant for all agencies and institutions of the state and, with the advice and consent of the Radiation Technical Advisory Council (RTAC), has the authority to promulgate rules and regulations (1) concerning the health and environ-

---

200 N.M. Stat. Ann. § 74-4A-7(A) (Repl. Pamp. 1993).

201 N.M. Stat. Ann. § 74-4A-7(C) (Repl. Pamp. 1993).

202 N.M. Stat. Ann. § 74-4A-7(D) (Repl. Pamp. 1993).

203 N.M. Stat. Ann. § 74-4A-7(B) (Repl. Pamp. 1993).

204 N.M. Stat. Ann. § 74-4A-7(E) (Repl. Pamp. 1993).

205 N.M. Stat. Ann. § 74-4A-8(A) (Repl. Pamp. 1993).

206 N.M. Stat. Ann. § 74-4A-8(B) (Repl. Pamp. 1993).

207 N.M. Stat. Ann. § 74-4A-8(C) (Repl. Pamp. 1993).

208 N.M. Stat. Ann. § 74-4A-8(D) (Repl. Pamp. 1993).

209 N.M. Stat. Ann. § 74-4A-8(E) (Repl. Pamp. 1993).

210 N.M. Stat. Ann. § 74-4A-1(A) (Repl. Pamp. 1993).

211 *Id.*

212 N.M. Stat. Ann. §§ 74-3-1 to -16 (Repl. Pamp. 1993). *See* Radioactive Materials and Waste Management Chapter.

mental aspects of radioactive material and radiation equipment, (2) prescribing license fees, (3) requiring the posting of a bond for licensed activities and (4) establishing continued care fund deposit requirements as otherwise provided for in the RPA.[213]

The Secretary of NMED may, as a condition of licensing or registration, enter at all reasonable times in or upon any private or public property when there is reasonable cause to believe there is radioactive material or radiation equipment present.[214]

13.1 RADIATION TECHNICAL ADVISORY COUNCIL

The Radiation Technical Advisory Council (RTAC) consists of seven members appointed by the Governor for five-year staggered terms.[215] EIB must, before enacting rules and regulations dealing with radioactivity, seek the advice and consent of RTAC.[216] The members of RTAC are to be individuals with scientific training in one or more of the following fields: (1) diagnostic radiology, (2) radiation therapy, (3) nuclear medicine, (4) radiation or health physics or (5) related sciences with specialization in radiation.[217] Four additional members sit as full council members on matters to which the Medical Radiation Health and Safety Act applies.[218] The additional members are radiologic technologists appointed by the Governor for staggered terms of five years each.[219]

RTAC is responsible for advising NMED and EIB on technical matters relating to radiation.[220]

13.2 EXEMPTIONS

The following activities are exempt from the provisions of the RPA: (1) radiation applied to a person for diagnostic or therapeutic purposes; (2) the transportation of any radioactive material in conformity with regulations of an agency of the federal government, or of any material or equipment owned by the United States and being used, stored or transported by or for the United States, except to the extent required or permitted by the authority in control of such materials or equipment and (3) the mining, extraction, processing, storage or transportation of radioactive ores or uranium concentrates that are regulated by the United States unless the authority is ceded to EIB.[221]

---

213 N.M. Stat. Ann. § 74-3-5(A) (Repl. Pamp. 1993).

214 N.M. Stat. Ann. § 74-3-5(C) (Repl. Pamp. 1993).

215 N.M. Stat. Ann. § 74-3-2(A) (Repl. Pamp. 1993).

216 N.M. Stat. Ann. § 74-3-5(A) (Repl. Pamp. 1993).

217 N.M. Stat. Ann. § 74-3-2(B) (Repl. Pamp. 1993).

218 N.M. Stat. Ann. § 74-3-2(C) (Repl. Pamp. 1993).

219 *Id.*

220 N.M. Stat. Ann. § 74-3-3 (Repl. Pamp. 1993).

221 N.M. Stat. Ann. § 74-3-10 (Repl. Pamp. 1993).

13.3 AGREEMENT WITH NUCLEAR REGULATORY COMMISSION

Pursuant to statutory authority[222] EIB and NMED entered into an agreement with the Nuclear Regulatory Commission (NRC), as provided in the Atomic Energy Act of 1954, as amended, transferring NRC authority to EIB and NMED[223] with respect to by-product materials, source materials and special nuclear materials in quantities not sufficient to form a critical mass. In 1986 the uranium mill tailings responsibilities were returned to NRC.

14.0 DEPARTMENT OF PUBLIC SAFETY ACT

The purpose of the Department of Public Safety Act (DPSA)[224] is to establish a single, unified department to consolidate state law enforcement and safety functions in order to provide better management, real coordination and more efficient use of state resources and manpower in responding to New Mexico's public safety needs and problems and to improve the professionalism of the state's law enforcement and investigative functions and personnel.[225]

14.1 PUBLIC SAFETY DEPARTMENT

The Public Safety Department (PSDept.) is a cabinet department consisting of four program divisions and one administrative division, as follows: (1) New Mexico State Police Division, (2) Special Investigation Division, (3) Training and Recruiting Division, (4) Technical and Emergency Support Division and (5) Administrative Services Division.[226]

14.2 SECRETARY

The administrative head of PSDept. is the Secretary of Public Safety (Secretary of PSDept.) who is appointed by the Governor with the consent of the Senate, and who serves in the Governor's executive cabinet.[227]

14.3 RESPONSIBILITY AND AUTHORITY OF THE SECRETARY

The Secretary of PSDept. is responsible to the Governor for the operation and management of PSDept. and for administering and enforcing the laws with which the Secretary or PSDept. is charged.[228]

---

222 N.M. Stat. Ann. § 74-3-15 (Repl. Pamp. 1993).

223 *See* Radioactive Materials and Waste Management Chapter.

224 N.M. Stat. Ann. §§ 9-19-1 to -11 (Repl. Pamp. 1991). *See* Community Right-to-Know and Emergency Planning Chapter.

225 N.M. Stat. Ann. § 9-19-3 (Repl. Pamp. 1991).

226 N.M. Stat. Ann. § 9-19-4 (Repl. Pamp. 1991).

227 N.M. Stat. Ann. § 9-19-5(A) (Repl. Pamp. 1991).

228 N.M. Stat. Ann. § 9-19-6(A) (Repl. Pamp. 1991).

14.4 TECHNICAL AND EMERGENCY SUPPORT DIVISION

The Technical and Emergency Support Division of PSDept. (TESD) consists of the Emergency Planning and Coordination Bureau of the PSDept., the personnel of the Hazardous Materials Emergency Response Program or Plan and the personnel of such other functions as communications, crime laboratory and records.[229]

The Director of TESD is responsible to the Secretary of PSDept. for carrying out the program for civil emergency preparedness authorized by law and serves as the Governor's authorized representative at the discretion of the Governor.[230]

14.5 EMERGENCY PLANNING AND COORDINATION BUREAU

The Emergency Planning and Coordination Bureau (EPCB) is created by the state's Civil Emergency Preparedness Act (CEPA).[231] The purposes of CEPA are to (1) authorize the creation of local offices of civil emergency preparedness in the political subdivisions of the state,[232] (2) confer upon the Governor and the governing bodies of the state civil emergency preparedness powers,[233] (3) provide a civil emergency preparedness plan for the protection of life and property adequate to cope with disasters resulting from acts of war or sabotage or from natural or man-made causes other than acts of war[234] and (4) provide for coordination of all civil emergency preparedness functions of New Mexico with the comparable functions of the federal government, other states and localities and private agencies.[235]

The EPCB chief directs and coordinates the civil emergency preparedness activities of all state departments, agencies and political subdivisions and maintains liaison and cooperates with civil emergency preparedness agencies and organizations of other states and the federal government.[236]

14.6 EMERGENCY MANAGEMENT ACT

The Legislature has concluded that the use of hazardous materials, including radioactive materials, and the transportation of such materials through or within New Mexico occurs on a daily basis and, no matter how safety-conscious facilities, users, shippers or carriers are, accidents may occur.[237] It is the purpose of the Emergency Management Act

---

229 N.M. Stat. Ann. § 9-19-7(D) (Repl. Pamp. 1991).

230 N.M. Stat. Ann. § 12-10-3(B) (Repl. Pamp. 1988 & Supp. 1993).

231 N.M. Stat. Ann. § 12-10-3(A) (Repl. Pamp. 1988 & Supp. 1993).

232 N.M. Stat. Ann. § 12-10-2(A) (Repl. Pamp. 1988 & Supp. 1993).

233 N.M. Stat. Ann. § 12-10-2(B) (Repl. Pamp. 1988 & Supp. 1993).

234 N.M. Stat. Ann. § 12-10-2(C) (Repl. Pamp. 1988 & Supp. 1993).

235 N.M. Stat. Ann. § 12-10-2(D) (Repl. Pamp. 1988 & Supp. 1993).

236 N.M. Stat. Ann. § 12-10-3(B) (Repl. Pamp. 1988 & Supp. 1993).

237 N.M. Stat. Ann. § 74-4B-2(A) (Repl. Pamp. 1993).

(EMA)[238] to (1) provide that adequate hazardous materials emergency management capability exists in the state to protect the health and safety of New Mexico citizens and the environment, (2) delineate state agencies responsible for responding to a hazardous materials accident and (3) provide for the formulation of a comprehensive hazardous materials emergency management plan.[239]

14.6.1 Responsibility of Secretary of PSDept.

The Secretary of PSDept. has final authority to administer the provisions of the EMA[240] and is responsible for central coordination and communication in the event of an accident.[241]

14.6.2 Responsible State Agencies

The state agencies responsible for responding to an emergency are (1) New Mexico State Police Division of PSDept. for coordination, law enforcement and traffic and crowd control, (2) NMED for assistance with accidents involving radioactive or hazardous materials or hazardous substances, (3) State Fire Marshall's office for assistance with any accident involving hazardous materials, (4) Emergency Medical Services Bureau of the Health Services Division of the Department of Health for assistance with accidents involving casualties, (5) EPCB and the Military Division of the Department of Military Affairs for assistance with accidents that require the evacuation of the vicinity of the accident or the use of the New Mexico National Guard and (6) State Highway and Transportation Department for assistance with road closures, designating alternate routes and related services.[242]

14.6.3 Emergency Management Task Force

An Emergency Management Task Force (EMTF) consisting of 11 members chosen essentially from each of the responsible state agencies was created for the purpose of developing and monitoring a comprehensive plan to deal with hazardous materials accidents.[243]

14.6.4 Hazardous Materials Safety Board

The Hazardous Materials Safety Board (HMSB) is composed of the training officers of the responsible state agencies[244] and is responsible for establishing a curriculum of accident response training for the personnel of each responsible state agency designed to

---

238 N.M. Stat. Ann. §§ 74-4B-1 to -14 (Repl. Pamp. 1993). *See* Community Right-to-Know and Emergency Planning Chapter.

239 N.M. Stat. Ann. § 74-4B-2(C) (Repl. Pamp. 1993).

240 N.M. Stat. Ann. § 74-4B-4(A) (Repl. Pamp. 1993).

241 N.M. Stat. Ann. § 74-4B-5(A) (Repl. Pamp. 1993).

242 N.M. Stat. Ann. § 74-4B-5(D) (Repl. Pamp. 1993).

243 N.M. Stat. Ann. § 74-4B-6 (Repl. Pamp. 1993).

244 N.M. Stat. Ann. § 74-4B-8(A) (Repl. Pamp. 1993).

implement the EMTF plan and for following through with a comprehensive training program.[245]

14.6.5 Hazardous Materials Emergency Response Administrator

The Hazardous Materials Emergency Response Administrator (HMERA) is a member of the TESD of the PSDept. and provides staff support to EMTF and HMSB.[246] HMERA is also responsible for maintaining relevant inventories, data bases and rosters as well as updating the EMTF plan and performing other duties requested by EMTF and HMSB.[247]

14.7 HAZARDOUS CHEMICALS INFORMATION ACT

The purpose of the Hazardous Chemicals Information Act (HCIA)[248] is to insure that current information on the nature and location of hazardous chemicals is available to local emergency planning committees (LEPCs), emergency responders and the public as required by the federal Emergency Planning and Community Right-to-Know Act of 1986 (EPCRA).[249]

14.7.1 State Emergency Response Commission

The State Emergency Response Commission (SERC) established by the HCIA consists of seven members appointed by the Governor, including representatives of private industry, federal facilities, public health and public safety.[250] SERC, together with PSDept., is responsible for carrying out the provisions of the HCIA.[251] SERC's responsibilities include the exercise of supervisory authority to implement the federal Emergency Planning and Community Right-to-Know Act of 1986 (Sara Title III) within New Mexico, the prescription of all reporting forms required by HCIA and the provision of direction to EMTF and HMSB.[252]

15.0 STATE AGRICULTURE DEPARTMENT

In addition to its other statutory duties, the New Mexico Department of Agriculture is given specific administration and enforcement responsibility with regard to the Pesticide Control Act, hazardous agricultural waste and the Petroleum Products Standards Act.

---

245 N.M. Stat. Ann. § 74-4B-8(B) (Repl. Pamp. 1993).

246 N.M. Stat. Ann. § 74-4B-6.1 (Repl. Pamp. 1993).

247 N.M. Stat. Ann. § 74-4B-6.1(B) (Repl. Pamp. 1993).

248 N.M. Stat. Ann. §§ 74-4E-1 to -9 (Repl. Pamp. 1993). *See* Community Right-to-Know and Emergency Planning Chapter.

249 N.M. Stat. Ann. § 74-4E-2 (Repl. Pamp. 1993).

250 N.M. Stat. Ann. § 74-4E-4(A) (Repl. Pamp. 1993).

251 N.M. Stat. Ann. § 74-4E-1 to -9 (Repl. Pamp. 1993).

252 N.M. Stat. Ann. § 74-4E-4(B) (Repl. Pamp. 1993).

15.1 PESTICIDE CONTROL ACT

The Pesticide Control Act (PCA)[253] is administered and enforced by the New Mexico Agriculture Department (AD), under the direction of the Board of Regents of New Mexico State University (Regents).[254] AD is responsible for administering and enforcing both the provisions of the PCA and the regulations promulgated by the Regents.[255]

The Regents may, after notice and public hearing, adopt regulations for carrying out the purpose and provisions of the PCA[256] that are consistent with regulations of EIB, WQCC and the laws administered by EPA.[257]

15.2 HAZARDOUS AGRICULTURAL WASTE

AD is responsible for the enforcement of all EIB regulations adopted pursuant to the Hazardous Waste Act regarding generators of hazardous agricultural waste.[258] NMED is required to enforce those EIB regulations pertaining to transporters, treaters, storers and disposers of hazardous agricultural waste.[259] In the exercise of its responsibilities, AD has the same authority as NMED.[260]

In adopting hazardous agricultural waste regulations, EIB must make a reasonable effort to consult with AD prior to the adoption of the regulations.[261] AD serves as the technical consultant to EIB on matters concerning hazardous agricultural waste.[262]

15.3 PETROLEUM PRODUCTS STANDARDS ACT

The Petroleum Products Standards Act (PPSA)[263] was enacted to guarantee adequate quality and quantity standards for petroleum products through a strong and comprehensive program involving inspection, testing and enforcement measures.[264]

---

253 N.M. Stat. Ann. §§ 76-4-1 to -39 (Repl. Pamp. 1981 & Supp. 1992). *See* Additional Environmental Laws Chapter.

254 N.M. Stat. Ann. § 76-4-2 (Repl. Pamp. 1981).

255 N.M. Stat. Ann. § 76-4-9 (Repl. Pamp. 1981).

256 N.M. Stat. Ann. § 76-4-9(A) (Repl. Pamp. 1981).

257 N.M. Stat. Ann. § 76-4-9(B) (Repl. Pamp. 1981).

258 N.M. Stat. Ann. § 74-4-4.1(A) (Repl. Pamp. 1993).

259 *Id.*

260 N.M. Stat. Ann. § 74-4-4.1(B) (Repl. Pamp. 1993).

261 N.M. Stat. Ann. § 74-4-4.1(C) (Repl. Pamp. 1993).

262 *Id.*

263 N.M. Stat. Ann. §§ 57-19-25 to -37 (Repl. Pamp. 1987 & Supp. 1993).

264 N.M. Stat. Ann. § 57-19-26 (Supp. 1993).

15.3.1 Board Duties

The Board of Regents at New Mexico State University (Regents)[265] is responsible for the administration and enforcement of the PPSA.[266] The Regents will adopt necessary rules and regulations, provide public notice and allow public comment on all proposed rules and regulations.[267]

15.3.2 Director Authority

The Director of the New Mexico Department of Agriculture (Director)[268] has authority to (1) inspect, investigate, analyze and take appropriate actions to administer and enforce the PPSA, (2) enter any commercial premises during normal business hours, (3) collect and test any petroleum products offered for sale, (4) issue and enforce stop-sale, hold and removal orders with respect to a petroleum product kept, offered or exposed for sale in violation of the PPSA, (5) require distributors and retailers to retain records for a period of not more than one year, (6) maintain and operate a petroleum product testing laboratory, (7) issue and enforce stop-use orders for measuring equipment or vehicle tanks used in violation of the PPSA and (8) delegate to authorized representatives any of the responsibilities for the proper administration of the PPSA.[269]

16.0 NATURAL RESOURCES TRUSTEE ACT

In 1993, the New Mexico Legislature enacted the Natural Resources Trustee Act (NRTA)[270] which establishes the position of the Natural Resources Trustee (Trustee). The Trustee is appointed by the Governor and acts on behalf of the public to protect and represent the state's interest under applicable federal laws regarding injury to, destruction of or loss of natural resources in the state.[271] The Trustee heads the Office of Natural Resources Trustee, which is administratively attached to NMED.[272]

16.1 TRUSTEE DUTIES AND AUTHORITY

Pursuant to the NRTA, the Trustee is required to take all actions necessary to (1) act on behalf of the public to protect New Mexico's natural resources by recovering damages for injury to, destruction of or loss of those resources, (2) investigate injury to, destruction of or loss of natural resources, (3) determine the amount and cause of injury to, destruction of or

---

265 N.M. Stat. Ann. § 57-19-27(A) (Supp. 1993).

266 N.M. Stat. Ann. § 57-19-28(A) (Supp. 1993).

267 *Id.*

268 N.M. Stat. Ann. § 57-19-27(D) (Supp. 1993).

269 N.M. Stat. Ann. § 57-19-28(B) (Supp. 1993).

270 N.M. Stat. Ann. §§ 75-7-1 to -5 (Supp. 1993). *Also see* Chapter X, Additional Environmental Laws, for more information on the NRTA.

271 N.M. Stat. Ann. § 75-7-2(A) (Supp. 1993).

272 N.M. Stat. Ann. § 75-7-2(B) (Supp. 1993).

loss of natural resources, (4) determine the liability of any person for injury to, destruction of or loss of natural resources, (5) assess and collect damages for injury to, destruction of or loss of natural resources and (6) expend monies for the purposes set forth in the NRTA.[273]

---

[273] N.M. Stat. Ann. § 75-7-3 (Supp. 1993).

CHAPTER II
AIR QUALITY MANAGEMENT

1.0 INTRODUCTION

New Mexico's air quality control statutes and regulations, like those in most states, are driven by the requirements of the federal Clean Air Act (CAA).[1] The CAA divides the country into two distinct areas known as attainment and non-attainment areas. An area is designated attainment if the air quality meets the primary and secondary National Ambient Air Quality Standards (NAAQS) established by the U.S. Environmental Protection Agency (EPA).[2] An area is designated non-attainment if it fails to meet one or more established NAAQS.[3] EPA has promulgated NAAQS for fine particulate matter (PM10), sulfur dioxide (SO_2), carbon monoxide (CO), nitrogen dioxide (NO_2), ozone (photochemical oxidants), and lead (Pb).[4]

Primary NAAQS are air quality standards which the EPA Administrator deems necessary to protect public *health*, factoring in an adequate margin of safety.[5] Secondary NAAQS are designed to protect public *welfare* from any known or anticipated adverse effects associated with the presence of a specific air contaminant in the ambient air.[6]

The CAA requires each state to submit a state implementation plan (SIP) to EPA demonstrating how the state proposes to implement, maintain, and enforce the primary and secondary NAAQS.[7] The SIP must include emissions limitations and other control measures, means, or techniques as well as schedules and timetables for compliance.[8] The CAA specifically places upon the states the primary responsibility for protecting air quality.[9] The State of New Mexico SIP was first officially submitted to EPA on January 27, 1972, and has been regularly supplemented and updated.[10] New Mexico's SIP establishes eight air quality control regions within the state: Albuquerque-Mid Rio Grande Intrastate, New Mexico Southern Border Intrastate, El Paso-Las Cruces-Alamogordo Interstate, Four Corners

---

1 42 U.S.C. §§ 7401 - 7671.

2 42 U.S.C. § 7407(d)(1).

3 *Id.*

4 40 C.F.R. Part 50.

5 42 U.S.C. § 7409(b)(1).

6 42 U.S.C. § 7409(b)(2).

7 42 U.S.C. § 7410(a)(1).

8 42 U.S.C. § 7410(a)(2).

9 42 U.S.C. § 7401(a)(3).

10 40 C.F.R. §§ 52.1620 - .1639.

Interstate, Northeastern Plains Intrastate, Pecos-Permian Basin Intrastate, Southwestern Mountains-Augustine Plains Intrastate, and Upper Rio Grande Valley Intrastate.[11]

While the CAA has greatly influenced the framework of the New Mexico air quality control program, New Mexico has initiated a more comprehensive regulatory approach pursuant to its authority under the New Mexico Air Quality Control Act (AQCA).[12] It has accomplished this principally through a comprehensive permitting program for all new or modified stationary sources that emit or have the potential to emit regulated air contaminants. New Mexico's Ambient Air Quality Standards and Air Quality Control Regulations (AQCRs) promulgated by the New Mexico Environmental Improvement Board (EIB) are designed not only to implement federal requirements established by the CAA but also to protect air quality in New Mexico as the state deems appropriate.[13]

This chapter addresses the regulation of stationary and mobile sources of air contaminants in New Mexico. The heart of the New Mexico program is the control of new stationary sources and modification of existing sources through the permit program. In the City of Albuquerque/Bernalillo County area, the largest metropolitan area in New Mexico, the state has delegated authority for air pollution control to a local air quality control board, the Albuquerque-Bernalillo County Air Quality Control Board (Board).[14] The Albuquerque/ Bernalillo County area has been designated by EPA as a non-attainment area for carbon monoxide emissions. The City of Albuquerque and Bernalillo County have, therefore, adopted motor vehicle emissions control ordinances and the Board has adopted extensive regulations implementing a motor vehicle emissions inspection program.[15]

2.0 THE NEW MEXICO AIR QUALITY CONTROL ACT

The AQCA was first adopted by the New Mexico Legislature in 1967. The AQCA provides the basic framework for air pollution control in New Mexico. NMED is established as the air pollution agency for all state purposes under federal legislation relating to air pollution.[16] The AQCA commands EIB or the Board, as appropriate, to adopt regulations to prevent or abate air pollution.[17]

---

11 40 C.F.R. § 52.1621.

12 N.M. Stat. Ann. §§ 74-2-1 to -17 (Repl. Pamp. 1993).

13 New Mexico has adopted state Ambient Air Quality Standards for total suspended particulates, SO_2, hydrogen sulfide, sulfur, CO, NO_x, photochemical oxidants and non-methane hydrocarbons. N.M. Air Quality Control Regulations § 201. (filed 6/15/81).

14 N.M. Stat. Ann. § 74-2-4 (Repl. Pamp. 1993).

15 *See* Albuquerque-Bernalillo County Air Quality Program Section of this Chapter.

16 N.M. Stat. Ann 74-2-5.2 (Repl. Pamp. 1993).

17 N.M. Stat. Ann. § 74-2-5(A) (Repl. Pamp. 1993).

New Mexico relies on an extensive permitting process to control the emission of air contaminants. EIB and the Board have authority to adopt regulations requiring persons constructing or modifying any source to obtain a permit prior to such construction or modification and requiring persons intending to operate any source for which an operating permit is required by the 1990 CAA amendments to obtain an operating permit.[18] Regulations must include requirements for submission of information ensuring that standards under the AQCA or the CAA will not be violated; specify deadlines for processing permit applications; implement a schedule of construction permit fees sufficient to cover the reasonable costs of administering, implementing, and enforcing the construction permits; and provide a schedule of emissions fees for operating permits consistent with the 1990 CAA amendments. For operating permits only, the regulations must provide for notice to, and review and comment by, EPA. The regulations must also contain provisions for renewal and specifications for termination, modification, or revocation and reissuance prior to the expiration of the permit's term.[19] If notice of objection is received from EPA, the permit must not be issued.

Regulations must require that NMED or the local agency may deny construction permit applications if it appears that the proposed construction or modification of an emissions source will not meet applicable requirements of the AQCA and the CAA or their regulations. As to operating permits, the regulations must require that NMED or the local agency may deny any application if the source will emit a hazardous air pollutant or any air contaminants in excess of a federal standard of performance or a regulation of the EIB or the local agency, or if it appears that the source will cause or contribute to air contaminant levels in excess of any NAAQS or local ambient air quality standard.[20]

NMED or the local agency may specify conditions for granting construction permits such as requirements, determined on a case by case basis, for the installation and operation of control technology sufficient to met the requirements of the AQCA, the CAA, and their regulations. For operating permits, conditions may include imposition of emission limits determined on a case by case basis as necessary to meet the requirements of the AQCA, the CAA, and their regulations; emission rates specified on the application; compliance with applicable federal standards of performance; other restrictions not relating to emission limits; or any combination of such conditions.[21] Any conditions placed upon a permit are enforceable to the same extent as a regulation.[22]

---

18 N.M. Stat. Ann. § 74-2-7(A) (Repl. Pamp. 1993).

19 N.M. Stat. Ann. § 74-2-7(B) (Repl. Pamp. 1993).

20 N.M. Stat. Ann. § 74-2-7(C) (Repl. Pamp. 1993).

21 N.M. Stat. Ann. § 74-2-7(D) (Repl. Pamp. 1993).

22 N.M. Stat. Ann. § 74-2-7(F) (Repl. Pamp. 1993).

Any person who participated in a permitting action is entitled to notice of action taken by NMED or the local agency.[23] Those adversely affected are entitled to request a hearing by making a written request to EIB or the Board, as appropriate, within 30 days after notice of the permit decision. Thereafter, it is required that EIB or the Board hold a hearing within 90 days.[24] If EIB or the Board determines that the subject of the petition substantially affects the public interest, it is required that the public receive notice of the date, time, and place of the hearing and that the public be given a reasonable opportunity to submit data, views, and arguments and to examine witnesses testifying at the hearing.[25] All hearings must be recorded and EIB or the Board may appoint a hearing officer to take evidence.[26] The burden of proof in such hearings is on the petitioner and EIB or the Board may sustain, modify, or reverse the action petitioned against.[27] Adversely affected persons may appeal administrative actions of EIB, the Board, the Secretary, or the local director by filing a notice of appeal with the New Mexico Court of Appeals within 30 days after the decision date. The appeal must be on the record made at the hearing and the Court of Appeals is directed to set aside the decision only if it is found to be arbitrary, capricious, or an abuse of discretion, not supported by substantial evidence in the record, or otherwise not in accordance with law.[28] After a hearing and a showing of good cause, a stay of the action appealed may be granted by either EIB, the Board, NMED, or the local agency or by the Court of Appeals if the administrative agencies deny or fail to act upon a stay application within 60 days after it is received.[29]

EIB and the Board, as appropriate, are authorized to grant variances from the limitations of the AQCA or Board regulations or any permit condition, when compliance will result in an arbitrary and unreasonable taking of property or will impose an undue economic burden and the grant of a variance will not result in injury to the health or safety of the public or cause or contribute to an air contaminant level in excess of a primary NAAQS.[30] When a variance is granted on the ground that there is no known practical means available for adequate air pollution control, the variance may exist only until a means of control becomes available. If a variance is granted on the ground that the air pollution control measures required must be spread over a considerable period of time because of their extent

---

23 N.M. Stat. Ann. § 74-2-7(G) (Repl. Pamp. 1993).

24 N.M. Stat. Ann. § 74-2-7(I) (Repl. Pamp. 1993).

25 *Id.*

26 N.M. Stat. Ann. § 74-2-7(J) (Repl. Pamp. 1993).

27 N.M. Stat. Ann. § 74-2-7(K) (Repl. Pamp. 1993).

28 N.M. Stat. Ann. § 74-2-9 (Repl. Pamp. 1993).

29 *Id.*

30 N.M. Stat. Ann. § 74-2-8(A) (Repl. Pamp. 1993).

or cost, the variance must be for a period not to exceed such time as deemed reasonable and the variance must contain a timetable for implementation of controls.[31] If the variance is granted on the ground that it is justified to prevent hardship, it must be limited to a one-year period.[32] The Secretary or local director must investigate the variance petition and make a recommendation to EIB or the Board, which will hold a public hearing if the recommendation favors the variance. If EIB or the Board is opposed to granting a variance, then a public hearing is held only upon request of the petitioner.

2.1 ENFORCEMENT OF THE AQCA

The Secretary or the local director have the power to issue compliance orders requiring compliance immediately or within a specified time period or assessing a penalty for any past or current violations. In the alternative, a civil action may be commenced in District Court for appropriate relief, including a temporary or permanent injunction.[33] Compliance orders may include a suspension or revocation of any permits and the assessment of a penalty not to exceed $15,000 per day of noncompliance for each violation.[34] A compliance order becomes final unless the person subject to the order submits a written request to the Secretary or the local director for a public hearing within 30 days after the date that the order is served. Upon such a request for hearing, the Secretary or local director must appoint an independent hearing officer to preside over the public hearing, who must make a complete record of the proceeding and forward a recommendation to the Secretary or the local director, who must make the final decision.

EIB and the Board have the power to implement a field citation program for minor violations providing for civil penalties not to exceed $1,000 per day of violation. The field citations may be issued by officers or employees of NMED or the local agency. Persons subject to a field citation may either pay the penalty assessment or request a hearing by the issuing agency.[35] In determining the amount of any penalty, it is required that the seriousness of the violation, any good-faith efforts to comply with applicable requirements, and other relevant factors be taken into account.[36]

The Secretary or the local director is authorized to issue emergency orders to reduce or cease immediately the emission of air contaminants creating emergency conditions. Such orders are enforceable for a 24-hour period. After 24 hours, an action in District Court must

---

31 N.M. Stat. Ann. § 74-2-8(C) (Repl. Pamp. 1993).

32 *Id.*

33 N.M. Stat. Ann. § 74-2-12(A) (Repl. Pamp. 1993).

34 N.M. Stat. Ann. § 74-2-12(B) (Repl. Pamp. 1993).

35 N.M. Stat. Ann. § 74-2-12(D), (E) (Repl. Pamp. 1993).

36 N.M. Stat. Ann. § 74-2-12(G) (Repl. Pamp. 1993).

be commenced whereupon the order will remain effective for an additional 48 hours or for such longer period as authorized by the court.[37]

Any person who violates any provision of the AQCA or any regulation, permit condition, or emergency order pursuant to the AQCA is subject to a civil penalty not to exceed $15,000 for each day during any portion of which a violation occurs.[38]

Persons who knowingly violate any regulation (1) relating to commercial or industrial incineration, (2) adopting any federal standard of performance, (3) relating to control of hazardous air pollutants, or (4) relating to control of toxic air pollutants are guilty of a fourth degree felony.[39] Persons who knowingly violate any other regulations of EIB or the Board are guilty of a misdemeanor.[40] Persons who knowingly make false statements or representations in any application, record, report, plan, or other document required to be maintained under the AQCA or who falsify, tamper with or knowingly render inaccurate any monitoring device required to be maintained under the AQCA or any ordinance or regulation adopted pursuant thereto are guilty of a petty misdemeanor and upon conviction are subject to punishment by a fine of not more than $10,000 or imprisonment for not more than six months, or both.[41] Any person who knowingly releases into the ambient air any hazardous air pollutant or extremely hazardous substance listed under federal laws and who knows at the time that the release creates a substantial danger of death or seriously bodily injury to another person is guilty of a second degree felony and, upon conviction, is subject to a term of imprisonment not to exceed nine years or a fine not to exceed $100,000, or both.[42]

Authorized employees of NMED or the local agency are authorized to enter any premises where an emission source or emissions records required to be maintained are located.[43] NMED employees are further empowered to have access to records which EIB or the Board require the source to maintain, to inspect any monitoring equipment or methods required to be installed, and to sample emissions.[44]

The Enforcement Unit of the Stationary Sources Section of the Air Pollution Control Bureau of NMED has the objective of ensuring that existing sources comply with the AQCA, the AQCRs and permit conditions. The Enforcement Unit accomplishes its objective through

---

[37] N.M. Stat. Ann. § 74-2-10 (Repl. Pamp. 1993).

[38] N.M. Stat. Ann. § 74-2-12.1 (Repl. Pamp. 1993).

[39] N.M. Stat. Ann. § 74-2-14(C) (Repl. Pamp. 1993).

[40] N.M. Stat. Ann. § 74-2-14(D) (Repl. Pamp. 1993).

[41] N.M. Stat. Ann. § 74-2-14(E) (Repl. Pamp. 1993).

[42] N.M. Stat. Ann. § 74-2-14(F) (Repl. Pamp. 1993).

[43] N.M. Stat. Ann. § 74-2-13 (Repl. Pamp. 1993).

[44] *Id.*

a number of source surveillance activities, including source tests, source inspections, material balances, compliance schedules, and visible emission readings.

3.0 PERMITTING AND REPORTING

The focus of New Mexico's regulatory control of air pollution is the permitting process. The basic framework for obtaining pre-construction permits from NMED with regard to new stationary sources, modifications of existing stationary sources, potential sources of toxic air pollutants and sources subject to New Source Performance Standards (NSPS) or National Emission Standards for Hazardous Air Pollutants (NESHAPs) is set forth at AQCR § 702.[45] The permit requirements of AQCR § 702 are in addition to permit requirements pertaining to prevention of significant deterioration (PSD), stationary sources within non-attainment areas, and operating permits.

3.1 PERSONS REQUIRED TO OBTAIN PERMITS

Any person constructing or modifying a stationary source which has a potential emission rate for regulated air contaminants greater than 10 pounds per hour or 25 tons per year must obtain a permit. Persons constructing or modifying (1) any stationary source subject to NSPS or NESHAPs, (2) temporary installations, (3) portable stationary sources, or (4) any stationary source with a potential emission rate for lead greater than five tons per year must also obtain a permit.[46] In addition, sources having potential emissions of toxic air pollutants may be required to obtain a permit.[47] Although it may be necessary for a source owner or operator to comply with several regulations pertaining to the AQCR permitting program, only one permit application is required, which must contain all information required pursuant to each applicable regulation. Source owners or operators may apply for revision to any terms or conditions of issued permits.[48]

3.2 PERMIT PROCESSING, DECISIONS, AND APPEALS

Permit applications must be submitted to NMED on approved forms and must contain, among other things, information sufficient to estimate the maximum quantities of any regulated air contaminants the source will emit and modeling or analysis to show that emissions will not violate any NSPS, NESHAPs, AQCR, NAAQS, or state ambient air quality standard.[49] An applicant is required to provide documentary proof that notice of the filing of the application has been provided to the public and other affected persons in accordance with the regulations.[50] When an application is complete, NMED is required to make it and

---

45 N.M. Air Quality Control Regulations EIB/AQCR, § 702, Part Two.A (filed 5/29/90).

46 N.M. Air Quality Control Regulations § 702, Part Two.A(2) - (3).

47 *See* Toxic Emissions Permits Section of this Chapter.

48 N.M. Air Quality Control Regulations § 702, Part Two.C.

49 N.M. Air Quality Control Regulations § 702, Part Two.D.

50 *Id.*

NMED's preliminary determination available for public inspection and allow at least 45 days for interested persons to submit written comments or evidence.[51] If the Secretary determines that there is significant public interest in an application, a public hearing is required.[52]

NMED has 30 days from the application submittal date to review the completeness of the application. After the application is deemed complete, NMED is required to grant the permit subject to conditions or deny the permit within 120 days, or within 180 days if a public hearing is ordered by the Secretary.[53] NMED must deny permits when it appears that any applicable regulations or standards will not be met.[54] NMED is authorized to impose permit conditions including individual emission limits, installation and operation of control technology, compliance with applicable NSPS and NESHAPs, and construction scheduling requirements.[55] Permit conditions are enforceable to the same extent as AQCRs.[56] An applicant dissatisfied with a NMED decision may submit a written request to the Secretary for a hearing before EIB within 30 days after notice of the decision. EIB is required to hold a hearing within 30 days after receipt of such a request.[57] EIB decisions may be appealed to the New Mexico Court of Appeals.[58]

Permits may be cancelled by NMED (1) when a source ceases operations for five years or more, (2) when source construction or modification is not commenced within two years from the permit issuance date, or (3) if construction or modification work is suspended for a total of one year.[59] Permittees are entitled to prior notice from NMED of a proposed cancellation and an EIB hearing may be requested.[60]

3.2.1 Source Class Streamlining

A permit streamlining process authorizes any source or class of sources to apply for exemption from the procedural requirements of AQCR § 702.[61] Such exemptions may be granted only after an EIB public hearing, and minimum exemption standards must be met. In general, no exemption can be granted unless EIB finds that air quality will be protected

---

51 N.M. Air Quality Control Regulations § 702, Part Two.G.

52 *Id.*

53 N.M. Air Quality Control Regulations § 702, Part Two.H.

54 N.M. Air Quality Control Regulations § 702, Part Two.I.

55 N.M. Air Quality Control Regulations § 702, Part Two.K.

56 *Id.*

57 N.M. Air Quality Control Regulations § 702, Part Two.H.

58 N.M. Stat. Ann. § 74-2-9 (Repl. Pamp. 1993).

59 N.M. Air Quality Control Regulations § 702, Part Two.L.

60 *Id.*

61 N.M. Air Quality Control Regulations § 702, Part Two.O.

at least as well through the streamlined process as by the full permit review process.[62] Protocols established for source class exemption must be submitted by NMED to EPA and are contingent upon EPA approval.[63] The streamlined process does not apply to sources subject to PSD requirements, non-attainment area regulation, NSPS, or NESHAPs.

In addition, source class permit streamlining is available to source categories of reciprocating internal combustion engines, including portable or temporary engines and turbines, used in connection with compressor stations whose primary functions are the extraction of crude oil, natural gas, or water from the earth.[64]

3.2.2 Filing and Permit Fees

A schedule of application filing and permit fees has been established for both stationary and portable sources.[65] The fee schedule includes fees pertaining to standard emissions permits as well as the permits required for PSD, non-attainment areas, NESHAPs, and toxic air pollutant emissions.[66] The fee schedule does not apply to operating permits under proposed AQCR § 770. Operating permit fees will be established under proposed AQCR § 771.[67]

3.2.3 Variances

Variance petitions must be submitted to the Secretary, who is required to issue a recommendation to EIB, which possesses the authority to grant a variance.[68] If EIB favors the granting of a variance, a public hearing is required for consideration of the variance petition. If EIB is initially opposed to the variance petition a public hearing is held only if, after receiving notice of EIB's opposition, the petitioner requests a public hearing. After a public hearing is held before EIB or before a hearing officer designated by EIB, the requested variance may be granted in whole or in part or denied.[69]

While a variance petition is pending, any enforcement action concerning the corresponding regulation is stayed unless the Secretary determines that despite the variance petition enforcement is reasonably necessary to protect the public interest.[70] A variance from compliance with PSD requirements, non-attainment area regulation, NSPS, and NESHAPs is not authorized.

---

62 *Id.*

63 *Id.*

64 N.M. Air Quality Control Regulations § 702, Part Four (filed 5/12/92).

65 N.M. Air Quality Control Regulations § 700 (filed 11/20/89).

66 *Id.*

67 *See* Operating Permits Section of this Chapter.

68 N.M. Air Quality Control Regulations § 701 (filed 10/7/75).

69 *Id.*

70 *Id.*

3.2.4 Schedules of Compliance

All stationary or mobile sources of air contaminants must operate under a schedule of compliance adopted by EIB unless the source has certified to EIB that it is complying with applicable AQCRs.[71] Schedules of compliance may be issued by EIB after the petition of a source owner or operator, which must be filed within 90 days of the effective date of the regulation to be complied with. A schedule of compliance can be adopted by EIB only following a public hearing.[72] The schedule of compliance must include increments of progress that the petitioner must meet to achieve compliance as expeditiously as practicable.[73]

3.2.5 Miscellaneous Permit Requirements

Permittees are required to provide notice to NMED concerning source start-ups and operator changes and may be required to undertake start-up and follow-up performance testing, the results of which must be provided to NMED in the form of written reports.[74]

Emergency permits are authorized when conditions threatening the public health, safety, or welfare require the rapid construction or modification of a source.[75]

In evaluating air quality impacts for proposed new sources or modifications of an existing source, for purposes of the permitting requirements of the AQCRs, no credits are given for emission reductions due to a source's stack height that exceeds good engineering practice or which is due to any other dispersion technique.[76]

Owners or operators of proposed new stationary sources with potential emission rates greater than 10 tons per year of any regulated air contaminants or one ton per year of lead must file a Notice of Intent with NMED, whether or not a permit is required, as a condition to construction.[77] Additionally, annual emissions inventories must be submitted to NMED by most owners or operators of stationary sources.[78] Emissions inventory submittal requirements are in addition to requirements that owners or operators of stationary sources maintain records of the nature and amount of emissions, which must be reported annually to NMED.[79]

---

71 N.M. Air Quality Control Regulations § 705 (filed 12/5/74).

72 *Id.*

73 *Id.*

74 N.M. Air Quality Control Regulations § 702, Part Two.M - .N.

75 N.M. Air Quality Control Regulations § 702, Part Two.P.

76 Additional details concerning stack requirements can be found in AQCR § 710 (filed 3/15/88).

77 N.M. Air Quality Control Regulations § 703.1, Part Two.A.

78 N.M. Air Quality Control Regulations § 703.1, Part Three.B.

79 N.M. Air Quality Control Regulations § 704 (filed 7/31/72).

The counties of Bernalillo, Chaves, Doña Ana, San Juan and Santa Fe have been designated as Air Quality Maintenance Areas because the current or projected air quality due to growth has the potential for exceeding a national ambient air quality standard.[80]

3.3 TOXIC EMISSIONS PERMITS

Any new source or source modification which has total potential emissions of a toxic air pollutant exceeding specified quantities and which meets other specified conditions must obtain a permit.[81] EIB has adopted a source-by-source permit-based approach due to the absence of approved toxic air pollutant ambient air standards in New Mexico. NMED is given limited authority to use Occupational Exposure Limits (OELs) as guides for evaluating permit applications.[82] Eight classes of sources are exempt from the permitting requirements for toxic air pollutants: (1) gasoline service stations, (2) automotive repair shops, (3) laundry, cleaning, and garment services, (4) domestic wood stoves and fireplaces, (5) oil and gas production facilities, (6) agricultural production and services, (7) containers that may emit toxic air pollutants used in connection with stationary sources and (8) non-process fugitive emissions of toxic air pollutants from stationary sources.[83]

Toxic air pollutant permit applications must include identification of all toxic air pollutants that may be emitted in excess of the specified pounds per hour standards and air quality modeling in accordance with EPA or NMED approved methods.[84] Health assessments for certain toxic air pollutants must be provided if air quality modeling shows average ambient concentrations of toxic air pollutants in excess of specified standards.[85] If an identified toxic air pollutant is a known or suspected human carcinogen and emissions concentrations exceed specified limits, the permit application must include information demonstrating that the source will install the best available control technology (BACT)[86] to control that pollutant.[87]

NMED toxic air pollutant permit decisions are controlled in part by the mandate that permits must be granted if ambient concentrations fall below certain specified limits, generally measured in terms of OELs or, with regard to known or suspected human carcinogens in which the emissions are projected to exceed OEL limits, if the applicant implements the best

---

80 N.M. Air Quality Control Regulations § 706 (filed 12/5/74).

81 N.M. Air Quality Control Regulations § 702, Part Three.C.

82 N.M. Air Quality Control Regulations § 702, Part Three.A.

83 N.M. Air Quality Control Regulations § 702, Part Three.C(3).

84 N.M. Air Quality Control Regulations § 702, Part Three.D(1).

85 N.M. Air Quality Control Regulations § 702, Part Three.D(2).

86 N.M. Air Quality Control Regulations § 702, Part Three.B(1).

87 N.M. Air Quality Control Regulations § 702, Part Three.D(3).

available control technology.[88] When projected emissions of non-carcinogens exceed an applicable OEL, NMED is required to prepare a Summary Review Statement including a recommendation on whether the emissions will or will not with reasonable probability injure human health.[89]

An applicant who does not agree with the recommendation contained in the Summary Review Statement can seek review by the Air Toxics Scientific Advisory Committee, a five-member expert committee appointed by the Secretary, which will evaluate the applicant's assessment and the Summary Review Statement and provide an advisory letter to NMED. NMED is then required to make a final decision after consideration of six specified factors and must deny any application if it is determined that the source will emit a toxic air pollutant in such quantities as may with reasonable probability injure human health.[90]

All stationary sources that have a potential emission rate for toxic air pollutants above specified levels, except those exempt from permitting requirements, are also subject to registration requirements.[91] The purpose of the registration requirements is to develop an emissions inventory for potential sources of toxic air pollutants.[92] The screening levels used in determining whether a source is required to be registered are tied to occupational health guidelines.[93]

3.4 PREVENTION OF SIGNIFICANT DETERIORATION

The Prevention of Significant Deterioration (PSD) program is designed to maintain the primary and secondary NAAQS established by EPA and requires pre-construction review of proposed major stationary sources[94] or of major modifications.[95] The PSD program

---

88 N.M. Air Quality Control Regulations § 702, Part Three.F.

89 *Id.*

90 *Id.*

91 N.M. Air Quality Control Regulations § 752 (filed 8/18/87).

92 N.M. Air Quality Control Regulations § 752.A.

93 *Id.*

94 N.M. Air Quality Control Regulations § 707 (filed 5/29/90). "Major stationary source" is defined in N.M. Air Quality Control Regulations § 707.P.26 as: (a) any stationary source listed in Table 1 [*See* Section 3.4.1 of this Chapter], which emits or has the potential to emit emissions equal to or greater than 100 tons per year of any regulated pollutant; or (b) any stationary source not listed in Table 1 and which emits or has the potential to emit 250 tons per year or more of any regulated pollutant; or (c) any physical change that would occur at a stationary source not otherwise qualifying under 26.(a) or (b) of this section if the change would constitute a major stationary source by itself; (d) any major stationary source or modification to an existing stationary source that is major for volatile organic compounds must be considered major for ozone.

95 N.M. Air Quality Control Regulations § 707.P(24).

requires that a pre-construction permit be obtained by any person constructing any new major stationary source or major modification that emits regulated pollutants in an attainment or unclassified area.[96] The program prohibits emissions increases from a proposed major source or modification which cause or contribute to air pollution in violation of any NAAQS or any applicable maximum allowable increase as shown in Table 4 of AQCR § 707.[97] New major stationary sources and major modifications are required to apply BACT for each regulated pollutant that would be emitted in amounts greater than specified significance levels.[98] In the alternative, NMED is authorized to approve innovative control technology[99] systems which would not contribute to an unreasonable risk to public health, welfare, or safety if the source owner or operator agrees to achieve a level of continuous emissions reductions by a specified date which is equivalent to that which would have been required under the BACT requirements.[100]

Applications for PSD permits must include an analysis of impairments to visibility, soils, and vegetation arising from the proposed emissions as well as from general commercial, residential, industrial, or other growth associated with the source.[101] Applications must also include an area-wide ambient air quality analysis when a source would potentially emit pollutants equal to or greater than the significance levels or when a major modification would result in a significant net emission increase.[102] Continuous air quality monitoring data for the area affected must be submitted to NMED for the one-year period prior to submittal of the permit application for all pollutants for which a NAAQS exists. NMED may also require post-construction ambient air monitoring to validate attainment of ambient air quality standards.[103] Additional monitoring may be required for visibility in any federal Class I[104] area where NMED determines an adverse impact on visibility may occur due primarily to the

---

96 N.M. Air Quality Control Regulations § 707.A.

97 N.M. Air Quality Control Regulations § 707.F.

98 N.M. Air Quality Control Regulations § 707, Table 2.

99 N.M. Air Quality Control Regulations § 707.P(22).

100 N.M. Air Quality Control Regulations § 707.E.

101 N.M. Air Quality Control Regulations § 707.G.

102 N.M. Air Quality Control Regulations § 707.I.

103 *Id.*

104 Federal Class I area means any of the following areas in New Mexico which were in existence on August 7, 1977: (1) national wilderness areas which exceed 5,000 acres in size and (2) national parks which exceed 6,000 acres in size. N.M. Stat. Ann. § 74-2-2(L) (Repl. Pamp. 1993). Nine Class I areas exist in New Mexico: Wheeler Peak Wilderness, San Pedro Parks Wilderness, Bandelier Wilderness, Pecos Wilderness, Gila Wilderness, Bosque del Apache Wilderness, White Mountain Wilderness, Salt Creek Wilderness, and Carlsbad Caverns National Park.

proposed new source or modification.[105] Sources impacting Class I areas are subject to additional restrictions and application submittal requirements.[106]

3.4.1 PSD Source Categories[107]

1. Fossil Fuel-fired steam electric plants of more than 250 million BTU/hr heat input
2. Coal cleaning plants (with thermal dryers)
3. Kraft pulp mills
4. Portland cement plants
5. Primary zinc smelters
6. Iron and steel mill plants
7. Primary aluminum ore reduction pollutants
8. Primary copper smelter
9. Municipal incinerators capable of charging more than 250 tons of refuse per day
10. Hydrofluoric acid plants
11. Sulfuric acid plants
12. Nitric acid plants
13. Petroleum refineries
14. Lime plants
15. Phosphate rock processing plants
16. Coke oven batteries
17. Sulfur recovery plants
18. Carbon black plants (furnace process)
19. Primary lead smelters
20. Fuel conversion plants
21. Sintering plants
22. Secondary metal production plants
23. Chemical process plants
24. Fossil fuel boiler (or combinations thereof) totaling more than 250 million BTU/hr heat input
25. Petroleum storage and transfer units with a total storage capacity exceeding 300,000 barrels
26. Taconite ore processing plants
27. Glass Fiber processing plants
28. Charcoal production plants

3.5 NON-ATTAINMENT AREAS

A non-attainment area is one which is shown by monitored data or calculated by air quality modeling to exceed any NAAQS.[108] The non-attainment designation is made separately for each air pollutant, and an area may be attainment for one air pollutant and

---

105 N.M. Air Quality Control Regulations § 707.I(5).

106 N.M. Air Quality Control Regulations § 707.O.

107 N.M. Air Quality Control Regulations § 707, Table 1 (filed 5/29/90).

108 N.M. Air Quality Control Regulations § 709.K(22) (filed 6/25/92).

non-attainment for another. Bernalillo County has been designated by EPA as a non-attainment area for carbon monoxide and an area within Grant County has been designated as non-attainment for SO_2.

Any new major stationary source (generally a source which emits or has the potential to emit 100 tons or more per year of a regulated pollutant) or major modification otherwise subject to AQCR § 702 which will be located within a non-attainment area and will emit a regulated pollutant for which the area is designated non-attainment must obtain a pre-construction permit from NMED.[109] In addition, major stationary sources or major modifications located within attainment or unclassified areas which will emit a regulated pollutant must obtain a permit if the ambient impact of such pollutant would exceed certain significance levels at locations that do not meet a NAAQS for that pollutant.[110]

In order for a non-attainment area permit to be granted, a major stationary source or major modification must be designed so that the lowest achievable emission rate (LAER) will be achieved for each regulated pollutant.[111] In addition, existing major stationary sources must be in compliance with all applicable emissions limitations, the CAA and all conditions of any federally enforceable permit.

Further, applicants must show that emissions reductions (offsets) at existing sources must occur prior to or concurrent with the start of the operation of the proposed stationary source or modification.[112] As a general rule, offsets must be at least 20 percent greater than the allowable emissions from the proposed new stationary source or modification.[113] At a minimum the new stationary source or modification must obtain sufficient offsets to compensate for adverse ambient impacts which would contribute to a violation of an NAAQS. Banking of emissions reductions is permitted so that any stationary source which decreases actual emissions of a regulated pollutant in excess of the regulation requirements may preserve such excess emission reductions for sale or future use.[114] Finally, a permit will not be granted unless the emissions offsets provide a net air quality benefit in the area where the NAAQS for a particular pollutant is violated and all applicable requirements of the SIP, NSPS, and NESHAPs will be met.[115]

Any stationary source or modification which will emit a regulated pollutant resulting in an excessive ambient concentration at a location which does not meet NAAQS for the

---

109 N.M. Air Quality Control Regulations § 709.A.

110 *Id.*

111 N.M. Air Quality Control Regulations § 709.D.

112 *Id.*

113 *Id.*

114 N.M. Air Quality Control Regulations § 709.H.

115 N.M. Air Quality Control Regulations § 709.D.

emitted pollutant must obtain emissions offsets for proposed emissions which will result in a net air quality benefit for the impacted location and satisfy other requirements.[116]

Additional requirements are imposed for sources impacting on federal Class I areas.[117]

3.6 OPERATING PERMITS

The 1990 CAA Amendments mandated that each state adopt a program for operating permits no later than November 15, 1993.[118] It is anticipated that EIB will promulgate operating permit regulations on or before that deadline. Draft regulations have been issued by NMED and as of the date of this writing are being considered in public hearings. The material in this section is based upon the draft regulations. Readers should refer to the final regulations as promulgated.

3.6.1 Applications and Permit Contents

Any source, including an area source, a major source, an acid rain source, or a source designated by EPA is required to obtain an operating permit.[119] The operating permit requirement is in addition to pre-construction permit requirements. Several specified source categories, including sources on Indian sovereign lands, are exempt from operating permit requirements.[120]

A source operator must submit a timely and complete application to NMED[121] or to the Air Pollution Control Division of the Albuquerque Environmental Health Department if the operator is located in Bernalillo County.[122] Generally, applications must be filed within 12 months after the effective date of the regulation.[123] Shorter application deadlines are required of certain oil and gas operations and specific deadlines are required for certain acid rain sources.[124] Unless NMED notifies an applicant that additional information is needed or that the application is incomplete within sixty days of the receipt of the application, the application must be deemed complete.

To be deemed complete, the application must contain information regarding the source's operator, its location, a description of its processes and products, all emissions information, calculations, and computations for each emissions unit, a citation and description

---

116 N.M. Air Quality Control Regulations § 702, Part Two.Q.

117 N.M. Air Quality Control Regulations § 709.E.

118 42 U.S.C. § 7661a(d).

119 Proposed N.M. Air Quality Control Regulations § 770, Part Two.A.

120 Proposed N.M. Air Quality Control Regulations § 770, Part Two.F.

121 Proposed N.M. Air Quality Control Regulations § 770, Part Three.A.

122 Proposed N.M. Air Quality Control Regulations § 770, Part Two.E.

123 Proposed N.M. Air Quality Control Regulation § 770, Part Three.A.

124 *Id.*

of all applicable air pollution control requirements, a certification of compliance, and an explanation of any proposed exemptions for otherwise applicable requirements.[125] For all major sources that have not submitted dispersion modeling analysis since January 1, 1986, submittal of dispersion modeling analysis showing whether ambient air impacts from emissions would contribute to violation of New Mexico or federal air quality standards is required.[126] For sources that are not in compliance with all applicable requirements at the time of the application, the application must also contain a compliance plan which describes how the source will achieve compliance and a schedule of remedial measures to achieve compliance.[127] Under the provisions of AQCR 110, NMED will review claims that the application contains confidential information.[128]

The operating permit must specify conditions, including emission limitations and operational requirements, to assure compliance with all applicable requirements.[129] The permit must contain a severability clause to ensure the validity of the various permit requirements in the event any portion of the permit is successfully challenged.[130] Each permit issued must, additionally, include provisions stating that noncompliance is grounds for enforcement action, in which case NMED may modify, revoke, reopen and reissue, or terminate the permit.[131]

Operational flexibility is provided for sources by allowing operational changes which contravene an express permit term but would not violate applicable requirements or permit terms and conditions that relate to monitoring, recordkeeping, reporting, or compliance certification and do not result in exceeding emissions limitations under the permit. These changes may be accomplished without applying for permit modification.[132] Permittees are required to provide notice to NMED and EPA at least seven days in advance of such proposed changes.

NMED may include in an operating permit a provision that compliance with permit conditions must be deemed compliance with any applicable requirements as of the date of permit issuance, provided such applicable requirements specifically are identified in the permit or NMED determines in writing that specifically identified requirements are not applicable

---

125 Proposed N.M. Air Quality Control Regulations § 770, Part Three.A.(4).

126 *Id.*

127 *Id.*

128 Proposed N.M. Air Quality Control Regulations § 770, Part Three.B.

129 Proposed N.M. Air Quality Control Regulations § 770, Part Three.C.

130 *Id.*

131 *Id.; see also* Proposed N.M. Air Quality Control Regulations § 770, Part Three.B.

132 Proposed N.M. Air Quality Control Regulation § 770, Part Three.C(8).

to the source. A permit that does not state expressly that a permit shield exists must be presumed not to provide such a shield.[133]

To assure that sources comply with permit conditions, authorized representatives of NMED must be allowed to enter the permittee's premises, have access to and copy records, inspect the facilities, equipment, practices or operations, and sample or monitor substances or parameters.[134] In certain instances, the source's application for an operating permit must contain an EPA approved modeling analysis showing whether the ambient air impacts from significant emissions, when combined with neighboring sources, would contribute to violation of any New Mexico ambient air quality standard for nitrogen oxides, sulfur oxides, or total suspended particulates or any NAAQS.[135]

The permit does not convey any property right or exclusive privilege.[136] Moreover, the issuance of a permit does not relieve an individual from civil or criminal liability concerning any applicable law or regulation.[137] Operating permits must be issued for a fixed term not to exceed 5 years.[138] Permits are also required to contain emissions monitoring procedures, recordkeeping, and reporting sufficient to assure and verify compliance, including submittal of compliance certification reports at least every 12 months.[139]

Instead of issuing operating permits on a case-by-case basis, NMED may, after notice and opportunity for public participation and EPA and affected program[140] review, issue general operating permits to cover numerous similar sources.[141] These sources must be similar in terms of operations, processes, and emissions and must be subject to similar requirements.[142]

---

133 *Id.*

134 Proposed N.M. Air Quality Control Regulation § 770, Part Three.C(7). Permittees must also submit periodical progress reports to the department. *Id.*

135 *Id.*

136 Proposed N.M. Air Quality Control Regulations § 770, Part Three.C(1).

137 *Id.*

138 Proposed N.M. Air Quality Control Regulations § 770, Part Three.C(2).

139 Proposed N.M. Air Quality Regulation § 770, Part Three.C(3) - (5).

140 "Affected programs" means all states, local air pollution control programs and Indian Tribes and Pueblos, that are within 50 miles of the source. Proposed N.M. Air Quality Control Regulations § 770, Part One.

141 Proposed N.M. Air Quality Control Regulations § 770, Part Three.D.

142 *Id.*

3.6.2 Permit Processing

Permits may be issued only if five basic conditions have been met: (1) NMED has received a complete application; (2) public participation procedures have been satisfied; (3) notification and response to affected programs has been accomplished; (4) permit conditions provide for compliance with all applicable requirements; (5) and EPA has received a copy of the permit and has not objected to its issuance.[143] NMED approval or disapproval of permits must be based upon information contained in the administrative record.

Generally, within 18 months after it has deemed an application to be complete, NMED must issue or deny the permit.[144] If the application is deemed complete, the applicant must submit a copy of the complete permit application directly to EPA and any affected program for review before the permit can be issued.[145] NMED is prohibited from issuing an operating permit until affected programs and EPA have had an opportunity to review the proposed permit. NMED is prohibited from issuing a permit when EPA objects to such issuance in writing within 45 days of receipt of the proposed permit and supporting information. If EPA does not object within 45 days, any person may within 60 days thereafter petition EPA to make such objection. If EPA then objects, NMED is prohibited from issuing a permit until the objection has been resolved. A petition to EPA for review does not stay the effectiveness of a permit issued after the end of the 45-day review period and prior to EPA objection. NMED is required as part of its submittal of proposed permits to EPA to notify EPA and any affected program in writing of refusal by NMED to accept all recommendations submitted by an affected program during the public review period.[146]

For sources in operation before the effective date of the regulation, NMED is required to take final action on one-third of such applications annually over a period not to exceed three years after such effective date. Any application containing an early reduction demonstration under the CAA must be acted on within nine months. Actions on acid rain portions of permits for acid rain sources must be taken in accordance with deadlines in Title IV of the 1990 CAA Amendments and regulations promulgated thereunder.[147]

The proceedings for all permit issuances, renewals, significant modifications, reopenings, revocations, and terminations must include public notice and provide opportunity for public comment. NMED must provide 30 days for comment.[148] In addition, NMED must hold a public hearing when there is significant public interest and provide 30 days

---

143 Proposed N.M. Air Quality Control Regulations § 770, Part Four.A(1).

144 Proposed N.M. Air Quality Control Regulations § 770, Part Four.A(3).

145 Proposed N.M. Air Quality Control Regulations § 770, Part Four.A(2),C.

146 Proposed N.M. Air Quality Control Regulations § 770, Part Four.C.

147 Proposed N.M. Air Quality Control Regulations § 770, Part Four.A(3).

148 Proposed N.M. Air Quality Control Regulations § 770, Part Four.B.

advance notice of the hearing.[149] Public notice of permit applications must be given by publication in a newspaper of general circulation in the area where the sources are located or in a state publication designed to give general public notice to persons on a mailing list developed by NMED. Public hearings must be held in the geographic area likely to be impacted by the source.[150]

Any person adversely affected by NMED permitting actions may file a petition for a hearing before EIB within 30 days from the date notice is given of such actions.[151] "Permitting action" includes the department's failure to take final action on an application for a permit within the specified time period.[152] Upon timely filing of a petition for hearing, NMED must certify the administrative record to EIB. Any person adversely affected by an EIB decision may appeal to the New Mexico Court of Appeals within 30 days after notice of the decision.[153] Additionally, any person may commence a civil action pursuant to the citizen suit provisions of the CAA.[154]

3.6.3 Permit Modifications

An operating permit may be modified.[155] A significant permit modification requires that the permittee meet all the requirements for permit issuance.[156] A permittee may, however, apply to NMED for a minor modification to its operating permit if it does not violate or relax any applicable regulation or standard.[157] Before issuing a permit modification, NMED must determine whether the application is complete and must provide EPA time to review the application.[158] The permittee may also request that NMED allow an administrative permit modification.[159] NMED may allow an administrative permit modification without providing notice to the public or affected programs as long as it designates the modifications as administrative and submits a copy of the revised permit to EPA.[160] The permittee may also make changes not addressed in or prohibited by the operating permit or other applicable requirements ("off-permit changes") by providing NMED

---

149 *Id.*

150 *Id.*

151 Proposed N.M. Air Quality Control Regulations § 770, Part Four.D.

152 *Id.*

153 *Id.*

154 Proposed N.M. Air Quality Control Regulations § 770, Part Four.G.

155 Proposed N.M. Air Quality Control Regulations § 770, Part Four.E.

156 Proposed N.M. Air Quality Control Regulations § 770, Part Four.E.(3).

157 Proposed N.M. Air Quality Control Regulations § 770, Part Four.E(2).

158 *Id.*

159 Proposed N.M. Air Quality Control Regulations § 770, Part Four.E(1).

160 *Id.*

with written notice of such changes.[161] Applicants and permittees may also seek a variance from the non-federally enforceable provisions pursuant to N.M. Stat. Ann. § 74-2-8 (Repl. Pamp. 1993).[162]

A permit will be reopened and revised, or revoked and reissued, when additional federal requirements become applicable, the permit contains a material mistake, or EPA determines that the permit must be revised or revoked and reissued to assure compliance with applicable requirements.[163]

Each owner or operator required to obtain an operating permit must pay an annual operating permit fee.[164] The amount of the fee depends on the type and amount of pollutant emitted by the source.[165] Proposed annual fees for each fee pollutant are $10.50 per ton and for hazardous pollutants are $150 per ton.[166] The amount of pollutant emissions is calculated based upon the allowable emission rate applicable to the source.[167] A maximum of 6,000 tons per year of any one fee pollutant is established in the fee calculation.[168] Fee rates are subject to annual adjustments based upon CPI increases. Failure to pay the required fee may result in civil penalties or suspension or revocation of the permit.

4.0 NEW SOURCE PERFORMANCE STANDARDS

New Mexico has adopted the New Source Performance Standards (NSPS) of EPA, contained in 40 C.F.R. Part 60 as amended through November 15, 1991, excluding only the Standards of Performance for New Residential Wood Heaters contained in 40 C.F.R. Part 60, Subpart AAA.[169] EPA delegated to New Mexico its authority to enforce the NSPS program.

A standard of performance under NSPS is an allowable emission limitation for a given category of sources which reflects the degree of emission limitation and the percentage reduction achievable through application of the best technological system of continuous emission reduction which (taking into consideration the cost of achieving such emission

---

161 Proposed N.M. Air Quality Control Regulations § 770, Part Three.C(9).

162 Proposed N.M. Air Quality Control Regulations § 770, Part Four.H.

163 Proposed N.M. Air Quality Control Regulations § 770, Part Four.F.

164 Proposed N.M. Air Quality Control Regulations § 771, Part Three.

165 *Id.*

166 Proposed N.M. Air Quality Control Regulations § 771, Part Five.A.; "Fee pollutant" and "hazardous pollutant" are defined in Proposed N.M. Air Quality Control Regulations § 771, Part One.

167 Proposed N.M. Air Quality Control Regulations § 771, Part Four.

168 *Id.*

169 N.M. Air Quality Control Regulations § 750 (filed 4/14/92).

reduction and any non-air quality, health and environmental impact and energy requirements) the EPA Administrator determines has been adequately demonstrated.[170] NSPS are promulgated for stationary sources which the EPA Administrator determines cause or contribute significantly to air pollution and which may reasonably be anticipated to endanger public health or welfare.[171]

5.0 HAZARDOUS AIR POLLUTANT EMISSION STANDARDS

New Mexico has adopted the National Emission Standard for Hazardous Air Pollutants (NESHAPs), contained in 40 C.F.R. Part 61 as amended through November 15, 1991, with the exception of 40 C.F.R. Part 61, Subparts B (Radon-222 Emissions from Underground Uranium Mines), H (Radionuclide Emissions from Department of Energy Facilities), I (Radionuclide Emissions from Facilities Licensed by the NRC and Federal Facilities not covered by Subpart H), R (Radon Emissions from Phosphogypsum Stacks), T (Radon Emissions From the Disposal of Uranium Mill Tailings), and W (Radon-222 Emissions from Licensed Uranium Mill Tailings).[172] New Mexico has been delegated the authority to implement and enforce NESHAPs.

A hazardous air pollutant is one to which no ambient air quality standard is applicable and which the EPA Administrator determines causes air pollution which may reasonably be anticipated to result in an increase in mortality or in serious or incapacitating illness.[173] NESHAPs are emission standards established by the EPA Administrator to provide an ample margin of safety to protect the public health.[174] If it is determined that establishing an emissions standard is not feasible, a design, equipment, work practice, or operational standard may be promulgated.[175] NESHAPs have been established for radon-222, beryllium, mercury, vinyl chloride, radionuclides, benzene, asbestos, and other substances.[176]

Any source owner or operator subject to a NESHAPs standard must obtain pre-construction approval from the Secretary and comply with other notification and reporting requirements.[177]

6.0 MISCELLANEOUS EXCESS EMISSIONS

Owners or operators of facilities which emit air contaminants are required to notify NMED in the event of excess air contaminant emissions arising from malfunction of or

---

170 42 U.S.C. § 7411(a).

171 42 U.S.C. § 7411(b)(1)(A).

172 N.M. Air Quality Control Regulations § 751 (filed 4/22/91).

173 42 U.S.C. § 7412(a)(1).

174 42 U.S.C. § 7412(b).

175 42 U.S.C. § 7412(e)(1).

176 40 C.F.R. Part 61.

177 40 C.F.R. Part 61, Subpart A.

damage to equipment, startup or shutdown of operations, or scheduled maintenance.[178] Failure to comply with notification requirements constitutes a violation of the applicable AQCR.[179] In order to avoid a violation, owners or operators must demonstrate to NMED that such excess emissions will be mitigated as much as practicable.[180] Facilities which start up or shut down frequently as part of their routine operations are exempt from notification requirements but are required to submit a written report to NMED which must include, among other things, the operating schedule and expected frequency of the startups or shutdowns.[181] Waivers of notification requirements are also available to facilities found to be in compliance with state emission standards on six successive inspections within an 18-month period and which have a record of complying with the notification requirements during such period.[182]

7.0 EMISSIONS CROSSING STATE BOUNDARIES

Air contaminant emissions generated from sources in New Mexico which cross the state boundary lines cannot exceed the standards and regulations of the bordering state, provided the bordering state has adopted reciprocal standards and regulations governing sources in that state whose emissions may travel into New Mexico.[183] Arizona, Colorado, and Texas have adopted federal standards and regulations regarding priority pollutants which are equivalent to those of New Mexico.

8.0 MUNICIPAL WASTE COMBUSTION

Owners or operators of any municipal waste combustion unit, which is defined as an incinerator, furnace, or boiler used to dispose of municipal waste by combustion either alone or with fossil fuel, must comply with emission limits, design and operational requirements, monitoring and testing, and recordkeeping and reporting standards established by regulation.[184]

Emission limits are established for particulate matter, SO_2, CO, NO_x, polychlorinated substances, total hydrocarbons, and various metals.[185] Compliance with emissions limits is required to be determined by emission monitor measurements and manual tests.[186]

---

178 N.M. Air Quality Control Regulations § 801.A (filed 5/29/81).

179 *Id.*

180 *Id.*

181 N.M. Air Quality Control Regulations § 801.C.

182 N.M. Air Quality Control Regulations § 801.E.

183 N.M. Air Quality Control Regulations § 901 (filed 1/27/70).

184 N.M. Air Quality Control Regulations § 2000 (filed 11/16/90).

185 N.M. Air Quality Control Regulations § 2000, Table 1.

186 N.M. Air Quality Control Regulations § 2000, § 301.

Applicable requirements of NSPS must also be complied with.[187] Design and operational requirements are established[188] and quarterly reporting to NMED is required. Municipal waste combustion units are not subject to the startup, shutdown, and maintenance notification requirements of AQCR § 801, but startup and shutdown restrictions are imposed and units are required to be equipped with a visual and audible alarm to notify the operator when required combustion temperatures have not been met.[189]

Handling and storage of ash must be conducted in a closed system which prevents ash from becoming airborne, and disposal of ash must be in compliance with applicable solid waste management regulations.[190] Operating personnel are subject to certification and training requirements.[191]

Waste material separation is mandated prior to combustion such that an overall reduction of at least 25 percent by weight on an annual basis is achieved.[192]

All applications for a municipal waste incinerator permit must include a formal assessment of risk to the population and the environment which may be affected by the incinerator.[193]

9.0 CONFIDENTIAL INFORMATION PROTECTION

Upon a satisfactory showing by any person that records, reports, or information to which NMED, EIB, or local boards or agencies have access under the AQCA, if made public, would divulge confidential business records or methods or processes entitled to protection as trade secrets, such record, report, or information must be considered confidential.[194]

The Confidential Information Protection regulation enacted in 1990 provides that items submitted by an applicant marked as confidential which concern processes or production techniques unique to the applicant or which relate to profits and costs not previously released to the public are not to be made a part of any public record without the express consent of the applicant. Confidentiality claims are subject to review by NMED. NMED confidentiality determinations are final for administrative purposes but are subject to judicial review.[195]

---

187 N.M. Air Quality Control Regulations § 2000, § 201.

188 N.M. Air Quality Control Regulations § 2000, Part IV.

189 N.M. Air Quality Control Regulations § 2000, Part VIII.

190 N.M. Air Quality Control Regulations § 2000, Part IX; *See also* N.M. Solid Waste Management Regulations § 707 (filed 5/29/90).

191 N.M. Air Quality Control Regulations § 2000, Part X.

192 N.M. Air Quality Control Regulations § 2000, Part XI.

193 N.M. Air Quality Control Regulations § 2000, Part XII.

194 N.M. Stat. Ann. § 74-2-11 (Repl. Pamp. 1993).

195 N.M. Air Quality Control Regulations § 110.

10.0 OPEN BURNING, SMOKE, AND VISIBLE EMISSIONS

Open burning is generally prohibited but is subject to numerous exceptions, including burning for recreational and ceremonial purposes, non-commercial cooking, burning of natural gas at gasoline plant and compressor stations, and burning of explosive materials when transportation of such materials to other facilities could be dangerous. Open burning also is permitted under certain conditions for communities having a population of less than 3,000 which do not have public refuse collection services. A permit for open burning may be obtained in a number of specified situations.[196]

The visual quality of the state's air is also specifically addressed by regulating particulate emissions from stationary combustion equipment not otherwise regulated. Visible emissions from such equipment may not exceed an opacity of 20 percent.[197]

11.0 INDUSTRY OR OPERATION-SPECIFIC REGULATIONS

EIB has adopted numerous AQCRs, which are described in this section, which apply to specific industries, industrial processes, and equipment.

11.1 WOODWASTE BURNERS

Emissions from woodwaste burners which equal or exceed an opacity of 20 percent are prohibited except during startup or daily burn-down.[198] Woodwaste burners must be equipped with continuous measure equipment to record the temperature of exiting gases. Woodwaste burner owners or operators are required to retain monitoring records for a period of six months from the date of each day's recordings.[199]

11.2 ASPHALT PROCESSING EQUIPMENT

Particulate matter emissions from asphalt processing equipment are limited. Fugitive dust control systems which limit all particulate emissions to the stack outlet are required.[200] NMED may suspend the regulation for portable asphalt processing equipment operated for not more than 90 days in rural areas when reasonably necessary for completion of a project.[201]

11.3 CEMENT KILNS

Cement kiln operators are prohibited from allowing particulate matter emissions in excess of 230 milligrams per cubic meter of exhaust gas.[202]

---

196 N.M. Air Quality Control Regulations § 301 (filed 7/24/84).

197 N.M. Air Quality Control Regulations § 401 (filed 7/15/86).

198 N.M. Air Quality Control Regulations § 402.A (filed 2/8/83).

199 N.M. Air Quality Control Regulations § 402.B (filed 2/28/83).

200 N.M. Air Quality Control Regulations § 501.C (filed 7/1/71).

201 N.M. Air Quality Control Regulations § 501.D.

202 N.M. Air Quality Control Regulations § 502 (filed 1/27/70).

11.4 GYPSUM PROCESSING PLANTS

Operators of equipment for gypsum processing are prohibited from allowing particulate matter emissions in excess of 690 milligrams per cubic meter of exhaust gas.[203]

11.5 COAL BURNING EQUIPMENT

Particulate matter emissions from coal burning equipment are regulated by establishing allowable emissions in pounds per million British thermal units (BTUs) input per hour.[204] The emissions limitations are divided into three categories depending on the rated heat capacity of the coal burning equipment. The rated heat capacity categories are: less than or equal to 250 million BTUs per hour; between 250 million and 5,000 million BTUs per hour; and equal to or greater than 5,000 million BTUs per hour.

SO_2 emissions from coal burning equipment are regulated.[205] All coal burning equipment with a power generating capacity in excess of 25 megawatts or a heat input of greater than 250 million BTUs per hour is subject to emissions limitations. The extent of emissions limitation is based upon the date on which the coal burning equipment began commercial operation. Owners and operators of coal burning equipment are required to maintain at least one NMED approved monitor for continuous measurement of SO_2 concentrations in the gases within each stack from which flue gases are released to the atmosphere.[206] In addition, owners and operators of coal burning equipment are required to submit quarterly emissions reports to NMED.[207]

NO_x emissions from coal burning equipment having a power burning capacity in excess of 25 megawatts or a heat input of greater than 250 million BTUs per hour are regulated. For coal burning equipment constructed after August 17, 1971, no NO_x emissions in excess of 0.7 pounds per million BTUs of heat input are permitted. For coal burning equipment constructed prior to December 31, 1963, no NO_x emissions to the atmosphere in excess of 0.85 pounds per million BTUs of heat input are permitted. For coal burning equipment constructed between December 31, 1963, and December 31, 1964, the coal burning equipment emissions limitation is 0.65 pounds per million BTUs of heat input.[208]

Effective April 30, 1992, total NO_x emissions from a facility with coal burning equipment constructed between December 31, 1963, and August 17, 1971, is limited to 335,000 pounds per day. Owners or operators of such coal burning equipment are required

---

203 N.M. Air Quality Control Regulations § 503.

204 N.M. Air Quality Control Regulations § 504 (filed 6/13/78).

205 N.M. Air Quality Control Regulations § 602 (filed 11/24/80). The reader should be aware that as of the date of this publication, NMED has proposed an amendment to AQCR § 602.

206 N.M. Air Quality Control Regulations § 602.D.

207 N.M. Air Quality Control Regulations § 602.E.

208 N.M. Air Quality Control Regulations § 603 (filed 7/9/91).

to maintain and operate continuous emissions monitoring and to submit quarterly emissions monitoring reports. These regulations are directed toward the Four Corners Power Plant.[209]

11.6 PUMICE, MICA, AND PERLITE PROCESS EQUIPMENT

Stack emissions from pumice, mica, or perlite processing equipment are regulated by establishing maximum stack emission rates in pounds per hour based upon the process rate pounds per hour. The process rate pounds per hour is derived by dividing the total process weight (the total of all materials including solid fuel but not including liquid or gaseous fuel introduced into any specific process) by the number of hours in the complete operation excluding equipment idle time.[210]

11.7 NON-FERROUS SMELTERS

Non-ferrous smelters constructed after September 1, 1971, are prohibited from emitting particulate matter to the atmosphere in excess of 0.03 grains per dry cubic foot of discharged gas.[211] Non-ferrous smelters fully constructed and operational prior to September 1, 1971, are subject to individual stack limitations for the stacks connected to the reverberatory furnace, stacks serving the acid plant, stacks serving the reverberatory feed dryer, and stacks serving the fire refining furnace.[212]

Fugitive particulate matter emissions from non-ferrous smelters are regulated. Non-ferrous smelter owners and operators are required to install and operate well-designed exhaust systems, to maintain and operate all furnaces and convertors to minimize fugitive particulate matter emissions to the maximum extent practicable, to maintain all ducts, flues, waste-heat boilers, and stacks in as near leak-free condition as practicable, and to control all transfers and conveyances of particulate matter from dry particulate control equipment by use of a non-dusting product within an enclosed system or by the use of hoods or enclosures and venting through fabric filters or other approved control systems.[213]

Storage piles for copper ore concentrate and precipitate, lime or limestone, and fine silica flux materials within the boundary of the smelter are prohibited unless the storage and associated materials handling areas are enclosed or other control methods approved by NMED are utilized.[214] All roadways and parking areas within the boundaries of a non-

---

209 *Id.*

210 N.M. Air Quality Control Regulations § 505 (filed 9/13/71).

211 N.M. Air Quality Control Regulations § 506.A (filed 11/21/78).

212 N.M. Air Quality Control Regulations § 506.D; *See also* N.M. Air Quality Control Regulations § 506.1 (filed 3/16/79).

213 N.M. Air Quality Control Regulations § 510 (filed 7/16/86).

214 N.M. Air Quality Control Regulations § 510.C.

ferrous smelter and associated facilities must be paved and frequently cleaned or used in connection with other control measures approved by NMED.[215]

Non-ferrous smelters operational prior to September 1, 1971, are prohibited from emitting SO_2 in excess of 7,000 lbs. per hour annual average emissions or 5,309 lbs. per hour median 3-hour running average during any 365-day compliance period.[216] In addition, the number of excess emission occurrences per year is also controlled. The release of fugitive sulfur emissions to the atmosphere must be minimized by the use of best engineering practices, which are specified in the regulation.[217]

Non-ferrous smelters constructed after September 1, 1971, are prohibited from emitting SO_2 to the atmosphere in excess of 10 lbs. of sulfur for every 100 lbs. of sulfur fed to the smelter.[218]

Owners and operators of non-ferrous smelters operational before September 1, 1971, are required to maintain monitors to record the SO_2 concentration and stack gas volume metric flow rates at least 95 percent of the time for any 12 consecutive calendar months and are required to submit quarterly emissions reports to NMED.[219]

11.8 OIL BURNING EQUIPMENT

Particulate matter, SO_2 and NO_x emissions from oil burning equipment are subject to regulation. Particulate matter emissions from oil burning equipment having a rated heat capacity greater than 250 million BTUs per hour, constructed after August 17, 1971, are limited to 0.03 lbs. per million BTUs of heat input, or visible emissions of an opacity of no more than 20 percent.[220] Emissions from oil burning equipment constructed prior to August 17, 1971, are limited based upon equipment function and date of construction.[221] NMED is authorized to mandate that owners or operators of oil burning equipment perform stack testing of emissions.[222]

SO_2 emissions from oil burning equipment having a heat input of greater than 1,000,000 million BTUs per year cannot exceed 0.34 lbs. per million BTUs of heat input.[223]

---

215 N.M. Air Quality Control Regulations § 510.D.

216 N.M. Air Quality Control Regulations § 652.A (filed 7/8/82).

217 *Id.*

218 N.M. Air Quality Control Regulations § 652.B.

219 N.M. Air Quality Control Regulations § 652.C, .G.

220 N.M. Air Quality Control Regulations § 507.A (filed 12/21/78).

221 N.M. Air Quality Control Regulations § 507.B.

222 N.M. Air Quality Control Regulations § 507.D.

223 N.M. Air Quality Control Regulations § 605 (filed 2/17/72).

NO_x emissions from oil burning equipment having a heat input of greater than 1,000,000 million BTUs per year cannot exceed 0.3 lbs. per million BTUs of heat input.[224]

11.9 POTASH, SALT, OR SODIUM SULFATE EQUIPMENT

There are limits on particulate matter emissions to the atmosphere from potash, salt, or sodium sulfate processing equipment. The emissions limits distinguish between equipment operative prior to January 1, 1979, and after that date. Emissions limits are also based to some extent on equipment functions. Circumvention of particulate matter concentration limits by increasing the volume of stack gas emissions is prohibited. Particulate matter emissions are generally required to pass through stacks equipped with sampling ports and platforms. Stack heights must meet standards for good engineering practice.[225]

11.10 LIME MANUFACTURING PLANTS

Owners and operators of lime manufacturing plants are required to equip and maintain plant equipment with emissions control systems to reduce and/or prevent the release of particulate matter emissions to the atmosphere. No particulate matter emissions except through stacks equipped with sampling ports and platforms are permitted. The extent of limitations on particulate matter emissions from lime manufacturing plants are partially dependent on whether the plant was constructed prior to or after May 3, 1977. Lime manufacturing plants constructed after May 3, 1977, are required to be equipped with continuous monitoring systems as specified in 40 C.F.R. Part 60, Subpart HH, § 60.343.[226]

11.11 KRAFT MILLS

Kraft mills are defined as industrial operations using an alkaline solution containing sulfur compounds for a cooking liquor in the pulping process.[227] Emissions of total reduced sulfur and particulate matter from recovery furnace stacks, lime kilns, and smelt tanks are limited in terms of emissions per ton of equivalent air dried kraft pulp.[228]

11.12 GAS BURNING EQUIPMENT

Gas burning equipment constructed prior to 1972 having a heat input of greater than 1,000,000 million BTUs per year is limited to NO_x emissions of 0.3 lbs. per million BTUs of heat input. Gas burning equipment constructed during 1972 and thereafter is limited to NO_x emissions of 0.2 lbs. per million BTUs of heat input.[229]

---

224 N.M. Air Quality Control Regulations § 606 (filed 2/17/72).

225 N.M. Air Quality Control Regulations § 508.H (filed 7/16/86).

226 N.M. Air Quality Control Regulations § 509 (filed 11/21/78).

227 N.M. Air Quality Control Regulations § 601 (filed 1/27/70).

228 *Id.*

229 N.M. Air Quality Control Regulations § 604 (filed 2/17/72).

11.13 NATURAL GAS PROCESSING PLANTS

The extent of permitted emissions of sulfur from natural gas processing plants is determined with reference to average daily sulfur release quantities and by the hydrogen sulfide content of the undiluted off-gas stream.[230] Gas coming off any off-gas sweetening regeneration unit or other sulfur releasing unit from a natural gas processing plant generally cannot be sent off-site for sulfur recovery or disposal, subject to certain exceptions.[231] All sulfur compounds must be emitted to the atmosphere from a stack of sufficient height to prevent concentrations which exceed any state or federal ambient air standard.[232] Allowable emissions differ depending on whether a natural gas processing plant was constructed on or after July 1, 1974.[233] Natural gas processing plant owners or operators are required to submit quarterly emissions reports to NMED.[234] Natural gas processing plants certified by NMED as declining emission natural gas[235] processing plants are exempt from a substantial portion of the regulations.[236]

11.14 PETROLEUM REFINERY AND PROCESSING FACILITIES

11.14.1 Emissions Limitations

Sulfur emissions limitations from petroleum refineries are established separately for refineries constructed before and after July 1, 1974.[237] Owners or operators of petroleum refineries are required to submit quarterly sulfur emissions reports to NMED.[238] No sulfur compound emissions are permitted unless such emissions are controlled by an NMED approved method to prevent concentrations near ground level which exceed state or federal ambient air standards.[239]

Mercaptan emissions from petroleum processing facilities are limited to 0.25 lbs. per hour. In the alternative, mercaptan emissions are permitted if a steam condenser and combustion device or other equivalent pollution control device is utilized to prevent mercaptan emissions to the atmosphere.[240]

---

230 N.M. Air Quality Control Regulations § 621 (filed 2/8/83).

231 N.M. Air Quality Control Regulations § 621.F.

232 N.M. Air Quality Control Regulations § 621.H.

233 N.M. Air Quality Control Regulations § 621.Y(3) - (4).

234 N.M. Air Quality Control Regulations § 621.L.

235 N.M. Air Quality Control Regulations § 621.N.

236 N.M. Air Quality Control Regulations § 621.M.

237 N.M. Air Quality Control Regulations § 622.E (filed 7/16/86).

238 N.M. Air Quality Control Regulations § 622.F.

239 N.M. Air Quality Control Regulations § 622.H.

240 N.M. Air Quality Control Regulations § 623 (filed 2/8/83).

CO emissions from petroleum processing facilities are regulated by separate CO emissions limitations for petroleum processing facilities constructed before and after July 1, 1974.[241]

Particulate matter emissions from petroleum processing facilities are regulated by separate emissions limits for petroleum processing facilities constructed before and after July 1, 1974, with regard to both quantity and opacity of emissions.[242]

Ammonia emissions from petroleum processing facilities are limited to 25 parts per million (ppm) by volume in the undiluted effluent gas stream.[243]

Hydrogen sulfide emissions from petroleum processing facilities or sulfur recovery plants, the feed stock of which is in whole or in part a product of petroleum processing, cannot exceed 10 ppm by volume in the undiluted effluent gas stream, or the effluent gas stream containing hydrogen sulfide must be passed through a device capable of oxidizing the hydrogen sulfide to SO_2.[244]

Petroleum processing facilities or sulfur recovery plants commencing operation after January 1, 1975, are required to maintain an alarm system connected to gas flares containing more than 10 ppm of hydrogen sulfide, which will signal non-combustion of the gas.[245]

Hydrocarbon discharges to the atmosphere from petroleum processing facilities are regulated by separate limitations established for facilities constructed prior to and after July 1, 1974.[246] No discharge of waste liquor containing hydrocarbons is permitted unless such discharge has first been treated in a hydrocarbon separation facility.[247]

11.14.2 Storage Facility Requirements

Storage of organic compounds in connection with petroleum processing facilities is regulated by separate standards for petroleum processing facilities constructed before and after July 1, 1974. For facilities constructed prior to July 1, 1974, utilizing stationary storage tanks with more than a 250,000 gallon storage capacity, such tanks generally must be pressure vessels capable of maintaining working pressures sufficient to minimize vapor or gas loss to the atmosphere.[248] When organic compounds with true vapor pressures of 3.0 to 11.0 lbs.

---

241 N.M. Air Quality Control Regulations § 624 (filed 2/8/83).

242 N.M. Air Quality Control Regulations § 625 (filed 7/24/84).

243 N.M. Air Quality Control Regulations § 626 (filed 2/8/83).

244 N.M. Air Quality Control Regulations § 627 (filed 2/8/83).

245 N.M. Air Quality Control Regulations § 628 (filed 2/8/83).

246 N.M. Air Quality Control Regulations § 629 (filed 7/24/84).

247 *Id.*

248 N.M. Air Quality Control Regulations § 630.A(1) (filed 7/24/84).

per square inch are stored, the tanks must be equipped with a floating roof, vapor-recovery system, or other equivalent devices.[249]

Petroleum processing facilities constructed after July 1, 1974, and utilizing storage tanks with a storage capacity of 65,000 gallons or more are subject to additional limitations, including requirements that tanks be equipped with gauging and sampling devices and conservation vents.[250]

Petroleum processing facilities constructed after July 1, 1974, are required to have loading and unloading facilities equipped with loading arms with vapor collection adapters and a means to prevent liquid organic compound drainage.[251] Pumping systems and blow-down systems to minimize hydrocarbon emissions to the atmosphere are also required.[252]

Hydrocarbon storage facilities associated with petroleum production or processing facilities and having a capacity of 20,000 gallons or more with a throughput of at least 30,000 gallons per week are required to use storage containers equipped to minimize hydrocarbon and hydrogen sulfide lost to the atmosphere.[253] Storage tanks within the corporate limits of a municipality which have a greater than 10,000 barrel per year throughput are prohibited from storing hydrocarbon liquids with vapor contents of more than 24 ppm of hydrogen sulfide unless the tank is equipped with a vapor-recovery system, floating roof, or other device at least as efficient to minimize the loss of sulfur-containing vapors or gases into the atmosphere.[254] These restrictions extend to storage facilities within five miles of the corporate limits of a municipality that has a population of 20,000 or greater.

For tanks installed after January 1, 1975, with a storage capacity of 65,000 gallons or greater, a floating roof and vapor-recovery system are required.[255] All tanks, regardless of storage capacity, located outside the Pecos-Permian Air Quality Control Region, located within the corporate limits of any municipality, or located within five miles of the corporate limits of any municipality with a population of 20,000 or more must be equipped with a well maintained vapor-recovery system.[256]

---

249 N.M. Air Quality Control Regulations § 630.A(2).

250 N.M. Air Quality Control Regulations § 630.B.

251 N.M. Air Quality Control Regulations § 630.C.

252 N.M. Air Quality Control Regulations § 630.D - E.

253 N.M. Air Quality Control Regulations § 631 (filed 2/8/83).

254 *Id.*

255 N.M. Air Quality Control Regulations § 631.D.

256 N.M. Air Quality Control Regulations § 631.E.

11.15 SULFUR RECOVERY PLANTS

Sulfur emissions not otherwise limited by the AQCRs are subject to the limitations contained in AQCR § 632 which, in addition to establishing sulfur emissions limitations, also requires owners or operators of sulfur recovery plants to submit quarterly emission reports to NMED.

11.16 SULFURIC ACID PRODUCTION UNITS

Separate limitations are established for SO_2 emissions, acid mist emissions, and visible emissions from sulfuric acid production units constructed before and after August 17, 1971.[257] Separate emissions limitations are also established for sulfuric acid production units located within the Pecos-Permian Basin Intrastate Air Quality Control Region.[258] NMED is authorized to require owners and operators to perform stack testing, maintenance of emission monitors, and retention of records for a period of two years from the measurement date and to conduct performance tests.[259] Owners and operators are also required to submit quarterly reports to NMED.[260]

11.17 GASIFICATION PLANTS

Gasification plants are defined as plants which manufacture synthetic gas. All emissions from gasification plants must pass through stacks equipped with sampling ports and platforms.[261]

Coal briquette forming facilities in conjunction with gasification plants are prohibited from emitting particulate matter to the atmosphere in excess of 0.03 grains per standard cubic foot of exhaust gas.[262] Any combination of hydrogen sulfide, carbon disulfide, and carbon oxysulfide emissions to the atmosphere in excess of 100 ppm by volume in the effluent gas stream is prohibited and the hydrogen sulfide components in such combined effluent gas streams must be limited to 10 ppm by volume.[263] Hydrogen cyanide emissions to the atmosphere in excess of 10 ppm by volume in the effluent gas stream are prohibited.[264]

---

257 N.M. Air Quality Control Regulations § 651.A - .B (filed 7/15/86). Readers should be aware that as of the date of this publication, NMED has proposed an amendment to AQCR § 651.

258 N.M. Air Quality Control Regulations § 651.B.

259 N.M. Air Quality Control Regulations § 651.D, .F, .G.

260 N.M. Air Quality Control Regulations § 651.H.

261 N.M. Air Quality Control Regulations § 670 (filed 2/8/83).

262 N.M. Air Quality Control Regulations § 671 (filed 7/24/84).

263 N.M. Air Quality Control Regulations § 673 (filed 7/24/84).

264 N.M. Air Quality Control Regulations § 674 (filed 2/8/83).

Any combination of hydrogen chloride and hydrochloric acid emissions to the atmosphere in excess of 5 ppm by volume in the effluent gas stream is prohibited.[265]

Gasification plant owners and operators are required to take reasonable precautions in material handling, transport, storage and disposal to prevent particulate matter from becoming airborne. Particulate matter emissions to the atmosphere in excess of 0.03 grains per cubic foot of effluent gas at standard conditions are prohibited.[266] Tanks or other containers containing ammonia must be equipped to prevent loss of ammonia to the atmosphere, and ammonia emissions in excess of 25 ppm by volume in the effluent gas stream are prohibited.[267]

Particulate matter emissions from gas burning boilers operated in conjunction with a gasification plant cannot exceed 0.03 lbs. per million BTUs of heat input.[268] Also, SO_2 emissions from such boilers cannot exceed 0.16 lbs. per million BTUs of heat input.[269]

Sulfur emissions from gasification plants cannot exceed 0.008 lbs. per million BTUs of heat input contained in the feed introduced into the plant.[270] Storage of phenols and organic compounds produced in the operation of gasification plants is limited by requiring that storage tanks or other storage containers must be designed with floating roofs, vapor-recovery systems, or other devices to prevent vapor or gas loss to the atmosphere.[271] Loading facilities, pumps, and blow-down systems must be equipped to dispose of such gases in a manner which will prevent hydrocarbon emissions to the atmosphere.[272]

When more than one fuel is fired simultaneously in a gasification plant boiler, the emissions limitations are required to be calculated by a specified formula.[273]

11.18 COAL MINES AND COAL PREPARATION PLANTS

Coal preparation plants are required to equip all crushers, conveyers, screens, cleaners, hoppers, and chutes with hoods, shields, or sprays to prevent particulate matter emissions to the atmosphere.[274] In addition, all persons operating coal mines are required

---

265 N.M. Air Quality Control Regulations § 675 (filed 2/8/83).

266 N.M. Air Quality Control Regulations § 676 (filed 2/8/83).

267 N.M. Air Quality Control Regulations § 677 (filed 2/8/83).

268 N.M. Air Quality Control Regulations § 678 (filed 2/8/83).

269 N.M. Air Quality Control Regulations § 679 (filed 7/24/84).

270 N.M. Air Quality Control Regulations § 680 (filed 7/24/84).

271 N.M. Air Quality Control Regulations § 681.A (filed 2/8/83).

272 *Id.*

273 N.M. Air Quality Control Regulations § 682 (filed 7/24/84).

274 N.M. Air Quality Control Regulations § 672.A (filed 11/16/73).

to treat main coal haulage roads to prevent particulate matter emissions to the atmosphere.[275]

11.19 BIOMEDICAL WASTE COMBUSTION

Emission limits for CO, particulate matter, SO_2, NO_x, hydrochloric acid (HCL), dioxins/furans and metals from biomedical waste combustion units are regulated by establishing allowable emissions tied to the charging capacity of the combustion unit and measured generally in terms of grains, milligrams, or nanograms per dry standard cubic foot or dry standard cubic meter.[276] The regulations apply to the owners or operators of any biomedical waste combustion unit located at a facility with a total charging capacity of less than 50 tons per day and do not apply to crematory incinerators. The regulations supplement federal regulations contained in 40 C.F.R. Part 60-Standards of Performance for New Stationary Sources.[277] Single chamber medical waste combustion units were required to be taken out of service on or before April 7, 1992. Material marked with radiation symbols as required by New Mexico's Radiation Protection Regulations or having a radioactivity level greater than background is prohibited from being combusted in a biomedical waste combustion unit. Hazardous waste may not be combusted unless a RCRA Permit has been obtained from the Hazardous and Radioactive Materials Bureau. Infectious wastes are subject to New Mexico Solid Waste Management Regulations. Biomedical waste combustion units located at a facility with a total charging capacity of 50 tons per day or more or which accept off-site municipal solid waste from a non-generator of biomedical waste must also meet the requirements of Municipal Waste Combustion Regulations.[278]

Continuous emission monitoring or manual testing is required, the results of which must be reported to the Air Quality Bureau of NMED. The Air Quality Bureau may, upon request by an owner or operator of a biomedical waste combustion unit located at a facility with a total charging capacity of up to 400 pounds per hour, issue a written exemption from applicable emission limits and emission monitoring requirements. The exemption is available if the owner or operator complies with emission limits for biomedical waste combustion units located at a facility with a total charging capacity of less than 200 pounds per hour and agrees to a condition in the written exemption limiting the operation of the unit to no more than six hours in any one day.[279]

All combustion units must be equipped with a secondary combustion chamber which provides for turbulent mixing to ensure that air within the combustion zone has sufficient

---

[275] N.M. Air Quality Control Regulations § 672.B.

[276] N.M. Air Quality Control Regulations § 2020 (filed 3/8/91).

[277] N.M. Air Quality Control Regulations § 2020, Part II.

[278] N.M. Air Quality Control Regulations § 2020, Part III.

[279] N.M. Air Quality Control Regulations § 2020, Part IV.

momentum to penetrate the combustion gases. Minimum combustion chamber temperatures must be maintained within both primary and secondary combustion chambers. Exhaust stack heights for all biomedical waste combustion units must be in accord with good engineering practice, which is defined in the regulation.[280]

Installation and operation of continuous emission monitors which measure oxygen, carbon monoxide, and opacity may be required depending upon total charging rates or total charging capacities of combustion units.[281] Annual performance tests to demonstrate compliance with emission standards must be conducted for pollutants, as specified in the regulations. Notice of the test date and a copy of the test protocol must be submitted to the Air Quality Bureau at least 30 days prior to the actual test date and the opportunity for an Air Quality Bureau representative to be present during all such emission tests is required. A written copy of all test results must be furnished to the Air Quality Bureau within 60 days from the test date.[282] Quarterly reports of combustion unit conditions must be submitted to the Air Quality Bureau and owners or operators must maintain records for all parameters contained in such reports for a period of three years.[283]

All handling and storage of fly ash and bottom ash must be conducted in a closed system which prevents ash from becoming airborne. Transporters of biomedical waste combustion ash must insure that transport vehicles are securely covered to prevent release of fugitive dust. Combustion unit operators must undergo training and trained operators must be present whenever waste is being combusted.[284]

12.0 ALBUQUERQUE-BERNALILLO COUNTY AIR QUALITY PROGRAM

Responsibility for the adoption of air pollution control programs for the City of Albuquerque and Bernalillo County is delegated to local government.[285]

12.1 AIR QUALITY CONTROL BOARD

The Albuquerque-Bernalillo County Air Quality Control Board (Board) was formed by separate Ordinances (Ordinance)[286] adopted by the City of Albuquerque and Bernalillo County. The Board consists of seven members, three appointed by the Bernalillo County Commission and four appointed by the Mayor of the City of Albuquerque.[287] At least a

280 N.M. Air Quality Control Regulations § 2020, Part V.

281 N.M. Air Quality Control Regulations § 2020, Part VI.

282 N.M. Air Quality Control Regulations § 2020, Part VII.

283 N.M. Air Quality Control Regulations § 2020, Part VIII.

284 N.M. Air Quality Control Regulations § 2020, Part IX.

285 N.M. Stat. Ann. § 74-2-4 (Repl. Pamp. 1993).

286 Albuquerque, N.M. Rev. Ordinances §§ 6-16-1 to -15 (1974 as amended through 1993), Bernalillo County Rev. Ordinance 88-45 (1988).

287 Albuquerque, N.M. Rev. Ordinances § 6-17-2.

majority of the members of the Board must be individuals who represent the public interest and do not derive any significant portion of their income from persons subject to or who appear before the Board.[288] The Board is empowered to administer and enforce the AQCA and its regulations applicable within Albuquerque and Bernalillo County, as well as to adopt its own regulations consistent with the AQCA to prevent or abate air pollution. Staff for administration and enforcement of the AQCA, the Ordinance and regulations pursuant thereto is provided by the City of Albuquerque Environmental Health Department (AEHD).[289]

The Board is authorized to adopt a permitting system requiring pre-construction permits for any construction or modification of new sources of air contaminants within the City of Albuquerque and Bernalillo County.[290] Appeals from Board decisions are filed directly with the New Mexico Court of Appeals, and such appeals are to be on the record made at Board hearings.[291]

AEHD is authorized to take enforcement action for violations of the AQCA, the Ordinance or any regulations of the Board, including permit conditions, by seeking injunctive relief or other appropriate relief in the District Court to secure abatement of the violation.[292] Violators of the Ordinance or any regulations adopted in accordance with the Ordinance may be found guilty of a misdemeanor and may be punished by fines and imprisonment.[293] Agents of AEHD are authorized to enter and inspect any premises in which an emission source is located or in which records related to emissions are located.[294]

In 1981, the Board adopted ambient air quality standards for the City and County designed to provide a level of air quality to protect human health, animal and plant life, and property.[295]

12.2 BOARD REGULATIONS

The Board has adopted regulations establishing NO_x, SO_2, volatile organic compounds, and particulate matter emission limits. The Board has also enacted regulations requiring

---

288 N.M. Stat. Ann. § 74-2-4(B) (Repl. Pamp. 1993).

289 Albuquerque, N.M. Rev. Ordinances § 6-16-3.

290 Albuquerque, N.M. Rev. Ordinances § 6-16-6.

291 Albuquerque, N.M. Rev. Ordinances § 6-16-6(J).

292 Albuquerque, N.M. Rev. Ordinances § 6-16-11.

293 Albuquerque, N.M. Rev. Ordinances § 6-16-11(D).

294 Albuquerque, N.M. Rev. Ordinances § 6-16-12.

295 Albuquerque-Bernalillo County Air Quality Control Board Standard, ABC/AQCB, No. 1, § 2.01 (filed 11/12/81).

general pre-construction permits for stationary sources,[296] as well as PSD permits.[297] New stationary sources within non-attainment areas under the jurisdiction of the Board must obtain an additional permit.[298] The Board has adopted the NSPS contained in 40 C.F.R. Part 60, as amended in the Federal Register through June 10, 1992,[299] and the NESHAPs contained in 40 C.F.R. Part 61, as amended in the Federal Register through June 3, 1992.[300] As of the date of this publication, the City of Albuquerque is considering amendments to the Ordinance to bring the Ordinance into conformity with the requirements of the 1990 CAA amendments. EPA has directly delegated to the Board and AEHD enforcement of the NSPS and NESHAPs in Bernalillo County.[301]

The Board has adopted a woodburning regulation which, among other things, allows the imposition of no-burn periods between October 1 and February 28 when it is determined that atmospheric conditions will not reasonably disperse woodsmoke.[302] The regulation provides exemptions required by a law mandating that any county or municipal ordinance adopting woodburning control laws provide an exemption procedure for indigent families who use woodburning as an essential form of cost-efficient heating.[303]

In 1991, the Board adopted an emissions trading regulation to encourage the reduction of air contaminants within Bernalillo County by replacing the current sources of air contaminants with sources producing fewer air contaminants.[304] As approved by AEHD, any person may establish a quantified program to permanently eliminate sources of air contaminants. The eliminated sources may be applied as emissions credits toward an authority-to-construct permit. The elimination of emissions sources must be realized no more than one year prior to the filing of the authority-to-construct permit application. Application for such emissions credits must be submitted in writing to AEHD and contain adequate

---

296 Albuquerque-Bernalillo County Air Quality Control Board Regulation No. 20 (filed 2/26/93).

297 Albuquerque-Bernalillo County Air Quality Control Board Regulation No. 29 (filed 2/26/93).

298 Albuquerque-Bernalillo County Air Quality Control Board Regulation No. 32 (filed 2/26/93).

299 Albuquerque-Bernalillo County Air Quality Control Board Regulation No. 30 (filed 4/22/93).

300 Albuquerque-Bernalillo County Air Quality Control Board Regulation No. 31 (filed 4/22/93).

301 54 Fed. Reg. 52031 (1989).

302 Albuquerque-Bernalillo County Air Quality Control Board Regulation No. 34 (filed 11/27/91).

303 N.M. Stat. Ann. § 74-2A-1 (Repl. Pamp. 1993).

304 Albuquerque-Bernalillo County Air Quality Control Board Regulation No. 38 (filed 6/03/91).

information to insure the permanent elimination of sources of applicable air contaminants in adequate amounts to produce a net air quality benefit of no less than 20% by weight. Provision is made for limitations, adjustments, or revocation of credits. Specific provision is made for hydrocarbon emissions trading by providing credits for the elimination of operable motor vehicle emissions sources.[305]

The Board has promulgated a regulation regarding the use of pathological waste destructors.[306] Pathological waste destructors may only be used to destroy pathological waste that has been generated at the site where the unit is located. No material marked with radiation symbols or having a radioactivity level greater than background, hazardous waste, or non-pathological waste may be burned in a pathological waste destructor. Limitations are established on emissions from such units. Design and operating requirements are also mandated. Monitoring, performance evaluation, and testing are also required.

The Board also requires that stationary source owners or operators which emit more than 2,000 lbs. of any air contaminant annually, or any amount of a hazardous air pollutant, obtain a registration certificate from AEHD.[307]

Variances from Board regulations or limitations may be sought by filing a written petition with the Director of AEHD, who must make a recommendation to the Board. If the Board favors the granting of a variance, a public hearing will be held before the Board issues its final order. If the Board initially opposes the granting of a variance, it must so notify the Petitioner and a public hearing will be held only if requested by the Petitioner.[308]

12.3 MOTOR VEHICLE EMISSIONS CONTROLS

The Albuquerque/Bernalillo County area has been designated by EPA as a non-attainment area for CO. In order to meet the source requirements of Section 172 of the Clean Air Act,[309] the City of Albuquerque adopted a Motor Vehicle Emissions Control Ordinance (Emissions Ordinance).[310] Bernalillo County soon thereafter adopted a similar ordinance. The Emissions Ordinance requires biennial mandatory inspection of 1975 or newer four-wheel motor vehicles weighing less than 26,000 lbs. Such motor vehicles are required to pass a visual emissions inspection and a tailpipe exhaust emissions test. Enforcement is enhanced by tying compliance with the Emissions Ordinance to the right to

---

305 Albuquerque-Bernalillo County Air Quality Control Board Regulation § 38.06.

306 Albuquerque-Bernalillo County Air Quality Control Board Regulation No. 39 (filed 6/16/92).

307 Albuquerque-Bernalillo County Air Quality Control Board Regulation No. 22 (filed 3/24/82).

308 Albuquerque-Bernalillo County Air Quality Control Board Regulation No. 24 (filed 11/27/91).

309 42 U.S.C. § 7502.

310 Albuquerque, N.M. Rev. Ordinances §§ 9-1-1 to -14 (1974 as amended through 1993).

register or transfer any vehicle, permission for which must be obtained from the New Mexico Motor Vehicle Division. Failure to have a vehicle inspection test constitutes a criminal misdemeanor.

The Board has adopted regulations to implement the Emissions Ordinance. The regulations establish emissions testing procedures, allowable carbon monoxide and hydrocarbon emissions levels, repair and adjustment requirements, and criteria for time extensions for obtaining required repairs. The regulations also establish certification and training requirements for emissions inspectors and mechanics.[311] The Emissions Ordinance contains exemptions for certain vehicles, as well as grace periods for obtaining any repairs necessary for a vehicle to pass inspection. As of the date of this publication, the Board is considering making substantial changes to the Emissions Ordinance regulations in order to conform with requirements of federal regulations promulgated under the 1990 CAA Amendments.

The Board has also adopted a regulation regarding the use of alternative fuels to reduce tailpipe emissions. Between November 1 and February 28 of each year, sellers of gasoline motor fuel within Bernalillo County are prohibited from selling fuel which has less than 2.7% oxygen content by weight.[312]

---

311 Albuquerque-Bernalillo County Air Quality Control Board Regulation No. 28 (filed 8/25/93).

312 Albuquerque-Bernalillo County Air Quality Control Board Regulation No. 35.02(A) (filed 6/25/92).

CHAPTER III
WATER QUALITY MANAGEMENT

1.0 INTRODUCTION

The New Mexico Legislature has divided responsibility for regulating water pollution among several entities. The Water Quality Act (WQA)[1] delegates primary authority to the Water Quality Control Commission (WQCC).[2] WQCC is charged with adopting a comprehensive water quality management program and continuing planning process,[3] adopting water quality standards for surface and ground waters,[4] and adopting regulations to prevent or abate water pollution and to govern the disposal of septage[5] and sludge.[6] In turn, WQCC assigns responsibility for administering its regulations to various agencies, including the New Mexico Environment Department (NMED).[7] Under the Environmental Improvement Act,[8] the Environmental Improvement Board (EIB) is responsible for promulgating regulations and standards for water supplies and liquid waste.[9] Finally, the Oil and Gas Act (OGA)[10] assigns to the Oil Conservation Division (OCD) responsibility for

---

1 N.M. Stat. Ann. §§ 74-6-1 to -17 (Repl. Pamp. 1993).

2 *See* N.M. Stat. Ann. § 74-6-4 (Repl. Pamp. 1993). The WQCC is the state water pollution control agency for New Mexico for all purposes of the federal Clean Water Act (CWA) and the wellhead protection and sole source aquifer programs of the federal Safe Drinking Water Act and may take all actions necessary and appropriate to secure to New Mexico, its political subdivisions or interstate agencies the benefits of that act and those programs. N.M. Stat. Ann. § 74-6-3(E) (Repl. Pamp. 1993).

3 N.M. Stat. Ann. § 74-6-4(B) (Repl. Pamp. 1993).

4 N.M. Stat. Ann. § 74-6-4(C) (Repl. Pamp. 1993).

5 No regulations have been issued as of the publication date of this Handbook. "Septage" is defined as the residual wastes and water periodically pumped from a liquid waste treatment unit or from a holding tank for maintenance or disposal purposes. N.M. Stat. Ann. § 74-6-2(M) (Repl. Pamp. 1993).

6 N.M. Stat. Ann. § 74-6-4(D) (Repl. Pamp. 1993). "Sludge" is defined as solid, semi-solid or liquid waste generated from a municipal, commercial, or industrial wastewater treatment plant, water supply treatment plant, or air pollution control facility that is associated with the treatment of these wastes. "Sludge" does not mean treated effluent from a wastewater treatment plant. N.M. Stat. Ann § 74-6-2(N) (Repl. Pamp. 1993).

7 N.M. Stat. Ann. § 74-6-4(E) (Repl. Pamp. 1993).

8 N.M. Stat. Ann. §§ 74-1-1 to -10 (Repl. Pamp. 1993).

9 N.M. Stat. Ann. § 74-1-8(A)(2),(3) (Repl. Pamp. 1993).

10 N.M. Stat. Ann. §§ 70-2-1 to -38 (Repl. Pamp. 1987 & Supp. 1993).

regulating water pollution that results from oil and gas activities.[11] The WQA does not apply to any activity or condition subject to the authority of OCD under the OGA and other laws conferring power on OCD to prevent or abate water pollution.[12]

1.1 FEDERAL-STATE RELATIONSHIP

Congress enacted the Clean Water Act (CWA)[13] in 1972. The CWA generally applies to "navigable waters,"[14] which it broadly defines as "the waters of the United States."[15] The United States Environmental Protection Agency (EPA), in turn, defines "waters of the United States" to encompass most surface waters, including navigable waters and their tributaries, interstate waters, and intrastate waters that can affect interstate or foreign commerce.[16] The CWA's reach does not extend to ground water pollution unless it affects surface waters.[17]

The CWA's regulatory regime includes water quality standards that each state must adopt[18] and a program of permits that governs discharge of pollutants (the National Pollutant Discharge Elimination System (NPDES)).[19] EPA may authorize a state to administer the NPDES within its boundaries,[20] but it has not so authorized New Mexico.[21] New Mexico does, however, certify that draft NPDES permits comply with applicable provisions of state and federal law, and the state can deny certification for specific reasons discussed in the Other General Provisions Section of this Chapter.[22] In addition, WQCC

---

11 N.M. Stat. Ann. § 70-2-12(B)(15) (Supp. 1993).

12 N.M. Stat. Ann. § 74-6-12(G) (Repl. Pamp. 1993).

13 Pub. L. No. 92-500, 86 Stat. 816 (1972) (codified as amended at 33 U.S.C. §§ 1251-1387).

14 *See, e.g.*, 33 U.S.C. §§ 1251(a)(1), 1252(a), 1313(c)(4), 1342(b), 1362(12).

15 33 U.S.C. § 1362(7).

16 40 C.F.R. § 122.2.

17 *Exxon Corp. v. Train*, 554 F.2d 1310, 1312, 1331 n.1 (5th Cir. 1977); *McClellan Ecological Seepage Situation v. Weinberger*, 707 F. Supp. 1182, 1193-96 (E.D. Cal. 1988); *Kelley ex rel. Michigan v. United States*, 618 F. Supp. 1103, 1107 (W.D. Mich. 1985).

18 33 U.S.C. § 1313.

19 33 U.S.C. § 1342.

20 33 U.S.C. § 1342(b).

21 New Mexico has never sought NPDES authority.

22 1993 Amendments to the WQA require the WQCC to adopt regulations establishing procedures for such certifications. N.M. Stat. Ann. § 74-6-5(B) (Repl. Pamp. 1993). The WQA also mandates circumstances under which a certification must be denied. *See* N.M. Stat. Ann. § 74-6-5(E). (Repl. Pamp. 1993).

has promulgated water quality standards for surface water in New Mexico.[23] Therefore, all persons who discharge into New Mexico's surface waters must ensure that they comply with both federal and state requirements.

1.2 ENFORCEMENT

NMED and other constituent agencies[24] have broad powers to carry out their responsibilities under the WQA, including the power to require the production of documents[25] and the power to enter, upon presentation of proper credentials and at reasonable times, any premises[26] in which a water contaminant source or records required to be maintained by regulations of the federal government or the WQCC are located, for the purpose of accessing and copying records, inspecting treatment works or monitoring equipment, or sampling any effluents, water contaminants, or receiving waters.[27]

Constituent agencies, including NMED, which determine that a requirement, regulation, or water quality standard adopted pursuant to the WQA, or a condition of a permit issued pursuant to that act, has been violated are empowered to issue compliance orders requiring compliance or imposing civil penalties, or both, and to commence a civil action in state District Court for appropriate relief, including an injunction.[28] Civil penalties assessed under a compliance order can reach $15,000 per day for violations of regulations or permits issued pursuant to N.M. Stat. Ann. § 74-6-5 (Repl. Pamp. 1993), and $10,000 per day for each violation of a provision of other sections of the WQA.[29] Failure to take corrective action required under a compliance order can result in a civil penalty of $25,000 for each day of continued noncompliance with the compliance order.[30]

---

23 Water Quality Standards for Interstate and Intrastate Streams in New Mexico (hereinafter cited as N.M. Water Quality Standards). *See* N.M. Stat. Ann. § 74-6-3(E) (Repl. Pamp. 1993).

24 Other constituent agencies are the State Engineer and the Interstate Stream Commission, the Department of Game and Fish, the Oil Conservation Commission, the State Park and Recreation Division of the Energy, Minerals and Natural Resources Department, the Department of Agriculture, the Soil and Water Conservation Commission, and the Bureau of Mines and Mineral Resources at the New Mexico Institute of Mining and Technology. N.M. Stat. Ann. § 74-6-2(J) (Repl. Pamp. 1993).

25 N.M. Stat. Ann. § 74-6-5(B).

26 Except private residences, entry into which requires a court order from a state District Court. N.M. Stat. Ann. § 74-6-9(E) (Repl. Pamp. 1993).

27 N.M. Stat. Ann. § 74-6-9(E) (Repl. Pamp. 1993).

28 N.M. Stat. Ann. § 74-6-10(A) (Repl. Pamp. 1993).

29 N.M. Stat. Ann. § 74-6-10(C) (Repl. Pamp. 1993).

30 N.M. Stat. Ann. § 74-6-10(F) (Repl. Pamp. 1993).

Penalties can also be imposed without compliance orders; these penalties address failure to comply. A failure to comply with the provisions of N.M. Stat. Ann. § 74-6-5 (Repl. Pamp. 1993), including any regulations or permits issued under that section, can result in civil penalties of up to $15,000 per day of noncompliance for each violation. Violations of any provision of the WQA other than those in § 74-6-5 or of any regulation, water quality standard, or compliance order adopted pursuant to the act can result in civil penalties of up to $10,000 per day for each violation.[31]

Knowingly discharging any water contaminant without a permit, violating a permit condition, making false statements or omissions of material fact in documents files submitted or required to be maintained under the WQA, tampering with monitoring devices or records, failing to monitor or sample as required by a permit and, under certain circumstances, introducing water contaminants or hazardous substances into a sewerage system or publicly owned treatment works, are fourth-degree felonies under the WQA.[32] A second or subsequent violation is a third-degree felony, as is a violation which causes a substantial adverse environmental impact.[33] If the person knowingly engaging in these acts also knows at the time that the action is creating a substantial danger of death or serious bodily injury to any other person, the person is guilty of a second-degree felony.[34]

A constituent agency with jurisdiction over a pollution source can commence an action in state District Court to restrain any person from causing or contributing to an imminent and substantial danger to human health.[35] If it is not practicable to assure prompt protection of public health solely by commencement of such an action, a constitucnt agency may issue any order it deems necessary to protect public health. Such an order is effective for no more than 73 hours unless the agency brings an action within that time. If an action is brought, the order is effective for 168 hours or for a longer period authorized by the court. A willful violation or failure or refusal to comply with such an order is punishable, upon conviction, by a fine of up to $5,000 for each day in which the violation, failure, or refusal occurs.[36]

---

31 N.M. Stat. Ann. § 74-6-10.1 (Repl. Pamp. 1993).

32 N.M. Stat. Ann. § 74-6-10.2(B) (Repl. Pamp. 1993). It is also a fourth-degree felony to knowingly cause or allow another person to undertake such actions. *Id.*

33 N.M. Stat. Ann. § 74-6-10.2(C) (Repl. Pamp. 1993). A substantial adverse environmental impact is an act or omission that causes harm or damage to human beings or that amounts to more than $10,000 in damage or mitigation costs to flora, aquatic life, waterfowl, livestock, or wildlife or their habitats, ground water or surface water, or the lands of the state. N.M. Stat. Ann. § 74-6-2(O) (Repl. Pamp. 1993).

34 N.M. Stat. Ann. § 74-6-10.2(E) (Repl. Pamp. 1993).

35 N.M. Stat. Ann. § 74-6-11(A) (Repl. Pamp. 1993).

36 N.M. Stat. Ann. § 74-6-11(C) (Repl. Pamp. 1993).

1.3 OTHER GENERAL PROVISIONS

WQCC requires that accidental discharges of contaminants in such quantity as may with reasonable probability injure or be detrimental to human health, animal or plant life, or property or unreasonably interfere with the public welfare or the use of property[37] be reported and cleaned up. The person in charge of the facility at which the discharge occurs must notify NMED orally within 24 hours after learning of the discharge.[38] Written notice must follow within one week.[39] The owner or operator of the facility must take immediate action to contain and remove or mitigate the damage caused by the discharge,[40] but only after consulting with NMED if that is feasible.[41] The owner or operator must file within 15 days a report with NMED that describes the discharge and corrective action,[42] which NMED will either approve or disapprove.[43]

Constituent agencies must deny an application for a discharge permit or deny the certification of a NPDES permit if (1) the effluent would not meet applicable state or federal regulations, standards of performance, or limitations,[44] (2) any provision of the WQA would be violated, (3) the discharge would cause or contribute to water contaminant levels in excess of any state or federal standard,[45] or (4) the applicant has within 10 years immediately preceding the date of submission of the permit application,[46] (a) knowingly misrepresented a material fact in an application for a permit, (b) refused or failed to disclose any information required under the WQA, (c) been convicted of a felony or other crime involving moral turpitude, (d) been convicted of a felony in any court for any crime defined by state or federal law as being a restraint of trade, price-fixing, bribery, or fraud, (e) exhibited a history of willful disregard for environmental laws of any state or the United

---

37 N.M. Water Quality Control Commission Regulations, WQCC, (hereinafter cited as N.M. Water Quality Regulations) § 1-203.A (as amended through 7/31/93).

38 N.M. Water Quality Regulations § 1-203.A(1).

39 N.M. Water Quality Regulations § 1-203.A(3).

40 N.M. Water Quality Regulations § 1-203.A(5).

41 N.M. Water Quality Regulations § 1-203.A(6).

42 *Id.*

43 N.M. Water Quality Regulations § 1-203.A(7).

44 N.M. Stat. Ann. § 74-6-5(E) (Repl. Pamp. 1993).

45 *Id.* Determination of the effect of the discharge on ground water will be measured at any place of withdrawal of water for present or reasonably foreseeable future use. Determination of the effect of the discharge on surface waters will be measured at the point of discharge. N.M. Stat. Ann. § 74-6-5(E)(3) (Repl. Pamp. 1993).

46 N.M. Stat. Ann. § 76-6-5(E)(4) (Repl. Pamp. 1993).

States, or (f) had an environmental permit revoked or permanently suspended for cause under any environmental laws of any state or the United States.[47]

A permit may be terminated or modified by the constituent agency that issued the permit prior to its date of expiration (1) for a violation of any condition of the permit, (2) if the permit was obtained by misrepresentation or a failure to fully disclose all relevant facts, (3) for a violation of any provision of the WQA or any applicable regulations, standard of performance, or water quality standard, (4) for a violation of any applicable state or federal effluent regulations or limitations, or (5) in the event a change in any condition that requires either a temporary or permanent reduction or elimination of the permitted discharge.[48]

Amendments to the WQA adopted in 1993 gave WQCC authority to adopt additional regulations in the area of water pollution.[49] First, WQCC is authorized to adopt regulations governing the disposal of septage and sludge and the use of sludge for beneficial purposes.[50] The regulations may include the use of tracking and permitting systems or other reasonable means necessary to assure that septage and sludge are designated for disposal in, and arrive at, disposal facilities[51] for which a permit or other authorization has been issued pursuant to the CWA or the WQA.[52] Second, WQCC may adopt regulations governing the construction and operation of new sewer systems, treatment works, or sewerage systems or extensions, modifications of, or additions to such systems now existing.[53] Third, WQCC may

---

47 N.M. Stat. Ann. § 74-6-5(E) (Repl. Pamp. 1993).

48 N.M. Stat. Ann. § 74-6-5(L) (Repl. Pamp. 1993).

49 As of the date of publication the WQCC had not adopted regulations. Rules, regulations, water quality standards, and administrative determinations pertaining to the WQA which existed prior to the effective date of the 1993 amendments to the WQA (June 18, 1993) will remain in full force and effect until repealed or amended, unless they conflict with, are prohibited by, or are inconsistent with the provisions of the WQA as amended. N.M. Stat. Ann. § 74-6-16 (Repl. Pamp. 1993).

50 N.M. Stat. Ann. § 74-6-4(D) (Repl. Pamp. 1993). The WQCC can also require that certain categories of applicants for a permit to dispose of or use septage or sludge file a disclosure statement on a form to be developed by the WQCC and the Department of Public Safety (PSDept.). N.M. Stat. Ann. § 74-6-5.1(A) - (E) (Repl. Pamp. 1993). PSDept. may prepare an investigative report on an applicant, based partly on the information contained in the disclosure statement, upon request of a constituent agency. The applicant is required to cooperate in preparing the investigative report and is charged with insuring that the disclosure report remains current. N.M. Stat. Ann. § 74-6-5.1(B),(D) (Repl. Pamp. 1993). A permit can be denied for any of the reasons set forth in N.M. Stat. Ann. § 74-6-5 (Repl. Pamp. 1993). Notice and appeal procedures are governed by N.M. Stat. Ann. § 74-6-5.1(F) (Repl. Pamp. 1993).

51 This does not include facilities on the premises where the septage and sludge is generated. N.M. Stat. Ann. § 74-6-4(D) (Repl. Pamp. 1993).

52 *Id.*

53 N.M. Stat. Ann. § 74-6-4(H) (Repl. Pamp. 1993).

adopt regulations requiring the filing of notices of intent by persons planning to introduce water pollutants or contaminants into the waters of the state.[54] Fourth, WQCC is now authorized to adopt regulations establishing pretreatment standards for pollutants to be introduced into publicly owned sewerage systems.[55] Fifth, WQCC may adopt regulations for the operation and maintenance of a permitted facility, including requirements for financial responsibility, including financial responsibility for corrective action.[56]

The 1993 amendments to the WQA also authorized WQCC to require a permit respecting the use of water in irrigated agriculture in a case where the employment of a specific practice in connection with such irrigation has, through documentation or actual case history, been shown to be hazardous to public health or the environment.[57]

Persons may petition WQCC for a variance from any of its regulations.[58] A petitioner generally must explain why compliance with the regulation will impose an unreasonable burden[59] and state the extent to which the petitioner wishes to vary from the regulation[60] and for what period of time the variance is desired.[61]

2.0 SURFACE WATER

WQCC has promulgated water quality standards for surface waters in New Mexico as well as effluent limitations for surface water discharges that EPA does not regulate.

2.1 WATER QUALITY STANDARDS

The purpose of the Water Quality Standards (Standards) is to designate the uses for which the surface waters of the state must be protected and to prescribe the water quality standards necessary to sustain the designated uses.[62] NMED implements the standards through an ongoing process of establishing and maintaining controls on the discharge of pollutants to surface waters.[63] The fundamental principle behind the Standards is to maintain the quality of the state's surface waters at a "fishable-swimmable" level. The Standards state that they are consistent with the CWA, which articulates a national goal that "whenever attainable, an interim goal of water quality which provides for the protection and

---

54 N.M. Stat. Ann. § 74-6-4(I) (Repl. Pamp. 1993).

55 N.M. Stat. Ann. § 74-6-4(J) (Repl. Pamp. 1993).

56 N.M. Stat. Ann. § 74-6-5(G) (Repl. Pamp. 1993).

57 N.M. Stat. Ann. § 74-6-4(K) (Repl. Pamp. 1993).

58 N.M. Water Quality Regulations § 1-210.

59 N.M. Water Quality Regulations § 1-210.A(8).

60 N.M. Water Quality Regulations § 1-210.A(7).

61 N.M. Water Quality Regulations § 1-210.A(9).

62 N.M. Water Quality Standards, WQCC 91-1, § 1-100.A (filed 6/29/91). The Standards apply to all water that falls within the ambit of the CWA.

63 N.M. Water Quality Standards § 1-101.B.

propagation of fish, shellfish, and wildlife and provides for recreation in and on the water be achieved."[64] The Standards also provide that, although agricultural, municipal, domestic, and industrial water supply are other essential uses of New Mexico's water, water contaminants resulting from these activities will not be allowed to lower the quality of streams below that which is required for recreation and maintenance of a fishery, where practicable.[65] The Standards also announce an anti-degradation policy:

> Degradation of waters the quality of which is better than the stream standards established by the New Mexico Water Quality Control Commission is not reasonable degradation and is subject to abatement under the authority granted the Commission by the New Mexico WQA, as amended, unless it is justifiable as a result of necessary economic and social development. Existing instream water uses and water quality necessary to sustain existing uses must be maintained and protected.... To protect the existing quality of water, the Commission under that Act will require the highest and best degree of effluent treatment practicable.[66]

The Standards contain general standards to sustain and protect waters that can support designated or attainable uses; they apply, in the absence of applicable specific standards, to all surface water that can be used for fishing, recreation, irrigation, or livestock or domestic water supply.[67] The Standards set forth limits on stream bottom deposits, floating solids, oil and grease, color, odor and taste of fish, plant nutrients, hazardous substances, radioactivity, pathogens, temperature, turbidity, salinity, and dissolved gases.[68] They also require that water courses must be free of any water contaminant in such quantity and of such duration as may with reasonable probability injure human health, animal or plant life, or property or unreasonably interfere with the public welfare or the use of property.[69] The applicability of the Standards may vary depending on stream flow; there are also provisions for mixing zones.[70] The Standards contain standards that apply to specific stretches of specific streams, rivers, and basins.[71] These include minimum and/or maximum permissible dissolved oxygen concentration, pH, temperature, salinity, fecal coliform bacteria, total dissolved solids, sulfates, and chlorides. The Standards also contain specific numeric standards for all waters with the attainable or designated uses of coldwater fishery, domestic

---

64 33 U.S.C. § 1251(a)(2), *quoted in* N.M. Water Quality Standards § 1-100.B.

65 N.M. Water Quality Standards § 1-100.B.

66 N.M. Water Quality Standards § 1-101.A.

67 N.M. Water Quality Standards § 1-102.

68 *Id.*

69 *Id.*

70 N.M. Water Quality Standards § 1-105.

71 N.M. Water Quality Standards §§ 2-100 to -805.

water supply, high quality coldwater fishery, irrigation, limited warmwater fishery, marginal coldwater fishery, primary contact recreation, warmwater fishery, and livestock or wildlife watering.[72]

The Standards are implemented in New Mexico through NPDES permits issued by the U.S. EPA under the CWA. However, the Standards must be observed even if the discharger has no NPDES permit.

2.2 EFFLUENT LIMITATIONS

WQCC effluent limitations[73] apply only to dischargers who are not subject to the federal NPDES or who have been on notice for more than 30 days that they are violating an NPDES permit.[74] They establish effluent limitations in the following areas: bio-chemical oxygen demand, chemical oxygen demand, settleable solids, fecal coliform bacteria, and pH.[75] They also specify stricter limitations in these same areas for a portion of the Rio Grande Basin.[76]

3.0 GROUND WATER

WQCC has promulgated standards for ground water quality.[77] Persons may not discharge effluent which may move into ground water[78] without submitting a discharge plan to the Secretary or to the OCD Director[79] and obtaining approval of it,[80] and the Secretary or OCD Director generally will not approve a plan if it will result in ground water that does not meet the standards.[81]

The stated purpose of the ground water standards delineates their scope:

> [T]o protect all ground water ... which has an existing concentration of 10,000 mg/l or less TDS [total dissolved solids], for present and potential future use as domestic and agricultural water supply, and to protect those segments of

---

72 N.M. Water Quality Standards § 3-101.

73 N.M. Water Quality Regulations §§ 2-100 to -102.

74 N.M. Water Quality Regulations § 2-100.

75 N.M. Water Quality Regulations § 2-101.

76 N.M. Water Quality Regulations § 2-102.

77 N.M. Water Quality Regulations § 3-103.

78 Ground water is interstitial water which occurs in saturated earth material and which is capable of entering a well in sufficient amounts to be utilized as a water supply. N.M. Water Quality Regulations § 1-101.Y.

79 References in this Section to the NMED Secretary may also include the Director of OCD. Generally, if the oil or gas industry is involved the OCD Director will be substituted for the Secretary.

80 N.M. Water Quality Regulations § 3-104. *See also* N.M. Stat. Ann. § 74-6-5(A) (Repl. Pamp. 1993).

81 N.M. Water Quality Regulations § 3-109.C(2).

> surface waters which are gaining because of ground water inflow, for uses designated in the New Mexico Water Quality Standards.[82]

Thus, the standards apply to all ground water, unless it is naturally high in TDS (usually salts), and they incorporate surface water standards where ground water and surface water are hydrologically connected. In contrast to the anti-degradation policy that is part of the surface water Standards, the ground water standards permit degradation if natural water quality is better than WQCC's standards.[83]

3.1 STANDARDS

The ground water standards specify limits for pH and a number of elements and compounds, both organic and inorganic.[84] There are three categories of standards: Human Health Standards, Other Standards for Domestic Water Supply, and Standards for Irrigation Use.[85]

3.2 DISCHARGE PLAN REQUIREMENT

Persons generally must obtain approval from the NMED Secretary (or OCD Director) of a discharge plan and comply with it if they discharge effluent into ground water:

> Unless otherwise provided by these regulations, no person must cause or allow effluent or leachate to discharge so that it may move directly or indirectly into ground water unless he is discharging pursuant to a discharge plan approved by the NMED Secretary. When a plan has been approved, discharges must be consistent with the terms and conditions of the plan.[86]

---

82 N.M. Water Quality Regulations § 3-101.A.

83 N.M. Water Quality Regulations § 3-101.A(1).

84 N.M. Water Quality Regulations § 3-103.

85 N.M. Water Quality Regulations § 3-103.A -.C. WQCC's assignment of a particular element or compound to one of these three categories has important consequences. Section 3-110 of the Water Quality Regulations authorizes WQCC to approve a discharge plan that will result in a violation of the § 3-103 standards only if the discharger can demonstrate that the discharges will not create a hazard to public health. N.M. Water Quality Regulations § 3-110.A. By definition, a hazard to public health exists any time the Human Health Standards (§ 3-103.A) are violated. Therefore, the variance provisions of § 3-110 can apply only to the other two categories of standards. Also, pursuant to a July 14, 1977, resolution, WQCC requires proof of compliance with the Irrigation Use Standards (§ 3-103.C) only if the contemplated discharge will be into water that has present or reasonably foreseeable agricultural use.

86 N.M. Water Quality Regulations § 3-104.

The Water Quality Regulations list 13 types of effluent or discharges that are exempt from this requirement.[87]

3.3 APPLICATION FOR DISCHARGE PLAN APPROVAL

Any person who intends to discharge into ground water, directly or indirectly, any contaminant listed in the ground water standards[88] or any toxic pollutant[89] must notify NMED.[90] The notice must provide the person's name and address, the location and quantity of the discharge, and an estimate of the concentrations of the contaminants.[91] Within 60 days, the Secretary will inform the person whether a discharge plan must be submitted.[92] For good cause shown, the Secretary may allow the person to discharge without an approved discharge plan for up to 120 days.[93]

The proposed discharge plan must set forth in detail the methods or techniques the discharger proposes to use or processes expected to naturally occur which will ensure compliance with the ground water regulations.[94] The plan must include information about the discharge, nearby watercourses, bodies of water and ground water locations, flooding potential, local geology, and sampling and measurement methods.[95] The Secretary may require the discharge plan to provide information about effluent and ground water

---

87 N.M. Water Quality Regulations § 3-105. These exemptions include "unpolluted" water, discharges from flood control systems, effluent that is subject to a NPDES permit, and effluent from septic tank systems that receive less than 2,000 gallons of liquid waste per day. These exemptions, however, generally do not apply to effluent disposal wells or in situ extraction wells. *See* N.M. Water Quality Regulations § 5-101.D.

88 N.M. Water Quality Regulations § 3-103.

89 "Toxic pollutant" means a water contaminant or combination of water contaminants in concentration(s) which, upon exposure, ingestion, or assimilation either directly from the environment or indirectly by ingestion through food chains, will unreasonably threaten to injure human health or the health of animals or plants which are commonly hatched, bred, cultivated, or protected for use by man for food or economic benefit. N.M. Water Quality Regulations § 1-101.Z.Z.

90 N.M. Water Quality Regulations § 3-106.B. A person who was discharging before June 1977 (four months after the effective date of the regulations) may continue to do so without a discharge plan until the Secretary notifies the person in writing that a discharge plan is required. N.M. Water Quality Regulations § 3-106.A.

91 N.M. Water Quality Regulations § 1-201.B.

92 N.M. Water Quality Regulations § 3-106.B.

93 *Id.*

94 N.M. Water Quality Regulations § 3-106.C.

95 *Id.*

monitoring, technology, and procedures.[96] The applicant must also, if requested, allow a representative of the Secretary to sample effluent and inspect the discharge site or facility as well as any relevant records.[97]

3.4 PROCEDURE FOR DISCHARGE PLAN APPROVAL

After the applicant has filed the proposed discharge plan, the Secretary sends notices of the application to the media, other governmental agencies, and persons who previously have requested notice.[98] Following this public notice, any member of the public may submit written comments to the Secretary and may also request a public hearing.[99] The Secretary must hold a public hearing on the application if the Secretary determines there is significant public interest in the application.[100]

Within 60 days after the public hearing or, if the Secretary decides not to hold a public hearing, within 60 days after the Secretary has received all required information, the Secretary must approve or disapprove the proposed discharge plan.[101] To receive approval,[102] the discharge plan must demonstrate first that neither a hazard to public health nor undue risk to property will result from the contemplated discharges.[103] The Secretary also must conclude that the contemplated discharge (1) will not affect ground water that has a total dissolved solids (TDS) concentration of 10,000 mg/l or less;[104] (2) will not result in concentrations that exceed the ground water quality standards[105] and will not result in the presence of any toxic pollutant at any place of withdrawal of water for present or reasonably

---

96 N.M. Water Quality Regulations § 3-107.A.

97 N.M. Water Quality Regulations § 3-107.D.

98 N.M. Water Quality Regulations § 3-108.A.

99 N.M. Water Quality Regulations § 3-108.C.

100 *Id.*

101 N.M. Water Quality Regulations § 3-109.A-.B.

102 1993 amendments to the WQA added three additional requirements for permit approval. *See* notes 45, 46 & 47 in this Chapter.

103 N.M. Water Quality Regulations § 3-109.C. A "hazard to public health" exists when water which is used or is reasonably expected to be used in the future as a human drinking water supply exceeds at the time and place of such use, one or more of the numerical [ground water quality] standards of Subsection 3-103.A, or the naturally occurring concentrations, whichever is higher, or if any toxic pollutant affecting human health is present in the water. N.M. Water Quality Regulations § 1-101.CC.

104 N.M. Water Quality Regulations § 3-109.C(1).

105 *See* N.M. Water Quality Regulations § 3-103.

foreseeable future use,[106] or (3) in certain circumstances, will meet differently articulated nitrogen and nitrate concentration limits and otherwise not result in contaminant concentrations that exceed the ground water quality standards.[107] The Secretary will not approve a proposed discharge plan if it does not provide for flow measurement and sampling, will result in the violation of the ground water quality standards, or otherwise may result in a hazard to public health.[108] The Secretary generally may approve a discharge plan for a maximum of five years.[109]

The N.M. Water Quality Regulations set forth a special procedure to obtain approval of a discharge plan even though it will result in contaminant concentrations that exceed WQCC's ground water quality standards.[110] The discharger may file with the Secretary a written petition that seeks WQCC's consideration of the discharge plan. The criteria that the Secretary and, ultimately, WQCC will consider are the extent to which the plan would violate the ground water quality standards[111] and whether the plan demonstrates either the maximum use of technology within the economic capability of the discharger or that there is no reasonable relationship between the economic and social costs and benefits (including meeting the ground water quality standards) to be obtained.[112] The discharger still must establish that discharges under the proposed plan would not create a hazard to public health or undue risk to property.[113]

---

106 N.M. Water Quality Regulations § 3-109.C(2). This alternative requirement expressly exempts contaminants that exist in the water before the discharger diverts it and contaminants that result from leaching through undisturbed natural materials. *See* N.M. Water Quality Regulations § 3-109.D.

107 N.M. Water Quality Regulations § 3-109.C(3). This alternative requirement expressly exempts contaminants that exist in the water before the discharger diverts it and contaminants that result from leaching through undisturbed natural materials. *See* N.M. Water Quality Regulations § 3-109.D.

108 N.M. Water Quality Regulations § 3-109.G(1). *See also* N.M. Stat. Ann. § 74-6-5(E) (Repl. Pamp. 1993).

109 N.M. Water Quality Regulations § 3-109.G(4). If discharges will not begin until after the approval date, the Secretary may approve a term of up to seven years, as long as the actual discharges are limited to a period of no more than five years. *Id. See also* N.M. Stat. Ann. § 74-6-5(H) (Repl. Pamp. 1993).

110 N.M. Water Quality Regulations § 3-110. As explained above, WQCC will never permit violation of the Human Health Standards. Section 3-110 also generally does not apply to effluent disposal wells and in situ extraction wells. *See* N.M. Water Quality Regulations § 5-101.E.

111 N.M. Water Quality Regulations § 3-110.B.

112 N.M. Water Quality Regulations § 3-110.A.

113 *Id.*

3.5 POST-APPROVAL ACTIONS

If, after approving the discharge plan, the Secretary determines that the discharger is violating any of the Water Quality Regulations or that the ground water quality standards are being or will be exceeded, the Secretary may direct the discharger to modify the plan to comply with the regulations.[114] The Secretary has the right to terminate the plan if the discharger fails to modify the plan in accordance with the Secretary's directions[115] or if any of the causes enumerated in N.M. Stat. Ann. § 74-6-5(L) (Repl. Pamp. 1993) exist.[116]

The Water Quality Regulations provide for transfer of ownership, control, and/or possession of a facility that is the subject of an approved discharge plan.[117] Before the transfer takes place, the transferor must send the transferee written notification that the discharge plan exists and must send a copy of the notice to the Secretary. Upon receipt of the notice, the transferee has a duty to review the plan. Once the transfer is accomplished, the transferee assumes the transferor's rights and responsibilities under the discharge plan.[118]

3.6 APPEALS

The WQA[119] and Water Quality Regulations[120] provide methods for any person who participated in a permitting action before NMED and who is adversely affected by such permitting action to appeal to WQCC. Anyone may appeal decisions of the Secretary with which they disagree by filing, within 30 days after receiving notice of the Secretary's action,[121] a petition for a hearing before WQCC.[122] WQCC must hold a hearing within 90 days after receipt of the petition.[123] The New Mexico Court of Appeals hears appeals from decisions of WQCC.[124] WQCC may stay an action of a constituent agency pending on appeal.[125]

---

114 N.M. Water Quality Regulations § 3-109.E(1).

115 N.M. Water Quality Regulations § 3-109.E(2). *See also* N.M. Stat. Ann. § 74-6-5(L) (Repl. Pamp. 1993).

116 *See* Other General Provisions Section of this Chapter.

117 N.M. Water Quality Regulations § 3-111.

118 *Id.*

119 N.M. Stat. Ann. §§ 74-6-5(M) to -5(P) (Repl. Pamp. 1993).

120 N.M. Water Quality Regulations §§ 3-112 to -113.

121 N.M. Stat. Ann. § 74-6-5(N) (Repl. Pamp. 1993).

122 *Id.*; N.M. Water Quality Regulations § 3-112.

123 N.M. Stat. Ann. § 74-6-5(O) (Repl. Pamp. 1993).

124 N.M. Stat. Ann. § 74-6-7 (Repl. Pamp. 1993); N.M. Water Quality Regulations § 3-113.

125 N.M. Stat. Ann. § 74-6-7(C) (Repl. Pamp. 1993).

4.0 INJECTION WELLS

WQCC has promulgated special regulations for effluent disposal wells and in situ extraction wells.[126] An "effluent disposal well" is:

> [A] well which is used for the disposal of fluids which may have the potential to cause water pollution. Wells used in the following practices are not effluent disposal wells: conventional mining, old stope leaching and sand backfilling. Wells where the emplacement of fluids is limited to natural ground water seeping or flowing into conventional mine workings are not effluent disposal wells. Barrier wells, drainage wells, recharge wells, and return flow wells are not effluent disposal wells if the discharger can demonstrate that the discharge will not adversely affect the health of persons, and
>
> 1. the injection fluid does not contain a contaminant which may cause an exceedance at any place of present or reasonable foreseeable future use of any primary state drinking water maximum contaminant level as specified in the "Water Supply Regulations" adopted by the Environmental Improvement Board under the Environmental Improvement Act; or
>
> 2. the discharger can demonstrate that the injection will result in an overall or net improvement in water quality as determined by the Director [Secretary].[127]

An "in situ" extraction well is a well which injects fluids for mineral extraction, except (1) conventional mines, (2) old stope leaching, (3) the extraction of oil, natural gas, or gas extracted from coal gasification, or (4) wells for which the discharger can demonstrate use as part of an experimental technology.[128]

4.1 GENERAL REQUIREMENTS

A person who intends to discharge fluid into the ground with an effluent disposal well or in situ extraction well must comply with WQCC's ground water pollution control regulations.[129] In particular, the Secretary's approval of a discharge plan must be obtained.[130] Under certain circumstances, the discharger may submit a project discharge plan that covers

---

126 N.M. Water Quality Regulations §§ 5-100 to -300.

127 N.M. Water Quality Regulations § 1-101.X.

128 N.M. Water Quality Regulations § 1-101.FF.

129 N.M. Water Quality Regulations § 5-101.A.

130 N.M. Water Quality Regulations § 5-101.B. Exceptions to this rule are discussed in the Exemptions and Waivers Section of this Chapter.

more than one well.[131] Operators of all other injection wells[132] must submit specified information to the Secretary and comply with the general ground water regulations.[133]

There are, however, additional requirements for an effluent disposal well or in situ extraction well discharge plan. First, the Secretary must consider additional information before approval is given.[134] Second, the discharger must include in the plan provisions for plugging and abandoning the well.[135] Third, the plan must contain the signature and certification of the discharger or, if the discharger is not an individual, an executive officer of the discharger.[136] Fourth, there are constraints on the type of ground water into which the effluent disposal well or in situ extraction well may discharge. The well may discharge into ground water that has a TDS concentration of 10,000 mg/l or more.[137] If the ground water has a TDS concentration of between 5,000 and 10,000 mg/l,[138] the discharger must obtain an aquifer designation[139] or, if the well is an in situ extraction well, the discharge plan may provide for restoration of the ground water at the conclusion of operations to WQCC's ground water quality standards.[140] If the ground water has a TDS concentration of less than 5,000 mg/l, effluent disposal wells are not permitted and in situ extraction wells are permitted only if the discharge plan provides for restoration.[141]

Finally, well operators must also meet certain requirements even before construction begins. Before construction begins on an effluent disposal well or conversion of an existing well to an effluent disposal well, the operator must obtain the Secretary's preliminary approval

---

131 N.M. Water Quality Regulations § 5-101.F.

132 Any well that results in the "subsurface emplacement of fluids" is an injection well. N.M. Water Quality Regulations § 1-101.DD.

133 N.M. Water Quality Regulations § 5-300.

134 N.M. Water Quality Regulations § 5-210.B. The Regulations also set forth detailed technical criteria and performance standards for effluent disposal wells and in situ extraction wells, by which the Secretary evaluates proposed discharge plans. N.M. Water Quality Regulations §§ 5-202 to -208.

135 N.M. Water Quality Regulations § 5-209.A.

136 N.M. Water Quality Regulations § 5-101.H.

137 N.M. Water Quality Regulations § 5-101.C.

138 N.M. Water Quality Regulations § 5-103.A.

139 N.M. Water Quality Regulations § 5-101.C(1).

140 N.M. Water Quality Regulations § 5-101.C(2).

141 *Id.* Effluent disposal wells, by their very nature, are incompatible with the notion of restoration. For that reason, they will be permitted only where the affected ground water cannot be used for any other purpose. In contrast, ground water affected by in situ extraction wells can be restored to the standards of § 3-103, and for that reason they will be allowed where the water has other potential uses.

of the discharge plan.[142] In contrast, the operator of an in situ extraction well must send written notice to the Secretary of the construction plans before the construction begins.[143] The notice must contain construction plans, specifications, and other information about the well,[144] including information showing the discharger is able to take measures to prevent ground water contamination.[145] Within 30 days after the notice is received, the Secretary must notify the discharger whether the information about the ability to take measures to prevent ground water contamination is acceptable or unacceptable.[146] If the Secretary has found the information unacceptable, construction may not begin.[147] Within the same 30-day period the Secretary will publicize the notice,[148] and public comment will be accepted during the following 30-day period.[149] At the end of the public comment period, the Secretary must comment in writing on the plans and specifications.[150] Finally, within 30 days after construction of the in situ extraction well is completed, the discharger must notify the Secretary whether the well was built in accordance with the original plan and specifications.[151]

4.2 DESIGNATED AQUIFERS

A person who wishes to discharge with an effluent disposal well into ground water that has a TDS concentration of 5,000 to 10,000 mg/l must obtain an aquifer designation.[152] A person who wishes to discharge with an in situ extraction well into such ground water has a choice of obtaining an aquifer designation or providing for restoration of water quality in his discharge plan.[153]

---

142 N.M. Water Quality Regulations § 5-102.A. Final approval will be contingent on additional information submitted after construction is finished. *Id.*; N.M. Water Quality Regulations § 5-210.C.

143 N.M. Water Quality Regulations § 5-102.B.

144 N.M. Water Quality Regulations § 5-102.B(1)(d).

145 N.M. Water Quality Regulations § 5-102.B(1)(d)(10).

146 N.M. Water Quality Regulations § 5-102.B(2).

147 *Id.*

148 N.M. Water Quality Regulations § 5-102.B(4).

149 *Id.*

150 N.M. Water Quality Regulations § 5-102.B(5). *See also* N.M. Water Quality Regulations § 5-102.B(3).

151 N.M. Water Quality Regulations § 5-102.B(6). If, after an in situ extraction well is constructed, the discharge plan is never approved or operation otherwise never begins, the discharger nevertheless must plug and abandon the well if it may cause ground water contamination. N.M. Water Quality Regulations § 5-103.B(7).

152 N.M. Water Quality Regulations § 5-103.A(1).

153 N.M. Water Quality Regulations § 5-103.A(2).

The discharger initiates the aquifer designation process by filing a written petition with the Secretary.[154] The petition must identify and describe the aquifer or aquifers,[155] state the extent to which the well would add water contaminants to ground water,[156] and demonstrate that:

> 1. It [the aquifer] is not currently used as a domestic or agricultural water supply; and
> 2. There is no reasonable relationship between the economic and social costs of failure to designate and benefits to be obtained from its use as a domestic or agricultural water supply because:
>   a) It is situated at a depth or location which makes recovery of water for drinking or agricultural purposes economically or technologically impracticable at present and in the reasonably foreseeable future; or
>   b) It is already so contaminated that it would be economically or technologically impracticable to render that water fit for human consumption or agricultural use at present and in the reasonably foreseeable future.[157]

If the petition concerns an in situ extraction well, it also must state whether, and to what extent, restoration will be carried out.[158]

The Secretary may deny the petition or refer it to WQCC with a recommendation that WQCC hold a public hearing.[159] If the Secretary refers it to WQCC, WQCC will undertake its own review and determine whether to grant or deny a public hearing.[160] If WQCC grants a public hearing, it will issue a public notice of the hearing,[161] conduct the hearing,[162] and then rule on the petition.[163] If WQCC grants the petition, the well operator still must comply with WQCC's other ground water regulations and insure that other aquifers will be protected.[164]

---

154 N.M. Water Quality Regulations § 5-103.A.

155 N.M. Water Quality Regulations § 5-103.B.

156 N.M. Water Quality Regulations § 5-103.D.

157 N.M. Water Quality Regulations § 5-103.C.

158 N.M. Water Quality Regulations § 5-103.D.

159 N.M. Water Quality Regulations § 5-103.E.

160 N.M. Water Quality Regulations § 5-103.F.

161 *Id.*

162 N.M. Water Quality Regulations § 5-103.H.

163 N.M. Water Quality Regulations § 5-103.J.

164 N.M. Water Quality Regulations § 5-103.K.

4.3 ACTION ON DISCHARGE PLANS

Discharge plans must provide for monitoring of wells and submission of the monitoring data to the Secretary.[165] If that data or other information available to the Secretary indicates that the discharge is violating or may violate the regulations, the Secretary may require modification of the discharge plan or the Secretary may terminate the plan.[166] The Secretary also may modify or terminate the plan if the discharger fails to comply with any of its provisions, if the discharger failed to disclose or misrepresented any relevant facts in connection with the discharge plan, or if operation of the well may cause a hazard to public health or undue risk to property and can only be regulated to acceptable levels by discharge plan modification or termination.[167]

The Secretary may approve a discharge plan for a period of up to five years.[168] At the end of the approval period, an operator of an effluent disposal well or an in situ extraction well must apply again to obtain the Secretary's approval of the plan. If the renewal application is submitted at least 180 days before the expiration date, however, the plan will continue in effect until the renewal application has been approved or disapproved, even if that process takes longer than 180 days.[169]

Special provisions govern transfer of effluent disposal well and in situ extraction well discharge plans.[170] The discharger must provide the Secretary with written notice of the transfer at least 30 days before the transfer date.[171] The notice must be signed by both the discharger and the proposed successor discharger, contain the proposed successor's acknowledgement that the proposed successor will be responsible for complying with the discharge plan after possession of the well is taken, identify the transfer date, and include information about the successor discharger's financial responsibility.[172] The Secretary must approve the proposed transfer before it can take effect.[173] The Secretary may require modification of the discharge plan and additional demonstration of adequate financial responsibility.[174]

---

165 N.M. Water Quality Regulations § 3-107.

166 N.M. Water Quality Regulations § 5-101.J.

167 *Id.*

168 N.M. Water Quality Regulations § 3-109.G(4).

169 N.M. Water Quality Regulations § 5-101.G.

170 N.M. Water Quality Regulations § 5-101.I.

171 N.M. Water Quality Regulations § 5-103.I(2)(a).

172 N.M. Water Quality Regulations § 5-103.I(3).

173 N.M. Water Quality Regulations § 5-103.I(2)(b).

174 *Id.*

4.4 EXEMPTIONS AND WAIVERS

The following effluent disposal wells or in situ extraction wells are exempt from WQCC's injection well regulations:[175] wells regulated by OCD pursuant to the OGA[176] or the Geothermal Resources Conservation Act,[177] wells regulated by the New Mexico Coal Surface Mining Bureau pursuant to the Surface Mining Act,[178] or wells used to dispose of less than 2,000 gallons per day of domestic sewage effluent, which the EIB regulates pursuant to its liquid waste disposal regulations.[179]

The Secretary may waive certain requirements for effluent disposal well and in situ extraction well discharge plans where the well does not penetrate or inject into or above ground water that has a TDS concentration of 10,000 mg/l or less.[180] In particular, the Secretary may approve a plan that has relaxed requirements for construction, mechanical integrity, operation, monitoring, and reporting.[181] If the plan concerns an in situ extraction well, the Secretary may even waive all the special regulations that apply to injection wells and require only that the discharger comply with the general ground water regulations.[182]

5.0 WATER SUPPLY REGULATIONS

The 1974 United States Safe Drinking Water Act[183] (SDWA) charged EPA with responsibility for preparing and implementing national drinking water regulations, prescribing maximum contaminant levels (MCLs)[184] for a variety of pollutants, and dictating criteria and

---

175 N.M. Water Quality Regulations § 5-101.D.

176 N.M. Stat. Ann. §§ 70-2-1 to -38 (Repl. Pamp. 1987 & Supp. 1993).

177 N.M. Stat. Ann. §§ 71-5-1 to -24 (Repl. Pamp. 1981 & Supp. 1989).

178 N.M. Stat. Ann. §§ 69-25A-1 to -36 (Repl. Pamp. 1979 & Supp. 1993).

179 *See* Liquid Waste Disposal Section of this Chapter.

180 N.M. Water Quality Regulations § 5-104. However, the Secretary may grant the waiver only if injection will not result in an increased risk of movement of fluids into ground water having 10,000 mg/l or less TDS, except for fluid movement approved pursuant to Section 5-103. N.M. Water Quality Regulations § 5-104.B.

181 N.M. Water Quality Regulations § 5-104.A(1).

182 N.M. Water Quality Regulations § 5-104.A(2).

183 21 U.S.C. § 349, 42 U.S.C. §§ 201, 300f to 300j-9. The SDWA was amended in 1986 to require MCLs for an additional 83 specified contaminants, with standards for additional contaminants to be issued on a three-year basis, to provide increased protection for sole source aquifers, and to regulate lead in drinking water. Also required by the amendments was the disinfection of all public water supplies and the filtration of all surface water systems.

184 "Maximum contaminant level" means the permissible level of a contaminant in water which is delivered to the free-flowing outlet of the ultimate user of a public water supply system, except in the case of turbidity and those contaminants listed in N.M. Water Supply Regulations § 203.D where the maximum permissible level is measured

procedures to assure supplies of drinking water which dependably comply with the MCLs.[185] The SDWA also authorized states to assume primary enforcement responsibility.[186] For its part the New Mexico Legislature in the Environmental Improvement Act[187] directed EIB to promulgate regulations and standards for water supplies.[188] NMED has the power to develop and enforce regulations for water supplies, known as the Water Supply Regulations (last amended April 16, 1991, effective May 17, 1991).[189] NMED has created a Drinking Water Bureau of the Field Operations Division to administer the regulations. As EPA continues to establish or modify MCLs for additional contaminants under the SDWA, EIB will amend the Water Supply Regulations to implement new federal regulations.

In 1993 the New Mexico Legislature imposed a 3¢/thousand gallon water conservation fee on every person which operates a public water supply system.[190] These fees are paid into a water conservation fund administered by NMED to be used in testing public water supplies as required under the SWDA, to perform vulnerability assessments, and to implement the requirements of the Utility Operators Certification Act.[191]

In addition, WQCC has adopted regulations authorized by the WQA[192] requiring most public water supply systems to be managed by certified operators; all such systems will be required to have certified operators by December 1, 1995.[193]

5.1 APPLICABILITY

The Water Supply Regulations are applicable to all public water supply systems. The Water Supply Regulations define "public water supply system" as a system for the provision

---

at the point of entry to the distribution system. Contaminants added to the water under circumstances controlled by the user, except those resulting from corrosion of piping and plumbing caused by water quality, are excluded from this definition. New Mexico Water Supply Regulations § 103. This definition expands the SDWA's definition of MCL: the maximum permissible level of a contaminant in water which is delivered to any user of a public water system. 42 U.S.C. § 300f(3).

185 42 U.S.C. § 300f.

186 42 U.S.C. §§ 300g-1, -2. New Mexico is authorized to exercise primary enforcement responsibility under the SDWA.

187 N.M. Stat. Ann. §§ 74-1-1 to -11 (Repl. Pamp. 1993).

188 N.M. Stat. Ann. § 74-1-8 (Repl. Pamp. 1993).

189 N.M. Stat. Ann. § 74-1-7 (Repl. Pamp. 1993).

190 N.M. Stat. Ann. § 74-1-13(A) (Repl. Pamp. 1993).

191 N.M. Stat. Ann. § 74-1-13(B),(C) (Repl. Pamp. 1993). The Utility Operators Certification Act is codified as N.M. Stat. Ann. §§ 61-33-1 to -10 (Repl. Pamp. 1993).

192 N.M. Stat. Ann. § 74-6-5(G) (Repl. Pamp. 1993).

193 N.M. Water Quality Regulations §§ 4-100 to -210. These regulations also provide for certification of operators of public wastewater facilities.

to the public of piped water for human consumption if the system has at least 15 service connections or regularly services an average of at least 25 individuals at least 60 days out of the year.[194] A public water supply system includes (1) any water supply source, treatment, storage, and distribution facilities under the control of the operator of the system and (2) any water supply source or pretreatment storage facilities not under such control which are used primarily in connection with such system. Water haulers and water wholesalers are included in this definition.[195] All public water supply systems must be managed and operated in compliance with the Water Supply Regulations,[196] and all operators of such systems must register with the New Mexico Taxation and Revenue Department in accordance with N.M. Stat. Ann. § 7-1-12 (Repl. Pamp. 1993).[197]

A public water supply system is either a community water system, a non-transient non-community water system or a non-community water system. These categories of public water supply systems must be carefully distinguished, as the applicability of the regulations varies depending on the type of water system involved. A community water system is a public water supply system which serves at least 15 service connections used by year-round residents or which regularly serves at least 25 year-round residences.[198] A non-transient non-community water system is a public water supply system that is not a community water system and that regularly serves at least 25 of the same persons for more than six months per year, including but not limited to schools and factories.[199] A non-community water system is a public water supply system that is not a community water system or a non-transient non-community water system. Such a system includes but is not limited to (1) seasonal facilities (such as children's camps and recreational camping areas) or (2) year-round facilities which serve more than 25 persons who are not residents thereof (such as gasoline service stations, marinas, rest areas, and restaurants) which are not served by a community water system.[200]

Finally, a private water supply system is a system for the provision of piped water for human consumption or domestic purposes, if such system does not have at least 15 service connections or does not regularly serve an average of 25 individuals at least 60 days during

---

194 N.M. Water Supply Regulations, (EIB/WSR) § 103 (as amended through 4/16/91). A functionally identical definition is found at N.M. Stat. Ann. § 74-1-13(G)(2) (Repl. Pamp. 1993).

195 *Id.*

196 N.M. Water Supply Regulations § 201.A.

197 N.M. Stat. Ann. § 74-1-13(F) (Repl. Pamp. 1993).

198 N.M. Water Supply Regulations § 103.

199 *Id.*

200 *Id.*

the year.[201] Except for well siting requirements, the Water Supply Regulations do not apply to these private systems.[202]

5.2 POWERS OF NMED SECRETARY

The powers of the Secretary or the Secretary's authorized representative are set forth in Section 201 of the Water Supply Regulations. The Secretary is authorized to take such actions as the Secretary deems necessary to protect the health of persons who are or may be users of a public water system, and the Secretary may respond to civil emergency situations involving public drinking water.[203] The Secretary may issue orders necessary to protect the health of persons who are or may be users of such systems, including travellers, and may commence civil actions for appropriate relief, including restraining orders or permanent or temporary injunctions.[204] Upon presentation of proper credentials and after receiving consent from the supplier of water, the Secretary is also empowered to inspect public water supply systems.[205] If permission to enter a public water supply system or otherwise make an inspection is denied, the Secretary may apply to a court for an inspection order allowing for such entry or inspection.[206] The supplier of water is authorized to accompany the Secretary during the inspection of the premises of the public water supply system.[207]

5.3 GENERAL OPERATING REQUIREMENTS

The Water Supply Regulations set out general operating requirements for all public water supply system owners or operators. These include (1) protection of water supply during repair work, (2) disinfection following repair or reconstruction, (3) disinfection of seasonally operated facilities, (4) security and protection of the water supply, (5) protection of water supply wells, (6) treatment requirements, (7) finished water storage facility requirements, (8) emergency operation requirements, (9) cross-connection requirements, (10) reservoir maintenance and disinfection, (11) chemical additives requirements, (12) lead pipe, solder, and flux prohibitions, and (13) prohibition on using iodine as a disinfectant.[208] In lieu of MCLs, the Water Supply Regulations also contain requirements for disinfection and filtration to

---

201 *Id.*

202 N.M. Water Supply Regulations §§ 104, 107.C(1).

203 N.M. Water Supply Regulations § 201.B.

204 *Id.* The EPA has separate enforcement powers under the SDWA which can be exercised against a public water supply system if the state does not take appropriate enforcement action. *See* 42 U.S.C. § 1414.

205 N.M. Water Supply Regulations § 109.A. "Supplier of water" means any person who owns or operates a public water supply system. N.M. Water Supply Regulations § 103.

206 N.M. Water Supply Regulations § 109.B.

207 N.M. Water Supply Regulations § 109.C.

208 N.M. Water Supply Regulations § 208.A-.M.

control Giardia lamblia, viruses, heterotrophic plate count bacteria, Legionella, and turbidity.[209]

5.4 MAXIMUM CONTAMINANT LEVELS

The Water Supply Regulations set Maximum Contaminant Levels (MCLs) for inorganic chemicals,[210] organic chemicals,[211] turbidity,[212] coliform bacteria,[213] and radioactivity.[214] Nitrate MCLs[215] apply to all public water supply systems. Other inorganic MCLs listed in the regulations apply only to community water systems,[216] as is the case with MCLs for specified insecticides,[217] herbicides,[218] and other organic contaminants.[219] The MCLs for trihalomethanes[220] applies only to community water systems serving a population of more than 10,000 individuals which add a disinfectant to the water in the treatment process.[221] MCLs for turbidity are applicable to all public water supply systems using surface water sources, excluding springs and infiltration galleries, in whole or in part, but only until June 29, 1993.[222] MCLs for coliform bacteria are also

---

209 N.M. Water Supply Regulations §§ 901-903.

210 N.M. Water Supply Regulations § 202.

211 N.M. Water Supply Regulations § 203.

212 N.M. Water Supply Regulations § 204.

213 N.M. Water Supply Regulations § 205.

214 N.M. Water Supply Regulations §§ 206-207.

215 N.M. Water Supply Regulations § 202. Compliance with the MCLs for nitrates is calculated pursuant to N.M. Water Supply Regulations § 304.

216 N.M. Water Supply Regulations § 202.A. Compliance with the MCLs for inorganic chemicals is calculated pursuant to N.M. Water Supply Regulations § 304.

217 N.M. Water Supply Regulations § 203.A. Compliance with the MCLs for herbicides is calculated pursuant to N.M. Water Supply Regulations § 305.

218 N.M. Water Supply Regulations § 203.B. Compliance with the MCLs for insecticides is calculated pursuant to N.M. Water Supply Regulations § 305.

219 N.M. Water Supply Regulations § 203.D. The MCLs set forth in § 203.D apply to non-transient non-community water systems as well as community water systems.

220 "Trihalomethane" means one of the family of organic compounds, named as derivatives of methane, wherein three of the four hydrogen atoms in methane are each substituted by a halogen atom in the molecular structure. N.M. Water Supply Regulations § 103.

221 N.M. Water Supply Regulations § 203. Compliance with the MCLs for trihalomethanes is calculated pursuant to N.M. Water Supply Regulations § 313.

222 N.M. Water Supply Regulations § 204.

applicable to all public water supply systems.[223] However, MCLs for radioactivity are applicable only to community water systems.[224]

All samples for MCLs must be collected, prepared, and examined using the most current methods for the examination of drinking water listed in the Code of Federal Regulations (40 C.F.R. Part 141) or by other methods for the examination of drinking water approved by EPA.[225] All samples for community and non-transient non-community water supply systems must be collected by either NMED (for a fee[226]) or persons holding a current sampling certificate issued by the Secretary, who must use NMED-approved supplies and equipment.[227] Analysis must be performed by a NMED-certified laboratory,[228] except that measuring turbidity or free-chlorine residual may be performed by any person acceptable to NMED.[229] NMED may validate the results of any monitoring done pursuant to the regulations and must validate results when it receives a positive bacterial sample.[230] NMED may also perform its own sampling and monitoring of water supplies.[231]

The Water Supply Regulations contain sampling and analytical requirements for (1) microbiological contaminants,[232] (2) systems utilizing surface water,[233] (3) inorganic chemicals,[234] (4) organic chemicals other than total trihalomethanes,[235] (5) radioactivity,[236] and (6) total trihalomethanes.[237]

There are special sampling requirements for certain specified organic chemicals applicable to all community water supply systems and non-transient non-community water systems.[238]

---

223 N.M. Water Supply Regulations § 205.

224 N.M. Water Supply Regulations §§ 206-207.

225 N.M. Water Supply Regulations § 301.

226 N.M. Water Supply Regulations § 301.I(2).

227 N.M. Water Supply Regulations § 301.E, .H, .I.

228 N.M. Water Supply Regulations § 309.A, .B.

229 N.M. Water Supply Regulations § 309.A.

230 N.M. Water Supply Regulations § 311.

231 N.M. Water Supply Regulations § 312.

232 N.M. Water Supply Regulations § 302.

233 N.M. Water Supply Regulations § 303.

234 N.M. Water Supply Regulations § 304.

235 N.M. Water Supply Regulations § 305.

236 N.M. Water Supply Regulations §§ 306-307.

237 N.M. Water Supply Regulations § 313.

238 N.M. Water Supply Regulations § 701.

5.5 VARIANCES

Variances from a maximum contaminant level for a public water supply system may be obtained from the Secretary. In order to grant a variance the Secretary must find (1) because of the characteristics of the raw water sources which are reasonably available, a system cannot meet an MCL despite application of the best technology, treatment techniques, or other means which the Secretary finds are generally available (taking costs into consideration) and (2) the granting of a variance will not result in an unreasonable risk to the health of the persons served by the system.[239] The Secretary may also grant a variance to a public water supply system from the requirements of a specified treatment technique upon a finding that the system has demonstrated that such a treatment technique is not necessary to protect the health of persons because of the nature of the raw water source of such system.[240] A variance is sought by filing a written request with the Secretary.[241] The Water Supply Regulations set forth the considerations which must be made by the Secretary in determining whether to grant the variance as well as timing, schedule of compliance, and public notification requirements.[242] There are specific regulations governing variances from the MCLs for total trihalomethanes, fluoride, synthetic organic chemicals, coliforms, and filtration and disinfection requirements.[243] The Secretary may also condition a variance (or exemption) for a public water supply system on the use of bottled water or point-of-use devices.[244]

5.6 EXEMPTIONS

An exemption from a maximum contaminant level or from a treatment technique requirement may be granted by the Secretary to a public water supply system upon a finding that (1) due to compelling factors (which include economic factors) the system is unable to comply with such contaminant level or treatment technique, (2) the system was in operation on the effective date of such contaminant level or treatment technique requirement, and (3) the granting of the exemption will not result in an unreasonable risk to health.[245] There are procedures for seeking an exemption, requirements for public notice, specified factors which the Secretary must consider in determining whether to grant such an exemption, and a prescribed method of disposition of exemption requests.[246] The Secretary must prescribe

---

239 N.M. Water Supply Regulations § 105.A.

240 N.M. Water Supply Regulations § 105.B.

241 N.M. Water Supply Regulations § 105.C.

242 N.M. Water Supply Regulations § 105.C, .F.

243 N.M. Water Supply Regulations § 107.

244 N.M. Water Supply Regulations § 108.

245 N.M. Water Supply Regulations § 106.A.

246 N.M. Water Supply Regulations § 106.B, .F.

a schedule for bringing the system into compliance; the Water Supply Regulations also provide a method for extending the date of compliance.[247]

5.7 REPORTS, NOTICE, AND RECORDS

There are reporting, public notification, and recordkeeping requirements applicable to all suppliers of water in a public water supply system.[248]

5.7.1 Reporting Requirements

Results of all analyses performed under the Water Supply Regulations must be provided to the appropriate NMED field office within 10 days after the analyses are performed, except as otherwise provided in the regulations.[249] Any failure to comply with the regulations must be reported to NMED within 48 hours.[250] A supplier of water is not required to report analytical results if the Scientific Laboratory Division of NMED performs the analysis or if the certified laboratory performing the analysis reports the results to NMED directly.[251] There are also reporting requirements for unregulated organic contaminants.[252]

5.7.2 Public Notification

The owner or operator must notify the public of violations of MCLs, treatment techniques, variances, or exemptions in the manner specified in the regulations.[253] The general content of the notice and, in certain circumstances, specific health effects language are mandated by the regulations.[254] All new billing units or new hookups must be given a copy of the most recent public notice for any outstanding violation of any MCL or any treatment technique by the owner or operator of a community water system prior to or at the time service begins.[255] NMED must be provided a representative copy of all public notices required for these violations within 10 days after completion of each public notification.[256]

---

247 N.M. Water Supply Regulations § 106.D(3), .G.

248 N.M. Water Supply Regulations §§ 401-406.

249 N.M. Water Supply Regulations § 401.A.

250 N.M. Water Supply Regulations § 401.B.

251 N.M. Water Supply Regulations § 401.C.

252 N.M. Water Supply Regulations § 702.

253 N.M. Water Supply Regulations § 402.A, .B.

254 N.M. Water Supply Regulations § 402.D, .E.

255 N.M. Water Supply Regulations § 402.C.

256 N.M. Water Supply Regulations § 401.D.

NMED may give the public notice on behalf of the owner or operator, but this does not relieve the supplier of water from the legal responsibilities for compliance with the public notice requirements.[257]

The Water Supply Regulations contain specific public notice requirements pertaining to lead and iodine applicable to all community water systems and non-transient non-community water systems. The regulations specify the manner and general content of the notice and require inclusion of specific mandatory health effects information.[258] The Water Supply Regulations also contain specific reporting and recordkeeping requirements for public water supply systems which utilize surface water.[259]

5.7.3 Recordkeeping

Public water supply system owners and operators must keep on the premises, or at a convenient location near the premises, the following records: (1) records of bacteriological and turbidity analyses, for not less than five years; (2) records of chemical analyses, for not less than 10 years;[260] (3) records of action taken to correct violations of federal and state drinking water regulations, for not less than three years after the last action taken with respect to the particular violation involved; (4) copies of any written reports, summaries, or communications relating to sanitary surveys of a system, for not less than 10 years after completion of the sanitary survey involved; and (5) records concerning a variance or exemption granted to the system, for not less than five years following the expiration of such variance or exemption.[261]

5.8 WATER SUPPLY SITING AND CONSTRUCTION

The Water Supply Regulations contain specific siting and construction requirements which are applicable to all new public water supply systems and to modifications of existing systems.[262] Section 501 requires approval by NMED before any construction or modification is commenced except for minor modifications[263] and Section 110 sets out specific site location requirements. Section 502 sets forth standards governing approval of construction or modification of public water supply systems. Appendix A to the Water Supply Regulations contains recommended review references pertaining to the design and preparation of engineering documents for public water supply systems.

---

257 N.M. Water Supply Regulations § 402.F.

258 N.M. Water Supply Regulations §§ 404-405.

259 N.M. Water Supply Regulations § 406.

260 Laboratory reports and data which must be kept may be kept in either original or tabular summary form. N.M. Water Supply Regulations § 403.A.

261 N.M. Water Supply Regulations § 403.A, .D.

262 N.M. Water Supply Regulations §§ 110, 501-502.

263 N.M. Water Supply Regulations § 502.C.

5.9 THE RURAL INFRASTRUCTURE ACT

The Water Supply Regulations also contain guidelines and regulations implementing the Rural Infrastructure Act (RIA).[264] The purpose of the Rural Infrastructure Act is to provide financial assistance for the construction or modification of water supply facilities to local authorities which will correct demonstrable hazardous or inadequate conditions.[265] The guidelines address NMED's rating criteria for proposed projects, while the regulations contain definitions and eligibility requirements, set forth responsibilities of NMED under RIA, set out loan and grant disbursement requirements and limitations, and authorize NMED to set water user rates to ensure repayment of loans under RIA.[266]

6.0 LIQUID WASTE DISPOSAL

Regulations governing liquid waste disposal were adopted by EIB under the authority of the Environmental Improvement Act.[267] The regulations, entitled New Mexico Environmental Improvement Board Liquid Waste Disposal Regulations-2 (LWDR-2), became effective on January 18, 1990. The purpose of the LWDR-2 is to protect the health and welfare of New Mexico citizens by preventing and abating public health hazards and surface and ground water contamination from on-site waste disposal practices. The regulations apply only to residential waste disposal and similarly composed nonresidential liquid waste systems.[268] A liquid waste system is a system which is designed to receive liquid waste and includes a liquid waste treatment unit and associated disposal system, or an enclosed system[269] which is designed to receive and which receives 2,000 gallons or less of liquid

---

264 N.M. Stat. Ann. §§ 75-1-3 to -6 (Repl. Pamp. 1991). *See* N.M. Water Supply Regulations §§ 601-602, 802-810. For further discussion of RIA, *see* Rural Infrastructure Act Section of Additional Environmental Laws Chapter.

265 N.M. Water Supply Regulations § 803.

266 N.M. Water Supply Regulations §§ 804-810.

267 N.M. Stat. Ann. §§ 74-1-1 to -10 (Repl. Pamp. 1993).

268 "Liquid waste" means human excreta and water-carried wastes from typical residential plumbing fixtures and activities, including but not limited to wastes from toilets, sinks, bathroom fixtures, clothes- and dish-washing machines, and floor drains. Water-carried wastes from non-residential sources must be considered liquid waste if the composition and concentrations of the waste do not differ from typical domestic wastewaters. Specifically excluded from the definition of liquid waste are commercial process wastewaters, roof drainage, and wastes containing high concentrations of stabilizing or deodorizing agents. N.M. Liquid Waste Disposal Regulations-2, EIB/LWDR-2, § 104.Y (filed 12/19/89).

269 N.M. Liquid Waste Disposal Regulations § 104.Z.

waste per day.[270] These regulations do not apply to liquid waste systems which are subject to an NPDES permit under the federal CWA.[271]

6.1 LIQUID WASTE SYSTEM PERMIT REQUIREMENTS

Any person[272] who wishes to install or have installed a new liquid waste disposal system or to modify an existing liquid waste system must first obtain a permit from NMED,[273] in addition to any other permits required under local, state, or federal law.[274] Permits are also required to install or modify a privy.[275]

Permits are obtained by filing an application with the field office of NMED on a form provided by NMED.[276] NMED must take action on the permit within 10 working days after receipt of the completed application and notify the applicant of the action taken.[277] If NMED finds that the liquid waste disposal system may cause a hazard to public health or the degradation of a body of water, it can impose additional requirements on the permit holder.[278]

An issued permit may be canceled if the installation or modification of the liquid waste system is not completed within one year of the issuance of the permit or if NMED determines that the application was materially inaccurate.[279]

6.1.1 Variances

NMED may issue a variance of the LWDR-2 if a petitioner can establish by clear and convincing evidence that (1) the proposed liquid waste system will, by itself or in combination with other liquid waste systems, neither cause a hazard to public health nor degrade any body of water and (2) granting the variance will result in public health and environmental

---

270 N.M. Liquid Waste Disposal Regulations § 103.

271 *Id.*

272 "Person" means any individual, partnership, firm, public or private corporation, association, trust, estate, the state or any political subdivision or agency, federal agency, or any other legal entity or their legal representative, agents, or assigns. N.M. Liquid Waste Disposal Regulations § 104.FF.

273 N.M. Liquid Waste Disposal Regulations § 201.A.

274 N.M. Liquid Waste Disposal Regulations § 201.B.

275 "Privy" means a receptacle for non-liquid-carried excreta allowing direct discharge to the soil. N.M. Liquid Waste Disposal Regulations § 104.HH.

276 N.M. Liquid Waste Disposal Regulations § 201.C.

277 N.M. Liquid Waste Disposal Regulations § 201.D.

278 N.M. Liquid Waste Disposal Regulations §§ 201.D, .E, 301.C.

279 N.M. Liquid Waste Disposal Regulations § 201.I.

protection equal to or greater than the minimum protection provided by the varianced requirement.[280]

Application for variances is made by a petition to the field office of NMED having jurisdiction, and it must be accompanied by documentation supporting the petition, including documentation demonstrating that all owners of adjacent property sharing a common border with the lot for which the variance is sought have been notified, unless all adjacent properties are more than 1,000 feet from the liquid waste system for which the variance is sought.[281]

Between 10 and 20 days after receipt of the completed petition NMED must grant or deny the variance or grant the variance subject to conditions and must notify the person in writing of its decision.[282]

6.1.2 Hearings

A hearing before the Secretary is available to any person dissatisfied with NMED's actions on a permit application or variance petition.[283] A request for a hearing must be made within 15 days after notice that NMED's action has been issued or the decision is final.[284]

Hearings are held within 15 days after receipt of the request. Notice of the hearing is made by certified mail to the affected person and all owners of adjacent property sharing a common border with the lot for which the variance is sought.[285] The burden of proof is on the person requesting the hearing. The rules of civil procedure and the technical rules of evidence do not apply, but hearings are to be conducted so that all relevant views, arguments, and testimony are amply and fairly presented.[286] Within 15 days following the closure of the hearing, the Secretary must issue a written order sustaining, modifying, or reversing the action of NMED.[287]

6.1.3 Inspection

Before making a decision on a permit application, NMED may perform site inspections. It may also perform inspections during and after the construction of the system. It can require inspection holes and documentation to determine soil types, percolation rates, and soil

---

280 N.M. Liquid Waste Disposal Regulations § 202.D.

281 N.M. Liquid Waste Disposal Regulations § 202.B.

282 N.M. Liquid Waste Disposal Regulations § 202.C.

283 N.M. Liquid Waste Disposal Regulations § 203.A.

284 *Id.*

285 N.M. Liquid Waste Disposal Regulations § 203.B.

286 N.M. Liquid Waste Disposal Regulations § 203.F.

287 N.M. Liquid Waste Disposal Regulations § 203.G.

and water table depths. NMED may also collect samples of soil, liquid waste, or water to determine compliance with the regulations.[288]

6.2 STANDARDS

The LWDR-2 prohibit the discharge of untreated liquid waste except into an enclosed system,[289] a liquid waste treatment unit,[290] or a public sewer system.[291] A privy may be used for the disposal of human excreta and toilet paper but not for the disposal of other liquid wastes. In turn, effluent from a liquid waste treatment unit can only be discharged to a liquid waste disposal system or to a public sewer.[292]

No one may discharge motor oil, gasoline, paint, varnish, solvents, pesticides, fertilizer, or other materials of a composition or concentration not generally associated with toilet flushing, food preparation, laundry, or personal hygiene to a liquid waste system. Nor may any chemical defined by WQCC as a toxic pollutant be discharged into a liquid waste system.[293]

The specific standards which apply to existing liquid waste systems depend on the date of initial installation. February 1, 1990, is the major changeover date to the LWDR-2 regulations. Liquid waste systems installed prior to February 1, 1990, must meet the requirements of the regulations in effect at the time of their initial installation or the requirements of LWDR-2, whichever are less stringent.[294] However, when the system design flow[295]

---

288 N.M. Liquid Waste Disposal Regulations § 204.

289 "Enclosed system" means a watertight liquid waste system which does not discharge to the soil including, but not limited to, holding tanks. N.M. Liquid Waste Disposal Regulations § 104.O.

290 "Treatment unit" means a watertight unit designed, constructed, and installed to retain solids and to stabilize liquid waste including, but not limited to, aerobic treatment units and septic tanks. N.M. Liquid Waste Disposal Regulations § 104.PP.

291 N.M. Liquid Waste Disposal Regulations § 301.A.

292 N.M. Liquid Waste Disposal Regulations § 301.B. "Disposal system" means a generally recognized system for disposing of the discharge from a liquid waste treatment unit including but not limited to, seepage pits, drain fields, evapotranspiration systems, sand mounds, and sand filters. N.M. Liquid Waste Disposal Regulations § 104.K.

293 N.M. Liquid Waste Disposal Regulations § 308.

294 N.M. Liquid Waste Disposal Regulations § 301.D.

295 "Design flow" means the flow rate for which a liquid waste system must be designed in order to assure acceptable system performance, assuming the use of conventional plumbing fixtures. For residential sources, the design flow must be calculated assuming two persons per bedroom for the first two bedrooms and one person per additional bedroom in a single family residential unit, and seventy-five gallons per person per day. Multiple family residential source design flows must be calculated as the sum of design flows for each single family unit included. Design flows for

is increased above that existing as of February 1, 1990, the system must meet the LWDR-2 requirements.[296] Liquid waste systems installed after February 1, 1990, must also meet the LWDR-2 requirements.[297]

Permissible sizes and locations for liquid waste systems which discharge to the soil and for evapotranspiration systems are determined by lot size, proposed design flow, and setback and clearance requirements as set forth by the regulations.[298]

6.2.1 Minimum Lot Size

Lot sizes must be no smaller than the minimum specified by the regulations,[299] based on total design flow.

6.2.2 Setback Requirements

Liquid waste systems must be located wholly on the same lot which is the site of the source served by the system.[300] Setback requirements must also be observed. These requirements vary according to whether the liquid waste system is a privy, an enclosed system, a liquid waste treatment unit, or a system discharging to the soil, and according to the nature of the object from which the liquid waste system must be setback.[301]

6.2.3 Clearance Requirements

Liquid waste systems must be situated so that they do not discharge liquid waste into soil when the clearance to the seasonal high ground water table, bedrock,[302] or other limiting layer[303] is less than four feet.[304] Unlined privy pits must have at least a two-foot clearance to the seasonal high ground water table, bedrock, or other limiting layer.[305]

---

nonresidential sources must be based on generally accepted references or based on professional engineering calculations, if more restrictive, and must include safety factors to account for peak flows. N.M. Liquid Waste Disposal Regulations § 104.I.

296 N.M. Liquid Waste Disposal Regulations § 301.D.

297 N.M. Liquid Waste Disposal Regulations § 301.E.

298 N.M. Liquid Waste Disposal Regulations §§ 302-304.

299 N.M. Liquid Waste Disposal Regulations § 302.E.

300 N.M. Liquid Waste Disposal Regulations § 302.B.

301 N.M. Liquid Waste Disposal Regulations § 303.

302 "Bedrock" means consolidated earth materials and includes fractured and cavernous rock. N.M. Liquid Waste Disposal Regulations § 104.B.

303 "Limiting layer" means layer of soil which is unsuitable for filtration or transmission of liquid waste including, but not limited to, soil with a percolation rate faster than 1 minute per inch or soil with a percolation rate slower than 120 minutes per inch. N.M. Liquid Waste Disposal Regulations § 104.W.

304 N.M. Liquid Waste Disposal Regulations § 304.A.

305 N.M. Liquid Waste Disposal Regulations § 304.B.

6.2.4 Holding Tank Requirements

Holding tanks[306] installed after February 1, 1990, may not serve any design flow greater than 375 gallons per day except to replace an existing holding tank.[307]

The total design flow on a property served by a holding tank installed after February 1, 1990, may not exceed 375 gallons per day.[308]

Holding tank owners must maintain records showing sufficient pumping and proper disposal of septage[309] from the tanks to prevent discharge.[310] NMED will supply forms for the records, which must be mailed on a semiannual basis to the NMED office having jurisdiction, kept for at least one year, and made available to NMED for inspection upon request.[311] NMED may perform site inspections periodically to ensure that a holding tank does not discharge.[312]

6.2.5 Septic Tank Requirements

The Construction Industries Division[313] (CID) of the New Mexico Regulation and Licensing Department has the authority to permit and inspect the construction and installation of private sewage disposal systems.[314] CID requires that the construction and installation of septic tanks meet the 1988 Uniform Plumbing Code. CID has requirements similar to NMED's with regard to setback and size and depth of the leach field.

CID provides diagrams and dimensions to homeowners who are building septic tanks. It also provides information on materials which can and cannot be used in the engineering and construction of septic tanks.

---

306 "Holding tank" means a watertight tank designed to receive and retain liquid waste for periodic pumping and disposal off-site. N.M. Liquid Waste Disposal Regulations § 104.U.

307 N.M. Liquid Waste Disposal Regulations § 305.A.

308 *Id.*

309 "Septage" means the residual wastes and water periodically pumped from a liquid waste treatment unit or from a holding tank for maintenance purposes. N.M. Liquid Waste Disposal Regulations § 104.LL.

310 N.M. Liquid Waste Disposal Regulations § 305.B.

311 N.M. Liquid Waste Disposal Regulations § 305.B.

312 N.M. Liquid Waste Disposal Regulations § 305.D.

313 N.M. Stat. Ann. § 60-13-7 (Repl. Pamp. 1989).

314 N.M. Stat. Ann. § 60-13-3 (Repl. Pamp. 1989).

CHAPTER IV
SOLID WASTE MANAGEMENT

1.0 THE SOLID WASTE ACT

The 1990 session of the New Mexico Legislature enacted New Mexico's first comprehensive Solid Waste Act (SWA)[1] which was signed by the Governor on March 6, 1990, taking effect immediately.

The SWA was enacted in order to (1) establish a comprehensive state-wide solid waste[2] management program, (2) provide technical, financial and program development assistance to counties and municipalities for solid waste management, (3) conserve, recover and recycle resources, (4) regulate the reduction, storage, collection, transportation, separation, processing, recycling and disposal of solid waste, (5) provide incentives for counties and municipalities to implement cost-effective and environmentally safe solid waste management at the local level, (6) require permits for the construction, operation, closure and post-closure maintenance of solid waste facilities, (7) promote source reduction, recycling, re-

---

1 The New Mexico Solid Waste Act is codified at N.M. Stat. Ann. § 74-9-1 to -42 (Repl. Pamp. 1993).

2 "Solid waste" means any garbage, refuse, sludge from a waste treatment plant, water supply treatment plant or air pollution control facility and other discarded material, including solid, liquid, semisolid or contained gaseous material resulting from industrial, commercial, mining and agricultural operations and from community activities. "Solid waste" does not include (1) drilling fluids, produced waters and other non-domestic wastes associated with the exploration, development or production, transportation, storage, treatment or refinement of crude oil, natural gas, carbon dioxide gas or geothermal energy; (2) fly ash waste, bottom ash waste, slag waste and flue gas emission control waste generated primarily from the combustion of coal or other fossil fuels and wastes produced in conjunction with the combustion of fossil fuels that are necessarily associated with the production of energy and that traditionally have been and actually are mixed with and are disposed of or treated at the same time with fly ash, bottom ash, boiler slag or flue gas emission control wastes from coal combustion; (3) waste from the extraction, beneficiation and processing of ores and minerals, including phosphate rock and overburden from the mining of uranium ore, coal, copper, molybdenum and other ores and minerals; (4) agricultural waste, including, but not limited to, manures and crop residues returned to the soil as fertilizer or soil conditioner; (5) cement kiln dust waste; (6) sand and gravel; (7) solid or dissolved material in domestic sewage or solid or dissolved materials in irrigation return flows or industrial discharges that are point sources subject to permits under § 402 of the Federal Water Pollution Control Act, 33 U.S.C. § 1342 or source, special nuclear or by-product material as defined by the Atomic Energy Act of 1954, 42 U.S.C. § 2011 *et seq.*; (8) densified-refuse-derived fuel; or (9) any material regulated by Subtitle C of the federal Resource Conservation and Recovery Act of 1976, substances regulated by the federal Toxic Substances Control Act or low-level radioactive waste. N.M. Stat. Ann. § 74-9-3(N) (Repl. Pamp. 1993).

use, treatment and transformation[3] of solid waste as viable alternatives to disposal of solid waste by landfill disposal methods and (8) require the state and its agencies to develop procurement policies that promote the development of recyclable materials.[4]

2.0 SOLID WASTE MANAGEMENT REGULATIONS

While the Environmental Improvement Board (EIB) had previously adopted solid waste management regulations pursuant to the Environmental Improvement Act (EIA), EIB adopted even more comprehensive regulations pursuant to the SWA on December 31, 1991, which took effect January 30, 1992. In addition to other substantive areas, the regulations address the following areas specified for regulation by the SWA: (1) solid waste facilities, (2) definition of solid wastes that are considered special wastes,[5] (3) detoxification and disposal of special wastes, (4) classification of solid waste facilities, (5) performance standards for the construction and operation of solid waste facilities, (6) transformation facilities, (7) permits for the modification of solid waste facilities, (8) commercial haulers, (9) a permit application fee schedule, (10) variances, (11) solid waste that shall not be treated or disposed of in solid waste facilities, (12) recordkeeping and (13) a solid waste facility operator certification program.[6] One notable limitation on EIB's regulatory authority is that it may not adopt a regulation that would allow NMED to permit the operation of any active solid waste facility larger than five hundred acres.[7]

2.1 GENERAL REQUIREMENTS

All solid waste must be processed or disposed of by means approved by the Secretary of the New Mexico Environment Department (Secretary) including, but not limited to, recycling, composting, transformation or landfilling in accordance with EIB regulations.[8]

The state, and each municipality, county, or cooperative association, must provide a means to dispose of solid waste generated within its respective jurisdiction which has been approved by the Secretary and complies with the solid waste management regulations.[9] While the state, municipality, county, or cooperative association may contract with any person for the collection, transportation, recycling, or disposal of solid waste, such action does not

---

3 "Transformation" means incineration, pyrolysis, distillation, gasification or biological conversion other than composting. N.M. Stat. Ann. § 74-9-3(S) (Repl. Pamp. 1993).

4 N.M. Stat. Ann. § 74-9-2 (Repl. Pamp. 1993).

5 "Special waste" means solid waste that has unique handling, transportation or disposal requirements to assure protection of the environment and the public health and safety. N.M. Stat. Ann. § 74-9-3(R) (Repl. Pamp. 1993).

6 N.M. Stat. Ann. § 74-9-8 (Repl. Pamp. 1993).

7 N.M. Stat. Ann. § 74-9-8(E) (Repl. Pamp. 1993).

8 N.M. Solid Waste Management Regulations § 106.A.

9 N.M. Solid Waste Management Regulations § 106.C.

relieve the state, municipality, county or cooperative association from responsibility for compliance with the solid waste management regulations.[10]

Any municipality with a population greater than 3,000 must provide collection at least once weekly or as often as otherwise necessary to comply with the requirements of the solid waste management regulations.[11]

2.2 INTERIM STATUS

There are detailed regulatory provisions pertaining to all non-permitted solid waste facilities existing as of January 31, 1992, which should be reviewed to determine the appropriate course of action depending on whether the facility as of January 31, 1992, (1) had a permit application pending,[12] (2) had no permit application pending,[13] or (3) in the case of landfills only, ceased operation after May 14, 1989, but had not had a closure and post-closure plan approved.[14]

Under certain circumstances and pursuant to certain conditions, an existing solid waste facility in operation prior to May 14, 1989, is deemed to have interim status and may continue to operate under such status until such status terminates or is revoked or suspended.[15] Similarly, there are provisions by which interim status may be obtained by non-permitted solid waste facilities in operation on January 31, 1992, with no permit application pending as of that date and by non-permitted landfills that ceased operation after May 14, 1989, but had not had a closure and post-closure plan approved as of January 31, 1992.[16] Interim status may be converted to permitted status upon the Secretary's final order on a permit application.[17]

While the siting criteria for landfills do not apply to any landfill having interim status, they do apply to the Secretary's final action on the permit application for such landfill unless a variance from the siting criteria is applied for and granted.[18]

---

10 N.M. Solid Waste Management Regulations § 106.D.

11 N.M. Solid Waste Management Regulations § 106.B.

12 N.M. Solid Waste Management Regulations § 213.A.

13 N.M. Solid Waste Management Regulations § 213.B.

14 *Id.*

15 N.M. Solid Waste Management Regulations § 213.A.1.

16 N.M. Solid Waste Management Regulations § 213.B.3.

17 N.M. Solid Waste Management Regulations § 213.D.(1)(d).

18 N.M. Solid Waste Management Regulations § 302.B.

3.0 SOLID WASTE MANAGEMENT PLAN

Pursuant to the statutory mandate of the SWA, the Secretary prepared and submitted a solid waste management plan (Plan)[19] to EIB on December 31, 1992. The EIB approved the Plan on July 9, 1993, and the Plan took effect August 8, 1993.[20] The Plan is to be used as a basis for developing a comprehensive statewide solid waste management program, including (1) source reduction and recycling, (2) environmentally safe transformation and (3) environmentally safe landfill disposal.[21] Regulations adopted by EIB, actions taken by the Secretary and grants to counties and municipalities under the SWA must all be consistent with the Plan.[22]

3.1 ESSENTIAL PLAN ELEMENTS

The Plan includes the following statutorily mandated elements: (1) waste characterization, (2) source reduction, (3) recycling, (4) composting, (5) solid waste facility capacity, (6) education and public information, (7) funding, (8) special waste and household hazardous waste, and (9) siting of facilities. The goal of the Plan is to divert 25 percent of all solid waste from solid waste disposal facilities by July 1, 1995, and 50 percent by July 1, 2000.[23]

3.2 INFORMATION REQUIRED FOR THE PLAN

As a basis for developing and preparing the Plan, the Secretary was required to request and use information from each county and municipality or combination thereof.[24] The Secretary also was required to prepare and distribute guidelines to assist the responding counties and municipalities in the preparation of information submittals for the Plan.[25] Some of the information required includes (1) documentation demonstrating the consideration of combining jurisdictional units to form a district for solid waste planning and implementation of state program elements and (2) information that corresponds generally to the required provisions of the Plan.[26] Counties and municipalities were required to furnish the documentation and information requested no later than July 1, 1992.[27] Failure to have furnished the required information may render the county or municipality ineligible for grants otherwise authorized under the SWA.[28]

---

19 N.M. Stat. Ann. § 74-9-4 (Repl. Pamp. 1993).

20 N.M. Stat. Ann. § 74-9-5 (Repl. Pamp. 1993).

21 N.M. Stat. Ann. § 74-9-4 (Repl. Pamp. 1993).

22 N.M. Stat. Ann. § 74-9-5 (Repl. Pamp. 1993).

23 N.M. Stat. Ann. § 79-9-6 (Repl. Pamp. 1993).

24 N.M. Stat. Ann. § 74-9-7 (Repl. Pamp. 1993).

25 N.M. Stat. Ann. § 74-9-7(B) (Repl. Pamp. 1993).

26 *Id.*

27 N.M. Stat. Ann. § 74-9-7(G) (Repl. Pamp. 1993).

28 N.M. Stat. Ann. § 74-9-7(H) (Repl. Pamp. 1993).

4.0 EIB REQUIRED ACTION FOLLOWING PLAN APPROVAL

The SWA requires that EIB take action in several areas following EIB approval of the Plan.

4.1 REVIEW AND ADOPTION OF REGULATIONS

EIB is required to review its initial solid waste regulations in order to make any modifications necessary to make the regulations consistent with the Plan[29] and to adopt regulations to establish source reduction and recycling programs consistent with the Plan.[30]

4.2 SOLID WASTE DISTRICTS

EIB is additionally required to adopt regulations to establish solid waste districts,[31] the boundaries of which must be contiguous within the state, although the boundaries may cross state lines[32] and need not be consistent with county or municipal boundaries.[33] In establishing districts EIB is required to take into account all relevant factors, including (1) impact of solid waste disposal on land, water and other resources, (2) financial impact to counties and municipalities of constructing and upgrading landfill disposal facilities, (3) risks associated with solid waste, (4) costs and risks of transportation of solid waste, (5) existing jurisdictional boundaries and commercial, industrial, transportation and population centers, and (6) existing landfill disposal agreements, service areas, facilities and collection systems.[34]

4.2.1 Solid Waste Assessment Fee

The SWA requires that a solid waste assessment fee be imposed upon the disposal of solid waste by a commercial hauler if the solid waste was generated outside the solid waste district in which the solid waste facility is located.[35]

EIB is to establish the amount of the fee and, in doing so, must take into account all factors relevant to the cost of disposal of the solid waste, including the (1) impact on air, water, land and other resources, (2) effect on the value of public and private property, (3) costs of protection of the public health, safety, welfare and the environment, (4) costs of out-of-district inspection and monitoring, (5) costs and risks of transportation and (6) administrative costs incurred by the collecting governmental entity.[36]

---

29 N.M. Stat. Ann. § 74-9-9 (Repl. Pamp. 1993).

30 N.M. Stat. Ann. § 74-9-10 (Repl. Pamp. 1993).

31 N.M. Stat. Ann. § 74-9-11(A) (Repl. Pamp. 1993).

32 N.M. Stat. Ann. § 74-9-11(B) (Repl. Pamp. 1993).

33 N.M. Stat. Ann. § 74-9-11(C) (Repl. Pamp. 1993).

34 N.M. Stat. Ann. § 74-9-11(A) (Repl. Pamp. 1993).

35 N.M. Stat. Ann. § 74-9-39(A) (Repl. Pamp. 1993).

36 N.M. Stat. Ann. § 74-9-39(B) (Repl. Pamp. 1993).

A commercial hauler is not required to pay the solid waste assessment fee if (1) the solid waste was generated in a commercial, industrial, transportation and population center in which the commercial hauler provided solid waste disposal service during the 1989 calendar year and (2) the solid waste is disposed of in a solid waste district in which the commercial hauler disposed of solid waste generated in that commercial, industrial, transportation and population center during the 1989 calendar year.[37]

5.0 SOLID WASTE AUTHORITY ACT

In 1993, the New Mexico Legislature enacted the Solid Waste Authority Act to allow small towns and municipalities to combine their resources for the creation of a unified solid waste authority.[38] A solid waste authority is considered a state political subdivision that serves the public use by acquiring, improving, maintaining and operating solid waste management-related projects.[39] A separate board of directors governs each solid waste authority.[40]

6.0 STATE SOLID WASTE MANAGEMENT PROGRAM

The Secretary is required to design a comprehensive state solid waste management program (Program) consistent with the Plan by December 1, 1993, to be fully implemented by July 1, 1994.[41] The Program is to be designed to achieve the following objectives: (1) reduction, recycling, collection, transportation, storage, separation, transformation and disposal of solid waste throughout the state, (2) coordinated regional activity for solid waste management within a solid waste district, (3) correction of deficiencies in present solid waste management processes, (4) financial, planning and technical assistance to counties and municipalities and others in order to achieve cost effective and environmentally safe solid waste management practices and (5) education and training in order to assure proper solid waste management.[42]

The Secretary is required to prepare a report for the legislature on the status of solid waste management efforts in the state by July 1, 1994, and yearly thereafter.[43]

7.0 NMED RESPONSIBILITY AND AUTHORITY

The New Mexico Environment Department (NMED) is responsible for the enforcement and implementation of EIB regulations and is further required to (1) develop

---

37 N.M. Stat. Ann. § 74-9-39(E) (Repl. Pamp. 1993).

38 N.M. Stat. Ann. § 74-10-1 to -100 (Repl. Pamp. 1993).

39 N.M. Stat. Ann. § 74-10-2(B), (C) (Repl. Pamp. 1993).

40 N.M. Stat. Ann. § 74-10-12 (Repl. Pamp. 1993).

41 N.M. Stat. Ann. § 74-9-12(A) (Repl. Pamp. 1993).

42 N.M. Stat. Ann. § 74-9-12(B) (Repl. Pamp. 1993).

43 N.M. Stat. Ann. § 74-9-13 (Repl. Pamp. 1993).

and implement the Program, (2) provide technical assistance to counties, municipalities and others, (3) promote source reduction, recycling and sensible solid waste facility siting systems, (4) assist in the development of regional solid waste management, (5) assist the Economic Development Department in encouraging development of commercial enterprises that (a) produce minimum solid waste, (b) engage in source reduction and recycling activities or (c) promote market activity and develop products made of recycled materials, (6) pursue alternative solid waste management methods, (7) pursue the development and expansion of markets for recyclable materials, (8) develop and manage a program of grants for source reduction and recycling programs, (9) cooperate in the development of a litter control program, (10) advise EIB about ground water protection devices, air quality monitoring devices and other devices or measures that may be required as a result of solid waste management operations, (11) increase public awareness of solid waste issues, (12) encourage public participation in the rule-making process, (13) determine monitoring requirements for solid waste facilities, (14) contract as necessary for implementation of appropriate parts of the solid waste management program, (15) enter into contracts necessary to fulfill its responsibilities, (16) receive and administer funds for the purpose of carrying out the provisions of the SWA and (17) participate in the adoption of uniform state laws and the formation of compacts with other states for the improved management, recycling and source reduction of solid waste.[44]

8.0 SOLID WASTE FACILITY GRANT FUND

The Solid Waste Facility Grant Fund (SWFGF) has been created in the state treasury.[45] NMED is responsible for administering the SWFGF and making grants from the SWFGF in accordance with the SWA. Monies credited to the SWFGF include earnings on balances in the SWFGF, federal funds, state appropriations,[46] proceeds from the collection of the solid waste assessment fee[47] and amounts collected in connection with the enforcement of the SWA.[48]

8.1 GRANT PROGRAM PURPOSE

NMED has established a program to make grants to counties and municipalities for the establishment or modification of solid waste facilities or for contracting for solid waste services,[49] and is required to prepare an annual report on the grants program[50] and to

---

44 N.M. Stat. Ann. § 74-9-14 (Repl. Pamp. 1993).

45 N.M. Stat. Ann. § 74-9-41(A) (Repl. Pamp. 1993).

46 *Id.*

47 N.M. Stat. Ann. § 74-9-39(F) (Repl. Pamp. 1993).

48 N.M. Stat. Ann. §§ 74-9-36(I) to -38 (Repl. Pamp. 1993).

49 N.M. Stat. Ann. § 74-9-40(A) (Repl. Pamp. 1993).

50 N.M. Stat. Ann. § 74-9-40(B) (Repl. Pamp. 1993).

award grants only to counties and municipalities that meet the criteria established by NMED.[51]

9.0 OTHER SWA MANDATED PROGRAMS

The SWA mandates that several specific programs be undertaken in order to promote the goals and objectives of the Plan and the Program. State government[52] and post-secondary educational institutions[53] are required to undertake specified activities in order to achieve source reduction and recycling. Further, NMED is required to develop an educational program in support of the state's source reduction and recycling goals.[54] The Secretary designated a household hazardous waste coordinator for the purpose of advising governmental entities that have implemented programs for household waste management.[55] NMED is also required to provide technical assistance with regard to household hazardous waste management programs[56] and to develop and implement a public information program on the proper disposal of household hazardous waste.[57] Further, the state purchasing agent and each central purchasing office are required to establish specifications, policies and practices in order to promote the prospect of governmental purchase of supplies and materials composed in whole or in part of recycled materials.[58]

10.0 SOLID WASTE FACILITY PERMIT

No person is entitled to construct, operate or close a solid waste facility[59] without

---

51 N.M. Stat. Ann. § 74-9-40(C) (Repl. Pamp. 1993).

52 N.M. Stat. Ann. § 74-9-15 (Repl. Pamp. 1993).

53 N.M. Stat. Ann. § 74-9-16 (Repl. Pamp. 1993).

54 N.M. Stat. Ann. § 74-9-17 (Repl. Pamp. 1993).

55 N.M. Stat. Ann. § 74-9-18(A) (Repl. Pamp. 1993).

56 N.M. Stat. Ann. § 74-9-18(B) (Repl. Pamp. 1993).

57 N.M. Stat. Ann. § 74-9-18(C) (Repl. Pamp. 1993).

58 N.M. Stat. Ann. § 74-9-19(A) (Repl. Pamp. 1993).

59 "Solid waste facility" means any public or private system, facility, location, improvements on the land, structures or other appurtenances or methods used for processing, transformation, recycling or disposal of solid waste, including landfill disposal facilities, transfer stations, resource recovery facilities, incinerators and other similar facilities not specified, but does not include: (1) equipment specifically approved by order of the Secretary to render medical waste generated on-site noninfectious, (2) a facility that is permitted pursuant to the provisions of the Hazardous Waste Act, (3) a facility fueled by a densified-refuse-derived fuel that accepts no other solid waste, (4) a facility that collects, transfers, or processes source separated household or commercial solid waste for recycling and has a design capacity of 25 tons or less per day and does not exceed 3 acres in size, (5) storage containers with a total capacity of 120 cubic yards or less, (6) that portion of a facility that refurbishes or re-sells used clothing, furniture or appliances for reuse, (7) scrap metal or auto salvage operations, (8) a

first obtaining a permit from the Secretary.[60] The application for a permit must be in the form and contain the information required by the Secretary.[61]

The Secretary is prohibited, by regulation, from issuing a permit for any active solid waste facility larger than 500 acres.[62] Permits are granted for the following periods of time for landfills, transfer stations, recycling or composting facilities depending on the ownership and operation of the facility: (1) the active life of the facility or twenty years, whichever is less, for a publicly owned and operated facility or a publicly owned and privately operated facility (if operated pursuant to a contract of no more than four years duration), or (2) the active life of the facility or ten years, whichever is less, for a privately owned facility or a publicly owned facility leased to, or operated by, a private person (pursuant to a contract of more than four years duration).[63] The terms of permits for other facilities are governed by EIB regulations which generally provide that a permit is valid for a period not longer than 10 years but may be renewed by submittal or a new application at least one year prior to expiration of the current permit.[64]

The Secretary must issue separate special waste permits for all solid waste facilities that transfer, process, transform, recycle or dispose of special waste pursuant to EIB regulations.[65]

10.1 GENERAL PERMIT APPLICATION REQUIREMENTS

Applicants for a permit, regardless of the type of solid waste facility for which a permit is sought, are required to furnish the following information: (1) name and address of the applicant, property owner and responsible party for the site operation, (2) legal description and maps of the proposed facility site (including land use and zoning of the surrounding area), (3) if exploration holes are drilled, a certification that the holes were plugged or sealed in accordance with the State Engineer's requirements for plugging or sealing of test holes,

---

composting facility other than those which compost municipal sewage sludge (mss), municipal solid waste (msw), or msw/mss combination which requires a processing area less than 5 acres and does not require additives other than water and utilizes manure in amounts less than 50% of the final mix, (9) manufacturing facilities that use recycled material in production of a new product, (10) facilities designed and operated to dispose of sludge on land such as land application or land injection, or (11) any facility accepting concrete and asphalt material for reuse. N.M. Solid Waste Management Regulations § 105.HHH.

60 N.M. Stat. Ann. § 74-9-20(A) (Repl. Pamp. 1993).

61 N.M. Stat. Ann. § 74-9-20(B) (Repl. Pamp. 1993).

62 N.M. Solid Waste Management Regulations § 301.

63 N.M. Stat. Ann. § 74-9-24(G)(1), (2) (Repl. Pamp. 1993).

64 N.M. Stat. Ann § 74-9-24(G)(3) (Repl. Pamp. 1993); N.M. Solid Waste Management Regulations § 212.A.

65 N.M. Stat. Ann. § 74-9-24(H) (Repl. Pamp. 1993).

(4) where a water supply is present at the facility, a description of the source and its location, and (5) other applicable information requested by NMED.[66]

Applicants also are required to include the following operational information: (1) the means of controlling and mitigating odors, (2) a listing and description of the equipment to be used, (3) a description of the general operating plan, (4) a plan for an alternative waste handling or disposal system and (5) the operating hours of the proposed facility.[67] Applicants must provide proof of public notice[68] and must provide plans for transportation to and from the facility, including but not limited to (1) the size and number of vehicles that will deliver waste to the facility daily, (2) employee traffic to and from the facility, (3) the routes that will be used, (4) the measures for controlling litter, dust and noise caused by traffic and (5) other impacts of traffic. [69]

Every applicant is required to file a disclosure statement with the information required by NMED simultaneously with the filing of the application for a permit.[70] The Secretary may request the Department of Public Safety to furnish an investigative report on the applicant and may also request information regarding any person who will be or could reasonably be expected to be involved in management activities of the solid waste facility or regarding any person who has a controlling interest in any permittee.[71]

If any information required in the disclosure statement changes or additional information should be added, the person required to file the disclosure statement must provide that information to the Secretary in writing.[72] Failure to provide the revised or additional information within 30 days may constitute the basis for revocation or denial of an application for a permit, but only if the applicant or permittee is given time within which to explain why the information was not provided as required.[73]

The disclosure statement is not required of an applicant that is a corporation that (1) has on file and in effect with the federal Securities and Exchange Commission a registration statement as required under the Securities Act of 1933 as amended, (2) submits to the Secretary with its application for a permit evidence of registration and a copy of the corporation's most recent annual Form 10-K or equivalent, and (3) submits to the Secretary on an

---

66 N.M. Solid Waste Management Regulations § 201.C.

67 N.M. Solid Waste Management Regulations § 201.D.

68 N.M. Solid Waste Management Regulations § 201.E

69 N.M. Solid Waste Management Regulations § 201.H.

70 N.M. Stat. Ann. § 74-9-21(A) (Repl. Pamp. 1993).

71 N.M. Stat. Ann. § 74-9-21(B) (Repl. Pamp. 1993).

72 N.M. Stat. Ann. § 74-9-21(D) (Repl. Pamp. 1993).

73 *Id.*

annual basis evidence of continued registration with the Securities and Exchange Commission and the corporation's most recent annual Form 10-K or equivalent.[74]

10.2 LANDFILLS

The following additional information is required on applications for a landfill permit: (1) a schedule of filling and methods of compaction of solid waste, (2) proof that all waste disposal and waste handling areas are at least 50 feet from the property boundaries and at least 500 feet from the nearest residence, school, hospital, institution or church, (3) the types and sources of daily and final cover, (4) maps or plans of the proposed facility indicating the location of (a) ground water monitoring wells and landfill gas monitoring points, (b) salvage operation(s), (c) borrow and fill areas, (d) water, gas and oil wells, (e) fire protection at the facility and (f) provisions for concealing the site from public view and reducing noise, (5) topographic maps, (6) a description of the geological regime, (7) a demonstration that the facility will not discharge contaminants in violation of WQCC regulations, (8) analysis of surface water flow including direction and rate with a demonstration that the landfill will not discharge contaminants in violation of WQCC regulations, (9) surface water control systems, (10) the distance of the facility site from the closest Federal Aviation Administration (FAA) airport and a demonstration of compliance with the most current FAA regulations, (11) the location and name of public and private water supplies within a one-mile radius of the site or three miles downstream from the site, (12) the location of high-tension power lines, pipelines, railroads and public and private roads within 300 feet of the proposed facility, (13) the location of proposed all-weather access roads to and within the proposed area, (14) the location of barriers, fences and similar structures, (15) the prevailing wind directions, (16) proof that the facility will not result in the destruction or adverse modification of the critical habitat of endangered or threatened species, (17) closure and post-closure plans and (18) contingency plans to cope with violations of any ground water, surface water, air quality, decomposition gas or any other applicable regulations.[75]

Unless otherwise approved by the Secretary, plans and specifications will be required for ground water monitoring systems[76] and gas monitoring programs.[77] If required or submitted, the following information also will be included in permit applications: (1) plans and specifications for vadose zone monitoring systems,[78] (2) plans and specifications for liner

---

[74] N.M. Stat. Ann. § 74-9-21(E) (Repl. Pamp. 1993).

[75] N.M. Solid Waste Management Regulations § 202.A.

[76] N.M. Solid Waste Management Regulations § 202.B.

[77] N.M. Solid Waste Management Regulations § 202.F.

[78] N.M. Solid Waste Management Regulations § 202.C.

systems,[79] (3) plans and specifications for leachate collection systems[80] and (4) plans for gas management.[81]

10.2.1 Locational Restrictions

The Secretary will not issue a permit for any landfill that is located (1) in a floodplain, within 500 feet of wetlands or within 200 feet of watercourses, (2) where depth to seasonal high water table will be closer than 100 feet to the bottom of the fill, (3) where subsurface mines are considered to be a problem or in an area subject to sink holes, (4) within 200 feet of a fault, (5) within historically or archaeologically significant sites, (6) within 1,000 feet of a public water supply well or a private well that pumps 100 gallons per minute or more, (7) within 350 feet of a public water supply well or a private well that pumps less than 100 gallons per minute, (8) within the distance set by FAA requirements, (9) within at least 50 feet from the nearest permanent residence, school, hospital, institution or church or (10) in an active alluvial fan.[82]

10.3 RECYCLING AND PROCESSING FACILITIES

The following additional information must be submitted on permit applications for recycling and processing facilities: (1) a description of the survey and analysis process used to determine such factors as characteristics of all solid waste expected to be processed, (2) plans of all structures used for processing, storage, alternate storage and disposal capability, (3) plans describing the sampling capability and safety designs, (4) plans describing methods for the containment or removal of residues and spills and (5) an operation and maintenance manual.[83]

10.4 TRANSFORMATION FACILITIES

The following additional information must be submitted on permit applications for transformation facilities: (1) the actual or expected physical and chemical composition of ash, residue or wash water produced by operation of the facility, (2) the proposed location and method for disposal, storage or processing of ash, residue or wash water, (3) the plan for separation, storage and ultimate disposal of unmarketable waste, (4) the minimum and maximum volumes of the types of material or solid waste to be stored prior to sale, reuse or disposal, and the minimum and maximum time that material or waste is to be stored, (5) detailed plans, drawings and information concerning the proposed facility, (6) a detailed description of the facility operation, (7) operation plans that illustrate the complete material and process sequence, (8) a comprehensive project construction schedule submitted fifteen

---

79 N.M. Solid Waste Management Regulations § 202.D.

80 N.M. Solid Waste Management Regulations § 202.E.

81 N.M. Solid Waste Management Regulations § 202.G.

82 N.M. Solid Waste Management Regulations § 302.A.

83 N.M. Solid Waste Management Regulations § 203.

days prior to commencement of work and (9) an identification of the landfill or landfills that will receive the residue and bypass waste and that facility's permit number(s).[84]

10.4.1 Locational Restrictions

The Secretary will not issue a permit for (1) an infectious waste incinerator having a throughput capacity of less than 1,000 pounds per hour or another transformation facility of equivalent size that is located within one mile of any residence, institution, school, church, hospital or other transformation facility[85] or (2) an infectious waste incinerator having a throughput capacity of 1,000 pounds per hour or greater or another transformation facility of equivalent size that is located within three miles of any residence, institution, school, church, hospital or other transformation facility.[86]

10.5 SPECIAL WASTE FACILITIES

The following additional information must be submitted on permit applications for facilities that accept special waste: (1) a complete description of the types of wastes to be accepted, (2) the anticipated amount and frequency of disposal of the wastes, (3) the method of disposal, (4) a copy of the disposal management plan for those special wastes not otherwise specified, (5) emergency and mitigation measures in case of a spill or leak and (6) any other information requested by NMED.[87]

10.6 COMPOSTING FACILITIES

The following additional information must be submitted on permit applications for composting facilities: (1) the method of measuring, shredding, mixing and proportioning input material, (2) a description of the temperature monitoring equipment and the location of all temperature and any other type of monitoring points, and the frequency of monitoring, (3) a description of any proposed additive material, (4) special precautions or procedures for operation during wind, heavy rain, snow and freezing conditions, (5) estimated composting time duration, (6) for windrow systems, the windrow construction, (7) the method of aeration, (8) a general description of the ultimate use for the finished compost and method for removal from the site and a plan for the disposal of the finished compost that cannot be used in the expected manner and (9) for in-vessel composting systems, a process flow diagram of the entire process.[88]

---

84 N.M. Solid Waste Management Regulations § 204.

85 N.M. Solid Waste Management Regulations § 304.A.

86 N.M. Solid Waste Management Regulations § 304.B.

87 N.M. Solid Waste Management Regulations § 205.

88 N.M. Solid Waste Management Regulations § 206.

10.6.1 Locational Restrictions

The Secretary will not issue a permit for any composting facility that is located (1) in a floodplain, within 500 feet of wetlands or within 200 feet of watercourses or (2) within 500 feet of any permanent residence, school, hospital, institution or church.[89]

10.7 TRANSFER STATIONS

Permit applications for transfer stations must include plans indicating (1) the location of building(s) currently in use by any person within 100 feet of the proposed facility, (2) the location of solid waste storage and loading areas, (3) the collection, treatment or disposal of rinse water and leachate from the facility and (4) the frequency of solid waste deposit and pick-up from the facility, the method of transport and the destination.[90]

10.8 NOTICE OF APPLICATION

Each application must include proof that the applicant has provided notice of the filing of the application to the public and other affected individuals and entities, including Indian tribes and pueblos.[91] The notice requirements of the SWA are very specific and include provisions for certified mail, publication and posting.[92]

10.9 APPLICATION DEEMED COMPLETE; HEARING

An application is deemed complete when the Secretary has received all information required.[93] Within 60 days of the determination that an application is complete, the Secretary must set a date, time and location for a hearing on the application and give notice in the same manner as required of an applicant upon filing an application for a permit.[94]

10.10 DECISION ON THE APPLICATION

The Secretary is required to make a decision on the application within 180 days after the application is deemed complete, following a public hearing.[95] The Secretary may issue a permit, issue a permit with terms and conditions or deny a permit application.[96] The SWA

---

89 N.M. Solid Waste Management Regulations § 303.A.

90 N.M. Solid Waste Management Regulations § 207.

91 N.M. Stat. Ann. § 74-9-22 (Repl. Pamp. 1993).

92 *Id.*

93 N.M. Stat. Ann. § 74-9-23(A) (Repl. Pamp. 1993).

94 N.M. Stat. Ann. § 74-9-23(B) (Repl. Pamp. 1993).

95 N.M. Stat. Ann. § 74-9-24(A) (Repl. Pamp. 1993). The Secretary is required to issue a final order no later than the earliest of (1) 30 days after receipt of the hearing officer's recommended decision, (2) 60 days after the hearing record is closed or (3) 180 days after the application was deemed complete. Rules Governing Hearings for Permits and Variances under the Solid Waste Act, NMED 91-1, § 502.A (filed June 18, 1991).

96 N.M. Stat. Ann. § 74-9-24(A) (Repl. Pamp. 1993).

and the New Mexico Solid Waste Management Regulations specify the grounds upon which a permit application may be denied or revoked.[97] However, if an applicant whose permit is being considered for denial or revocation on the basis of certain specified prior bad acts[98] has submitted an affirmative action plan, approved in writing by the Secretary, that provides a period of operation under a conditional permit or license that will allow the applicant to affirmatively demonstrate its rehabilitation, the Secretary may issue a conditional license for a reasonable period of time.[99]

10.10.1 Prerequisite to Permit Validity

A permit is not valid until the permit or a notice of the permit and a legal description of the property on which the facility is located are filed and recorded in the office of the county clerk in each county in which the facility is located.[100]

11.0 FINANCIAL RESPONSIBILITY

Owners or operators who are state or federal government entities are not required to provide financial assurances.[101] Neither private persons who contract with the State of New Mexico nor political subdivisions of the State are entitled to the government exemption from financial assurances.[102] All permit applicants must provide proof to assure that there are adequate sources of funds to provide for (1) closure, post-closure inspection and maintenance, and environmental monitoring and control, (2) removal and disposal of buildings, fences, roads and other improvements, (3) reclamation of affected or contaminated lands and waters, (4) construction of any solid waste cover or containment system required as a condition of any solid waste facility permit, (5) stabilization, removal and off-site treatment or disposal of any contaminated material that is being stored or treated, (6) decontamination, dismantling and removal of any solid waste storage, treatment or disposal equipment and (7) operation of any required environmental monitoring systems or pollution control systems.[103] Sources of funds provided to meet financial responsibility requirements must be available during the operating life of the solid waste facility and for a post-closure period to be set by EIB.[104]

---

97 N.M. Stat. Ann. § 74-9-24(A), (B) (Repl. Pamp. 1993); N.M. Solid Waste Management Regulations § 212.

98 N.M. Stat. Ann. § 74-9-24(B) (Repl. Pamp. 1993).

99 N.M. Stat. Ann. § 74-9-24(D) (Repl. Pamp. 1993).

100 N.M. Stat. Ann. § 74-9-24(F) (Repl. Pamp. 1993).

101 N.M. Stat. Ann. § 74-9-35(E), (Repl. Pamp. 1993); *See also* § 74-9-35.1.

102 *Id.*

103 N.M. Solid Waste Management Regulations § 208.C.

104 N.M. Solid Waste Management Regulations § 208.D.

Acceptable methods of furnishing evidence of financial responsibility, which are to be specified by EIB, include evidence of trust funds, performance bonds, insurance and irrevocable letters of credit.[105] EIB has, to date, established a financial assurance procedure allowing either a trust fund or a performance bond with a standby trust fund for operators seeking to evidence financial responsibility.[106] However, local governments may employ all methods approved by the federal Environmental Protection Agency in evidencing financial responsibility.[107]

The financial assurances are submitted upon initial application for a permit and are updated yearly to adjust for inflation and/or facility modification that would affect closure or post-closure costs.[108] Financial assurance cost estimates are based on a third party performing closure and post-closure care.[109]

12.0 GENERAL OPERATION REQUIREMENTS

The operators of all solid waste facilities must (1) locate and operate the facility so that it does not cause a public nuisance or create a potential hazard to public health or welfare, (2) post signs, (3) have a certified operator or representative present during operating hours, (4) implement a plan that will check loads to detect and prevent the disposal of regulated hazardous and unauthorized special waste, (5) maintain written records of all inspections and (6) upon discovery of the receipt of unauthorized waste, the operator will (a) notify NMED, the hauler and the generator within 24 hours, (b) restrict the area from the public and facility personnel and (c) assure proper cleanup, transport and disposal of the waste.[110] In the event of an emergency, the Secretary may permit temporary changes in operation or facility design when necessary to protect human health or the environment.[111] All facilities must be operated in accordance with conditions and plans approved by NMED as part of the permits for the facilities.[112]

Multiple facilities may be operated under one permit provided that all the requirements are met for each facility.[113]

---

105 N.M. Stat. Ann. § 74-9-35(D) (Repl. Pamp. 1993).

106 N.M. Solid Waste Management Regulations § 208.H.

107 N.M. Stat. Ann. § 74-9-35(D) (Repl. Pamp. 1993).

108 N.M. Solid Waste Management Regulations § 208.D.

109 N.M. Solid Waste Management Regulations § 208.B.

110 N.M. Solid Waste Management Regulations § 401.B.

111 N.M. Solid Waste Management Regulations § 401.C.

112 N.M. Solid Waste Management Regulations § 401.D.

113 N.M. Solid Waste Management Regulations § 201.G.

12.1 LANDFILLS

In addition to the general operation requirements applicable to all solid waste facility operators, landfill operators also must (1) utilize the principles of sanitary engineering to confine the solid waste to the smallest practical area and to reduce it to the smallest practical volume, (2) assure through monitoring and demonstrations that methane and other decomposition gases do not migrate laterally from the landfill, (3) prevent unauthorized access by the public and entry by large animals to the active portion of the landfill, (4) control entry of run-on water, (5) prohibit scavenging, (6) provide adequate means to prevent and extinguish fires, (7) direct the deposit of hot waste[114] to a remote area of the landfill, (8) if recycling operations are conducted, (a) perform them in a sanitary and convenient manner and (b) remove all recyclable materials daily or safely store them, (9) provide and maintain access roads, (10) assure that there are sufficient unloading areas, (11) control run-off from the site, (12) control litter, vectors and odors, (13) not excavate a closed cell unless approved by the Secretary, (14) for Class A landfills,[115] cover the cell with a six-inch layer of earth or alternate daily cover, (15) for all landfills, provide intermediate cover as necessary that is (a) one foot thick, (b) placed on all areas of a landfill that will not receive further waste for one month or greater, but have not reached final elevation, (c) stabilized with vegetation on any areas that will be left for more than two years and (d) placed, inspected and maintained to prevent erosion and infiltration, (16) for Class B landfills,[116] dispose of dead animals in separate trenches and immediately cover upon arrival, (17) for Class B or C landfills,[117] cover the fill with a minimum of six inches clean earth at least once each week during the period of April 1 through October 31, and at least once each two weeks during the period of November 1 through March 31 and (18) for Class D landfills,[118] cover the fill with a six-inch layer of earth or other appropriate material at the end of each day's operation or at other intervals as approved by the Secretary.[119]

---

[114] "Hot waste" means any waste that is on fire or smoldering when delivered to the facility. N.M. Solid Waste Management Regulations § 105.DD.

[115] "Class A landfill" means a sanitary landfill serving a population of 3,000 or more. N.M. Solid Waste Management Regulations § 105.L.

[116] "Class B landfill" means a sanitary landfill serving a population of less than 3,000. N.M. Solid Waste Management Regulations § 105.M.

[117] "Class C landfill" means any sanitary landfill that is to receive only construction and demolition waste. N.M. Solid Waste Management Regulations § 105.N.

[118] "Class D landfill" means an industrial on-site disposal operation, including those industrial sites that are disposing of industrial process waste on-site, but does no include farms and ranches. N.M. Solid Waste Management Regulations § 105.O.

[119] N.M. Solid Waste Management Regulations § 402.

12.1.1 Closure and Post-Closure Requirements

Landfill facility operators must comply with the following closure and post-closure requirements: (1) placement of a compacted layer of not less than two feet of suitable material over the entire surface of each portion of the final lift[120] not later than 60 days following the placement of refuse in the final lift, (2) the side slopes of all above-grade landfills may not exceed a 25 percent grade, (3) submission of a proposed final land use plan to the Secretary, (4) submission of a schedule for completion of all closure work, (5) upon completion of closure, a detailed description of the use of the site, including a plat, must be filed with the appropriate county land recording authority for the county in which the site is located, (6) submission of a proposed post-closure care and monitoring plan for a 25-year period which may be extended at the discretion of the Secretary and (7) submission of reports of monitoring performed and data collected to the Secretary at the end of each calendar year.[121]

The Secretary may extend the post-closure care period if the Secretary finds that the extended period is necessary to protect human health and the environment.[122] The operator may amend the post-closure plan by submitting a request to the Secretary 30 days prior to the proposed change.[123]

12.2 TRANSFER STATIONS

In addition to the general operation requirements applicable to all solid waste facility operators, transfer station operators also must (1) accept only those special wastes they are permitted to accept, (2) use leak-proof, non-biodegradable containers, (3) provide adequate means to prevent and extinguish fires, (4) conduct recycling operations in a safe and sanitary manner, (5) provide sufficient unloading areas, (6) for transfer stations that handle less than 250 cubic yards of solid waste per day, (a) confine solid waste to as small an area as possible, (b) empty all containers and/or trailers at least every other day and (c) not park uncleaned transfer vehicles containing putrescible materials on public streets or roads except in emergencies, (7) for stations that handle more than 250 cubic yards of solid waste per day, not leave any solid waste at the end of the operating day, (8) clean each station daily of all loose materials and litter and (9) provide separate storage areas if bulky wastes such as brush, junk vehicles, white goods and tires are accepted.[124]

---

120 "Lift" means an accumulation of refuse which is compacted into a cell and over which compacted cover is placed. N.M. Solid Waste Management Regulations § 105.JJ.

121 N.M. Solid Waste Management Regulations § 501.A&B.

122 N.M. Solid Waste Management Regulations § 501.C.

123 N.M. Solid Waste Management Regulations § 501.D.

124 N.M. Solid Waste Management Regulations § 403.

12.2.1 Closure and Post-Closure Requirements

Transfer station operators must comply with the following closure requirements: (1) cleanup of the area, (2) dismantling and removal of any improvements related to solid waste handling or disposal if required by NMED, (3) testing of soils and ground water for contamination if required by NMED and (4) any other condition of the permit.[125] Post-closure inspection and maintenance is not required if the facility demonstrates that all requirements of closure have been met and there is no evidence of contamination. However, post-closure inspection and maintenance is required before closure if the Secretary determines that it is necessary to protect human health and the environment.[126]

12.3 TRANSFORMATION FACILITIES

In addition to the general operation requirements applicable to all solid waste facility operators, transformation facility operators also must (1) control dust in the unloading and charging areas, (2) maintain appropriate fire-fighting equipment, (3) conduct recycling operations in a safe and sanitary manner, (4) provide sufficient unloading areas and (5) provide sufficient training for all new employees.[127] All transformation operators must establish an ash testing program prior to start-up.[128] All products remaining after transformation must be disposed of in a properly permitted landfill.[129]

12.3.1 Closure and Post-Closure Requirements

Transformation facility operators must comply with the following closure requirements: (1) cleanup of the area, (2) dismantling and removal of any improvements related to solid waste handling or disposal if required by NMED, (3) testing of soils and ground water for contamination if required by NMED and (4) any other condition of the permit.[130] Post-closure inspection and maintenance is not required if the facility demonstrates that all requirements of closure have been met and there is no evidence of contamination. However, post-closure inspection and maintenance is required before closure if the Secretary determines that it is necessary to protect human health and the environment.[131]

12.4 RECYCLING AND PROCESSING FACILITIES

In addition to the general operation requirements applicable to all solid waste facility operators, recycling and processing facility operators also must (1) post operational procedures, (2) store special wastes in covered buildings, covered leak-proof containers or tanks,

---

125 N.M. Solid Waste Management Regulations § 503.A.

126 N.M. Solid Waste Management Regulations § 503.B.

127 N.M. Solid Waste Management Regulations § 404.A.

128 N.M. Solid Waste Management Regulations § 404.B.

129 N.M. Solid Waste Management Regulations § 404.C.

130 N.M. Solid Waste Management Regulations § 503.A.

131 N.M. Solid Waste Management Regulations § 503.B.

(3) provide audible signals to alert operating personnel of critical operating unit malfunctions, (4) provide sampling sites of each process stream that do not interfere with normal facility operation, (5) provide separate areas for storage of special wastes while the wastes await processing or transport, (6) mark storage areas for special wastes, (7) store residues in a manner that prevents the containers or material from falling, leaking or blowing away, (8) store in separate areas all materials that are physically, chemically or biologically incompatible, (9) provide storage for special waste by-products generated during the initial start-up characterization period, (10) provide for the wash-down or other cleanup of the facility and for the disposal of wastewaters in accordance with all applicable state and federal regulations, (11) move all oils, polychlorinated biphenyls (PCBs), battery acid or other liquids that have the potential of being generated or spilled to a covered, substance-compatible, beamed containment pad and (12) keep a schedule and contacts for removal of stored wastes.[132]

12.4.1 Closure and Post-Closure Requirements

Recycling and processing facility operators must comply with the following closure requirements: (1) cleanup of the area, (2) dismantling and removal of any improvements related to solid waste handling or disposal if required by NMED, (3) testing of soils and ground water for contamination if required by NMED and (4) any other condition of the permit.[133] Post-closure inspection and maintenance is not required if the facility demonstrates that all requirements of closure have been met and there is no evidence of contamination. However, post-closure inspection and maintenance is required before closure if the Secretary determines that it is necessary to protect human health and the environment.[134]

12.5 COMPOSTING FACILITIES

In addition to the general operating requirements applicable to all solid waste facility operators, composting facility operators also must (1) maintain daily operational records which include temperature data and quantity of material processed, (2) process within two years all materials collected for the purpose of processing, (3) dispose properly all materials not destined for processing, (4) stabilize finished compost so that it can be stored or applied to land without creating a nuisance, environmental threat or hazard to health, (5) if windrowed, assure construction and turning frequency sufficient to maintain aerobic conditions and produce a compost product in the desired time frame, (6) assure that finished compost contains no sharp objects and (7) assure that all facilities utilizing municipal sewage sludge, septate or sludge/MSW commingled solid waste meet the requirements of applicable New

---

132 N.M. Solid Waste Management Regulations § 405.

133 N.M. Solid Waste Management Regulations § 503.A.

134 N.M. Solid Waste Management Regulations § 503.B.

Mexico Water Quality Control Commission Regulations and Appendix II of 40 C.F.R. § 257.[135]

12.5.1 Closure and Post-Closure Requirements

Within 30 days of closure, all composting facility operators must (1) remove all windrows and in-vessel compost material on the facility property, (2) remove or revegetate compacted compost material left on the land, (3) drain ponds or leachate collection systems, backfill, and assure removed contents were properly disposed, and (4) provide cover if necessary.[136] Following closure, all composting facility operators must (1) maintain ground water monitoring, if required, to detect possible migration of contaminants and (2) inspect and maintain any cover material.[137] The post-closure care period is 25 years, but the Secretary may decrease the period if there is no evidence of present or likely pollution or contamination.[138] The Secretary also may extend the post-closure period if necessary to protect human health and the environment.[139]

12.6 REMEDIAL ACTION; CONTINGENCY PLAN

NMED requires remedial action in connection with the operation of all solid waste facilities in the event that there is an increase in contaminants as evidenced in the water quality monitoring data.[140] The particular remedial action required depends on the type of contaminant.[141] If NMED determines that remedial action is necessary, NMED may require the following from operators: (1) written acknowledgement that a contaminant exists, (2) additional information pertaining to the monitoring and facility design and operation, (3) submittal of a remediation plan within 120 days of acknowledgement, (4) any other information NMED may require and (5) if drinking water supply has been contaminated, replacement of the water supply within seven days of being notified.[142] Additionally, NMED may require operators to (1) revise operational procedures, (2) change the design or construction, (3) provide an alternate method of waste treatment, processing or disposal, (4) temporarily close a facility or (5) restore ground water to safe standards.[143]

---

135 N.M. Solid Waste Management Regulations § 406.

136 N.M. Solid Waste Management Regulations § 502.A.

137 N.M. Solid Waste Management Regulations § 502.B.

138 N.M. Solid Waste Management Regulations § 502.C.

139 N.M. Solid Waste Management Regulations § 502.D.

140 N.M. Solid Waste Management Regulations § 801.A.

141 N.M. Solid Waste Management Regulations § 801.A-E.

142 N.M. Solid Waste Management Regulations § 802.A.

143 N.M. Solid Waste Management Regulations § 802.B

Each owner or operator must have a contingency plan for each solid waste facility in order to minimize hazards to human health or the environment.[144] The provisions of the plan will be carried out immediately in case of a fire, explosion or any unplanned release of contaminants or hazardous waste.[145] A copy of the plan must be submitted to all local police and fire departments, hospitals and state and local emergency response teams.[146] The plan must be revised if (1) the facility permit is revised or modified, (2) the plan fails in an emergency, (3) the facility changes design, construction, operation or maintenance, (4) the list of emergency coordinators changes or (5) the list of emergency equipment changes.[147]

13.0 SPECIAL WASTES

Special wastes are those wastes that have unique handling, transportation and disposal requirements to assure both public health and safety and environmental protection.[148] These wastes must either be treated prior to disposal or be isolated in their disposal to ensure a minimum amount of public exposure.[149] Special waste must be (1) disposed of at authorized facilities only,[150] (2) stored at authorized facilities only,[151] and (3) stored for no longer than 45 days.[152] A manifest must accompany each load of specified special waste that originates or is to be disposed of in New Mexico.[153] The physical and chemical characteristics of all special wastes must be documented.[154] All containers of special waste to be stored or disposed of must be labeled clearly, indicating the contents and potential hazards.[155]

13.1 ASBESTOS WASTE

No transporter may accept or transport asbestos waste unless the waste has been properly wetted and containerized.[156] A transporter must ensure that the asbestos waste is properly contained in leak-proof containers with appropriate labels and that the outsides

---

144 N.M. Solid Waste Management Regulations § 803.B.

145 N.M. Solid Waste Management Regulations § 803.C.

146 N.M. Solid Waste Management Regulations § 803.E.

147 N.M. Solid Waste Management Regulations § 803.F.

148 N.M. Solid Waste Management Regulations § 105.JJJ.

149 N.M. Solid Waste Management Regulations § 701.

150 N.M. Solid Waste Management Regulations § 702.A.

151 N.M. Solid Waste Management Regulations § 703.A.

152 N.M. Solid Waste Management Regulations § 703.B.

153 N.M. Solid Waste Management Regulations § 702.C.

154 N.M. Solid Waste Management Regulations § 703.D.

155 N.M. Solid Waste Management Regulations § 703.C.

156 N.M. Solid Waste Management Regulations § 705.A(1).

of the containers are not contaminated with asbestos debris adhering to the containers.[157] The transporter must ensure that the asbestos waste containers are loaded into the transport vehicle in a manner which prevents the breaking of the containers and that they are transferred at the disposal site in such a manner as to avoid fiber release.[158] If the transporter discovers that asbestos waste is not properly containerized, the transporter must immediately clean up the contaminated area and repair or reseal the container.[159] NMED must be notified of any release.[160] Vehicles used for transport of containerized asbestos waste must have an enclosed carrying compartment.[161] All asbestos containers must be tagged with a warning label.[162]

The transporter of the asbestos waste is required to notify the landfill operator that the load contains asbestos. The landfill operator must then inspect the load to verify that the asbestos waste is properly contained and labeled appropriately. The operator must notify the Secretary if he believes that the asbestos waste may cause significant fiber release during disposal. If the waste is not properly containerized and the landfill operator accepts the load, the operator must thoroughly soak the asbestos, rinse out the truck and immediately cover the waste with non-waste material which prevents fiber release prior to compacting the waste in the landfill.[163]

In order to dispose of and cover the asbestos the operator must prepare a separate trench to receive only asbestos waste which must be as narrow as possible while complying with all applicable trenching regulations and other solid waste management regulations pertaining to the covering of a trench containing asbestos.[164] In order to close an asbestos-containing cell, the landfill operator must cover the trench with an additional 30 inches of compacted non-waste-containing material to provide a 36-inch final cover to the original grade.[165]

The operator must provide barriers adequate to control public access to the asbestos portion of the landfill.[166] The operator is also required to have present when asbestos waste is being disposed at least one employee who has received at least 24 hours of course

---

157 N.M. Solid Waste Management Regulations § 705.A(2)(a).

158 N.M. Solid Waste Management Regulations § 705.A(2)(b).

159 N.M. Solid Waste Management Regulations § 705.A(2)(c).

160 *Id.*

161 N.M. Solid Waste Management Regulations § 705.A(3).

162 N.M. Solid Waste Management Regulations § 705.B(1).

163 N.M. Solid Waste Management Regulations § 705.C(1).

164 N.M. Solid Waste Management Regulations § 705.C(2).

165 N.M. Solid Waste Management Regulations § 705.C(3).

166 N.M. Solid Waste Management Regulations § 705.C(4).

work in an EPA-certified training course dealing with the identification, hazards and management of asbestos waste.[167]

13.2 INFECTIOUS WASTE

The generator of infectious waste which, by definition, carries a probable risk of transmitting disease to humans[168] must treat or dispose of such waste by incineration, sterilization, discharge to a sewage treatment system that provides secondary treatment of waste (only if the waste is liquid or semi-solid), or by any other methods approved by the Secretary.[169] Waste consisting of human anatomical remains, including human fetal remains, must be disposed by incineration or interment.[170] Infectious waste and sharps must be properly contained in appropriate containers prior to disposal.[171] All bags used for containment purposes must be red or orange and clearly identified.[172] There are stringent requirements pertaining to the transportation of infectious waste.[173]

13.3 ASH

No transporter may accept or transport ash[174] unless it has been treated or is securely covered to prevent release of fugitive dust.[175] Transporters must cover and line or seal vehicles in such a manner as to prevent leakage of liquids and fugitive dust during transport.[176]

The landfill operator attending to the disposal of ash must prepare a separate trench to receive non-hazardous ash[177] and take other prescribed measures to prevent the escape of fugitive emissions during the handling and covering process.[178] In order to close a cell containing ash, the landfill operator must cover the ash with additional compacted non-ash-containing material to provide a 36-inch final cover to the original grade.[179]

---

167 N.M. Solid Waste Management Regulations § 705.C(5).

168 N.M. Solid Waste Management Regulations § 105.GG.

169 N.M. Solid Waste Management Regulations § 706.E.

170 N.M. Solid Waste Management Regulations § 706.D.

171 N.M. Solid Waste Management Regulations § 706.C.

172 *Id.*

173 N.M. Solid Waste Management Regulations § 706.F.

174 "Ash" is defined as ash from the incineration or transformation of solid waste, including fly ash, bottom ash and ash from the incineration of refuse-derived fuel. N.M. Solid Waste Management Regulations § 105.G.

175 N.M. Solid Waste Management Regulations § 707.A(1).

176 N.M. Solid Waste Management Regulations § 707.A(2)-(3).

177 N.M. Solid Waste Management Regulations § 707.B(1).

178 N.M. Solid Waste Management Regulations § 707.B.

179 N.M. Solid Waste Management Regulations § 707.C(1).

The landfill operator is also required to provide barriers adequate to control public access to ash including, at a minimum, limiting access to the ash site to no more than two entrances by gates that can be locked when left unattended or by isolating trenches used at a Class A landfill.[180]

Ash that is temporarily stored must be stored in a manner so as to prevent fugitive dust emissions.[181]

13.4 CONTAMINATED SOILS

All soils that are to be disposed of at a landfill or that are suspected of being contaminated with petroleum products or other contaminants must be tested.[182] Soils containing free liquid will not be accepted at a landfill.[183] Soil may be stored temporarily on-site in a bermed area on an impermeable liner or in a manner that does not contaminate ground water, surface water, air or uncontaminated soil.[184] Soil will be spread no greater than six inches thick, may be required to be lined with an impermeable material and will be turned or disced once every two weeks until remediation is determined to be adequate.[185] The operator must provide a report to NMED documenting remediation.[186]

13.5 MANIFEST REQUIREMENT

A manifest must accompany each load of special waste originating or to be disposed of in New Mexico. The manifest contains the following information: (1) name of the generator, (2) name of the transporter, (3) name and identification number of the solid waste facility to which the waste is being delivered, (4) type of waste, (5) quantity of waste, (6) special handling instructions, and (7) date and location of delivery of the waste.[187]

The manifest must be signed by the generator and the transporter of the special waste and by the landfill operator, acknowledging both delivery and receipt of the waste.[188] Upon discovery of any significant discrepancy in the manifest, the person discovering the discrepancy must notify NMED, the generator, transporter and operator within 24 hours.[189] A copy of

---

180 N.M. Solid Waste Management Regulations § 707.D.

181 N.M. Solid Waste Management Regulations § 707.E.

182 N.M. Solid Waste Management Regulations § 708.A.

183 N.M. Solid Waste Management Regulations § 708.B.

184 N.M. Solid Waste Management Regulations § 708.C.

185 N.M. Solid Waste Management Regulations § 708.D.

186 N.M. Solid Waste Management Regulations § 708.F.

187 N.M. Solid Waste Management Regulations § 711.A.

188 N.M. Solid Waste Management Regulations § 711.B.

189 N.M. Solid Waste Management Regulations § 711.C.

the manifest must be maintained permanently by the generator, transporter and operator of the landfill.[190]

14.0 OPERATOR CERTIFICATION

All operators of landfills, transfer stations, processing facilities and transformation facilities must be certified by January 31, 1994.[191] All prospective operators must (1) meet the minimum educational requirements,[192] (2) complete all required training courses[193] and (3) pass an examination accompanying each training course.[194]

15.0 RECORD KEEPING AND ANNUAL REPORTS

Operators[195] of solid waste facilities are required to keep a written daily record during the operating life of the facility containing the following information: (1) the type and weight or volume of the solid waste, (2) the state, county and municipality in which the solid waste originated, (3) the commercial haulers of the solid waste, (4) the type and weight or volume of the special waste received, (5) the description of solid waste or special waste handling problems or emergency disposal activities, (6) the record of deviations from the approved design or operational plans, and (7) for a transfer station, the origin and destination of the solid waste.[196]

Operators must submit annual reports to the Secretary within 45 days after each anniversary date of the permit, registration or other approval.[197] Records of the annual reports must be retained at least throughout the post-closure period for landfills, and at least seven years after closure for all other solid waste facilities.[198]

All records, including plans, required by the regulations must be furnished upon request and made available at all reasonable times for inspection by the Secretary.[199]

---

190 N.M. Solid Waste Management Regulations § 711.E.

191 N.M. Solid Waste Management Regulations § 601.A.

192 N.M. Solid Waste Management Regulations § 602.

193 N.M. Solid Waste Management Regulations §§ 603-607.

194 N.M. Solid Waste Management Regulations § 608.

195 "Operator" means any person responsible for the operation of all or any portion of a solid waste facility. N.M. Solid Waste Management Regulations § 105.QQ. "Solid waste facility" means any public or private system, facility, location, improvements or structures used for processing, transformation, recycling or disposal of solid waste. N.M. Solid Waste Management Regulations § 105.HHH.

196 N.M. Solid Waste Management Regulations § 109.A-B.

197 N.M. Solid Waste Management Regulations § 109.C.

198 N.M. Solid Waste Management Regulations § 109.E.

199 N.M. Solid Waste Management Regulations § 109.D.

16.0 INSPECTION OF FACILITIES

The Secretary or any authorized representative is entitled to take the following actions with regard to solid waste facilities: (1) enter at any reasonable time for the purpose of making an inspection of solid waste management practices, (2) enter, inspect and monitor any solid waste compaction facilities that compact solid waste for disposal in a solid waste district different from the district in which the compaction facility is located, (3) take samples of the waste, soil, air or water in order to detect the nature and concentration of contaminants and (4) monitor or test the equipment, contents or surrounding soils, air, surface water or ground water at a solid waste facility.[200] The Secretary is required to make reasonable periodic inspections without prior notice at every solid waste facility and may conduct inspections of solid waste in transit at weigh stations or other adequate sites or facilities.[201]

Any commercial hauler that disposes of waste in a solid waste facility must allow inspection of its vehicles, transfer stations, collection facilities or any other facilities designed for the collection or transportation of solid waste.[202]

Any records, reports or information obtained by NMED are available to the public except information entitled to protection under the provisions of 18 U.S.C. § 1905.[203] The referenced federal statute deals with prohibitions on the disclosure of confidential information by employees of the United States and protects specified types of information such as trade secrets, processes, operations, style of work or apparatus, confidential statistical data, amount or source of income and income returns or abstracts thereof. A person required to provide data under the SWA may (1) designate the data the person believes is entitled to protection under 18 U.S.C. § 1905 and (2) submit such designated data separately from other data submitted under the SWA.[204]

17.0 PROHIBITED ACTS

Except as otherwise provided, no person may (1) dispose of solid waste in a manner that the person knows or should know will harm the environment or will endanger public health or safety, (2) dispose of solid waste in a place other than a permitted or otherwise authorized solid waste facility, (3) dispose of solid waste in a solid waste facility when the disposal of that particular type of solid waste is prohibited in that facility, (4) construct, operate or close a solid waste facility without a permit from NMED, (5) modify a solid waste

---

200 N.M. Stat. Ann. § 74-9-33(A)(1) to (4) (Repl. Pamp. 1993); N.M. Solid Waste Management Regulations § 110.A(1)-(4).

201 N.M. Stat. Ann. § 74-9-33(A)(5) (Repl. Pamp. 1993); N.M. Solid Waste Management Regulations § 110.A(5).

202 N.M. Stat. Ann. § 74-9-33(B) (Repl. Pamp. 1993); N.M. Solid Waste Management Regulations § 110.B.

203 N.M. Stat. Ann. § 74-9-33(C) (Repl. Pamp. 1993).

204 N.M. Stat. Ann. § 74-9-33(E) (Repl. Pamp. 1993).

facility without permission from the Secretary, (6) dispose of petroleum waste, sludge which does not meet required criteria, domestic sewage, treated domestic sewage, or septage at any solid waste facility, (7) dispose of certain hazardous wastes at any solid waste facility, unless properly permitted, (8) dispose of bulk liquids at any landfill, (9) process, recycle, transfer, transform, or dispose of radioactive waste in a solid waste facility except as otherwise provided, (10) dispose of lead-acid batteries at any landfill or incinerator, or (11) dispose of solid waste in a manner that the person knows or should know will be harmful to the environment or endanger the public health or safety.[205]

17.1 EXCEPTIONS

The following activities are not prohibited: (1) the disposal of solid waste on property where the waste is generated by a homeowner, residential tenant or agricultural enterprise, (2) the disposal of domestic solid waste on property where the waste is generated by a person occupying the property if the property is located so that it is not feasible to dispose of the solid waste in a permitted facility and the disposal does not harm the environment or otherwise violate any applicable SWA provision or regulation or (3) the disposal of construction and demolition debris or yard refuse on property where the debris or refuse is generated by a person in possession if the disposition does not violate any provision of the SWA or any regulation adopted pursuant to the SWA.[206]

18.0 EXEMPTIONS

Exemptions from the application of the provisions of the SWA may be granted if EIB determines after a hearing that the applicant or group of applicants is subject to requirements or regulations under an applicable federal or state law that imposes requirements as stringent as or more stringent than those provided for in the SWA.[207] EIB must deny the application unless the petitioner establishes by clear and convincing evidence that the applicable law cited by the petitioner is as stringent as or more stringent than the SWA or the Solid Waste Management Regulations.[208]

---

205 N.M. Stat. Ann. § 74-9-31(A) (Repl. Pamp. 1993); N.M. Solid Waste Management Regulations § 107.A.

206 N.M. Stat. Ann. § 74-9-31(B) (Repl. Pamp. 1993); N.M. Solid Waste Management Regulations § 108.

207 N.M. Stat. Ann. § 74-9-32 (Repl. Pamp. 1993).

208 N.M. Solid Waste Management Regulations § 902.G.

19.0 VARIANCES

Any person seeking a variance[209] from the requirements contained in the Solid Waste Management Regulations must do so by filing a written petition with the Secretary.[210]

The Secretary must deny the variance petition unless the petitioner establishes evidence that (1) application of the regulation would result in an arbitrary and unreasonable taking of the applicant's property or would impose an undue economic burden upon any lawful business, occupation or activity and (2) granting the variance will not result in any condition injurious to human health, safety or welfare or the environment.[211] However, no variance may be granted without consideration of the relative interests of the applicant, other owners of property likely to be affected, and the general public.[212]

Even if a variance is granted, the limitations on the grant of variance are significant. If the variance is granted on the grounds there are no practicable means known or available for the adequate prevention of degradation of the environment or the risk to public health, safety or welfare, it will continue only until the necessary means for the prevention of the degradation or risk become known and available.[213] If the variance is granted on other grounds, it may be granted for no more than one year.[214]

NMED is required to maintain a file of all variances issued and denied, which file is open for public inspection.[215]

20.0 NON-ADJUDICATORY ACTIONS

The following non-adjudicatory actions by EIB are subject to prior hearing: (1) approval or modification of the Plan, (2) designation of solid waste districts and changes in boundaries of solid waste districts, (3) adoption of any solid waste assessment fees to be charged and (4) adoption of substantive and procedural regulations.[216]

20.1 HEARING PROCEDURE

EIB's procedural regulations pertaining to hearings on non-adjudicatory actions must provide, at a minimum, for (1) public hearings, (2) notice, (3) a list of persons desiring notice,

---

209 "Variance" means any waiver from one or more provisions of the Solid Waste Management Regulations on any grounds other than those set forth in N.M. Stat. Ann. § 74-9-32 for an exemption. N.M. Solid Waste Management Regulations § 105.QQQ.

210 N.M. Solid Waste Management Regulations § 901.A.

211 N.M. Solid Waste Management Regulations § 901.C.

212 N.M. Solid Waste Management Regulations § 901.D.

213 N.M. Solid Waste Management Regulations § 901.E.(1).

214 N.M. Solid Waste Management Regulations § 901.E.(2).

215 N.M. Solid Waste Management Regulations § 901.F.

216 N.M. Stat. Ann. § 74-9-26 (Repl. Pamp. 1993).

(4) an opportunity for persons to be heard, (5) a hearing officer, (6) a record and (7) an appropriate place for the hearing.[217]

Actions by EIB are required to be (1) written, stating the reasons for the action, (2) made public, (3) communicated to all persons that have requested notification of the action taken and (4) taken not more than 60 days after the closing of the hearing or the day of submission of a report by a hearing officer.[218]

21.0 ADJUDICATORY ACTIONS

In addition to specific hearing requirements and procedures under other provisions of the SWA, the following adjudicatory actions by NMED are subject to prior hearing: (1) issuance, refusal to issue or modify and revocation of permits for solid waste facilities, (2) administrative enforcement actions and (3) actions on requests for variances and exceptions.[219] In any adjudicatory hearing, subpoenas may be issued for the attendance and testimony of witnesses and the production of documentary evidence.[220]

21.1 HEARING PROCEDURE

The Secretary has adopted procedural regulations for hearings on adjudicatory actions of the Secretary which provide for (1) public hearings, (2) notice, (3) a list of persons desiring notice, (4) an opportunity for persons to be heard, (5) discovery, (6) procedural due process, (7) a hearing officer, (8) a record, and (9) an appropriate place for the hearing.[221] In furtherance of this mandate, NMED has adopted Rules Governing Hearings for Permits and Variances under the Solid Waste Act[222] and Rules Governing Appeals from Compliance Orders under the Hazardous Waste Act and the Solid Waste Act.[223]

Actions by the Secretary following a hearing on an adjudicatory action must be (1) written, stating the reasons for the action, (2) made public, (3) communicated to all persons that have requested notification of the action taken and (4) taken not more than 30 days after the closing of the hearing or the date of submission of a report by a hearing officer.[224]

---

217 N.M. Stat. Ann. § 74-9-27(A) (Repl. Pamp. 1993).

218 N.M. Stat. Ann. § 74-9-27(B) (Repl. Pamp. 1993).

219 N.M. Stat. Ann. § 74-9-28(A) (Repl. Pamp. 1993).

220 N.M. Stat. Ann. § 74-9-28(B) (Repl. Pamp. 1993).

221 N.M. Stat. Ann. § 74-9-29(A) (Repl. Pamp. 1993).

222 NMED 91-1 (filed June 18, 1991).

223 HED 90-10 (EID) (filed Oct. 16, 1990).

224 N.M. Stat. Ann. § 74-9-29(B) (Repl. Pamp. 1993).

22.0 LIABILITY

The following persons[225] are strictly liable for the costs[226] of removal or remedial action incurred by New Mexico or any of its counties or municipalities because of a release or threatened release of contaminants from a solid waste facility: (1) the owner of the solid waste facility, (2) the operator of the solid waste facility, (3) any person having a permit for the solid waste facility issued under the SWA or the Environmental Improvement Act or otherwise authorized to accept solid waste, (4) any person who, at the time of disposal, owned, operated or had a permit or registration certificate to operate the solid waste facility, (5) any person who arranged for disposal, treatment or transportation for disposal or treatment of solid waste owned or possessed by that person and disposed of in the solid waste facility, (6) any generator[227] and (7) any person who accepted any solid waste for transfer to the solid waste facility.[228]

A person otherwise liable is not liable if the person can establish by a preponderance of the evidence that (1) the release of contaminants and the damages resulting therefrom were caused solely by an act of God or an act of war or (2) he or she is an owner who (a) at the time he or she acquired the property did not know and had no reason to know that the property had been used for a solid waste facility, (b) is a governmental entity that acquired the property by escheat, through any other involuntary transfer or acquisition or through the exercise of eminent domain authority, or (c) acquired the property by inheritance or devise.[229]

If any responsible party[230] that is liable for a release or threatened release fails without sufficient cause to take remedial action upon order of the Secretary, that person will be liable for punitive damages in an amount at least equal to and not more than three times the amount of any costs incurred as a result of the failure to take proper action.[231]

---

225 "Person" means an individual or any entity, including federal, state and local governmental entities, however organized. N.M. Stat. Ann. § 74-9-3(I) (Repl. Pamp. 1993).

226 N.M. Stat. Ann. § 74-9-34(A)(3) (Repl. Pamp. 1993).

227 "Generator" means the United States or a state, including New Mexico, or any agency, department, instrumentality, office, institution or political subdivision of a state in which any solid waste disposed of in a solid waste facility in New Mexico originated. N.M. Stat. Ann. § 74-9-34(A)(1) (Repl. Pamp. 1993).

228 N.M. Stat. Ann. § 74-9-34(B) (Repl. Pamp. 1993).

229 N.M. Stat. Ann. § 74-9-34(C) (Repl. Pamp. 1993).

230 "Responsible party" means any person other than a generator upon whom liability is imposed under § 74-9-34(B). N.M. Stat. Ann. § 74-9-34(A)(2) (Repl. Pamp. 1993).

231 N.M. Stat. Ann. § 74-9-34(D) (Repl. Pamp. 1993).

In the event a civil action is brought, the court must apportion an award of costs or damages, or both, in accordance with equitable principles among the defendants found liable.[232]

23.0 ENFORCEMENT

Whenever the Secretary determines that any person has violated, is violating or threatens to violate any requirement of the SWA, any regulation promulgated pursuant to the SWA or any condition of a permit issued under the SWA, the Secretary may (1) issue a compliance order or (2) commence a civil action.[233]

A compliance order may include a suspension or revocation of any permit previously issued.[234] Any penalty assessed in the order may not exceed $5,000 per day of noncompliance for each violation.[235]

If a violator fails to take corrective action within the time specified in the compliance order, the Secretary may (1) assess a civil penalty of not more than $10,000 for each day of continued noncompliance and (2) suspend or revoke any permit previously issued.[236]

Whenever the Secretary determines that there is or has been a release of contaminants, the Secretary may issue an order requiring corrective action, including action beyond a solid waste facility's boundaries, or the Secretary may commence an action in district court for appropriate relief, including a temporary or permanent injunction.[237]

Any order issued must state with reasonable specificity the nature of the required corrective action or other response measure, together with a time for compliance, and may include a suspension or revocation of a permit.[238] If any person named in an order fails to comply, the Secretary may assess a civil penalty in an amount not to exceed $5,000 for each day of noncompliance.[239]

Any enforcement proceeding or any claim for personal or property injury may be issued to or taken against the insurer or guarantor of an owner or operator if (1) the owner or operator is in bankruptcy, reorganization or arrangement pursuant to the federal bankruptcy code or (2) jurisdiction in any state or federal court cannot with reasonable diligence be obtained over an owner or operator likely to be solvent at the time of judgment.[240]

---

232 N.M. Stat. Ann. § 74-9-34(E) (Repl. Pamp. 1993).

233 N.M. Stat. Ann. § 74-9-36(A) (Repl. Pamp. 1993).

234 N.M. Stat. Ann. § 74-9-36(B) (Repl. Pamp. 1993).

235 *Id.*

236 N.M. Stat. Ann. § 74-9-36(C) (Repl. Pamp. 1993).

237 N.M. Stat. Ann. § 74-9-36(D) (Repl. Pamp. 1993).

238 N.M. Stat. Ann. § 74-9-36(E) (Repl. Pamp. 1993).

239 *Id.*

240 N.M. Stat. Ann. § 74-9-36(F) (Repl. Pamp. 1993).

Any order issued becomes final unless the person(s) named therein submits a written request to the Secretary for a public hearing within 30 days after the order is served.[241] Upon such a request, the Secretary will promptly arrange for a public hearing and appoint an independent hearing officer to preside.[242] The hearing officer will make and preserve a record of the proceedings and forward his or her recommendation based thereon to the Secretary, who makes the final decision.[243] The Secretary has adopted rules for discovery procedures and may issue subpoenas for the attendance and testimony of witnesses and the production of documents.[244]

24.0 CIVIL PENALTY

Any person who disposes of solid waste in a manner prohibited by the SWA or who violates any related regulation adopted pursuant to the SWA may be assessed a civil penalty not to exceed $5,000 for each day during any portion of which a violation occurs.[245]

25.0 CRIMINAL PENALTIES

Any person who disposes of solid waste in a manner prohibited by the SWA is guilty of a misdemeanor if the cost of cleanup is less than $10,000[246] and of a fourth-degree felony if the cost of cleanup is $10,000 or greater.[247] Any person who willfully fails to disclose or makes an intentional false disclosure under the provisions of the SWA permit application procedure is guilty of a fourth-degree felony.[248]

26.0 JUDICIAL REVIEW

Any person adversely affected by an administrative action of EIB or the Secretary may appeal to the New Mexico Court of Appeals.[249] The appeal is based on the record made at the hearing.[250]

---

241 N.M. Stat. Ann. § 74-9-36(G) (Repl. Pamp. 1993).

242 *Id.*

243 *Id.*

244 N.M. Stat. Ann. § 74-9-36(H) (Repl. Pamp. 1993); Rules Governing Appeals from Compliance Order Under the Hazardous Waste Act and the Solid Waste Act, HED 90-10 (EID), pt. III (filed Oct. 16, 1990).

245 N.M. Stat. Ann. § 74-9-38 (Repl. Pamp. 1993).

246 N.M. Stat. Ann. § 74-9-37(A) (Repl. Pamp. 1993).

247 N.M. Stat. Ann. § 74-9-37(B) (Repl. Pamp. 1993).

248 N.M. Stat. Ann. § 74-9-37(C) (Repl. Pamp. 1993).

249 N.M. Stat. Ann. § 74-9-30(A) (Repl. Pamp. 1993).

250 *Id.*

On appeal, the court of appeals will set aside the administrative action only if it is found to be (1) arbitrary, capricious or an abuse of discretion, (2) not supported by substantial evidence in the record or (3) otherwise not in accordance with law.[251]

27.0 NO PREEMPTION OF LOCAL AUTHORITY

Nothing in the SWA limits the authority of any county or municipality to adopt and enforce solid waste management requirements more stringent than those in the SWA or the authority of any county or municipality to exercise its planning and zoning authority.[252]

28.0 MUNICIPAL ENVIRONMENTAL SERVICES TAX

In order to afford municipalities the financial capability to comply with the provisions of the SWA, the Legislature enacted a municipal environmental services gross receipts tax.[253] The majority of the members of the governing body of a municipality may enact an ordinance imposing an excise tax on any person engaging in business, at the rate of one-sixteenth of one percent of the gross receipts of the person engaging in business. The imposition of this tax is not subject to referendum of any kind unless required by a municipal charter.[254]

The governing body is required, at the time of enacting an ordinance imposing the tax, to dedicate the revenue for acquisition, construction, operation and maintenance of solid waste facilities, water facilities, wastewater facilities, sewer systems and related facilities.[255]

29.0 COUNTY ENVIRONMENTAL SERVICES TAX

In order to afford counties the financial capability to comply with the provisions of the SWA, the Legislature enacted a county environmental services gross receipts tax.[256] The majority of the members of the governing body of a county may enact an ordinance imposing an excise tax on any person engaging in business in the county area, for the privilege of engaging in business, at the rate of one-eighth of one percent of the gross receipts of the person engaging in business in the county area.[257] The imposition of this tax is not subject to referendum of any kind unless required by the county charter.[258]

---

[251] N.M. Stat. Ann. § 74-9-30(B) (Repl. Pamp. 1993).

[252] N.M. Stat. Ann. § 74-9-42 (Repl. Pamp. 1993).

[253] N.M. Stat. Ann. § 7-19D-10 (Repl. Pamp. 1993).

[254] N.M. Stat. Ann. § 7-19D-10(A) (Repl. Pamp. 1993).

[255] N.M. Stat. Ann. § 7-19D-10(C) (Repl. Pamp. 1993).

[256] N.M. Stat. Ann. § 7-20E-17 (Repl. Pamp. 1993).

[257] N.M. Stat. Ann. § 7-20E-17(A) (Repl. Pamp. 1993).

[258] N.M. Stat. Ann. § 7-20E-17(C) (Repl. Pamp. 1993).

The governing body is required to dedicate the entire amount of revenue produced by the tax for the acquisition, construction, operation and maintenance of solid waste facilities, water facilities, wastewater facilities, sewer systems and related facilities.[259]

[259] N.M. Stat. Ann. § 7-20E-17(D) (Repl. Pamp. 1993).

CHAPTER V
HAZARDOUS WASTE MANAGEMENT

1.0 INTRODUCTION

The Hazardous Waste Act (HWA)[1] establishes the State of New Mexico's program for hazardous waste management and control. Since its initial adoption in 1977, the HWA has been substantially amended in 1981, 1987, and 1989 in order to bring its provisions more closely into conformity with the 1980[2] and 1984[3] amendments to the federal Resource Conservation and Recovery Act (RCRA).[4] In large measure, the major provisions of the HWA have been taken directly from Subtitle C (Hazardous Waste Management)[5] and Subtitle I (Regulation of Underground Storage Tanks)[6] of the RCRA.

The Environmental Improvement Board (EIB) is charged with promulgating regulations establishing New Mexico's hazardous waste program, and the New Mexico Environment Department (NMED) is responsible for administering and, with one exception, enforcing the regulations.[7] EIB has adopted virtually all the regulations promulgated by the United States Environmental Protection Agency (EPA) under Subtitle C of the RCRA , as revised through July 1, 1992. Because the HWA regulations are extremely detailed and voluminous, this Chapter will not attempt to present a detailed analysis of the hazardous waste program that they establish. Rather, this Chapter focuses on the main elements of New Mexico's hazardous waste program and briefly describes the kinds of requirements that may be applicable in a given area. For specific issues with regard to hazardous waste regulation, reference to the regulations adopted under the HWA and found in 40 C.F.R. Parts 260-266, 268 and 270 or to a reference guide is recommended.[8]

---

1 N.M. Stat. Ann. §§ 74-4-1 to -13 (Repl. Pamp. 1993).

2 Solid Waste Disposal Act Amendments of 1980, Pub. L. No. 96-482, 94 Stat. 2334 (1980).

3 Hazardous & Solid Waste Amendments of 1984, Pub. L. 98-616, 98 Stat. 3221 (1984).

4 Pub. L. No. 94-580, 90 Stat. 2795 (1976), codified at 42 U.S.C. §§ 6901-6987.

5 42 U.S.C. §§ 6921-6979.

6 42 U.S.C. §§ 6991-6991(i). For a discussion of the applicability of HWA to underground storage tanks, *see* Underground Storage Tank Management Chapter.

7 The New Mexico Department of Agriculture is responsible for the enforcement of all regulations adopted by EIB pursuant to the HWA regarding generators of hazardous agricultural waste. N.M. Stat. Ann. § 74-4-4.1 (Repl. Pamp. 1993). *See* Farmers and Waste Section of this Chapter.

8 An excellent overview and analysis of the federal regulations can be found in R. Hall, R. Schwartz, N. Bryson, R. Davis, B. Donohue, *The RCRA Hazardous Wastes Handbook.* 10th ed. Rockville, MD, Government Institutes, Inc., 1993.

1.1 RELATIONSHIP TO THE FEDERAL RCRA

In enacting the RCRA in 1976, Congress directed EPA to develop a federal program for the management and control of hazardous wastes from creation to ultimate disposal. Congress amended the RCRA in 1980 and again in 1984. The 1980 amendments strengthened the enforcement powers of EPA, provided for special treatment of certain types of waste, and clarified certain administrative aspects of the original act.[9] The Hazardous and Solid Waste Amendments of 1984 (1984 Amendments), sometimes referred to as "HSWA," expanded the scope of wastes to which the RCRA applied and restricted the use of landfills for hazardous waste disposal.[10] As discussed below, the 1984 Amendments have an important impact on the scope of the authorization of New Mexico's hazardous waste program.

The RCRA provides that states may be authorized by EPA to develop and carry out their own hazardous waste programs in lieu of the federal program[11] administered by EPA.[12] In order to obtain authorization, a state must submit an application to the Administrator of EPA and must demonstrate to the Administrator that the state program (1) is equivalent to the federal program, (2) is consistent with the federal or state programs applicable in other states, and (3) provides adequate enforcement of compliance with the requirements of the federal program.[13]

New Mexico applied for and received authorization to administer a hazardous waste program in lieu of the federal RCRA program on January 11, 1985[14] (sometimes referred to by federal and state agencies as the "base RCRA program"). Additional authorizations expanding the scope of the initial authorization were granted on April 10, 1990,[15] on July 25, 1990,[16] and on October 5, 1992.[17] The HWA meets requirements (1) and (2) above

---

9 Pub. L. No. 96-482, 94 Stat. 2334 (1980).

10 Pub. L. No. 98-616, 98 Stat. 3221 (1984).

11 The federal program is established and described in the federal regulations promulgated by EPA pursuant to the RCRA . These regulations are set forth at 40 C.F.R. Parts 124 and 260-272. In addition, certain provisions of the 1984 Amendments were self-implementing and did not require promulgation of regulations by EPA to be effective. Consequently, these self-implementing provisions of the 1984 Amendments constitute a portion of the federal program.

12 RCRA § 3006(b), 42 U.S.C. § 6926(b).

13 *Id.*

14 50 Fed. Reg. 1515 (1985).

15 55 Fed. Reg. 4604 (1990).

16 55 Fed. Reg. 28397 (1990).

17 57 Fed. Reg. 45717 (1992). On October 12, 1993, EPA published notice of the authorization status of New Mexico's hazardous waste program and of the hazardous waste statutes and regulations of New Mexico that EPA will enforce under the RCRA Section 3008. 58 Fed. Reg. 52677 (1993).

by providing that EIB shall adopt regulations for the management of hazardous waste equivalent to, and no more stringent[18] than, federal regulations adopted by EPA pursuant to the RCRA . As to requirement (3), New Mexico submitted the required documents.[19]

EIB may adopt hazardous waste regulations by reference to the federal regulations without setting forth the provisions of the federal regulations.[20] On October 8, 1992, effective November 21, 1992, EIB adopted, with a few substitutions and minor exceptions, the entire body of Parts 260-266 and 268-270 of EPA's Subtitle C Regulations, as set forth in 40 C.F.R. through July 1, 1992.[21] *See* Chart I on page 149 for a description of the relationship of these New Mexico regulations to the federal EPA regulations. It is likely that EIB will continue the practice of adopting the federal regulations as amended through June of the previous year, since the federal program requires as a condition of continued authorization of the base RCRA program that states modify their programs to reflect changes to the federal program occurring during the twelve months preceding the previous July 1.[22]

New Mexico's authorization to carry out a hazardous waste program in lieu of the federal program administered by EPA does not extend at this time to the regulations promulgated by EPA pursuant to the 1984 Amendments.[23] Nevertheless, most of these regulations are contained in the regulations adopted by EIB on October 8, 1992. New Mexico has applied for authorization to administer some of the federal regulations mandated by the 1984 Amendments, but as of November 1, 1993, the state has not received final authorization to administer these regulations.[24] A further complication is the "lag time" that exists because EIB has not yet adopted the federal regulations promulgated by EPA after July 1, 1992. This

---

18 N.M. Stat. Ann. § 74-4-4(A) (Repl. Pamp. 1993). The 1993 New Mexico Legislature amended the HWA to provide that EIB may adopt regulations for the management of hazardous waste and hazardous waste transformation that are more stringent than federal regulations adopted by the EPA pursuant to the RCRA , if EIB determines, after notice and public hearing, that such federal regulations are not sufficient to protect public health and the environment. N.M. Stat. Ann. § 74-4-4(D) (Repl. Pamp. 1993). "Transformation" means an incinerator, pyrolysis, distillation, gasification, or biological conversion other than composting. *Id.*

19 *See* 40 C.F.R. § 271.5. This provision constitutes EPA's implementation and specification of the congressional requirements for state authorization.

20 N.M. Stat. Ann. § 74-4-4(D) (Repl. Pamp. 1993).

21 N.M. Hazardous Waste Management Regulations, EIB/HWMR-7 (filed Oct. 21, 1992).

22 40 C.F.R. § 271.21(e)(2)(ii).

23 The Subtitle C regulations promulgated by EPA are found in 40 C.F.R. Parts 260-266, 268-270, as revised through July 1, 1992.

24 For more detailed information regarding the areas of respective state and federal jurisdiction, consultation with the Hazardous and Radioactive Materials Bureau of NMED and Region 6 of EPA is advised.

lag time will remain a consideration as EIB adopts, presumably on a yearly basis, the federal regulations effective through June 30 of the previous year. The practical effects of the authorized and non-authorized aspects of New Mexico's hazardous waste program are that (1) EPA will continue to administer that portion of the federal program promulgated pursuant to the 1984 Amendments until New Mexico receives authorization to do so, and (2) the most recently adopted federal regulations (other than those promulgated pursuant to the 1984 Amendments) will not be administered by EPA nor by the State of New Mexico until adopted by EIB.

1.2 HAZARDOUS WASTE MANAGEMENT SYSTEM

Section 101 of the New Mexico Hazardous Waste Management Regulations (HWMR-7) incorporates the EPA regulations set forth in 40 C.F.R. Part 260 (Hazardous Waste Management System: General),[25] which provide definitions of terms, general standards, and overview information applicable to Parts 260 through 265 and 268 of Subtitle C of the RCRA In addition, Part 260 addresses the availability or confidentiality of information, mandates that certain hazardous waste recycling activities be regulated on a case-by-case basis, and specifies the procedures for such regulation.[26]

1.2.1 Availability or Confidentiality of Information

Any information provided to NMED under Parts 260 through 265 and 268 of the regulations will be made available to the public to the extent and in the manner authorized by New Mexico laws governing inspection of public records.[27] A claim of business confidentiality covering part or all of any information provided to NMED under Parts 260 through 266 and 268 of the regulations may be asserted by following specified procedures.[28]

1.2.2 Substitutions, Omissions, and Additions

Terms related to the State of New Mexico are substituted in place of the corresponding federal terms, in order to accomplish the administration of the New Mexico program by New Mexico officials rather than EPA officials.[29] Thus "Administrator" or "Regional Administrator," in the federal regulations means the Secretary of NMED (Secretary) or the

---

25 Subject to certain substitutions, omissions, and additions, as provided for in § 102 of Hazardous Waste Management Regulations-7.

26 The hazardous waste recycling activity referred to involves recyclable materials from which precious metals are reclaimed. Such materials may not be "accumulated speculatively." For definition of this term, *see* Solid Waste Defined Section of this Chapter.

27 N.M. Stat. Ann. §§ 14-2-1 to -3, 14-3A-1 to -2 (Repl. Pamp. 1988); N.M. Stat. Ann. § 74-4-4.3(D) (Repl. Pamp. 1993).

28 40 C.F.R. § 260.2(b).

29 N.M. Hazardous Waste Management Regulations-7 § 102.

CHART I
NEW MEXICO HAZARDOUS WASTE ACT REGULATIONS-7
(adopted October 8, 1992)

	New Mexico Section(s)	Adopts Federal 40 C.F.R. Part	Omits Federal 40 C.F.R. Section(s)
Part I			
Hazardous Waste Management General	101	260	
	102		260.1(b)(6) 260.22 260.30 260.31 260.32 260.33
Part II			
Identification & Listing of Hazardous Waste	201	261	
Part III			
Standards Applicable to Generators	301	262	
Part IV			
Standards Applicable to Transporters	401	263	
	402		263.20(e)
Part V			
Standards for Owners & Operators of Treatment, Storage & Disposal Facilities	501	264	
	502		264.149 264.150
Part VI			
Interim Status Standards for Owners & Operators of Treatment, Storage & Disposal Facilities	601	265	
	602		265.149 265.150
Part VII			
Standards for Management of Specific Hazardous Wastes & Specific Types of Hazardous Waste Management Facilities	701	266	
Part VIII			
Land Disposal Restrictions	801	268	
Part IX			
Hazardous Waste Permit Program	901	270	
	902		
Part X			
Miscellaneous	1001-1007		

Secretary's designee.[30] Other substitutions of a significant nature are (1) "Freedom of Information Act" or "FOIA" means the New Mexico act governing inspection of public records[31] and (2) references to 40 C.F.R. Part 124 (Procedures for Decision Making on Permits) within the text of HWMR-7 are construed to mean Section 902 (Permitting Procedures) of HWMR-7.[32]

Certain sections of 40 C.F.R. Part 260 are omitted from the state's hazardous waste regulations, including the following:

(1) Procedures for seeking to exclude a waste at a particular generating facility from the hazardous waste lists in Subpart D of Part 261;

(2) Variances for certain recycled materials from classification as a solid waste;

(3) Standards and criteria for variances for recycled materials from classification as solid waste;

(4) Standards for variances for certain enclosed devices using controlled-flame combustion to be classified as boilers, even though they do not otherwise meet the definition of boiler contained in Section 260.10;[33] and

(5) Procedures for variances from classification as a solid waste or to be classified as a boiler.[34]

The effect of omission is that the specified exclusion or variance must be sought from EPA rather than from the Secretary of NMED (Secretary).

An additional definition not found in the federal regulations but included in the state's regulations, is "hazardous substance incident" which is defined to mean any emergency incident involving a chemical or chemicals, including but not limited to transportation wrecks, accidental spills or leaks, fires, or explosions, which incident creates the reasonable probability of injury to human health or property.[35]

1.2.3 Change In Counterpart to an HWA Regulation

If EPA should suspend any federal hazardous waste regulation having a direct counterpart to an HWA regulation, the counterpart and the HWA regulation is automatically

---

30 N.M. Hazardous Waste Management Regulations-7 § 102.A(1).

31 N.M. Hazardous Waste Management Regulations-7 § 102.B(7). As to inspection of public records, *see* N.M. Stat. Ann. §§ 14-2-1 to -3, 14-3A-1 to -2 (Repl. Pamp. 1988); N.M. Stat. Ann. § 74-4-4.3(D) (Repl. Pamp. 1993).

32 N.M. Hazardous Waste Management Regulations-7 § 1003.

33 40 C.F.R. § 260.10 contains the definitions of terms applicable to Parts 260 through 266 and Part 268 of the federal hazardous waste regulations.

34 N.M. Hazardous Waste Management Regulations-7 § 102.C.

35 N.M. Hazardous Waste Management Regulations-7 § 102.B(8). This definition repeats the language of the HWA. N.M. Stat. Ann. § 74-4-3(H) (Repl. Pamp. 1993).

deemed suspended[36] and if any federal regulation incorporated by reference in the HWA regulations is stayed, invalidated, or otherwise rendered unenforceable by EPA, in whole or in part, by action of a federal court, such incorporated federal regulation is enforceable by NMED only to the extent it is enforceable by EPA.[37]

2.0 IDENTIFICATION OF HAZARDOUS WASTE

New Mexico's hazardous waste program, like its federal counterpart, places the responsibility for determining whether or not a material is a hazardous waste subject to regulation on the person handling the material.[38]

2.1 STATUTORY DEFINITION

A hazardous waste is any solid waste or combination of solid wastes which because of their quantity, concentration or physical, chemical or infectious characteristics may (1) cause or significantly contribute to an increase in mortality or an increase in serious irreversible or incapacitating reversible illness or (2) pose a substantial present or potential hazard to human health or environment when improperly treated, stored, transported, disposed of or otherwise managed.[39] Hazardous waste may also include any material imported into the State of New Mexico for the purpose of disposal which is defined or classified as hazardous waste in the state of origin.[40]

2.2 STATUTORY EXCLUSIONS

The following materials are excluded from the definition of hazardous waste until EIB determines that they are subject to Subtitle C of the RCRA : drilling fluids, produced waters and other wastes associated with the exploration, development or production of crude oil or natural gas or geothermal energy, any fly ash waste, bottom ash waste, slag waste, flue gas emission control waste generated primarily from the combustion of coal or other fossil fuels, solid waste from the extraction, beneficiation or processing of ores and minerals, including phosphate rock and overburden from the mining of uranium ore, or cement kiln dust waste.[41] As of November 1, 1993, EIB has not made such a determination.

A second set of exclusions precludes the HWA's applicability to specified activities or substances which are subject to the Federal Water Pollution Control Act, the Safe Drinking Water Act, or the Atomic Energy Act of 1954, as amended, except to the extent that such

---

36 N.M. Hazardous Waste Management Regulations-7 § 1001.

37 N.M. Hazardous Waste Management Regulations-7 § 1005.

38 *See, e.g.,* 40 C.F.R. § 262.11.

39 N.M. Stat. Ann. § 74-4-3(I) (Repl. Pamp. 1993).

40 N.M. Stat. Ann. § 74-4-3.3 (Repl. Pamp. 1993).

41 *See* RCRA § 3001, 42 U.S.C. § 6921. *See also* 40 C.F.R. 261.4(b)(7) for restrictions on certain categories of this exclusion.

application or regulation is not inconsistent with the requirements of such acts.[42] The HWA does not apply to the treatment, storage or disposal of wastes under a permit issued pursuant to the Surface Mining Act[43] or the Federal Surface Mining Control and Reclamation Act of 1977, as amended, or to any farmer disposing of waste pesticides from his own use, provided he triple rinses each emptied pesticide container and disposes of the pesticide residues on his own farm in a manner consistent with the disposal instructions on the pesticide label.[44]

2.3 SOLID WASTE DEFINED

A waste must be a solid waste before it can be a hazardous waste. Solid waste is:

> ... any garbage, refuse, sludge from a waste treatment plant, water supply treatment plant or air pollution control facility and other discarded material, including solid, liquid, semisolid or contained gaseous material resulting from industrial, commercial, mining and agricultural operations, and from community activities...[45]

Excluded from this statutory definition are solid or dissolved materials in domestic sewage or solid or dissolved materials in irrigation return flows or industrial discharges which are point sources subject to permits under Section 402 of the Federal Water Pollution Control Act, as amended,[46] or source, special nuclear or by-product material as defined by the Atomic Energy Act of 1954, as amended.[47] The regulations further exclude from the definition of solid waste[48] (1) materials subjected to in-situ mining techniques which are not removed from the ground as part of the extraction process, (2) pulping liquors (*i.e.*, black liquor) that are reclaimed in a pulping liquor recovery furnace and then reused in the pulping process, unless accumulated speculatively,[49] (3) spent sulfuric acid used to produce virgin sulfuric

---

42 N.M. Stat. Ann. § 74-4-3.1 (Repl. Pamp. 1993).

43 N.M. Stat. Ann. §§ 69-25A-1 to -35 (Repl. Pamp. 1979 & Supp. 1993).

44 N.M. Stat. Ann. § 74-4-3.1 (Repl. Pamp. 1993).

45 N.M. Stat. Ann. § 74-4-3(M) (Repl. Pamp. 1993).

46 Codified as amended at 33 U.S.C. § 1342.

47 *See* Atomic Energy Act of 1954, ch. 1073, 68 Stat. 921, 923 (1954). Codified as amended at 42 U.S.C. §§ 2011 *et seq.*

48 40 C.F.R. Part 261 addresses the identification of hazardous waste and solid waste.

49 A material is "accumulated speculatively" if it is accumulated before being recycled. A material is not accumulated speculatively, however, if the person accumulating it can show that the material is potentially recyclable and has a feasible means of being recycled and that during the calendar year (commencing on January 1) the amount of material that is recycled, or transferred to a different site for recycling, equals at least 75 percent by weight or volume of the amount of that material accumulated at the beginning of the period. 40 C.F.R. § 261.1(c)(8). The regulations also specify how the calculations for the percentage of turnover are to be performed. *Id.*

acid, unless accumulated speculatively, (4) secondary materials that are reclaimed and returned to the original process or processes in which they were generated, subject to specified conditions, (5) spent wood preserving solutions that have been reclaimed and are reused for their original intended purpose together with waste waters from the wood preserving process that have been reclaimed and are reused to treat wood, (6) decanter tank tar sludge from coking operations and any waste from the coke byproducts processes, subject to specified conditions, and (7) non-wastewater splash condenser dross residue from treatment of K061[50] in high temperature metals recovery units, provided it is shipped in drums (if shipped) and not land disposed before recovery.[51]

The most inclusive term in the solid waste definition above is "discarded material," which is defined as any material which is abandoned, recycled, or considered inherently waste-like.[52] Materials are abandoned by being disposed of, burned or incinerated, or by being accumulated, stored or treated (but not recycled) before or in lieu of being disposed of, burned, or incinerated.[53] Materials are solid waste if they are recycled -- or accumulated, stored, or treated before recycling -- as specified in the regulations,[54] with certain exceptions.[55] Certain materials when they are recycled are also identified by the regulations as solid waste because of their inherent waste-like characteristics.[56]

2.4 HAZARDOUS WASTE DEFINED BY THE REGULATIONS

A solid waste is generally a hazardous waste if it is not excluded from regulation as a hazardous waste,[57] is a listed hazardous waste, exhibits any of the characteristics of hazardous waste (characteristic waste), or is a mixture of solid waste and a hazardous waste.[58]

2.4.1 Exclusions from Regulation as a Hazardous Waste

In addition to the statutorily mandated exclusions, the regulations provide that the following solid wastes are also excluded as hazardous wastes: (1) household waste,[59] (2) agri-

---

50 This listed waste from a specific source is identified as emission control dust/sludge from the primary production of steel in electric furnaces. 40 C.F.R. § 261.32

51 40 C.F.R. § 261.4(a)(5)-(11).

52 40 C.F.R. § 261.2(a)(2).

53 40 C.F.R. § 261.2(b).

54 40 C.F.R. § 261.2(c).

55 40 C.F.R. § 261.2(e).

56 40 C.F.R. § 261.2(d).

57 As specified in 40 C.F.R. § 261.4(b).

58 40 C.F.R. § 261.3(a).

59 "Household waste" means any material including garbage, trash and sanitary waste in septic tanks, derived from households (including single and multiple residences, hotels

cultural wastes from the growing and harvesting of agricultural crops and the raising of animals, including animal manures, which are returned to the soils as fertilizers, (3) mining overburden returned to the mine site, (4) certain chromium-bearing wastes, (5) certain wastes produced by the leather tanning and finishing industry, (6) solid waste from the extraction, beneficiation, and processing of ores and minerals (including coal) including phosphate rock and overburden from the mining of uranium ore, provided certain definitions and standards are met as provided for in the regulations, (7) wood or wood products which fail the test for the Toxicity Characteristic solely for arsenic and which are not a hazardous waste for any other reason, if the waste is generated by persons who utilize the arsenical-treated wood and wood products for their intended use, (8) petroleum-contaminated media and debris that fail the test for the Toxicity Characteristic and that are subject to the corrective action regulations applicable to underground storage tanks, (9) injected ground water that is hazardous only because it exhibits the Toxicity Characteristic, subject to conditions specified in the regulations, (10) used chlorofluorocarbon refrigerants from total enclosed heat transfer equipment, provided the refrigerant is reclaimed for further use, (11) non-terne-plated used oil filters that are not mixed with listed wastes if these oil filters have been gravity hot-drained using a specified method, [60] (12) wastes that are generated in certain types of units (generally enclosed) until such time as the waste exits the unit in which it is generated,[61] (13) waste samples that are collected and sent to an analytical laboratory for testing or to a testing facility for treatability studies, subject to specified handling requirements,[62] (14) waste samples collected for the purpose of conducting treatability studies, subject to specified handling requirements,[63] (15) samples undergoing treatability studies at laboratories and testing facilities, subject to specified conditions,[64] (16) residues of hazardous wastes in containers or liners, provided the container meets the regulatory definition of "empty" and that certain specified conditions are met as provided for in the regulations,[65] and (17) PCB-containing dielectric fluid and electrical equipment containing such fluid whose disposal is regulated under the Toxic Substances Control Act and that are hazardous only because they fail the test for the Toxicity Characteristic.[66]

---

and motels, bunk houses, ranger stations, crew quarters, camp grounds, picnic grounds and day use recreation areas). 40 C.F.R. § 261.4(b)(1).

[60] 40 C.F.R. § 261.4(b).

[61] 40 C.F.R. § 261.4(c).

[62] 40 C.F.R. § 261.4(d).

[63] 40 C.F.R. § 261.4(e).

[64] 40 C.F.R. § 261.4(f).

[65] 40 C.F.R. § 261.7.

[66] 40 C.F.R. § 261.8.

2.4.2 Listed Wastes

There are lists of solid wastes that have been determined to be hazardous wastes because the waste meets one of the following criteria: (1) it exhibits certain specified characteristics of hazardous waste, (2) it is found to be fatal to humans in low doses[67] or is otherwise capable of causing or significantly contributing to an increase in serious irreversible or incapacitating reversible illness, or (3) it contains any of certain specified toxic constituents.[68] As to these "listed wastes," the regulations assign an EPA hazardous waste number which must be used in complying with notification and reporting requirements.[69]

The listed hazardous wastes are divided into the following subgroups, depending upon origin: (1) hazardous waste from nonspecific sources,[70] (2) hazardous waste from specific sources,[71] and (3) discarded commercial chemical products, off-specification species, container residues, and spill residues.[72]

If generators of wastes from wood preserving processes at plants that do not resume or initiate use of chlorophenolic preservatives to meet specified conditions, such waste will not meet the listing definition for EPA waste F032.[73] These wastes may, however, continue to meet another hazardous waste listing description or may exhibit one or more of the hazardous waste characteristics.[74]

2.4.3 Characteristic Wastes

Characteristic hazardous wastes are solid wastes which exhibit one or more of the following characteristics:[75] ignitability,[76] corrosivity,[77] reactivity,[78] or toxicity.[79] The first two terms are self-explanatory. A waste that is unstable, reacts violently, forms potentially explosive mixtures with water, or is capable of explosive reaction without being deton-

---

67 In the absence of data on human toxicity, the regulations specify criteria based on the testing of animals. 40 C.F.R. § 261.11(a)(2).

68 40 C.F.R. 261.11(a)(3).

69 40 C.F.R. § 261.30(c).

70 40 C.F.R. § 261.31.

71 40 C.F.R. § 261.32.

72 40 C.F.R. § 261.33.

73 40 C.F.R. § 261.35(a).

74 *Id.*

75 40 C.F.R. § 261.20.

76 40 C.F.R. § 261.21.

77 40 C.F.R. § 261.22.

78 40 C.F.R. § 261.23.

79 40 C.F.R. § 261.24.

ated is considered reactive.[80] A solid waste exhibits the characteristic of toxicity if, using the test methods prescribed in the regulations, the extract from a sample of the waste contains concentrations of contaminates in excess of those allowed, as specified in the regulations.[81] Solid wastes that are not listed wastes and exhibit one or more of these four characteristics are commonly referred to as "characteristic wastes."

3.0 GENERATORS

EIB has adopted *in toto* 40 C.F.R. Part 262,[82] which deals with standards applicable to generators of hazardous waste. A generator is any person producing hazardous waste.[83] The regulations amplify this statutory definition by defining generator as any person,[84] by site, whose act or process produces hazardous waste identified or listed in the regulations or whose act first causes a hazardous waste to become subject to regulation.[85]

3.1 WASTE ANALYSIS

A person who generates a solid waste must determine whether that waste is a hazardous waste by the following process: (1) determine whether the waste is excluded from regulation; (2) if not, determine whether the waste is a listed hazardous waste; (3) if not, and for the purpose of complying with the land disposal restrictions,[86] determine whether the waste is a characteristic waste by either (a) testing the waste according to the specified method or according to an equivalent method approved by the Secretary or (b) applying knowledge of the hazardous characteristic of the waste in light of the materials or the processes used.[87] If the waste is determined to be hazardous, the generator must consult the regulations for possible exclusions or restrictions pertaining to management of the waste.[88]

3.2 CLASSES OF GENERATORS

There are five classes of generators that are subject to varying degrees of regulation, depending upon the volume and type of hazardous waste accumulated on-site and whether

---

80 40 C.F.R. § 261.23.

81 40 C.F.R. § 261.24.

82 N.M. Hazardous Waste Management Regulations-7 Part III-Standards Applicable to Generators of Hazardous Waste.

83 N.M. Stat. Ann. § 74-4-3(F) (Repl. Pamp. 1993).

84 A "person" is defined as any individual, trust, firm, joint stock company, federal agency, corporation including a government corporation, partnership, association, state, municipality, commission, political subdivision of a state or any interstate body. N.M. Stat. Ann. § 74-4-3(K) (Repl. Pamp. 1993).

85 40 C.F.R. § 260.10.

86 *See* Land Disposal Restrictions Section of this Chapter.

87 40 C.F.R. § 262.11(a) - (c).

88 40 C.F.R. § 262.11(d).

the hazardous waste generated is also stored, treated or disposed of by the generator. The classes of generators are (1) conditionally exempt small quantity generators (generate no more than 100 kilograms of hazardous waste or 1 kilogram of acutely hazardous waste in a calendar month), (2) small quantity generators (generate more than 100 kg and less than 1,000 kg of hazardous waste and no more than 1 kg of acutely hazardous waste in any calendar month), (3) generators of 1,000 kg or more of hazardous waste per calendar month or more than 1 kg of acutely hazardous waste in any calendar month, (4) farmers who generate waste pesticides which are hazardous wastes, and (5) a generator who treats, stores, or disposes of hazardous waste on-site.

3.2.1 Conditionally Exempt Small Quantity Generator

A conditionally exempt small quantity generator generates no more than 100 kilograms of hazardous waste or 1 kilogram of acutely hazardous waste in a calendar month.[89] Such a generator is not subject to the extensive regulation governing generators of larger volumes of hazardous waste, provided the generator complies with waste analysis, accumulation, and disposal requirements. As to waste analysis, such generator should follow procedures described above. As to accumulation, such generator may not accumulate on-site (1) more than 100 kg of hazardous waste in a calendar month, (2) more than 1 kg of acutely hazardous waste in a calendar month, (3) more than 100 kg of any residue or contaminated soil, waste or other debris resulting from the cleanup of a spill of any acute hazardous waste in a calendar month, or (4) at any one time more than 1,000 kg of hazardous waste.[90]

As to disposal, the conditionally exempt small quantity generator must treat or dispose of the hazardous waste in an on-site facility or insure delivery to an off-site treatment, storage or disposal facility, either of which, if located in the United States, is (1) a facility with a permit under Part 270 of the regulations,[91] (2) an interim status facility,[92] (3) authorized to manage hazardous waste by a state with a hazardous waste management program approved under Part 271 of the federal EPA regulations, (4) permitted, licensed, or registered by a state to manage municipal or industrial solid waste, or (5) a facility which (a) beneficially uses or reuses or legitimately recycles or reclaims its waste or (b) treats its waste prior to beneficial use or reuse or legitimately recycles or reclaims.[93]

If a conditionally exempt small quantity generator's wastes are mixed with used oil, the mixture is subject to regulation as used oil burned for energy recovery if in fact the

---

89 *See* 40 C.F.R. § 261.5.

90 40 C.F.R. § 261.5.

91 *See* Permit System Section of this Chapter.

92 *Id.*

93 40 C.F.R. § 261.5(f) - (g).

mixture is destined to be burned for energy recovery.[94] Any material produced from such a mixture by processing, blending, or other treatment is also so regulated if it is destined to be burned for energy recovery.[95]

3.2.2 Small Quantity Generator

A second class of generators includes generators, sometimes referred to as small quantity generators, that produce between 100 and 1,000 kg of hazardous waste per month. Such generators are subject to substantial regulation, which requires that the generator (1) determine whether solid waste produced is hazardous waste and if so comply with requirements in connection with land disposal restrictions, (2) obtain an EPA identification number, (3) observe accumulation and storage restrictions and requirements on hazardous waste, (4) comply with the manifest system for hazardous waste that is transported, treated, stored, or disposed of off-site, (5) observe recordkeeping requirements, (6) submit biennial reports, and (7) follow export notification requirements. These requirements are discussed in greater detail below.

3.2.2.1 Identification of Hazardous Waste

The small quantity generator is required to make the same hazardous waste determination as a conditionally exempt small quantity generator.[96] In addition, if the waste is determined to be hazardous, this generator must comply with the requirements related to the land disposal restrictions.[97]

3.2.2.2 EPA Identification Number

A generator must not treat, store, dispose of, transport or offer for transportation hazardous waste without having received an EPA identification number,[98] which may be obtained by application to the Secretary using EPA form 8700-12.[99] A generator may not offer hazardous waste to transporters or to treatment, storage or disposal facilities which do not have EPA identification numbers.[100]

---

94 40 C.F.R. § 261.5(j).

95 *Id.*

96 *See* 40 C.F.R. § 262.11. For a description of the process involved in this determination, *see* Waste Analysis in this Section and Waste Analysis in the Land Disposal Restrictions Section of this Chapter.

97 40 C.F.R. §§ 262.11(d), 262.34(d)(4).

98 40 C.F.R. § 262.12(a).

99 The application for the EPA identification number is submitted to NMED; however, EPA's Regional Office 6 actually furnishes the number after NMED reviews the application.

100 40 C.F.R. § 262.12(c).

3.2.2.3 Accumulation and Storage Restrictions

A small quantity generator may accumulate up to 6,000 kg of hazardous waste on-site for a period of up to 180 days without a permit,[101] or for a period of up to 270 days[102] if the waste must be transported over 200 miles to a treatment, storage or disposal facility (TSDF). A general storage permit exemption is provided for all hazardous waste generators, including small quantity generators, when they store any amount of hazardous waste on-site in tanks or containers for a period of 90 days or less, provided they comply with labeling requirements and operating standards as specified in the regulations.[103] A generator may also accumulate without a permit as much as 55 gallons of hazardous waste or one quart of acutely hazardous waste[104] in containers at or near any point of generation where waste initially accumulates, provided that the container is properly labeled and certain requirements are fulfilled regarding the condition of the container, the compatibility of waste with the container and the management of the container.[105] Finally, small quantity generators and generators of hazardous waste in excess of 1,000 kg per month must also comply with emergency planning and preparedness requirements and must provide for an emergency coordinator who is responsible for coordinating all emergency response measures.[106]

A generator who exceeds the accumulation and storage limits for hazardous waste or who treats or disposes of hazardous waste on-site is required to submit an application for and to receive a permit.[107]

3.2.2.4 Manifest Requirements

The HWA mandates the use of the manifest system for generators of hazardous waste.[108] A manifest is the form used for identifying the quantity, composition, origin, routing and destination of hazardous waste during transportation from point of generation to point of disposal, treatment, or storage.[109] This form is a shipping document which the generator must fill out and which must accompany hazardous waste that is shipped off-site

---

101 40 C.F.R. § 262.34(d).

102 40 C.F.R. § 262.34(e).

103 40 C.F.R. § 262.34(a).

104 40 C.F.R. § 261.33(e).

105 40 C.F.R. § 262.34(c).

106 40 C.F.R. § 262.34(d).

107 *See* Permit System Section of this Chapter for a description of these requirements.

108 N.M. Stat. Ann. § 74-4-4(A)(2)(h) (Repl. Pamp. 1993). The regulations do not require use of the manifest system by conditionally exempt small quantity generators, as described earlier in this Chapter.

109 N.M. Stat. Ann. § 74-4-3(J) (Repl. Pamp. 1993).

to its ultimate destination. The hazardous waste generator, the transporter(s),[110] and the treatment, storage, or disposal facility (TSDF) operator must each sign this document and keep a copy. The TSDF operator must return a signed copy of the manifest to the generator in order to notify the generator of the receipt of the hazardous waste.[111] A small quantity generator must notify the Secretary in writing in the event a completed manifest is not received within 60 days of the date the waste was accepted by the initial transporter.[112]

The manifest form requires two certifications. The generator must initially certify that the contents are, in accordance with the regulations, fully and accurately described, properly classified, packed, marked and labeled, and in a condition appropriate for the mode of transportation being used. The second certification requires a statement that the generator has made a good faith effort to minimize waste generation and has selected the best waste management method that is available which he can afford.[113]

3.2.2.5 Recordkeeping

A small quantity generator is required to retain a signed copy of the manifest covering each shipment of hazardous waste for three years or the fully signed-off manifest from the TSDF for three years.[114]

3.2.2.6 Biennial Reports

A generator who ships any hazardous waste off-site to a TSDF within the United States must prepare and submit a single copy of a Biennial Report by March 1 of each even-numbered year. New Mexico requires such information as the identity of the generator, the transporters, and TSDFs used by the generator for hazardous waste shipped off-site during the reporting year, the types of hazardous waste that were shipped off-site, changes in the volume and toxicity of the generator's waste in relation to previous years, and the efforts undertaken to reduce the volume or toxicity of the hazardous waste that was generated.[115] Generators who treat, store or dispose of hazardous waste on-site are also subject to this reporting requirement.[116]

3.2.2.7 Exports and Imports of Hazardous Waste

In order to export hazardous waste out of the United States, the generator must notify in writing, in addition to the Secretary, EPA's Office of International Activities at least

---

110 40 C.F.R. § 263.20.

111 40 C.F.R. §§ 264.71, 265.71.

112 40 C.F.R. § 262.42(b).

113 *See* Uniform Hazardous Waste Manifest, Form 8700-22, 40 C.F.R. Part 262 app.

114 40 C.F.R. § 262.40(a).

115 40 C.F.R. § 262.41.

116 40 C.F.R. § 262.41(b).

60 days before the initial shipment.[117] The receiving foreign country must have expressed its written consent to receive the hazardous waste before shipment. Shipment of the hazardous waste is prohibited until EPA has received and transmitted to the exporter the consent of the receiving foreign country.[118]

Any person who imports hazardous waste from a foreign country into New Mexico, must comply with special manifest requirements, as provided in the regulations.[119]

3.2.3 Larger Quantity Generator

The generator of more than 1,000 kg of hazardous waste per month (large quantity generator) must comply with all the requirements imposed on small quantity generators, with the following exceptions and additions:

(1) As to accumulation requirements, such generator can remain exempt from the permit requirement when it stores any amount of hazardous waste in containers or tanks for a period of 90 days or less at the site of generation, provided it complies with the labeling and operating requirements identified above for small quantity generators.[120] In addition, the large quantity generator may also store hazardous waste on drip pads[121] provided the generator complies with the requirements governing drip pads[122] and maintains specified records.[123] The large quantity generator may not take advantage of the accumulation exemption of the small quantity generator, which allows a small quantity generator to accumulate up to 6,000 kg of hazardous waste over a 180- or 270-day period.

(2) The large quantity generator may make use of the exemption from permitting, which allows accumulation of up to 55 gallons of hazardous waste or one quart of acutely hazardous waste in containers at or near the initial point of generation in accordance with the

---

117 40 C.F.R. § 262.53(a) - (b).

118 40 C.F.R. §§ 262.52 - .53. Special requirements on manifests, exception reports, annual reports, and record keeping are applied to exporters of hazardous waste. 40 C.F.R. §§ 262.54 -.57.

119 40 C.F.R. § 262.60.

120 40 C.F.R. § 262.34(a).

121 A "drip pad" is an engineered structure consisting of a curbed, free-draining base, constructed of non-earthen materials and designed to convey preservative kick-back or drippage from treated wood, precipitation, and surface water run-on to an associated collection system at wood preserving plants. 40 C.F.R. § 260.10.

122 Subpart W of 40 C.F.R. Part 265.

123 40 C.F.R. § 262.34(a)(1) - (2). Due to an ambiguity in the numbering of the subparagraphs in 40 C.F.R. § 262.34, it is unclear whether the regulations governing drip pads apply to small quantity generators. *See* 40 C.F.R. § 262.34 Editorial Note.

conditions identified in accumulation and storage restrictions for small quantity generators.[124]

(3) Under the manifest system, if a signed manifest has not been received within 45 days of the initial transporter's acceptance of the hazardous waste shipment, then the large quantity generator must submit an Exception Report to the Secretary.[125]

(4) If a large quantity generator accumulates hazardous waste in tanks or containers or on drip pads for more than 90 days, such a generator becomes an operator of a storage facility and is subject to the requirements of the general standards for TSDFs.[126]

(5) On the manifest form the large quantity generator must sign the same certification that a small quantity generator signs regarding the contents of the hazardous waste shipment. However, a second certification is required which is more stringent, requiring a statement that such generator has a program in place to reduce the volume and toxicity of waste generated to a degree which has been determined to be economically practicable, and that the generator has selected the method of treatment, storage or disposal currently available to the generator which minimizes the present and future threat to human health and the environment.[127]

3.2.4 Farmers and Waste

There is a special category of waste and a special kind of exemption for farm activities that involve the use of pesticides. The HWA does not apply to any farmer disposing of waste pesticides from the farmer's own use, provided the farmer triple rinses each emptied pesticide container and disposes of the pesticide residues on the farmer's own farm in a manner consistent with the disposal instructions on the pesticide label.[128]

The New Mexico Department of Agriculture is the entity responsible for the enforcement of all regulations adopted pursuant to the HWA regarding generators of hazardous agricultural waste.[129] Hazardous agricultural waste is defined as hazardous waste generated as part of the licensed activity by any person licensed under the Pesticide Control Act[130] or any hazardous waste designated as hazardous agricultural waste by EIB but does not include animal excrement in connection with farm, ranch or feedlot operations.[131] NMED

---

124 40 C.F.R. § 262.34(c)(1) - (2).

125 40 C.F.R. § 262.42(a)(2).

126 40 C.F.R. § 262.34(b).

127 *See* Uniform Hazardous Waste Manifest, Form 8700-22, 40 C.F.R. Part 262 app.

128 N.M. Stat. Ann. § 74-4-3.1 (Repl. Pamp. 1993). The regulations provide for a similar exclusion. *See* 40 C.F.R. § 262.70.

129 N.M. Stat. Ann. § 74-4-4.1 (Repl. Pamp. 1993).

130 N.M. Stat. Ann. §§ 76-4-1 to -39 (Repl. Pamp. 1981 & Supp. 1992).

131 N.M. Stat. Ann. § 74-4-3(G) (Repl. Pamp. 1993).

enforces EIB regulations pertaining to transporters, treaters, storers and disposers of hazardous agricultural waste.

As of November 1, 1993, EIB had not adopted any regulations specifically addressing the handling of hazardous agricultural waste, other than the regulations regarding the disposal of waste pesticides.[132]

3.2.5 On-Site Disposal

Unless a generator is a conditionally exempt small quantity generator who satisfies the requirements of on-site facility disposal for conditionally exempt small quantity generators, a generator of hazardous waste that disposes of hazardous wastes on-site must comply with all standards applicable to TSDFs except the manifest requirements, which are applicable to hazardous waste that is moved from the point of generation to an off-site place of storage, treatment, or disposal.[133]

4.0 TRANSPORTERS

EIB has established standards applicable to a transporter of hazardous waste[134] or of fuel produced from any such waste or of fuel from such waste and any other material (Transporter)[135] by adopting as Part IV of the HWMR-7 the federal regulations set forth in 40 C.F.R. Part 263, with one omission[136] which will be discussed below.

4.1 GENERAL REQUIREMENTS

A Transporter is required to obtain an EPA identification number before shipping hazardous waste.[137]

Transporters are subject to United States Department of Transportation (DOT) regulations regarding the transportation of hazardous materials.[138] The DOT regulations

---

132 40 C.F.R. § 262.70.

133 40 C.F.R. §§ 264.70, 265.70.

134 The HWA defines "transporter" as a person engaged in the movement, not including movement at the site of generation, disposal, treatment or storage, of hazardous waste. N.M. Stat. Ann. § 74-4-3(P) (Repl. Pamp. 1993). This definition does not apply to on-site transportation of hazardous waste by generators or by owners or operators of permitted hazardous waste management facilities. *See* 40 C.F.R. § 263.10.

135 By including fuel produced from any such hazardous waste or fuel produced from such waste in any other material, the HWA incorporates the 1984 Amendments to the RCRA . N.M. Stat. Ann. § 74-4-4(A)(3) (Repl. Pamp. 1993). *See* RCRA § 3003(a), 42 U.S.C. § 6923(a).

136 N.M. Hazardous Waste Management Regulations-7, Part IV.

137 40 C.F.R. § 263.11 Such a number may be obtained by submitting a completed copy of EPA form 8700-12 to NMED, which reviews the form and then submits the form to EPA for review and issuance of the number.

138 40 C.F.R. § 263.10(a) Note.

concern, among other things, labeling, marking, placarding, using proper containers, and reporting discharges.[139] Use of and compliance with the DOT regulations insures consistency of the HWA requirements with the requirements of DOT and avoids duplicate or conflicting requirements.[140]

A Transporter may have to comply with the requirements imposed upon a generator if one or both of the following instances occur: (1) the Transporter ships hazardous waste into the United States from abroad or (2) the Transporter mixes hazardous wastes of different DOT shipping descriptions by placing them into a single container.[141] Transporters may also be subject to extensive regulation as a TSDF unless the Transporter meets certain packing requirements[142] and the hazardous waste is stored for a period of 10 days or less.[143]

4.2 MANIFEST REQUIREMENTS

A Transporter may not accept hazardous waste from a generator unless the waste is accompanied by a manifest signed by the generator.[144] Special requirements apply to hazardous waste that is to be exported.[145] Before transporting a hazardous waste, the Transporter must (1) sign and date the manifest acknowledging acceptance of the hazardous waste from the generator and return a signed copy to the generator before leaving the generator's property[146] and (2) insure that the manifest accompanies the hazardous waste. A Transporter who delivers the hazardous waste to another Transporter or to the designated facility must (1) obtain the date of delivery and the handwritten signature of that Transporter or of the owner or operator of the designated facility on the manifest, (2) retain one copy of the manifest in accordance with recordkeeping requirements discussed below, and (3) give the remaining copies of the manifest to the accepting Transporter or designated facility.[147] An exemption exists for rail shipments, provided certain conditions are fulfilled.[148]

---

139 *See* 49 C.F.R. Parts 171-179.

140 *See* 40 C.F.R. § 263.10(a) Note.

141 40 C.F.R. § 263.10(c).

142 40 C.F.R. § 262.30 requires packing of hazardous waste material in accordance with DOT regulations on packaging under 49 C.F.R. §§ 173, 178-179.

143 40 C.F.R. § 263.12.

144 40 C.F.R. § 263.20(a).

145 *Id.*

146 40 C.F.R. § 263.20(b).

147 40 C.F.R. § 263.20(d).

148 40 C.F.R. § 263.20(f). A second exemption from the manifest requirements involves the bulk shipment of hazardous waste by a vessel on waterways. This exception granted by the federal regulations has not been adopted by EIB, presumably because

The Transporter must deliver the entire quantity of hazardous waste which has been transported from a generator or a previous Transporter to (1) the designated facility listed on the manifest, (2) the alternate designated facility if the hazardous waste cannot be delivered to the designated facility because an emergency prevents delivery, (3) the next designated Transporter, or (4) the place outside the United States designated by the generator.[149] If the hazardous waste cannot be delivered to these designated locations, the Transporter must contact the generator for further directions and must revise the manifest according to the generator's instructions.[150]

4.3 RECORDKEEPING REQUIREMENTS

A Transporter must keep a copy of the manifest signed by the generator, the Transporter, and the next designated Transporter, or the owner or operator of the designated facility, for a period of three years from the date the hazardous waste was accepted by the initial Transporter.[151]

4.4 HAZARDOUS WASTE AND SUBSTANCE INCIDENTS

In the event of a discharge of hazardous waste during transportation, a Transporter must take appropriate, immediate action to protect human health and the environment (*e.g.*, notify local authorities, dike the discharge area).[152] A Transporter must also clean up any hazardous waste discharge that occurs during transportation or take such action as may be required or approved by federal, state or local officials so that the hazardous waste discharge no longer presents a hazard to human health or the environment.[153] The HWA additionally requires corrective action for "hazardous substance incidents," defined as any emergency incident involving a chemical or chemicals, including but not limited to transportation wrecks, accidental spills or leaks, fires or explosions, which creates the reasonable probability of injury to human health or property.[154] NMED is authorized to take any action necessary or appropriate to protect persons from injury or other harm which might arise from hazardous substance incidents, including but not limited to providing for cleanup and disposal and coordinating the activities of other public officials. NMED may also assess charges against persons responsible for hazardous substance incidents for the cost NMED incurs in cleanup

---

New Mexico has no waterways available for such a method of transportation. *See* Hazardous Waste Management Regulations-7 § 402.

149 40 C.F.R. § 263.21(a).

150 40 C.F.R. § 263.21(b).

151 40 C.F.R. § 263.22. For special recordkeeping requirements for transporters of hazardous waste by rail within the United States, *see* 40 C.F.R. § 263.22(c).

152 40 C.F.R. § 263.30.

153 40 C.F.R. § 263.31.

154 N.M. Stat. Ann. § 74-4-3(H) (Repl. Pamp. 1993).

of hazardous substance incidents and disposal of hazardous substances and for damage to state property.[155]

5.0 TSDF REGULATION

EIB has established performance standards and permitting requirements applicable to owners and operators of facilities for the treatment, storage or disposal of hazardous waste[156] by adopting, with a few minor exceptions,[157] the entire body of federal regulations regarding operating standards and permit requirements for TSDFs.[158] This Section and the following Sections, which address general standards for TSDFs, standards for specific types of TSDFs, and standards for specific wastes, provide a general overview of the regulatory program for TSDFs.

5.1 TSDF IDENTIFICATION

A "facility" means all contiguous land and structures, other appurtenances, and improvements on the land used for treating, storing, or disposing of hazardous waste.[159] A facility may consist of several treatment, storage or disposal operational units (*e.g.*, one or more landfills, service impoundments, or combinations of them).[160] "Treatment" means any method, technique or process, including neutralization, designed to change the physical, chemical or biological character or composition of any hazardous waste so as to neutralize such waste, or so as to recover energy or material resources from the waste, or so as to render such waste nonhazardous or less hazardous, safer to transport, store, or dispose of, or amenable for recovery, amenable for storage or reduced in volume.[161] The term includes any activity or processing designed to change a physical form or chemical composition of hazardous waste so as to render it nonhazardous.[162] "Storage" means the containment of hazardous waste, either on a temporary basis or for a period of years, in such a manner as not to constitute disposal of such hazardous waste.[163] "Disposal" means the discharge, deposit,

---

155 N.M. Stat. Ann. § 74-4-7(C)(Repl. Pamp. 1993). Amounts received in payment of such assessments are to be deposited in the Hazardous Waste Emergency Fund. A person who is assessed such charges may appeal the assessment to the District Court within 30 days of notice of the assessment. *Id.*

156 N.M. Stat. Ann. § 74-4-4(A)(5) (Repl. Pamp. 1993). This portion of the HWA borrows heavily from the RCRA § 3004, 42 U.S.C. § 6924.

157 *See* Chart I in Relationship to Federal RCRA Section of this Chapter.

158 This includes 40 C.F.R. §§ 264-266, 268, 270.

159 40 C.F.R. § 260.10.

160 *Id.*

161 *Id.*

162 N.M. Stat. Ann. § 74-4-3(Q) (Repl. Pamp. 1993).

163 N.M. Stat. Ann. § 74-4-3(N) (Repl. Pamp. 1993).

injection, dumping, spilling, leaking, or placing of any solid waste or hazardous waste into or on any land or water so that the solid waste or hazardous waste or a constituent thereof may enter the environment or be emitted into the air or discharged into any waters, including ground waters.[164] A "disposal facility" is a facility or part of a facility at which hazardous waste is intentionally placed into or on any land or water, and at which waste will remain after closure.[165] The broader scope of the combination of the definitions of "facility" and "disposal" subjects the unintentional disposal of hazardous waste into the environment to hazardous waste regulation (including notification and cleanup requirements), while the narrower definition of "disposal facility" identifies those facilities required to follow the operating standards and permit requirements provided in the regulations.

5.2 THE PERMIT SYSTEM

The centerpiece of the regulatory program for hazardous waste in New Mexico is the permit requirement for TSDFs. The three avenues of compliance available to meet this requirement are (1) interim status, (2) permitted status, and (3) permit by rule.

5.2.1 Interim Status

Any person owning or operating a hazardous waste facility who has met the requirements for interim status[166] under the RCRA is deemed to have interim status under the HWA.[167] Owners or operators of TSDFs who can meet the following conditions are granted interim status: (1) the facility was in existence on November 19, 1980, or is in existence on the effective date of statutory or regulatory changes under the RCRA that render the facility subject to the requirement to have a permit, (2) the owner or operator has complied with notification requirements,[168] and (3) the operator has made an application for a permit.[169] Interim status facilities must comply with interim status standards[170] and with the representations made in the permit application.[171]

Interim status is terminated on the following bases: (1) final administrative disposition of a permit application,[172] (2) failure to submit in a timely fashion a Part B application,[173]

---

164 N.M. Stat. Ann. § 74-4-3(C) (Repl. Pamp. 1993).

165 40 C.F.R. § 260.10.

166 RCRA § 3005; 42 U.S.C. § 6925.

167 N.M. Stat. Ann. § 74-4-9 (Repl. Pamp. 1993).

168 RCRA § 3010(a); 42 U.S.C. § 6930(a).

169 RCRA § 3005(e), 42 U.S.C. § 6925(e). *See* Permitted Facilities Section of this Chapter.

170 40 C.F.R. § 270.71(b).

171 40 C.F.R. 270.71(a).

172 40 C.F.R. § 270.73(a).

173 40 C.F.R. § 270.73(b). *See* Permitted Facilities Section of this Chapter.

(3) for owners or operators of land disposal facilities granted interim status prior to November 8, 1984, termination on November 8, 1985, unless specified conditions are fulfilled,[174] (4) for owners or operators of each land disposal facility which is in existence on the effective date of statutory or regulatory amendments under the HWA that renders the facility subject to the requirement to have a permit and which is granted interim status, termination 12 months after the date on which the facility first becomes subject to such permit requirement, unless specified conditions are fulfilled,[175] (5) for owners or operators of any land disposal unit that is granted authority to operate when certain specified changes occur at the facility, termination on the date 12 months after the effective date on which permit requirements apply to such changes, unless the owner or operator certifies that such unit is in compliance with all applicable ground water monitoring and financial responsibility requirements,[176] (6) for owners or operators of each incinerator facility, termination on November 8, 1989,[177] unless the owner or operator of such facility submitted a Part B application for a RCRA permit for an incinerator facility by November 8, 1986, and (7) for owners or operators of any facility other than a land disposal or incinerator facility, termination on November 8, 1992, unless the owner or operator of the facility has submitted a Part B application for a RCRA permit for the facility by November 8, 1988.[178]

An owner or operator of an interim status facility may make specified changes at the facility, including among others, changes to types of hazardous waste handled, processes employed or design capacities observed and addition of newly regulated units, provided a revised Part A permit application reflecting such changes is submitted prior to such changes, and provided such changes do not amount to a reconstruction of the hazardous waste management facility,[179] subject to certain exceptions.[180]

5.2.2 Permitted Facilities

There is a detailed procedure for applying for and obtaining an HWA permit. An HWA permit application consists of two parts, Part A and Part B.[181] Existing hazardous

---

174 These conditions include having submitted a Part B application for a permit and having certified that the facility is in compliance with all applicable ground water monitoring and financial responsibility requirements. 40 C.F.R. § 270.73(c).

175 40 C.F.R. § 270.73(d).

176 40 C.F.R. § 270.73(e).

177 40 C.F.R. § 270.73(f).

178 40 C.F.R. § 270.73(g).

179 Reconstruction occurs when the capital investment in the changes to the facility exceeds 50% of the capital cost of a comparable entirely new hazardous waste management facility. 40 C.F.R. § 270.72(b).

180 40 C.F.R. § 270.72.

181 40 C.F.R. § 270.1(b).

waste facilities must file Part A applications in order to receive interim status. The Part A application requires information regarding (1) the activities conducted by the applicant which required it to obtain an HWA permit, (2) name, mailing address and location of the facility, (3) standard industrial classification (SIC) codes reflecting the principal products or services provided by the facility, (4) the operator's name, address, and telephone number, (5) the name, address, and telephone number of the owner of the facility, (6) whether the facility is located on Indian lands, (7) whether the facility is new or existing and whether the application is a first or revised application, (8) scale drawings and photographs of the facility, (9) a description of the processes to be used for treating, storing and disposing of hazardous waste, (10) specification of the hazardous waste, estimate of quantity to be handled, and a general description of the processes to be used, (11) a list of all permits or construction approvals received or applied for, (12) a map locating the facility within a one-mile area, and (13) a brief description of the nature of the business.[182]

The Part B application requires extensive information that must be submitted in narrative form. Certain technical data in a Part B application, such as design drawings and specifications and engineering studies, are required to be certified by a registered professional engineer.[183] Information required under a Part B application includes chemical and physical analyses of the hazardous waste to be handled at the facility, a description of security procedures and equipment, a copy of the general inspection schedule for the facility, a copy of the emergency contingency plan, a description of procedures for the handling of hazardous waste, a description of traffic patterns, volumes, and access to the facility, seismic and flood plain information, closure and post-closure plans, including ground water monitoring, and indicia of financial responsibility.[184] In addition, there are specific information requirements for specified types of TSDFs.[185]

A treatment, storage or disposal facility that was not in existence on November 19, 1980,[186] must submit a Part A and Part B application at least 180 days before physical construction of the facility is to begin.[187] Thus, no "new" facility can operate as a TSDF without an approved HWA permit.[188] Hazardous waste permits issued after April 8, 1987,

---

182 40 C.F.R. § 270.13.

183 40 C.F.R. § 270.14.

184 *Id.*

185 40 C.F.R. §§ 270.15 - .26.

186 RCRA § 3005; 42 U.S.C. § 6925.

187 40 C.F.R. § 270.1(b).

188 40 C.F.R. § 270.10(f). An exception exists for a facility constructed for the incineration of PCBs. *See* 40 C.F.R. § 270.10(f)(3).

shall require corrective action for all releases of hazardous waste or constituents from any solid waste management unit at a TSDF seeking a permit.[189]

5.2.2.1 General Application Requirements for Permits

When a facility or activity is owned by one person but is operated by another person, it is the operator's duty to obtain a permit, but the owner must also sign the permit application.[190] Applicants must keep records of all data used to complete permit applications and any supplemental information for a period of at least three years from the date that the application is signed.[191] The regulations specify who may sign on behalf of a corporation, partnership, municipality or other federal agency.[192] The individual signing the application must certify that the application and all attachments were prepared under the direction or supervision of the signer in accordance with a system properly designed to assure that qualified personnel properly gathered and evaluated the information submitted.[193]

Any information submitted to NMED may be claimed as confidential by the submitter, provided that such claim is asserted at the time of submission in the manner prescribed on the application form.[194] If no claim is made at the time of submission, NMED may make the information available to the public without further notice.[195] Claims of confidentiality for the name and address of any permit applicant or permittee will be denied.[196]

5.2.2.2 Permitting Procedures

In addition to adopting 40 C.F.R. § 270 (EPA's federal permit program process) as part of Part IX of the HWMR-7, EIB also adopted Section 902, which provides the permitting procedures in New Mexico once an application, Part A and Part B, has been submitted.

Once an application is complete, the Secretary must decide whether to prepare and issue a Draft Permit or a Notice of Intent to Deny.[197] A Draft Permit must contain all conditions, compliance schedules, monitoring requirements and technical standards for treatment, storage and/or disposal.[198] A Notice of Intent to Deny must contain the Secretary's

---

189 N.M. Stat. Ann. § 74-4-4.2(B) (Repl. Pamp. 1993).

190 40 C.F.R. § 270.10(b).

191 40 C.F.R. § 270.10(i).

192 40 C.F.R. § 270.11.

193 40 C.F.R. § 270.11(d).

194 40 C.F.R. § 270.12(a).

195 *Id.*

196 40 C.F.R. § 270.12(b).

197 N.M. Hazardous Waste Management Regulations-7 § 902.A(1).

198 N.M. Hazardous Waste Management Regulations-7 § 902.A(1)(a).

reasons for the intended denial.[199] Any Draft Permit or Notice of Intent to Deny is to be accompanied by a fact sheet based on the administrative file, and copies of this fact sheet are to be sent to the applicant and any applicable state or federal agency and to any other person upon request.[200] The Secretary must give public notice that a Draft Permit or Notice of Intent to Deny has been prepared and must allow 45 days for public review and comment, including requests for public hearing.[201] If the Secretary issues a Draft Permit and a timely written notice of opposition to the Draft Permit and a request for public hearing are received, NMED, acting in conjunction with the applicant, will respond to the request in an attempt to resolve the issues giving rise to the opposition. If such issues are resolved to the satisfaction of the opponent, the opponent may withdraw the request for a public hearing.[202] No ruling shall be made on permit issuance or denial without an opportunity for a public hearing, at which all interested persons are to be given a reasonable chance to submit significant data, views or arguments orally or in writing and to examine witnesses.[203] A public hearing is mandated if (1) the Secretary issues a Notice of Intent to Deny and a timely request for public hearing is received from the applicant, (2) the Secretary issues a Draft Permit and a timely request for public hearing is received from any person opposed to the granting of the permit, and such person does not subsequently withdraw the request, or (3) the Secretary determines no later than five days following the end of the 45-day comment period that a public hearing should be held notwithstanding the absence of a timely request for a public hearing.[204]

When ruling on permit issuance, the Secretary may disapprove in whole or in part or make reasonable conditions to any permit, if it appears that the permit applied for will not meet the requirements of the regulations.[205] The Secretary is required, at the time any final permit decision is issued, to issue a response to comments, which must specify the provisions, if any, of the Draft Permit that have been changed in the final permit decision and the reasons for the change and must briefly describe and respond to all significant comments on the Draft Permit or the permit application raised during the public comment period or during any hearing.[206] The Secretary's response to the comments is to be available to the

---

199 N.M. Hazardous Waste Management Regulations-7 § 902.A(1)(b).

200 N.M. Hazardous Waste Management Regulations-7 § 902.A(2).

201 N.M. Hazardous Waste Management Regulations-7 § 902.A(3).

202 N.M. Hazardous Waste Management Regulations-7 § 902.A(4).

203 N.M. Hazardous Waste Management Regulations-7 § 902.A(5).

204 N.M. Hazardous Waste Management Regulations-7 § 902.A(5)(a) - (c).

205 N.M. Hazardous Waste Management Regulations-7 § 902.A(8).

206 N.M. Hazardous Waste Management Regulations-7 § 902.A.9(a) - (b).

public.[207] A final permit decision becomes effective 30 days after notice of the decision has been served on the applicant, or at such later time as the Secretary may specify.[208] Approval of a permit does not relieve any person from the responsibility of complying with applicable state or federal laws and regulations.[209]

The HWA provides that the Secretary may deny any permit application or modify, suspend or revoke any permit issued pursuant to the HWA if the applicant or permittee has: (1) knowingly and willfully misrepresented a material fact in the application for a permit; (2) refused to disclose required information; (3) been convicted in any court, within ten (10) years immediately preceding the date of submission of the permit application, of (a) a felony or other crime involving moral turpitude or (b) a crime defined by state or federal statutes as involving or being in restraint of trade, price-fixing, bribery or fraud; (4) exhibited a history of willful disregard for environmental laws of any state or the United States; (5) had any permit revoked or permanently suspended for cause under the environmental laws of any state or the United States; or (6) violated any provision of the HWA, any regulation adopted and promulgated pursuant to the HWA or any condition of a permit issued under the HWA.[210] If the Secretary makes any finding of (1) - (6) above, the Secretary may consider aggravating and mitigating factors.[211] If an applicant or permittee whose permit is being considered for denial or revocation has submitted an action plan that has been approved in writing by the Secretary, and plan approval includes a period of operation under a conditional permit that will allow the applicant or permittee a reasonable opportunity to demonstrate its rehabilitation, the Secretary may issue a conditional permit for a reasonable period of time in accordance with specified considerations.[212] Two exceptions to the foregoing denial or revocation procedure are that (1) a research, development and demonstration permit may be terminated upon the determination by the Secretary that termination is necessary to protect human health or the environment and (2) a permit may be modified at the request of the permittee for just cause as demonstrated by the permittee.[213]

5.2.2.3 Permit Termination, Modification, and Revocation and Reissuance

The Secretary may terminate any permit issued (1) for noncompliance with any permit condition, (2) for failure in the application or during the permit issuance process to totally

---

207 N.M. Hazardous Waste Management Regulations-7 § 902.A(9)(c).

208 N.M. Hazardous Waste Management Regulations-7 § 902.A(10). This provision does not extend the time for appeal of a permanent decision as provided by the HWA. *Id.*

209 N.M. Hazardous Waste Management Regulations-7 § 902.A(11).

210 N.M. Stat. Ann. § 74-4-4.2(D) (Repl. Pamp. 1993).

211 N.M. Stat. Ann. § 74-4-4.2(E) (Repl. Pamp. 1993).

212 N.M. Stat. Ann. § 74-4-4.2(F) (Repl. Pamp. 1993).

213 N.M. Stat. Ann. § 74-4-4.2(G) (Repl. Pamp. 1993).

disclose all relevant facts, or misrepresentation of any relevant facts at any time, or (3) upon the determination that termination is necessary to protect human health and the environment.[214] The regulations provide for permit modifications at the request of a permittee, grouping the modifications into certain specified classes (i.e., Class 1, Class 2 and Class 3) and providing for the procedures and notifications required for each of the requested class modifications.[215]

The Secretary may modify or, when the permittee requests or agrees, revoke and reissue a permit when (1) there have been material and substantial alterations to the facility, (2) new information becomes available to the Secretary that was not previously available, (3) new statutory or regulatory requirements have become applicable to the facility, (4) events occur over which the permittee has little or no control which create a need for modification of a compliance schedule, or (5) when the required review of a permit for a land disposal facility is conducted,[216] the Secretary determines that modification is required to assure compliance with applicable regulations.[217] The Secretary may modify or revoke and reissue a permit in the event of a proposed transfer of the permit or for the same reasons that the Secretary may terminate a permit.[218] The Secretary may modify, suspend, revoke or terminate a permit upon initiative or if, after NMED's investigation of the facts and circumstances, pursuant to the request of any interested person, such action is deemed warranted.[219] All requests for permit modification, suspension, revocation or termination must be in writing and contain facts or reasons supporting the request.[220] If the Secretary decides that the request is not justified, the permittee will be notified in writing explaining the reason for denial. Denials of requests for modification, revocation and reissuance, or termination are not subject to public notice, comment, or hearings.[221] If the Secretary tentatively decides to modify or revoke and reissue a permit for the reasons stated above, a Draft Permit must be prepared incorporating the proposed changes.[222] The Secretary may request additional information and, in the case of a modified permit, may require the submission of an updated application. In the case of a revoked and reissued permit, the Secretary must require the submission of

---

214 N.M. Hazardous Waste Management Regulations-7 § 902.B. 40 C.F.R. § 270.43.

215 40 C.F.R. § 270.42.

216 40 C.F.R. § 270.50 requires the Secretary to review a permit for a land disposal facility five years after the date of permit issuance or reissuance.

217 40 C.F.R. § 270.41(a)(1) - (5).

218 40 C.F.R. § 270.41(b)(1) - (2).

219 N.M. Hazardous Waste Management Regulations-7 § 902.B(2).

220 N.M. Hazardous Waste Management Regulations-7 § 902.B(3).

221 N.M. Hazardous Waste Management Regulations-7 § 902.B(4).

222 N.M. Hazardous Waste Management Regulations-7 § 902.B(5).

a new application.[223] In a permit modification, only those conditions to be modified are considered when a new Draft Permit is prepared, and all other aspects of the existing permit remain in effect for the duration of the unmodified permit.[224] However, when a permit is revoked and reissued, the entire permit is reopened just as if the permit had expired and were being reissued.[225] Finally, when the Secretary tentatively decides to terminate a permit for the reasons stated above, a notice of intent to terminate must be issued.[226] A notice of intent to terminate is a type of Draft Permit which follows the same procedures applicable to any Draft Permit.[227]

5.2.2.4 Public Notices

Public notice of the issuance of a Draft Permit or a Notice of Intent to Deny, and of any scheduled public hearing, is required by publication in a newspaper of general circulation in the area affected, by broadcasts over local radio stations, and by mailing copies of the notice to the permit applicant, those individuals on NMED's mailing list of persons interested in hazardous waste permit actions, and any units of local, state and federal government as may be applicable.[228] Certain specified minimum information must be included in the notice.[229]

A fact sheet must be prepared for every Draft Permit for a hazardous waste management facility or activity.[230] Specific types of information are required upon the fact sheet, including the principal facts and the significant factual, legal, methodological and policy questions considered in preparing the Draft Permit.[231] The fact sheet is available at the time the public notice is published.[232]

5.2.2.5 Hearings

Public notice of any public hearing must be given at least 30 days prior to the scheduled date of the hearing. A hearing officer may be designated by the Secretary to take evidence at the hearing. At the hearing, which is to be recorded by a certified court reporter, the rules of civil procedure and the technical rules of evidence are not applied, but the hearing is to be conducted so that all relevant views, arguments, and testimony are amply and

---

223 *Id.*

224 N.M. Hazardous Waste Management Regulations-7 § 902.B(6).

225 *Id.*

226 N.M. Hazardous Waste Management Regulations-7 § 902.B(7).

227 *Id.*

228 N.M. Hazardous Waste Management Regulations-7 § 902.C(1).

229 N.M. Hazardous Waste Management Regulations-7 § 902.C(2).

230 N.M. Hazardous Waste Management Regulations-7 § 902.D(1).

231 N.M. Hazardous Waste Management Regulations-7 § 902.D(2).

232 N.M. Hazardous Waste Management Regulations-7 § 902.D(3).

fairly received without undue repetition.[233] The burden of proof at hearings on permit issuance or modification is on the applicant or permittee; at hearings on permit suspension or revocation, the burden of proof is on NMED.[234]

5.2.2.6 Appeal

Any person adversely affected by a decision of the Secretary concerning the issuance, modification, suspension or revocation of a permit may appeal the decision by filing a notice of appeal with the New Mexico Court of Appeals within 30 days after the date the decision is made.[235] The record on appeal includes the transcript of the hearing, all related correspondence, any response to comments, and all other information relied upon by the Secretary in deciding upon the permanent action.[236] The filing of an appeal does not act as a stay of any action required by the Secretary's decision.[237]

5.2.2.7 Reapplication

Any TSDF with an effective permit shall submit a new application at least 180 days before the expiration date of the effective permit, unless permission for a later date has been granted by the Secretary. A permit is issued for a fixed period of time not to exceed 10 years.[238]

5.2.2.8 Hazardous Waste Fees

The HWA mandates that EIB provide a schedule of fees for businesses generating hazardous waste or seeking a permit for the management of hazardous waste, to be deposited to the credit of the Hazardous Waste Fund.[239] This mandate includes, but is not limited to: (1) a hazardous waste business fee applicable to any business engaged in a regulated hazardous waste activity, which shall be an annual flat fee based on the type of activity; (2) a hazardous waste generation fee applicable to any business generating hazardous waste, which shall be based on the quantity of hazardous waste generated annually;[240] and (3) a hazardous waste permit application fee, not exceeding the estimated cost of investigating the application and issuing the permit, to be paid at the time of the Secretary notifies the appli-

---

233 N.M. Hazardous Waste Management Regulations-7 § 902.E(1), (3) - (5).

234 N.M. Hazardous Waste Management Regulations-7 § 902.E(6).

235 N.M. Stat. Ann. § 74-4-4.2(G) (Repl. Pamp. 1993).

236 N.M. Hazardous Waste Management Regulations-7 § 902.G(2).

237 N.M. Hazardous Waste Management Regulations-7 § 902.G(1).

238 40 C.F.R. § 270.50(a).

239 N.M. Stat. Ann. § 74-4-4.2(J) (Repl. Pamp. 1993).

240 When certain specified materials are determined by EIB to be subject to regulation under Subtitle C of the RCRA , EIB may set a generation fee under this paragraph for that waste based on its volume, toxicity, mobility and economic impact on the regulated entity. N.M. Stat. Ann. § 74-4-4.2(J)(2) (Repl. Pamp. 1993).

cant by certified mail that the application has been deemed administratively complete and a technical review is scheduled.[241]

EIB is scheduled to consider, in November 1993, regulations proposed by NMED that would establish business fees referred to in (1) and hazardous waste generation fees referred to in (2) above. The proposed hazardous waste business fees would be based upon and assessed against every generator and owner or operator of a treatment storage or disposal facility engaged in a regulated hazardous waste activity.[242] The fees would vary and be based on the number of sites and the number of units involved at each site. The proposed generation fees will be based upon the quantity of waste generated, with large quantity generators paying one cent per pound and small quantity generators paying between $35 and $250 a year, depending upon the amount of waste generated.[243]

EIB has promulgated Hazardous Waste Fee Regulations (HWFR-1) to establish fee schedules for permits, permit renewals, modifications, revisions, and special expanded public participation permits. The fee schedules and their accompanying tables establish permit fees for the following: (1) "basic permit," which covers the numerous subjects common to all permits,[244] (2) storage permit,[245] (3) treatment permit,[246] (4) disposal permit,[247] (5) post-closure care permit for land disposal units,[248] (6) permit renewal,[249] (7) permit modification,[250] (8) expanded public participation permit,[251] and (9) permit application revision.[252] A final permit consists of a basic permit plus a permit for each operating

241 N.M. Stat. Ann. § 74-4-4.2(J) (Repl. Pamp. 1993).

242 Proposed Annual Hazardous Waste Fee Regulations, EIB/AHWFR-1 Part IV.

243 Proposed Annual Hazardous Waste Fee Regulations, EIB/AHWFR-1 Part II.

244 N.M. Hazardous Waste Fee Regulations-1, EIB/HWFR-1 § 200 (Filed 10/28/88).

245 N.M. Hazardous Waste Fee Regulations-1 § 201.

246 N.M. Hazardous Waste Fee Regulations-1 § 202.

247 N.M. Hazardous Waste Fee Regulations-1 § 203.

248 N.M. Hazardous Waste Fee Regulations-1 § 204.

249 N.M. Hazardous Waste Fee Regulations-1 § 205.

250 N.M. Hazardous Waste Fee Regulations-1 § 206.

251 N.M. Hazardous Waste Fee Regulations-1 § 207. An expanded public participation permit is a facility permit that has a substantial impact or generates considerable public interest and therefore is subject to extra efforts to solicit public participation in the permit process, thereby requiring significant NMED staff time. *Id.*

252 N.M. Hazardous Waste Fee Regulations-1 § 208. Permit application revision involves revisions to an application after it has been deemed administratively complete but before a Draft Permit has been advertised for public review. Revisions deemed minor by NMED may be made without charge; such revisions are ones which do not require detailed analysis. *Id.*

unit[253] of the facility for which a permit application is made.[254] The total fee will be the sum of the fees for the basic permit plus the fees for each operating unit plus, if appropriate, a fee for public participation.[255] The fees are due and payable at the time an application for a permit is made and are not refundable.[256]

5.2.2.9 Effect of an HWA Permit

Compliance with an HWA permit during its term constitutes compliance for purposes of enforcement with the HWA, except for those requirements not included in the permit which become effective by statute, which are promulgated by regulations[257] that restrict the placement of hazardous wastes in or on the land, or which are promulgated under Part 264 of the regulations[258] regarding leak detection systems for new and replacement surface impoundment, waste pile, and landfill units, and lateral expansions of surface impoundment, waste pile, and landfill units.[259] However, the issuance of a permit does not authorize any injury to persons or property, invasion of other private rights, or infringement of state or local law or regulations.[260]

5.2.3 Permit by Rule

Certain types of TSDFs, subject to regulation under other federal or state statutes, are "deemed" to have an HWA permit if they meet certain specified conditions. These facilities include ocean disposal barges or vessels having permits authorized by the Marine Protection, Research, and Sanctuaries Act, as amended, owners or operators of underground injection wells with underground injection control (UIC) permits issued under the Safe

---

253 A "unit" means "hazardous waste management unit" which is defined as a contiguous area of land on or in which hazardous waste is placed, or the largest area in which there is significant likelihood of mixing hazardous waste constituents in the same area. Examples of hazardous waste management units include a surface impoundment, a waste pile, a land treatment area, a landfill cell, an incinerator, a tank and its associated piping and underlying containment system and a container storage area. A container alone does not constitute a unit; the unit includes containers and the land or pad upon which they are placed. 40 C.F.R. § 260.10; N.M. Hazardous Waste Fee Regulations-1 § 102.B.

254 N.M. Hazardous Waste Fee Regulations-1 § 101.B.

255 *Id.*

256 N.M. Hazardous Waste Fee Regulations-1 § 101.C.

257 *See* 40 C.F.R. Part 268.

258 40 C.F.R. Part 264 establishes standards for hazardous waste TSDFs.

259 40 C.F.R. § 270.4(a).

260 40 C.F.R. § 270.4(c).

Drinking Water Act, and publicly owned treatment works having a National Pollutant Discharge Elimination System (NPDES) permit under the Clean Water Act.[261]

5.2.4 Other Special Permits

A number of special permits may be issued by the Secretary under specified circumstances: (1) an emergency permit on a temporary basis to a non-permitted facility when the Secretary finds that an imminent and substantial endangerment to human health or the environment justifies issuance of a permit,[262] (2) a short-term permit for a hazardous waste incinerator in order to allow the incinerator to conduct trial burns so that the actual operating conditions of the hazardous waste incinerator may be reflected in the final permit that is issued,[263] (3) a permit for land treatment demonstrations using field tests or laboratory analysis in order to allow the applicant to establish that the proposed land treatment method is in fact effective,[264] and (4) owners and operators of new boilers and industrial furnaces that burn hazardous waste in order to establish appropriate operating conditions.[265]

Special interim permits for UIC wells may be issued under specified conditions.[266] The Secretary may also issue a research, development and demonstration permit for any hazardous waste treatment facility which proposes to utilize an innovative and experimental hazardous waste treatment technology or process for which permit standards have not been promulgated.[267]

5.2.5 Exemptions from Permit Requirements

Exemptions or partial exemptions exist for certain persons and facilities that might otherwise be construed as required to have an HWA permit.[268] These include (1) generators who accumulate hazardous waste on-site for less than specified time periods,[269] (2) farmers who dispose of hazardous waste pesticides from their own use in accordance with the manner prescribed by the regulations,[270] (3) persons who own or operate a facility solely for the treatment, storage or disposal of hazardous waste, if the only hazardous waste handled by the facility is excluded from regulation pursuant to the special exemption for conditionally

---

261 40 C.F.R. § 270.60.

262 40 C.F.R. § 270.61(a).

263 40 C.F.R. § 270.62(a).

264 40 C.F.R. § 270.63.

265 40 C.F.R. § 270.66.

266 40 C.F.R. § 270.64.

267 40 C.F.R. § 270.65.

268 40 C.F.R. § 270.1(c)(2).

269 *See* 40 C.F.R. § 262.34.

270 40 C.F.R. § 262.70.

exempt small quantity generators or is otherwise excluded,[271] (4) owners or operators of totally enclosed treatment facilities,[272] (5) owners and operators of elementary neutralization units,[273] (6) owners and operators of wastewater treatment units,[274] (7) Transporters storing manifested shipments of hazardous waste in containers in accordance with specified conditions[275] at a transfer facility for a period of 10 days or less, and (8) persons adding absorbent material to waste in a container,[276] provided that these actions occur at the time waste is first placed in a container and certain specified conditions are met.[277] Also exempt are persons engaged in treatment or containment activities during immediate response to a discharge or imminent and substantial threat of a discharge of hazardous waste.[278]

In addition to the exemptions described above, certain recyclable materials are exempted from TSDF permitting requirements. The ordinary presumption is that the recyclable materials, which are defined by the regulations as "hazardous wastes that are

---

271 40 C.F.R. § 261.5. *See* Conditionally Exempt Small Quantity Generator Section of this Chapter. 40 C.F.R. § 261.4 *See* Exclusions from Regulation as a Hazardous Waste, Section 2.4.1 of this Chapter.

272 "Totally enclosed treatment facility" is defined as a facility for the treatment of hazardous waste which is directly connected to an industrial production process and which is constructed and operated in a manner which prevents the release of any hazardous waste or any constituent thereof into the environment during treatment. An example is a pipe in which waste acid is neutralized. 40 C.F.R. § 260.10.

273 "Elementary neutralization unit" is defined as a device which (1) is used for neutralizing wastes that are hazardous only because they exhibit the corrosivity characteristic... or are listed [hazardous waste] only for this reason; and, (2) meets the definition of tank, tank system, container, transport vehicle or vessel. 40 C.F.R. § 260.10.

274 "Wastewater treatment unit" is defined as a device which (1) is part of a wastewater treatment facility which is subject to regulation under either § 402 or § 307(b) of the Clean Water Act, (2) receives and treats or stores an influent wastewater which is a hazardous waste as defined in § 261.3 [the section of Regulations which defines hazardous waste], or generates and accumulates a wastewater treatment sludge which is a hazardous waste as defined in § 261.3, or treats or stores a wastewater treatment sludge which is a hazardous waste as defined in § 261.3, and (3) meets the definition of tank or tank system as specified in the Regulations. 40 C.F.R. § 260.10.

275 40 C.F.R. § 262.30.

276 40 C.F.R. § 260.10 defines "container" as "any portable device in which a material is stored, transported, treated, disposed of, or otherwise handled."

277 40 C.F.R. §§ 264.17(b), 264.171 - .172 establish these conditions.

278 40 C.F.R. §§ 264.1(e)(8)(i), 265.1(c)(11)(i). Any person who continues or initiates hazardous waste treatment or containment activities after the immediate response is over is subject to full HWA regulation.

recycled,"[279] are fully subject to regulation as hazardous wastes. However, subject to specified conditions,[280] some recyclable materials are exempt from the permit requirements, including (1) certain types of recyclable materials used in a manner constituting disposal,[281] (2) used oil burned for energy recovery,[282] (3) recyclable materials utilized for precious metal recovery,[283] (4) spent lead-acid batteries being reclaimed,[284] (5) hazardous waste burned in boilers and industrial furnaces[285] (6) industrial ethyl alcohol that is reclaimed,[286] (7) used batteries (or used battery cells) returned to a battery manufacturer for regeneration,[287] (8) used oil that exhibits one or more of the characteristics of hazardous waste but is recycled in some other manner than being burned for energy recovery,[288] (9) scrap metal,[289] (10) fuels produced from the refining of oil-bearing hazardous wastes along with normal process streams at a petroleum refining facility,[290] (11) oil reclaimed from hazardous waste resulting from normal petroleum refining, production, and transportation practices,[291] (12) hazardous waste fuel and reclaimed oil produced from oil-bearing hazardous waste from petroleum refining, production, or transportation practices,[292] and (13) petroleum coke produced from petroleum refinery hazardous waste-containing oil at the same facility at which such wastes were generated.[293]

---

279 40 C.F.R. § 261.6(a)(1).

280 The specified conditions are found in two places in the regulations. *See* 40 C.F.R. Part 266, Subparts C, E-G, 40 C.F.R. § 261.6(a)(2)(i) - (v), (3)(i) - (ix). The materials described in 40 C.F.R. § 261.6(a)(2)(i) - (v) may have a permit requirement depending upon when and by whom they are handled. *See* Recyclable Materials Section of this Chapter.

281 40 C.F.R. Part 266, Subpart C; 40 C.F.R. § 261.6(a)(2)(i).

282 40 C.F.R. Part 266, Subpart E; 40 C.F.R. § 261.6(a)(2)(iii).

283 40 C.F.R. Part 266, Subpart F; 40 C.F.R. § 261.6(a)(2)(iv).

284 40 C.F.R. Part 266, Subpart G; 40 C.F.R. § 261.6(a)(2)(v).

285 40 C.F.R. Part 266, Subpart H.

286 40 C.F.R. § 261.6(a)(3)(i).

287 40 C.F.R. § 261.6(a)(3)(ii).

288 40 C.F.R. § 261.6(a)(3)(iii).

289 40 C.F.R. § 261.6(a)(3)(iv).

290 40 C.F.R. § 261.6(a)(3)(v).

291 40 C.F.R. § 261.6(a)(3)(vi).

292 40 C.F.R. § 261.6(a)(3)(vii).

293 40 C.F.R. § 261.6(a)(3)(viii).

6.0 TSDF GENERAL STANDARDS

Separate parts of the regulations govern permitted TSDFs and interim status TSDFs. 40 C.F.R. Part 264 sets forth the permit program requirements which serve as the basis for issuing the HWA permits to TSDFs, while Part 265 sets forth the requirements applicable to interim status TSDFs. This Section will address the general requirements for TSDFs, and the following Section will discuss the standards for specific types of TSDFs.

6.1 IDENTIFICATION NUMBER AND NOTICES

All TSDFs are required to have an EPA identification number, which is obtained from EPA although the application form is submitted to NMED.[294] Generators of hazardous waste are required to use this number in filling out the manifest form to identify the TSDF that is to receive the hazardous waste.[295]

Certain notices must be given under specified circumstances. Notice must be given to the EPA Regional Administrator and to NMED at least four weeks before a TSDF is to receive hazardous waste from a foreign source.[296] Before transferring ownership or operation of a TSDF, the owner or operator of a TSDF must notify the prospective owner in writing of the HWA requirements that pertain to the TSDF.[297] The owner or operator of a permitted TSDF that receives hazardous waste from an off-site source (except where the owner or operator is also the generator) must inform the generator in writing that the owner or operator has the appropriate permit(s) for, and will accept, the waste the generator is shipping. The owner or operator must keep a copy of this written notice as part of the operating record.[298]

6.2 WASTE ANALYSIS

In order to properly manage a hazardous waste, an owner or operator of a TSDF must have sufficient knowledge about the waste to enable the facility to handle it properly. Consequently, before an owner or operator treats, stores or disposes of any hazardous waste, or any non-hazardous wastes in a landfill, land treatment or surface impoundment unit after final receipt of hazardous wastes at that unit (subject to specified conditions), the owner or operator must obtain a detailed chemical and physical analysis of a representative sample of the waste.[299] At a minimum, this analysis must contain all the information which must be known to treat, store or dispose of the waste in accordance with the requirements of the

---

294 40 C.F.R. §§ 264.11, 265.11.

295 *See* Appendix to 40 C.F.R. Part 262.

296 40 C.F.R. §§ 264.12(a), 265.12(a).

297 40 C.F.R. §§ 264.12(c), 265.12(b).

298 40 C.F.R. § 264.12(b).

299 40 C.F.R. §§ 264.13(a), 265.13(a).

regulations.[300] A comment in the regulations states that the owner or operator of an off-site facility may arrange for the generator of the hazardous waste to supply part or all of the required information, except as otherwise specified in 40 C.F.R. 268.7(b) and (c) relating to requirements under the land disposal restrictions.[301] The analysis must be repeated as necessary to ensure that it is accurate and up to date, and the owner or operator of an off-site facility must inspect, and if necessary analyze, each hazardous waste shipment received at the facility to determine whether it matches the identity of the waste specified on the accompanying manifest or shipping paper.[302] Finally, the owner or operator must develop and follow a written waste analysis plan which describes the procedures which will be carried out to comply with the waste analysis requirements. Such a plan must be kept at the facility.[303]

6.3 SECURITY

The owner or operator of a TSDF must prevent the unknowing entry, and minimize the possibility for the unauthorized entry, of persons or livestock onto the active portion of the TSDF, subject to certain specified exceptions.[304] Entry into the facility may be controlled either by the use of a 24-hour surveillance system or by erection of a fence or other barrier which completely surrounds the active portion of the facility.[305] Unless exempt, the owner or operator must also post signs bearing the legend "Danger - Unauthorized Personnel Keep Out" at each entrance to the active portion of the facility and at other locations in sufficient numbers to be seen from any approach to the active portions.[306] The warning signs must be legible from a distance of at least 25 feet and written in English and any other language that is predominant in the area in which the facility is located.[307]

6.4 GENERAL INSPECTION REQUIREMENTS

The owner or operator of a TSDF must inspect the facility for malfunctions and deterioration, operating errors, and discharges which may be causing, or may lead to, release of hazardous waste constituents to the environment or a threat to human health.[308] A

---

300 *Id.*

301 40 C.F.R. §§ 264.13(a)(2), 265.13(a)(2).

302 40 C.F.R. §§ 264.13(a)(4), 265.13(a)(4).

303 For the minimum requirements of the plan, *see* 40 C.F.R. §§ 264.13(b)-(c), 265.13(b)-(c).

304 40 C.F.R. §§ 264.14(a), 265.14(a).

305 40 C.F.R. §§ 264.14(b), 265.14(b).

306 40 C.F.R. §§ 264.14(c), 265.14(c).

307 *Id.*

308 40 C.F.R. §§ 264.15(a), 265.15(a).

written schedule for inspection is required and the records of inspection must be kept for three years.[309]

6.5 PERSONNEL TRAINING

TSDF personnel must have training in the handling of hazardous waste, and the owner or operator is responsible for implementing a program to accomplish this training.[310] At a minimum, the training program must be designed to ensure that facility personnel are able to respond effectively to emergencies by familiarizing the personnel with emergency procedures, emergency equipment, and emergency systems.[311] The general elements of such a training program are specified and certain records must be kept regarding the training program.[312]

6.6 IGNITABLE, REACTIVE, OR INCOMPATIBLE WASTES

The owner or operator of a TSDF must take precautions to prevent accidental ignition or reaction of ignitable or reactive waste.[313] This waste must be separated and protected from sources of ignition or reaction.[314] The treatment, storage, or disposal of ignitable or reactive waste, and the mixture or commingling of incompatible wastes[315] or incompatible wastes and other materials, must be conducted so that it does not (1) generate extreme heat or pressure, fire or explosions, or violent reactions, (2) produce uncontrolled toxic mists, fumes, dusts, or gases in sufficient quantities to threaten human health or the environment, (3) produce uncontrolled flammable fumes or gases in sufficient quantities to pose a risk of fire or explosions, (4) damage the structural integrity of the device or facility, or (5) through other like means threaten human health or the environment.[316]

---

309 40 C.F.R. §§ 264.15(b),(d), 265.15(b),(d).

310 40 C.F.R. §§ 264.16(a), 265.16(a).

311 *Id.*

312 40 C.F.R. §§ 264.16(a)-(d), 265.16(a)-(d).

313 40 C.F.R. §§ 264.17(a), 265.17(a).

314 *Id.*

315 "Incompatible waste" means a hazardous waste which is unsuitable for (1) placement in a particular device or facility because it may cause corrosion or decay of containment materials (*e.g.*, container inner liners or tank walls) or (2) commingling with another waste or material under uncontrolled conditions because the commingling might produce heat or pressure, fire or explosion, violent reaction, toxic dusts, mists, fumes, or gases, or flammable fumes or gases. 40 C.F.R. § 260.10.

316 40 C.F.R. §§ 264.17(b), 265.17(b).

6.7 LOCATION STANDARDS

Location standards for TSDFs include seismic considerations and restrictions applicable to floodplains, salt dome formations, salt bed formations, underground mines, and caves.[317]

A permit will not be issued to portions of new TSDFs where treatment, storage, or disposal of hazardous waste will be conducted within 61 meters (200 feet) of a fault which has had displacement in Holocene time.[318]

A permitted facility located in a 100-year floodplain[319] must be designed, constructed, operated and maintained to prevent washout of any hazardous waste by a 100-year flood, unless the owner or operator can meet certain specified conditions.[320] While the seismic restrictions will apply only to new TSDFs, the floodplain restrictions will apply to interim status TSDFs when they receive their HWA permits. The floodplain restriction requirements are not contained in the interim status facility regulations.

Finally, the placement of any non-containerized or bulk liquid hazardous waste in any salt dome formation, salt bed formation, underground mine, or cave is prohibited for permitted facilities.[321] This prohibition does not apply to the Department of Energy Waste Isolation Pilot Project (WIPP) in New Mexico.[322] The prohibition as applied to interim status facilities is worded in a slightly different fashion: "The placement of any hazardous waste in a salt dome, salt bed formation, underground mine or cave is prohibited, except for the Department of Energy Waste Isolation Pilot Project in New Mexico."[323]

6.8 CONSTRUCTION QUALITY ASSURANCE PROGRAM

A construction quality assurance (CQA) program is required for all surface impoundment, waste pile, and landfill units required to comply with specified portions of the regulations.[324] The program must insure that the construction unit meets or exceeds all design criteria and specifications in the permit.[325] The program must be developed and imple-

---

317 *See* 40 C.F.R. §§ 264.18, 265.18.

318 40 C.F.R. § 264.18(a). Appendix VI to 40 C.F.R. Part 264 provides a list of areas where such faults are known to exist.

319 "100-year floodplain" means any land area which is subject to a one percent or greater chance of flooding in any given year from any source. 40 C.F.R. § 264.18(b)(2)(i).

320 40 C.F.R. § 264.18(b)(1).

321 40 C.F.R. § 264.18(c).

322 *Id.*

323 40 C.F.R. § 265.18.

324 40 C.F.R. §§ 264.19(a), 265.19(a).

325 *Id.*

mented under the direction of a CQA officer who is a registered professional engineer.[326] The owner or operator of units subject to the CQA program must develop and implement a written CQA plan.[327] The plan must identify steps that will be used to monitor and document the quality of materials and the condition and manner of their installation.[328] Waste must not be received in a unit until the owner or operator has submitted to the Secretary by certified mail or hand-delivery a certification signed by the CQA officer that the approved CQA plan has been successfully carried out and that the unit meets the specified requirements.[329]

6.9 PREPAREDNESS AND PREVENTION

TSDFs must be designed, constructed, maintained and operated to minimize the possibility of fire, explosion, or any unplanned sudden or non-sudden release of hazardous waste or hazardous waste constituents into the environment.[330] Also required are (1) the presence of certain kinds of emergency equipment at the facility, (2) the testing and maintenance of the equipment, (3) access to communications or alarm systems, (4) the maintenance of aisle space for the movement of equipment and personnel, and (5) arrangements with local authorities including police, fire and hospital personnel regarding the hazardous waste operation at the facility.[331]

6.10 CONTINGENCY PLAN AND EMERGENCY PROCEDURES

Each owner or operator of a TSDF must have a contingency plan for the facility, which must be designed to minimize hazards to human health or the environment from fires, explosions, or any unplanned sudden or non-sudden release of hazardous waste or hazardous waste constituents to air, soil, or surface water.[332] The provisions of the plan must be carried out immediately whenever there is a fire, explosion, or release of hazardous waste or hazardous waste constituents which could threaten human health or the environment.[333] A copy of the contingency plan and all revisions to the plan must be maintained at the facility and submitted to all local police departments, fire departments, hospitals and state and local emergency response teams that may be called upon to provide emergency services.[334] There are also requirements pertaining to the amendment of the contingency plan, the

---

326 *Id.*

327 40 C.F.R. §§ 264.19(b), 265.19(b).

328 *Id.*

329 40 C.F.R. §§ 264.19(d), 265.19(d).

330 40 C.F.R. §§ 264.31, 265.31.

331 40 C.F.R. §§ 264.32 - .37, 265.32 - .37.

332 40 C.F.R. §§ 264.51(a), 265.51(a).

333 40 C.F.R. §§ 264.51(b), 265.51(b).

334 40 C.F.R. §§ 264.53, 265.53.

designation of an emergency coordinator, and the requirements for emergency procedures.[335]

6.11 MANIFEST SYSTEM, RECORDKEEPING, AND REPORTING

When a facility receives hazardous waste that must be accompanied by a manifest (off-site hazardous waste), the owner or operator, or their agent, must (1) sign and date each copy of the manifest to certify that the hazardous waste covered by the manifest was received, (2) note any significant discrepancies in the manifest on each copy of the manifest, (3) immediately give the Transporter at least one copy of the signed manifest, (4) within 30 days after the delivery, send a copy of the manifest to the generator, and (5) retain at the facility a copy of each manifest for at least three years from the date of delivery.[336] Other requirements include the following: (1) certain actions must be taken with regard to significant manifest discrepancies as defined in the regulations,[337] (2) an operating record of the facility must be maintained at the facility,[338] (3) certain records must be retained and be available for inspection by NMED,[339] (4) biennial reports must be submitted containing specified information,[340] (5) certain steps must be taken and a report submitted to NMED when unmanifested waste is received by the facility;[341] and (6) additional reports must be submitted as required by the regulations.[342] There are special requirements for a facility that receives hazardous waste from a rail Transporter.[343]

6.12 GROUND WATER MONITORING AND RELEASES

With respect to ground water, the regulations for interim status facilities are less extensive than those for permitted facilities. The owner or operator of a surface impoundment, landfill, or land treatment facility which is used to manage hazardous waste must implement a ground water monitoring program capable of determining the facility's quality of ground water in the uppermost aquifer underlying the facility, unless a specified exception applies.[344] The regulations specify what the ground water monitoring system must consist

---

335 40 C.F.R. §§ 264.54 - .56, 265.54 - .56.

336 40 C.F.R. §§ 264.71(a), 265.71(a).

337 40 C.F.R. §§ 264.72, 265.72.

338 40 C.F.R. §§ 264.73, 265.73.

339 40 C.F.R. §§ 264.74, 265.74.

340 40 C.F.R. §§ 264.75, 265.75.

341 40 C.F.R. §§ 264.76, 265.76.

342 40 C.F.R. §§ 264.77, 265.77.

343 40 C.F.R. §§ 264.71(b), 265.71(b).

344 40 C.F.R. § 265.90.

of[345] and mandate that the owner or operator develop and follow a ground water sampling and analysis plan, which must be kept at the facility.[346] An owner or operator must also prepare an outline of a ground water quality assessment program and perform certain analyses and notifications to NMED, should hazardous waste discharges to the ground water be suspected.[347]

EIB has established a three-stage ground water monitoring program for permitted facilities, unless the facility qualifies for a narrow exception.[348] All surface impoundments, waste piles, land treatment units, and landfills that receive hazardous waste after July 26, 1982, are subject to this program.[349] The first stage is a detection monitoring program which is designed to monitor ground water wells in order to determine if leachate from the facility is entering the ground water.[350] The second stage, which occurs when hazardous constituents from a facility are detected in the ground water within certain limits, is termed a "compliance monitoring program."[351] The third stage occurs if and when the ground water protection standard is violated and involves a corrective action program, if necessary.[352] The details for each stage of a facility's ground water program will be developed in the course of the HWA permitting process.

While the different stages of the ground water program apply to surface impoundments, waste piles, land treatment units, and landfills, the owner or operator of any TSDF seeking a permit must institute corrective action as necessary to protect human health and the environment for all releases of hazardous waste or constituents from any solid waste management unit at the facility, regardless of the time at which waste was placed in such unit.[353] Corrective action beyond the facility property boundary must also be taken where necessary to protect human health and the environment, unless the owner or operator demonstrates to the satisfaction of the Secretary that, despite the owner or operator's best efforts, the owner or operator was unable to obtain the necessary permission to undertake such actions.[354]

---

345 40 C.F.R. § 265.91.

346 40 C.F.R. § 265.92.

347 40 C.F.R. § 265.93.

348 40 C.F.R. § 264.90(b).

349 40 C.F.R. § 264.90(a)(2).

350 40 C.F.R. §§ 264.91(a)(4), 264.98.

351 40 C.F.R. §§ 264.91(a)(1), 264.99.

352 40 C.F.R. §§ 264.91(a)(2) - (3); 264.100.

353 40 C.F.R. § 264.101(a); N.M. Stat. Ann. § 74-4-4(A)(5)(h) (Repl. Pamp. 1993).

354 40 C.F.R. § 264.101(c); *see* N.M. Stat. Ann. § 74-4-4(A)(5)(i) (Repl. Pamp. 1993).

6.13 AIR EMISSIONS STANDARDS FOR PROCESS VENTS

EIB has adopted regulations, subject to specified exceptions, applicable to TSDF operations with process vents[355] associated with distillation, fractionation, thin-film evaporation, solvent extraction, or air or steam stripping operations that manage hazardous wastes with organic concentrations of at least 10-ppmw, if these operations are conducted in (1) units that are subject to the permitting requirements of Part 270 or (2) hazardous waste recycling units that are located on hazardous waste management facilities otherwise subject to the permitting requirements of Part 270.[356] As to permitted facilities, the air emissions standards for process vents must be incorporated into a permit that is reissued or reviewed pursuant to the requirements of the regulations if the owner or operator has received a permit prior to December 21, 1990.[357]

The owner or operator of a facility with process vents associated with distillation, fractionation, thin-film evaporation, solvent extraction, or air or steam stripping operations managing hazardous wastes with organic concentrations of at least 10-ppmw is required to (1) reduce total organic emissions from all affected process vents at the facility below 1.4 kg/h (3lb/h) and 2.8 Mg/yr (3.1 ton/yr) or (2) reduce, by use of a control device,[358] total organic emissions from all affected process vents at the facility by 95 weight percent.[359] Owners or operators must utilize closed vent systems[360] and control devices to comply with the air emissions standards.[361]

To accomplish the required reductions in air emissions, an owner or operator of a TSDF subject to the air emissions standards is required to (1) prepare an implementation

---

355 "Process vent" is defined as any open-ended pipe or stack that is vented to the atmosphere either directly, through a vacuum-producing system, or through a tank (e.g., distillate receiver, condenser, bottoms receiver, surge control tank, separator tank, or hot well) associated with hazardous waste distillation, fractionation, thin-film evaporation, solvent extraction, or air or steam stripping operations. 40 C.F.R. §§ 264.1031, 265.1031.

356 40 C.F.R. §§ 264.1030(b), 265.1030(b).

357 40 C.F.R. § 264.1030(c).

358 "Control device" means an enclosed combustion device, vapor recovery system, or flare. Any device the primary function of which is the recovery or capture of solvents or other organics for use, reuse, or sale (e.g., a primary condenser on a solvent recovery unit) is not a control device. 40 C.F.R. §§ 264.1031, 265.1031.

359 40 C.F.R. §§ 264.1032(a), 265.1032(a).

360 A "closed vent system" means a system that is not open to the atmosphere and that is composed of piping, connections and, if necessary, flow-inducing devices that transport gas or vapor from a piece or pieces of equipment to a control device. 40 C.F.R. §§ 264.1031, 265.1031.

361 40 C.F.R. §§ 264.1033(a), 265.1033(a).

schedule for installation and startup of the system,[362] (2) observe technical performance, operational and design standards for the various control devices utilized,[363] (3) observe test method and procedures requirements,[364] and (4) observe detailed recordkeeping requirements regarding design, installation, inspection, monitoring, performance, and repair of such control devices.[365]

Owners and operators of permitted facilities subject to the air emission standards for process vents are required to submit a semiannual report to the Secretary, which should include (1) the EPA identification number and name and address of the facility and (2) dates when the control device exceeded or operated outside the design specifications, together with other specified information.[366] If, during the semiannual reporting period, the control device does not exceed or operate outside the design specifications for more than 24 hours or a flare does not operate with visible emissions as defined in the regulations, a report to the Secretary is not required.[367]

6.14 AIR EMISSION STANDARD FOR EQUIPMENT LEAKS

EIB has adopted regulations providing air emission standards for equipment leaks that apply to equipment that contains or contacts hazardous wastes with organic concentrations of at least 10% by weight in (1) units that are subject to the permitting requirements of Part 270 or (2) hazardous waste recycling units that are located on hazardous waste management facilities otherwise subject to the permitting requirements of Part 270.[368] As to permitted facilities, the air emission standards for equipment leaks must be incorporated into a permit that is reissued or reviewed pursuant to the requirements of the regulations, if the owner or operator has received a permit prior to December 21, 1990.[369] Each piece of equipment subject to the air emission standards for equipment leaks must be marked in such a manner that it can be distinguished readily from other pieces of equipment.[370]

In connection with such equipment, there are standards for the design, inspection and operation of (1) pumps in liquid service,[371] (2) compressors,[372] (3) pressure relief devices

---

362 40 C.F.R. §§ 264.1033(a), 265.1033(a).

363 40 C.F.R. §§ 264.1033(b) - (l), 265.1033(b) - (k).

364 40 C.F.R. §§ 264.1034, 265.1034.

365 40 C.F.R. §§ 264.1035, 265.1035.

366 40 C.F.R. § 264.1036(a).

367 40 C.F.R. § 264.1036(b).

368 40 C.F.R. §§ 264.1050(b), 265.1050(b).

369 40 C.F.R. § 264.1051(c).

370 40 C.F.R. §§ 264.1050(d), 265.1050(c).

371 40 C.F.R. §§ 264.1052, 265.1052.

372 40 C.F.R. §§ 264.1053, 265.1053.

in gas/vapor service,[373] (4) sampling connecting systems,[374] (5) open-ended valves or lines,[375] (6) valves in gas/vapor service or in light liquid service,[376] and (7) pumps and valves in heavy liquid service, pressure relief devices in light liquid or heavy liquid service, and flanges and other connectors.[377] Delay in repair of equipment for which leaks have been detected is allowed under certain circumstances.[378] There are also alternative standards under specified conditions for valves in gas/vapor service or in light liquid service.[379]

Owners and operators of TSDFs utilizing equipment subject to the air emission standards for equipment leaks are required to follow specified test methods and procedures[380] and are subject to extensive recordkeeping requirements regarding such matters as equipment design, inspection, testing, maintenance, and repair.[381]

Owners and operators of permitted facilities subject to the air emission standards for equipment leaks are required to submit a semiannual report to the Secretary, which should include (1) the EPA identification number and name and address of the facility and (2) for each month during the semiannual reporting period, the equipment identification number of each valve, pump, or compressor for which a leak was not repaired as required by the regulations, (3) dates of hazardous waste management unit shutdowns, and (4) dates when the control device exceeded or operated outside the design specifications, together with other specified information.[382] If, during the semiannual reporting period, leaks from valves, pumps, and compressors were repaired as required by the regulations and the control device did not exceed or operate outside the design specifications for more than 24 hours, a report to the Secretary is not required.[383]

6.15 CLOSURE AND POST-CLOSURE REQUIREMENTS

The owner or operator of a TSDF must close the facility in a manner that minimizes the need for further maintenance and that controls, minimizes or eliminates, to the extent necessary to protect human health and the environment, post-closure escape of hazardous waste, hazardous constituents, leachate, contaminated run-off, or hazardous waste decomposi-

---

373 40 C.F.R. §§ 264.1054, 265.1054.

374 40 C.F.R. §§ 264.1055, 265.1055.

375 40 C.F.R. §§ 264.1056, 265.1056.

376 40 C.F.R. §§ 264.1057, 265.1057.

377 40 C.F.R. §§ 264.1058, 265.1058.

378 40 C.F.R. §§ 264.1059, 265.1059.

379 40 C.F.R. §§ 264.1061, 265.1061; 40 C.F.R. §§ 264.1062, 265.1062.

380 40 C.F.R. §§ 264.1063, 265.1063.

381 40 C.F.R. §§ 264.1064, 265.1064.

382 40 C.F.R. § 264.1065(a).

383 40 C.F.R. § 264.1065(b).

tion products to the ground or surface waters or to the atmosphere.[384] Each TSDF must have a written closure plan that identifies the steps necessary to achieve partial or final closure of the facility at any point during its active life.[385] For interim facilities, this plan must be furnished to the Secretary upon request.[386] If an owner or operator decides to close an interim status facility and does not have a plan approved by the Secretary, the closure plan must be submitted to the Secretary for approval at least 180 days prior to the date on which the owner or operator expects to begin closure of the first surface impoundment, waste pile, land treatment, or landfill unit, or final closure if it involves such a unit, and at least 45 days prior to the date on which the owner or operator expects to begin partial or final closure of a boiler or industrial furnace or final closure of a facility with only tanks, container storage, or incinerator units.[387] If the owner or operator has an approved plan, the 180-day notification period is reduced to 60 days and the 45-day notification period remains the same.[388] For permitted facilities, the closure plan will be a condition of the HWA permit.[389]

Once closure is initiated, the owner or operator must treat, remove from the unit or facility, or dispose of on-site all hazardous wastes in accordance with the approved closure plan. Closure itself must be completed within six months of receiving the last shipment of hazardous waste or, subject to specified condition, of non-hazardous waste.[390] The Secretary may approve a longer period if the owner or operator can meet specified conditions.[391] At a minimum, the contents of a closure plan must include (1) a description of how each hazardous waste management unit at the facility will be closed, (2) a description of how final closure of the facility will be conducted, (3) an estimate of the maximum inventory of hazardous waste ever on site over the active life of the facility, (4) a detailed description of the steps needed to remove or decontaminate all hazardous waste residues and contaminated containment system components and equipment, (5) a description of other activities necessary during the closure period to ensure that all performance standards are met, (6) a schedule for closure of each unit and for final closure of the facility, and (7) for certain facilities, an estimate of the expected year of final closure.[392]

---

384 40 C.F.R. §§ 264.111, 265.111.

385 40 C.F.R. §§ 264.112, 265.112.

386 40 C.F.R. § 265.112(a).

387 40 C.F.R. § 265.112(d).

388 *Id.*

389 40 C.F.R. § 270.14(b)(13).

390 40 C.F.R. §§ 264.113(b), 265.113(b).

391 40 C.F.R. §§ 264.113(a), 265.113(a).

392 40 C.F.R. §§ 264.112(b), 265.112(b).

A written post-closure plan is required for all hazardous waste disposal facilities and for certain waste piles, surface impoundments and tank systems.[393] The post-closure care requirements include a written post-closure plan that should, at a minimum, describe the planned monitoring activities and the planned maintenance activities that will ensure the integrity of the containment system and the proper functioning of the facility monitoring equipment.[394] The plan must also identify the name, address, and phone number of the person or office to contact about the hazardous waste disposal unit or facility during the post-closure care period.[395] Similar to the requirements of the closure plan, the post-closure plan for an interim status facility must be submitted to the Secretary for approval at least 180 days prior to the date the owner or operator expects to begin closure.[396] The post-closure plan for a permitted TSDF will be approved at the time the HWA permit is issued. The owner or operator and a registered professional engineer must execute a certification that the post-closure care was performed in accordance with the plan.[397]

The post-closure care program includes certain notice requirements.[398] A survey plat, indicating the location and dimensions of landfill cells or other disposal areas and containing a record of the types, location, and quantities of hazardous wastes disposed within each cell or disposal unit, must be submitted to the local zoning authority and to the Secretary.[399] In addition, the owner or operator must record a notice on the deed to the property or in some other instrument which is normally examined during the title search that the land had been used to manage hazardous waste, that its use is restricted, and that a survey plat bearing the information described above has been filed with the local zoning authority and with the Secretary.[400] Such a deed or notice must be filed in the real property records of the county in which the property is located and must be properly signed and acknowledged.[401]

6.16 FINANCIAL RESPONSIBILITY REQUIREMENTS

Financial responsibility requirements have been established for both interim status and permitted TSDFs to ensure that the funds needed to implement closure and post-closure

---

393 40 C.F.R. §§ 264.110, 265.110.

394 40 C.F.R. §§ 264.118(b)(1) - (2), 265.118(c)(1) - (2).

395 40 C.F.R. §§ 264.118(b)(3), 265.118(c)(3).

396 40 C.F.R. § 265.118(e).

397 40 C.F.R. §§ 264.120, 265.120.

398 40 C.F.R. §§ 264.119, 265.119.

399 40 C.F.R. §§ 264.119(b), 265.119(b).

400 *Id.*

401 *Id.*

plans are available.[402] The owner or operator must have a detailed written estimate in current dollars of the cost of closing the facility, and the estimate must equal the cost of final closure at the point in the facility's active life when the extent and manner of its operation would make closure the most expensive.[403] An owner or operator of each TSDF must also establish financial assurance for closure of the facility. A number of options are available, including a trust fund, surety bond, letter of credit, insurance policy, use of a financial test and corporate guarantee, or use of multiple financial mechanisms.[404]

Owners or operators of TSDFs must demonstrate financial responsibility for bodily injury and property damage to third-parties caused by sudden accidental occurrences arising from operations of the facility or group of facilities.[405] Owners or operators of a surface impoundment, landfill, or land treatment facility which is used to manage hazardous waste, or a group of such facilities, must demonstrate financial responsibility for bodily injury and property damage to third-parties caused by non-sudden accidental occurrences arising from such operations.[406] Approved methods of demonstrating this aspect of financial responsibility include the use of insurance, financial tests, financial guarantee, letter of credit, surety bond, and trust fund.[407] An owner or operator of a TSDF is required to notify the Secretary in writing within 30 days whenever (a) a claim for bodily injury or property damage caused by the operation of a TSDF is made against the owner or operator or the instrument providing financial assurance or (b) the amount of financial assurance for liability is reduced.[408]

EIB did not adopt as part of the New Mexico regulations 40 C.F.R. § 264.149 and § 265.149, which provide for the substitution of a state-required financial mechanism for the federally required mechanism, so long as the state-required mechanism is at least equivalent to the financial mechanisms of the federal program. EIB also did not adopt 40 C.F.R. § 264.150 and § 265.150, which provide that if the state either assumes legal responsibility for an owner's or operator's compliance with the closure, post-closure care, or liability requirements or assures that funds will be available from state sources to cover those requirements, the owner or operator will be in compliance with the financial responsibility requirements for

---

402 40 C.F.R. §§ 264.140 - .151, 265.140 - .151.

403 40 C.F.R. §§ 264.142(a), 265.142(a).

404 40 C.F.R. §§ 264.143(a), (b), (d) - (g), 265.143(a) - (f). Permitted facilities are also allowed use of a performance bond. 40 C.F.R. § 264.143(c). The regulations provide the specific wording for each of these instruments in 40 C.F.R. §§ 264.151 and 265.151.

405 40 C.F.R. §§ 264.147(a), 265.147(a).

406 40 C.F.R. §§ 264.147(b), 265.147(b).

407 40 C.F.R. § 264.147(a) - (b), § 265.147(a) - (b).

408 *Id.*

closure and post-closure if the EPA Regional Administrator determines that the state's assumption of responsibility is at least equivalent to the financial mechanisms specified in the federal regulations.[409]

7.0 STANDARDS FOR SPECIFIC TYPES OF TSDFS

EIB has promulgated specific standards for specific types of TSDFs regulated under the HWA. These facilities include containers, tank systems, surface impoundments, waste piles, land treatment facilities, landfills, incinerators, thermal treatment facilities, chemical, physical and biological treatment facilities, drip pads and underground injection wells.[410]

The technical standards for permitted TSDFs are set forth in 40 C.F.R. Part 264, Subparts I through O, and W. The technical standards for interim status TSDFs are set forth in 40 C.F.R. Part 265, Subparts I through R, and W. The interim status standards address thermal treatment, chemical, physical, and biological treatment and underground injection, while the permitted standards do not. Conversely, the permitted standards address "miscellaneous units," while the interim status standards do not.

The remainder of this Section will provide a brief overview of the type of requirements that apply to each of the specified types of TSDFs and the one "miscellaneous units" category. Since the permitted facilities standards generally reflect and incorporate the standards for interim facilities, a separate discussion on interim status standards as distinguished from permitted facility standards will not be included unless there are significant differences.

7.1 USE AND MANAGEMENT OF CONTAINERS

A container is any portable device in which a material is stored, transported, treated, disposed of, or otherwise handled.[411] Requirements with regard to containers include (1) the container be in good condition, (2) the material composition of the container be compatible with the waste to be stored,[412] (3) the container be closed during storage, except when it is necessary to add or remove waste, (4) the container be inspected on a weekly basis, (5) a container holding ignitable or reactive waste be located at least 15 meters (50 feet) from the facility's property line, and (6) incompatible waste or incompatible waste and mater-

---

409 *See* N.M. Hazardous Waste Management Regulations-7 §§ 502, 602.

410 In addition, EIB has adopted regulations for "miscellaneous units" that establish performance standards and provide for monitoring, analysis, inspection, response, reporting, corrective action and post-closure care. EIB has also adopted regulations for underground storage tanks for "regulated substances" as defined by HWA. UST regulations are discussed in the Underground Storage Tank Management Chapter.

411 40 C.F.R. § 260.10.

412 An "incompatible waste" is defined in the Ignitable, Reactive, or Incompatible Wastes Section of this Chapter.

ials[413] not be placed in the same container unless specified conditions are met.[414] There are also design and operational standards for permitted facilities.[415]

7.2 TANK SYSTEMS

A tank is a stationary device, designed to contain an accumulation of hazardous waste, which is constructed primarily of non-earthen materials (*e.g.*, wood, concrete, steel, plastic) which provide structural support.[416] A tank system is a hazardous waste storage or treatment tank and its associated ancillary equipment and containment system.[417] Areas addressed with respect to tanks and tank systems include (1) design and installation standards for new tank systems or components,[418] (2) assessment of the existing tank system's integrity, (3) provision for secondary containment and detection of releases,[419] (4) specified operational standards, (5) daily inspection of specified portions of the tank system, (6) response to leaks or spills and disposition of leaking or unfit-for-use tank systems, (7) closure and post-closure care, and (8) observance of certain standards or prohibitions with regard to ignitable, reactive, or incompatible wastes.[420]

For interim status tanks and tank systems there are special requirements for generators of more than 100 kg but less than 1,000 kg of hazardous waste in a calendar month (small quantity generators) that accumulate hazardous waste in tanks for less than 180 days (or 270 days if a generator must ship the waste greater than 200 miles) and do not accumulate more than 6,000 kg on-site at any time.[421]

7.3 SURFACE IMPOUNDMENTS

A surface impoundment is a facility or part of a facility which is a natural topographic depression, man-made excavation or diked area formed primarily of earthen materials (although it may be lined with man-made materials), which is designed to hold an accumulation of liquid wastes or wastes containing free liquids, and which is not an injection well. Examples of surface impoundments are holding, storage, settling, and aeration pits, ponds, and

---

413 *See* Appendix V to 40 C.F.R. Parts 264 and 265 for examples.

414 *See* 40 C.F.R. §§ 264.170 - .178, 265.170 - .177.

415 40 C.F.R. § 264.175.

416 40 C.F.R. § 260.10.

417 *Id.*

418 A "new tank system" and "new tank component" are defined as facilities for which installation commenced after July 14, 1986. 40 C.F.R. § 260.10.

419 The regulations contain an exemption from this requirement for tanks that are used to store or treat hazardous waste containing no free liquids and that are situated inside a building with an impermeable floor. 40 C.F.R. §§ 264.190, 265.190.

420 *See* 40 C.F.R. §§ 264.190 - .199, 265.190 - .199

421 40 C.F.R. § 265.201.

lagoons.[422] Areas addressed with respect to surface impoundments include (1) standards for design and operation, including the installation of liners and a leachate collection system, unless exempted by the Secretary, (2) action leakage rate, including a response plan and required actions in the event the rate is exceeded,[423] (3) monitoring and inspection, (4) closure and post-closure care, and (5) certain procedures and/or prohibitions with regard to ignitable, reactive or incompatible wastes or other specified wastes.[424]

7.4 WASTE PILES

"Waste pile" is not defined. However a "pile" is defined as any non-containerized accumulation of solid, non-flowing hazardous waste that is used for treatment or storage.[425] Areas addressed with respect to waste piles[426] include (1) design and operating standards, including liner leachate collection systems and protection against run-off and wind dispersal, (2) action leakage rate, including a response plan and required actions in the event the rate is exceeded, (3) inspection and monitoring, (4) special procedures and prohibitions with respect to ignitable, reactive or incompatible wastes or other specified wastes, and (5) closure and post-closure care.[427] As to permitted facilities, certain hazardous wastes must not be placed in waste piles that are not enclosed unless the owner or operator operates the waste pile in accordance with a management plan for these specified wastes that is approved by the Secretary pursuant to specified standards.[428] As to interim facilities, certain waste analysis procedures are also required.[429]

7.5 LAND TREATMENT

A land treatment facility is a facility or part of a facility at which hazardous waste is applied onto or incorporated into the soil surface; such facilities are disposal facilities if the waste will remain after closure.[430] For interim status facilities the placement of hazardous waste in or on a land treatment facility is prohibited unless the waste can be made less

---

422 40 C.F.R. § 260.10.

423 40 C.F.R. §§ 264.222 -.223, 265.222 -.223. The action leakage rate is the maximum design flow rate that the leak detection system (LDS) can remove without the fluid head on the bottom liner exceeding one foot. *Id.*

424 *See* 40 C.F.R. §§ 264.220 - .231, 265.220 - .230.

425 40 C.F.R. § 260.10.

426 The regulations in Subpart L of Parts 264 and 265 apply to owners and operators of facilities that store or treat hazardous waste in piles. For waste piles that are closed with wastes left in place, the regulations under Subpart N of Parts 264 and 265 (Landfills) apply. *See* 40 C.F.R. §§ 264.250, 265.250.

427 *See* 40 C.F.R. §§ 264.250 - .258, 265.250 - .258.

428 40 C.F.R. § 264.259.

429 40 C.F.R. § 265.252.

430 40 C.F.R. § 260.10.

hazardous or nonhazardous by degradation, transformation, or immobilization processes occurring in or on the soil.[431] The owner or operator of an interim status facility must also perform certain waste analyses before placing hazardous waste in or on a land treatment facility.[432] For a permitted facility, for each waste that will be applied to the treatment zone, the owner or operator must demonstrate, prior to the application of the waste, that hazardous constituents in the waste can be completely degraded, transformed, or immobilized in the treatment zone.[433] The following areas for both interim status facilities and permitted facilities are also addressed: (1) requirements for land treatment facilities that may be used for the growth of food-chain crops, (2) unsaturated zone monitoring, (3) recordkeeping, (4) closure and post-closure care, and (5) certain procedures and/or prohibitions with regard to ignitable, reactive, or incompatible wastes.[434] For permitted facilities, certain hazardous wastes must not be placed in a land treatment unit unless the owner or operator operates the facility in accordance with a management plan for these wastes that is approved by the Secretary pursuant to specified standards.[435]

7.6 LANDFILLS

A landfill is a disposal facility or part of a facility where hazardous waste is placed in or on land and which is not a pile, a land treatment facility, a surface impoundment, an underground injection well, a salt dome formation, a salt bed formation, an underground mine, or a cave.[436] Subject to two specified exceptions, a permitted landfill must have a liner system for all portions of the landfill (except for existing portions of such landfill).[437] The first exception involves a grant of exemption by the Secretary on the basis of meeting certain specified standards.[438] The second exception requires the owner or operator of each new landfill unit on which construction commences after January 29, 1992, each lateral expansion of a landfill unit on which construction commences after July 29, 1992, and each replacement of an existing landfill unit that is to commence reuse after July 29, 1992, to install two or more liners and a leachate collection and removal system above and between such liners.[439]

---

431 40 C.F.R. § 265.272.

432 40 C.F.R. § 265.273.

433 40 C.F.R. § 264.272.

434 *See* 40 C.F.R. §§ 264.276 - .282, 265.276 - .282.

435 40 C.F.R. § 264.283.

436 40 C.F.R. § 260.10.

437 40 C.F.R. § 264.301(a).

438 40 C.F.R. § 264.301(b).

439 40 C.F.R. § 264.301(c). This double liner requirement may be waived by the Secretary for any monofill if specified conditions are satisfied. 40 C.F.R. § 264.301(e).

As to facilities seeking interim status, the owner or operator of each new landfill unit on which construction commences after January 29, 1992, each lateral expansion of a landfill unit on which construction commences after July 29, 1992, and each replacement of an existing landfill unit that is to commence reuse after July 29, 1992, must install two or more liners and a leachate collection and removal system above and between such liners and operate the leachate collection and removals systems in accordance with specified standards.[440] The owner or operator of each such unit must notify the Secretary at least 60 days prior to receiving waste.[441] The owner or operator of each facility submitting notice must file a Part B application within six months of the receipt of such notice.[442] An exemption is provided if the owner or operator meets specified requirements.[443] Additional areas addressed with regard to landfills include (1) control of run-on and run-off and wind dispersal, (2) action leakage rate and the submittal of an action leakage rate response plan, (3) monitoring and inspection, (4) surveying and recordkeeping requirements, (5) closure and post-closure care, (6) special procedures and/or prohibitions with respect to ignitable, reactive, or incompatible wastes, (7) special requirements for bulk and containerized liquids, (8) special requirements for containers, and (9) special requirements for disposal of small containers of hazardous waste and overpacked drums (lab packs).[444] As with permitted waste piles and land treatment units, certain hazardous wastes must not be placed in a permitted landfill unless the owner or operator operates the landfill in accordance with a management plan for these wastes that is approved by the Secretary pursuant to specified standards.[445]

7.7 INCINERATORS

An incinerator is any enclosed device that (1) uses controlled flame combustion and neither meets the criteria for classification as a boiler nor is listed as an industrial furnace or (2) meets the definition of infrared incinerator or plasma arc incinerator.[446] The owner or operator of a permitted hazardous waste incinerator may burn only waste specified in the

---

440 40 C.F.R. § 265.301(a).

441 40 C.F.R. § 265.301(b).

442 *Id.*

443 40 C.F.R. § 265.301(c)-(h).

444 *See* 40 C.F.R. §§ 264.301 - .316, 265.301 - .316.

445 40 C.F.R. § 264.317.

446 40 C.F.R. § 260.10. For definition of "boiler" and "industrial furnace," *see id.* An "infrared incinerator" means any enclosed device that uses electric powered resistance heaters as a source of radiant heat and which is not listed as an industrial furnace. *Id.* A "plasma arc incinerator" means any enclosed device using high intensity electrical discharge or arc as a source of heat and which is not listed as an industrial furnace. *Id.*

permit and only under specified operating conditions for certain wastes.[447] Certain incinerator facilities are exempt from the mainstream of regulations if the waste to be burned meets specified criteria.[448] Areas addressed with regard to incinerators include (1) waste analyses, (2) general operating requirements, (3) monitoring, inspecting, and recordkeeping requirements, and (4) closure requirements.[449]

As to interim status incinerators, the owners or operators may burn certain wastes if they receive a certification from the Secretary that they can meet the performance standards applicable to permitted facilities when they burn the specified wastes.[450]

7.8 THERMAL TREATMENT

Thermal treatment is the treatment of hazardous waste in a device which uses elevated temperatures as a primary means to change the chemical, physical, or biological character or composition of the hazardous waste. Examples of thermal treatment processes are incineration, molten salt, pyrolysis, calcination, wet air oxidation, and microwave discharge.[451] The requirements for thermal treatment are very similar to the requirements for incinerators[452] and include such areas as general operating requirements, waste analysis, monitoring and inspections, and closure.[453] The open burning of hazardous waste is prohibited except for the open burning and detonation of waste explosives.[454]

Owners or operators of thermal treatment devices may burn certain specified wastes if they receive certification from the Secretary that they can meet the performance standards for permitted incinerators when they burn the specified wastes.[455]

---

447 40 C.F.R. § 264.344.

448 40 C.F.R. §§ 264.340(a)-(c), 265.340(a)-(b).

449 *See* 40 C.F.R. §§ 264.340 - .351, 265.340 - .352. A comment to the regulations on closure provides that unless the owner or operator can demonstrate that the residue removed from the incinerator is not a hazardous waste, the owner or operator becomes a generator of hazardous waste and must manage it in accordance with all the requirements applicable to generators. 40 C.F.R. §§ 264.351, 265.351.

450 40 C.F.R. § 265.352.

451 40 C.F.R. § 260.10.

452 *See* Subpart O of 40 C.F.R. Part 265.

453 40 C.F.R. §§ 265.370 - .381. The regulations for thermal treatment are found in Subpart P of Part 265 (interim status facilities) and are not included in the regulations for permitted facilities.

454 40 C.F.R. § 265.382. This regulation describes what is meant by the "detonation of waste explosives" and the circumstances under which burning or detonation is permitted.

455 40 C.F.R. § 265.383.

7.9 CHEMICAL, PHYSICAL, AND BIOLOGICAL TREATMENT

The interim status facility regulations provide requirements for owners and operators of facilities that treat hazardous waste by chemical, physical, or biological methods in other than tanks, surface impoundments, and land treatment facilities. Areas addressed include general operating requirements, waste analysis and trial tests, inspections and recordkeeping, closure, and special requirements for ignitable, reactive or incompatible wastes.[456]

7.10 UNDERGROUND INJECTION

Underground injection is the subsurface emplacement of fluids through a bored, drilled or driven well or through a dug well where the depth of the dug well is greater than the largest surface dimension.[457] An "injection well" is a well into which fluids are injected.[458] A "well" is a shaft or pit dug or bored into the earth, generally of a cylindrical form, and often walled with bricks or tubing to prevent the earth from caving in.[459] The owner or operator of an interim status facility which disposes of hazardous waste by underground injection[460] is excluded from the requirements of closure and post-closure care and financial requirements generally applicable to interim status facilities.[461]

7.11 DRIP PADS

A drip pad is an engineered structure consisting of a curbed, free-drained base, constructed of non-earthen materials and designed to convey preservative kick-back or drippage from treated wood, precipitation, and surface water run-on to an associated collection system at wood preserving plants.[462] Owners and operators of facilities that use new or existing drip pads to convey treated wood drippage, precipitation, and/or surface water run-on to an associated collection system are subject to specified requirements.[463] Existing drip pads are those constructed before December 6, 1990, and those for which the owner or operator has a design and has entered into binding financial or other agreements for construction prior to December 6, 1990. All other drip pads are new drip pads.[464] For each exist-

---

456 40 C.F.R. §§ 265.400 - .406.

457 40 C.F.R. § 260.10.

458 *Id.*

459 *Id.*

460 The regulations in 40 C.F.R. Part 265, Subpart R apply to the owners and operators of interim status hazardous underground injection wells which are classified as Class I wells or Class IV wells under EPA's underground injection control (UIC) program regulations promulgated under the authority of the Safe Drinking Water Act (42 U.S.C. §§ 300f *et seq.*). Those regulations are set forth at 40 C.F.R. Parts 144 - 147.

461 40 C.F.R. § 265.430.

462 40 C.F.R. § 260.10.

463 40 C.F.R. §§ 264.570(a), 265.440(a).

464 *Id.*

ing drip pad, the owner or operator must evaluate the drip pad and determine that it meets all specified requirements.[465] The owner or operator must obtain and keep on file at the facility a written assessment of the drip pad, reviewed and certified by an independent, qualified registered professional engineer, that attests to the results of the evaluation.[466] The assessment must be reviewed, updated and re-certified annually until all upgrades, repairs or modifications necessary to achieve regulatory compliance are complete.[467] Areas addressed for drip pads include design and installation of new drip pads, design and operating requirements, inspections, and closure.[468]

7.12 MISCELLANEOUS UNITS

A miscellaneous unit is a hazardous waste management unit where hazardous waste is treated, stored, or disposed of and that is not a container, tank, surface impoundment, pile, land treatment unit, landfill, incinerator, boiler, industrial furnace, or specified underground injection well. A miscellaneous unit may also be a unit eligible for a research, development, and demonstration permit.[469] The regulations for permitted facilities address owners and operators of facilities that treat, store, or dispose of hazardous waste in miscellaneous units.[470] The basic requirement is that a miscellaneous unit must be located, designed, constructed, operated, maintained, and enclosed in a manner that will ensure protection of human health and the environment.[471] Permits for miscellaneous units are to contain such terms and provisions as are necessary to protect human health and the environment, including but not limited to, as appropriate, design and operating requirements, detection and monitoring requirements, requirements for responses to releases of hazardous waste or hazardous constituents from the unit and post-closure care requirements.[472]

8.0 STANDARDS AND REQUIREMENTS FOR SPECIFIC WASTES

This Section will address the management standards that EIB has established for certain recyclable wastes, as found in Part 266 of the regulations, and for hazardous wastes that are restricted from land disposal, as found in Part 268 of the regulations.

---

465 40 C.F.R. §§ 264.571, 265.441.

466 *Id.*

467 *Id.*

468 40 C.F.R. §§ 264.572-575, 265.442-445.

469 40 C.F.R. § 260.10. *See* Other Special Permits, Section 5.24 of this Chapter.

470 40 C.F.R. §§ 264.600 - .603.

471 40 C.F.R. § 264.601.

472 40 C.F.R. §§ 264.600 -.603.

8.1 RECYCLABLE MATERIALS - INTRODUCTION

Hazardous wastes that are recycled, termed "recyclable materials" by the regulations, are subject to the requirements for generators, transporters, and storage facilities unless specifically excluded or unless subject to the special standards.[473] Any waste which is subject to the requirements of Part 266 is not regulated under requirements for generators and transporters of hazardous wastes, or TSDFs handling hazardous wastes, unless Part 266 so provides.[474]

8.1.1 Disposal of Recyclable Materials

Subpart C of Part 266 applies to recyclable materials that are applied to or placed on the land (1) without mixing with any other substance(s) or (2) after mixing or combination with any other substance(s). Such recyclable materials are referred to as "materials used in a manner that constitutes disposal."[475] Subject to the exemptions described below, the following standards apply to materials used in a manner that constitutes disposal: (1) generators and transporters of such materials are subject to the full standards for generators and Transporters of hazardous waste and must fill out EPA Form 8700-12 in order to fulfill notification requirements, (2) owners and operators of facilities which store such materials are subject to the full standards promulgated for hazardous waste storage facilities including permitting procedures and must comply with the notification requirements embodied in the submittal of EPA Form 8700-12, and (3) owners or operators of facilities that use recyclable materials in a manner that constitutes disposal are subject to the general standards for TSDFs,[476] permitting requirements, as well as the notification requirements embodied in EPA Form 8700-12.[477] In addition, the use of waste oil or used oil or other material which is contaminated with dioxin or any other hazardous waste (other than a waste identified solely on the basis of ignitability) for dust suppression or road treatment is prohibited.[478]

Two types of materials are exempted from the special requirements for materials used in a manner constituting disposal. The first exemption covers products produced for the use of the general public that are used in a manner that constitutes disposal and that contain recyclable materials if (a) the recyclable materials have undergone a chemical reaction in the course of producing the product so as to become inseparable by physical means and (b) the product meets the applicable treatment standard in Subpart D of Part 268 (the Land Disposal

---

473 40 C.F.R. § 261.6(a)(1). *See* Exemptions from Permit Requirements, Section 5.25 of this Chapter.

474 40 C.F.R. § 261.6(a)(2).

475 40 C.F.R. § 266.20(a).

476 *See* 40 C.F.R. Parts 264 - 265, Subparts A through N.

477 *See* 40 C.F.R. §§ 266.21 - .23(a).

478 40 C.F.R. § 266.23(b).

Restrictions).[479] The second exemption is for certain commercial fertilizers containing recyclable materials that are produced for the use of the general public.[480]

8.1.2 Used Oil Burned for Energy Recovery

Subpart E of Part 266 applies to used oil that is burned for energy recovery in any boiler or industrial furnace that is not regulated under Subpart O (Incinerators) of Part 264 (Standards for Permitted TSDFs) or 265 (Standards for Interim Status TSDFs), unless exempt. Used oil that is burned for energy recovery, termed "used oil fuel," includes any fuel produced from used oil by processing, blending, or other treatment.[481] Used oil in turn is defined as any oil that has been refined from crude oil, used, and as a result of such use is contaminated by physical or chemical impurities.[482] Used oil burned for energy recovery is subject to regulation under Subpart E of Part 266 rather than as a hazardous waste fuel under Subpart H if it is a hazardous waste solely because it (1) exhibits a characteristic of hazardous waste and thus is a characteristic waste, provided it is not mixed with a hazardous waste,[483] or (2) contains hazardous waste generated only by a person subject to the special requirements for conditionally exempt small quantity generators.[484] Except as provided in the preceding sentence, used oil burned for energy recovery, and any fuel produced from used oil by processing, blending, or other treatment, is subject to regulation under Subpart E unless it is shown not to exceed any of the allowable levels of specified constituents and properties.[485] Used oil that meets these specifications is subject only to specified analysis and recordkeeping requirements.[486]

A number of prohibitions and restrictions apply to used oil fuel, including the following: (1) a person may market off-specification used oil[487] for energy recovery only to burners or other marketers who have provided the required notification to NMED and who have an EPA identification number or to burners who burn the used oil in an industrial

---

479 40 C.F.R. § 266.20(b).

480 *Id.*

481 40 C.F.R. § 266.40(a).

482 40 C.F.R. § 266.40(b).

483 The criteria for the characteristics of hazardous wastes are found in Subpart C of Part 261. *See* Characteristic Wastes Section of this Chapter for discussion of this matter.

484 40 C.F.R. § 266.40(d).

485 40 C.F.R. § 266.40(e),(g).

486 *Id.*

487 The regulations define used oil fuel that exceeds any specification level as "off-specification used oil fuel." 40 C.F.R. § 266.40(e).

furnace or boiler allowed by the regulations[488] and (2) off-specification used oil may be burned for energy recovery only in devices specified by the regulations.[489]

The following standards have been established with respect to used oil fuel: (1) generators who market used oil directly to a burner are subject to the standards applicable to marketers, and generators who burn used oil are subject to the standards applicable to burners of used oil; otherwise, generators are not subject to the standards contained in Subpart E of Part 266;[490] (2) persons who market used oil fuel[491] are subject to notification requirements, an invoice system, and specified recordkeeping practices;[492] and (3) owners and operators of facilities that burn used oil fuel are termed burners by the regulations and are subject to notification, used oil fuel analysis, and recordkeeping requirements.[493] There is one exception to the applicability of the Subpart E regulations to used oil burned for energy recovery involving used oil that is mixed with hazardous waste and burned for energy recovery. Such used oil is subject to regulation as hazardous waste fuel under Subpart H of Part 266,[494] unless it satisfies one of two specified conditions.[495]

8.1.3 Recyclable Materials Utilized for Precious Metal Recovery

Subpart F of Part 266 applies to recyclable materials that are reclaimed to recover economically significant amounts of gold, silver, platinum, palladium, iridium, osmium, rhodium, ruthenium, or any combination of these substances.[496] Persons who generate, transport, or store such recyclable materials are required (1) to notify NMED through use of EPA Form 8700-12 and (2) to observe the manifest requirements for generators, transport-

---

488 40 C.F.R. § 266.41(a).

489 40 C.F.R. § 266.41(b).

490 40 C.F.R. § 266.42.

491 Marketers include generators who market used oil fuel directly to a burner, persons who receive used oils from generators and produce, process or blend used oil fuel from these used oils (including persons sending blended or processed used oil to brokers or other intermediar-ies) and persons who distribute but do not process or blend used oil fuel. 40 C.F.R. § 266.43(a). The regulations also contain two exceptions to this general definition. *Id.*

492 40 C.F.R. § 266.43(b).

493 40 C.F.R. § 266.44.

494 40 C.F.R. § 266.40(c). *See* Hazardous Waste Burned in Boilers and Industrial Furnaces Section of this Chapter.

495 *I.e.*, if it is a hazardous waste solely because it (1) exhibits a characteristic of hazardous waste and thus is a characteristic waste, provided it is not mixed with a hazardous waste, or (2) contains hazardous waste generated only by a person subject to the special requirements for conditionally exempt small quantity generators. 40 C.F.R. § 266.40(d)(1) - (2).

496 40 C.F.R. § 266.70(a).

ers, and storers of such recyclable materials.[497] Persons who store such recycled materials must keep records of the following information to document that they are not accumulating these materials speculatively:[498] (1) the volume of these materials stored at the beginning of the calendar year, (2) the amount of these materials generated or received during the calendar year, and (3) the amount of materials remaining at the end of the calendar year.[499] Recyclable materials that are accumulated speculatively are subject to full regulation for generators, Transporters, and TSDFs handling hazardous waste.[500]

8.1.4 Spent Lead-Acid Batteries Being Reclaimed

Subpart G of Part 266 applies to persons who reclaim spent lead-acid batteries that are recyclable materials; these are referred to as "spent batteries" in the regulations.[501] Persons who generate, transport or collect spent batteries or who store spent batteries but do not reclaim them are not subject to the regulations applicable to generators, Transporters, or TSDFs handling hazardous waste and also are not required to notify NMED through the use of EPA Form 8700-12.[502]

Owners or operators of facilities that store spent batteries before reclaiming them are subject to the following requirements: (1) notification of hazardous waste activity to NMED through the use of EPA Form 8700-12 and (2) all applicable provisions of standards for permitted and interim status TSDFs,[503] excluding the requirements regarding waste analysis and the use of the manifest and manifest discrepancies.[504]

---

497 *See* 40 C.F.R. §§ 262.20 - .23 for generators, §§ 263.20 - .21 for Transporters, and §§ 265.71 -.72 for persons who store.

498 *See* Solid Waste Defined Section of this Chapter for meaning of "accumulated speculatively."

499 40 C.F.R. § 266.70(c).

500 40 C.F.R. § 266.70(d).

501 40 C.F.R. § 266.80(a).

502 *Id.*

503 These provisions include Subparts A-L of 40 C.F.R. Parts 264 and 265. The general subject matter of these Subparts is as follows: A - General, B - General Facility Standards, C - Preparedness and Prevention, D - Contingency Plan and Emergency Procedures, E - Manifest System, Recordkeeping and Reporting, F - Releases from Solid Waste Management Units, G - Closure and Post-Closure, H - Financial Requirements, I - Use and Management of Containers, J - Tank Systems, K - Surface Impoundments, L - Waste Piles.

504 40 C.F.R. § 266.80(b). *See* 40 C.F.R. §§ 264.13 and 265.13 for waste analysis requirements; 40 C.F.R. §§ 264.71 - .72 and 265.71 - .72 for use of the manifest and manifest discrepancies.

8.1.5 Hazardous Waste Burned in Boilers and Industrial Furnaces

Subpart H of Part 266 applies to hazardous waste burned or processed in a boiler[505] or industrial furnace[506] irrespective of the purpose of burning or processing, subject to stated exceptions.[507] The term "burn" means burning for energy recovery or destruction, or processing for materials recovery or as an ingredient.[508]

Hazardous waste in facilities that are not subject to regulation under Subpart H includes: (1) used oil burned for energy recovery that is also a hazardous waste solely because it exhibits a characteristic of hazardous waste;[509] (2) gas recovered from hazardous or solid waste landfills when such gas is burned for energy recovery; (3) hazardous wastes that are specifically exempt from regulation[510] and hazardous wastes that are subject to the special requirements for conditionally exempt small quantity generators; and (4) ovens, if the only hazardous waste burned is EPA hazardous waste No. KO87 (decanter tank tar sludge from coking operations).[511] Owners and operators of specified smelting, melting, and refining furnaces that process hazardous waste solely for metal recovery are conditionally exempt from regulation subject to specified exceptions.[512]

Generators and Transporters of hazardous waste that is burned in a boiler or industrial furnace are subject to full regulation.[513] Owners and operators of facilities that store hazardous waste that is burned in a boiler or industrial furnace are subject to all applic-

---

505 "Boiler" means an enclosed device using controlled flame combustion and having the following characteristics: (1)(a) The unit must have physical provisions for recovering and exporting thermal energy in the form of steam, heated fluids, or heated gases; (b) the unit's combustion chamber and primary energy recovery section(s) must be of integral design; (c) while in operation, the unit must maintain a thermal energy recovery efficiency of at least 60%; and (d) the unit must export and utilize at least 75% of the recovered energy, calculated on an annual basis; or (2) the unit is one which the Secretary has determined, on a case-by-case basis, to be a boiler, after considering specified standards. 40 C.F.R. § 260.10.

506 "Industrial furnace" means any of twelve specified devices that are integral components of manufacturing processes and that use thermal treatment to accomplish recovery of materials or energy. In addition to the specified devices, the Secretary may, after notice and comment, add to the list of approved devices, after considering factors specified in the regulations. 40 C.F.R. § 260.10.

507 40 C.F.R. § 266.100(a).

508 *Id.*

509 Such used oil is subject to regulation under Subpart E of Part 266. 40 C.F. R. § 266.100(b)(1).

510 *See* 40 C.F.R. §§ 261.4, 261.6(a)(3)(v-viii).

511 40 C.F.R. § 266.100(b)(1)-(4).

512 40 C.F.R. § 266.100(c).

513 40 C.F.R. § 266.101(a), (b).

able requirements for permitted or interim status TSDFs.[514] Owners and operators of facilities that burn, in an on-site boiler or industrial furnace exempt from regulation under the small quantity burner provisions, hazardous waste that they generate are exempt from regulation under Subparts A-L of Parts 264 and 265, and Part 270, with respect to the storage of mixtures of hazardous waste and the primary fuel to the boiler or industrial furnace in tanks that feed the fuel mixture directly to the burner.[515]

Subpart H contains detailed regulations that address the following areas: (1) permit standards for burners (2) interim status standards for burners, (3) standards to control organic emissions, (4) standards to control particulate matter, (5) standards to control metals emissions, (6) standards to control hydrogen chloride (HCl) and chlorine gas (CL_2) emissions, (7) an exemption for a small quantity on-site burner, (8) an exemption for low risk waste, (9) a waiver of a destruction and removal efficiency (DRE) trial burn for boilers, (10) standards for direct transfer, and (11) regulation of residues.[516]

8.2 LAND DISPOSAL RESTRICTIONS

40 C.F.R. Part 268 identifies hazardous wastes that are restricted from land disposal and defines those limited circumstances under which an otherwise prohibited waste may continue to be land disposed. The requirements apply to persons who generate or transport hazardous waste and owners and operators of TSDFs.[517] Land disposal is defined as "the placement in or on the land and includes, but is not limited to, placement in a landfill, surface impoundment, waste pile, injection well, land treatment facility, salt dome formation, salt bed formation, underground mine or cave, or placement in a concrete vault or bunker intended for disposal purposes."[518]

The Part 268 regulations were originally promulgated by EPA in response to the 1984 amendments to the RCRA .[519] In these amendments, Congress mandated a ban on land disposal of hazardous wastes, to take effect automatically and according to a set schedule, if EPA did not promulgate treatment standards to diminish the toxicity of the hazardous waste

---

514 40 C.F.R. § 266.101(c). Applicable requirements are found in 40 C.F.R. Part 264, Subparts A-L and 40 C.F.R. Part 265, Subparts A-L and Part 270, dealing with permit requirements. These standards apply to storage by the burner as well as to storage facilities operated by intermediaries (processors, blenders, distributors, etc.) between the generator and the burner. *Id.*

515 40 C.F.R. § 266.101(c)(2). However, storage of hazardous waste prior to mixing with the primary fuel is subject to regulation under Subparts A-L of Parts 264 and 265, and Part 270. *Id.*

516 40 C.F.R. §§ 266.102-.112.

517 40 C.F.R. § 268.1(b).

518 40 C.F.R. § 268.2(a).

519 RCRA § 3004(m); 42 U.S.C. § 6924(m).

or to reduce substantially the likelihood that the hazardous constituents of the waste would enter the environment.[520] EPA promulgated regulations pursuant to the mandate of Congress and restricted the land disposal of hazardous wastes, unless certain conditions could be met, in accordance with the timetable specified by Congress. EIB has adopted *in toto* EPA's Part 268 regulations restricting land disposal of hazardous waste.

8.2.1 Exceptions to Land Disposal Restrictions

Exceptions to the restrictions against land disposal of hazardous waste include (1) persons generating, treating, storing, or disposing of a hazardous waste who have been granted an extension to the effective date of a prohibition by applying for and receiving from the Secretary an extension of up to one year, subject to renewal for a second year, to continue to land dispose the prohibited waste,[521] (2) persons who have been granted an exemption from a prohibition by submitting a petition to the Secretary demonstrating, to a reasonable degree of certainty, that there will be no migration of hazardous constituents from the disposal unit or injection zone for as long as the wastes remain hazardous,[522] (3) wastes that are hazardous only because they exhibit a hazardous characteristic, if the wastes are disposed into a non-hazardous or hazardous injection well pursuant to EPA's regulations under its underground injection control program and if such wastes do not exhibit any prohibited characteristic of hazardous waste at the point of injection,[523] (4) wastes generated by small quantity generators of less than 100 kg of non-acute hazardous waste per month or less than 1 kg of acute hazardous waste per month,[524] (5) farmers disposing of waste pesticides,[525] (6) waste identified or listed as hazardous after November 8, 1984, for which NMED has not promulgated land disposal prohibitions or treatment standards,[526] and (7) wastes otherwise prohibited from land disposal which are treated in a surface impoundment or series of impoundments provided certain technical requirements are complied with.[527] The requirements of the land disposal restrictions are not to affect the availability of a waiver under

---

520 *Id.*

521 40 C.F.R. § 268.1(c)(1). 40 C.F.R. § 268.5 provides the procedures whereby such an extension may be applied for and, if approved, received.

522 40 C.F.R. § 268.1(c)(2). 40 C.F.R. § 268.6 provides the procedures for applying for this petition and defines the standards under which such a petition will be reviewed.

523 40 C.F.R. § 268.1(c)(3).

524 40 C.F.R. § 268.1(e)(1).

525 40 C.F.R. § 268.1(e)(2). *See* the Farmers and Waste Section of this Chapter.

526 40 C.F.R. § 268.1(e)(3).

527 40 C.F.R. § 268.4.

Section 121(d)(4) of the Comprehensive Environmental Response, Compensation and Liability Act of 1980.[528]

8.2.2 Dilution Prohibition

Dilution as a substitute for treatment of a waste restricted from land disposal is prohibited, with one exception.[529] Dilution of wastes that are hazardous only because they exhibit a characteristic in a treatment system which treats wastes subsequently discharged to a water of the United States pursuant to a permit issued under section 402 of the Clean Water Act or which treats wastes for purposes of pretreatment requirements under section 307 of the Clean Water Act is not impermissible dilution unless a method has been specified as the treatment standard in the regulations, or unless the waste is a D003 reactive cyanide wastewater or non-wastewater.[530]

8.2.3 Waste Analysis

Subject to a limited exception,[531] if a generator's waste is a listed waste, a generator must test the waste or test an extract using an approved method, or use knowledge of the waste, to determine if the waste is restricted from the land disposal. Subject to the same limited exception, if a generator's waste exhibits one or more of the characteristics set out at 40 C.F.R. Part 261, Subpart C (a characteristic waste), the generator must test an extract used in the test method prescribed, or use knowledge of the waste, to determine if the waste is restricted from land disposal.[532] If the generator determines that the waste being managed does not meet the applicable treatment standards or exceeds applicable prohibition levels, the generator must with each shipment of the waste notify the treatment or storage facility in writing of the appropriate treatment standards. The notice should include the EPA hazardous waste number and, with certain exceptions, the treatment standards for the restricted waste may be referenced by including on the notification the subcategory and subdivision of the waste, the treatability group(s) of the waste(s), the C.F.R. section(s) and paragraphs where the treatment standards appear, the manifest number associated with the shipment of the waste, and waste analysis data, where available.[533] If the generator determines that the managed waste can be land disposed without further treatment the generator must certify that the waste meets the applicable treatment standard as set forth in the land disposal restrictions.[534] The regulations contain specific requirements for generators handling waste

---

[528] 42 U.S.C. § 9621(d)(4). *See* 40 C.F.R. § 268.1(d).

[529] 40 C.F.R. § 268.3(a).

[530] 40 C.F.R. § 268.3(b).

[531] *See* 40 C.F.R. § 268.32.

[532] 40 C.F.R. § 268.7(a).

[533] 40 C.F.R. § 268.7(a)(1).

[534] 40 C.F.R. § 268.7(a)(2).

exempt from land disposal restrictions, for waste managed in tanks or containers, and for lab packs.[535] Certain recordkeeping practices are required to be observed.[536]

Treatment facilities must test their waste according to the frequency specified in their waste analysis plans as required by the regulations.[537] Treatment facilities are also required to submit certifications to the land disposal facility stating that the waste or treatment residue conforms to the requirements of the regulations.[538] If the waste or treatment residue will be further managed at a different treatment or storage facility, the treatment, storage or disposal facility sending the waste or treatment residue off-site must comply with the notice and certification requirements applicable to generators.[539]

8.2.4 Special Rules Regarding Wastes Exhibiting a Characteristic

The initial generator of a solid waste must determine each EPA Hazardous Waste Number (waste code) applicable to the waste in order to determine the applicable treatment standards under the land disposal restrictions.[540] The waste will carry the waste code for any applicable listing under the listed waste category. In addition, the waste will carry one or more of the waste codes under the characteristic waste category, except in the case when the treatment standard for the listed waste operates in lieu of the standard for the characteristic waste.[541] Where a prohibited waste is both listed and exhibits a characteristic, the treatment standard for the waste code listed in Subpart D (listed waste) will operate in lieu of the standard for the Subpart C (characteristic waste), provided the treatment standard for the listed waste includes a treatment standard for the constituent that caused the waste to exhibit the characteristic; otherwise the waste must meet the treatment standards for all applicable listed and characteristic codes.[542] In addition to any applicable standards determined from the initial point of generation, no prohibited characteristic waste may be land disposed unless the waste complies with the treatment standards set forth in the land disposal restrictions.[543] Finally, wastes that exhibit a characteristic are also subject to specified waste analysis, notification, and recordkeeping requirements, except that once the waste is no longer hazardous, for each shipment of such waste to a subtitle D facility (solid waste facility), the initial generator

---

535 40 C.F.R. § 268.7(a)(3) - (10).

536 *Id.*

537 40 C.F.R. § 268.7(b). *See* Waste Analysis under TSDF General Standards Section of this Chapter.

538 40 C.F.R. § 268.7(b)(5).

539 40 C.F.R. § 268.7(b)(6).

540 40 C.F.R. § 268.9(a).

541 *Id.*

542 40 C.F.R. § 268.9(b).

543 40 C.F.R. § 268.9(c).

or the treatment facility need not meet the specified waste analysis, notification and record-keeping requirements, provided certain other requirements are satisfied.[544]

8.2.5 Land Disposal Prohibition and Treatment Standards

A schedule is established for reviewing the listed wastes subject to restrictions on land disposal and for establishing treatment standards for such wastes. Three groups of specified wastes are mandated to be evaluated by specified deadlines. The first group of wastes was to be evaluated by August 8, 1988,[545] the second group by June 8, 1989,[546] and the third group by May 8, 1990.[547] The third group also includes waste identified as hazardous based on a characteristic alone, along with other specified wastes.[548]

8.2.6 Prohibitions on Land Disposal

Treatment standards and effective dates for land disposal prohibitions are established for certain (1) solvent wastes, subject to certain exceptions governing both type of waste and date of disposal prohibition,[549] (2) dioxin-containing wastes, subject to certain exceptions governing both type of waste and date of disposal prohibition,[550] and (3) wastes identified as "California list wastes", subject to certain conditions and exemptions.[551] Unless specified treatment standards are met, land disposal prohibitions are established that are specific to certain identified hazardous wastes, commonly referred to under groupings as the "First Third Wastes," the "Second Third Wastes," and the "Third Third Wastes."[552]

8.2.7 Treatment Standards

There are three types of treatment standards for hazardous wastes restricted from land disposal, each of which applies to a particular set of wastes. These treatment standards include treatment standards expressed as concentrations in waste extract,[553] treatment standards expressed as specified technologies,[554] and treatment standards expressed as waste concentrations.[555] If the appropriate standard is met, the waste can be disposed of on land.

---

544 40 C.F.R. § 268.9(d).

545 40 C.F.R. § 268.10.

546 40 C.F.R. § 268.11.

547 40 C.F.R. § 268.12(a).

548 40 C.F.R. § 268.12(b) - (g).

549 40 C.F.R. § 268.30.

550 40 C.F.R. § 268.31.

551 40 C.F.R. § 268.32.

552 40 C.F.R. § 268.33 - .35.

553 40 C.F.R. § 268.41.

554 40 C.F.R. § 268.42.

555 40 C.F.R. § 268.43.

A petition to the Secretary for a variance from the treatment standards under specified conditions is allowed.[556]

8.2.8 Prohibitions on Storage

The storage of hazardous wastes restricted from land disposal is prohibited unless certain conditions are met, including (1) a generator must store such wastes in tanks or containers on-site solely for the purpose of accumulating such quantities of hazardous waste as are necessary to facilitate proper recovery, treatment, or disposal and must comply with the requirements governing accumulation of waste on-site,[557] (2) (a) an owner or operator of a hazardous waste TSDF must store such wastes in tanks or containers solely to accumulate sufficient quantities of hazardous waste to facilitate proper recovery, treatment, or disposal, (b) each container must be clearly marked to identify its contents and the date each period of accumulation begins, (c) each tank must be clearly marked with a description of its contents, the quantity of each hazardous waste received, and the date such period of accumulation begins, or such information for the tank must be maintained in the facility operating record, and (d) the owner or operator must comply with EIB's facility operating record requirements,[558] and (3) a Transporter must store manifested shipments of such wastes at a transfer facility for 10 days or less.[559] The regulations also provide in specified circumstances certain exceptions to the prohibition against storing hazardous wastes restricted from land disposal.[560]

9.0 ENFORCEMENT MECHANISMS

NMED has a wide range of mechanisms to insure compliance with and enforcement of the elements of the hazardous waste program established by the HWA and the regulations promulgated thereunder. These compliance mechanisms and enforcement mechanisms are discussed below.

9.1 RIGHT OF ENTRY AND AVAILABILITY OF RECORDS

For the purposes of developing or assisting in the development of any regulations, conducting any study, taking any corrective action, or enforcing the provisions of the HWA, upon request of the Secretary or the Secretary's authorized representative, any person who generates, stores, treats, transports, disposes of or otherwise handles or has handled hazardous wastes must furnish information relating to such hazardous wastes and permit the Secretary or the Secretary's authorized representative (1) to enter at reasonable times any establishment

---

556 40 C.F.R. § 268.44.

557 40 C.F.R. § 268.50(a)(1). *See* Classes of Generators Section and the Sections immediately following for a description of these requirements.

558 40 C.F.R. § 268.50(a)(2).

559 40 C.F.R. § 268.50(a)(3).

560 40 C.F.R. § 268.50(c) - (f).

or other place maintained by any person where hazardous wastes are or have been generated, stored, treated, disposed of, or transported from or where an underground storage tank is located[561] and (2) to inspect and obtain samples from any person of any hazardous wastes and samples of any containers or labeling for the wastes.[562] Any person owning property to which access is necessary in order to investigate or clean up a facility where hazardous waste is generated, stored, treated or disposed of, or where underground storage tanks are located, must permit the Secretary or the Secretary's authorized representative to obtain samples of soil or ground water or both, at reasonable times, and shall provide access to such property for structures or equipment necessary to the monitoring or cleanup of hazardous wastes or leakage from underground storage tanks under the condition that such structures or equipment do not unreasonably interfere with the owner's use of the property, or else the owner is entitled to compensation for such interference.[563]

Each inspection performed by the Secretary or the Secretary's authorized representative is to be commenced and completed with reasonable promptness.[564] If the Secretary or the Secretary's representative obtains any samples, the owner, operator or agent in charge must be given a receipt describing the sample prior to leaving the premises and, if requested, a portion of each sample equal in volume or weight to the portion retained must be furnished. If analysis is made of the samples, a copy of the results of the analysis is to be given to the owner, operator, or agent in charge.[565]

Any records, reports or information obtained by NMED pursuant to the aforementioned powers of inspection are available to the public. However, a confidentiality exception to such materials is available upon a showing satisfactory to NMED that such materials or a particular part thereof, if made public, would divulge information entitled to protection under Section 1905 of Title 18 of the United States Code.[566] In submitting data under the HWA, a person required to provide such data may identify the data that the person believes is entitled to confidentiality and submit this data separately from other data submitted under the HWA. A designation of confidentiality must be made in writing and in such manner as the

---

[561] The New Mexico Court of Appeals has ruled that in the event consent to enter and inspect a premises for compliance is denied, an administrative search warrant is required. *New Mexico Envtl. Improvement Div. v. Climax Chem. Co.*, 105 N.M. 439, 733 P.2d 1322 (Ct. App. 1987).

[562] N.M. Stat. Ann. § 74-4-4.3(A)(1) (Repl. Pamp. 1993).

[563] N.M. Stat. Ann. § 74-4-4.3(B) (Repl. Pamp. 1993).

[564] N.M. Stat. Ann. § 74-4-4.3(C) (Repl. Pamp. 1993).

[565] *Id.*

[566] N.M. Stat. Ann. § 74-4-4.3(D) (Repl. Pamp. 1993). There also exists an exception to this exception. Such materials may be disclosed to officers, employees, or authorized representatives of the United States concerned with carrying out the RCRA , or when relevant in any proceedings under HWA. *Id.*

Secretary may prescribe.[567] Any person not subject to the provisions of Section 1905 of Title 18 of the United States Code who knowingly and willfully divulges or discloses any information entitled to confidentiality is subject, upon conviction, to a fine of not more than $5,000 or to imprisonment not to exceed one year, or both.[568]

9.2 HAZARDOUS WASTE FUNDS

The HWA creates two separate funds in the state treasury related to the purposes of the Hazardous Waste Act. The Hazardous Waste Fund (HWF) was created to meet necessary expenses in the administration and operation of the hazardous waste and underground storage tank programs. Funds for the HWF are generated pursuant to a schedule of fees for businesses generating hazardous waste (that is to be developed by EIB), and in accordance with an existing schedule of fees for businesses seeking a permit for management of hazardous waste.[569]

The Hazardous Waste Emergency Fund (HWEF) is to be used for cleanup of hazardous substance incidents, disposal of hazardous substances, and necessary repairs to or replacement of state property. The HWEF may also be used for the state's share of any response action taken under the Comprehensive Environmental Response, Compensation and Liability Act of 1980.[570] Amounts received in payment of assessed charges against persons responsible for hazardous substance incidents for costs NMED incurs in cleanup of hazardous substance incidents, disposal of hazardous substances, and for damages to state property are a source of income for HWEF, along with penalties collected pursuant to an administrative order.[571]

9.3 ENFORCEMENT - COMPLIANCE ORDERS

The HWA grants broad enforcement powers to the Secretary. Whenever the Secretary determines on the basis of any information that any person has violated, is violating, or threatens to violate any requirement of the HWA, any regulation promulgated pursuant to the HWA, or any condition of a permit issued under the HWA, the Secretary may (1) issue a compliance order stating with reasonable specificity in nature of the violation or threatened violation and requiring compliance immediately or within a specified time period or assessing

---

567 N.M. Stat. Ann. § 74-4-4.3(F) (Repl. Pamp. 1993).

568 N.M. Stat. Ann. § 74-4-4.3(E) (Repl. Pamp. 1993).

569 N.M. Stat. Ann. § 74-4-4.5 (Repl. Pamp. 1993). *See* Hazardous Waste Fees Subsection of this Chapter.

570 40 U.S.C. §§ 9601-9675. In addition, the administrative and technical expenses of maintaining an emergency response program within NMED will be reimbursable on a quarterly basis from HWEF. Any penalties collected by NMED shall be credited to HWEF. N.M. Stat. Ann. § 74-4-8 (Repl. Pamp. 1993).

571 N.M. Stat. Ann. §§ 74-4-7(C), -10(J) (Repl. Pamp. 1993).

a civil penalty for any past or current violation, or both, or (2) commence a civil action in district court for appropriate relief, including a temporary or permanent injunction.[572]

Any order issued in the circumstances described above may include a suspension or revocation of any permit issued by the Secretary. Any penalty assessed in the order shall not exceed $10,000 per day of noncompliance for each violation. In assessing the penalty, the Secretary is required to take into account the seriousness of the violation and any good-faith efforts to comply with the applicable requirements.[573]

If a violator fails to take corrective action within the time specified in the compliance order, the Secretary may (1) assess a civil penalty of not more than $25,000 for each day of continued noncompliance with the order and (2) suspend or revoke any permit issued to the violator pursuant to the HWA.[574]

If a research, development, and demonstration permit previously has been granted, the Secretary is authorized to order an immediate termination of all research, development, and demonstration operations upon the determination that immediate termination is necessary to protect human health and the environment.[575]

Whenever, on the basis of any information, the Secretary determines that there is or has been a release of hazardous waste into the environment from an interim status TSDF, the Secretary may issue an order requiring corrective action, including corrective action beyond the facility's boundaries or such other response as deemed necessary to protect human health and the environment.[576] Such an order may include a suspension or revocation of authorization to operate as an interim status facility, shall state with reasonable specificity the nature of the required corrective action or other response measure, and shall specify a time for compliance.[577] Alternatively, the Secretary may commence an action in District Court in the district in which the facility is located for appropriate relief, including a temporary or permanent injunction.[578] If the Secretary issues an order and the person fails to comply with the order, the Secretary may assess a civil penalty in an amount not to exceed $10,000 for each day of noncompliance.[579]

An order or enforcement proceeding described above, or any claim for personal or property injury arising from any conduct for which evidence of financial responsibility must

---

[572] N.M. Stat. Ann. § 74-4-10(A) (Repl. Pamp. 1993).

[573] N.M. Stat. Ann. § 74-4-10(B) (Repl. Pamp. 1993). For violations related to underground storage tanks, "per violation" means per tank. *Id.*

[574] N.M. Stat. Ann. § 74-4-10(C) (Repl. Pamp. 1993).

[575] N.M. Stat. Ann. § 74-4-10(D) (Repl. Pamp. 1993).

[576] N.M. Stat. Ann. § 74-4-10(E) (Repl. Pamp. 1993).

[577] N.M. Stat. Ann. § 74-4-10(F) (Repl. Pamp. 1993).

[578] N.M. Stat. Ann. § 74-4-10(E) (Repl. Pamp. 1993).

[579] N.M. Stat. Ann. § 74-4-10(F) (Repl. Pamp. 1993).

be provided, may be issued to or taken against the insurer or guarantor of an owner or operator of a TSDF or underground storage tank if (1) the owner or operator is in bankruptcy, reorganization, or arrangement pursuant to the federal bankruptcy code, or (2) jurisdiction in any state or federal court cannot by reasonable diligence be obtained over an owner or operator likely to be solvent at the time of judgment.[580] Any such order by the Secretary becomes final unless, no later than 30 days after the order was served, the person or persons named in the order submit a written request to the Secretary for a public hearing.[581] Upon such request, the Secretary must promptly conduct a public hearing and shall appoint an independent hearing officer to preside over the hearing.[582] The hearing officer is required to make and preserve a complete record of the proceedings and forward a recommendation based on the record to the Secretary, who must make the final decision.[583] The Secretary is empowered by the HWA in connection with any such proceeding to issue subpoenas for the attendance and testimony of witnesses and the production of relevant papers, books, and documents and may promulgate rules for discovery procedures.[584] The Secretary has promulgated detailed rules governing appeals from compliance orders, including rules for discovery procedures.[585]

9.4 MONITORING, ANALYSIS AND TESTING

The Secretary is authorized to require hazardous waste monitoring, analysis and testing under certain circumstances. Specifically, if the Secretary determines that (1) the presence of any hazardous waste at a facility or site at which hazardous waste is or has been stored, treated or disposed of or (2) the release of any such waste from such facility or site may present a substantial hazard to human health or the environment, the Secretary may issue an order requiring the owner or operator of the facility to conduct such monitoring, testing, analysis, and reporting with respect to the facility or site as the Secretary deems reasonable to ascertain the nature and extent of the hazard.[586] In the case of any facility or site not in operation at the time a determination is made under the above conditions, if the Secretary finds that the owner of the facility or site could not reasonably be expected to have actual

---

580 N.M. Stat. Ann. § 74-4-10(G) (Repl. Pamp. 1993).

581 N.M. Stat. Ann. § 74-4-10(H) (Repl. Pamp. 1993).

582 *Id.*

583 *Id.*

584 N.M. Stat. Ann. § 74-4-10(I) (Repl. Pamp. 1993).

585 Rules Governing Appeals from Compliance Orders Under the Hazardous Waste Act and the Solid Waste Act. HED 90-10 (EID) (filed Oct. 16, 1990). These Rules consist of six Parts: Part I - General Provisions, Part II - Document Requirements, Part III - Prehearing Procedures and Discovery, Part IV - Hearing Procedures, Part V - Post-Hearing Procedures, and Part VI - Miscellaneous Provisions.

586 N.M. Stat. Ann. § 74-4-10.1(A) (Repl. Pamp. 1993).

knowledge of the presence of hazardous waste at the facility or site and of its potential for release, the Secretary may issue an order requiring the most recent previous owner or operator of the facility or site who could reasonably be expected to have actual knowledge to carry out the monitoring, testing, analysis, and reporting.[587] A person to whom such an order has been issued must submit to the Secretary, within 30 days from the issuance of the order, a proposal for carrying out the required monitoring, testing, analysis, and reporting.[588] In response the Secretary may, after providing the person with an opportunity to confer with the Secretary respecting the proposal, require the person to carry out such monitoring, testing, analysis, and reporting in accordance with the proposal and such modifications in the proposal as the Secretary deems reasonable to ascertain the nature and extent of the hazard.[589]

NMED may conduct the monitoring, testing, or analysis or any combination thereof, or may authorize a local authority or other person to carry out any such action, under three sets of circumstances: (1) if the Secretary determines that no owner or operator is able to conduct monitoring, testing, analysis, or reporting satisfactory to the Secretary; (2) if the Secretary deems any such action carried out by the owner or operator to be unsatisfactory; or (3) if the Secretary cannot initially determine whether there is an owner or operator who is able to conduct such monitoring, testing, analysis, or reporting.[590] In the event that NMED itself conducts the monitoring, testing, or analysis or authorizes a local authority or other person to carry out these actions, the Secretary may require, by order, the owner or operator of the site (or the most recent previous owner or operator as described above) to reimburse NMED or other authority or person for the costs of such activity. Any reimbursement to NMED is to be deposited to the credit of the Hazardous Waste Fund.[591]

The Secretary may commence a civil action to enforce such an order against any person who fails or refuses to comply with monitoring, testing, analysis and reporting requirements. Such an action must be brought in the district court of the county in which the defendant is located, resides, or is doing business. The court has jurisdiction to require compliance with the order and to assess a civil penalty not to exceed $5,000 for each day during which the failure or refusal occurs.[592]

9.5 PENALTY - CRIMINAL

There are four types of criminal violations of the HWA. The first violation involves any person who knowingly violates any major element of the hazardous waste program and

---

587 N.M. Stat. Ann. § 74-4-10.1(B) (Repl. Pamp. 1993).

588 N.M. Stat. Ann. § 74-4-10.1(C) (Repl. Pamp. 1993).

589 *Id.*

590 N.M. Stat. Ann. § 74-4-10.1(D) (Repl. Pamp. 1993).

591 *Id.*

592 N.M. Stat. Ann. § 74-4-10.1(E) (Repl. Pamp. 1993).

the regulations promulgated thereunder, including but not limited to (1) transporting hazardous waste to a non-permitted facility, (2) treating, storing, or disposing of hazardous waste without a permit, in violation of a permit, or in violation of interim status regulations, (3) omitting material information or making a false statement or representation in an application, label, manifest, record, report, permit, or other filed document, (4) destroying, altering, concealing or failing to file required documents, (5) transporting hazardous waste without a manifest, or (6) improperly exporting hazardous waste.[593] Such a person, upon conviction, is guilty of a fourth degree felony and will be punished by a fine of not more than $10,000 per violation per day or by imprisonment for a definite term of not more than eighteen months, or both. For a second conviction, such a person is guilty of a third degree felony and will be punished by a fine of not more than $25,000 per violation per day or by imprisonment for not more than three years, or both.[594]

The second violation involves any person who knowingly transports, treats, stores, disposes of or exports any hazardous waste in violation of (1) - (6) as described above and who knows at the time of the violation that such person creates a substantial danger of death or serious bodily injury to another person. Such a violator is guilty of a second degree felony and will be sentenced to a term of imprisonment not to exceed nine years or a fine not to exceed $100,000, or both. Any person other than an individual that knowingly transports, treats, stores, disposes of or exports any hazardous waste in violation of (1) - (6) as described above and knows at that time that it places an individual in imminent danger of death or serious bodily injury is guilty of a second degree felony and shall be fined in an amount not to exceed $250,000.[595]

The third violation involves any person who knowingly violates any underground storage tank regulation. Such a person is guilty of a misdemeanor and upon conviction will be punished by a fine of not more than $5,000 per violation per day or by imprisonment for a definite term of one year or both.[596]

The fourth violation involves any person who knowingly transports, treats, stores, disposes of or exports any hazardous waste in violation of (1) - (6) as described above, and who knows at the time of the violation that such person creates a substantial danger of a substantial adverse environmental impact, is guilty of a third degree felony if the violation causes a substantial environmental impact.[597] A "substantial adverse environmental impact" exists when an act or omission of a person causes harm or damage to (1) human beings, or

---

593 N.M. Stat. Ann. § 74-4-11(A) (Repl. Pamp. 1993).

594 N.M. Stat. Ann § 74-4-11(B) (Repl. Pamp. 1993).

595 N.M. Stat. Ann § 74-4-11(F) (Repl. Pamp. 1993).

596 N.M. Stat. Ann. § 74-4-11(C) (Repl. Pamp. 1993). For violations related to underground storage tanks "per violation" means per tank. *Id.*

597 N.M. Stat. Ann. § 74-4-11(D) (Repl. Pamp. 1993).

(2) to flora, wildlife, fish or other aquatic life or water fowl; to the habitats of wildlife, fish, other aquatic life, water fowl or livestock; to agricultural crops; to any ground water or surface water; or to the lands and waters of the state where such harm or damage amounts to more than $10,000.[598]

9.6 PENALTY - CIVIL

Any person who violates any provision of the HWA, any regulation made pursuant to the HWA, or any compliance order may be assessed a civil penalty not to exceed $10,000 for each day during any portion of which a violation occurs.[599]

9.7 IMMINENT HAZARDS

Whenever the Secretary receives evidence that the past or current handling, storage, treatment, transportation, or disposal of any solid waste or hazardous waste or the condition or maintenance of any underground storage tank may present an imminent and substantial endangerment to health or the environment, the Secretary may bring suit in the appropriate district court against any person, including any past or present generator, past or present Transporter, or past or present owner or operator of a treatment, storage, or disposal facility who has contributed or is contributing to such activity, to restrain such person immediately or to require the person to take such other action as may be necessary, or both.[600] If the transportation of such waste was under a sole contractual arrangement arising from a published tariff and acceptance for carriage by common carrier by rail and the Transporter exercised due care in the past or present handling, storage, treatment, transportation, and disposal of such waste, then the Transporter shall not be deemed to have contributed or be contributing to the handling, storage, treatment, or disposal taking place after the solid waste or hazardous waste has left the possession or control of the Transporter.[601]

Any person who willfully violates or fails or refuses to comply with any order of the Secretary described in the above paragraph may, in an action brought in the appropriate district court to enforce such order, be fined not more than $5,000 for each day in which the violation occurs or the failure to comply continues.[602]

The Secretary is mandated, upon receipt of information that there is a hazardous waste at any site which has presented an imminent and substantial endangerment to human health or the environment, to provide immediate notice to the appropriate local government

---

598 N.M. Stat. Ann. § 74-4-11(E) (Repl. Pamp. 1993).

599 N.M. Stat. Ann. § 74-4-12 (Repl. Pamp. 1993). For violations related to underground storage tanks, "per violation" means per tank. *Id.*

600 N.M. Stat. Ann. § 74-4-13(A) (Repl. Pamp. 1993).

601 *Id.*

602 N.M. Stat. Ann. § 74-4-13(B) (Repl. Pamp. 1993).

agencies of such endangerment. In addition, the Secretary shall require notice of endangerment to be promptly posted at the site where the waste is located.[603]

10.0 NATURAL RESOURCES TRUSTEE AND AGREEMENTS WITH FEDERAL AGENCIES

The State of New Mexico has no legislation or regulations that correspond to the federal Comprehensive Environmental Response, Compensation, and Liability Act of 1980 (CERCLA) (commonly referred to as the "Superfund Act"),[604] as amended by the Superfund Amendments and Reauthorization Act of 1986 (SARA),[605] and EPA regulations[606] - promulgated thereunder. However, on April 7, 1993, the 1993 New Mexico Legislature enacted the Natural Resources Trustee Act, effective immediately. This Act created the position of Natural Resources Trustee whose responsibilities include representing the state's interest under applicable federal laws, including CERCLA as amended by SARA, regarding injury to, destruction of, or loss of natural resources in the state.[607]

NMED has entered into three agreements with EPA whereby the Groundwater Protection and Remediation Bureau under its own Superfund Program administers a portion of the Federal Superfund Program. NMED also has entered into agreements with the Department of Defense, the Department of Energy and the Bureau of Land Management that address NMED's oversight responsibilities with regard to facilities and lands subject to the jurisdiction of these three federal agencies.

10.1 AGREEMENTS WITH EPA

The first agreement, a Multi-Site Cooperative Agreement (MSCA), allows NMED to assist EPA in evaluating potential hazardous waste sites in New Mexico, identifying those sites which require remedial action under the CERCLA and the SARA, performing early stage remedial investigation and feasibility tasks, and reviewing and evaluating remedial investigation, feasibility study, and remedial design work at National Priorities List (NPL) sites. This agreement was first signed in 1986 and has been renewed annually. The current MSCA expires in 1994.

The second agreement, the Core Program Cooperative Agreement (CPCA), funds non-site-specific management activities and cost recovery activities. This agreement provides the state with EPA approval to manage, administer, and plan the MSCA and to improve

---

603 N.M. Stat. Ann. § 74-4-13(C) (Repl. Pamp. 1993).

604 42 U.S.C. §§ 9601-9675.

605 Pub. L. No. 99-499, 100 Stat. 1613 (1986).

606 40 C.F.R. Parts 300 - 372.

607 N.M. Stat. Ann. § 75-7-2(A) (Repl. Pamp. 1991 & Supp. 1993). Refer to Section 5.0 of Chapter X, Additional Environmental Laws, for more information regarding the duties of the Natural Resources Trustee.

existing mechanisms to meet the complex financial recordkeeping and reporting requirements of the MSCA. The CPCA authorizes NMED to oversee, supervise, plan, and write the Hazardous Waste Capacity Assurance Plan (CAP). The CPCA also provides funds to enable NMED Superfund staff to have access to legal opinions or interpretations regarding special studies, wastes, the CERCLA petroleum exclusion, state and federal compliance with the National Oil and Hazardous Substances Pollution Contingency Plan (NCP), preparation of an interstate agreement as part of New Mexico's CAP, determination of Applicable or Relevant and Appropriate Requirements (ARARs) and other provisions of the CERCLA, the SARA, and the NCP. This agreement was first signed in 1988 and has been renewed annually. The current agreement expires in 1994.

The third agreement, the Site-Specific Cooperative Agreement (SSCA) provides funding and authority for NMED to conduct a Remedial Investigation and Feasibility Study (RI/FS) at the Cleveland Mill NPL site. The SSCA permits NMED to hire contractors to perform site characterization, environmental risk assessment, feasibility studies, and community relations, and provides mechanisms for NMED to oversee the contractor's work. The SSCA was signed in 1990 and it is anticipated that it will remain in effect through 1994.

The three agreements provide for the majority of the funding of the Superfund Program of the Ground Water Protection and Remediation Bureau; the remaining funding for the Section comes from the State's general fund.

The State of New Mexico currently has 9 NPL sites and two additional sites proposed for such listing. The nine NPL sites are: (1) Atchison, Topeka & Santa Fe site in Clovis, Curry County; (2) Cal West Metals site in Lemitar, Socorro County; (3) Cimarron Mining & Milling site in Carrizozo, Lincoln County; (4) Cleveland Mill site near Silver City, Grant County; (5) Homestake Mining Company site near Milan, Cibola County; (6) Lee Acres Landfill site near Farmington, San Juan County; (7) Prewitt Refinery site in Prewitt, McKinley County; (8) South Valley site in Albuquerque, Bernalillo County; and (9) United Nuclear Corporation site in Church Rock, McKinley County.

10.2 AGREEMENT WITH DEPARTMENT OF DEFENSE

In June of 1990 the State of New Mexico signed a Memorandum of Agreement (MOA) with the Defense Department which provides an explicit mechanism for state oversight of the Department of Defense's equivalent to Superfund environmental remediation, the Installation Restoration Program. Pursuant to the MOA, the state's comments are requested on specific work plans and contract documents, and a formal mechanism is provided to ensure that remedial actions comply with state regulations. Provision is also made for reimbursement of most state costs incurred in connection with oversight of the Installation Restoration Program.

The Agreement applies to Installation Restoration Program activities at Holloman, Cannon, and Kirtland Air Force Bases, Melrose Air Force Range, Air Force Plant 83 in Albuquerque, Fort Wingate Army Depot, the portion of Fort Bliss that extends into New

Mexico, and White Sands Missile Range. The Agreement also applies to remedial actions at formerly used Defense Department sites, the currently most active of which is the former Walker Air Force Base near Roswell, New Mexico. Primary responsibility for implementation of the MOA has been delegated to the Ground Water Protection and Remediation Bureau, although considerable coordination among several NMED Bureaus is also required.

10.3 AGREEMENT WITH DEPARTMENT OF ENERGY

In October, 1990 the State of New Mexico signed an Agreement in Principle (AIP) with the Department of Energy (DOE) to provide for state oversight of DOE facilities located in New Mexico. The Oversight program established under the AIP involves four bureaus of NMED: the Air Quality Bureau, the Ground Water Protection and Remediation Bureau, the Hazardous and Radioactive Materials Bureau and the Surface Water Quality Bureau. The AIP not only specifies oversight and monitoring tasks to be performed by NMED but also specifies "deliverables" (specific assessments/evaluations or information) to be completed by NMED and DOE. DOE facilities included under the AIP in New Mexico are the Inhalation Toxicology Research Institute, Los Alamos National Laboratory, Sandia National Laboratory and the Waste Isolation Pilot Plant (WIPP). Under the Oversight Program state AIP technical staff, instead of functioning in a regulatory role, offers technical comment and guidance on regulatory compliance to the DOE facilities.

10.4 AGREEMENT WITH THE BUREAU OF LAND MANAGEMENT

In April, 1993 the State of New Mexico signed a Cooperative Agreement (CA) with the Bureau of Land Management (BLM) to provide for a cooperative program for the management of hazardous materials and hazardous waste consistent with the CERCLA, the SARA, the NCP, the RCRA , and New Mexico State law, on BLM managed public lands in the state. Pursuant to the CA, BLM provides funding to NMED, and NMED provides technical and regulatory input on BLM hazardous materials management issues in order to accomplish timely evaluation and cleanup of sites. Primary responsibility for the CA's implementation has been delegated to the Ground Water Protection and Remediation Bureau, Remediation Section. The CA requires yearly renewal by both parties and such renewals are expected to extend the life of the CA until September 30, 1998.

CHAPTER VI
UNDERGROUND STORAGE TANK MANAGEMENT

1.0 INTRODUCTION

The history of underground storage tank (UST) management in New Mexico is both complicated and evolving. This Introduction will describe the history of UST regulation, while the balance of this Chapter will outline the regulatory scheme as it presently exists. UST owners and operators are advised to maintain contact with the UST Bureau of the New Mexico Environment Department (NMED) to obtain copies of all regulations and to get on the mailing list for future materials.

The United States Environmental Protection Agency (EPA) is authorized by the Resource Conservation and Recovery Act (RCRA), as amended, to develop a comprehensive regulatory program for USTs.[1] These federal legislation provides incentives, including the provision of funds for remediation of leaking underground storage tanks that meet EPA minimum requirements. EPA regulations were finalized during the latter part of 1988. These federal regulations established minimum standards for USTs and authorized individual states to adopt UST programs.

The 1987 New Mexico Legislature amended the Hazardous Waste Act (HWA)[2] in response to the federal grant of authority.[3] The amendment authorizes the New Mexico Environmental Improvement Board (EIB) to "adopt regulations concerning underground storage tanks that are equivalent to, and no more stringent than, federal regulations."[4]

In response to both federal and state legislative authorizations, EIB adopted UST regulations which address virtually every aspect of the ownership and operation of a UST system.[5] Administration of the regulations is vested in NMED. The statutory and regulatory schemes have the strong public policy purpose of protecting the public health and welfare and the lands and waters of the state through the exercise of the state's police power.[6] The UST

---

1 42 U.S.C.A. §§ 6991 - 6991i.

2 N.M. Stat. Ann. §§ 74-4-1 to -14 (Repl. Pamp. 1993).

3 1987 N.M. Laws ch. 179.

4 N.M. Stat. Ann. § 74-4-4(C) (Repl. Pamp. 1993).

5 Federal approval of the state regulations, which must occur for the state regulations to be effective as the only regulations with which UST owners and operators must be concerned, was granted in September, 1990. Final federal authorization for the New Mexico UST program became effective November 16, 1990. 55 Fed. Reg. 38064 (1990).

6 N.M. Underground Storage Tank Regulations § 100.

regulations were originally filed by EIB on March 15, 1988,[7] and were refiled with amendments on September 12, 1988, and February 14, 1989. In response to concerns expressed by the regulated industry, EIB held a public hearing and repealed Parts IV-IX (except § 505.A-.C) of the previously adopted regulations and adopted the corresponding federal regulations by reference on March 9, 1990. Corrective action regulations (Part XV of the UST Regulations) for prioritizing UST leak sites for expenditures were filed on June 18, 1991, and became effective on July 18, 1991.

The 1988 New Mexico Legislature enacted the Petroleum Storage Cleanup Act (PSCA)[8] to address the problem of leaking USTs in the state. The PSCA provided authority for (1) the regulation of hazards associated with leaks and spills from USTs, (2) containment and remediation of pollution incidents, and (3) funding for some remediation actions. The 1990 New Mexico Legislature repealed the PSCA and adopted the Ground Water Protection Act (GWPA)[9] to address corrective action measures undertaken in response to UST leaks and to create a Corrective Action Fund (CAF) to provide revenue sources to fund ground water protection activities. The GWPA has been amended a number of times to specify the circumstances under which monies from the CAF are to be paid for clean-up and for reimbursement to private parties performing corrective action.[10] CAF regulations under GWPA have been adopted by the Secretary which specify under what circumstances NMED will (a) provide cost reimbursement for costs associated with minimum site assessments and corrective action, (b) determine compliance as a basis for cost reimbursement, and (c) determine eligibility of costs for reimbursement.[11]

2.0 DEFINITIONS

A UST is defined as a tank or combination of tanks, including underground connecting pipes, used to contain a regulated substance, so long as the volume of the tanks and connecting pipes is at least ten percent beneath the surface of the ground.[12] A tank is defined as a stationary device constructed of non-earthen materials (e.g., concrete, steel, plastic) designed to contain an accumulation of regulated substances.[13] The regulations do

---

7 All regulations adopted by an administrative agency, to be valid and enforceable, must be filed with the State Records Center. N.M. Stat. Ann. § 14-4-5 (Repl. Pamp. 1988).

8 N.M. Stat. Ann. §§ 74-4D-1 to -8 (Repl. Pamp. 1989); repealed by 1990 N.M. Laws, ch. 124, § 23.

9 N.M. Stat. Ann. §§ 74-6B-1 to -14 (Repl. Pamp. 1993).

10 *Id.*

11 N.M. Ground Water Protection Act Corrective Action Fund Regulations, NMED-92-1 (filed 9/24/92).

12 N.M. Stat. Ann. § 74-6B-3(K) (Repl. Pamp. 1993); N.M. Underground Storage Tank Regulations § 102.CCC.

13 N.M. Underground Storage Tank Regulations § 102.YY.

not explicitly address above-ground storage tanks, which are ostensibly subject to provisions of the HWA and the New Mexico Water Quality Act (WQA).[14]

The UST regulations apply only to tanks which contain regulated substances. A regulated substance is any substance defined in Section 101(14) of the Comprehensive Environmental Response, Compensation and Liability Act (CERCLA)[15] as well as petroleum products, including crude oil or any fraction thereof which is liquid at standard conditions of temperature and pressure of 60° Fahrenheit and 14.7 pounds per square inch absolute.[16] The definition of regulated substance does not include any substance regulated as a hazardous waste under Subtitle C of the RCRA.[17]

The UST regulations apply to any owner and operator of an underground storage tank as defined in the regulations. A UST owner, in the case of a UST in use on November 8, 1984, or brought into use after that date, means any person who owns an underground storage tank used for storage, use, or dispensing of regulated substances. In the case of an underground storage tank in use before November 8, 1984, but no longer in use on that date, an owner means any person who owned the tank immediately before discontinuation of its use.[18] An operator is defined as any person in control of, or having responsibility for, the daily operation of the UST system.[19]

The definition of UST is not intended to cover specific systems,[20] and the regulations do not apply under certain circumstances to what might otherwise be considered a UST system. The term UST does not include (1) farm, ranch, or residential tanks of 1,100 gallons or less used for storing fuel or oil for non-commercial purposes, (2) septic tanks, (3) pipeline facilities regulated under the federal Natural Gas Pipeline Safety Act of 1968, (4) surface impoundments, pits, ponds, or lagoons, (5) storm water or wastewater collection systems, (6) flow-through process tanks, (7) liquid traps, gathering lines, or equipment used in connection with the exploration, development, or production of oil and natural gas, (8) storage tanks

---

14 N.M. Stat. Ann. §§ 74-6-1 to -17 (Repl. Pamp. 1993).

15 Codified at 42 U.S.C. §§ 9601-9657.

16 N.M. Underground Storage Tank Regulations § 102.NN (1) - (2).

17 *Id.* The list of regulated substances is set out in 40 C.F.R. § 302.4, and the list of excluded substances can be found at 40 C.F.R. Part 261.

18 N.M. Stat. Ann. § 74-6B-3(E) (Repl. Pamp. 1993); N.M. Underground Storage Tank Regulations § 102.HH. The term "owner" for purposes of registration requirements under the regulations excludes any person who (1) had a tank taken out of operation on or before January 1, 1974, or (2) had a tank taken out of operation after January 1, 1974, and removed from the ground prior to November 8, 1984. *Id.*

19 N.M. Stat. Ann. § 74-6B-3(D) (Repl. Pamp. 1993); N.M. Underground Storage Tank Regulations § 102.FF.

20 N.M. Stat. Ann. § 74-6B-3(K) (Repl. Pamp. 1993); N.M. Underground Storage Tank Regulations § 102.CCC.

situated in an underground area, such as a basement, cellar, mine working drift, shaft, or tunnel, if the storage tank is situated upon or above the surface of the floor, or (9) pipes connected to any tank described in the preceding list.[21]

The UST regulations do not apply to (1) wastewater treatment tanks, (2) sumps, (3) UST systems containing radioactive waste, (4) electrical equipment, (5) hydraulic lift tanks, and (6) any UST system with a capacity of 110 gallons or less.[22] The regulations provide, however, that no person may install a UST system listed in the preceding sentence for the purpose of storing regulated substances unless the UST system will prevent releases due to corrosion or structural failure for the operational life of the tank, the system is cathodically protected against corrosion or designed in a manner to prevent the release or threatened release of any stored substance, and the material used in the construction or lining of the tank is compatible with the substance to be stored.[23]

3.0 UST REGISTRATION

Tank owners were required to register any tank or tanks with the Underground Storage Tank Bureau of NMED by July 14, 1988.[24] The GWPA sets a registration fee of $100 per year for each tank owned or operated, which is to be paid by the owner or operator and deposited into the Underground Storage Tank Fund.[25] Annual renewal is required for each tank, with a late fee charged in the event the fee is not paid when due.[26] Upon receipt of the application for registration and payment of the annual fee, NMED will issue a validated registration certificate which must be displayed on the premises of the UST system at all times.[27] Application forms for registration of USTs are available at NMED offices or by writing to the Underground Storage Tank Bureau of NMED.

Registration requirements are imposed with respect to any change of ownership, installation or substantial modification of a UST. If ownership of a UST system changes, the new owner must re-register the tank with NMED within 30 days of ownership transfer.[28] If an owner intends to install any new tank or UST system or modify substantially an existing UST system, the owner must notify NMED in writing at least 30 days before installation or modification. The owner of a new UST system must register any new tank or UST system

---

21 *Id.*

22 N.M. Underground Storage Tank Regulations § 103.C.

23 N.M. Underground Storage Tank Regulations § 103.D.

24 N.M. Underground Storage Tank Regulations § 200.A.

25 N.M. Stat. Ann. § 74-6B-9 (Repl. Pamp. 1993).

26 N.M. Underground Storage Tank Regulations §§ 200.B, 302.

27 N.M. Underground Storage Tank Regulations § 207.A.

28 N.M. Underground Storage Tank Regulations § 201.

with NMED prior to placing it into service.[29] Emergency repairs or replacements of UST systems may be made in the event an emergency situation presents a threat to the public health, provided that notice is telephoned to NMED within 24 hours after the repair.[30] Written notice must be submitted to NMED within seven days of the incident.[31]

4.0 UST DESIGN, CONSTRUCTION, AND INSTALLATION

The UST regulations impose minimum performance standards on both new and upgraded UST systems, including piping, to prevent releases due to structural failure or corrosion for as long as the UST system is utilized.[32] The regulations address the material which can be utilized in the construction of the tank, provide for cathodic protection of steel tanks, and mandate compliance with industry codes of practice pertaining to corrosion protection. Tanks and piping that routinely contain regulated substances must conform to one of the following: (1) fiberglass-reinforced plastic construction, (2) steel construction with cathodic protection, (3) steel-fiberglass-reinforced-plastic composite, or (4) metal construction without corrosion protection if the site is certified by a corrosion expert as not corrosive enough to cause a release during the operating life of the tank.[33] Other tank materials may be used if the construction and corrosion protection are determined by NMED to be adequately designed to prevent releases.[34] Reference should be made to the industry codes and standards set forth in the regulations.

Owners and operators must utilize spill and overfill prevention equipment on UST systems unless the system is filled by transfers of no more than 25 gallons at one time.[35] Spill prevention equipment must prevent the release of product to the environment when the transfer hose is detached from the fill pipe (i.e., a spill catchment basin).[36] Overfill prevention equipment must automatically shut off flow into a tank when the tank is no more than 95 percent full or must alert the operator when the tank is no more than 90 percent full by restricting flow or triggering a high-level alarm.[37] Alternative equipment may be used if approved by NMED.[38]

---

29 N.M. Underground Storage Tank Regulations §§ 202-203.

30 N.M. Underground Storage Tank Regulations §§ 204 - 205.

31 N.M. Underground Storage Tank Regulations § 204.B.

32 N.M. Underground Storage Tank Regulations § 400.

33 N.M. Underground Storage Tank Regulations § 400(a)(1)-(4).

34 N.M. Underground Storage Tank Regulations § 400(a)(5).

35 N.M. Underground Storage Tank Regulations § 400(c)(2)(ii).

36 N.M. Underground Storage Tank Regulations § 400(c)(1)(i).

37 N.M. Underground Storage Tank Regulations § 400(c)(1)(ii)(B).

38 N.M. Underground Storage Tank Regulations § 400(c)(2)(i).

All tanks and piping must be properly installed in accordance with industry codes of practice developed by a nationally recognized association or independent testing laboratory and in accordance with the manufacturer's instructions.[39] Owners and operators must certify compliance with installation standards by providing a certificate of compliance on a notification form.[40] The certification must demonstrate one of the following: (1) the installer has been certified by tank and piping manufacturers, (2) the installer has been certified or licensed by NMED, (3) the installation has been inspected and certified by a registered professional engineer with education and experience in UST system installation, (4) the installation has been inspected and approved by NMED, (5) all work listed in the manufacturer's installation checklist has been completed, or (6) the owner or operator has complied with another certification method approved by NMED.[41]

The regulations also provide for the upgrading of all existing UST systems by December 22, 1998. UST system upgrade requirements can be met by upgrading existing systems to comply with specified performance standards for new UST systems.[42] Upgrading requirements for steel tanks may be met by one of the following: (1) internal lining of tanks if the lining is installed in accordance with specified requirements and the internal lining is internally inspected within 10 years of installation and every 5 years thereafter,[43] (2) cathodic protection with inspection and monitoring,[44] or (3) internal lining combined with cathodic protection.[45] Piping upgrading must provide cathodic protection in accordance with industry codes of practice.[46] All existing UST systems must comply with new UST system spill and overfill prevention equipment requirements no later than December 22, 1998.[47] Failure to meet the upgrade requirements by the deadline will require the owner or operator to close the UST system.[48]

Any owner who brings a new UST system into use must submit notification of the installation of the system to NMED 30 days before installation and must register the new tank

---

39 N.M. Underground Storage Tank Regulations § 400(d). Publications and industry codes specified in the regulations should be consulted.

40 N.M. Underground Storage Tank Regulations § 400(e).

41 *Id.*

42 N.M. Underground Storage Tank Regulations § 401(a)(1).

43 N.M. Underground Storage Tank Regulations § 401(b)(1).

44 N.M. Underground Storage Tank Regulations § 401(b)(2).

45 N.M. Underground Storage Tank Regulations § 401(b)(3).

46 N.M. Underground Storage Tank Regulations § 401(c).

47 N.M. Underground Storage Tank Regulations § 401(a), (d).

48 N.M. Underground Storage Tank Regulations § 401(a)(3).

or UST system with NMED prior to placing it into service.[49] In the notification, all owners and operators must certify compliance with installation requirements, requirements for cathodic protection of steel tanks and piping, financial responsibility requirements, and release detection requirements.[50] Any seller of a tank intended for UST use must notify the purchaser of the owner's notification obligations.[51]

5.0 OPERATING REQUIREMENTS

All owners and operators of USTs have a duty to insure that releases due to spills or overfills do not occur.[52] Owners and operators must ensure that the volume available in the tank is greater than the volume of product to be transferred to the tank and that the transfer is monitored constantly to prevent overfilling and spilling.[53] In addition, owners and operators are required to report, investigate, and clean up any spills or overfills.[54]

Specific requirements dealing with corrosion protection are set forth with respect to owners and operators of steel UST systems.[55] The regulations impose inspection, testing, and record maintenance requirements. Owners and operators are required to use a UST system made of, or lined with, materials that are compatible with the substance stored in the system.[56]

Owners and operators of UST systems are authorized to repair the systems but must ensure that the repairs will prevent releases due to structural failure or corrosion.[57] Repairs must be properly conducted in accordance with industry codes.[58] Tank owners must replace any piece of metal pipe section or fitting from which a release has occurred.[59] Repaired tanks and piping must undergo tank tightness testing within 30 days of the repair.[60] Tank

---

49 N.M. Underground Storage Tank Regulations § 202.

50 N.M. Underground Storage Tank Regulations § 402(a)(1).

51 N.M. Underground Storage Tank Regulations § 402(c).

52 N.M. Underground Storage Tank Regulations § 500(a).

53 *Id.*

54 N.M. Underground Storage Tank Regulations § 500(b).

55 N.M. Underground Storage Tank Regulations § 501.

56 N.M. Underground Storage Tank Regulations § 502. "Compatible" substances have the ability to maintain their respective physical and chemical properties upon contact with one another for extended periods of time and under varied environmental conditions (i.e., at different temperatures). N.M. Underground Storage Tank Regulations § 102.H.

57 N.M. Underground Storage Tank Regulations § 503.

58 N.M. Underground Storage Tank Regulations § 503(a).

59 N.M. Underground Storage Tank Regulations § 503(c).

60 N.M. Underground Storage Tank Regulations § 503(d).

testing is not required if (1) the repaired tank is internally inspected in accordance with an industry recognized code of practice, (2) the repaired portion is monitored monthly for releases, or (3) another test method approved by NMED is used.[61] Cathodic protection systems must be tested in accordance with regulation requirements within six months of any repair to any cathodically protected system.[62]

NMED has broad power to inspect, monitor, and test UST systems. All UST system owners and operators are required to cooperate fully with inspections, monitoring, and testing conducted by NMED. UST system installation, repair, modification, and inventory records must either be maintained on-site and be available for immediate inspection by NMED or be maintained at a readily available alternative site so long as inspection is available upon request.[63] NMED is authorized to enter at reasonable times any establishment or place where a UST is located, inspect the UST system and obtain samples of its contents, and conduct monitoring or testing of the tanks, associated equipment, or surrounding soils, air, or ground water.[64] If NMED obtains any samples from the testing, it is required to provide the owner or operator with a receipt describing the sample obtained and, if requested, a portion of each sample equal in volume or weight to the portion retained. A copy of the results of any analysis conducted on any sample must be provided promptly to the owner, operator, or agent in charge of the UST system.[65] Owners and operators are required to permit NMED representatives to be present at and inspect all UST system installations, replacements, repairs, substantial modifications, installations of leak detection systems, and system closures. Oral notice of the commencement of any identified procedure must be given at least 24 hours in advance. NMED inspectors may require that critical junctures be performed during regular business hours.[66]

---

61 *Id.*

62 N.M. Underground Storage Tank Regulations § 503(e).

63 N.M. Underground Storage Tank Regulations § 504(c).

64 N.M. Underground Storage Tank Regulations § 505(a).

65 N.M. Underground Storage Tank Regulations § 505(b).

66 N.M. Underground Storage Tank Regulations § 505(c). A "critical juncture" can involve virtually any activity associated with the installation or repair of a UST, including excavation preparation, setting tanks or pipes, making piping component connections, pressure testing, backfilling excavations, repair, testing, tank cleaning and devaporizing, tank or piping removal, and assessment of a tank site for releases. *Id.*

6.0 RELEASE DETECTION

All UST systems are required to have a method or combination of methods of release detection with respect to tanks.[67] The objective of the release detection requirements is to provide for a release detection system capable of detecting a release from any portion of the UST system.[68] Any UST system that cannot implement an approved method of release detection by the required date must complete closure procedures.[69]

Owners and operators of petroleum UST systems must provide release detection for tanks and piping.[70] Allowable release detection systems for tanks include (1) product inventory control, (2) manual tank gauging, (3) tank tightness testing, (4) automatic tank gauging, (5) vapor monitoring, (6) ground water monitoring, or (7) interstitial monitoring between a UST system and a secondary barrier under limited circumstances.[71] Other types of release detection methods, or a combination of methods, may be used if detection criteria are met and approved by NMED.[72] Tanks which meet new UST system performance standards and monthly inventory control requirements may use tank tightness testing every five years until December 22, 1998, or until 10 years after installation, whichever is later.[73] Tanks which do not meet new UST system performance standards may use monthly inventory controls and annual tank tightness testing until December 22, 1998, when all tanks must meet

---

67 The regulations require leak detection for tanks *and* pressurized piping by the following dates:

A. All new installations since Dec. 22, 1988, must have leak detection;
B. Tanks installed before 1965 or date unknown - Dec. 22, 1989;
C. Tanks installed 1965-69 - Dec. 22, 1990;
D. Tanks installed 1970-74 - Dec. 22, 1991;
E. Tanks installed 1975-79 - Dec. 22, 1992;
F. Tanks installed 1980-88 - Dec. 22, 1993;
G. Pressurized piping - Dec. 22, 1990.

N.M. Underground Storage Tank Regulations § 600(c).

68 N.M. Underground Storage Tank Regulations § 600(a)(1).

69 N.M. Underground Storage Tank Regulations § 600(d).

70 N.M. Underground Storage Tank Regulations § 601.

71 N.M. Underground Storage Tank Regulations § 603(a)(g). The regulations allow new and existing tanks to use tank tightness testing combined with inventory control for 10 years after installation or upgrading or until December 22, 1998, whichever is later. N.M. Underground Storage Tank Regulations § 601.

72 N.M. Underground Storage Tank Regulations § 603(h).

73 N.M. Underground Storage Tank Regulations § 601(a)(1).

new UST system standards.[74] Tanks with a capacity of 550 gallons or less may use weekly tank gauging.[75]

Underground piping that routinely contains regulated substances must be monitored for releases.[76] Pressurized piping must be equipped with an automatic line leak detector and have either an annual line tightness test or monthly monitoring.[77] Suction piping must either have a line tightness test every three years or use monthly monitoring.[78] No release detection is required for suction piping designed and constructed to meet specific standards.[79]

Owners and operators of hazardous substance tank systems[80] must provide release detection that meets the requirements for petroleum UST systems.[81] By December 22, 1998, all existing hazardous substance UST systems must meet release detection requirements for new hazardous substance systems, which include secondary containment systems which can contain regulated substances until they are detected and removed;[82] installation of double-walled tanks;[83] installation of external liners,[84] and use of secondary containment on underground piping.[85] Another method may be used if the owner or operator satisfies NMED of its effectiveness.[86]

All UST system owners and operators must maintain records demonstrating compliance with all applicable requirements. All written performance claims pertaining to release detection systems must be maintained for five years unless otherwise specified by NMED.[87]

---

74 N.M. Underground Storage Tank Regulations § 601(a)(2).

75 N.M. Underground Storage Tank Regulations § 601(a)(3).

76 N.M. Underground Storage Tank Regulations § 601(b).

77 N.M. Underground Storage Tank Regulations § 601(b)(1).

78 N.M. Underground Storage Tank Regulations § 601(b)(2).

79 *Id.*

80 A "hazardous substance tank system" means an underground storage tank system that contains an accumulation of hazardous substances defined in Section 101(14) of the CERCLA (but not including any substance regulated as a hazardous waste under Subtitle C of the RCRA) or any mixture of such substances and petroleum in which hazardous substances comprise greater than 50% of the weight or volume of the mixture. N.M. Underground Storage Tank Regulations § 102(u).

81 N.M. Underground Storage Tank Regulations § 602.

82 N.M. Underground Storage Tank Regulations § 602(a), (b)(1).

83 N.M. Underground Storage Tank Regulations § 602(b)(2).

84 N.M. Underground Storage Tank Regulations § 602(b)(3).

85 N.M. Underground Storage Tank Regulations § 602(b)(4).

86 N.M. Underground Storage Tank Regulations § 602(b)(5).

87 N.M. Underground Storage Tank Regulations § 605(a).

Results of any sampling, testing, or monitoring must be maintained for one year unless otherwise specified by NMED.[88] Documentation on all calibration, maintenance, and repair of release detection equipment must be maintained for at least one year, unless otherwise specified by NMED, except that schedules of required calibration and maintenance provided by the manufacturer must be maintained for five years from the date of installation.[89]

7.0 REPORTING, CORRECTIVE ACTION REQUIREMENTS, AND UST GUIDELINES

Prior to adoption of the GWPA and the current UST regulations which are now in effect, NMED addressed UST releases and subsequent remedial action under the HWA, the WQA, and the PSCA and regulations adopted pursuant to those statutes. The regulations imposed notification and cleanup requirements on "any person in charge of a facility" and required notification within 24 hours where the person in charge of a facility had notice or knowledge of a discharge or a hazardous substance incident.[90] Both emergency and non-emergency regulatory enforcement procedures are authorized under these statutes.[91] These regulations and statutes should be consulted, depending on the timing of the incident, release, or suspected release, in the event notification or corrective action issues arise.[92]

7.1 REPORTING

The current UST regulations require that notice of several conditions be provided to NMED within 24 hours unless otherwise specified. The conditions sufficient to trigger a notification requirement include the discovery of regulated substances at the UST site, unusual operating conditions (such as erratic behavior of product dispensing equipment or sudden loss of product) unless system equipment is found to be defective but not leaking, and monitoring results from a leak detection method that indicate a release may have occurred

---

88 N.M. Underground Storage Tank Regulations § 605(b).

89 N.M. Underground Storage Tank Regulations § 605(c).

90 New Mexico Water Quality Regulations § 203.A(1). A "hazardous substance incident" is an emergency incident involving chemicals, including but not limited to transportation wrecks, accidental spills or leaks, fires, or explosions, which creates a reasonable probability of injury to human health or property. N.M. Stat. Ann. § 74-4-3(H) (Repl. Pamp. 1993).

91 *See* the Hazardous Waste Management and Water Quality Management Chapters.

92 At least one observer has argued that discharges occurring prior to February 17, 1974, are exempt from WQCC regulations and that any discharge should be governed by the law or regulation in existence at the time of discharge. *See* T. Hnasko, "Claims Arising Under State and Federal Laws and Regulations," paper presented at Natural Resource Law Section of New Mexico State Bar Convention, October 1988. There is no New Mexico case law governing this question.

unless (1) the monitoring device is defective and immediately replaced or repaired or (2) in the case of inventory control, a second month of data does not confirm the initial result.[93]

Unless corrective action is initiated, owners and operators must immediately investigate and confirm all suspected releases within seven days unless otherwise specified by NMED. Confirmation of a release may be made utilizing an appropriate system check or site check.[94] Other procedures may be used if approved by NMED.[95] NMED may require investigation to determine if the UST system is the source of off-site impacts.[96]

7.2 CORRECTIVE ACTION FOR PETROLEUM UST SYSTEMS[97]

All releases, including those for which full compliance with the requirements of Part XII of the UST Regulations (Corrective Action for UST Systems containing Petroleum) is not required, must be cleaned up through soil remediation, ground and surface water remediation and other appropriate procedures in a manner protective of health, public welfare, and the environment as guided by the regulations.[98] Owners and operators of petroleum UST systems must comply with the requirements of Part XII of the regulations depending upon the volume, depth to ground water, or actual impact on ground or surface water at the site.[99] Notice of all releases and reports must be mailed to the UST Bureau of NMED.[100] Time deadlines are computed from the date of confirmation or other identification of a release unless another event is specified in the regulations.[101] If a release constitutes a hazardous substance incident under the HWA, the HWA's provisions or regulations may apply in addition to the corrective action regulations.[102]

7.2.1 Notification and Abatement

Upon confirmation or identification of a release, the owner and operator must notify NMED within 24 hours pursuant to Section 204 of the UST regulations, notify local fire authorities, when available, and take immediate action to prevent any further release from

---

93 N.M. Underground Storage Tank Regulations § 700.

94 N.M. Underground Storage Tank Regulations § 702.

95 *Id.*

96 N.M. Underground Storage Tank Regulations § 701.

97 A similar regulatory scheme is set forth in Part XIII of the regulations for Hazardous Substance UST Systems. See also UST Soil/Water Sampling and Disposal Guidelines Section of this Chapter.

98 N.M. Underground Storage Tank Regulations § 1200.A.

99 N.M. Underground Storage Tank Regulations § 1200.B.

100 N.M. Underground Storage Tank Regulations § 1200.C.

101 N.M. Underground Storage Tank Regulations § 1200.D.

102 N.M. Underground Storage Tank Regulations § 1200.F.

the UST system by whatever means necessary.[103] Unless NMED directs otherwise, the owner and operator must undertake initial abatement and site investigation procedures within 72 hours of the confirmation or other identification of the release, including an assessment of water supply impacts, investigation to determine whether potentially explosive or harmful vapors are present in any building, utility corridor, basement or other surface or subsurface structure on or adjacent to the release site, installation of a vapor venting system if vapors are present, and operation of a vapor venting system until safe levels are attained.[104] The owner and operator must also remove any exposed petroleum products and mitigate any other fire and safety hazard as soon as possible but in no case later than 72 hours after the confirmation or other identification of the release.[105]

The owner and operator or their representative must make an oral report summarizing the abatement procedures undertaken and the results of their initial investigation to NMED within 72 hours of the confirmation or other identification of the release.[106] The owner, operator or representative must submit a written report to NMED within seven days, along with the written notice required under Section 204 of the regulations. The report must summarize all work done and include information about private and public water supplies, well logs, and construction and location information for any on-site wells, information about any known or suspected water supply impacts and actions taken to abate such impacts, information concerning vapors, information about fire and safety hazards and actions taken to abate such hazards, and information about the current and past ownership of the UST system, the substance stored in the system, and the property on which the UST system is located.[107]

7.2.2 On-Site Investigation

The owner and operator must conduct an on-site investigation of the release site within 30 days unless the owner and operator can demonstrate that ground water has not been contaminated and that either the release is cleaned up to standards set out in the regulations within 72 hours or the release is permanently contained and it can be demonstrated that the release has not moved beyond the excavation area.[108] The purpose of the on-site investigation is to determine whether ground or surface water has been impacted or threatened, whether other hazardous conditions exist as a result of the release, and whether immediate mitigation procedures are necessary to prevent the spread of or to remove or

---

103 N.M. Underground Storage Tank Regulations § 1202.A.

104 N.M. Underground Storage Tank Regulations § 1203.A - .B.

105 N.M. Underground Storage Tank Regulations § 1203.C.

106 N.M. Underground Storage Tank Regulations § 1204.A.

107 N.M. Underground Storage Tank Regulations § 1204.B.

108 N.M. Underground Storage Tank Regulations § 1205.A.

reverse ongoing contamination.[109] The on-site investigation must determine the horizontal and vertical extent of soil contamination and whether the release has impacted ground water, identify the location of all underground utilities and other subsurface structures which may be impacted by the release, and identify all surface water courses within a one-half mile radius of the site.[110] Movement of exposed or free product into surface water must be stopped within 24 hours of discovery and further movement must be prevented. Immediate action must be taken to stop the movement of petroleum-contaminated ground water into surface water.[111]

The owner, operator, or their representative must submit a letter or informal report summarizing the results of the on-site investigation within 30 days of the date of confirmation or other identification of the release. The report must include information about the contamination or threatened contamination of ground or surface water, results of the utility site check, records of tightness tests, repairs to the UST system, and other pertinent records from the UST system.[112] The owner, operator, or their representative must submit a written report describing the results of the on-site investigation within 45 days of the date of confirmation or other identification of the release, which must include information about the extent of soil contamination, preliminary information about soil and aquifer characteristics in the vicinity of the release, a description of any actions taken, a brief description of plans for future actions to recover petroleum products released from the system, a report on the removal of highly contaminated soils, drawings of the release site, monitoring well data, and a statement signed by the owner, operator or representative (for the owner or operator) stating that he or she is personally familiar with the information submitted in the report and attached documents.[113] The owner or operator must also allow NMED an opportunity to take split samples from the site and must notify NMED at least 48 hours prior to the collection of any soil or water samples. NMED may request to be present at the collection of the samples. All samples must be collected, stored, and transported appropriately.[114]

7.2.3 Hydrogeologic Investigation

Specific provisions are included in the regulations dealing with free product removal[115] and the treatment of highly contaminated soils.[116] The owner, operator, or

---

109 N.M. Underground Storage Tank Regulations § 1205.B.

110 N.M. Underground Storage Tank Regulations § 1205.C.

111 N.M. Underground Storage Tank Regulations § 1205.C(4).

112 N.M. Underground Storage Tank Regulations § 1206.A.

113 N.M. Underground Storage Tank Regulations § 1206.B.

114 N.M. Underground Storage Tank Regulations § 1207.

115 N.M. Underground Storage Tank Regulations § 1208.

116 N.M. Underground Storage Tank Regulations § 1209. *See also* UST Soil/Water

representative must complete and submit to NMED a hydrogeologic investigation report within 75 days if any one of the following determinations is made: (1) the release of petroleum has impacted ground or surface water and contamination levels are above state standards, (2) free product has been found on the water table, (3) the release threatens to impact ground or surface water before cleanup is completed, or (4) the release otherwise threatens health, public welfare, or the environment.[117] The hydrogeologic report must define or describe specific features of the site[118] and must contain a statement signed by the owner, operator, or representative (for the owner or operator) stating that he or she is personally familiar with the information submitted in the report and the attached documents.[119] NMED must, within 30 days of its receipt of the hydrogeologic investigation report, notify the owner and operator in writing of any inadequacies, at which time the owner or operator has 15 days to modify and resubmit the report to NMED for review and written approval or disapproval.[120]

7.2.4 Reclamation Proposal

If the owner or operator determines that free product has been found on the water table or that a release has otherwise contaminated ground or surface water, that a release threatens to contaminate ground or surface water, or that a release otherwise threatens health, public welfare, or the environment, the owner and operator must submit a reclamation proposal to NMED.[121] The reclamation proposal must, where appropriate, contain provisions for ground or surface water reclamation, treatment of contaminated soils, or treatment of other conditions existing at the site.[122] Three copies of the proposal must be submitted to NMED within 30 days of the date the hydrogeologic investigation report was submitted, or within 30 days of the date of the revised report if such was submitted, but in no event later than 120 days following the confirmation or identification of the release.[123] The reclamation proposal must include (1) a description of the corrective action system to be used at the site, (2) timetables for the initiation of containment and calculations demonstrating containment, (3) performance standards and timetables for aquifer and soil restoration, (4) monitoring schedules, (5) maintenance commitments, (6) engineering plans and specifications for the corrective action plan, (7) contingency commitments, and (8) copies of all pertinent applica-

---

Sampling and Disposal Guidelines Section of this Chapter.

117 N.M. Underground Storage Tank Regulations § 1210.A.

118 N.M. Underground Storage Tank Regulations § 1210.C.

119 N.M. Underground Storage Tank Regulations § 1210.D.

120 N.M. Underground Storage Tank Regulations § 1211.

121 N.M. Underground Storage Tank Regulations § 1212.A.

122 N.M. Underground Storage Tank Regulations § 1212.B.

123 N.M. Underground Storage Tank Regulations § 1212.C.

tions and access agreements required to initiate reclamation.[124] The owner and operator must publish a legal notice of the submission or planned submission of the reclamation proposal at least twice in a paper of general circulation in the state or county(ies) in which soil or water has been contaminated. The regulations set out various requirements for the notice.[125]

The regulations provide for a review of the reclamation proposal by NMED and set out the procedure to be followed in the event NMED determines the proposal is inadequate.[126] The Secretary of NMED has discretion, if the public interest so requires, to provide notice of the submission of a reclamation proposal to persons other than the owner and operator and provide for public participation in the proposal review process.[127] Prior to NMED's approval of the reclamation proposal, owners and operators may implement the reclamation proposal or take other corrective actions not specifically provided for in the regulations so long as they notify NMED of their intention, comply with any conditions imposed by NMED, incorporate self-initiated cleanup measures into the reclamation proposal, and report quarterly on the self-initiated cleanup measures.[128] The owner and operator must install and operate the corrective action system in accordance with the reclamation proposal as soon as possible, but no later than 30 days after the approval of the proposal by NMED.[129] The owner and operator must continue to implement the reclamation proposal and operate all aspects of the corrective action system until reclamation is terminated. The owner and operator must submit quarterly reports to NMED on the continuing implementation of the reclamation proposal. A first quarterly report is due 120 days after the date the reclamation proposal is approved, but not later than 180 days after the date the reclamation proposal is submitted.[130] The corrective action system must be evaluated by the owner, operator, and NMED during the second year of operation to determine its effectiveness. Alternative treatment technologies must be proposed if it is determined that the corrective action system or any part of the system is not effectively mitigating the contamination.[131] The owner or operator may petition NMED to approve a modification of the reclamation proposal for good cause.[132]

---

124 N.M. Underground Storage Tank Regulations § 1212.D.

125 N.M. Underground Storage Tank Regulations § 1213.

126 N.M. Underground Storage Tank Regulations § 1214.A.

127 N.M. Underground Storage Tank Regulations § 1214.C.

128 N.M. Underground Storage Tank Regulations § 1215.C.

129 N.M. Underground Storage Tank Regulations § 1215.A.

130 N.M. Underground Storage Tank Regulations § 1216.B.

131 N.M. Underground Storage Tank Regulations § 1217.

132 N.M. Underground Storage Tank Regulations § 1218.

7.2.5 Reclamation

Reclamation will be complete when all the following criteria are met: (1) no floating product is present on the water table; (2) after pumping is ceased, New Mexico Water Quality Control Commission (WQCC) ground water quality standards are met for all petroleum product constituents for eight consecutive quarters in at least four compliance wells at the site; (3) standards for other additives or constituents are met; (4) soil contamination has been reduced to a level which will not recontaminate ground water; (5) no petroleum odors are apparent in water which is a public or private water supply; and (6) any other conditions which threaten health, public welfare, or the environment have been remediated.[133] Termination of reclamation pursuant to this section does not relieve the owner and operator of any other liability or responsibility they may have under these regulations or any other state or federal law or regulations.[134] An owner and operator may terminate reclamation if they can demonstrate technical infeasibility of continued remediation.[135] The regulations provide that NMED may extend any time limit under the regulations for good cause shown.[136] NMED may finally grant a variance from any provision of these regulations whenever it is found by a preponderance of the evidence that the methods, technologies, operations, and procedures used by the owner and operator, although not conforming to a regulation, will in fact protect health, the public welfare, and the environment to a degree which is equal to or greater than that provided by the regulations.[137] A written request must be made to trigger the variance process.[138]

7.3 UST SOIL/WATER SAMPLING AND DISPOSAL GUIDELINES

NMED has issued UST soil and water sampling and disposal guidelines whose purpose is to clarify lead program responsibilities at leaking UST sites, tank removal methodologies, soil and ground water sampling protocols, and analyses and procedures for investigating and remediating soil and ground water contaminated with petroleum hydrocarbons, hazardous substances, and wastes from UST systems.[139]

---

133 N.M. Underground Storage Tank Regulations § 1219.A.

134 N.M. Underground Storage Tank Regulations § 1219.B.

135 N.M. Underground Storage Tank Regulations § 1220.

136 N.M. Underground Storage Tank Regulations § 1221.

137 N.M. Underground Storage Tank Regulations § 1222.A.

138 N.M. Underground Storage Tank Regulations § 1222.B.

139 The New Mexico Environment Department, *UST Soil/Water Sampling & Disposal Guidelines*, revised December 7, 1992. (hereinafter "Guidelines").

7.3.1 Lead Programs

The UST Bureau is the lead program at all sites where a petroleum hydrocarbon release has occurred from a UST.[140] There are exceptions to this rule, however. When a UST has been used to store hazardous waste not commingled with petroleum products, this situation should be referred to the Hazardous and Radioactive Materials Bureau.[141] Situations involving petroleum release from a non-UST source, such as an above-ground storage tank, should be referred to the Remediation Section of the Ground Water Protection and Remediation Bureau.[142] If a situation exists in which a facility uses both above-ground storage tanks and USTs and one of the sources of release is a UST, the matter should be referred to the UST Bureau, which will apprise the Ground Water Protection and Remediation Bureau of the situation. A joint decision will be made regarding which bureau will be the Lead Program.[143] Petroleum releases whose source is on tribal lands will be referred to the Environmental Protection Agency.[144]

7.3.2 Soil and Water Sample Methods at Tank Removals

Owners of USTs must measure for the presence of a release before permanent closure or a change in service is completed.[145] The only exception to this requirement is if vapor monitoring or ground water monitoring is operating at the time of closure and these processes indicate that no release has occurred.[146] However, if a release is either suspected or confirmed even when one of these procedures is in operation, a soil sampling should be conducted.[147]

Sampling locations and numbers are dependent upon the size and characteristics of the USTs. For tanks with a two thousand gallon or less capacity, one sample under the center of each tank should be taken.[148] If there are two or more tanks of this capacity in a single pit, samples from the bottom of the pit in each corner (or each wall midpoint) and

---

140 Guidelines I.

141 Guidelines I.A. The UST Bureau will handle hazardous wastes commingled with petroleum products pursuant to RCRA Subtitle C and the UST Regulations Part XIII. *Id.*

142 Guidelines I.B.

143 *Id.*

144 Guidelines I.C. Sites on Navajo lands are referred to Region IX in San Francisco, California; all sites on other tribal lands are referred to Region 6 in Dallas, Texas. *Id.*

145 N.M. Underground Storage Tank Regulations § 802; Guidelines II.A.

146 Guidelines II.A.; *See* N.M. Underground Storage Tank Regulations § 603(e) - (f).

147 Guidelines II.A.

148 Guidelines II.B(1).

in the center of the pit must be taken.[149] Tanks with a capacity greater than two thousand gallons require one sample under each end of the tank.[150] When there are more than three of these tanks in a single pit, samples must be taken at the bottom of the pit in each corner (or each wall midpoint) and in the center of the pit.[151] In addition, sampling locations should also be based on these considerations: area(s) of highest contamination, type of closure, type of soil, backfill material, and system configuration.[152] Soil should also be sampled where holes or releases have occurred in tanks or where overfill spill has occurred.[153] If ground water is encountered, samples of the water should be collected in a clean container and then decanted into 40 ml VOA/VOC vials for lab analysis.[154] Samples should be taken as close as possible to the time the tanks are removed and before there are any disturbances to the pit bottom. Samples must be taken a minimum of one (1) foot below the bottom of the tank(s) or pit, whichever is deeper.[155]

Results of all lab analyses must be submitted to the UST Bureau field inspector to determine if a release has occurred. All samples above or below acceptable limits must be reported to the Remedial Action Section of the UST Bureau.[156] The Guidelines should be consulted for field and laboratory analytical methodologies and protocols for both soil and ground water samples.[157]

7.3.3 Handling, Disposal, and Remediation of Contaminated Soil/Water

The guidelines for handling and remediating both contaminated soils and highly contaminated soils are found in Section 1209 of the UST Regulations. In addition, it should be noted that a responsible party may have to obtain one or more permits before remediating, disposing of, or handling petroleum hydrocarbon-contaminated soils and water.[158] Responsible parties should contact the Ground Water Protection & Remediation Bureau for ground water discharge permits, the Surface Water Quality Bureau for surface water discharge permits, the Air Quality Bureau for air quality permits, and the Solid Waste Bureau for waste disposal permits prior to implementing any handling, disposal, or remediation

---

149 *Id.*

150 Guidelines II.B(2).

151 *Id.*

152 Guidelines II.B(3).

153 *Id.*

154 Guidelines II.B(4).

155 Guidelines II.B.

156 Guidelines II.C.

157 Guidelines II.D. - .E, III A. - .B.

158 Guidelines IV.A.

actions.[159] In addition, landfill/landfarm and asphalt plant owners and operators must contact the appropriate NMED bureau to determine if a permit or modification of an existing permit is required prior to accepting petroleum hydrocarbon-contaminated soils and water.[160] The Guidelines provide specific instructions for remediating and disposing of contaminated soils in accordance with the provisions of Section 1209 of the UST Regulations.[161] Disposing or remediating contaminated soils by mixing with clean soils is not allowed, as dilution is not considered to be an appropriate remediation method.[162]

Remediation and treatment of contaminated ground water can be accomplished through various technologies including air sparging, carbon filtration, and pump and treat systems.[163] Owners and operators responsible for contaminated water should consult an environmental consultant with experience in remcdiating and treating contaminated water before implementing any program.[164] The Guidelines set out the steps that must be followed when disposing of or remediating contaminated water.[165] If the Guidelines do not cover a situation that has arisen, responsible parties should contact the UST Bureau.[166]

8.0 CORRECTIVE ACTION FUND AND COST REIMBURSEMENT UNDER THE GWPA

The GWPA provides broad power to NMED to address UST contamination sites within the state. The stated purpose of the GWPA is to provide substantive provisions and funding mechanisms that will enable the state to take corrective action at sites contaminated by leakage from USTs.[167]

8.1 CORRECTIVE ACTION AND THE CORRECTIVE ACTION FUND

The GWPA creates the Corrective Action Fund (CAF) to provide for financial assurance coverage required by federal law and to be used by NMED to take corrective action in response to a release, to pay for the cost of a minimum site assessment in excess of $10,000, to pay the state's share of federal leaking underground storage tank trust fund clean-up costs as required by the RCRA, and to make payments to or on behalf of owners and

---

159 *Id.*

160 *Id.*

161 Guidelines IV.B.

162 Guidelines IV.B(5).

163 Guidelines IV.D.

164 *Id.*

165 *Id.*

166 Guidelines IV. Endnote.

167 N.M. Stat. Ann. § 74-6B-2.(C) (Repl. Pamp. 1993).

operators in accordance with the cost reimbursement program.[168] EIB, upon recommendation from the UST Committee,[169] is authorized to adopt regulations for establishing priorities for corrective action at sites contaminated by USTs. Priorities must be based upon public health, safety, and welfare and environmental concerns.[170]

On June 18, 1991, EIB adopted Ground Water Protection Act Regulations (Part XV of the UST regulations) pursuant to the GWPA mandate. The scheme adopted by EIB includes a three-tiered priority approach depending upon the nature and extent of the release or contamination. Funds are to be applied to sites based upon the priority ranking.[171] NMED is authorized to make expenditures from the CAF, including payment of agency legal and administrative costs, in accordance with regulations adopted by EIB and to take corrective action at sites in the order of priority on the priority list, except when an emergency threat to public health, safety, and welfare or to the environment exists.[172]

NMED is authorized to bring legal action against an owner or operator to recover expenses it incurs under the GWPA.[173] The GWPA provides that all owners and operators of sites contaminated by a UST are strictly liable for NMED's costs of taking corrective action at a site.[174] Strict liability means that an owner or operator will be liable for cleanup costs irrespective of fault considerations.[175] Involvement as an owner or operator with a con-

---

168 N.M. Stat. Ann. § 74-6B-7.A (Repl. Pamp. 1993). The fund is not available for use by owners and operators as evidence of financial assurance to satisfy third-party claims. N.M. Stat. Ann. § 74-6B-7.A (Repl. Pamp. 1993). The GWPA does not prohibit existing or future third-party damage claims based upon a UST release. N.M. Stat. Ann. § 74-6B-6 (Repl. Pamp. 1993).

169 N.M. Stat. Ann. § 74-6B-4 (Repl. Pamp. 1993) establishes an advisory UST Committee composed of seven members, including the Secretary of NMED and six members appointed by the Governor.

170 N.M. Stat. Ann. § 74-6B-7(B) (Repl. Pamp. 1993); N.M. Underground Storage Tank Regulations § 1505.

171 N.M. Underground Storage Tank Regulations § 1506.

172 N.M. Stat. Ann. § 74-6B-7(C) (Repl. Pamp. 1993) (the GWPA does not define the term "emergency threat"); N.M. Underground Storage Tank Regulations § 1504.

173 N.M. Stat. Ann. § 74-6B-8(C) (Repl. Pamp. 1993).

174 N.M. Stat. Ann. § 74-6B-8(A) (Repl. Pamp. 1993). The GWPA definition of owners and operators is identical to that contained in N.M. Underground Storage Tank Regulations §§ 102.FF and 102.HH. N.M. Stat. Ann. § 74-68-3(D), (E) (Repl. Pamp. 1993).

175 Strict liability has been the rule under federal environmental statutes for some time. *New York v. Shore Realty Corp.*, 759 F.2d 1032 (2d. Cir. 1985) (purchaser of property contaminated with hazardous waste held liable for environmental response costs notwithstanding fact that buyer had not participated in generation or disposal of any waste on the property); *United States v. Maryland Bank & Trust Co.*, 632 F. Supp. 573 (D. Md. 1986) (foreclosing bank held liable for environmental response costs relating

taminated site may result in the imposition of liability whether or not the owner or operator caused or contributed to the contamination. An owner or operator will not be liable to NMED for money expended from the corrective action fund if the owner or operator (a) is in compliance with all requirements and provisions of regulations adopted by EIB pursuant to the HWA,[176] (b) has paid all underground storage tank fees required by the HWA and the GWPA, (c) has conducted a minimum site assessment and, if contamination is found, has taken action to prevent continuing contamination, and (d) has cooperated in good faith with NMED and has granted access to NMED for investigation, clean-up, and monitoring.[177] A minimum site assessment requires that the owner and operator (1) report, investigate, and confirm the release pursuant to Part VII of the UST regulations and (2) determine the immediate extent, impact, and magnitude of the release.[178] Cost reimbursements for assessments are set out in the GWPA.[179] For sites where USTs have been removed or properly abandoned prior to March 7, 1990, an owner will not be liable for money expended from the corrective action fund if it is established that the owner (a) has paid all underground storage tank fees required by the HWA and a $200 fee per site, (b) has conducted a minimum site assessment as required by the UST regulations, and (c) has cooperated in good faith with NMED and has granted access to NMED for investigation, clean-up, and monitoring.[180]

NMED may bring an action against an owner or operator of a site to recover reasonable and necessary expenses incurred by NMED for corrective action and may recover expenditures of federal funds from the leaking underground storage tank trust fund. Recoverable expenses include but are not limited to costs of investigating a release and undertaking corrective action, administrative costs, and reasonable attorneys' fees. Expenses recovered, excepting any recovered federal funds, must be deposited into the CAF.[181] NMED has a right of subrogation to any insurance policies in existence at the time of the release and to proceeds due under those policies. The right of subrogation applies even if

---

to property upon which it foreclosed despite bank's lack of involvement with actions that led to release of hazardous wastes); *United States v. Argent Corp.,* 21 Env't. Rep. Cas. (BNA) 1354 (D.N.M. 1984) (landowner-lessor liable for cleanup of hazardous waste at facility contaminated by lessee's silver recovery business).

176 Reference is made in the GWPA to N.M. Stat. Ann. §§ 74-4-4 and 74-4-4.4 (Repl. Pamp. 1993).

177 N.M. Stat. Ann. § 74-6B-8 (B)(1) (Repl. Pamp. 1993); N.M. Underground Storage Tank Regulations § 1508.

178 N.M. Underground Storage Tank Regulations § 1508.A.

179 N.M. Stat. Ann. § 74-6B-13 (Repl. Pamp. 1993).

180 N.M. Stat. Ann § 74-6B-8(B)(2) (Repl. Pamp. 1993).

181 N.M. Stat. Ann. § 74-6B-8(C) (Repl. Pamp. 1993).

the owner or operator establishes non-liability under the factors discussed in the preceding paragraph.[182]

In connection with the GWPA's corrective action provisions, an incentive grace period was established for reporting contamination incidents. The grace period began on the effective date of the GWPA (March 7, 1990) and ended two years thereafter. The 1993 Legislature repealed the provision granting this two-year grace period.[183]

Nothing in the GWPA creates an insurance company or an insurance fund, and the CAF is specifically exempted from the provisions of the New Mexico Insurance Code.[184]

The New Mexico Tax Administration Act authorizes a distribution to the CAF of the net receipts attributable to the petroleum products loading fee.[185] The imposition of the fee is to cease on the first day of the month following the expiration of 90 days from the end of the month for which the unencumbered balance of the CAF is certified to equal or exceed $50,000,000 and for every month thereafter until the unencumbered balance is certified by the Secretary to be less than or equal to $12,000,000 at the end of any month.[186] In that event the imposition of the petroleum products loading fee must be reinstated on the first day of the month following the expiration of the (90) days after the end of the month for which the certification was made and the distribution of the fee must be returned to the CAF.[187] The petroleum products loading fee is a one-time fee of $80 per load (1¢ per gallon) of gasoline or special fuel imported into the state for resale or consumption.[188]

8.2 COST REIMBURSEMENT

The GWPA was amended by the 1992 Legislature in two significant respects. First, NMED was authorized to pay for costs of a minimum site assessment in excess of $10,000 with monies from the CAF.[189] Second, if owners or operators can demonstrate compliance with the requirements of Section 74-6B-8 of the GWPA (tank fees, minimum site assessment, investigation, clean-up, and monitoring) an owner or operator may apply to NMED for payment for the costs of corrective action, provided specified conditions are satisfied.[190]

---

182 N.M. Stat. Ann. § 74-6B-8(D) (Repl. Pamp. 1993).

183 1993 N.M. Laws, ch. 298, § 5.

184 N.M. Stat. Ann. § 74-6B-10 (Repl. Pamp. 1993).

185 N.M. Stat. Ann. § 7-1-6.25 (Repl. Pamp. 1993).

186 *Id.*

187 *Id.*

188 N.M. Stat. Ann. § 7-13A-3(C) (Repl. Pamp. 1993). A "load" means 8,000 gallons of gasoline or special fuel. The fee is imposed on each load on which the fee has not previously been paid. N.M. Stat. Ann. § 7-13A-3(B) (Repl. Pamp. 1993).

189 N.M. Stat. Ann § 74-6B-13(A) (Repl. Pamp. 1993).

190 N.M. Stat. Ann. § 74-6B-13(B) (Repl. Pamp. 1993).

The payment of the cost of corrective action, including the cost of a minimum site assessment, must be made by NMED following application and proper documentation of the costs and in accordance with regulations adopted by the Secretary establishing eligible and ineligible costs.[191] Eligible costs for payment are those reasonable and necessary costs actually incurred after March 7, 1990, in the performance of a site assessment and for corrective action that are consistent with NMED's fee schedule.[192] Ineligible costs include attorneys' fees, repair or upgrade of tanks, loss of revenue, and costs of monitoring a contractor.[193] The Secretary adopted regulations, effective September 22, 1992, implementing the mandates of the 1992 GWPA amendments.[194] These regulations (1) address (a) what constitutes compliance for reimbursement purposes and (b) eligibility and ineligibility of costs associated with minimum site assessments and corrective action, (2) specify the application payment and reimbursement procedures, and (3) prescribe an administrative review process.

With respect to compliance determinations, the regulations provide that the director of the Environmental Protection Division of NMED (Director) determines compliance on a case by case basis and must notify the owner or operator in writing of the determination, the reasons therefor, and the right to an administrative appeal of the determination.[195] With respect to minimum site assessments, the compliance determination is made in accordance with UST Regulations Section 1508, which specifies the requirements for a minimum site assessment. When an owner or operator applies to NMED for reimbursement or payment of corrective action costs, NMED must determine whether the owner or operator is in compliance with the requirements of N.M. Stat. Ann. § 74-6B-8(B). during the term of ownership or operation for all USTs owned and/or operated at the site where the corrective action was or is being taken.[196] Compliance is to be determined for the period from March 7, 1990, and every day continuously thereafter to the date the application for payment or reimbursement submitted by the owner or operator is deemed complete.[197] The owner or operator seeking a determination of compliance has the burden of establishing each point of fact relevant to such determination.[198] A compliance determination must be made by the

---

191 N.M. Stat. Ann. § 74-6B-13(C) (Repl. Pamp. 1993).

192 *Id.*

193 *Id.*

194 N.M. Ground Water Protection Act Corrective Action Fund Regulations, NMED-92-1 (filed 9/24/92).

195 N.M. Ground Water Protection Act Corrective Action Fund Regulations § 201.B.

196 N.M. Ground Water Protection Act Corrective Action Fund Regulations § 201.A.(3).

197 *Id.*

198 N.M. Ground Water Protection Act Correction Action Fund Regulations § 203.C.

Director within 30 days following NMED's determination of the submission as "complete."[199] The Director may make a separate compliance determination for each phase of corrective action other than a minimum site assessment for which payment or reimbursement is requested.[200]

Only reasonable and necessary eligible costs in excess of $10,000 actually incurred to complete a minimum site assessment will be paid by NMED.[201] Payment or reimbursement must not be paid for work performed on or after September 22, 1992, if the owner or operator does not obtain NMED approval of proposed work plans and associated cost estimates for the minimum site assessment before the costs are incurred.[202] The regulations provide costs that are ineligible for reimbursement which include, *inter alia*, costs incurred prior to March 7, 1990, and those costs incurred on or after September 22, 1992, that exceed those in the NMED fee schedule in effect at the time the work was performed.[203]

With respect to corrective action, payment or reimbursement will be made only for reasonable and necessary costs incurred to complete corrective action other than a minimum site assessment.[204] Before making any payment or reimbursement, NMED must determine that (a) all costs submitted for payment or reimbursement are eligible costs, (b) the owner or operator has filed a claim with its insurers and has pursued payment of the claim in good faith, (c) the owner or operator has reimbursed NMED for all of the leaking underground storage tank trust funds expended for contractual services at the site, and (d) the owner or operator has been determined by the Director to be in compliance as required by the regulations.[205] Payment or reimbursement will not be made for work performed on or after September 22, 1992, if the owner or operator does not obtain NMED approval of proposed work plans and associated cost estimates before costs are incurred.[206] A list of ineligible costs for reimbursement is provided which include, *inter alia*, costs incurred on or after September 22, 1992, that exceed those in NMED's fee schedule in effect at the time the work was performed, costs paid or reimbursed by insurance companies or any other third party, costs incurred prior to March 7, 1990, and economic losses and liability to third parties.[207]

---

199 N.M. Ground Water Protection Act Corrective Action Fund Regulations § 203.D.

200 *Id.*

201 N.M. Ground Water Protection Act Corrective Action Fund Regulations § 301.A. *But see* 1993 GWPA Amendment Section of this Chapter.

202 N.M. Ground Water Protection Act Corrective Action Fund Regulations § 301.D.

203 N.M. Ground Water Protection Act Collection Action Fund Regulations § 301.D.

204 N.M. Ground Water Protection Act Corrective Action Fund Regulations § 302.A.

205 *Id.*

206 N.M. Ground Water Protection Act Corrective Action Fund Regulations § 302.C.

207 N.M. Ground Water Protection Act Corrective Action Fund Regulations § 302.D.

An application for payment or reimbursement must be typed or printed and submitted by the owner or operator on a form provided by NMED. The application must include copies of all release investigation reports for the site submitted to NMED, with copies of invoices showing the work performed for the minimum site assessment and for each phase of corrective action for which payment or reimbursement is sought.[208] Applicants must also include a certification of truthfulness of all of the matters and facts contained in the application and state that the invoices reflect actual costs paid or otherwise incurred.[209] Claims for costs incurred prior to September 22, 1992, must have been received, by NMED prior to June 30, 1993. All other claims must be received by NMED within six months of the date the costs are incurred.[210] NMED must review all written submissions in the order received and must, within thirty days of receipt, notify the owner or operator in writing of any inadequacies in the submittal.[211] If, after the Director has made a determination of compliance, NMED determines that the balance in the CAF is insufficient to cover the amount requested for payment or reimbursement, NMED must promptly notify the owner or operator.[212] Payment or reimbursement for eligible costs must occur when sufficient amounts are available in the CAF.[213] Unless the balance of the CAF is insufficient, payment or reimbursement for eligible costs must occur not later than ninety days after NMED deems the submittal complete.[214]

The following actions of the Director are subject to the right of an administrative appeal by an owner or operator who has completed an application for payment or reimbursement: (a) a determination of compliance in accordance with the regulations, (b) a determination of whether a minimum site assessment was performed in accordance with the regulations, or (c) a determination of eligibility for costs for which payment or reimbursement was requested.[215] The appealing party must file a written request for a hearing with the hearing clerk designated by the Secretary within thirty days after notice of the determination has been received by the party.[216] The appellant must attach to the request for hearing a copy of the determination for which review is sought along with a response to the determination.[217]

---

208 N.M. Ground Water Protection Act Corrective Action Fund Regulations § 401.A.

209 N.M. Ground Water Protection Act Corrective Action Fund Regulations § 401.A(2).

210 N.M. Ground Water Protection Act Corrective Action Fund Regulations § 401.A(3).

211 N.M. Ground Water Protection Act Corrective Action Fund Regulations § 401.C.

212 N.M. Ground Water Protection Act Corrective Action Fund Regulations § 401.D.

213 *Id.*

214 N.M. Ground Water Protection Act Corrective Action Fund Regulations § 401.E.

215 N.M. Ground Water Protection Act Corrective Action Fund Regulations § 501.A.

216 N.M. Ground Water Protection Act Corrective Action Fund Regulations § 501.B.

217 N.M. Ground Water Protection Act Corrective Action Fund Regulations § 501.C.

The response must admit or deny each of the factual assertions contained in the determination; where the appellant has no knowledge of a particular factual assertion and so states, the assertion may be denied on that basis. Any allegation of the determination not specifically denied is deemed admitted.[218] Except as otherwise provided, notice of docketing and hearing officer assignment, motions, pre-hearing procedures and discovery, and hearing and post-hearing procedures must be governed by NMED's Rules Governing Appeals From Compliance Orders Under The Hazardous Waste Act and Solid Waste Act.[219] The hearing officer must schedule a hearing for no later than ninety days after service of the Notice of Docketing.[220]

8.3 1993 GWPA AMENDMENT

The 1993 Legislature amended the GWPA to require NMED to adopt regulations to provide for payments from the CAF to persons who cannot afford to pay all or a portion of the initial $10,000 cost of a minimum site assessment otherwise required under GWPA.[221] NMED is mandated to develop a financial assistance means test, including a sliding scale of financial relief as NMED deems appropriate, that allows some or all of the minimum site assessment costs to be paid from the CAF.[222] This financial assistance relief is to be made available to owners or operators who performed or made arrangements to perform corrective action after March 7, 1990.[223]

9.0 REMOVAL OR CLOSURE OF UST SYSTEMS

Owners and operators of a UST system who plan to take the system out of service while leaving regulated substances in the tank must nevertheless continue to meet the requirements of the UST regulations, including operation of release detection systems and notification of releases or suspected releases.[224] Additional requirements are set forth if a UST is taken out of service for a period of between three and 12 months.[225] If a UST system is taken out of service for longer than 12 months, it must be closed permanently unless the system meets either new UST system performance standards or upgraded requirements, except that spill and overfill requirements do not have to be met.[226] Permanent closure is

---

218 N.M. Ground Water Protection Act Corrective Action Fund Regulations § 501.C.

219 N.M. Ground Water Protection Act Corrective Action Fund Regulations § 502.A.

220 N.M. Ground Water Protection Act Corrective Action Fund Regulations § 502.B.

221 N.M. Stat. Ann. § 74-6B-13(D) (Repl. Pamp. 1993).

222 *Id.*

223 *Id.*

224 N.M. Underground Storage Tank Regulations § 800(a).

225 N.M. Underground Storage Tank Regulations § 800(b).

226 N.M. Underground Storage Tank Regulations § 800(c).

required at the end of the 12-month period unless NMED grants a 12-month extension.[227] At least 30 days prior to permanent closure, the owner of a UST system must notify NMED of its plan for closure, including plans for assessing the excavation area.[228] Owners and operators are required to measure for a release by taking samples.[229] Any contamination discovered during excavation must be treated and reported like any other release.[230] Tanks permanently taken out of service must be emptied and removed from the ground in compliance with industry recognized procedures or filled with inert material.[231] All UST system owners must maintain records pertaining to the closure procedure.[232] Owners may continue to use a UST system to store a non-regulated substance as long as the tank is emptied and cleaned and a site assessment is performed.[233]

10.0 FINANCIAL RESPONSIBILITY

Owners of USTs are required to assure financial responsibility with respect to corrective action necessitated by releases from USTs and to third party damage claims arising from releases from USTs.[234] On October 29, 1992, the Secretary determined that the CAF is an acceptable financial assurance mechanism under the UST regulations for corrective action.[235] The Secretary also determined that the CAF cannot be used as evidence of financial assurance to satisfy claims of third parties.[236] Within 60 days following the October 29, 1992 determinations, NMED was required to send each tank owner and operator

---

227 *Id.*

228 N.M. Underground Storage Tank Regulations § 801(a).

229 N.M. Underground Storage Tank Regulations § 802. *See* Soil and Water Sample Methods at Tank Removals Section of this Chapter for sampling guidelines.

230 N.M. Underground Storage Tank Regulations § 802(b).

231 N.M. Underground Storage Tank Regulations § 801(b).

232 N.M. Underground Storage Tank Regulations § 804.

233 N.M. Underground Storage Tank Regulations § 801(c).

234 N.M. Underground Storage Tank Regulations § 903(a). The financial responsibility regulations do not apply to operators or owners of wastewater treatment tanks, sumps, UST systems containing radioactive waste, electrical equipment, hydraulic lift tanks, or UST systems with capacity of 110 gallons or less. N.M. Underground Storage Tank Regulations § 103.C.

235 New Mexico Environment Department Determination of Acceptability of the Ground Water Protection Act Corrective Action Fund as a State Fund Assuring Financial Responsibility for Corrective Action (Determination), Conclusion No. 1. N.M. Reg. 11/30/92. *See* N.M. Underground Storage Tank Regulations § 911. Thus the CAF provides financial assurance at least equivalent to the financial mechanism specified in the federal and state regulations and therefore can be used by tank owners and operators to demonstrate financial responsibility for corrective action.

236 Determination, Conclusion No. 2.

for which financial responsibility is being assumed a letter or certificate describing the nature of the assumption of responsibility.[237] The letter or certificate must have the facility's name and address and the amount of funds for corrective action that is assured by the state.[238] In the event that the CAF can no longer provide financial assurance for tank owners and operators, NMED must, 60 days prior to the termination of fund coverage, notify all owners and operators that coverage is terminating and advise them that they must obtain other financial responsibility coverage to satisfy their obligations under Part IX of the UST regulations.[239]

As to the requirement for demonstrating financial responsibility for third-party damage claims, the regulations set out minimum insurance coverage requirements based upon the volume of petroleum handled and the number of USTs owned. For UST owners that either are located at petroleum marketing facilities or handle an average of more than 10,000 gallons of petroleum per month based on annual throughput for the previous calendar year, a $1,000,000 per occurrence minimum coverage requirement is established, while a $500,000 per occurrence minimum is established for all other owners of USTs.[240] For owners of one to 100 petroleum underground storage tanks, $1,000,000 per occurrence coverage minimums are required, while for owners of 101 or more USTs a $2,000,000 per occurrence minimum is established.[241]

The regulations provide a number of mechanisms by which a UST owner may demonstrate financial responsibility. First, an owner may satisfy the financial responsibility requirements by passing a financial test of self insurance in combination with a guarantee, but only if the financial statements of the owner or operator are not consolidated with those of the guarantor.[242] The self insurance standards may be met by showing a tangible net worth of at least $10,000,000 or by showing a tangible net worth in excess of the applicable aggregate insurance amounts described in the previous paragraph. A tangible net worth of at least ten times the sum of corrective action cost estimates will also suffice.[243] In addition, the owner must either file financial statements annually with an identified agency or report annually the firm's tangible net worth to Dun & Bradstreet. The firm's year-end financial statements cannot include an adverse auditor's opinion, a disclaimer of opinion, or a "going concern"

237 Determination, Conclusion No. 3.

238 *Id.*

239 Determination, Conclusion No. 4.

240 N.M. Underground Storage Tank Regulations § 903(a).

241 N.M. Underground Storage Tank Regulations § 903(b).

242 N.M. Underground Storage Tank Regulations § 905.

243 N.M. Underground Storage Tank Regulations § 905(b).

qualification.[244] Owners are required to sign a letter form specified by regulation to demonstrate self insurance and are required to obtain alternative coverage if the owner at any point fails to meet the financial tests set out in the regulation.[245]

An owner may satisfy the financial responsibility requirements by obtaining (1) a guarantee subject to specified conditions,[246] (2) liability insurance,[247] (3) coverage from a risk retention group chartered, licensed, and authorized to operate in New Mexico,[248] or, (4) a surety bond.[249] Letters of credit may also be used to satisfy the financial responsibility requirements.[250] Substitution of financial assurance mechanisms is allowed as long as the owner maintains an effective financial assurance mechanism or a combination of mechanisms to satisfy the financial responsibility requirements.[251]

The regulations limit the ability of a provider of financial assurance to cancel or fail to renew an assurance mechanism.[252] Except in the event of bankruptcy of the owner or provider of financial assurance, if a provider of financial assurance cancels or fails to renew its coverage and the owner fails to obtain alternative coverage within 60 days after receipt of the notice of termination, the owner must notify NMED in writing.[253] The regulations impose financial responsibility reporting requirements on an owner after an identified release or suspected release and before placing a new tank in service.[254]

An owner is required to maintain evidence of all financial assurance mechanisms used to demonstrate financial responsibility until released from the requirements of the financial responsibility section.[255] As to financial responsibility for taking corrective action, the

---

[244] N.M. Underground Storage Tank Regulations § 905(b)(5).

[245] N.M. Underground Storage Tank Regulations § 905(d)-(e).

[246] N.M. Underground Storage Tank Regulations § 906.

[247] N.M. Underground Storage Tank Regulations § 907. The insurance policy must contain an endorsement as specified in the regulations.

[248] N.M. Underground Storage Tank Regulations § 907. An endorsement specified by NMED must be included as part of the policy.

[249] N.M. Underground Storage Tank Regulations § 908. An owner using a surety bond authorized by regulation must establish a standby trust fund. N.M. Underground Storage Tank Regulations § 908(d). *See* N.M. Underground Storage § 913.

[250] N.M. Underground Storage Tank Regulations § 909.

[251] N.M. Underground Storage Tank Regulations § 914. The regulation does not require notice of the substitution itself, but notification requirements applicable to any specific method of proving financial assurance would likely apply.

[252] N.M. Underground Storage Tank Regulations § 915.

[253] N.M. Underground Storage Tank Regulations §§ 915(6), 916.

[254] N.M. Underground Storage Tank Regulations § 916(a)-(b).

[255] N.M. Underground Storage Tank Regulations § 917(a).

Secretary required NMED to send, within 60 days after October 29, 1992, the date of the financial assurance determination, to each tank owner and operator for which NMED was assuming financial responsibility, a letter or certificate describing the nature of the assumption of responsibility.[256] In the event that the CAF can no longer provide financial assurance for the tank owners and operators in New Mexico, NMED must, 60 days prior to termination of CAF coverage, notify all owners and operators that coverage is terminating and advise them that they must obtain other financial responsibility coverage to satisfy their obligations under Part IX of the UST regulations.[257] Recordkeeping generally involves maintaining documentation evidencing financial responsibility.[258] Records must be maintained either on-site or at a readily available alternative site for inspection on 24 hours notice.[259] An owner may be released from the financial responsibility requirements following closure of the tank and completion of any required corrective action.[260]

11.0 ADMINISTRATIVE REVIEW

The UST regulations provide that an owner or operator of a UST who is aggrieved by a decision made by NMED staff pursuant to the regulations, may obtain review of the decision by submitting a written request for informal review to NMED. The request must be postmarked within 15 days of the date of the decision[261] and must specify the grounds upon which the petitioner objects to the decision.[262] An informal conference will be held at which the petitioner may present his or her views and arguments.[263] NMED may either affirm, modify, or reverse the original decision and must furnish the petitioner with a written notification of its determination.[264] Within 20 days after a determination made by NMED pursuant to the aforementioned procedure, a petitioner may appeal the determination to the Secretary by requesting a review of the written record. This request also must be in writing and must specify the grounds upon which the petitioner objects to NMED's determination.[265] NMED staff then have an opportunity to respond to the petition.[266] The Secretary's action on the request must be based upon the written materials and documentation

---

256 Determination, Conclusion No. 3.

257 Determination, Conclusion No. 4.

258 N.M. Underground Storage Tank Regulations § 917(b).

259 N.M. Underground Storage Tank Regulations § 917(a).

260 N.M. Underground Storage Tank Regulations § 919.

261 N.M. Underground Storage Tank Regulations § 1000.A.

262 N.M. Underground Storage Tank Regulations § 1000.C.

263 N.M. Underground Storage Tank Regulations § 1000.B.

264 N.M. Underground Storage Tank Regulations § 1000.E.

265 N.M. Underground Storage Tank Regulations § 1001.A.

266 N.M. Underground Storage Tank Regulations § 1001.D.

submitted unless, in the Secretary's discretion, the Secretary schedules a conference or hearing.[267] The Secretary's action on the request must be by written order which states the decision and the reason therefor.[268] The Secretary has discretion to provide for public participation in the review process.[269]

12.0 CERTIFICATION OF TANK INSTALLERS

Part XIV of the UST Regulations provides for the regulation of persons installing and repairing underground storage tank systems which contain regulated substances. The purpose of the regulations is to assure that UST systems are being installed and repaired in a manner which will not encourage or facilitate leaking and which will protect the public health and welfare and the lands and waters of the state.[270] The regulations apply to all persons who perform installation or repair services on UST systems within the state.[271]

The regulations essentially require that no person may install or repair UST systems in this state unless the person is, or employs, an individual who has been certified by NMED to install and repair UST systems.[272] The process for contractor and individual certification requires experience and the passing of a written examination and an on-site examination.[273] The certification regulations impose duties and obligations on certified contractors and installers, including the duty to report to NMED any and all releases, suspected releases, or spills as those terms are defined in the UST Regulations.[274] NMED is authorized to receive written complaints against a certified installer and to undertake investigations and take such actions as it deems necessary to insure compliance with the provisions of the regulations, including the initiation of proceedings to suspend or revoke an installer's certificate.[275]

---

267 N.M. Underground Storage Tank Regulations § 1001.B.

268 N.M. Underground Storage Tank Regulations § 1001.E.

269 N.M. Underground Storage Tank Regulations § 1002.

270 N.M. Underground Storage Tank Regulations § 1400.

271 N.M. Underground Storage Tank Regulations § 1403.A. The regulations do not apply to the installation or repair of wastewater treatment tanks, sumps, UST systems containing radioactive waste, electrical equipment, hydraulic lift tanks, and any UST system with a capacity of 110 gallons or less. N.M. Underground Storage Tank Regulations § 1403.B.

272 N.M. Underground Storage Tank Regulations § 1404.

273 N.M. Underground Storage Tank Regulations §§ 1405 - 1409.

274 N.M. Underground Storage Tank Regulations § 1413.

275 N.M. Underground Storage Tank Regulations §§ 1415 - 1416.

CHAPTER VII
MINING AND OIL AND GAS

1.0 MINE REGISTRATION AND REPORTING

New Mexico Energy, Minerals and Natural Resources Department (EMNRD) Rule EMNRD MMD 89-1 (Rule 89-1) requires that before operations start at any mine, mill, smelter, or other treatment plant, the operator must register the facility with the Mining and Minerals Division (MMD) of EMNRD on the MMD Mine/Mill/Smelter Registration form.[1]

Rule 89-1 also requires operators of such facilities to file with MMD, before February 15 of each year, an annual report on the MMD form for the commodity mined or processed.[2] In addition, operators of underground and solution mines must at the same time file with MMD "a current and accurate map of all workings" prepared "by a competent surveyor."[3]

Operators of underground and in situ leach operations which are to be "suspended permanently or for an indefinite period" must have a competent surveyor prepare a complete and final survey of all workings which shows the exact relations of the most advanced workings to the boundary of the property; a copy of the survey must be filed with MMD.[4]

The operator of a mine, mill, smelter, or other treatment plant must file an MMD Change of Registration form at least ten days prior to any change in ownership, operator name, mine name, address, or operational status.[5] Change in operational status may include the cancellation of registration, suspension of operations, and/or abandonment.[6]

2.0 COAL MINING REGULATION

Surface mining of coal is defined as the extraction of coal from the earth by such methods as excavation, auger mining or strip mining, and underground mining. It could include strip mining, mountaintop removal, and open pit mining.[7] Surface coal mining activities may include blasting operations, in situ distillation or retorting, leaching or other chemical or physical processing, and the processing or preparation of coal at or near the mine

---

1 N.M. Mine Registration, Reporting and Safeguarding Regulations, Rule EMNRD MMD 89-1, Part 1, § 2.1 (filed 8/18/89).

2 N.M. Mine Registration, Reporting and Safeguarding Regulations, Part 1, § 3.1.

3 N.M. Mine Registration, Reporting and Safeguarding Regulations, Part 1, § 3.2.

4 N.M. Mine Registration, Reporting and Safeguarding Regulations, Part 1, § 3.3.

5 N.M. Mine Registration, Reporting and Safeguarding Regulations, Part 1, § 4.1.

6 *Id.*

7 N.M. Surface Coal Mining Regulations, CSMC Rule 80-1, § 1-5 (as amended through Feb. 1993).

site.[8] The regulatory framework for these activities consists of the Surface Mining Act (SMA)[9] and regulations promulgated thereunder by the New Mexico Coal Surface Mining Commission (CSMC). All New Mexico rules and regulations must be consistent with the Federal Surface Mining Control and Reclamation Act (SMCRA), which regulates surface and underground coal exploration and mining.[10] MMD administers CSMC regulations.[11]

2.1 COAL MINING AND RECLAMATION PERMIT REQUIREMENTS

A permit from the MMD Director (Director) is required in order to carry out both surface and underground coal mining and reclamation operations on non-Indian lands.[12] In most cases, a permit is not required to explore for coal, but the explorer must file a notice of intent to explore with MMD and is limited to extracting 250 tons of coal from the land. Exploration must be conducted pursuant to the applicable performance standards.[13] Approval from the Director is required before conducting exploration that removes more than 250 tons.[14]

Applications for mining and reclamation permits must be filed with MMD. The application must identify the applicant, owners and operators of the land, property interests, current or previous mining permits and the applicant's past record of compliance with environmental regulations. It must describe the proposed mining site in relation to areas designated unsuitable for mining and the environmental resources at the site, including hydrology, geology, ground and surface water, and alternative water supply information. Environmental information must also include data on the climate, existing vegetation, fish and wildlife resources, soil composition, water, and past land use. Further, the application must describe the operating plan, including details of plans to prevent or minimize air pollution and to protect fish and wildlife, and the reclamation plan.[15] Applicants desiring to use experimental practices, mountaintop removal, or steep slope mining techniques must meet additional requirements.[16]

When an applicant submits an application to MMD, the applicant must also advertise in a local newspaper of general circulation in the county where the proposed mine is to be

---

8 N.M. Stat. Ann. § 69-25A-3(P) (Supp. 1993).

9 N.M. Stat. Ann. §§ 69-25A-1 to -35 (Repl. Pamp. 1979 & Supp. 1993).

10 *See* 30 U.S.C. § 1201.

11 N.M. Stat. Ann. § 69-25A-8 (Repl. Pamp. 1979).

12 N.M. Stat. Ann. §§ 69-25A-9(A), 69-11-1 to -3 (Repl. Pamp. 1979 & Supp. 1993).

13 N.M. Surface Coal Mining Regulations, §§ 6-11 to -15.

14 N.M. Surface Coal Mining Regulations, § 6-12.

15 N.M. Surface Coal Mining Regulations, §§ 5-11, -23.

16 N.M. Surface Coal Mining Regulations, §§ 10-13 to -16.

located at least once a week for four consecutive weeks.[17] This advertisement must include a map or description of the proposed permit area, the applicant's name and address, the location where a copy of the application may be reviewed, and the name and address of the Director, to whom written comments, objections, or requests for an informal conference should be sent.[18] If the mine would be within 100 feet of the outside right-of-way of a public road or if a public road would be relocated, the advertisement must contain details on the road and the proposed relocation.[19] After receiving the completed application, MMD will notify federal, state, and local government agencies and authorities.[20] Agencies which have received such notification may submit written comments on the application, which will be received by the Director and made available for public review together with the application.[21] Any interested person may file written objections within 30 days after the last publication of the newspaper advertisement. Further, any person may request an informal conference with the Director not later than 30 days after the last publication.[22] The informal conference may be used by the Director as the public hearing, if one is required by the regulations.[23] If a public hearing is held, it will be advertised and held in the county in which the mining is to be conducted.[24]

No permit may be approved unless the application is accurate and complete, the mining and reclamation operations are feasible, the hydrologic balance will not be damaged, and the proposed permit area is suitable for mining.[25] Before the permit is issued, the applicant must meet bonding and insurance requirements.[26]

The Director's decision to approve or deny a permit is subject to administrative and judicial review. Within 30 days after a final decision, the applicant, permittee, or any interested person may request a hearing before the Director on the reasons for the decision.[27] After a hearing on the record, an aggrieved person may appeal to CSMC. Notice must be filed with both CSMC and the Director within 30 days of the Director's decision. The appeal

---

17 N.M. Stat. Ann. § 69-25A-17(A) (Repl. Pamp. 1979).

18 N.M. Surface Coal Mining Regulations, § 11-11(a).

19 N.M. Surface Coal Mining Regulations, § 11-11(a)(5).

20 N.M. Surface Coal Mining Regulations, § 11-11(c).

21 N.M. Surface Coal Mining Regulations, § 11-12.

22 N.M. Surface Coal Mining Regulations, §§ 11-12 to -14.

23 N.M. Surface Coal Mining Regulations, § 11-14(d), (f).

24 N.M. Surface Coal Mining Regulations, § 11-14(e)(3).

25 N.M. Surface Coal Mining Regulations, § 11-19. *See* § 11-19(d), which lists general restrictions on lands which may be mined.

26 N.M. Surface Coal Mining Regulations, Part 14.

27 N.M. Surface Coal Mining Regulations, § 12-10.

hearing will generally be limited to the record before the Director.[28] However, CSMC is not bound by the Director's findings of fact and may order that additional evidence be presented if it is material and there was good reason for its omission in the initial hearing.[29] Parties aggrieved by a CSMC decision may seek review in the District Court of Santa Fe County. A petition for review must be filed with the court within 30 days after CSMC renders its decision.[30] The court may reverse the CSMC decision if the decision affects substantial rights and is found to be unlawful, arbitrary or capricious, or unsupported by substantial evidence on the entire record.[31]

2.2 ENVIRONMENTAL PROTECTION STANDARDS FOR COAL MINES

All permits issued under the SMA require the operator to meet applicable performance standards designed to maximize the recovery of coal while minimizing the impact on the land during and after mining.[32] In general, these standards are intended to maximize the use and recovery of coal so that the land need not be disturbed again and to restore the land to as close to its original condition as possible.[33]

Once mining begins, all topsoil and subsoil that is to be used as topdressing or that is suitable for root development must be removed and segregated.[34] If it will not be immediately redistributed, it must be protected from erosion and contamination so it can sustain vegetation in the future.[35] If removing the topsoil or vegetative growth could result in accelerated erosion or cause air or water pollution, the topsoil may be removed only from a limited area at any one time and must be redistributed at times when its physical and chemical properties can be protected and erosion minimized. MMD and, for farmland, the United States Secretary of Agriculture may require other measures as well.[36]

Mining must be conducted to minimize changes in the prevailing hydrologic balance.[37] The operator may not violate any federal or state water quality statutes or other laws. Operations must be conducted to minimize water pollution, changes in water quality

---

28 N.M. Surface Coal Mining Regulations, § 12-11.

29 N.M. Surface Coal Mining Regulations, § 12-11(b), (c).

30 N.M. Surface Coal Mining Regulations, § 12-12.

31 N.M. Stat. Ann. § 69-25A-30(C) (Repl. Pamp. 1979).

32 N.M. Stat. Ann. § 69-25A-19 (Repl. Pamp. 1979).

33 N.M. Stat. Ann. § 69-25A-19(B) (Repl. Pamp. 1979).

34 N.M. Surface Coal Mining Regulations, §§ 20-22, -23.

35 N.M. Surface Coal Mining Regulations, § 20-23; N.M. Stat. Ann. § 69-25A-19(B)(5) (Repl. Pamp. 1979).

36 N.M. Surface Coal Mining Regulations, Rule 80-1, § 20-22(f); N.M. Stat. Ann. § 69-25A-19(B)(7) (Repl. Pamp. 1979).

37 N.M. Surface Coal Mining Regulations, § 20-41.

and quantity, depth to ground water, and location of drainage channels.[38] Operators may with the approval of MMD divert water flowing over the land and shallow ground water if diversion is necessary to minimize erosion, reduce the volume of water to be treated or avoid acid-forming or toxic-forming materials.[39] Similarly, the operator may with the approval of MMD construct diversions of perennial and intermittent streams.[40] The operator must meet performance standards for sediment control[41] and prevent acid-forming and toxic-forming spoils[42] from draining into the ground and surface water.[43] The operator may not construct permanent impoundments without permission of MMD.

Other authorized means of protecting the hydrology in the mine area include locating backfilled materials so as to minimize contamination of ground water, protecting the recharge capacity for ground water, and monitoring surface and ground water.[44] Mining within 100 feet of a perennial stream or a stream with a biological community is subject to special restrictions.[45] With a few specified exceptions, every exposed underground opening, including exploration holes, bore holes, shafts, and wells, must be cased, sealed, or otherwise managed in order to protect ground and surface water from acid or toxic drainage and to minimize disturbance to the pre-existing hydrologic balance. This requirement is intended to ensure that people, livestock, fish, and wildlife are safe.[46] The exceptions to this rule are holes used only for blasting[47] or approved for use as water wells.[48] All operators must comply with any water replacement plan approved by the State Engineer and with applicable New Mexico water laws and regulations.[49]

Mine wastes, tailings, coal processing wastes, and other wastes in areas other than the mine workings or excavations must be compacted and stabilized in piles at designated areas within the site.[50] Eventually, the operator must revegetate the piles and assure that their

---

38 *Id.*

39 N.M. Surface Coal Mining Regulations, § 20-43.

40 N.M. Surface Coal Mining Regulations, § 20-44.

41 N.M. Surface Coal Mining Regulations, §§ 20-45, -46.

42 Spoils are the overburden or underground development waste material. N.M. Surface Coal Mining Regulations, § 1-5.

43 N.M. Surface Coal Mining Regulations, § 20-48.

44 N.M. Surface Coal Mining Regulations, §§ 20-50 to -52.

45 N.M. Surface Coal Mining Regulations, § 20-57.

46 N.M. Surface Coal Mining Regulations, § 20-13.

47 *Id.*

48 N.M. Surface Coal Mining Regulations, § 20-15.

49 N.M. Surface Coal Mining Regulations, § 20-54.

50 N.M. Stat. Ann. § 69-25A-19(B)(11) (Repl. Pamp. 1979).

contour is compatible with natural surroundings.[51] Coal processing waste may also be returned to underground mine workings in accordance with a program approved by the Director and the Mine Safety and Health Administration (MSHA) of the United States Department of Labor.[52] Spoil must be handled and placed within the permit area in a way that assures mass stability, prevents erosion and filtration of water into the pile, and meets other specified criteria.[53] Wastes defined as hazardous wastes must be disposed of pursuant to the New Mexico Hazardous Waste Act (HWA).[54]

Additional regulations govern the surface effects of underground coal mining. These regulations are promulgated under the SMA and recognize the distinct difference between surface and underground coal mining. Generally, underground mining is not allowed where it will endanger inhabitants of urbanized areas, cities, towns, and communities. Operators are required, to the extent possible, to prevent subsidence which could cause material damage, seal unneeded openings between the surface and mine, fill exploratory holes, return wastes to the mine, and stabilize waste piles. In addition, the operator must protect surface and ground water on and off the site from degradation, revegetate affected areas, and eliminate hazardous conditions. Furthermore, the operator must minimize disturbances and adverse impacts of the operations on fish, wildlife, and related environmental values and achieve enhancement of such resources where possible.[55]

2.3 COAL MINE RECLAMATION

Reclamation refers to backfilling, grading, topdressing, and revegetating land that has been disturbed by surface coal mining.[56] A reclamation plan must be submitted as part of the permit application. It must describe the pre-mining condition of the land and how the proposed land use or uses after mining will be achieved.[57]

The plan must include results of pre-mining tests and analyses of the land and its resources. It must also include engineering techniques to be used in mining and reclamation, surface water drainage and impoundment, and soil stabilization and revegetation, cost estimates, and a detailed timetable. It must describe proposed means of compliance with applicable air and water quality laws and health and safety standards.[58]

---

51 *Id.*

52 N.M. Surface Coal Mining Regulations, § 20-88.

53 N.M. Stat. Ann. § 69-25A-19(B)(22) (Repl. Pamp. 1979).

54 N.M. Surface Coal Mining Regulations, § 20-89(e).

55 *See generally* N.M. Stat. Ann. § 69-25A-20 (Repl. Pamp. 1979).

56 N.M. Surface Coal Mining Regulations, § 20-100.

57 N.M. Stat. Ann. § 69-25A-12(A)(1) to -12(A)(4) (Repl. Pamp. 1979).

58 N.M. Stat. Ann. § 69-25A-12(A) (Repl. Pamp. 1979).

Reclamation should be conducted as nearly contemporaneously as possible with mining operations.[59] In general, reclamation involves backfilling and grading disturbed areas and returning them to their approximate original contour.[60] The recontoured area must be covered with diverse, effective, and permanent vegetative cover, usually with a species that is native to the area or appropriate for the post-mining land use. The vegetation should be capable of stabilizing the soil and minimizing erosion.[61]

2.4 COAL MINE INSPECTION AND ENFORCEMENT

Permittees must establish and maintain records and have monitoring and evaluation procedures. Permittees must collect data on surface drainage, precipitation, and ground water. Permittees must make quarterly hydrologic reports to MMD.[62] MMD must inspect coal mining sites partially at least once a month and completely at least once each calendar quarter.[63] In addition, a citizen may request MMD to inspect such sites by submitting a signed, written statement presenting the grounds therefor.[64]

If an inspection reveals violations that do not create an imminent danger or harm, MMD must issue a written notice of violation which sets forth the nature of the violation, the required remedial action, the time in which the violation should be abated, and notice of opportunity for review. A notice of violation will be terminated when all violations have been abated.[65] If an inspection reveals the existence of any condition or practice which creates or can be expected to cause imminent environmental harm or if the permittee fails to abate a notice of violation, the Director may issue a cessation order. MMD may also require the operator to take affirmative steps if the cessation order will not completely abate the danger.[66]

If a pattern of violations is caused by an unwarranted failure to comply with requirements or conditions or is willfully caused, the Director must require the permittee to show cause as to why the permit should not be suspended or revoked.[67]

A person who receives a notice of violation or a cessation order may request a conference by notifying MMD in writing within 15 days of receiving the notice.[68] For violations,

---

59 *Id.*

60 N.M. Surface Coal Mining Regulations, § 20-102.

61 N.M. Surface Coal Mining Regulations, §§ 20-111, -112.

62 N.M. Surface Coal Mining Regulations, § 20-52.

63 N.M. Surface Coal Mining Regulations, § 29-11.

64 N.M. Surface Coal Mining Regulations, § 29-12.

65 N.M. Surface Coal Mining Regulations, § 30-12(i).

66 N.M. Surface Coal Mining Regulations, § 30-11.

67 N.M. Surface Coal Mining Regulations, § 30-13.

68 N.M. Surface Coal Mining Regulations, Part 31.

there is a civil penalty assessment system. The Director must determine the amount of penalty and serve the operator with a notice of assessment.[69] The operator charged may request a hearing,[70] but if the operator does not request a hearing, the proposed assessment will become final.

2.5 CITIZEN SUITS - COAL MINING

The SMA permits a citizen to bring a civil action against the Director or CSMC alleging a violation of the SMA or of a rule, regulation, order or permit or a failure to perform a nondiscretionary act. A citizen may also sue any person alleged to be violating a rule, regulation, order, or permit. These provisions are limited in that an action may not be brought if the Director or CSMC is already prosecuting a civil action in court. However, a person whose interest is adversely affected may intervene in such an action.[71]

The plaintiff must give written notice to the Director, attorney general, CSMC, and violator 60 days before bringing suit. If there is an immediate threat, the action may be brought immediately after giving notice.[72] The Director or CSMC may intervene in any citizen suit.

3.0 HARD ROCK MINING REGULATION

The New Mexico Mining Act[73] (NMMA) regulates what has been traditionally known as "hard rock" mining, such as copper and gold mining.[74] Explicitly exempted from regulation under the NMMA are the exploration and extraction of potash, sand, gravel, caliche, borrow dirt and quarry rock used as aggregate in construction, liquid or gaseous petroleum, coal, geothermal resources, and materials which are regulated by the Nuclear Regulatory Commission.[75] The purposes of the NMMA include promoting the responsible utilization and reclamation of lands affected by exploration, mining, or mineral extraction that are vital to the welfare of New Mexico.[76]

---

69 N.M. Surface Coal Mining Regulations, § 30-15.

70 N.M. Surface Coal Mining Regulations, § 31-19.

71 N.M. Stat. Ann. § 69-25A-24 (Repl. Pamp. 1979).

72 N.M. Stat. Ann. § 69-25A-24(B) (Repl. Pamp. 1979).

73 N.M. Stat. Ann. §§ 69-36-1 to -20 (Repl. Pamp. 1993).

74 NMMA defines "mining" as the process of obtaining useful minerals from the earth's crust or from previously disposed of or abandoned mining wastes, including exploration, open-cut mining and surface operation, the disposal of refuse from underground and in situ mining, mineral transportation, concentrating, milling, evaporation, leaching and other processing. The NMMA excludes from the definition of mining the exploration and extraction of the substances enumerated in the text immediately below. N.M. Stat. Ann. § 69-36-3(H) (Repl. Pamp. 1993).

75 *Id.*

76 N.M. Stat. Ann. § 69-36-2 (Repl. Pamp. 1993).

The NMMA is administered by the MMD. The New Mexico Environment Department (NMED) also has a role under the NMMA in certifying the environmental compliance of new mining operations and new and expanded units at existing mining units.[77]

Regulations necessary to implement the NMMA and to coordinate the roles of agencies responsible for other permitting requirements applicable to hard rock mines must be adopted by the Mining Commission ("Commission") by June 18, 1994.[78] The Commission, created by the NMMA, consists of seven voting members and two non-voting members.[79] The voting members are the Director of the Bureau of Mines and Mineral Resources at the New Mexico Institute of Mining and Technology (or an academic from a mining-related field), the Secretary of Environment or designee, the State Engineer or designee, the Commissioner of Public Lands or designee, the Director of the Department of Game and Fish or designee, and two public members and an alternate for each.[80] The non-voting, ex officio members are the Chairman of the Soil and Water Conservation Commission and the Director of the Agricultural Experiment Station of New Mexico State University or their designees.[81]

The NMMA categorizes mining operations as exploration, existing mining operations, or new mining operations. Each category of mining operation is subject to different statutory and regulatory requirements, with new mining operations being subject to the most comprehensive requirements. A permit is required for any mining operation and involves public notice and hearing requirements.[82] However, mining operations, including exploration, which have minimal impact on the environment may be permitted without notice and hearing and are subject to lesser permitting requirements.[83]

Operators may designate as confidential exploration maps, financial information, information concerning the grade or location of ore reserves, or trade secret information.[84]

---

77 N.M. Stat. Ann. §§ 69-36-7(P)(2), -11(B)(4) (Repl. Pamp. 1993).

78 N.M. Stat. Ann. § 69-36-7 (Repl. Pamp. 1993).

79 N.M. Stat. Ann. § 69-36-6 (Repl. Pamp. 1993).

80 As of the date of publication the Governor had not appointed the two public members.

81 N.M. Stat. Ann. § 69-36-6(A), (B) (Repl. Pamp. 1993).

82 N.M. Stat. Ann. § 69-36-7(K) (Repl. Pamp. 1993). Other activities which require public notice and an opportunity for hearing include renewal or modification of a permit for a new or existing mining operation which would have a significant environmental impact, an application for standby status or exploration, or a variance or release from financial assurance. *Id.*

83 N.M. Stat. Ann. § 69-36-7(L) (Repl. Pamp. 1993).

84 N.M. Stat. Ann. § 69-36-10 (Repl. Pamp. 1993).

Regulations to be promulgated under the NMMA must provide mechanisms for operators of new and existing mining operations to apply for standby status or a variance and to transfer permits.[85]

3.1 EXPLORATION MINING OPERATIONS

Exploration, a subcategory of mining under the NMMA, means searching for or investigating a mineral deposit.[86] It includes sinking shafts, tunneling, drilling core and bore holes, digging pits, making cuts and other work for the purpose of extracting samples before starting extraction operations. It does not include activities that cause no, or very little, surface disturbance, such as airborne surveys and photographs, use of instruments or devices that are hand carried or otherwise transported over the surface to perform magnetic, radioactive or other tests and measurements, boundary or claim surveying, location work or other work that causes no greater disturbance than is caused by ordinary lawful use of the area by persons not engaged in exploration.[87]

After December 31, 1994, an exploration permit will be required.[88] Permits may not be issued for more than one year, although they are renewable annually.[89] An applicant for an exploration permit must pay applicable fees, provide adequate financial assurance, certify that the applicant is not in violation of any other obligation under the NMMA or its regulations, and agree to reclaim any surface area damaged during exploration. If the impacted area is later incorporated into a new mining operation, however, its reclamation may be postponed.[90]

3.2 EXISTING MINING OPERATIONS

An existing mining operation is an extraction operation that produced marketable minerals for a total of at least two years between January 1, 1970 and June 18, 1993.[91] Existing mining operations must submit site assessments to the Director on or before June 30, 1994 or if reclamation is complete, they may apply for determination that the reclamation

---

85 N.M. Stat. Ann. § 69-36-7(O), (T) (Repl. Pamp. 1993).

86 N.M. Stat. Ann. § 69-36-3(F) (Repl. Pamp. 1993).

87 *Id.*

88 N.M. Stat. Ann. § 69-36-13 (Repl. Pamp. 1993). Note that a permit application must be submitted by September 1, 1994 in order to be approved by December 31, 1994. *Id.*

89 Applications to renew the exploration permit should be submitted 30 days before the current permit expires. *Id.*

90 N.M. Stat. Ann. § 69-36-13 (Repl. Pamp. 1993).

91 N.M. Stat. Ann. § 69-36-3(E) (Repl. Pamp. 1993).

satisfies the NMMA's requirements. If so, the operator or owner of the existing mining operation must be released from further requirements under the NMMA.[92]

The site assessment must describe existing permits and regulatory requirements, the permit area, and the surface and ground water at or adjacent to the mining operation and must analyze the impact of mining on that water. It must also describe the underlying and adjacent geologic regimes; describe the piles and accumulations of materials at the site and analyze their impact; describe and analyze the mining operation's impact on local communities, surrounding wildlife, and wildlife habitat; and describe the design limits for each mining unit.[93]

An existing mining operation must submit a permit application to the Director by December 31, 1994. This application must include a proposed compliance schedule for submitting a closeout plan before December 31, 1995, unless there is good cause for an extension of time.[94] The closeout plan must be based on site-specific characteristics, provide for compliance with regulatory performance standards, and specify the work necessary to reclaim the physical environment of the permit area to a condition that allows for the reestablishment of a self-sustaining ecosystem appropriate for the life zone of the surrounding areas, unless this would conflict with the approved post-mining land use.[95] The Director may grant an existing mining operation a waiver of the requirement to achieve a self-sustaining ecosystem or post-mining land use if measures will be taken to ensure that the open pit or waste unit will meet all applicable federal and state laws and regulations for air, surface water, and ground water protection following closure and will not pose a current or future hazard to public health or safety.[96] Operators of existing mining operations will be required to provide financial assurance adequate to assure the completion of the performance requirements of the closeout plan.[97]

A permit for an existing mining operation must be modified for each new discrete processing, leaching, excavation, storage, or stockpile unit located within the existing permit area and not previously identified and for each expansion of such a unit that exceeds the design limits specified in the permit. If the modification will have significant environmental

---

92 N.M. Stat. Ann. § 69-36-5(E) (Repl. Pamp. 1993). This submittal may not be made until after regulations are adopted. *Id.*

93 N.M. Stat. Ann. § 69-36-5(B) (Repl. Pamp. 1993). "Design limits" and "unit" are not defined in the NMMA.

94 N.M. Stat. Ann. § 69-36-11 (Repl. Pamp. 1993).

95 *Id.* Regulations under the NMMA must further define the terms "self-sustaining ecosystem appropriate for the life zone of the surrounding areas" and "approved post-mining land use."

96 N.M. Stat. Ann. § 69-36-11(B)(3) (Repl. Pamp. 1993).

97 N.M. Stat. Ann. § 69-36-7(Q) (Repl. Pamp. 1993).

impact, public notice and an opportunity for public hearing will be required.[98] Permit modifications should facilitate contemporaneous reclamation consistent with the closeout plan.[99] An existing mining operation may seek a permit modification in order to incorporate an approved closeout plan[100] or to obtain stand-by status.[101]

3.3 NEW MINING OPERATIONS

A new mining operation is a mining operation which engages in development or extraction operations after June 18, 1993, but which does not meet the definition of an existing mining operation.[102] A new mining operation may continue until it is either granted or denied a permit, provided that the operator submits before June 30, 1994, either a site assessment or a notice of intent to close.[103] A new mining operation that files a notice of intent to close must comply with the requirements for reclaiming of new mining operations.[104]

A permit application for a new mining operation must be based on site-specific information.[105] It must include baseline data on the proposed permit area and affected areas.[106] It must provide that the mining operation be designed and operated using the most appropriate technology and best management practices and that it assure protection of human health and safety, the environment, wildlife, and domestic animals. It must provide for reclamation measures that will achieve a self-sustaining ecosystem appropriate for the life zone of surrounding areas following closure unless conflicting with the approved post-mining land use, and it must provide for reduction of acid and other toxic drainage.[107] An application must identify ownership and the identity of other mining operations within the United States, the mining and engineering techniques proposed, the anticipated starting and termination dates of each phase of the operation and the land to be affected, detailed environmental

---

98 Significant environmental impact must be further defined and developed through regulations.

99 N.M. Stat. Ann. § 69-36-7(D) (Repl. Pamp. 1993).

100 N.M. Stat. Ann. § 69-36-7(G) (Repl. Pamp. 1993).

101 N.M. Stat. Ann. § 69-36-7(E) (Repl. Pamp. 1993).

102 N.M. Stat. Ann. § 69-36-3(I) (Repl. Pamp. 1993).

103 N.M. Stat. Ann. § 69-36-5(A) (Repl. Pamp. 1993).

104 N.M. Stat. Ann. § 69-36-5(C) (Repl. Pamp. 1993).

105 N.M. Stat. Ann. § 69-36-7(H) (Repl. Pamp. 1993).

106 "Affected area" means the area outside the permit area where the land surface, surface water, ground water and air resources are impacted by mining operations within the permit area. N.M. Stat. Ann. § 69-36-3(A) (Repl. Pamp. 1993).

107 N.M. Stat. Ann. § 69-36-7(I) (Repl. Pamp. 1993).

information, data about the ore body and a reclamation plan.[108] The applicant must demonstrate that the mining operation will comply with regulatory performance standards and that other applicable state and federal permits will be issued, provide a determination by the New Mexico Secretary of Environment that the applicant has demonstrated that the activities will be expected to comply with all applicable other environmental standards, and file financial assurance adequate to assure the completion of the performance requirements of the permit.[109] Before the Director may approve or deny a permit for a new mining operation, the Director must prepare an environmental evaluation which includes an analysis of the reasonably foreseeable impacts of proposed activities on the premining and post-mining environment and the local community, including other past, present, and reasonably foreseeable future actions, regardless of the agency or persons that undertake the other actions or whether the actions are on private, state, or federal land.[110] The Director must issue a permit for a new mining operation if the Director finds that the permit application is complete, the permit application fee has been paid, the financial assurance is adequate and has been provided, reclamation in accordance with the proposed reclamation plan is economically and technically feasible, and the operation is designed to meet without perpetual care all applicable environmental requirements imposed by the NMMA and its regulations.[111] Before issuing the permit the Director must also find that the applicant, the operator and/or the owner, or persons or entities directly controlled by the applicant, operator and/or owner, are not currently in violation of the terms of another Department permit or in violation of any substantive environmental law or regulation at a mining operation in the United States which is unabated and not the subject of appeal, have not forfeited financial assurance for any other mining permit in the United States, and have not demonstrated a pattern of willful violations of the NMMA or other New Mexico environmental statutes.[112]

The term of a new mining operation may not exceed twenty years; the term of renewal may not exceed ten years.[113]

3.4 INSPECTION AND ENFORCEMENT

The NMMA requires the Director to inspect mining operation sites, although the frequency of inspections will vary with the type of operations.[114] The Director has the

---

108 *Id.*

109 The NMMA provides for the release of financial assurance as reclamation work proceeds. *See generally* N.M. Stat. Ann. § 69-36-7(R) (Repl. Pamp. 1993).

110 N.M. Stat. Ann. § 69-36-9(G) (Repl. Pamp. 1993).

111 N.M. Stat. Ann. § 69-36-12(B) (Repl. Pamp. 1993).

112 *Id.*

113 N.M. Stat. Ann. § 69-36-7(C) (Repl. Pamp. 1993).

114 N.M. Stat. Ann. § 69-36-7(S) (Repl. Pamp. 1993).

power to order the immediate cessation of an operation if a violation creates an imminent danger to the health or safety of the public or if it will cause significant environmental harm.[115] If a violation does not meet these standards, the Director must issue a notice fixing a reasonable time, not exceeding 60 days, for the abatement of a violation. If the violation is not timely abated, the Director must order the operations to stop. Where there is a pattern of violations or where the violations are willful or caused by an unwarranted failure to comply with the law, the Director must order the permittee to show cause why the permit should not be suspended or revoked.[116]

The NMMA provides for citizen suits, administrative review, and judicial review. Citizen suits for injunctive relief to compel compliance with the NMMA may be brought against a person who is alleged to be in violation of a rule, regulation, order, or permit or against NMED, EMNRD, or the Commission. A citizen suit may not be brought if one of these agencies is already prosecuting a civil or administrative proceeding or until 60 days after the plaintiff gives written notice to NMED, EMNRD, the Commission, the New Mexico Attorney General, and the alleged violator. If there is an immediate threat to the health or safety of the plaintiff or the violation would immediately and irreversibly impair the plaintiff's legal interest, an action may be brought immediately after notice to the proper parties.[117]

Administrative review is available for any order, penalty assessment, or issuance or denial of a permit. A written petition for review must be filed within 60 days from the date of notice of the order or decision.[118]

Judicial review is available to any person who is or may be affected by a regulation of the Commission. In most cases, a notice of appeal must be filed with the New Mexico Court of Appeals within 30 days from the date the regulation is filed with the State Records Center. However, a person who shows good cause for not appearing at the public hearing on the regulation may appeal a decision of the Commission by filing a notice of appeal with the Court of Appeals within 45 days after entry of the Commission's decision.[119] Those who are or may be affected by a final action other than a regulation may file an appeal in the District Court of the First Judicial District in Santa Fe within 30 days from the date of the Commission's action.[120] A regulation, order, or other action may be set aside by a court

---

115 N.M. Stat. Ann. § 69-36-7(S) (Repl. Pamp. 1993).

116 *Id.*

117 N.M. Stat. Ann. § 69-36-14 (Repl. Pamp. 1993).

118 N.M. Stat. Ann. § 69-36-15 (Repl. Pamp. 1993).

119 N.M. Stat. Ann. § 69-36-16(B) (Repl. Pamp. 1993).

120 N.M. Stat. Ann. § 69-36-16(C) (Repl. Pamp. 1993).

only if it is arbitrary, capricious, or an abuse of discretion, not supported by substantial evidence in the record, or otherwise not in accordance with law.[121]

The Director or the Commission may assess a civil penalty of up to $10,000 per day for each violation of the NMMA, regulations, orders, or a permit condition.[122] The knowing or willful violation of the NMMA, regulations, or a permit condition or a failure or refusal to comply with a final decision or order of the Commission or the Director is a misdemeanor and is subject to a fine of up to $10,000 per day of violation or imprisonment of up to one year or both.[123]

3.5 MISCELLANEOUS NMMA PROVISIONS

The NMMA does not supersede current or future requirements and standards of any other applicable federal or state law.[124]

After June 18, 1993, and until the Commission adopts regulations to carry out the NMMA, county mining laws or ordinances shall apply to mining within their jurisdictions.[125]

Administration, implementation, enforcement, investigation, and permitting under the NMMA will be funded by annual fees on mining operations.[126] The NMMA creates a mining act fund which receives all moneys paid by permit applicants, permit holders, the federal government, other state agencies, or legislative appropriations. The fund will be used to carry out the purposes of the NMMA.[127] The NMMA also creates an inactive or abandoned non-coal mine reclamation fund, into which will be paid all money received from administrative or court-ordered penalties, and from which money will be drawn to conduct reclamation activities on abandoned or inactive non-coal mining areas.[128]

The NMMA does not limit any right that any person may have pursuant to any statute or common law to seek enforcement of the NMMA or of regulations issued under the NMMA or to seek any other relief.[129]

---

121 N.M. Stat. Ann. § 69-36-16(F) (Repl. Pamp. 1993).

122 N.M. Stat. Ann. § 69-36-17 (Repl. Pamp. 1993).

123 N.M. Stat. Ann. § 69-36-18 (Repl. Pamp. 1993).

124 N.M. Stat. Ann. § 69-36-4 (Repl. Pamp. 1993).

125 N.M. Stat. Ann. § 69-36-4(B) (Repl. Pamp. 1993).

126 N.M. Stat. Ann. § 69-36-7(M) (Repl. Pamp. 1993).

127 N.M. Stat. Ann. § 69-36-19(A) (Repl. Pamp. 1993).

128 N.M. Stat. Ann. § 69-36-19 (Repl. Pamp. 1993).

129 N.M. Stat. Ann. § 69-36-20 (Repl. Pamp. 1993).

4.0 ABANDONED MINE RECLAMATION

The New Mexico Abandoned Mine Reclamation Act (AMRA)[130] requires the Director to (1) prepare a state plan for reclaiming land and water mined or affected by mining and abandoned or inadequately reclaimed before August 3, 1977; (2) submit the plan to the United States Secretary of the Interior for approval; and (3) administer funds from the plan received from the United States pursuant to Title IV of SMCRA. If the owner of land or water subject to the plan is not known or readily available or will not give the Director permission to reclaim the property, the Director may, after making certain findings and giving notice, restore the affected property.[131] AMRA also authorizes the Director to acquire affected land by purchase or donation, to sell such land after it has been reclaimed,[132] and to create a lien upon reclaimed land, the surface of which was owned by a person prior to May 2, 1977, who neither consented to, participated in, nor exercised control over the coal mining which resulted in the reclamation.[133] A lien is created by filing in the office of the appropriate county clerk a statement itemizing the amount of money spent for reclamation. The size of the lien may not exceed the amount of the increase in the market value of the land resulting from the reclamation.[134] Such a lien has priority from the date money was spent for reclamation.[135]

5.0 SAFEGUARDING MINE SURFACE OPENINGS

Before either the permanent suspension of mining operations or the temporary suspension of mining operations when an office with a responsible person at all times is not maintained at a mine, mill, smelter, or other treatment plant at which are located mine surface openings including shafts, adits, or auger boreholes, the operator must complete and file with MMD a Notice of Intention to Suspend Operations form. The Notice must include a plan to effectively close or fence off all surface mine openings.[136] The operator may not lawfully start such safeguarding operations until the operator has received an approved copy of the submitted form signed by the Director.[137] Safeguarding plans rejected by the Director must be amended and re-submitted.[138] When approved safeguarding procedures are

---

130 N.M. Stat. Ann. §§ 69-25B-1 to -12 (Supp. 1993).

131 N.M. Stat. Ann. § 69-25B-7(A) (Supp. 1993).

132 N.M. Stat. Ann. § 69-25B-7(C) to -7(F) (Supp. 1993).

133 N.M. Stat. Ann. § 69-25B-8(A) (Supp. 1993).

134 *Id.*

135 N.M. Stat. Ann. § 69-25B-8(C) (Supp. 1993).

136 N.M. Mine Registration, Reporting and Safeguarding Regulations, Part 2, § 2.1.

137 *Id.*

138 N.M. Mine Registration, Reporting and Safeguarding Regulations, Part 2, § 3.1.

completed, the operator must complete and file with MMD a Report of Safeguarding on the MMD form.[139]

MMD has adopted non-mandatory Guidelines for the Safeguarding of Mine Surface Openings (Guidelines), which are Attachment A to Rule 89-1. The Guidelines, unlike Rule 89-1, state that all closures must be monitored and maintained throughout the period of suspension. The Guidelines also state that the most effective way of [permanently] safe-guarding shafts, adits, and auger boreholes is to backfill them with earth or waste rock, that adits should be filled a distance of 30 ft. into the opening, and that shafts should be filled to a level above the surrounding ground to allow for settling. The Guidelines indicate that highwalls in pits which are to be permanently closed should be safeguarded by (1) having the highwalls dozed or blasted down so that the slope of the embankment does not exceed 2h:lv or 50% gradient, (2) backfilling up against the highwall, or (3) installing rigid guardrails at the top of the highwall.[140]

When adit operations are to be suspended for an indefinite period, the Guidelines suggest that surface openings be sealed with a steel reinforced concrete or masonry wall bolted or otherwise keyed into the sides of the opening. Shafts in which operations are to be suspended for an indefinite time can be sealed with a steel reinforced concrete slab or cable net closure.

The Guidelines indicate that when operations are expected to be suspended for a short period of time, surface openings may be fenced with securely anchored wire, cable, or heavy rope.[141]

MMD has the right to enter mines for the purpose of determining compliance with Rule 89-1.[142] If following either such an inspection or a complaint by any affected party the Director determines that there is a violation of statutes, rules, and regulations applicable to safeguarding mine surface openings and a party responsible for such safeguarding can be identified, the Director must issue a written notice of non-compliance to the responsible party.[143] The responsible party must respond in writing to the Director within ten days after it receives such a notice of non-compliance.[144] A failure to respond in a timely manner must be deemed a failure to properly safeguard and may result in referral by the Director to the appropriate District Attorney for prosecution.

---

139 N.M. Mine Registration, Reporting and Safeguarding Regulations, Part 2, § 2.1.

140 N.M. Mine Registration, Reporting and Safeguarding Regulations, Rule 89-1, Attachment A, Guidelines for the Safeguarding of Mine Surface Openings. (1/11/90).

141 *Id.*

142 N.M. Mine Registration, Reporting and Safeguarding Regulations, Part 2, § 4.1.

143 N.M. Mine Registration, Reporting and Safeguarding Regulations, Part 2, § 5.1.

144 *Id.*

Each individual failure either to comply with a statute, rule, or regulation relating to safeguarding surface mine openings or to respond to a notice of non-compliance will constitute a separate unlawful act that may be prosecuted.[145] Each unlawful act may be punished by a fine of not more than $200 and/or by imprisonment for three months in the county jail.[146] In addition, the Director may seek an injunction requiring compliance.[147]

If the Director determines that an immediate danger to public health and safety exists due to the lack of or ineffective safeguarding of surface mine openings, the Director may take appropriate actions necessary to effectively safeguard the mine and to recover reasonable costs for such work from the owner of the mine, either by negotiation or by litigation.[148]

6.0 SANTA FE COUNTY REGULATION

In 1991, Santa Fe County adopted County Ordinance No. 1991-2, establishing a complex system for regulating mining and oil and gas exploration and production in the County. Generally, the Ordinance prohibits exploration or production without a County permit and conditions the issuance of a permit upon the submission of detailed environmental assessments, master plans, and reclamation plans which must be reviewed and approved at several levels of County government. In 1993, the County enacted Ordinance No. 1993-3, which imposes more detailed regulations. Subsequently, the New Mexico Mining Act was passed. Section 4(B) of the NMMA provides that "[a]fter the effective date of the ... Act and until the commission adopts regulations necessary to carry out the provisions of [the Act], county mining laws or ordinances must apply to mining within their jurisdictions in New Mexico."[149] Whether, or to what extent, this statutory language preempts County Ordinance No. 1993-3 has not been determined in court.

7.0 COMMISSIONER OF PUBLIC LANDS

The Commissioner of Public Lands, who is directly elected by the voters for a four-year term,[150] is responsible for administering most lands owned by the state.[151] The Commissioner directs the State Land Office.[152] The Commissioner is authorized to sell

---

145 *Id.*

146 *Id.*

147 *Id.*

148 N.M. Mine Registration, Reporting and Safeguarding Regulations, Part 2, § 6.1.

149 N.M. Stat. Ann. §§ 69-36-1 to -20 (Repl. Pamp. 1993).

150 N.M. Const. art. V, § 1 (Repl. Pamp. 1992).

151 N.M. Const. art. XIII, §§ 1-2 (Repl. Pamp. 1992); N.M. Stat. Ann. § 19-1-2 (Repl. Pamp. 1985).

152 N.M. Stat. Ann. § 19-1-1 (Repl. Pamp. 1985).

state lands[153] and to lease such lands for oil and gas,[154] coal,[155] geothermal resources,[156] other minerals,[157] agricultural and grazing,[158] and other purposes. Oil and gas lessees are required by statute to comply with laws, rules, regulations, ordinances, and other requirements relating to conservation, aesthetics, pollution, cultural properties, fire, and ecology.[159] The Commissioner routinely includes similar provisions in other leases and in documents granting easements and rights of way.

8.0 OIL CONSERVATION DIVISION

The Oil Conservation Division (OCD) is a division of EMNRD.[160] The primary duty of OCD is to prevent waste of oil and gas[161] by regulating:

> the inefficient, excessive or improper, use or dissipation of the reservoir energy ... and the locating, spacing, drilling, equipping, operating or producing, of any well or wells in a manner to reduce or tend to reduce the total quantity of crude petroleum oil or natural gas ultimately recovered from any pool, and the use of inefficient underground storage of natural gas,[162]

and

> the unnecessary or excessive surface loss or destruction without beneficial use ... of natural gas of any type or in any form or crude petroleum oil, or any product thereof, but including the loss or destruction, without beneficial use, resulting from evaporation, seepage, leakage or fire, especially such loss or destruction incident to or resulting from the manner of spacing, equipping, operating or producing well or wells, or incident to or resulting from the use of inefficient storage or from the production of crude petroleum oil or natural gas in excess of the reasonable market demand.[163]

OCD also has more typical environmental responsibilities. OCD is charged with protecting fresh water (defined, with a few specified exceptions, to include "water in lakes and playas, the surface water of all streams regardless of the quality . . ., and all underground waters

---

153 N.M. Stat. Ann. § 19-7-9 (Repl. Pamp. 1985 & Supp. 1993).

154 N.M. Stat. Ann. §§ 19-10-1 to -70 (Repl. Pamp. 1985 & Supp. 1993).

155 N.M. Stat. Ann. §§ 19-9-9 to -16 (Repl. Pamp. 1985 & Supp. 1993).

156 N.M. Stat. Ann. §§ 19-13-1 to -28 (Repl. Pamp. 1985).

157 N.M. Stat. Ann. §§ 19-8-4, -10, -12, -14 (Repl. Pamp. 1985).

158 N.M. Stat. Ann. § 19-7-28 (Repl. Pamp. 1985).

159 N.M. Stat. Ann. §§ 19-10-4.1(17), -4.2(16), -4.3(16) (Repl. Pamp. 1985).

160 N.M. Stat. Ann. § 70-2-4 (Repl. Pamp. 1987).

161 N.M. Stat. Ann. § 70-2-2 (Repl. Pamp. 1987).

162 N.M. Stat. Ann. § 70-2-3(A) (Repl. Pamp. 1987).

163 N.M. Stat. Ann. § 70-2-3(B) (Repl. Pamp. 1987).

containing 10,000 milligrams per liter . . . or less of total dissolved solids . . . .").[164] OCD may make rules, regulations, and orders requiring dry or abandoned wells to be plugged so as to confine oil, gas, or water to the strata in which they are found.[165] OCD is charged with regulating the methods and devices employed for storing oil or gas or their products,[166] regulating the disposition of water produced and used in connection with drilling for or producing oil or gas in a manner that will afford reasonable protection against contamination of fresh water supplies,[167] governing the Oil and Gas Reclamation Fund,[168] regulating the construction and operation of oil treating plants, requiring the posting of bonds for reclaiming plant sites after operations stop, and regulating the disposition of non-domestic wastes resulting from the exploration, development, production, storage, transportation, treatment and refining of oil and gas and from the oil field service industry.[169] OCD's Environmental Bureau has developed guidelines for a number of the environmental permits required by OCD.[170]

8.1 NEW MEXICO WATER QUALITY ACT

The New Mexico Water Quality Act (WQA)[171] does not apply to any activity or condition subject to the authority of the Oil Conservation Commission (OCC) under the Oil and Gas Act (OGA),[172] and other laws conferring power on the OCC to prevent or abate water pollution."[173] In turn, the Oil and Gas Act assigns to the Oil Conservation Division (OCD) responsibility for regulating water pollution that results from oil and gas activities.[174] The Water Quality Control Commission (WQCC) has allocated duties and responsibilities relating to water pollution control between OCD and the New Mexico Environment Department (NMED).

8.1.1 NMED and OCD Responsibilities

Pursuant to WQCC's allocation, OCD will, as a general rule, administer and enforce both applicable WQCC and OCD regulations pertaining to surface and ground water dis-

---

164 N.M. Oil Conservation Division Rules and Regulations, Rules 0.1, 1(A), 2, and 3(A) (effective 3/1/91).

165 N.M. Stat. Ann. § 70-2-12(B)(1), (B)(2) (Repl. Pamp. 1987 & Supp. 1993).

166 N.M. Stat. Ann. § 70-2-12(B)(13) (Repl. Pamp. 1987 & Supp. 1993).

167 N.M. Stat. Ann. § 70-2-12(B)(15) (Repl. Pamp. 1987 & Supp. 1993).

168 N.M. Stat. Ann. § 70-2-12(B)(18) (Repl. Pamp. 1987 & Supp. 1993).

169 N.M. Stat. Ann. § 70-2-12(B)(20) -(22) (Repl. Pamp. 1987 & Supp. 1993).

170 N.M. Oil Conservation Division Environmental Regulations.

171 N.M. Stat. Ann. §§ 74-6-1 to -17 (Repl. Pamp. 1993).

172 N.M. Stat. Ann. §§ 70-2-1 to -19, -21 to -38 (Repl. Pamp. 1987 & Supp. 1992).

173 N.M. Stat. Ann. § 74-6-12(G) (Repl. Pamp. 1993).

174 N.M. Stat. Ann. § 70-2-12(B)(15) (Repl. Pamp. 1993).

charges at oil and gas drilling and production sites, oil refineries, natural gas processing plants, geothermal installations, carbon dioxide facilities, oil and natural gas pipelines and compressor stations. OCD will generally also administer and enforce applicable WQCC and OCD regulations pertaining to activities of the oil field service industry.[175]

Jurisdiction over activities associated with transportation of oil and gas before refining and storage and treatment of oil and gas or oil or gas products on refinery premises is also allocated to OCD.[176] OCD has discretion as to which regulations relating to water pollution to enforce in any particular situation.[177] OCD administers and enforces WQCC regulations at brine operations, including brine production wells and holding ponds and tanks, and has jurisdiction over all manufactured brine after it is transported, used, or disposed of away from brine plant premises for use in or directly related to oil and gas operations regulated by OCD.[178] OCD regulates subsurface fluid injection through its Class II Underground Injection Control Program if the fluid is produced as a result of, or used in drilling for, production of oil and gas. NMED regulates fluid injection if the fluid is used or disposed of for other purposes.[179] OCD has general jurisdiction over the oil field service industry, even with respect to activities that would ordinarily be regulated by NMED.[180]

NMED regulates several matters associated with the oil and gas industry, including air emissions, underground storage tanks used to store gasoline, diesel and new or waste oil (except those at OCD-regulated facilities which contain wastewater or are considered flow-through process tanks), the generation, transportation, and storage of hazardous waste, radioactive materials which fall above the WQCC standard of 30.0 pCi/l for Radium-226 and Radium-228, sewage discharges (except discharges comingled with oil and gas wastes at an OCD-regulated facility), naturally occurring radioactive materials (NORM), and solid waste (except waste produced by oil and gas operations at an OCD-regulated facility).[181]

8.2 TANKS AND LINED PITS

Lined pits and below-grade tanks may, with the exceptions discussed below, be used to contain produced water, sediment oil, tank bottoms, miscellaneous hydrocarbons, and other

---

175 N.M. Oil Conservation Division Rules and Regulations, Appendix, Water Quality Control Comm'n, § 1 (7/21/89).

176 *Id.*

177 *Id.*

178 N.M. Oil Conservation Division Rules and Regulations, Appendix, Water Quality Control Comm'n, § 1 (7/21/89).

179 *Id.*; N.M. Oil Conservation Division Environmental Regulations, Tab 1.

180 N.M. Oil Conservation Division Rules and Regulations, Appendix, Water Quality Control Comm'n, § 2(H) (7/21/89); N.M. Oil Conservation Division Environmental Regulations, Tabs 1, 6b.

181 N.M. Oil Conservation Division Environmental Regulations, Tab 2.

fluids subject to the jurisdiction of OCD, but only after application and approval of OCD.[182] Tanks exceeding 16 feet in diameter and exposed pits and ponds must be screened, netted, or covered to protect migratory birds unless an exception is granted by OCD.[183] Oil must be removed immediately from all pits used for drilling, completion, blowdown, workover, or in an emergency after the pits are no longer in use, or the pits must be screened, netted, or covered to protect migratory birds.[184]

Unless removal of fluids or cuttings from the drill site is permitted by an OCD district supervisor, operators must provide adequate pits for the accumulation of drill cuttings and dispose of drilling fluids and drill cuttings at the well site so as to prevent contamination of surface and ground water.[185]

Storage of oil in earthen reservoirs or open receptacles is prohibited.[186] Fire walls must be built and maintained around permanent oil tanks within the corporate limits of a municipality, within 150 feet of any producing oil or gas well, within 500 feet of any highway or inhabited dwelling, within 1,000 feet of any school or church, or where such tanks are located as to be deemed an objectionable hazard by OCD. Required fire walls must provide reservoir capacity one-third larger than the capacity of the enclosed tanks.[187]

Oil tanks, tank batteries, automatic custody transfer systems, tanks used for brine collection or disposal, and tanks used for treating sediment oil must be identified by a sign posted on or not more than 50 feet from the tank. Such signs must be of durable construction and legible at 50 feet and must identify the name of the operator, the name of the lease or leases being served by the tank, and the 40-acre tract in which the tank is located.[188]

Except in an emergency, liquid hydrocarbons which are not merchantable through normal channels may not be cleaned from tanks, removed from leases, destroyed, or delivered to treating plants or other facilities without the prior approval of the appropriate OCD district office.[189] Reports are required in connection with the cleaning and removal of

---

182 N.M. Oil Conservation Division Rules and Regulations, Rule 8.A.

183 N.M. Oil Conservation Division Rules and Regulations, Rules 8.B., 105.B., 312.A(12), 313; OCD Order No. R-8952 (6/20/89); OCD Memorandum, "Implementation of Migratory Bird Protection Regulations" (7/26/89).

184 N.M. Oil Conservation Division Rules and Regulations, Rule 105.B.

185 N.M. Oil Conservation Division Rules and Regulations, Rule 105.A.

186 N.M. Oil Conservation Division Rules and Regulations, Rule 310.A.

187 *Id.*

188 N.M. Oil Conservation Division Rules and Regulations, Rule 310.B.

189 N.M. Oil Conservation Division Rules and Regulations, Rule 311.

sediment oil from tanks and leases.[190] When an emergency requires delivery of hydrocarbons to a treating plant or other facility prior to OCD approval, the transporter is required to notify the appropriate OCD division office of the nature and extent of such emergency on the first working day following the emergency and to file OCD Form C-117-A within two working days after the emergency.[191]

If tank bottoms are removed to surface pits, the pits must be fenced and the fence must be maintained.[192]

8.3 DRILLING

During the drilling of any oil, injection, or service well, all oil, gas, and water strata above the producing and/or injection horizon must be sealed or separated in order to prevent their contents from passing into other strata.[193] All fresh water and water of present or probable future value for domestic, commercial, or stock purposes must be confined to its strata and adequately protected by methods approved by OCD. Special precautions by methods satisfactory to OCD must be taken in drilling and abandoning wells to guard against (a) any loss of artesian water from the strata in which it occurs and (b) the contamination of artesian water by objectionable water or by oil or gas.[194]

All water must be excluded from the various oil- and gas-bearing strata which are penetrated. Such exclusion will ordinarily be by cementing.[195]

Oil and gas wells must have such surface and intermediate casing strings and cementing as are necessary to effectively seal and isolate all water-, oil-, and gas-bearing strata and other strata encountered in the well down to the casing point. Unless OCD allows an exception when known conditions in a given area render compliance impracticable, sufficient cementing must be used on surface casings to fill the annular space behind the casing to the top of the hole.[196] Unless another method is expressly authorized by OCD, cementing must be by the pump and plug method and done with conventional hard-setting cement to which additives (lighteners, densifiers, extenders, accelerators, retarders, etc.) have been added to suit well conditions. Casing strings, except conductor pipe, must be tested after cementing and before commencing any other well operations.

---

190 *Id.* "Sediment oil" is defined as tank bottoms and any other accumulations of liquid hydrocarbons on an oil and gas lease, which hydrocarbons are not merchantable through normal channels. *Id.*

191 *Id.*

192 N.M. Oil Conservation Division Rules and Regulations, Rule 313.

193 N.M. Oil Conservation Division Rules and Regulations, Rules 106.A, 107, 108.

194 N.M. Oil Conservation Division Rules and Regulations, Rule 106.

195 N.M. Oil Conservation Division Rules and Regulations, Rule 106.C.

196 N.M. Oil Conservation Division Rules and Regulations, Rule 107.B.

8.4 WELL PLUGGING

OCD rules and regulations set forth plugging and abandonment requirements for oil, gas, and service wells.[197]

Owners and drillers of oil, gas, and service wells on private and state lands must obtain OCD approval of a surety or cash bond on an OCD form in favor of the state, subject to the condition that the well be plugged and abandoned in compliance with OCD rules and regulations.[198] The bond will remain effective until either it is replaced by another bond approved by OCD or OCD has approved the plugging and abandonment of the well to which the bond relates.

Before plugging operations start, the owner of the well or his agent must file with OCD a notice of intention to plug.[199] Before a well is abandoned, it must be plugged so as to permanently confine all oil, gas, and water in the separate strata originally containing them by using mud-laden fluid, cement, and plugs approved by OCD.[200] The location of an abandoned well must be shown by a steel marker at least four inches in diameter set in concrete and extending at least four feet above mean ground level. Within 30 days after plugging is completed, the well owner must file a report with OCD. The appropriate district office of OCD inspects plugged wells and approves plugging reports.

An OCD permit is required before a well can be temporarily abandoned.[201] OCD will not issue such a permit without evidence that the well condition is such as will prevent damage to the producing zone, migration of hydrocarbons or water, contamination of fresh water or other natural resources, or leakage of any substance at the surface.[202]

A well need not be plugged and abandoned when it may safely be used as a fresh water well and such use is desired by the land owner, provided that written agreement has been secured from the land owner and filed with OCD.[203]

8.5 TREATING PLANTS

Treating plants are plants constructed or being used wholly or partially for reclaiming, treating, processing, or in any manner making tank bottoms or other waste oil marketable.[204] Tank bottoms are the accumulation of hydrocarbon material and other substances

197 N.M. Oil Conservation Division Rules and Regulations, Rules 201-204.

198 N.M. Oil Conservation Division Rules and Regulations, Rule 101.

199 N.M. Oil Conservation Division Rules and Regulations, Rule 202.A.

200 N.M. Oil Conservation Division Rules and Regulations, Rule 202.B.

201 N.M. Oil Conservation Division Rules and Regulations, Rule 203.A.

202 N.M. Oil Conservation Division Rules and Regulations, Rule 203.B.

203 N.M. Oil Conservation Division Rules and Regulations, Rule 204.

204 N.M. Oil Conservation Division Rules and Regulations, Rule 0.1.

which settle naturally below crude oil in tanks and receptacles that are used in handling and storing crude oil and which contain in excess of two percent basic sediment and water.[205]

Treating plants may not be constructed without an OCD permit.[206] To obtain such a permit, an application showing the location of the proposed plant, describing the plant and its design capacity, containing a diagrammatic plan of the plant layout and a description of any containment dikes and pits, and demonstrating that any unmerchantable solids or liquids resulting from the operation of the plant will be disposed of at an OCD approved site must be filed with OCD. The applicant must also file with OCD evidence that the applicant has given written notice of the application to the owners of the surface of the plant site and the area within half a mile of the plant site and, in addition, evidence that the applicant has published an advertisement in a newspaper of general circulation in the county where the treating plant is to be located. Finally, the application must include a surety or cash bond in the amount of $25,000, on an OCD form, conditioned upon compliance with New Mexico law and OCD rules and regulations and on satisfactory site cleanup when operation of the plant stops.[207]

After a complete application has been filed, the OCD Director may issue a treating plant permit if no party has objected within 20 days after the filing. If there has been a timely objection or the OCD Director elects to do so, the Director may schedule an application for a treating plant permit for public hearing.[208]

When operation of a treating plant stops for six consecutive months, the operator must complete cleanup and restoration of the plant site within another six months, unless an extension of time is granted by the OCD Director. Cleanup must be in accordance with a plan acceptable to the OCD Director and may include removal or demolition of buildings, removal of tanks, vessels, equipment or hardware, containment and removal of fluids and chemicals, back-filling and grading of pits, removal of contaminated soil, and reclamation of the plant site. The surety or cash bond required to be filed with OCD with an application for a treating plant permit will not be released until OCD inspects the treating plant site to determine that restoration is adequate.[209]

On April 2, 1991, EPA issued at the request of operators in Southeast New Mexico and West Texas a preliminary determination that wastes generated by crude oil and tank bottom reclamation facilities are exempt from the Subtitle C (Hazardous Waste) provisions of the Resource Conservation and Recovery Act (RCRA). OCD has stated that the EPA

---

205 *Id.*

206 N.M. Oil Conservation Division Rules and Regulation, Rule 312.A; *see* N.M. Oil Conservation Division Environmental Regulations, Tab 5.

207 *Id.*

208 *Id.*

209 *Id.*

determination indicates that treating plants in New Mexico permitted by OCD can receive and treat production wastes (but not used motor oil or refined product tank bottoms) without complying with RCRA Subtitle C, but that RCRA regulated solvents may not be used to treat production wastes in such plants.

8.6 INJECTION

The injection of gases and liquids into hydrocarbon reservoirs to maintain reservoir pressure, for secondary or other enhanced recovery, or for water disposal, is strictly regulated.[210] All such injections require OCD approval. Applicants for approval must furnish, by certified or registered mail, a copy of the application to the owner of the surface of the land under which each injection or disposal well will be located and to each lease operator within one-half mile of the well site.[211]

OCD may in its discretion approve an injection or disposal well application without a hearing if the applicant publishes a notice of the application in a newspaper of general circulation in the county in which the proposed well will be located and no objection to the well is received by OCD within 15 days after OCD receives a complete application, evidence of mailing, and proof of publication.[212] If OCD receives timely written objection, or if a hearing is deemed advisable by the OCD Director, the application will be set for hearing and notice thereof will be given by OCD.[213]

All applications for approval of pressure maintenance and water flood projects must be set for hearing.[214] The OCD Director may waive this requirement for salt water disposal wells when the waters to be disposed of are mineralized to the extent that they are unfit for domestic, stock, irrigation, or other general use, such waters are to be disposed of into a formation older than Triassic (Lea County only), and no objections have been received.[215]

The OCD Director may without a hearing grant a permit for the underground storage of liquified petroleum gas or liquid hydrocarbons in secure caverns within massive salt beds.[216]

Injection wells must be cased with safe and adequate casing or tubing so as to prevent leakage. Such casing or tubing must be so set and cemented as to prevent the movement of formation or injected fluids from the injection zone into any other zone or to the surface

---

210 N.M. Oil Conservation Division Rules and Regulations, Rules 701-708; N.M. Oil Conservation Division Environmental Regulations, Tab 1.

211 N.M. Oil Conservation Division Rules and Regulations, Rule 701.B.

212 N.M. Oil Conservation Division Rules and Regulations, Rule 701.C.

213 N.M. Oil Conservation Division Rules and Regulations, Rule 701.D.

214 N.M. Oil Conservation Division Rules and Regulations, Rule 701.F, .G.

215 N.M. Oil Conservation Division Rules and Regulations, Rule 701.E.

216 N.M. Oil Conservation Division Rules and Regulations, Rule 701.H.

around the outside of any casing string.[217] Injection wells must also be equipped, operated, monitored, and maintained to permit periodic testing, to prevent significant leaks and vertical fluid movement, to confine injected fluids to the approved interval, and to prevent surface damage or pollution.[218]

Periodic testing of injection wells is required.[219] Wells must be equipped so that injection and annular pressures and volumes may be determined at least monthly.[220] Immediately upon the commencement of injection operations in any well and within 30 days after permanent cessation of gas or liquified petroleum gas storage operations or discontinuance of injection operations, the operator must notify OCD.[221]

Temporary abandonment of an injection well for more than six months without prior OCD approval is prohibited unless the injection interval has been isolated by use of a cement or bridge plug.[222] OCD approval is required before any injection well is plugged.[223]

Without an extension approved by the OCD Director, whenever there is a continuous six-month period of non-injection into any injection project, storage project, salt water disposal well, or special purpose injection well, such project or well is considered abandoned, and authority for injection automatically terminates.[224]

Injection well operators must keep accurate records and make monthly reports of gas or liquid volumes injected, stored, and/or produced.[225]

8.7 PRODUCED WATER

Produced water means water produced in conjunction with the production of crude oil and/or natural gas which is commonly collected at field storage, processing, or disposal facilities, including but not limited to lease tanks, commingled tank batteries, burn pits, lease automatic custody transfer units, and community or lease salt water disposal systems, or which may be collected in gas processing plants, pipeline drips, and other processing or transportation facilities.[226] Produced water may not be removed from a lease, central tank battery, or other facility without OCD approval.[227]

---

217 N.M. Oil Conservation Division Rules and Regulations, Rule 702.

218 N.M. Oil Conservation Division Rules and Regulations, Rule 703.

219 N.M. Oil Conservation Division Rules and Regulations, Rule 704.A.

220 N.M. Oil Conservation Division Rules and Regulations, Rule 704.B.

221 N.M. Oil Conservation Division Rules and Regulations, Rule 705.

222 N.M. Oil Conservation Division Rules and Regulations, Rule 705.B(2).

223 N.M. Oil Conservation Division Rules and Regulations, Rule 705.B(3).

224 N.M. Oil Conservation Division Rules and Regulations, Rule 705.B.

225 N.M. Oil Conservation Division Rules and Regulations, Rule 706.

226 N.M. Oil Conservation Division Rules and Regulations, Rule 0.1.

227 N.M. Oil Conservation Division Rules and Regulations, Rule 709.

OCD has published guidelines for the installation of below-grade produced water tanks and sumps and requires that plans and specifications for such facilities be submitted to it for approval prior to installation. Plans and specifications may deviate from OCD's guidelines if it can be shown that the design integrity is such that the installation will not affect any present or future sources of fresh ground water.[228]

EPA General Permit NMG320000 prohibits discharges of produced water into waters of the United States, as broadly defined in 40 C.F.R. Part 122.2. OCD prohibits the disposition of produced water onto the surface, into any pit, pond, lake, depression, draw, streambed, arroyo, or water course, or in any other place or in any manner which will constitute a hazard to any fresh water supplies.[229] OCD district office supervisors may grant temporary exceptions to this prohibition for emergency situations, for use of produced water in road construction or maintenance, or for use of produced water for other construction purposes.[230] The delivery of produced water to approved salt water disposal facilities, secondary recovery or pressure maintenance injection facilities, or to a drill site for use in drilling fluid will not be considered as constituting a hazard to fresh water supplies if the produced water is placed in tanks or other impermeable storage at such facilities.[231]

In response to reports of illegal dumping of produced water in the San Juan Basin in Northwestern New Mexico, on November 8, 1990, OCD published Memorandum No. 3-90 in order to curtail illegal dumping. Memorandum No. 3-90 asks transporters of produced water to monitor closely driver transportation records to detect improper or inconsistent entries, report to OCD discrepancies in record keeping together with what action the company has taken to investigate possible improper disposal and to resolve the problem to prevent reoccurrence, and perform additional driver education on the need to follow established procedures for safe transport and proper disposal of water and other wastes.[232]

OCC Order Nos. R-3221 and R-3221-C generally prohibit the disposal of produced water on the surface of the ground, in any pit, pond, lake, depression, draw, streambed, or arroyo, or in any watercourse, or in any other place or in any manner which will constitute a hazard to any fresh water supplies in the Southeastern New Mexico Counties of Chaves, Eddy, Lea, and Roosevelt, but allow disposal under some circumstances of produced water in properly maintained impervious lined surface pits used before April 19, 1967, for which OCD has issued a permit and disposal of small quantities of produced water in unlined

---

228 N.M. Oil Conservation Division Environmental Regulations, Tab 7a.

229 N.M. Oil Conservation Division Rules and Regulations, Rule 710.A.

230 N.M. Oil Conservation Division Rules and Regulations, Rule 710.C. *See* N.M. Oil Conservation Division Environmental Regulations, Tab 7a.

231 N.M. Oil Conservation Division Rules and Regulations, Rule 710.B. *See* N.M. Oil Conservation Division Environmental Regulations, Tab 7a.

232 OCD Memorandum No. 3-90, "Produced Water Hauling/Disposal" (11/8/90).

surface pits. OCC Order Nos. R-3221-B and R-3221-B-1 modify Order No. R-3221 to permit the disposal of produced water in unlined surface pits in specified sections of land in the Clayton Basin and Nash Draw areas of Eddy and Lea Counties. OCC Order No. R-3221-C provides that OCD may under some circumstances issue a permit allowing the evaporation or storage of produced water in lined pits constructed after April 19, 1969. OCC Order No. R-3221-D adopts guidelines for seeking exceptions to the rules adopted in Order Nos. R-3221, R-3221-B, and R-3221-C. Generally, an exception will be granted only when the applicant demonstrates that potentially usable ground water will not be affected.[233]

In addition to the R-3221 series of orders discussed above, which are generally applicable in Chaves, Eddy, Lea, and Roosevelt Counties, OCC has adopted orders prohibiting disposal of produced water in unlined pits within certain limited areas in Chaves and Lea Counties. Order No. 1224-A applies to the Hobbs, Monument, and other oil pools within the Lea County Underground Water Basin. Order No. R-2526 applies to oil pools of Pennsylvanian and Wolf Camp geologic age in Lea County. Order No. R-2788 applies to an area 12 miles long within two miles of the Pecos River in Chaves County, and Order No. 12-3164 applies to the Vacuum Oil Field in Lea County.[234]

OCC Order Nos. R-7940 and R-7940-C define a Vulnerable Area within the Northwestern New Mexico Counties of McKinley, Rio Arriba, San Juan, and Sandoval and adopt special rules and regulations for the disposal of produced water and oil and natural gas wastes in the Vulnerable Area. The Vulnerable Area consists of:

> (i) areas within the valleys of the San Juan, Animas, and La Plata Rivers bounded by the topographic line on either side of the river that is 100 vertical feet above the river channel measured perpendicularly to the river channel;
>
> (ii) those alluvial areas which lie within 50 vertical feet, measured perpendicularly to the drainage channel, of all major perennial and ephemeral creeks, canyons, washes, arroyos, and draws located within the oil and gas producing areas of the San Juan Basin;
>
> (iii) areas between the San Juan, Animas, and La Plata Rivers and the following ditches: Highland Park, Hillside Thomas, Cunningham, Farmers, Halford Independent, Citizens, and Hammond; and
>
> (iv) other areas in which ground water is subsequently found to be within 50 feet of the ground surface, including but not limited to 29 specified sections of land in Townships 28-32 North, Ranges 8, 10-13, 15, 16, 18, and 19 West.[235]

Generally, the rules and regulations adopted by Order Nos. R-7940 and R-7940-C prohibit, with several specified exceptions, (1) the disposal within the Vulnerable Area of

---

233 N.M. Oil Conservation Commission Environmental Regulations, Tab 8a.

234 N.M. Oil Conservation Division Environmental Regulations, Tabs 1, 8a.

235 N.M. Oil Conservation Division Environmental Regulations, Tab 8c.

produced water in unlined pits or on the surface, (2) the disposal of oil and natural gas wastes produced within the Vulnerable Area onto the surface or into unlined pits, and (3) the disposal or storage of oil and natural gas wastes in below-grade tanks or lined pits within the Vulnerable Area except after application to and approval by OCD upon a proper showing that the tank or lined pit will be constructed and operated in such a manner as to safely contain the wastes to be placed therein and to detect leakage therefrom. Regulations pursuant to Order Nos. R-7940 and R-7940-C also provide for the elimination, according to a specified schedule, of discharges of oil and natural gas wastes produced outside the Vulnerable Area to unlined pits within the Vulnerable Area and require the submission to OCD for approval of applications or plans to close existing unlined pits not later than 60 days after the date scheduled for the elimination of the discharge.

8.8 COMMERCIAL SURFACE WASTE DISPOSAL FACILITIES

A commercial surface waste disposal facility is any facility that receives compensation for collection, disposal, evaporation, or storage of produced water, drilling fluids, drill cuttings, completion fluids, or other approved oil field-related waste in surface pits, ponds, or below-grade tanks. Such facilities may not be operated without an OCD permit. Applications for such permits must be filed with the Santa Fe office of OCD. Permit applicants must give written notice of the application to the surface owner of the site sought to be used for the facility, and a notice of the application must be published in a newspaper of general circulation in the county in which the facility would be located. Applications must be accompanied by a surety or cash bond in the amount of $25,000 on an OCD form and conditioned upon compliance with New Mexico law, OCD rules and regulations, and satisfactory site cleanup after the end of operations.[236]

The OCD Director may issue a permit if a complete application has been filed and no significant objections have been filed within 30 days following the publication of public notice. In other cases, a public hearing is required.[237]

Operators are required to file certain forms and to maintain certain records. Facilities may not be used except when an attendant is on duty.[238]

Operators must notify OCD when operations cease. After operations have ceased for six consecutive months, the operator must begin to clean up constructed facilities and to restore the facility site within the following six months unless an extension of time is granted by the OCD Director. Such cleanup and restoration must be in accordance with a closure plan approved by the OCD Director and may include removal or demolition of buildings,

---

236 N.M. Oil Conservation Division Rules and Regulations, Rule 711.A; N.M. Oil Conservation Division Environmental Regulations, Tabs 1, 4; *see* N.M. Oil Conservation Division Environmental Regulations, Tabs 1, 4, 4a, 4b (permit application guidelines).

237 *Id.*

238 *Id.*

removal of all tanks, vessels, equipment or hardware, containment and removal of fluids and chemicals, back-filling and grading of pits, removal of contaminated soil, aquifer restoration (if necessary), and reclamation of the facility site. Prior to releasing the required surety or cash bond, OCD will inspect the site to determine that restoration is adequate.[239]

Commercial surface waste disposal facilities permitted by OCD may not accept hazardous waste. Oil field-related wastes which are not subject to RCRA Subtitle C do not need OCD approval to be disposed of at a permitted commercial surface waste disposal facility. Wastes which are subject to RCRA Subtitle C, but which do not exhibit hazardous waste characteristics, must receive OCD approval prior to disposal. Such approval may be sought either by the operator of the facility or by the generator of the waste.[240]

OCD has published guidelines for the preparation of waste disposal permit applications and for facility design and construction. Designs may deviate from the guidelines if it can be shown that the design integrity is such that construction of impoundments will not affect any present or future sources of protectable ground water, and the facility is protective of public health and the environment.[241]

9.0 GROUND WATER DISCHARGE PLANS

Operators must prepare and obtain OCD approval of a discharge plan describing the techniques they will use to comply with Water Quality Control Commission (WQCC) Regulations 3-106 and 3-107 and the requirements of the OGA concerning the transfer and storage of fluids and the proper disposal of waste liquids and solids[242] at natural gas processing plants, oil refineries, gas compressor stations,[243] and brine extraction facilities.[244] Even if the operator does not intend to discharge liquids, a discharge plan must be approved.[245] After receiving the proposed plan, OCD will publish a public notice and allow 30 days for public comment. If there is significant public interest, a public hearing will be held.[246]

---

239 *Id.*

240 N.M. Oil Conservation Division Environmental Regulations, Tab 4.

241 N.M. Oil Conservation Division Rules and Regulations, Rule 711.A; N.M. Oil Conservation Division Environmental Regulations, Tabs 1, 4; *see* N.M. Oil Conservation Division Environmental Regulations, Tabs 1, 4, 4a and 4b. (permit application guidelines).

242 N.M. Oil Conservation Division Environmental Regulations, Tab 6a.

243 *Id.*

244 N.M. Oil Conservation Division Environmental Regulations, Tab 6c.

245 N.M. Oil Conservation Division Environmental Regulations, Tab 6a, 6c. For example, the discharge plan would address surface facility operations, including storage pits, tankage, and loading areas. *Id.* If good cause is shown, a discharger may be allowed to operate without an approved plan for 120 days. *Id.*

246 N.M. Oil Conservation Division Environmental Regulations, Tab 6a at 2.

9.1 NATURAL GAS PROCESSING PLANTS, OIL REFINERIES, AND GAS COMPRESSOR STATIONS

OCD has prepared guidelines to assist applicants and expedite the discharge plan review process. In general, the review is expedited when (1) the liquids are routed to tanks, Class II injection wells, or lined ponds with underdrains for leak detection; (2) monitoring and testing procedures will detect leaks from below-grade or underground tanks and plant pipelines; and (3) adequate contingency plans for accidental spills and leaks are in place.[247] A longer review period may be required when operators seek to use procedures that have a high probability of allowing effluent and leachate to infiltrate and move to the subsurface.[248] A non-refundable filing fee payable to the Water Quality Management Fund must be submitted with the proposed discharge plan; an additional fee based on the type of facility and the application will be due when the plan is approved.[249]

A proposed discharge plan must identify the type of operation, the processes occurring at the operation, the operator or the legally responsible party and a local representative, the location of the operation, and the landowners of record. It must also include detailed geographic, hydrologic, and water quality information, as well as a diagram of the facility.[250] Information on soil types, aquifer characteristics, flooding potential, and flooding protection must also be submitted.[251]

The proposed plan must identify, for each source,[252] the type of major effluent; estimated quantity in barrels or gallons per month; the type and volume of major additives; concentration analyses for total dissolved solids, major cations/anions and pH; hydrocarbon analyses; and analyses for any remaining WQCC Regulation § 3-103 standards not already discussed. The plan must also identify toxic pollutants (or their absence), sampling protocols, and variable flow rates. In some cases, an operator may satisfy these requirements by submitting information on the chemical characteristics of commingled effluent or process streams.[253] The proposed discharge plan must discuss the collection and storage systems

---

247 *Id.*

248 *Id.*

249 *Id.* at 3.

250 *Id.* at 5-7.

251 *Id.* at 12-13.

252 Examples of sources include separators, boilers, engine cooling waters, cooling towers, commingled sewage, waste lubrication and motor oils, waste and slop oil, used filters, tank solids and sludges, cleaning operations using solvents/degreasers, washing of tanks, trucks, and drums, and other liquid and solid wastes. N.M. Oil Conservation Division Environmental Regulations, Tab 6a.

253 *Id.* at 5-6.

for each source, provide water and wastewater flow schematics to show individual treatment and process units, and comply with OCD design criteria.[254]

The proposed plan must describe existing on-site facilities used for effluent disposal and provide technical data on the design elements of each disposal method. If off-site disposal is to be used, the proposed plan must identify the general composition of the material to be disposed of, method of shipment, shipping agent, receiving facility, and final disposition.[255] Procedures for inspection, maintenance, and reporting must be described and a contingency plan which describes accident prevention, detection, containment, mitigation, and notification must be prepared.[256] Finally, the plan must include any additional information necessary to demonstrate that approval of the discharge plan will not result in concentrations in excess of the standards of WQCC Regulation § 3-103 or the presence of any toxic pollutant at any place where the withdrawal of water for use is presently or reasonably foreseeable.[257]

9.2 BRINE EXTRACTION FACILITIES

Brine extraction facilities must have an approved discharge plan. Existing facilities operating under an approved plan, however, may receive an extension of time to renew if their renewal application is submitted to OCD at least 180 days before the plan expires and if they are in compliance with the existing plan on the original expiration date.[258] After the application is accepted, the administrative review procedure is similar to that employed by OCD for other types of discharge plans. Similarly, the review process may vary in length depending on the procedures proposed.[259]

The proposed plan must identify the name of the facility and indicate whether the application is new or for a renewal. It must identify the name of the operator or legally responsible party, the local representative, and the landowners of record. Additionally, the proposed plan must include the legal location of the facility and detailed geographic, hydrographic, and water quality information, including the location of the injection well, storage tanks or ponds, process equipment, relevant objects, and property boundaries.[260] The proposed plan must list all fluids used or stored at the facility and identify the source, average daily volume produced, estimated volume stored, location, and type of containers.

---

254 *Id.* at 7-8.

255 *Id.* at 10-11.

256 *Id.* at 10-12.

257 *Id.* at 13.

258 N.M. Oil Conservation Division Environmental Regulations, Tab 6c.

259 *See* Section 9.0 of this Chapter.

260 N.M. Oil Conservation Division Environmental Regulations, Tab 6c at 5.

The proposed plan must provide information about the transfer, storage, and disposal of fluids and solids which is adequate to determine what water contaminants may be discharged to the surface and subsurface within the facility. Such information could include identification of the method of transfer, storage and disposal (tankage, surface impoundment, leach field, or solids disposal), whether tanks, piping, and pipelines are pressurized, and fluid flow schematics in sufficient detail to show individual units. In addition, the proposed plan must describe existing and proposed measures to prevent or retard seepage, provide the location and design of sites and methods available for sampling and measurement or calculation of flow, and describe the existing or proposed monitoring system. If off-site disposal is proposed, the general composition of the materials, method of shipment, receiving facility, and final disposition should be included. The plan must also provide for routine inspection, monitoring, and maintenance and include a contingency plan to prevent, detect, mitigate, and report accidental leaks or spills.[261]

Operators of in-situ brine extraction wells must meet the requirements of Part 5 of the WQCC Regulations and other applicable WQCC and OCD requirements. Before beginning to drill, deepen, or plug back a well, the operator must file with OCD various documents including Form C-101 Application for Permit to Drill, Deepen, or Plug Back; Notice of Intent to Discharge (new facilities only); maps and other information showing the location of producing oil and gas wells, ground water, and abandoned wells; maps and cross-sections of the geology and geologic structure of the local area; proposed formation testing program; schematic drawings of surface and subsurface construction; proposed drilling, evaluation, and testing programs; the proposed stimulation, injection, and operation procedures; and a plan for plugging and abandonment.[262] A plugging bond will also be required before drilling can begin.[263]

A discharge plan for a brine extraction well must also include evaluation, completion, and workover information; proposed maximum and average injection pressures and volumes; proposed mechanical integrity testing program; analysis of injection fluid and brine; and a comparison of volumes of fresh water injected to volumes of brine in order to detect underground losses.[264] Applications to renew a discharge plan for facilities in operation over 15 years must also provide information on the size and extent of the solution cavern and geologic/engineering data demonstrating that continued brine extractions will not cause subsidence or a catastrophic collapse.[265]

---

261 *Id.* at 5-7, 11.

262 *Id.*

263 *Id.* at 8-10.

264 *Id.* at 10.

265 *Id.* at 11.

In all cases, OCD reserves the right to request additional information to demonstrate that the approval of the discharge plan will not result in applicable standards being exceeded or the presence of any toxic pollutant at any place where water is or may be withdrawn for use.[266]

10.0 GUIDELINES FOR CLOSURE OF UNLINED SURFACE IMPOUNDMENTS

Although OCD has not required operators to close all unlined surface impoundments immediately, it has issued detailed guidelines covering site assessment, soil and water remediation levels, soil and water sampling procedures, remediation options and requirements, and final closure.[267] These guidelines apply to the closure of unlined produced water pits, dehydrator pits, blowdown pits, tank drain pits, pipeline drip collector pits, compressor scrubber pits, flare pits, and all unlined pits which receive exploration, production, and processing wastes regulated by OCD but do not apply to pits for drill cuttings and drilling fluids, which are regulated by OCD Rule 105.[268]

A plan for closure must be submitted to and approved by OCD before the impoundment is closed. An operator may seek approval for a deviation from specified procedures if the operator's proposed alternative will remove or isolate contaminants in a way that will not impact fresh waters, public health, and the environment.[269]

11.0 GUIDELINES FOR REMEDIATION OF LEAKS, SPILLS, AND RELEASES

Operators must take corrective action for leaks, spills, or releases or any material that has a reasonable probability of injuring or being detrimental to public health, fresh waters, animal or plant life, or property or that may unreasonably interfere with the public welfare or use of property. As a result, OCD has issued remediation guidelines for use on all federal, state, and fee lands. Compliance with these guidelines alone, however, will not ensure that an operator has complied with all applicable regulations.[270]

The operator must notify OCD of any leaks, spills, and releases of any wastes or products from oil field operations. This notice must include the names of the responsible party and local contact and facility, time and description of the incident, type and quantity of the discharge, site characteristics, and any immediate corrective action that was taken. Subsequently, the operator must take steps to eliminate the source of the leak, spill, or release and secure the site; contain the materials that were leaked, spilled, or released; and stabilize the site, provided that no safety hazard would result.[271] The operator will then be responsible

---

266 *Id.* at 12.

267 N.M. Oil Conservation Division Environmental Regulations, Tab 7b.

268 *Id.* at 2.

269 *Id.* at 2.

270 N.M. Oil Conservation Division Environmental Regulations, Tab 7d.

271 *Id.* at 2-3.

for site assessment and remediation actions until the site is closed. Throughout this process, all responsible agencies should be consulted and necessary approvals obtained in order to comply with all applicable laws.[272]

12.0 CENTRALIZED AND COMMERCIAL LANDFARMS

A permit is required for a commercial or a centralized landfarm for treating oil field solids that are either exempt from RCRA Subtitle C Regulations or are nonhazardous by characteristic testing. These permits are reviewed and approved pursuant to OCD Rule 711, which applies to commercial surface waste facilities generally.[273] Landfarm operations may also be conducted at individual well sites with prior approval from the district OCD office.[274]

---

272 *See generally id.*

273 N.M. Oil Conservation Division Environmental Regulations, Tab 7e.

274 *Id.*

CHAPTER VIII
RADIOACTIVE MATERIALS AND WASTE MANAGEMENT

1.0 INTRODUCTION

New Mexico has been an "Agreement State" with the Federal Nuclear Regulatory Commission (NRC) since 1974.[1] Agreement State status means that NRC has ceded its regulatory authority to New Mexico with respect to by-product materials,[2] source materials,[3] and special nuclear materials in quantities not sufficient to form a critical mass.[4] NRC conducts audits and reviews New Mexico's regulations in order to assure these remain compatible with federal standards. Since 1986, when New Mexico returned licensing and regulatory authority over uranium mills to NRC, the New Mexico Environment Department (NMED) has not enforced its uranium regulations. Although the regulations have not been repealed, federal law controls and NRC should be consulted.

New Mexico has implemented its authority through a variety of statutes and regulations. The primary statutes pertaining to radioactive materials and radioactive waste are the Radioactive and Hazardous Materials Act,[5] the Radiation Protection Act (RPA),[6] and the Medical Radiation Health and Safety Act (MRHSA).[7] In addition, statutory provisions cover the transportation of radioactive materials.[8] Radiation protection regulations cover licensing and registration procedures, radiation protection standards, safety requirements, land disposal,

---

1 This agreement was entered with NRC pursuant to the provisions of the Atomic Energy Act of 1954, as amended.

2 "By-product material" is defined as any radioactive material (except special nuclear material) yielded in or made radioactive by exposure to the radiation incident to the process of producing and utilizing special nuclear material, and the tailings or wastes produced by the extraction or concentration of uranium or thorium from any ore processed primarily for its source material content. N.M. Radiation Protection Regulations, EIB/RPR 1, § 1-102.G (filed March 10, 1989).

3 "Source material" is defined as uranium or thorium, or any combination thereof, in any physical or chemical form, or ores which contain by weight 0.05 percent or more of uranium, thorium, or any combination thereof. Source material does not include special nuclear material. N.M. Radiation Protection Regulations § 1-102.ZZ.

4 "Special nuclear material in quantities not sufficient to form a critical mass" means uranium enriched in the isotope U-235 in quantities not exceeding 350 grams of contained U-235, uranium 233 in quantities not exceeding 200 grams, or plutonium in quantities not exceeding 200 grams. N.M. Radiation Protection Regulations § 1-102.BBB.

5 N.M. Stat. Ann. §§ 74-4A-2 to -14 (Repl. Pamp. 1993).

6 N.M. Stat. Ann. §§ 74-3-1 to -16 (Repl. Pamp. 1993).

7 N.M. Stat. Ann. §§ 61-14E-1 to -12 (Repl. Pamp. 1993).

8 N.M. Stat. Ann. § 74-4A-1 (Repl. Pamp. 1993).

and transportation. These regulations are in the process of being amended to cover the possession, use, transfer, transport, storage, and disposal of naturally occurring radioactive materials (NORM) associated with the oil and gas industry.[9]

New Mexico is also a member of two interstate compacts. The Western Interstate Nuclear Compact[10] was established to provide a framework for cooperative efforts in nuclear and related fields in order to enhance the western economy and contribute to the well-being of the region's population. Other members of this compact are Alaska, Arizona, Colorado, Idaho, Nevada, Oregon, Utah, Washington, and Wyoming.[11] The second compact of which New Mexico is a member is the Rocky Mountain Low-Level Radioactive Waste Compact.[12] This compact is intended to provide for the establishment and operation of regional low-level radioactive waste disposal facilities. At present, no such facility exists in New Mexico. Other members of the Rocky Mountain Low-Level Radioactive Waste Compact are Nevada and Colorado.[13]

NMED is responsible for maintaining and enforcing certification standards for medical technologies that involve radioactive materials, establishing and maintaining educational programs, establishing procedures for licensing and registration of radioactive materials, and establishing standards for the handling of radioactive materials.[14] It is also responsible for developing, maintaining, and enforcing other radiation control regulations.[15] However, responsibility for promulgating regulations and standards for radiation control is vested in the Environmental Improvement Board (EIB).[16] EIB must seek the advice and consent of the Radiation Technical Advisory Council prior to adopting regulations pursuant to the RPA.[17] EIB has independent authority to promulgate regulations pursuant to the MRHSA.[18] The State Highway Commission has exclusive authority to designate routes for transportation of

---

9 N.M. Radiation Protection Regulations § 14-101 (Draft Aug. 18, 1993). These draft regulations are discussed in more detail in the Regulation and Licensing of NORM in the Oil & Gas Industry Section of this Chapter.

10 N.M. Stat. Ann. §§ 11-9-1 to -3 (Repl. Pamp. 1983).

11 N.M. Stat. Ann. § 11-9-1, compiler's note (Repl. Pamp. 1983).

12 N.M. Stat. Ann. §§ 11-9A-1 to -3 (Repl. Pamp. 1983).

13 Wyo. Stat. Ann. § 9-6-201 *et seq.*; Nev. Rev. Stat. § 459.007 *et seq.*; Colo. Rev. Stat. § 24-60-2201 *et seq.*

14 N.M. Stat. Ann. § 61-14E-6 (Repl. Pamp. 1993).

15 N.M. Stat. Ann. § 74-1-7(A) (Repl. Pamp. 1993).

16 N.M. Stat. Ann. § 74-1-8(A) (Repl. Pamp. 1993).

17 N.M. Stat. Ann. § 74-3-3 (Repl. Pamp. 1993). The Radiation Technical Advisory Council is an appointed body charged to advise NMED and EIB on technical matters related to radiation.

18 N.M. Radiation Protection Regulations § 3-480.

radioactive materials, except as preempted by federal law.[19] EIB, however, retains the authority to promulgate regulations pertaining to the transportation of radioactive materials on the highway.[20] Should these regulations be violated, NMED may impose fines of up to $1,000.[21]

1.1 GENERAL RADIATION PROTECTION STANDARDS

The general rule of radiation protection is that the "ALARA" concept should be met. In other words, levels of radiation should be kept "as low as is reasonably achievable" taking into account the state of technology and the economics of improvements in relation to benefits to the public health and safety and in relation to the utilization of ionizing radiation in the public interest.[22]

This rule is implemented through a regulatory scheme that requires everyone who receives, uses, possesses, transfers, or acquires a minimum amount of specific radioactive materials to hold a license.

NMED may revoke, suspend, or modify any license on a number of grounds. These grounds include the making of material false statements or the violation of or failure to follow statutory terms and conditions, license conditions, or NMED rules and regulations. Before NMED may act, however, the licensee is entitled to notice and an opportunity to comply.[23] Violating provisions of the RPA, the MRHSA, and related regulations is a misdemeanor.[24]

2.0 RADIOACTIVE MATERIALS

Exempt quantities of radioactive materials are not covered by the regulations governing receivers, users, possessors, transferors, or acquirers. If radioactive materials are possessed in greater quantities, the regulations determine whether a general license or specific license is appropriate.

2.1 EXEMPT QUANTITIES

Certain quantities of radioactive material are exempt from licensing requirements, except distribution licensing.[25] Quantities of source material that are by weight less than 0.05 percent of any chemical mixture, compound, solution, or alloy need not be licensed.[26] Items such as glass mantels, vacuum tubes, electric lamps, and so forth that contain source

---

19 N.M. Stat. Ann. § 74-4-1(A) (Repl. Pamp. 1993).

20 *Id.*

21 N.M. Stat. Ann. § 74-4A-1(C) (Repl. Pamp. 1993).

22 N.M. Radiation Protection Regulations § 4-100.B.

23 N.M. Radiation Protection Regulations § 3-480.

24 N.M. Stat. Ann. §§ 74-3-12, 61-14E-12 (Repl. Pamp. 1993).

25 N.M. Radiation Protection Regulations § 3-340.B.

26 N.M. Radiation Protection Regulations § 3-110.

material are exempt from the licensing regulations. The regulations also define exempt concentrations of radioactive material that is not source material. Further, the regulations do not require persons to be licensed in order to receive, possess, use, or transfer unrefined or unprocessed ore that contains source material.[27]

2.2 GENERAL LICENSES

General licensees do not need to file an application or to receive a licensing document, but they may need to register with NMED. Manufacturers or distributors of generally licensed materials or devices are required to notify NMED of who received what type of radiation device.[28] Common and contract carriers and private carriers have a general license for intrastate transportation of radioactive material in the regular course of their carriage for another or storage incident thereto, unless they are transporting nuclear waste. Carriers with a general license are subject to the applicable federal Department of Transportation (DOT) regulations for loading, storage, placarding, and reporting of incidents.[29] Private physicians who transport radioactive material for use in their practice do not need to comply with DOT requirements.[30]

The regulations grant a general license to use and transfer not more than 6.8 kilograms of source material at any one time to pharmacists, physicians and their patients, commercial, industrial, research, educational and medical institutions, and state and local governments for research and development, educational, commercial or operational purposes.[31] Such general licensees may not receive more than 68 kilograms of source material per year.[32] Holders of a general license to possess source material are exempt from the general radiation protection standards of Part 4 and the worker safety and inspection requirements of Part 10 of the regulations.[33]

In addition, physicians may hold a general license for radioactive material for diagnostic purposes after filing a certificate with NMED and obtaining a certification number.[34] Subsequently, the physician may possess a limited amount of radioactive material at one time. This material must be obtained only in prepackaged individual doses and transferred only to

---

27 *Id.*

28 N.M. Radiation Protection Regulations § 3-340.J(4).

29 N.M. Radiation Protection Regulations § 3-230. Carriers of exempt quantities of radioactive material do not need a license. *Id.*

30 N.M. Radiation Protection Regulations § 3-230.B(2). Transportation of radioactive material is discussed in more detail in the Transportation Section of this Chapter.

31 N.M. Radiation Protection Regulations § 3-210.

32 N.M. Radiation Protection Regulations § 3-210.A.

33 N.M. Radiation Protection Regulations §§ 3-210.B, 3-220.E(5).

34 N.M. Radiation Protection Regulations § 3-220.E.

authorized recipients.[35] The physician need not comply with the general radiation protection standards of Part 4 and the worker safety and inspection requirements of Part 10 of the regulations.[36]

A general license is also available for *in vitro* and clinical laboratory testing. The potential licensee must file a certificate with NMED for *in vitro* testing and receive a validated copy and a certification number in return. The general license applies only to *in vitro* clinical and laboratory testing and does not extend to tests involving the internal or external administration of radioactive materials or radiation to humans or animals.[37] The licensee may transfer the testing materials only to a licensed person, and only in labeled, packaged units.[38] This general licensee does not need to comply with the radiation protection standards or worker notice and inspection requirements.[39]

Holders of a specific license that authorizes the receipt, possession, use, and transfer of special nuclear material concurrently hold a general license to possess limited amounts of calibration and reference sources. Special nuclear material includes enriched uranium and plutonium.[40] This general licensee must observe NMED labeling, reporting, testing, recordkeeping, inspection, transfer, transportation, reporting, and radiation protection regulations.[41]

There is also a general license to receive, acquire, possess, use, or transfer depleted uranium contained in industrial products or devices. However, within 30 days of receiving or acquiring such a device, the licensee must register it with NMED.[42] This general licensee may not introduce the depleted uranium into other materials. The licensee may not abandon the device and must transfer or dispose of it in accordance with the regulations. If the general licensee under this part transfers the device to another, the transferor must report the name and address of the transferee to NMED within 30 days.[43]

A general license is available for possession of luminous safety devices for aircraft. This general licensee is generally exempt from precautionary procedures and reporting and inspection requirements, with the exception that radiation incidents, theft, or loss of licensed

---

35 *Id.*

36 *Id.*

37 N.M. Radiation Protection Regulations § 3-220.F(1). A specific license pursuant to § 3-320 is necessary.

38 N.M. Radiation Protection Regulations § 3-220.F(3)(d).

39 N.M. Radiation Protection Regulations § 3-220.F(6).

40 *See* N.M. Radiation Protection Regulations § 1-102.BBB.

41 N.M. Radiation Protection Regulations § 3-220.D(4).

42 N.M. Radiation Protection Regulations § 3-210.E.

43 *Id.*

material must be reported to NMED. Reports of theft or loss must be made immediately by telephone and in writing. Major radiation incidents must be reported immediately, while less serious incidents may be reported within 24 hours by telephone and in writing.[44]

A measuring, gauging, or controlling device may be owned or received under a general license. This general licensee must see that labels are not removed, test the device regularly, maintain records for at least two years, and not abandon the device. Furthermore, the general licensee may transfer the device only to a specific licensee, unless the device will still be used at the same location. In either case, the transfer must be reported to NMED within 30 days.[45]

Ice detection devices may be owned and used under a general license.[46] These general licensees must comply with waste disposal requirements.[47] They must also report the theft or loss of the device and notify NMED of radiation incidents.[48]

A general license also exists for the ownership of static elimination devices and ion generating tubes. This licensee is subject to NMED recordkeeping, inspection, testing, and other requirements.[49]

Watchmakers using radium-containing luminous compounds do so under a general license. They must keep records and obtain radioactive material from licensed distributors.[50]

2.3 SPECIFIC LICENSES

Specific licensees must apply for and receive a license from NMED.[51] Specific licensees as well as registrants must ensure that all information supplied to NMED is kept current. Licenses are reciprocal in New Mexico under certain specified circumstances.[52]

Applicants for a specific license must file a signed application with NMED. If the application is for a commercial radioactive waste disposal site, it must be accompanied by an environmental report, a showing that title to the land is transferable to the state or the United States, and assurances of financial ability to cover costs throughout the facility's life and closure. Other applicants may be required to file an environmental report if NMED finds there is a significant impact on the environment or public health and safety.[53] Appli-

---

44 N.M. Radiation Protection Regulations § 3-220.C.

45 N.M. Radiation Protection Regulations § 3-220.B.

46 N.M. Radiation Protection Regulations § 3-220.G(1).

47 N.M. Radiation Protection Regulations § 2-220.G(2).

48 *Id.*

49 N.M. Radiation Protection Regulations § 3-220.A.

50 N.M. Radiation Protection Regulations § 3-220.H.

51 N.M. Radiation Protection Regulations § 3-200.B.

52 N.M. Radiation Protection Regulations § 3-600.A.

53 N.M. Radiation Protection Regulations § 3-300.

cants for a disposal site must show that financial surety arrangements and continued care requirements will be met.[54]

After receipt of the application, NMED will provide notice to the public and other interested government and private parties. A 60-day comment period will generally ensue during which any member of the public can make a written request for a hearing. If the application was for a disposal site, the public has 120 days in which to request a hearing. The Secretary of NMED (Secretary) has the discretion to call a hearing on 30 days notice. The parties are given the opportunity to submit data, argument, and views and to examine witnesses at a hearing which will be recorded.[55]

In order to receive a specific license, the applicant must show, at a minimum, that (1) the applicant has sufficient training and experience, (2) the radioactive material will be used for the requested purpose in accordance with the regulations and in a manner that minimizes dangers to the public health and safety or property, (3) the applicant possesses adequate equipment, facilities and procedures, (4) issuance of the specific license will not be inimical to the public health and safety, and (5) special requirements, if any, have been met.[56] A specific license may be revoked if these requirements were not met or are later violated.[57]

A specific licensee may terminate the license by written request to NMED.[58] Within 30 days before leaving the premises that may have been contaminated with radioactive materials as a result of a specific licensee's activities, the licensee must notify NMED of the intent to vacate. NMED may require the licensee to decontaminate the premises.[59] A specific license cannot be transferred without written consent of NMED.[60]

Before transferring radioactive materials, the transferor must verify that the transferee is authorized to receive radioactive material. However, a transferee may transfer radioactive material to NMED, U.S. Department of Energy, exempt persons, and licensees or other authorized persons. In other cases, written authorization from NMED is necessary prior to the transfer.[61]

---

54 N.M. Radiation Protection Regulations §§ 3-315 to -316.

55 N.M. Radiation Protection Regulations § 3-312.D - .H.

56 N.M. Radiation Protection Regulations § 3-310.

57 N.M. Radiation Protection Regulations § 3-480.B.

58 N.M. Radiation Protection Regulations § 3-480.D.

59 N.M. Radiation Protection Regulations § 4-460.

60 N.M. Radiation Protection Regulations § 3-410.B.

61 N.M. Radiation Protection Regulations § 3-490.

A specific license is necessary to distribute radioactive materials, even in exempt quantities.[62] These materials must be labeled and records kept. The distributor must report to NMED annually.[63]

Each holder of a specific license for distribution of radioactive materials must give the transferee a copy of the general license issued under the regulations. In addition, the specific licensee must report the transfer to NMED. This report must identify the transferee, a person who may serve as a point of contact between NMED and the transferee, the device transferred, and the quantity and type of radioactive material it contained. The distributor must keep records that reflect this information.[64]

A specific license is needed to introduce exempt quantities of radioactive material into products or materials that will be transferred to others and to incorporate radioactive material that is not source or by-product material into gas and aerosol detectors. Similarly, a specific license is needed to manufacture and distribute measuring, gauging, and controlling devices, to manufacture, assemble and repair luminous aircraft safety devices, and to manufacture calibration sources containing radioactive material.[65] Manufacturers of ice detection equipment must obtain a special license pursuant to the New Mexico regulations and must also comply with federal regulations.[66] A specific license is necessary to manufacture, assemble, repair, and distribute devices containing depleted uranium or other radioactive materials.[67]

Manufacturers and distributors of industrial products that contain depleted uranium must hold a specific license. In addition to other requirements, the application must list the expected dose and the utility of the product or device to be manufactured and must provide reasonable assurance that unique benefits will accrue to the public.[68] These specific licensees are also subject to specific labeling and transfer requirements. In general, they must label each unit to identify the manufacturer, the license number under which the unit was manufactured, the fact that the unit contains depleted uranium, and the quantity thereof. Each transferee must receive a copy of the general license that enables the transferee to possess the device. The specific licensee must also report transfers to NMED, and in some cases to NRC, on a quarterly basis.[69]

---

62 N.M. Radiation Protection Regulations § 3-340.B.

63 *Id.*

64 N.M. Radiation Protection Regulations § 3-340.D(4).

65 N.M. Radiation Protection Regulations § 3-340.

66 N.M. Radiation Protection Regulations § 3-340.I.

67 N.M. Radiation Protection Regulations § 3-340.J - .K.

68 N.M. Radiation Protection Regulations § 3-340.J.

69 N.M. Radiation Protection Regulations § 3-340.J(4).

Manufacturers and distributors of radioactive material that will be used by physicians for medical purposes must possess a specific license.[70] These materials must be manufactured, labeled and packaged in accordance with the federal regulations for new drugs or biological products. In addition, these materials must be properly labeled. Similarly, manufacturers and distributors of radioactive material for *in vitro* clinical or laboratory testing must observe size limitations for each packaged unit and labeling requirements as to the contents, include the radiation caution symbol, and provide handling, storage and disposal instructions.

2.4 LICENSES FOR INDUSTRIAL AND SCIENTIFIC USE

Industrial radiography means using radiation to examine the macroscopic structure of materials. Its tools are radiation machines, sealed sources, particle accelerators, and analytical and cabinet x-ray machines. As a rule, every radiation machine must be registered and its operator must be licensed. The regulations discussed here supplement general registration requirements, safety standards, and transportation regulations.

2.4.1 Sealed Sources

In order to obtain a specific license to use a sealed source for industrial radiography purposes, the applicant must show that a training program exists for the radiographers and their assistants. In addition, written operating and emergency procedures must exist to cover the handling and use of radioactive sources, radiation surveys, controlled access, personnel monitoring, transportation, accident procedures, and notification and recordkeeping. Finally, it is NMED policy to examine the overall organizational structure of the company or licensee, their leak testing procedures, and the inspection and maintenance program prior to granting the license.

Specific licensees are subject to continuing license conditions. Only authorized personnel may replace, repair, test, or otherwise modify a sealed source. The licensee must have each sealed source tested for leaks twice annually. Leaks must be corrected and reported to NMED within five days after results are known. The licensee must label the sealed source if it is not fastened to or contained within a radiographic exposure device.[71] Furthermore, the specific licensee must regularly inventory the sealed sources and maintain a log of who possesses each source and where and when it was last used.[72] All radiographic exposure devices and storage containers must be inspected and maintained.[73]

Industrial licensees must also comply with posting, surveying, and recordkeeping requirements. They must see that radiographers and their assistants wear film badges or thermal luminous dosimeters plus a pocket dosimeter or a pocket chamber. The pocket

---

70 N.M. Radiation Protection Regulations § 3-340.G.

71 N.M. Radiation Protection Regulations § 5-240.

72 N.M. Radiation Protection Regulations §§ 5-250 to -260.

73 N.M. Radiation Protection Regulations § 5-270.

dosimeter or pocket chamber must be read daily. If exposures are above a certain level, the film badge or thermal luminescent dosimeter must be developed promptly.[74]

2.4.2 X-Ray Equipment

All analytical x-ray equipment that is used for industrial or scientific purposes must be equipped with safety devices (unless exempted by NMED), warning devices, warning labels, and other mechanisms that promote safety and prevent the unsafe operation of the equipment.[75] Licensees using analytical x-ray equipment must also ensure that radiation levels do not exceed dose limits, conduct radiation surveys, and comply with posting requirements.

Cabinet x-ray machines must be registered with NMED. In addition, the regulations contain specific safety rules and requirements for personnel monitoring that must be observed. Industrial radiography performed with cabinet machines and in shielded rooms is generally exempt from these requirements.

2.4.3 Particle Accelerators

Users of particle accelerators in industrial applications must register with NMED.[76] In addition, the regulations contain special radiation safety requirements specific to the use of particle accelerators, which must be complied with by all licensees.

2.5 BROAD LICENSE

A special type of specific license is that which is known as a "specific license of broad scope" or a "broad license."[77] There are three types of broad license, known as type A, type B, and type C. In general, a broad license authorizes the receipt, acquisition, possession, use, and transfer of any chemical or physical form of a specified radioactive material in limited quantities. In order to receive one of these broad licenses, an applicant must satisfy the general requirements for a specific license and also meet certain requirements concerning experience and administrative oversight. Broad licenses are not a substitute for specific licenses for therapy, diagnostic uses, manufacture, assembly, repair, or distribution of commodities that have radioactive material in them.[78]

A specific license is also required before using radioactive materials for certain medical purposes and before opening a disposal site. Because of the detail involved in each of these areas, they will be discussed separately.

---

74 N.M. Radiation Protection Regulations § 5-320.

75 N.M. Radiation Protection Regulations § 8-120.

76 N.M. Radiation Protection Regulations §§ 9-100 to -210.

77 N.M. Radiation Protection Regulations § 3-330.

78 N.M. Radiation Protection Regulations § 3-330.E.(1)(c).

3.0 MEDICAL USES

The use of radiation or radioactive materials in the healing arts falls generally into two categories: the use of sealed sources on or in humans and the use of x-rays. The regulations require that the user be certified and possess a materials license.

3.1 CERTIFICATION

Only a department-certified radiologic technologist[79] may use ionizing radiation on humans or engage in any radiology specialties.[80] Licensed medical practitioners or auxiliary or health practitioners who are certified by an independent board are exempt from this requirement, as are students under the supervision of a licensed practitioner or certified radiologic technologist.[81]

A certificate may be denied, revoked or suspended by EIB in the event that an applicant used fraud or deceit to procure or attempt to procure a certificate, was convicted of a felony after certification, is found to be unfit, incompetent, habitually intemperate, addicted to habit-forming drugs, or medically incompetent or guilty of unprofessional or unethical conduct. Additional grounds for the denial or revocation of a certificate are aiding and abetting the practice of a non-certificate holder, practicing beyond the scope of authorized activity, or interpreting a diagnostic imaging procedure for a patient or the patient's family. Finally, a license may be denied, revoked, or suspended for the willful or repeated public violation of the MRHSA.[82] It is a misdemeanor for a person knowingly or willfully to employ a person who is required to have a certificate or who practices without a certificate or exemption or otherwise to violate the MRHSA.[83] NMED has supervisory authority over this area.

All fees paid by radiologic technicians go into the radiologic technology fund in the state treasury, which is used for enforcement and promoting education and standards for radiologic technology.[84]

---

79 A radiologic technologist is a person other than a person licensed to practice medicine, dentistry, podiatry, chiropractic, or osteopathy who applies radiation to humans for diagnostic or therapeutic purposes or applies radiopharmaceutical agents to humans for diagnostic or therapeutic purposes. It includes radiographers, radiation therapy technologists, and nuclear medicine technologists. N.M. Stat. Ann. § 61-14E-4(I) (Repl. Pamp. 1993).

80 N.M. Stat. Ann. § 61-14E-7 (Repl. Pamp. 1993).

81 N.M. Stat. Ann. § 61-14E-7(C) (Repl. Pamp. 1993).

82 N.M. Stat. Ann. § 61-14E-11 (Repl. Pamp. 1993).

83 N.M. Stat. Ann. § 61-14E-12 (Repl. Pamp. 1993).

84 N.M. Stat. Ann. § 61-14E-10 (Repl. Pamp. 1993).

3.2 LICENSING

A specific license is necessary to use a sealed source on a human for medical purposes.[85] The licensee must have specialized training or equivalent experience. In addition, if the licensee is an individual, he or she must have access to a hospital with adequate facilities to hospitalize and monitor patients. The licensee must have extensive experience in handling and administering radioactive materials and in clinical management, where appropriate.[86] If the applicant is an institution, there must be a medical isotope committee that evaluates all proposals for research, diagnosis, and therapeutic uses of radioactive material. In addition, the institution must be adequate for the clinical care of patients and the medical users must have substantial experience in the handling and administering of radioactive materials and the clinical management of radioactive patients. The applicant's staff must have substantial experience in the use of a variety of radioactive materials for a variety of human uses.[87]

Licensees are subject to recordkeeping and physical inventory requirements,[88] regular testing for leakage,[89] radiation survey requirements, and posting requirements. In particular, the institution must post signs on the bed or room warning others of the presence of radioactive sources in the patient. The exception to this rule is that if personnel are present who will take precautions to prevent exposure to radioactive sources in excess of limits then there is no need to post signs.[90] A patient who has been treated with a sealed source may not be released until all implants have been removed and their removal confirmed with a source count and a radiation survey of the patient.[91]

Medical personnel who use sealed sources through teletherapy must also meet the applicable standards for equipment, operations, and testing procedures.[92]

Each x-ray machine used for medical purposes must be registered with NMED, and operators must be adequately instructed in the competent and safe use of the equipment. These operators are subject to occupational exposure limits and must wear protective clothing and monitoring devices when necessary.[93] Workers must have access to written procedures. X-ray machines must also bear warning labels and be inspected regularly. Before buildings

---

85 N.M. Radiation Protection Regulations § 3-320.D.

86 N.M. Radiation Protection Regulations § 3-320.B.

87 N.M. Radiation Protection Regulations § 3-320.A.

88 N.M. Radiation Protection Regulations § 7-200.

89 *Id.*

90 *Id.*

91 N.M. Radiation Protection Regulations § 7-200.E.

92 N.M. Radiation Protection Regulations § 7-300.

93 N.M. Radiation Protection Regulations § 6-120.A.

that will contain x-ray equipment are constructed or remodeled, NMED must review the floor plan and equipment arrangement.[94]

If radiation is misadministered in a therapeutic procedure, NMED and the referring physician must be notified by telephone within 24 hours of discovering the error. In addition, unless the physician believes it would be harmful, the patient or responsible relative or guardian must be notified. Within 15 days, a written report must be filed with NMED. If radiation is misadministered in diagnosis, the referring physician and NMED must be notified in writing within 10 days after the end of the calendar quarter in which the misadministration occurs.[95] Licensees must maintain records of all misadministrations of radiopharmaceuticals and radiation from teletherapy or brachytherapy sources.[96]

4.0 RADIATION HEALTH AND SAFETY

Radiation health and safety requirements range from specific limits on exposures for workers to inspection, reporting, and recordkeeping requirements. Laws and regulations concerning the transportation and disposal of radioactive materials are also relevant to public health and safety. These topics are discussed separately, however, because of their importance.

4.1 ALLOWABLE DOSE REQUIREMENTS

NMED has set limits on the concentration of radioactive materials in restricted areas and the amounts that can be inhaled, ingested, or taken up through the skin by workers. The following are the maximum doses per quarter for a worker within a restricted area: whole body -- 1 1/4 rems; hand/forearms, feet/ankles -- 18 3/4 rems; skin of the whole body -- 7 1/2 rems.[97] These dose limits are not used in every situation, however, and the regulations must be consulted for definitive information. More stringent standards limit the exposure of minors and the concentrations of airborne material and doses.

In unrestricted areas, individual doses may not exceed two mrems per hour or 100 mrems in seven days.[98] These limits may be exceeded with NMED permission if the licensee can show that the higher limit is not likely to cause an individual dose to the whole body greater than 0.5 rems per year.[99] Further, the licensee must seek NMED permission

---

94 N.M. Radiation Protection Regulations § 6-120.B.

95 N.M. Radiation Protection Regulations §§ 4-430 to -440.

96 N.M. Radiation Protection Regulations § 4-445.

97 N.M. Radiation Protection Regulations § 4-110.A. "Rem" means a measure of the dose of radiation to body tissue in terms of its estimated biological effect relative to a dose received from an exposure to one roentgen of x-rays. *Id.* § 102.uu. A roentgen is a special unit of exposure. *Id.* § 102.xx.

98 A millirem (mrem) is 0.001 rem. N.M. Radiation Protection Regulations § 102.uu.

99 N.M. Radiation Protection Regulations § 4-150.

before using radioactive materials in a manner which would release radioactive materials to unrestricted areas in excess of regulatory limits.[100]

4.2 WORKER SAFETY REQUIREMENTS

Requirements designed specifically to protect workers and other users of radioactive material generally consist of monitoring and reporting requirements, labeling standards, and inspection requirements. Allowable dose requirements (discussed above) also protect both workers' areas and the general public, as do all safety standards covering radioactive materials.

4.2.1 Right-To-Know

Those who work in restricted areas must be informed of the storage, transfer, and use of radioactive material or radiation. They must be instructed about potential health problems and protective devices and regulations, know the proper response to warning signals, and understand radiation exposure reports.[101]

4.2.2 Protective Measures

The licensee must see that precautionary measures such as process and engineering control, surveillance, limited working time, and respiratory protective equipment are available to limit worker exposure.[102] The licensee must ensure that alarms and locks limit access to high radiation areas and that workers cannot enter areas when radiation levels are very high. A licensee is responsible for meeting additional requirements to protect workers in areas in which an individual could receive a dose in excess of 500 rems per hour.

4.2.3 Monitoring and Reporting

Licensees and registrants must supply personnel monitoring equipment to workers and require all workers who enter high radiation areas or restricted areas to use this equipment.[103] Before the licensee or registrant discontinues the use of personnel monitoring equipment, NMED must receive 30 days written notice. Personal dosimetry services must report exposures greater than 400 mrems per month to NMED within 10 days.[104] The licensee must notify individuals of radiation exposure data and the results of measurements. If the worker so requests, the licensee must advise the worker of his or her annual exposure.

---

100 N.M. Radiation Protection Regulations § 4-160.

101 N.M. Radiation Protection Regulations § 10-120.

102 N.M. Radiation Protection Regulations § 4-130.D, .H. Except in an emergency, NMED must be notified in writing at least 30 days before respiratory protective equipment is used.

103 N.M. Radiation Protection Regulations § 4-210.

104 N.M. Radiation Protection Regulations § 2-130.E.

4.2.4 Labeling and Posting

Licensees must also observe labeling and posting requirements.[105] Documents that must be posted include the worker protection and radiation protection sections of the New Mexico Radiation Protection Regulations, the applicable license or registration certificate, operating procedures, and any notices of violation, NMED orders, and responses. In addition, NMED's Form 045 "Notice to Employees" must be posted.

Radiation machines and x-ray machines must be properly labeled to indicate that radiation is produced when the machine is operated. Rooms and areas in which radioactive material is stored must be labeled with caution signs.[106] Similarly, containers of radioactive material must be properly labeled. Radiation areas must be indicated by the radiation caution symbol plus a sign stating "Caution -- Radiation Area." The only exceptions to the posting requirements are (1) rooms with a sealed source in which the level of radiation approximately 30 centimeters away from the source is less than five mrems per hour, (2) rooms where patients containing radioactive materials are, and (3) rooms under a licensee's control in which radioactive materials will be present for fewer than eight hours and will constantly be under a licensee's control. General licensees are also exempted from these posting requirements.

4.3 INSPECTION REQUIREMENTS

NMED may inspect materials, machines, activities, facilities, premises, and records at any time.[107] In addition, NMED may meet privately with workers and be accompanied by a worker's representative during inspections. A worker may request an inspection if he or she believe a violation of the RPA, regulations, or license condition exists. The licensee or registrant may accompany inspectors on this inspection. The licensee or registrant is also required to make records available upon reasonable notice.[108]

4.4 REPORTING AND RECORDKEEPING REQUIREMENTS

Licensees and registrants must maintain records of the receipt, transfer, and disposal of all sources of radioactivity.[109] In addition, they must keep and retain records of individual exposures, bioassays, survey and monitoring results, and disposal until NMED authorizes their disposition. In some cases, survey and monitoring results may be disposed of after

---

105 N.M. Radiation Protection Regulations § 4-220.

106 The radiation caution symbol that must be used is the traditional three-bladed purple or magenta symbol on a yellow background. *See* N.M. Radiation Protection Regulations § 4-220.

107 N.M. Radiation Protection Regulations § 1-112.

108 N.M. Radiation Protection Regulations §§ 1-112, 10-140, 10-160.

109 N.M. Radiation Protection Regulations § 1-111.

two years. If a licensee discontinues or curtails its activities, NMED may accept these records and relieve the licensee of its recordkeeping responsibilities.[110]

If radioactive materials are stolen or lost, the licensee must immediately report to NMED by telephone and in writing. Incidents involving radioactive waste must be reported within 24 hours. If the incident is serious, it must be reported immediately.[111]

5.0 TRANSPORTATION

Transporters of radioactive materials fall into two groups: general licensees and specific licensees. General licensees are those private carriers, common carriers, and contract carriers who are not subject to the rules and regulations of DOT or the United States Postal Service. These carriers have a general license to transport and store radioactive material in the regular course of their intrastate carriage, if they observe DOT's loading, storage, placarding, and incident-reporting rules and regulations.[112] In contrast, interstate transporters of nuclear waste on the highway into, from, within, or through New Mexico must obtain a specific license from NMED.[113]

Both general and specific licensees must follow applicable regulations in preparing radioactive materials for transportation. If the carrier is subject to DOT or United States Postal Service regulations, then these apply. Other licensees must comply with DOT regulations for packaging, monitoring, marking, and labeling.[114] In addition to these requirements, the licensee must ensure that safe opening and closing procedures exist and that the consignee is aware of special opening procedures, if any.[115]

Before the recipient may open a package, he or she must monitor the package for excess levels of radiation soon after its receipt. If removable contamination levels are greater than 0.01 microcurie per hundred square centimeters on the package surface, the recipient must notify NMED by telephone and in writing. NMED must also be notified, as well as the delivering carrier, if the external surface radiation is greater than 200 mrems per hour or 10 mrems per hour at a distance of three feet away.[116] The only packages that are exempt from monitoring are those that contain exempt quantities of radioactivity.[117]

In addition to holding a specific license for the transportation of nuclear waste, the carrier must notify the Governor in writing, in advance, of any shipment, revised schedules,

---

110 N.M. Radiation Protection Regulations § 4-400.

111 N.M. Radiation Protection Regulations § 4-420.

112 N.M. Radiation Protection Regulations § 3-700.A.

113 N.M. Radiation Protection Regulations § 3-700.C.

114 N.M. Radiation Protection Regulations § 3-700.A.

115 N.M. Radiation Protection Regulations § 3-700.A(3).

116 N.M. Radiation Protection Regulations § 4-260.

117 *Id.*

and canceled schedules.[118] Further, the carrier must travel on approved routes[119] and report incidents to NMED immediately by telephone and in writing within 24 hours.

6.0 DISPOSAL OF RADIOACTIVE MATERIALS

This section briefly reviews a licensee's obligation to see that radioactive materials are disposed of properly. It does not cover the disposal of transuranic waste, which is discussed in the Waste Isolation Pilot Plant (WIPP) Section of this Chapter.

6.1 LICENSEE DISPOSAL OBLIGATIONS

Radioactive materials (excluding certain exempt quantities) may only be disposed of in an authorized manner at a licensed disposal facility.[120] Release into a sanitary sewer system is only allowed for soluble materials that do not exceed specified concentrations.[121] Disposal by incineration is only allowed if NMED specifically approves the proposed procedures and the emissions meet regulatory standards.[122] Containers or handling devices for radioactive materials must be disposed of as if they were radioactive unless a radiation survey shows that the activity of the items is essentially background level, radiation symbols are removed or unrecognizable, and the items are stored in an area secured from the general public.[123]

Radioactive material may be disposed of by burial in the soil if specifically approved by NMED[124] and at a licensed disposal site,[125] if the waste is received from other persons. The disposer must see that the waste is properly packaged according to the conditions of the site operator's licensee and labeled as to whether it is Class A, B or C waste. The waste form must be structurally stable with a minimum number of void spaces.[126] The licensee must provide a manifest to the intended recipient, send a copy with the shipment and retain a copy.[127] Should the recipient not acknowledge receipt of the shipment in due time, the licensee must investigate.[128] The licensee must file a report with NMED within two weeks

---

118 N.M. Radiation Protection Regulations § 3-720.

119 N.M. Radiation Protection Regulations § 3-800.D, .E.

120 N.M. Radiation Protection Regulations § 4.300.

121 N.M. Radiation Protection Regulations § 4-320.

122 N.M. Radiation Protection Regulations §§ 4-340, 4-160, 4-310.

123 N.M. Radiation Protection Regulations § 4-350.

124 N.M. Radiation Protection Regulations § 4-330.

125 N.M. Radiation Protection Regulations § 13-100.

126 N.M. Radiation Protection Regulations § 4-380.B.

127 N.M. Radiation Protection Regulations § 4-391.

128 N.M. Radiation Protection Regulations § 4-391.

of completing the investigation. The site operator must acknowledge receipt of the waste within one week.[129]

6.2 LICENSING REQUIREMENTS FOR DISPOSAL FACILITIES

A potential operator of a disposal facility must obtain a license before beginning construction.[130] The application must include the applicant's technical qualifications, technical information about the site, design of the facility, the applicable codes and standards, and construction and operation plans. It must also describe the site closure plan, quality control program, and radiation safety program.[131] The application must describe the environmental monitoring program, including the results of a preoperational monitoring program conducted prior to filing the application,[132] and must contain assurances that the land will be transferred to a federal or state agency if it is not already owned by the government and that an agency is prepared to accept transfer of the license upon site closure.[133]

The application must include financial information that demonstrates the applicant's ability to conduct all the licensed activities throughout the facility's life, to carry out site closure and stabilization activities, and to pay for monitoring and required maintenance after closure.[134]

NMED will issue a license if it will not constitute an unreasonable risk to the health and safety of the public[135] and if other regulatory requirements are met. After issuance, disposal cannot begin until after NMED inspects the facility.[136] A license may not be transferred without the permission of NMED. The licensee must meet recordkeeping and reporting requirements, allow tests, and permit inspection.[137]

The licensee must obtain an amendment to the license in order to close the site. The closure application must include the details of the site closure plan, including post-closure observation and maintenance plans.[138] After closure and the completion of the post-closure monitoring period, the licensee may apply to amend the license for transfer to the federal or state agency that owns the land.

---

129 N.M. Radiation Protection Regulations § 4-391.G.

130 N.M. Radiation Protection Regulations § 13-300.B.

131 N.M. Radiation Protection Regulations § 13-600.

132 N.M. Radiation Protection Regulations § 13-2500.

133 N.M. Radiation Protection Regulations § 13-800.

134 N.M. Radiation Protection Regulations § 13-3000.

135 N.M. Radiation Protection Regulations § 13-1000.

136 N.M. Radiation Protection Regulations § 13-1100.F.

137 N.M. Radiation Protection Regulations §§ 13-3100 to -3300.

138 N.M. Radiation Protection Regulations §§ 13-1300 to -1400.

A licensee can apply to terminate the license after it has been transferred to the site owner and all the necessary institutional controls are in place.[139] Permanent markers must also be in place to warn against intrusion.[140]

7.0 REGULATION AND LICENSING OF NORM IN THE OIL AND GAS INDUSTRY

NMED is in the process of developing regulations to cover naturally occurring radioactive materials (NORM) found in connection with oil and natural gas exploration and production in New Mexico.[141] NORM may be found in sludges, scale deposits, deposits in soil and water or at facilities. Because NMED has proposed regulations but the rulemaking process has not been completed,[142] the following discussion is not definitive. NMED should be consulted before making any decisions concerning NORM.

The proposed regulations establish a level at which NORM will be exempt from regulation. NORM concentrations less than 5 picocuries per gram of radium, above background, for soil averaged over 100 square meters are exempt. Concentrations are higher for soil below the surface and for radionuclides other than radium.[143] For equipment, the threshold is a radiation exposure reading that does not exceed 50 microroentgens per hour, including background, or removable surface NORM contamination that does not exceed 1,000 DPM/100 cm^2. Produced water disposed of in an approved manner[144] and natural gas and crude oil used as fuels are also exempt.[145]

Where these levels are exceeded, NORM will be considered "Regulated NORM," and the regulations will apply to anyone who extracts, transfers, transports, stores, or disposes of Regulated NORM or who enhances NORM in a manner that alters its chemical properties or physical state or potential exposure pathways to humans.[146]

The draft regulations follow the same licensing scheme used elsewhere in the Radiation Protection Regulations. Thus, a general license would be issued to extract, receive, possess, own, use, process, and transport Regulated NORM in any quantity, store Regulated NORM for 90 days or less, dispose of Regulated NORM in plugged and abandoned wells and, in some circumstances, dispose of Regulated NORM in Class I or Class II underground

---

139 N.M. Radiation Protection Regulations § 13-1600.C.

140 N.M. Radiation Protection Regulations § 13-1600.C(3).

141 New Mexico Environmental Department Rationale, Regulation and Licensing of Naturally Occurring Radioactive Materials (NORM) in the Oil and Gas Industry, Part 14 (Aug. 17, 1993).

142 Memorandum from Ron Curry, NMED Deputy Secretary, to NMED NORM Committee, interested parties of August 19, 1993.

143 *Id.*

144 N.M. Radiation Protection Regulations § 14-104.C - .E (Draft Aug. 18, 1993).

145 N.M. Radiation Protection Regulations § 14-104.B (Draft Aug. 18, 1993).

146 N.M. Radiation Protection Regulations § 14-102.A-C (Draft Aug. 18, 1993).

injection wells. A general licensee's ability to transfer facilities and equipment containing Regulated NORM, however, would be subject to some restrictions.[147] A specific license would be required to manufacture and distribute any material or product containing Regulated NORM, decontaminate equipment or facilities, transfer Regulated NORM for long-term storage, treatment, and/or disposal, store Regulated NORM for more than 90 days, and dispose of Regulated NORM.

In addition to obtaining a general or specific license, the operator must prepare a Worker Protection Plan pursuant to NMED guidelines.[148] An important difference from the general radiation protection standards is that proposed regulations limit the total critical organ radiation dose received by an oil and gas industry worker in any one year to 10% of the limits specified for other workers.[149] This lower exposure limit recognizes the probability that those workers will not be monitored for radiation exposure as other radiation workers would be.[150] Operators must also post caution signs at facilities where NORM is present.[151]

Regulated NORM must be disposed of in accordance with both the Worker Protection Plan and a Regulated NORM Management Plan and Report. The draft regulations require current operators to submit a Regulated NORM Management Plan and Report to NMED within 12 months of the promulgation of the regulations. Operators must conduct baseline radiation surveys of equipment and facilities and report the results to NMED in their Regulated NORM Management Plan and Report. The initial survey must be conducted within 12 months after the regulations are promulgated and confirmed at five-year intervals, as well as whenever there is a major change in operation or an addition to a facility.[152] In contrast, operators need not submit the Worker Protection Plan to NMED although employees must be notified of, and have access to, this Plan.[153]

The draft regulations identify approved disposal methods, including disposal in non-retrieved flowlines and pipelines, disposal at commercial and centralized facilities, disposal in plugged and abandoned wells, disposal by injection, or disposal by transfer of the Regulated NORM to a licensed land disposal facility. The draft also permits NMED to consider alterna-

---

147 N.M. Radiation Protection Regulations § 14-110 (Draft Aug. 18, 1993).

148 N.M. Radiation Protection Regulations § 14-106.A. (Draft Aug. 18, 1993). These guidelines would be issued by NMED after the regulations are final. § 14-106.B.

149 N.M. Radiation Protection Regulations § 14-106.E. (Draft Aug. 18, 1993).

150 N.M. Environment Department Rationale Regulation and Licensing of Naturally Occurring Radioactive Materials (NORM) in the Oil and Gas Industry, Part 14 at 9 (Aug. 17, 1993).

151 N.M. Radiation Protection Regulations § 14-106.C. (Draft Aug. 18, 1993).

152 N.M. Radiation Protection Regulations § 14-109. (Draft Aug. 18, 1993).

153 N.M. Radiation Protection Regulations § 14.106.A.2. (Draft Aug. 18, 1993).

tive disposal methods, provided the applicant demonstrates that those methods will protect the environment, public health, and fresh waters and are otherwise consistent with applicable regulations.[154]

8.0 WASTE ISOLATION PILOT PLANT

The Waste Isolation Pilot Plant (WIPP) was authorized in 1979 for the express purpose of providing a research and development facility to demonstrate the safe disposal of radioactive wastes resulting from the defense activities and programs of the United States exempted from regulation by the Nuclear Regulatory Commission.[155] The WIPP site is located in southern New Mexico, about 26 miles southeast of Carlsbad. The repository itself will be situated 2,150 feet below ground level in the middle of a nearly 3,000-foot-thick bedded salt layer known as the Salado Formation. After meeting legal and regulatory requirements, WIPP will be the first site in the United States for the permanent disposal of transuranic (TRU)[156] wastes resulting from nuclear weapons research, development, and production. Most of these wastes are mixed wastes,[157] which are radioactive wastes contaminated with other hazardous waste.

No waste is currently in place at WIPP. Although construction is complete, the test phase[158] may not begin until the requirements of the Waste Isolation Pilot Plant Land Withdrawal Act (LWA) are satisfied.[159]

---

154 N.M. Radiation Protection Regulations § 14-108.E. (Draft Aug. 18, 1993).

155 Department of Energy National Security & Military Applications of Nuclear Energy Authorization Act of 1980, Pub. L. No. 96-164, § 213(a) (uncodified).

156 "Transuranic waste" is defined as waste which results from plutonium reprocessing and fabrication as well as research activities at DOE defense installations. It is material contaminated with alpha-emitting radionuclides that are heavier than uranium with half-lives greater than 20 years and in concentrations greater than 100 nanocuries per gram. Final Supplemental Environmental Statement, WIPP, DOE/EIS-0026-FS, January 1990, Vol. 1, p. Glo-18.

157 Mixed wastes are defined as any mixture of hazardous waste regulated under the Hazardous Waste Act and radioactive waste regulated under the federal Atomic Energy Act of 1954. N.M. Stat. Ann. § 74-4A-4(G) (Repl. Pamp. 1993).

158 U.S. DOE, Draft Plan for the Waste Isolation Pilot Plant Test Phase: Performance Assessment and Operations Demonstration, DOE/WIPP 89-011, April 1989, executive summary. Based on Key Decision No. 4 of the Energy Systems Acquisition Advisory Board, Under Secretary John C. Tuck, DOE, authorized closeout of the construction phase in a memorandum dated March 29, 1991. In general, the test phase will examine performance assessment and the physical operation of WIPP. The performance assessment will involve calculations and experiments to determine the ability of the repository to meet applicable federal and state regulations. Operation assessment will examine the interrelated steps involved in taking the waste from the waste generation or storage site to final disposal in the WIPP facility. *Id.*

159 Waste Isolation Pilot Plant Land Withdrawal Act of 1992 (LWA), Pub. L.No. 102-

Although the federal statute first authorizing WIPP did not require that the United States Department of Energy (DOE) develop and operate WIPP in compliance with federal environmental standards, this situation changed in October 1992 with the passage of the LWA. The LWA withdrew and reserved the federal land where WIPP is located and transferred jurisdiction from the Secretary of the Interior to the Secretary of Energy.[160] In general, the LWA requires that WIPP be operated in compliance with generally applicable standards for the management and storage of spent fuel, high-level waste, and transuranic waste and with federal environmental laws[161] including the Clean Air Act,[162] the Solid Waste Disposal Act,[163] the Safe Drinking Water Act,[164] the Toxic Substance Control Act,[165] and the Comprehensive Environmental Response, Compensation and Liability Act.[166] The LWA confirms that neither high-level waste nor spent fuel may be transported to or emplaced at WIPP.[167] The LWA provides that DOE cannot begin the test phase unless EPA issues final disposal regulations, determines that DOE has complied with the terms and conditions of the no-migration determination,[168] and approves both the test phase and retrieval plans. Recent changes in DOE policy, however, mean that the immediate effect of these requirements is uncertain because DOE does not currently plan to conduct tests using TRU waste at WIPP. Instead, DOE will conduct a revised testing program in laboratories rather than at the WIPP site and will not submit test phase and retrieval plans to EPA. DOE hopes to submit its revised test strategy to EPA in late 1993 and submit its draft compliance application to EPA by Spring, 1995.[169] Had this change not occurred, the DOE would have been subject to provisions in the LWA that limited the volume of waste that could be transported to WIPP during the test phase to 0.5% of WIPP's total

---

579, § 5(d), 106 Stat. 4777, 4782 (1992).

160 The LWA § 3(a), 106 Stat. at 4779.

161 *See* the LWA § 9(a), 106 Stat. at 4788.

162 40 U.S.C. § 7401 et seq.

163 42 U.S.C. § 6901 et seq.

164 42 U.S.C. 300f et seq.

165 15 U.S.C. § 260 et seq.

166 42 U.S.C. § 9601 et seq.

167 The LWA § 12, 106 Stat. at 4791.

168 DOE received a conditional no-migration variance determination from EPA pursuant to 40 C.F.R. § 268.6, which permits the disposal of the hazardous constituents of mixed waste during the test phase.

169 "DOE Announces Revised Test Strategy for Waste Isolation Pilot Plant," *DOE News*, R-93-215 (Oct. 21, 1993).

capacity[170] and required that the waste remain retrievable during the test phase and as long thereafter as necessary.[171] The LWA also requires the Secretary of Labor to certify that the emergency response training programs comply with 29 CFR Section 1910.120 and that safety concerns, including room stability, have been met before waste can be transported to WIPP.[172] Finally, the LWA addresses health, safety, and transportation issues and takes steps toward providing financial assistance to the state and local communities.[173]

Waste cannot be permanently disposed at WIPP until the EPA certifies that the facility will comply with applicable disposal regulations and approves DOE decommissioning and post-decommissioning plans. Other prerequisites are that DOE must notify Congress that it is in compliance with specified federal laws and a subsequent 180-day waiting period must expire; DOE must also acquire the two remaining federal oil and gas leases or obtain a determination from EPA that their acquisition is not necessary, conduct a survey identifying all transuranic waste types at all sites, and prepare a comprehensive recommendation and a timetable for the disposal of all transuranic waste under DOE control.

8.1 STATE JURISDICTION OVER WIPP

Before passage of the Land Withdrawal Act, the State of New Mexico had entered into agreements with DOE giving New Mexico a right to the timely provision and exchange of information from the DOE concerning WIPP and establishing a formal conflict resolution procedure. These agreements, which resulted from negotiations and litigation between DOE and the state, are set forth in the Agreement for Consultation and Cooperation Between the Department of Energy and the State of New Mexico on the Waste Isolation Plant (Agreement). In general, DOE must identify key events and milestones in the WIPP project and consult and cooperate with the state as the project continues. DOE must notify the state in writing before beginning a key event, coordinate its environmental monitoring plans and programs, and provide environmental data and documentation.[174]

If a significant level of radiation is released by any WIPP-related activity, or if WIPP-related radiation-induced health effects are detected in surrounding communities, along transportation routes, or among the WIPP work force, the state has the right under the

---

170 The LWA § 6(c)(1), 106 Stat. at 4783. Under this limit, a maximum of approximately 4200 drums of waste would be allowed during the test phase. WIPP Land Withdrawal Act: *Section by Section Analysis*, prepared by C.J. Wentz, N.M. Radioactive Waste Consultation Task Force. (undated).

171 The LWA § 10, 106 Stat. at 4789.

172 The LWA § 6, 106 Stat. at 4783-84.

173 The LWA §§ 5, 13, 106 Stat. at 4782, 4791.

174 Supplemental Stipulated Agreement Resolving Certain State Off-Site Concerns Over WIPP at 24-25, *State ex rel. Bingaman v. United States Dep't of Energy*, No. Civ. 81-363JB (D.N.M. filed Dec. 28, 1982) [hereinafter Supplemental Stipulated Agreement].

Agreement to conduct short-term and long-term health studies through an independent agency or a contractor. If financial help from other federal agencies is unavailable, DOE will fund such studies, subject to the condition that they are scientifically justified. Disputes as to whether these studies are justified will be resolved by a panel of scientific peers.[175] Section 21 of the LWA provides that it will not affect New Mexico's rights under these agreements except as explicitly stated in the LWA.[176] The LWA also gives New Mexico the right to be consulted on the management of the land that was withdrawn from the public domain for WIPP.[177] The state has a right to comment upon DOE's biennial performance assessment report, receive a written response, and receive free and timely access to data relating to health, safety, and environmental issues at WIPP and has a right, to the extent practicable, to attend expert and peer review meetings.[178] The state is specifically entitled to receive documentation of EPA's continued compliance with final disposal regulations[179] and to enforce its applicable laws.[180]

The LWA also authorizes annual appropriations of $20,000,000 adjusted for inflation for fifteen years beginning when transportation of wastes to WIPP begins.[181] DOE must also, to the extent funded, provide technical assistance and funds for training emergency responders[182] and help the state acquire necessary equipment and provide other transportation safety assistance.

New Mexico's right to invoke the conflict resolution procedure is specifically mentioned with respect to DOE's compliance with applicable radiation protection standards,[183] the assurances of retrievability of the waste,[184] and adequacy of emergency medical response training.[185] This conflict resolution procedure begins with a meeting between the state and DOE (specifically, the manager of the Albuquerque office) to discuss the matter in detail. DOE must then inform the state within in 10 days, in writing, of the action it intends to take.

---

175 Supplemental Stipulated Agreement, p. 28.

176 The LWA § 21, 106 Stat. at 4795.

177 The LWA § 4, 106 Stat. at 4780-81.

178 The LWA §17, 106 Stat. at 4794-95.

179 The LWA § 8(f), 106 Stat. at 4787-88.

180 The LWA §§ 9(d), 14, 106 Stat. at 4789, 4791.

181 The LWA § 15, 106 Stat. at 4791.

182 The LWA § 16(c), 106 Stat. at 4792-93.

183 The LWA § 8(e), 106 Stat. at 4787.

184 The LWA § 10(c), 106 Stat. at 4790.

185 The LWA § 16(g), 106 Stat. at 4794.

If this is not satisfactory, the Governor must notify the United States Secretary of Energy within 10 days that the conflict resolution procedure will be invoked.[186]

The state and DOE will then agree upon an independent expert who will serve as the conflict resolution hearing officer. The officer will consider written statements submitted by the state and DOE. The officer also has the discretion to hear oral arguments and accept written public comments. The hearing officer must then make written recommendations based on this record to the Secretary of Energy, the principal representative of the state, and the manager of the Albuquerque DOE office. The state and the manager of the Albuquerque DOE office may also submit comments and recommendations to the Secretary of Energy which will be incorporated into the record. Within 25 days of receiving the record, the Secretary of Energy must issue a written decision.[187] This decision is a final agency action[188] for purposes of judicial review. The existence of this conflict-resolution procedure does not, however, preclude the state from exercising its right to judicial review of DOE actions with respect to WIPP.[189]

8.1.1 State Jurisdiction Over Transuranic Radioactive Wastes

State statutory authority over the regulation of non-mixed radioactive wastes is limited. The Radiation Protection Act does not apply "to any material or equipment owned by the United States and being used, stored or transported by or for the United States or any department, agency or instrumentality thereof, except to the extent required or permitted by the authority in control of such materials or equipment."[190] Since the wastes to be disposed of at the WIPP site are owned by DOE, federal law and agreements between DOE and the state control.

8.1.2 State Jurisdiction Over Mixed Wastes

The state has authority over transuranic wastes that are contaminated with hazardous wastes because HWA applies to mixed wastes to be stored or disposed of at WIPP.[191]

---

186 Agreement for Consultation & Cooperation Between Dept. of Energy & the State of N.M. on the Waste Isolation Pilot Plant (updated April 18, 1988), Art. IX, ¶ A, p.6 [hereinafter Consultation & Cooperation Agreement].

187 Consultation & Cooperation Agreement, Art. IX, ¶¶ A-J, M, p. 11.

188 Consultation & Cooperation Agreement, Art. IX, ¶ I, p. 11.

189 Consultation & Cooperation Agreement, Art. IX, ¶ N, p. 12.

190 N.M. Stat. Ann. § 74-3-10(B) (Repl. Pamp. 1993).

191 In 1989 the New Mexico Legislature repealed N.M. Stat. Ann. § 74-4-3.2, which had provided that "nothing in the Hazardous Waste Act must be construed to apply to any radioactive waste processed and certified for emplacement in the mined geologic repository at the Waste Isolation Pilot Plant." 1989 N.M. Laws, ch. 4, § 1. The Hazardous Waste Regulations currently apply to WIPP as the state received authority from EPA to regulate mixed wastes, effective July 25, 1990. 55 Fed. Reg. 28397 (1990).

Under HWA, NMED has authority to regulate hazardous waste.[192] NMED received EPA authority to regulate radioactive mixed waste in New Mexico, effective July 25, 1990.[193] Although DOE has applied for a permit under the Hazardous Waste Act, on October 21, 1993, it requested NMED to delay activities regarding issuance of the permit while the effect of the decision that tests using TRU waste would not be conducted at WIPP.[194] but has not yet received it.

8.2 TRANSPORTATION TO WIPP

Transportation of waste to the WIPP site must be in compliance with Department of Transportation and Nuclear Regulatory Commission regulations.[195] Contact-handled waste will be shipped to WIPP in containers known as the TRUPACT-II that are certified as to design and quality assurance program by the Nuclear Regulatory Commission through a Certificate of Compliance.[196] The Certificate of Compliance was certified in August of 1989.[197] Remote-handled transuranic waste may be shipped in a container known as NUPAC 72B.[198]

Although shipment of waste to WIPP by railroad is possible, it is not currently planned.[199] The LWA directs DOE to study transportation alternatives, however, including environmental impacts, emergency response capabilities, and comparative costs.[200]

EIB has the exclusive authority to promulgate regulations prescribing conditions for the transportation of radioactive material on the highways of the state.[201] The State Highway Commission has exclusive authority within New Mexico to designate routes for the transportation of radioactive material on highways, except as specifically preempted by federal law.[202]

---

192 N.M. Stat. Ann. § 74-4-4(A) (Repl. Pamp. 1993).

193 55 Fed. Reg. 28397 (1990).

194 Letter from Arlen Hunt, DOE Albuquerque Operations Office, to Judith Espinosa, Director, NMED (Oct. 21, 1993).

195 Second Modification Agreement, p. 5; LWA § 16, 106 Stat. at 4792-94.

196 Second Modification Agreement, p. 5.; LWA § 16(a), 106 Stat. at 4792.

197 Project Manager's Progress Report for August 1989, p. 19.

198 The LWA prohibits the shipping to or emplacement of remote-handled waste during the test phase. It also requires DOE to analyze the impact of such waste on the performance assessment of WIPP and compare this waste with contact-handled waste on issues such as gas generation, flammability, explosiveness, solubility, and brine and geochemical interactions. LWA § 6(c).

199 Final Supplement Environmental Impact Statement, WIPP Vol. I, 3.1.1.3, p. 3-17.

200 LWA § 16(e), 106 Stat. at 4793.

201 N.M. Stat. Ann. § 74-4A-1(A) (Repl. Pamp. 1993).

202 *Id.*

Federal transportation regulations require that "any motor vehicle which contains a radioactive material for which placarding is required [be] operated on routes that minimize radiological risks"[203] unless there is only one "practicable" highway route available or the vehicle is operated on a "preferred highway."[204] The regulations define preferred highway as either an interstate highway or a state-designated route selected by a state routing agency.[205] In New Mexico, the State Highway Commission is the appropriate routing agency. Preferred transportation routes have been designated.[206] No waste may be shipped from Los Alamos National Laboratory until funds sufficient to construct a road bypassing Santa Fe have been made available and the bypass has been completed or EPA has certified that WIPP will comply with the final disposal regulations.[207] Before any transuranic waste is transported to or from WIPP, moreover, DOE must notify the states and Indian tribes through whose jurisdiction the waste will pass.[208]

Once waste destined for WIPP enters New Mexico, the state has the power to inspect and monitor radiation levels and the condition of the drivers, the trucks, and the TRUPACT-II containers at entry and exit points. The Commercial Vehicle Safety Alliance (CVSA) has, however, established a cooperative agreement with the DOE to develop both mechanical and radiological inspection criteria and corresponding procedures for application to spent fuel, high-level, and transuranic radioactive waste shipments. These criteria and procedures, were developed in consultation with the state and the Conference of Radiation Control Program Directors (CRCPD). The objective of this integration is to establish and test inspection procedures that can be implemented by states to promote the uniform and reciprocal inspection of vehicles carrying highway route controlled quantity (HRCQ) radioactive waste.[209]

The state also may send an inspector to the point of origin of the waste to monitor the condition of the waste, trucks, and containers.[210] The state has the right to timely notice prior to shipment of the waste into the state and the right to independently monitor the transportation of the waste to and from the site within New Mexico. The monitoring system (TRANSCOM) to be used has been provided to the state by DOE. In addition, the

---

203 49 C.F.R. § 177.825(a).

204 *Id.*

205 *Id.*

206 49 C.F.R. § 177.825.

207 The LWA § 16(e), 106 Stat. at 4793.

208 The LWA § 16, 106 Stat. at 4792-94.

209 DOE Office of Civilian Radioactive Waste Management and CVSA Cooperative Agreement titled "CVSA Pilot Study of Highway Vehicle Inspection Procedures for the Transportation of Radioactive Materials" DE-FC04-85AL20533 (1986, extended 1989).

210 Supplemental Stipulated Agreement, p. 20.

state has the right to review shipping records and documents concerning the type, source, curie content, and nature of the waste shipped and to conduct unannounced and announced inspections of vehicles, drivers, containers, and records. The state is not obliged to fund road improvements necessary for the transportation of radioactive waste.[211]

8.3 EMERGENCIES AND STATE LIABILITY

Emergency response under state law is fully discussed in the Emergency Planning and Community Right-to-Know Chapter of this Handbook. DOE has committed to pay for the cleanup and removal of radioactive wastes and the decontamination of any areas within the state exposed to radiation as a result of a transportation accident involving shipments of waste to or from WIPP.[212] Furthermore, if New Mexico requests assistance in dealing with any WIPP-related radiological accident or emergency within the state, DOE will provide all appropriate and reasonably available federal emergency response resources within its control at the earliest possible time. DOE will continue to provide this aid until all significant radiological risks have been eliminated and the damages mitigated to the maximum extent possible.[213]

DOE has addressed the issue of New Mexico's liability in the event of a radiation or WIPP-related accident by agreeing that Price-Anderson Act[214] indemnity coverage extends to New Mexico in the WIPP context. DOE has agreed that the Price-Anderson Act covers transportation through New Mexico to and from the WIPP site and that the state, its political subdivisions, and municipalities are indemnified under the Price-Anderson Act.[215] DOE has also agreed that New Mexico need not exhaust its own liability insurance before being indemnified.[216] Similarly, DOE has agreed not to deplete the Price-Anderson Act fund by investigating or settling claims and defending suits before paying claimants.[217]

A training program is in progress to ensure that emergency personnel within the state are prepared to respond to emergencies involving radioactive materials before WIPP receives any waste. The Radioactive Waste Section of the Hazardous and Radioactive Materials Bureau of NMED has developed a training seminar to address issues related to a hospital

---

211 Supplemental Stipulated Agreement, p. 30.

212 Supplemental Stipulated Agreement, p. 8.

213 Supplemental Stipulated Agreement, p. 8.

214 Price-Anderson Amendments Act of 1988, Pub. L. No. 100-408, 102 Stat. 1066 (1988) (codified as amended in scattered sections of 42 U.S.C.). The Act sets up a federal insurance fund which can be used in response to a WIPP-related incident, among other things. Should an incident occur at or en route to WIPP, the federal government would assume liability for all damage claims up to $7.3 million.

215 Supplemental Stipulated Agreement, pp. 5-7.

216 Supplemental Stipulated Agreement, p. 7.

217 Supplemental Stipulated Agreement, p. 8.

facility having to treat a radiologically contaminated patient. Other programs include a course designed for first responders, who must be able to respond to an incident while avoiding unnecessary exposure or damage to the public, emergency personnel, and the environment, and another course, mitigation, intended to reach those who must evaluate the impact of the accident and monitor cleanup. Its curriculum will include skills such as gathering samples, operating instruments, and evaluating the actions taken during the initial response. The program also includes a command and control personnel course which will cover establishment of a command post, compliance with existing emergency response plans, and responses if radioactive contamination occurs.[218]

DOE will provide funds to reimburse local emergency response personnel to attend these courses. Moreover, funding has been made available to enable the state to improve its expertise in health physics and further develop an emergency response plan. Funds for equipment, including anticontamination equipment, a four-wheel drive vehicle, and sampling and monitoring equipment have also been provided. DOE will also provide equipment, including emergency response kits and a personal computer for tracking waste shipments.[219]

Although DOE sponsors this training, it is monitored by the state Hazardous Materials Safety Board.[220] This board is primarily responsible for reviewing accidents that the emergency management team responded to and for developing the curriculum for hazardous materials emergency response training.

8.4 OVERSIGHT OF THE WIPP PROJECT

Several state and independent groups conduct technical and environmental monitoring of WIPP. One such group is the Environmental Evaluation Group (EEG), which was established in 1978 as an independent entity with the mission of reviewing, evaluating, and commenting on the environmental health and safety aspects of WIPP. Its mission is to review and evaluate WIPP's design, construction, and operations independently as these relate to the public health and safety and the environment.[221] The EEG is the only full-time oversight panel concerned with WIPP. It is funded wholly by DOE but is not subject to DOE or state control. EEG publishes its reports and makes them available to the public. There are also part-time review groups on the federal and state level. The National Academy of Sciences

---

218 NMED Radioactive Waste Section. Information sheet on Emergency Response Training.

219 *Id. See also* LWA § 16(c), 106 Stat. at 4792-93.

220 N.M. Stat. Ann. § 74-4B-8 (Repl. Pamp. 1993).

221 National Defense Authorization Act, Fiscal Year 1989, Pub. L. No. 100-456, § 1433(a) 102 Stat. 1918, 2073 (1988); *see also*, N.M. Stat. Ann. § 74-4A-4(C) (Repl. Pamp. 1993) (defining "environmental evaluation group" as the independent state review facility administratively attached to New Mexico Institute of Mining and Technology funded by the United States Department of Energy.).

has appointed a WIPP Review Panel. This independent panel meets several times each year and makes its reports available to the public.[222]

Federally funded review committees have included the Blue Ribbon Panel, which consisted of five experts charged with reviewing the project and identifying what must be done before WIPP can open. Each member of this panel wrote an independent report for submission to the Secretary of Energy. In addition, the Advisory Committee on Nuclear Facility Safety is charged with reviewing all DOE facilities, including WIPP, and reporting upon their status.[223] Finally, the Defense Nuclear Facilities Safety Board is an independent group within the executive branch charged to "review and evaluate the content and implementation of the standards relating to the design, construction, operation and decommissioning of defense nuclear facilities."[224] The board must submit a written report annually and may issue periodic reports.[225] Finally, the LWA encourages the appointment of an advisory group of health professionals and other experts to review emergency response training programs for incidents involving transuranic waste being transported to WIPP.[226] This group was appointed in June 1993.[227]

At the state level, the Radioactive and Hazardous Materials Committee provides legislative oversight of WIPP.[228] This is a joint committee, composed equally of members from the House and Senate. The Radioactive Waste Consultation Task Force was formed in 1979 to provide guidance and advice to the executive branch of state government.[229] It is charged to represent the state in negotiations with the federal government concerning disposal of radioactive waste.[230] The task force also coordinates information and keeps the Governor informed of developments pertaining to WIPP.[231]

---

222 Conversation with Mr. Robert Neill, Director, Environmental Evaluation Group, January 8, 1990.

223 *Id.*

224 42 U.S.C. § 2286a.

225 42 U.S.C. § 2286e.

226 The LWA § 16(g), 106 Stat. at 4994.

227 Executive Order #93-16, June 23, 1993.

228 N.M. Stat. Ann. § 74-4A-9 to 11 (Repl. Pamp. 1993).

229 N.M. Stat. Ann. §§ 74-4A-6 to -7 (Repl. Pamp. 1993).

230 N.M. Stat. Ann. § 74-4A-7(A) (Repl. Pamp. 1993).

231 N.M. Stat. Ann. § 74-4A-7(D) (Repl. Pamp. 1993).

CHAPTER IX
COMMUNITY RIGHT-TO-KNOW AND EMERGENCY PLANNING

1.0 HAZARDOUS CHEMICALS INFORMATION ACT

New Mexico's Hazardous Chemicals Information Act (HCIA)[1] was enacted in compliance with the mandate of the federal Emergency Planning and Community Right-To-Know Act of 1986 (EPCRA), also known as Title III of the Superfund Amendments and Reauthorization Act.[2] As its title implies, the EPCRA has two purposes. First, it establishes state-level systems of emergency planning and notification to deal with releases of extremely hazardous substances. Each state is required to create a State Emergency Response Commission (SERC).[3] In turn, each SERC is charged with creating local emergency planning committees (LEPCs)[4] which, under guidance from SERC, are responsible for preparing, reviewing annually, and if necessary implementing emergency plans in the event of a release of hazardous chemicals.[5]

The second purpose of the EPCRA is to provide a means whereby members of the public can learn of the presence of hazardous chemicals used in their communities and of any releases of those chemicals. Facilities[6] which use hazardous chemicals must report their inventories and provide notice of any releases to the Public Safety Department (PSDept.), the appropriate LEPCs, and the local fire department having jurisdiction. With limited trade secret and chemical location exceptions, these notices and reports are available to the general public.

New Mexico's SERC[7] is responsible for exercising supervisory authority to implement the EPCRA in the state[8] but does not determine the types or quantities of hazardous substances which may be subject to the EPCRA reporting requirements. This power is reserved in the EPCRA to the federal Environmental Protection Agency (EPA). Therefore, while the

---

1 N.M. Stat. Ann. §§ 74-4E-1 to -9 (Repl. Pamp. 1993).

2 42 U.S.C. §§ 11001 - 11050. The HCIA refers to the EPCRA as Title III. N.M. Stat. Ann. § 74-4E-3(H) (Repl. Pamp. 1993).

3 42 U.S.C. § 11001.

4 *Id.*; N.M. Stat. Ann. § 74-4E-3(F) (Repl. Pamp. 1993). New Mexico has 28 LEPCs. Of those, only 11 were actually active as of September 16, 1993. Telephone conversation with Max Johnson, SARA Title III Coordinator, PSDept. (September 16, 1993).

5 42 U.S.C. § 11001. SERC must review each LEPCs' emergency plan. 42 U.S.C. § 11003(e).

6 The term "facility" is defined at 40 C.F.R. § 370.2. For purposes of emergency release notification, the term includes motor vehicles, rolling stock, and aircraft.

7 N.M. Stat. Ann. § 74-4E-4 (Repl. Pamp. 1993).

8 N.M. Stat. Ann. § 74-4E-4(B) (Repl. Pamp. 1993).

HCIA implements the EPCRA in New Mexico, facility owners or operators must consult the EPCRA and its regulations to determine their responsibilities under the HCIA.

PSDept. is responsible for promulgating policies and procedures for receiving and processing requests by the public for the release of information submitted by industry under the HCIA.[9] PSDept. is the designated recipient for the notices and forms which facility owners or operators are required to file with SERC.[10] PSDept. also sets deadlines for filing reports and can adopt other regulations for the enforcement of the HCIA.[11]

1.1 NOTICES AND REPORTS

The HCIA requires facility owners or operators to file with PSDept., the appropriate LEPCs, and the local fire department, one or more notices or forms, depending on the types and quantities of hazardous chemicals[12] stored at or released from the facility, the facility's

---

9 N.M. Stat. Ann. § 74-4E-6 (Repl. Pamp. 1993).

10 N.M. Stat. Ann. § 74-4E-5(A) (Repl. Pamp. 1993).

11 N.M. Stat. Ann. § 74-4E-5 (Repl. Pamp. 1993).

12 N.M. Stat. Ann. § 74-4E-3(D) (Repl. Pamp. 1993) defines "hazardous chemical" as any hazardous chemical, extremely hazardous substance, toxic chemical, or hazardous material as defined by Title III [EPCRA]. "Hazardous chemical," "extremely hazardous substance," and "toxic chemical," are defined in the EPCRA and are applicable to particular sections of the EPCRA. "Hazardous material" in the HCIA's definition of "hazardous chemical" is not used in the EPCRA. The HCIA uses the term "hazardous material" in implementing the EPCRA's requirement that "hazardous chemical" inventory forms be filed yearly. "Hazardous material" may have the same meaning as the EPCRA's "hazardous chemical," given the context of the term's use in the HCIA, but this point is not clear. In defining "hazardous chemical," the EPCRA adopts, in modified form, the Occupational Safety and Health Administration's definition of "hazardous chemical" as any chemical which is a physical hazard or a health hazard. *See* 29 C.F.R. § 1200(c). However, the EPCRA differs from OSHA's definition by excluding from the definition of "hazardous chemical" (1) any food, food additive, color additive, drug, or cosmetic regulated by the Food and Drug Administration; (2) any substance present as a solid in any manufactured item to the extent exposure to the substance does not occur under normal conditions of use; (3) any substance to the extent it is used for personal, family, or household purposes, or is present in the same form and concentration as a product packaged for distribution and use by the general public; (4) any substance to the extent it is used in a research laboratory or a hospital or other medical facility under the direct supervision of a technically qualified individual; and (5) any substance to the extent it is used in routine agricultural operations or is a fertilizer held for sale by a retailer to the ultimate customer. 42 U.S.C. § 11021(e). The EPCRA defines "extremely hazardous substances" as those listed by EPA pursuant to 42 U.S.C. § 11002(a)(2). This list can be found at 40 C.F.R. Part 355, Apps. A & B. Finally, "toxic chemical" is defined in the EPCRA as a chemical listed in Committee Print No. 99-169 of the Senate Committee on Environment and Public Works, titled "Toxic Chemicals Subject to Section 313 of EPCRA, [as revised by EPA.]" *See* 42 U.S.C. § 11023(c).

size, and its standard industrial classification (SIC) code.[13] There are five types of notices or forms required under the HCIA.

1.1.1 Presence of Extremely Hazardous Substance

The first notice is given by owners and operators to PSDept. when an extremely hazardous substance[14] at or above a specified quantity[15] is present at a facility.[16]

The owners or operators of the facility are not required to identify to PSDept. the specific hazardous substance involved but only to report that the facility is subject to the HCIA because a regulated substance is present at or above threshold planning quantities.[17] However, since the purpose of this notice is to allow LEPCs, under the guidance of SERC, to develop emergency preparedness plans in the event of a release of an extremely hazardous substance, the owners or operators of a facility are required to designate a representative to participate in the preparation of local emergency plans with the appropriate LEPCs. LEPCs can request additional information from the owner or operator necessary to develop and implement its emergency plan.[18] Any relevant changes at the facility must be reported to the appropriate LEPCs to be incorporated into the emergency plan.[19]

1.1.2 Release of Hazardous or Extremely Hazardous Substance

A second type of notice must be given whenever a release[20] of certain kinds of chemical substances[21] has occurred at or above reportable quantities.[22] If a reportable

---

13 N.M. Stat. Ann. § 74-4E-5 (Repl. Pamp. 1993); 42 U.S.C. §§ 11002, 11004, 11021 - 11023.

14 N.M. Stat. Ann. § 74-4E-5(A)(1) (Repl. Pamp. 1993); 42 U.S.C. § 11002.

15 This quantity, defined as a "threshold planning quantity" by 42 U.S.C. § 11002(a)(3), is determined for each extremely hazardous substance by EPA. *See* 40 C.F.R. Part 355, Apps. A & B.

16 N.M. Stat. Ann. § 74-4E-5(A)(1) (Repl. Pamp. 1993), implementing the EPCRA § 302. 42 U.S.C. § 11002(c).

17 42 U.S.C. § 11002(c). If EPA adds new chemicals to its list of extremely hazardous substances, or if the threshold planning quantity is changed, the owners or operators of facilities have 60 days after the change to make the notification. *Id.*

18 42 U.S.C. § 11003(d).

19 *Id.*

20 The HCIA defines "release" as any spilling, leaking, pumping, pouring, emitting, emptying, discharging, injecting, escaping, leaching, dumping, or disposing into the environment of any hazardous chemical, extremely hazardous substance, or toxic chemical and includes the abandonment or discarding of barrels, containers, and other closed receptacles. N.M. Stat. Ann. § 74-4E-3(G) (Repl. Pamp. 1993). The EPCRA's definition is nearly identical. 42 U.S.C. § 11049(8).

21 "Chemical substance" is not defined in the HCIA nor used in the EPCRA.

22 N.M. Stat. Ann. § 74-4E-5(A)(2) (Repl. Pamp. 1993), implementing the EPCRA §

quantity of either an extremely hazardous substance[23] or a hazardous substance designated under Section 102 of the federal Comprehensive Environmental Response, Compensation, and Liability Act (CERCLA)[24] is released, telephonic or personal notice of the release must immediately be given to SERC of any state that might be affected by the release and to the community emergency coordinator of the local LEPCs.[25] If the release is a "transportation-related release," notice may be given to the "911" or "O" operator,[26] and if it can be done without delay, the notice of release must include eight categories of information.[27] A written follow-up of the emergency notice must also be made, setting forth, if necessary, and updating the eight categories of information in the oral notice and including additional information.[28] In the event of a release of a hazardous substance regulated under the CERCLA, the CERCLA notification reporting requirements must also be observed.[29]

1.1.3 Inventory Forms for Hazardous Chemicals

In addition to the required emergency planning and response notices, the HCIA also requires a third type of notice, which is designed to notify SERC, LEPCs, and fire departments of inventories and releases of hazardous chemicals in the state.[30] The impact of the HCIA's inventory requirement is widespread, affecting the owners or operators of any facility

---

304, 42 U.S.C. § 11004.

23 The reportable quantity of the EPCRA extremely hazardous substances is listed in 40 C.F.R. Part 355, Apps. A & B.

24 The reportable quantity of the CERCLA hazardous substances is listed in 40 C.F.R. 302.4, Table.

25 42 U.S.C. § 11004(b)(1). In New Mexico, notice is given to PSDept. N.M. Stat. Ann. 74-4E-5(Repl. Pamp. 1993).

26 40 C.F.R. § 355.40(b)(4)(ii). "Transportation-related release" means a release during transportation or storage incident to transportation if the stored substance is moving under active shipping papers and has not reached the ultimate consignee. *Id.* 42 U.S.C. § 11004 is the only section of the EPCRA applicable to the transportation of chemicals. 42 U.S.C. § 11047.

27 (1) The chemical name or identity of any substance involved in the release; (2) whether the substance is listed by EPA as an extremely hazardous substance; (3) an estimate of the quantity of the substance released; (4) the time and duration of the release; (5) into what the release occurred; (6) any anticipated health risks associated with the emergency and, where appropriate, advice regarding medical attention necessary for exposed individuals; (7) proper precautions to take as a result of the release, including evacuation; and (8) the name and telephone number of the persons to be contacted for further information. 42 U.S.C. § 11004(b)(2).

28 42 U.S.C. § 11004(c); 40 C.F.R. § 355.40(b)(2), (3).

29 42 U.S.C. § 11004(a); 40 C.F.R. Part 302.

30 N.M. Stat. Ann. § 74-4E-5(A)(3) (Repl. Pamp. 1993), implementing the EPCRA § 311, 42 U.S.C. § 11021.

who are required to prepare or have available Material Safety Data Sheets (MSDS)[31] for hazardous chemicals under New Mexico's Occupational Health and Safety Act[32] and the federal Occupational Safety and Health Act of 1970.[33] MSDS, the contents of which are specified in the state and federal occupational health acts and regulations,[34] must be submitted to PSDept.[35] if the regulated chemical is present above a threshold quantity.[36]

In lieu of MSDS, the owner or operator may submit a list of the hazardous chemicals to PSDept., the local LEPC, and the fire department having jurisdiction.[37] However, upon request from an LEPC, the owner or operator of a facility must submit MSDS for any hazardous chemical on the list. MSDS and chemical lists must be updated within three months following discovery by an owner or operator of a facility of significant new information concerning an aspect of a hazardous chemical for which an MSDS was previously submitted to an LEPC.[38]

Along with a one-time submission of MSDS for a hazardous chemical, the HCIA requires owners or operators of facilities who have submitted MSDS to file an Emergency and Hazardous Chemical Inventory form with PSDept., the appropriate LEPC, and the fire

---

31 N.M. Stat. Ann. § 50-9-3(L) (Repl. Pamp. 1993) defines "material safety data sheet" as written or printed material concerning a hazardous chemical which contains information on the identity listed on the label, the chemical and common names of the hazardous ingredients, the physical and health hazards, the primary route of entry, the exposure limits, any generally applicable control measures, any emergency or first aid procedures, the date of preparation, and the name, address, and telephone number of the chemical manufacturer, importer, employer, or other responsible party preparing or distributing the material safety data sheet. *See also* 29 C.F.R. § 1910.1200(g).

32 N.M. Stat. Ann. §§ 50-9-1 to -25 (Repl. Pamp. 1993).

33 42 U.S.C. § 11021. The federal Occupational Safety and Health Act is at 29 U.S.C. 651, et. seq. Under the broad scope of the federal Occupational Safety and Health Act's regulations, nearly every business which uses chemicals could be subject to these reporting requirements. For a discussion of the federal Occupational Safety and Health Act's hazard communication regulations, adopted in New Mexico, which incorporate MSDS requirements, *see* the Workplace Hazard Communication Standard Section of this Chapter.

34 N.M. Stat. Ann. § 50-9-3(L) (Repl. Pamp. 1993); 29 C.F.R. § 1910.1200(g).

35 N.M. Stat. Ann. § 74-4E-5 (Repl. Pamp. 1993).

36 42 U.S.C. § 11021(b). The threshold quantity is 10,000 lbs. for "hazardous chemicals" and the lower of 500 lbs. or the threshold planning quantity for all § 302 "extremely hazardous substances." 40 C.F.R. § 370.20.

37 42 U.S.C. § 11021(a). 42 U.S.C. § 11021(a)(2) specifies the contents of the list and should be consulted if this alternative is desired.

38 42 U.S.C. § 11021(d)(2).

department with jurisdiction over the facility on or before March 1 of each year.[39] This is the fourth type of notice required under the EPCRA. The HCIA does not describe the required contents of the annual inventory forms, but this information can be found in the EPCRA.[40]

In New Mexico, owners or operators must file a "Tier II" Emergency and Hazardous Chemicals Inventory form. The required Tier II information includes (1) the name of the hazardous chemical, (2) estimates of the amount of hazardous chemical present in the past calendar year, (3) a description of the manner of hazardous chemical storage, (4) the location of the hazardous chemical, and (5) whether the owner or operator elects to withhold the location of a specific hazardous chemical from disclosure to the public under 42 U.S.C. § 11044.[41]

1.1.4 Toxic Chemical Release Inventory Forms

The fifth form which an owner or operator of a facility may be required to submit under the HCIA is a Toxic Chemical Release Inventory form.[42] This requirement is only applicable to facilities that have 10 or more employees and that fall in SIC codes 20 through 39, as in effect on July 1, 1985.[43] These SIC codes cover most manufacturing facilities. Furthermore, the EPCRA sets threshold reporting amounts, which differ depending on whether a toxic chemical is used at a facility (10,000 lbs. of the toxic chemical per year) or if it is manufactured or processed there (25,000 lbs. per year for the period July 2, 1989, forward).[44]

If a facility is subject to the notices and reporting requirements of the HCIA and the toxic chemical threshold amount is exceeded, then the owner or operator must annually, on or before July 1,[45] submit a Form "R"[46] containing information on the toxic chemical to

---

39 N.M. Stat. Ann. § 74-4E-5(A)(3) (Repl. Pamp. 1993), implementing the EPCRA § 312, 42 U.S.C. § 11022. The HCIA uses the term "hazardous material" inventory form, rather than "hazardous chemical" inventory form.

40 42 U.S.C. § 11022.

41 42 U.S.C. § 11022(d) - (f). The form is published at 40 C.F.R. § 370.41.

42 N.M. Stat. Ann. § 74-4E-5(A)(4) (Repl. Pamp. 1993), implementing the EPCRA § 313, 42 U.S.C. § 1023.

43 *Id.*

44 42 U.S.C. § 11023. If a facility is subject to this provision of the HCIA, 40 C.F.R. Part 372 should be consulted.

45 N.M. Stat. Ann. § 74-4E-5(A)(4) (Repl. Pamp. 1993).

46 *See* 40 C.F.R. § 372.85.

EPA and to PSDept.[47] Owners and operators must also report on their source reduction and recycling activities.[48]

1.2 ACCESS TO INFORMATION OR FACILITIES

Citizens may obtain information submitted under the HCIA[49] unless it has been defined as confidential under the EPCRA. The EPCRA contains a provision authorizing any person required to submit information with regard to a hazardous chemical, an extremely hazardous substance, or a toxic chemical to apply to have the specific chemical identity of that substance withheld as a trade secret.[50] Otherwise, every emergency response plan, MSDS, chemical list under 42 U.S.C. § 11021(a)(2), inventory form, toxic chemical release form and follow-up emergency notice is available to the public during normal working hours at a location designated by PSDept., SERC, or the local LEPCs, as appropriate.[51] PSDept., SERC, and LEPCs must respond to requests for Tier II information within 45 days of receipt of the request.[52]

Health professionals can, subject to the requirement of entering into a confidentiality agreement, override trade secret protection[53] and obtain information regarding hazardous

---

47 42 U.S.C. § 11023(g)(1). The form contains (1) the name, location, and principal business activities at the facility; (2) certification, signed by a senior official with management responsibility for the persons completing the report, regarding the accuracy and completeness of the report; and (3) for each listed toxic chemical known to be present at the facility (a) whether the toxic chemical at the facility is manufactured, processed, or otherwise used and the general category or categories of use of the chemical, (b) an estimate of the maximum amounts (in ranges) of the toxic chemical present at the facility at any time during the preceding calendar year, (c) for each waste stream, the waste treatment or disposal methods employed and an estimate of the treatment efficiency typically achieved by such methods for that waste stream, and (d) the annual quantity of the toxic chemical entering each environmental medium.

48 42 U.S.C. § 13106.

49 N.M. Stat. Ann. § 74-4E-6 (Repl. Pamp. 1993).

50 42 U.S.C. § 11042. If trade secret protection is sought, this section of the EPCRA should be carefully analyzed for its requirements, exceptions, and penalties for frivolous requests for trade secret protection.

51 42 U.S.C. §§ 11021(c), 11044. Upon request of an owner or operator, however, SERC and local LEPCs must withhold from disclosure the location at a facility of any specific chemical disclosed in a Tier II report. 42 U.S.C. § 11044(a). *See also* 40 C.F.R. § 370.30.

52 42 U.S.C. § 11022(e)(3)(D).

53 42 U.S.C. §§ 11042(e), 11043. A request for information under this section can be enforced under a court order if needed. 42 U.S.C. § 11045(e).

chemicals based on a statement of need or in the case of a medical emergency. PSDept., under the HCIA, has adopted the EPCRA's public notice provisions.[54]

It should also be noted that local fire departments may request access to any facility which files an inventory form for the purpose of conducting an inspection.[55] Owners or operators must also provide location information on hazardous chemicals to local fire departments[56] and, in the case of facilities where extremely hazardous substances are present, to LEPCs.[57]

1.3 FEES AND PENALTIES

There is a fee of $25 for each inventory form filed, with a maximum fee of $250 per facility owner per year. Federal, state, and local agencies are exempt from these fee requirements. There is a $5,000 penalty per violation for any facility owner or operator who knowingly, willfully, and intentionally fails to file any notice, form, or report or to pay any fee required.[58] In addition, the EPCRA contains provisions for civil, administrative, and criminal penalties for failure to comply with the EPCRA.[59] The EPCRA can be enforced by EPA or through citizen suits, which may be commenced by an individual or by a state or local government, including SERC and LEPCs.[60] The HCIA has no similar citizen suit provision.

2.0 EMERGENCY MANAGEMENT ACT

New Mexico has assumed responsibility for the emergency management of accidents involving hazardous materials[61] under the Emergency Management Act

---

54 Under the authority of N.M. Stat. Ann. § 74-4E-6(B) (Repl. Pamp. 1993).

55 42 U.S.C. § 11022(f); 40 C.F.R. § 370.25(d).

56 *Id.*

57 40 C.F.R. § 355.30(d).

58 N.M. Stat. Ann. § 74-4E-9 (Repl. Pamp. 1993).

59 42 U.S.C. § 11045.

60 42 U.S.C. § 11046.

61 The EMA defines "hazardous materials" as hazardous substances, radioactive materials, or a combination of hazardous substances and radioactive materials. N.M. Stat. Ann. § 74-4B-3(I) (Repl. Pamp. 1993). In turn, the EMA defines "hazardous substances" as flammable solids, semi-solids, liquids or gases, poisons, corrosives, explosives, compressed gases, reactive or toxic chemicals, irritants, or biological agents. N.M. Stat. Ann. § 74-4B-3(J), (Repl. Pamp. 1993). The EMA also defines "radioactive materials" as any material or combination of materials that spontaneously emits ionizing radiation. Materials in which the estimated specific activity is not greater than 0.002 microcuries per gram of material are not considered to be radioactive materials unless determined to be so by the Hazardous and Radioactive Materials Bureau of the Water and Waste Management Division of the New Mexico Environment Department for purposes of emergency response pursuant to the EMA. N.M. Stat. Ann. § 74-4B-3(M) (Repl. Pamp. 1993).

(EMA).[62] The EMA created an Emergency Management Task Force which developed and distributed to emergency response personnel a comprehensive plan for assessing and managing hazardous materials spills, drawing on the resources of a number of state agencies.[63] The EMA also created a Hazardous Materials Safety Board (Board), composed of members of various state agencies. The Board is responsible for training appropriate state agency personnel and conducting post-accident review.[64] The EMA also created the position of Hazardous Materials Emergency Response Administrator within PSDept.[65] The administrator maintains inventories and data bases relevant to the Board activities, maintains rosters of emergency response personnel, and updates the comprehensive plan at the Task Force's direction.[66]

2.1 REPORTING REQUIREMENTS

In the event of an accident involving hazardous materials that may cause injury to persons or property, the driver of the vehicle carrying the materials, or any owner, shipper, or carrier of the hazardous materials who has knowledge of the accident, or the owner of the building, premises, or facility where the accident occurred, must immediately notify the New Mexico State Police Division of PSDept. by the quickest means of communication available.[67] If a law enforcement officer is the first to respond to an accident, the officer must immediately notify the State Police District Emergency Response Officer in the area, who in turn must notify the State Police Emergency Response Center. The Response Center is charged with evaluating and determining the scope of the accident, instructing the first responder on how to proceed at the accident scene, notifying the responsible state agency, and advising the state agency of the necessary response.[68]

---

62 N.M. Stat. Ann. §§ 74-4B-1 to -14 (Repl. Pamp. 1993). The federal government retains primary responsibility for weapons-related shipments and acts as an additional resource for emergency management when the state determines that its capacity has been exceeded. In addition, the U.S. Department of Energy has agreed to provide all appropriate and reasonably available federal emergency response resources in the event of an emergency related to the Waste Isolation Pilot Plant (WIPP). N.M. Hazardous Materials Emergency Response Plan, Part IIIC.

63 The Task Force expired Dec. 31, 1990, pursuant to N.M. Laws 1986, Ch. 62, § 8(B).

64 N.M. Stat. Ann. § 74-4B-8 (Repl. Pamp. 1993).

65 N.M. Stat. Ann. § 74-4B-6.1 (Repl. Pamp. 1993).

66 *Id.*

67 N.M. Stat. Ann. § 74-4B-5(F) (Repl. Pamp. 1993).

68 N.M. Stat. Ann. § 74-4B-5(C) (Repl. Pamp. 1993).

2.2 RESPONSIBILITY FOR CLEANUP; ORPHAN HAZARDOUS MATERIALS; IMMUNITY

The state's actions after a hazardous material spill do not relieve the hazardous material owner, shipper, or carrier of responsibility or liability.[69]

Hazardous materials whose owners cannot be identified are defined as "orphan hazardous materials."[70] The PSDept. may assess charges against persons responsible for orphan hazardous materials for costs incurred in cleanup of the orphan hazardous materials and for damage to state property. Amounts received in payment of assessments for cleanup of orphan hazardous materials are deposited into an "orphan material recovery fund"[71] in the State Treasury. Amounts received in payment of assessments for damage to state property are to be used to repair the damage. Persons assessed charges may appeal to a state District Court within 30 days of receipt of notice of the assessment.[72]

The EMA contains a good samaritan provision, which grants immunity from civil liability to anyone who provides assistance or advice in mitigating or attempting to mitigate the effects of a release of hazardous materials.[73] However, there is no immunity for gross negligence, recklessness, or wanton or intentional misconduct.[74] In addition, the person(s) whose acts or omissions caused the release of hazardous materials and persons who receive compensation for their services in rendering assistance or advice, other than out-of-pocket expenses, do not enjoy immunity under this provision.[75]

3.0 WORKPLACE HAZARD COMMUNICATION STANDARD

In 1983, the United States Occupational Safety and Health Administration (OSHA), acting under the authority granted in Section 6(b)(7) of the Occupational Safety and Health

---

[69] N.M. Stat. Ann. § 74-4B-10 (Repl. Pamp. 1993).

[70] N.M. Stat. Ann. § 74-4B-3(K) (Repl. Pamp. 1993).

[71] N.M. Stat. Ann. § 74-4B-13 (Repl. Pamp. 1993).

[72] N.M. Stat. Ann. § 74-4B-14 (Repl. Pamp. 1993).

[73] N.M. Stat. Ann. § 74-4B-10.1 (Repl. Pamp. 1993).

[74] *Id.*

[75] *Id.*

Act,[76] adopted the workplace Hazard Communication Standard.[77] The purpose of the Hazard Communication Standard is to ensure that the hazards of chemicals in the workplace are communicated to employees.[78] New Mexico's Occupational Health and Safety Act[79] (OHSA) was amended in 1987 to incorporate federal OSHA's Hazard Communication Standard. In adopting the Hazard Communication Standard, the New Mexico Legislature found that the proliferation of hazardous chemicals in the environment posed a growing threat to the public health, safety, and welfare and that it was in the public interest to establish a comprehensive program for the disclosure of information about hazardous substances in places of employment and to provide a procedure whereby employees could gain access to that information.[80]

By letter agreement, New Mexico has also assumed responsibility for enforcing federal OSHA's Hazard Communication Standard. The New Mexico Environmental Improvement Board (EIB), under the state's letter agreement with federal OSHA, and under authority granted in state OHSA,[81] adopted the federal OSHA's Hazard Communication Standard regulations in their entirety[82] with two exceptions.[83] The New Mexico Environment Department (NMED) has the responsibility for implementing and enforcing the federal and state hazard communication standards and regulations.[84]

---

76 29 U.S.C. § 655(b)(7).

77 29 C.F.R. § 1910.1200. First effective in 1985, the standard was amended in 1987 to expand its coverage from only the manufacturing sector to cover all employees exposed to hazardous chemicals. *See* 52 Fed. Reg. 31852 (1987).

78 29 C.F.R. 1910.1200(a)(1)-(2).

79 N.M. Stat. Ann. §§ 50-9-1 to -25 (Repl. Pamp. 1993).

80 N.M. Stat. Ann. § 50-9-2.1 (Repl. Pamp. 1993).

81 N.M. Stat. Ann. § 50-9-7 (Repl. Pamp. 1993).

82 N.M. Stat. Ann. § 50-9-13 (Repl. Pamp. 1993); N.M. Occupational Health and Safety Regulations § 200.A.

83 N.M. Occupational Health and Safety Regulations § 200.B.12. With these exceptions, all subsequent references to the regulations will be to the Code of Federal Regulations.

84 N.M. Stat. Ann. § 50-9-4 (Repl. Pamp. 1993).

3.1 HAZARD COMMUNICATION REQUIREMENTS

The Hazard Communication Standard applies to any employer[85] which uses hazardous chemicals[86] in its workplace. The methods for informing employees[87] about hazardous chemicals are labels, MSDS, written hazard communication programs, and employee training.

3.1.1 Labeling

Under federal OSHA regulations, manufacturers, importers and distributors of hazardous chemicals[88] are required to label their products as hazardous.[89] New Mexico employers

---

85 N.M. Stat. Ann. § 50-9-3(C) (Repl. Pamp. 1993) defines "employer" as any person who has one or more employees, but does not include the United States. OHSA's regulations further refine this definition to include only those persons engaged in a business where chemicals are either used, distributed, or produced for use or distribution, including a contractor or subcontractor. 29 C.F.R. § 1910.1200(c).

86 N.M. Stat. Ann. § 50-9-3(I) (Repl. Pamp. 1993) defines "hazardous chemical" as any chemical or combination of chemicals which has been labeled hazardous by the chemical manufacturer, importer, or distributor in accordance with regulations promulgated by the federal Occupational Safety and Health Act of 1970. These regulations define "hazardous chemical" as any chemical which is a physical hazard or a health hazard. 29 C.F.R. § 1910.1200(c). The regulations define "health hazard" as a chemical for which there is statistically significant evidence based on at least one study conducted in accordance with established scientific principles that acute or chronic health effects may occur in exposed employees, including carcinogens, toxic or highly toxic agents, reproductive toxins, irritants, corrosives, sensitizers, hepatotoxins, nephrotoxins, neurotoxins, agents which act on the hematopoietic system, and agents which damage the lungs, skin, eyes, or mucous membranes. *Id.* Appendix A to 29 C.F.R. § 1910.1200 provides further definitions and explanations of the scope of health hazards covered by this section, and Appendix B describes the criteria to be used to determine whether or not a chemical is to be considered hazardous for the purposes of this standard. "Physical hazard" means a chemical for which there is scientifically valid evidence that it is a combustible liquid, a compressed gas, explosive, flammable, an organic peroxide, an oxidizer, pyrophoric, unstable (reactive), or water-reactive. *Id. See also* 29 C.F.R. § 1910.1200(d).

87 N.M. Stat. Ann. § 50-9-3(B) (Repl. Pamp. 1993) defines "employee" as an individual who is employed by an employer, but does not include a domestic employee or a volunteer nonsalaried firefighter. The regulations refine the statutory definition. "Employee" in the regulations means a worker who may be exposed to hazardous chemicals under normal operating conditions or in foreseeable emergencies. Workers such as office workers or bank tellers who encounter hazardous chemicals only in non-routine, isolated instances are not covered. 29 C.F.R. § 1910.1200(c).

88 The process whereby a chemical is determined to be hazardous is set forth in 29 C.F.R. § 1910.1200(d). Only chemical manufacturers and importers are required to evaluate chemicals to determine whether they are hazardous. Employers are not required to make this evaluation unless they choose not to rely on the evaluation performed by the chemical manufacturer or importer. *Id.*

89 29 C.F.R. 1910.1200(f). This section also includes label content requirements.

may not remove labels indicating that a chemical is hazardous unless the container is immediately marked with the required information.[90]

3.1.2 Material Safety Data Sheets

Each employer is required to obtain MSDS from manufacturers, importers, or distributors and to maintain MSDS for each hazardous chemical used in the place of employment.[91] The information on MSDS must be readily available to all employees, including employees at mobile work sites.[92] If an employer does not receive MSDS from the manufacturer, importer, or distributor of a hazardous chemical, the employer must take affirmative action to immediately obtain the MSDS.[93]

3.1.3 Written Hazard Communication Programs

Each employer must develop and implement a written hazard communication program.[94] The program must set out how the labeling, MSDS, and employee training requirements will be satisfied. The program must also include the following information: (1) a list of the hazardous chemicals known to be present, referenced to the appropriate MSDS (the list may be compiled for the place of employment as a whole or for individual work areas); (2) the methods the employer will use to inform employees of the hazards of non-routine tasks, for example, the cleaning of reactor vessels and the hazards associated with chemicals contained in unlabeled pipes in their work areas; and (3) the methods the employer will use to inform any contract employers whose employees work in the employer's place of business of the hazardous chemicals their employees may be exposed to while performing their work

---

90 N.M. Stat. Ann. § 50-9-5.1(A) (Repl. Pamp. 1993). *See also* 29 C.F.R. § 1910.1200(f)(8).

91 N.M. Stat. Ann. § 50-9-5.1(B) (Repl. Pamp. 1993). MSDS content requirements are found at 29 C.F.R. § 1910.1200(g)(2).

92 N.M. Stat. Ann. § 50-9-3(L) (Repl. Pamp. 1993) defines "mobile work site" as any place of employment in standard industrial classification codes 13, oil and gas extraction, and 15 through 17, construction, where work is performed in a different location than the principal office in a fixed location used by the employer. *See also* 29 C.F.R. § 1910.1200(g)(9). For these workers, the MSDS may be kept in a central location at the primary workplace facility. The employer must assure that employees can immediately obtain the required information in an emergency. In adopting this section of federal OSHA regulations, EIB expanded federal OSHA regulations by specifying that the information in the MSDS be readily accessible by telephone, two-way communication, computer, or actual copies of the MSDS. *See* N.M. Occupational Health and Safety Regulations § 200.B.12(b). This is one of the two variations to the otherwise verbatim adoption of federal OSHA Hazard Communication Standard regulations by EIB.

93 N.M. Stat. Ann. § 50-9-5.1(B) (Repl. Pamp. 1993).

94 N.M. Stat. Ann. § 50-9-5.1(D) (Repl. Pamp. 1993).

and any suggestions for appropriate protective measures.[95] The program must be supplied upon request to employees, their designated representatives, and NMED.[96]

NMED has prepared a sample Hazard Communication Program, which is available to all new employers.[97] An employer may adopt this sample program or other existing hazard communication programs, as long as the program meets state OHSA requirements.[98]

3.1.4 Employee Information and Training

Employers must provide employees with information and training on hazardous chemicals they use or may become exposed to during the course of employment by providing them information about label contents, MSDS, and the actions needed to avoid or minimize exposure to the chemicals.[99] However, this training requirement does not apply to any hazardous chemicals received by an employer in a sealed package if it is subsequently sold or transferred with the seal intact.[100] The training requirements also do not apply if an employer can demonstrate that a new employee has received training regarding the same hazards within the past 12 months.[101]

3.2 PENALTIES

Willful or repeated violations of state OHSA or its regulations can result in the assessment of a civil penalty not to exceed $70,000 for each violation, provided that a civil penalty must not be less than $5,000 for each willful violation.[102] Serious[103] violations and

---

95 *Id. See also* 29 C.F.R. § 1910.1200(e) for additional specifics.

96 N.M. Stat. Ann. § 50-9-5.1(D) (Repl. Pamp. 1993).

97 For copies of the sample Hazard Communication Program, contact the N.M. Occupational Health and Safety Bureau, New Mexico Environment Department, P.O. Box 26110, Santa Fe, New Mexico 87502-6110.

98 N.M. Stat. Ann. § 50-9-5.1(D) (Repl. Pamp. 1993).

99 N.M. Stat. Ann. § 50-9-5.1(E) (Repl. Pamp. 1993). 29 C.F.R. § 1910.1200(h).

100 N.M. Stat. Ann. § 50-9-5.1(F) (Repl. Pamp. 1993).

101 N.M. Occupational Health and Safety Regulations § 200.B.12(c). This is the second exception to the otherwise verbatim adoption of federal OSHA hazard communication standard regulations by EIB.

102 N.M. Stat. Ann. § 50-9-24(A) (Repl. Pamp. 1993). If a willful violation results in the death of an employee, the employer can be punished by a fine of $10,000 or imprisonment for six months or both; for a second offense, the maximum fine increases to $20,000 and the period of imprisonment extends up to one year. N.M. Stat. Ann. § 50-9-24(J) (Repl. Pamp. 1993).

103 A "serious violation" is deemed to exist in a place of employment if there is a substantial probability that death or serious physical harm could result from a condition which exists or from one or more practices, means, methods, operations, or processes which have been adopted or are in use in the place of employment, unless the employer did not or could not with the exercise of reasonable diligence know of the

non-serious violations can both result in the assessment of a civil penalty not to exceed $7,000 for each violation.[104] Failure to correct a violation for which a citation has been issued can result in the assessment of a civil penalty not to exceed $7,000 for each day during which the violation continues.[105]

presence of the violation. N.M. Stat. Ann. § 50-9-24(F) (Repl. Pamp. 1993).

104 N.M. Stat. Ann. § 50-9-24(B), (C). (Repl. Pamp. 1993).

105 N.M. Stat. Ann. § 50-9-24(D) (Repl. Pamp. 1993).

CHAPTER X
ADDITIONAL ENVIRONMENTAL LAWS

1.0 AEROSOL PRODUCTS

While New Mexico presently does not have legislation in effect which requires or prohibits the sale of aerosol products, the state Legislature has enacted certain legislative findings and conclusions pertaining to the dangers posed by the use of aerosol products.[1]

1.1 DANGER FROM INHALATION

The Legislature has concluded that the deliberate inhalation of aerosol spray products presents an immediate danger to the public health, safety, and welfare of the citizens and future citizens of New Mexico.[2] This conclusion is based on the following findings: (1) the deliberate inhalation of certain aerosol products has become so widespread in New Mexico, particularly among children and young adults from low income backgrounds, that it is now a leading drug problem in some areas; (2) an increasing number of individuals have died from such deliberate inhalation; (3) other known effects from such deliberate inhalation are permanent brain, lung, liver, and kidney damage; and (4) the best available scientific information indicates the specific components of aerosol spray products which are dangerous.[3]

1.2 DANGER FROM RELEASE INTO THE ATMOSPHERE

The Legislature has also concluded that the release of aerosol spray products into the atmosphere is a significant hazard to the public health, safety, and welfare of the citizens and future citizens of New Mexico.[4] This conclusion is based on the following findings: (1) available scientific information indicates a substantial possibility that fluoroalkanes, a major component of certain aerosol spray products, when discharged into the atmosphere, dissipate or impair the earth's protective layer of ozone; (2) the dissipation or impairment of even a small portion of the ozone layer is likely to decrease the screening of ultraviolet radiation; (3) any significant increase in human exposure to ultraviolet radiation is likely to increase the risk of skin cancer and other serious illness; and (4) any significant increase in exposure of the environment to ultraviolet radiation may endanger the environment.[5]

---

1 N.M. Stat. Ann. § 30-29-2 (Repl. Pamp. 1989); N.M. Stat. Ann. § 74-5-1 (Repl. Pamp. 1993).

2 N.M. Stat. Ann. § 74-5-1(A) (Repl. Pamp. 1993).

3 *Id.*

4 N.M. Stat. Ann. § 74-5-1(B) (Repl. Pamp. 1993).

5 *Id.*

2.0 PESTICIDE CONTROL ACT

The New Mexico Department of Agriculture (AD) administers and enforces the Pesticide Control Act[6] (PCA) under the direction of the Board of Regents of New Mexico State University (Regents).[7] The PCA regulates the registration, labeling, use, storage, transportation, and disposal of both pesticides and herbicides,[8] as well as the licensing of pesticide dealers, consultants, applicators, and operators.[9] It also regulates and provides for the inspection of commercial pesticide application equipment.[10]

Since 1974, under a cooperative agreement with the U.S. Environmental Protection Agency (EPA), AD has had primary certification authority for the Federal Insecticide, Fungicide and Rodenticide Act (FIFRA),[11] and since 1979 it has had primary enforcement authority as well. The PCA is patterned after the FIFRA (as amended in 1978), and its requirements are at least as strict as the FIFRA. The PCA incorporates pesticide registration regulations similar to those in place under the FIFRA.[12] AD usually treats pesticide violations as a matter to be dealt with under the PCA, not the FIFRA. However, if a violation involves significant violation of federal law or health or property damage, EPA will be notified.

2.1 LABELING, DISPLAY, STORAGE, AND DISPOSAL

All pesticides and devices[13] distributed in the state are required to be properly

---

6 N.M. Stat. Ann. §§ 76-4-1 to -39 (Repl. Pamp. 1981 & Supp. 1992). Definitions for the PCA are found at N.M. Stat. Ann. § 76-4-3 (Repl. Pamp. 1981) and New Mexico Department of Agriculture (AD) Pesticide Control Act (PCA) Regulatory Order No. 5, November 2, 1979, pp. 2-4.

7 *See* N.M. Stat. Ann. §§ 76-4-1, -3(B), -3(C), -9 (Repl. Pamp. 1981).

8 PCA's definition of pesticides includes herbicides. *See* note 13, *infra*.

9 N.M. Stat. Ann. §§ 76-4-3(N), -4 to -6, -13 to -20.1, -30 (Repl. Pamp. 1981).

10 N.M. Stat. Ann. §§ 76-4-3(A), -26 (Repl. Pamp. 1981).

11 7 U.S.C. §§ 136 to 136y.

12 The Regents are authorized to issue regulations under the PCA by N.M. Stat. Ann. § 76-4-9(A) (Repl. Pamp. 1981).

13 N.M. Stat. Ann. § 76-4-3(N) (Repl. Pamp. 1981) defines "pesticide" as any substance or mixture of substances intended for: (1) preventing, destroying, repelling or mitigating any pest; (2) causing the leaves or foliage to drop from a plant, with or without causing abscission; (3) artificially accelerating the drying of plant tissue; or (4) accelerating or retarding the rate of growth or rate of maturation, or for otherwise altering the behavior of ornamental or crop plants or the produce thereof, through physiological action, but not including substances that are intended as plant nutrients, trace elements, nutritional chemicals, plant inoculants or soil amendments. N.M. Stat. Ann. § 76-4-3(D) (Repl. Pamp. 1981) defines "device" as any instrument or contrivance other than a firearm which is intended for trapping, destroying, repelling or mitigating any pest or any other form of life except man and except bacteria, viruses

labeled.[14] Each must bear the name and address of the producer, registrant, or person for whom produced, the name, brand or trademark under which the pesticide is distributed, an ingredient statement, directions for use and a warning or caution statement, net weight, EPA assigned producer, establishment and product registration numbers, and a statement of use classification, as required by federal regulation.[15] The label of any pesticide or herbicide which contains any substance in a quantity highly toxic to humans, if so determined by the Regents, must bear (1) the skull and crossbones or any other EPA required symbol, (2) the word "POISON" prominently printed in red on a contrasting background, and (3) a statement of antidote or practical treatment in case of poisoning.[16] Labels for spray adjuvants must state the type or function of the functioning agents.[17]

All of the foregoing information must appear on the pesticide label or labeling with such conspicuousness and in such terms as to render it likely to be read and understood by the ordinary individual under customary conditions of purchase and use.[18] Labels may be required by EPA or the Regents to be printed in both English and Spanish.[19]

Pesticides intended for distribution or sale must be stored within an enclosed building or fenced area and in a manner that will reasonably insure that foods, drugs, fertilizers, seeds, or clothing will not be contaminated. Pesticides may not be sold in damaged containers or in cartons with damaged or obscured labels.[20] No one may discard, transport, or distribute any pesticide or pesticide container in a manner that may cause injury to humans, vegetation, crops, livestock, wildlife, or beneficial insects or pollute any waterway.[21]

2.2 REGISTRATION

Each pesticide or device distributed in the state or transported in intrastate commerce or between points within the state through any point outside the state must be registered with

---

or other microorganisms in or on any living thing except plants. The term "device" does not include equipment used to apply pesticides which is sold separately from the pesticides, or predator or rodent traps, or sterilization using dry heat or steam.

14 N.M. Stat. Ann. § 76-4-4 (Repl. Pamp. 1981).

15 *Id. See* 7 U.S.C. § 136a(a)-(d).

16 N.M. Stat. Ann. § 76-4-4(H) (Repl. Pamp. 1981). To date the Regents have never made this determination, because EPA has already required such warnings to be put on these types of pesticides as restricted use pesticides.

17 N.M. Stat. Ann. § 76-4-4(J) (Repl. Pamp. 1981).

18 N.M. Stat. Ann. § 76-4-4(D) (Repl. Pamp. 1981).

19 N.M. Stat. Ann. § 76-4-4(K) (Repl. Pamp. 1981). Neither the Regents nor EPA has taken this step.

20 AD PCA Regulatory Order No. 5, p. 10.

21 N.M. Stat. Ann. § 76-4-5(B) (Repl. Pamp. 1981).

AD.[22] Registration is not required if the pesticide is shipped from one plant or warehouse to another plant or warehouse operated by the same person and if it is used solely at such plant or warehouse as a constituent part to make a pesticide which is registered under the PCA.[23]

An applicant for registration must file a statement with the Regents which includes the applicant's name and address and the name and address of the person whose name will appear on the pesticide's label if not the applicant, the name of the pesticide or device, a complete copy of the labeling accompanying the pesticide or device, a statement of all claims, including the directions and precautions for use, the use classification of the pesticide, as required by federal regulations, and any other necessary information required for completion of the application for registration form.[24]

While it has never done so, AD can require the submission of the complete formula of the pesticide and a full description of the tests and results on which the claims for the pesticide or device were made. AD has requested this information from numerous applicants wishing to register ultrasonic pest control devices. Since no submitted test data has proven the efficacy of the devices to AD's satisfaction, none of these devices has ever been registered in New Mexico.[25] It is a violation of law for any person to use for his or her own advantage or to reveal any information relative to formulas of any products acquired under the authority of the PCA, except in a medical emergency or by court order.[26]

Registrations expire on the December 31 following issuance[27] and can be renewed annually. Re-registration forms are mailed to registrants by AD at least 30 days prior to the due date.[28]

Registration can be denied if it appears to AD that the pesticide or device does not warrant the proposed claims or if the pesticide or device or its labeling does not comply with the PCA or its regulations.[29]

Field testing of unregistered pesticides requires experimental use permits issued by AD.[30]

---

22 N.M. Stat. Ann. § 76-4-6 (Repl. Pamp. 1981).

23 *Id.*

24 *Id.*

25 *Id.*

26 N.M. Stat. Ann. § 76-4-5(B)(4) (Repl. Pamp. 1981).

27 AD PCA Regulatory Order No. 5, p. 6.

28 N.M. Stat. Ann. § 76-4-6(F) to -6(H) (Repl. Pamp. 1981).

29 N.M. Stat. Ann. § 76-4-8 (Repl. Pamp. 1981).

30 N.M. Stat. Ann. § 76-4-7 (Repl. Pamp. 1981).

If AD determines that an already registered pesticide or device or its labeling does not comply with the PCA or its regulations, the registration will be canceled. If AD determines that during the time required for cancellation the continued use of a pesticide would result in unreasonable adverse effects on the environment, the registration can be suspended immediately on AD's own motion.[31]

2.3 LICENSING AND INSPECTIONS

AD licenses and certifies pesticide dealers,[32] pest management consultants,[33] public pest management consultants,[34] commercial pesticide applicators and operators,[35] public applicators,[36] and noncommercial applicators.[37] Private applicators are certified by the Cooperative Extension Service under authority of AD.[38] Licenses and certifications for commercial applicators, public applicators, private applicators, noncommercial applicators, and pest management consultants are classified by AD by category of pest control, and applicants for such licenses or certification must pass a separate written exam for each classification.[39] A licensee's classification limits the scope of operations which may be performed.[40]

AD requires that all licensees notify its Secretary in writing of any change of employment, ownership of the firm, the firm name or address, or any pertinent data on the application, including changes in licensed employees. A pesticide license is nontransferable.[41]

---

31 N.M. Stat. Ann. § 76-4-8 (Repl. Pamp. 1981).

32 N.M. Stat. Ann. § 76-4-13 (Repl. Pamp. 1981).

33 N.M. Stat. Ann. § 76-4-14 (Repl. Pamp. 1981).

34 N.M. Stat. Ann. § 76-4-15 (Repl. Pamp. 1981). As an AD policy, applicants for this license are issued public applicator licenses.

35 N.M. Stat. Ann. §§ 76-4-17 to -18 (Repl. Pamp. 1981).

36 N.M. Stat. Ann. § 76-4-19 (Repl. Pamp. 1981).

37 N.M. Stat. Ann. § 76-4-20.1 (Repl. Pamp. 1981).

38 N.M. Stat. Ann. § 76-4-20 (Repl. Pamp. 1981). License application and examination procedures are found at AD PCA Regulatory Order No. 5, p. 11.

39 N.M. Stat. Ann. §§ 76-4-16, -17, -19, -20, -20.1 (Repl. Pamp. 1981). In contrast, private applicator licenses are not issued for specific categories. Licensed private applicators can use any restricted use pesticide on their property for the production of an agricultural commodity.

40 N.M. Stat. Ann. § 76-4-32 (Repl. Pamp. 1981); AD PCA Regulatory Order No. 5, p. 4. The license categories are as follows: agricultural pest control; agricultural weed control; animal pest control; forest pest control; ornamental and turf pest control: insecticides and fungicides; ornamental and turf pest control; herbicides; seed treatment; aquatic pest control; right-of-way pest control; structural pest control; vertebrate animal control; fumigation; wood destroying pest control; public health pest control; regulatory pest control; demonstration and research pest control.

41 AD PCA Regulatory Order No. 5, p. 10.

2.3.1 Pesticide Dealers

Only licensed pesticide dealers may distribute highly toxic or restricted use pesticides.[42] A restricted use pesticide is a pesticide or device designated by EPA or the Regents as requiring specific restrictions to prevent unreasonable adverse effects on the environment.[43] In addition to creating a list of restricted use pesticides specifically for New Mexico, the Regents have incorporated EPA's classifications of restricted use pesticides into New Mexico's list of restricted use pesticides.[44]

Pesticide dealers must obtain a license for each location from which pesticides are distributed.[45] The license expires on the December 31 following issuance.[46]

Dealer licenses are not required for licensed pesticide applicators who sell pesticides only as an integral part of their application service and which are dispensed only through their own pesticide apparatus.[47] Further, federal, state, and city agencies or municipalities which provide pesticides only for their own programs are not required to obtain pesticide dealer licenses.[48]

Dealers must provide adequate facilities for the storage or distribution of restricted use pesticides and must keep a record of the sale of all restricted use pesticides.[49] Sales of restricted use pesticides can only be made to licensed applicators.[50]

2.3.2 Commercial Pesticide Applicators and Operators

Persons who are engaged in the business of applying restricted use or general use pesticides to land not owned or occupied by them must obtain a commercial pesticide application license, which expires on the October 31[51] following issuance. Commercial applicators who apply pesticides to control wood-destroying pests are subject to special regulations.[52] Before being licensed, applicants must furnish proof of at least two years of pesticide application experience in the license categories or related categories for which application is being made, or a year of experience and not less than 20 college credit hours in biological or

---

42 N.M. Stat. Ann. § 76-4-13(A) (Repl. Pamp. 1981).

43 N.M. Stat. Ann. § 76-4-3(R) (Repl. Pamp. 1981).

44 AD Rule No. 89-2.

45 N.M. Stat. Ann. § 76-4-13(A) (Repl. Pamp. 1981).

46 AD PCA Regulatory Order No. 5, p. 6 (11/2/79).

47 N.M. Stat. Ann. § 76-4-13(C) (Repl. Pamp. 1981).

48 *Id.*

49 AD PCA Regulatory Order No. 5, p. 10.

50 AD PCA Regulatory Order No. 5, p. 11.

51 AD PCA Regulatory Order No. 5, p. 6.

52 AD Rule NMDA, No. 89-1 (5/1/89).

agricultural sciences.[53] An applicant must also furnish proof of financial responsibility in the form of liability insurance or a surety bond.[54] Operators are defined as employees of commercial pesticide applicators who apply pesticides and include agricultural pilots and servicemen. Applicants must pass a written examination covering label comprehension, pesticide safety, and environmental protection before obtaining an operator's license.[55] A commercial pest control operator may perform any category of pest control for which his supervising commercial pesticide applicator is certified.

Commercial pesticide applicators' service vehicles must be identified with the commercial applicator's business name and license numbers.[56] Properly decontaminated and functional protective equipment must be provided to all employees who apply pesticides, if the pesticide label so requires.[57]

2.3.3 Public Applicators

Public applicators are employees of a federal, state, county, or city agency or a municipal corporation who use or supervise the use of any restricted use pesticides.[58] Public applicators are subject to examination before being licensed.[59] Their free, limited licenses are valid only when the applicator is acting in his capacity as a public employee.[60] Government researchers are exempt from the public applicator licensing requirements when applying general use pesticides to experimental plots.[61]

2.3.4 Pest Management Consultants

Pest management consultants are persons who offer or supply technical advice or make recommendations to the users of highly toxic or restricted use pesticides.[62] An

---

53 N.M. Stat. Ann. § 76-4-17 (Repl. Pamp. 1981).

54 N.M. Stat. Ann. § 76-4-24 (Repl. Pamp. 1981); AD PCA Regulatory Order No. 7, p. 1 (11/2/79).

55 N.M. Stat. Ann. § 76-4-18 (Repl. Pamp. 1981). However, the regulations allow operators to work under temporary permits for up to 30 days. AD PCA Regulatory Order No. 5, pp. 11-12.

56 AD PCA Regulatory Order No. 5, p. 10.

57 *Id.*, p. 9.

58 N.M. Stat. Ann. § 76-4-3(V) (Repl. Pamp. 1981).

59 N.M. Stat. Ann. § 76-4-19 (Repl. Pamp. 1981).

60 *Id.*

61 *Id.*

62 A public pest management consultant is any individual who is employed by a governmental agency or municipality to act as a pest management consultant. N.M. Stat. Ann. § 76-4-15 (Repl. Pamp. 1981).

applicant must pass a written examination in order to be issued a license.[63] Federal and state pesticide researchers are exempt from the pesticide management consultant licensing requirements.[64] Private pest management consultant licenses expire on the December 31 following issuance; public pest management consultant licenses expire on the June 30 following issuance.[65]

2.3.5 Private Applicators

Private applicators are persons who use or supervise the use of restricted use pesticides on land leased or owned by them, or on land of another person, for no compensation other than the trading of personal services between producers of agricultural commodities.[66] Private applicators must pass a written examination and be certified and in some cases must obtain user permits prior to the purchase and use of restricted use pesticides.[67] Certifications are valid until the December 31 of the fifth year following certification.[68] Unlike other applicators, private applicators are certified by the Cooperative Extension Service. Private applicator licensees holding licenses for use of M-44 sodium cyanide are subject to special regulation.[69]

A farmer or rancher who does not use restricted use pesticides is exempt from state pesticide licensing requirements as long as the person (1) operates farm or ranch property and operates or maintains pesticide application equipment primarily for his or her own use, (2) is not regularly engaged in the business of applying pesticides for hire, or (3) operates pesticide application equipment only in the vicinity of his or her own property and for the accommodation of his or her neighbors.[70]

2.3.6 Noncommercial Applicators

Persons who are not private applicators, commercial applicators, or public applicators,[71] or a person working under their direct supervision, and who wish to use a restricted

---

63 N.M. Stat. Ann. § 76-4-16 (Repl. Pamp. 1981).

64 N.M. Stat. Ann. § 76-4-15 (Repl. Pamp. 1981).

65 AD PCA Regulatory Order No. 5, p. 6.

66 N.M. Stat. Ann. § 76-4-3(U) (Repl. Pamp. 1981).

67 N.M. Stat. Ann. § 76-4-20 (Repl. Pamp. 1981); AD Rule No. 89-2.

68 AD PCA Regulatory Order No. 5, p. 6.

69 AD PCA Regulatory Order No. 5, p. 7.

70 N.M. Stat. Ann. § 76-4-28 (Repl. Pamp. 1981).

71 Public applicators are certified applicators who are employed by a federal, state, county, or city agency or municipal corporation and who use restricted use pesticides. N.M. Stat. Ann. § 76-4-3(V) (Repl. Pamp. 1981).

use pesticide must obtain a noncommercial applicator license,[72] which expires on the April 30 following issuance.[73]

2.3.7 Fees, Inspections, and Recordkeeping

Fees for licensing and inspections are set by regulation.[74]

AD conducts annual inspections of equipment used by commercial pest applicators and can require repairs or other changes.[75] Equipment which fails an inspection cannot be put in service until repaired.[76] All licensed apparatus is to be identified by a license plate or decal supplied by AD.[77]

Licenses, permits, and certifications may be suspended or revoked by AD if it has reason to believe that the holder has taken any action in violation of the PCA or its regulations.[78]

Each commercial applicator, noncommercial applicator, and public applicator is required to keep detailed pesticide application records for a period of two years following application, must open these records for inspection when required, and must furnish AD with a copy upon written request. Customers may also request a copy of the record of each application of pesticide upon their land.[79]

2.4 ENFORCEMENT, DAMAGES, ACCESS, AND PENALTIES

AD is charged with administration and enforcement of the PCA and the regulations issued by the Regents.[80] If AD has reasonable cause to believe that a pesticide or device is being distributed, used, stored, or transported in violation of the PCA or its regulations, it may issue a written "stop sale, use or removal" order to the owner or custodian of the pesticide or device.[81] Thereafter, the pesticide or device may not be distributed, used, or moved until the PCA has been complied with and AD has released the pesticide or device under

---

72 N.M. Stat. Ann. § 76-4-20.1 (Repl. Pamp. 1981).

73 AD PCA Regulatory Order No. 5, p. 6.

74 N.M. Stat. Ann. § 76-4-22 (Repl. Pamp. 1981); AD Rule No. 88-2 (5/1/88).

75 N.M. Stat. Ann. § 76-4-26 (Repl. Pamp. 1981). AD PCA Regulatory Order No. 5, pp. 7-8 sets out inspection standards.

76 *Id.*

77 N.M. Stat. Ann. § 76-4-27 (Repl. Pamp. 1981).

78 N.M. Stat. Ann. § 76-4-23 (Repl. Pamp. 1981). *See also* AD PCA Regulatory Order No. 5, p. 11.

79 N.M. Stat. Ann. § 76-4-33 (Repl. Pamp. 1981); AD PCA Regulatory Order No. 5, pp. 6-7.

80 N.M. Stat. Ann. §§ 76-4-2, -9 (Repl. Pamp. 1981).

81 N.M. Stat. Ann. § 76-4-11 (Repl. Pamp. 1981).

specified conditions, or until the violation has been disposed of by a court of competent jurisdiction.[82]

Either AD or a person served with a "stop sale, use or removal" order may file an action for adjudication of the alleged violation. The court may issue such orders as it deems advisable, including issuing temporary or permanent injunctions and ordering condemnation of the pesticide or device.[83]

A person suffering a loss or damage from the use or application of pesticide by another shall file a verified report of loss with AD within 60 days of the loss or damage becoming known to the claimant. AD may notify the licensee or the owner or lessee of the land of the claimed damage and must inspect damage wherever possible.[84] If AD determines that the complaint has sufficient merit, it shall make the information available to the person claiming damage and the person alleged to have caused the damage.[85]

Failure to file a report does not bar a court action against the person alleged to have caused the damage, nor is it a violation of the PCA.[86] However, if the person failing to file the report is the only one injured, AD may, when it is in the public interest, refuse to hold a hearing for the denial, suspension, or revocation of a license or permit.[87] A person claiming damage must permit AD, the licensee, and the licensee's representatives to observe the damage, or the claim against the licensee will be automatically barred.[88]

AD is authorized to enter any public or private premises, with the consent of the owner or by court order, for the purpose of carrying out the provisions of the PCA.[89] AD may inspect any apparatus subject to the PCA, inspect land and storage or disposal areas, investigate complaints of injury, sample pesticides, or sample lands or agricultural products for pesticide residues.[90] If AD finds that an apparatus fails to comply with the PCA and institutes proceedings against any person, it must notify the person of the contemplated proceedings beforehand.[91] If AD determines that the PCA or its regulations have been violated, it may refer a copy of its findings to the district attorney of the county where the

---

82 *Id.*

83 N.M. Stat. Ann. § 76-4-12 (Repl. Pamp. 1981).

84 N.M. Stat. Ann. § 76-4-25(B) (Repl. Pamp. 1981).

85 *Id.*

86 N.M. Stat. Ann. § 76-4-25(C) (Repl. Pamp. 1981).

87 N.M. Stat. Ann. § 76-4-25(D) (Repl. Pamp. 1981).

88 N.M. Stat. Ann. § 76-4-25(E) (Repl. Pamp. 1981).

89 N.M. Stat. Ann. § 76-4-31 (Repl. Pamp. 1981).

90 N.M. Stat. Ann. §§ 76-4-10, -31 (Repl. Pamp. 1981).

91 N.M. Stat. Ann. § 76-4-31 (Repl. Pamp. 1981).

violation occurred. In turn, the district attorney is under a duty to cause appropriate proceedings to be instituted and prosecuted without delay in a court of competent jurisdiction.[92]

Violation of the PCA or its regulations is a petty misdemeanor. In addition to any other penalties imposed, willful or repeated violations may subject the offender to a civil penalty not to exceed $1,000 for each violation.[93]

3.0 ENVIRONMENTAL COMPLIANCE ACT

The purpose of the Environmental Compliance Act (ECA)[94] is to implement a systematic procedure to review compliance with environmental regulations by providing for an environmental auditing procedure. Other purposes of the ECA include (1) fostering a sensitivity to the environment, (2) improving industry's compliance with environmental regulations while still pursuing the industrial and technological development of New Mexico, and (3) improving the environmental regulatory process by enhancing communication between industry and regulatory agencies.[95]

3.1 THE ENVIRONMENTAL AUDIT

The New Mexico Environmental Improvement Board (EIB) is responsible for developing and maintaining regulations and standards regarding environmental auditing programs[96] and for promulgating such other regulations as may be necessary to carry out the provisions of the ECA.[97] The environmental audit called for in the ECA is a systematic assessment, analysis, and evaluation by a regulated entity of its compliance with environmental laws and regulations administered by EIB and the New Mexico Environment Department (NMED) applicable to its operation.[98] The regulated community, members of which perform the environmental audit, is broadly defined as any person, partnership, corporation, firm, association, governmental or other entity organized and engaging in any business or activity in New Mexico which deals with or has an impact on the environment of New Mexico or which must by law comply with federal or state environmental protection regulations.[99]

---

92 *Id.*

93 N.M. Stat. Ann. § 76-4-34 (Repl. Pamp. 1981). N.M. Stat. Ann. § 76-4-35 (Repl. Pamp. 1981) sets out certain classes of persons who are exempt from the PCA's penalty provisions. Serious violations may also subject the offender to sanctions under the federal act, which would be administered by EPA.

94 N.M. Stat. Ann. §§ 74-7-1 to -8 (Repl. Pamp. 1993).

95 N.M. Stat. Ann. § 74-7-2 (Repl. Pamp. 1993).

96 N.M. Stat. Ann. § 74-7-4(A) (Repl. Pamp. 1993).

97 N.M. Stat. Ann. § 74-7-4(B) (Repl. Pamp. 1993).

98 N.M. Stat. Ann. § 74-7-3(D) (Repl. Pamp. 1993).

99 N.M. Stat. Ann. § 74-7-3(E) (Repl. Pamp. 1993).

3.2 ADOPTION OF REGULATIONS

No regulations are to be adopted pursuant to the ECA until after a public hearing by EIB.[100] Any amendment or repeal of a regulation constitutes a regulation.[101]

Notice of the hearing must be given at least 30 days prior to the hearing date. The notice must (1) state the subject, time, and place of the hearing and the manner in which interested persons may present their views, (2) state where interested persons may secure copies of any proposed regulation, and (3) be published in a newspaper of general circulation in the area affected. A reasonable effort must be made to give notice to all persons who have made a written request to EIB for advance notice of hearings.[102]

At the hearing, all interested persons are allowed reasonable opportunity to submit data, views, or arguments, orally or in writing, pertaining to the feasibility of conducting environmental audits.[103]

In adopting a regulation, EIB is to give all relevant facts and circumstances presented at the hearing the weight it deems appropriate.[104] Facts and circumstances considered relevant include (1) the protection of the health and welfare of both the general public and the individual worker and the maintenance of the ecological balance, (2) the necessity for and technical practicability and economic reasonableness of taking action with respect to environmental auditing programs, (3) the need to protect private proprietary processes, (4) the level of management support within the specific regulated entity for the environmental auditing program, (5) a regulated entity's established procedures to ensure compliance and correction of any environmental standards that are violated, and (6) compliance with the requirements of the following federal laws and their associated standards, regulations, and state implementing directives: (a) the National Environmental Policy Act of 1969 (NEPA), (b) the Federal Water Pollution Control Act, (c) the Safe Drinking Water Act (SDWA), (d) the Resource Conservation and Recovery Act of 1976 (RCRA), (e) the Used Oil Recycling Act of 1980, (f) the Clean Air Act (CAA), (g) the Toxic Substances Control Act (TSCA), (h) the Occupational Safety and Health Act of 1970, (i) the Noise Control Act of 1972, (j) the Hazardous Materials Transportation Act, and (k) the Comprehensive Environmental Response, Compensation and Liability Act of 1980 (CERCLA).[105]

No regulation or amendment or repeal thereof becomes effective until 30 days after its filing pursuant to the State Rules Act.[106]

---

100 N.M. Stat. Ann. § 74-7-5(A) (Repl. Pamp. 1993).

101 *Id.*

102 N.M. Stat. Ann. § 74-7-5(B) (Repl. Pamp. 1993).

103 N.M. Stat. Ann. § 74-7-5(C) (Repl. Pamp. 1993).

104 N.M. Stat. Ann. § 74-7-5(A) (Repl. Pamp. 1993).

105 N.M. Stat. Ann. § 74-7-5(A) (Repl. Pamp. 1993).

106 N.M. Stat. Ann. § 74-7-5(D) (Repl. Pamp. 1993).

Any person who is affected by a regulation adopted by EIB may appeal to the New Mexico Court of Appeals.[107] All appeals are upon the transcript made at the hearing and must be taken within 30 days after filing of the regulation.[108]

3.2.1 Development of Environmental Auditing Programs

NMED is responsible for establishing guidelines for regulated entities concerning environmental auditing programs pursuant to rules and regulations adopted by EIB.[109] Regulated entities may, in cooperation with NMED, develop environmental auditing programs in compliance with rules and regulations adopted by EIB and may then apply to NMED for certification of the programs developed.[110] These programs are entitled to certification upon NMED's determination of compliance with established rules and regulations.[111]

The regulated entities are allowed a reasonable time, as determined by NMED, to correct any potential problem areas identified in the environmental auditing process.[112] EIB and NMED are each required to develop incentives to encourage regulated entities to participate in the ECA.[113]

4.0 FINANCING OF ENVIRONMENTAL PROJECTS

The following New Mexico statutes authorize financing for environmental projects: (1) the Rural Infrastructure Act (RIA) provides financial assistance for the construction or modification of water supply facilities; (2) the Wastewater Facility Construction Loan Act (WFCLA) provides financial assistance in the construction of wastewater facilities; (3) the New Mexico Community Assistance Act (NMCAA) assists in providing water, sewage treatment, power, transportation, and communication facilities; (4) the Pollution Control Revenue Bond Act (PCRBA) authorizes municipalities to acquire, own, lease, or sell projects in order to reduce, abate, or prevent pollution; and (5) the County Pollution Control Revenue Bond Act (CPCRBA) authorizes counties to acquire, own, lease or sell projects in order to reduce, abate or prevent pollution. Each of these statutes is discussed below.

---

107 N.M. Stat. Ann. § 74-7-5(E) (Repl. Pamp. 1993).

108 *Id.*

109 N.M. Stat. Ann. § 74-7-6 (Repl. Pamp. 1993).

110 N.M. Stat. Ann. § 74-7-7 (Repl. Pamp. 1993).

111 *Id.*

112 N.M. Stat. Ann. § 74-7-8 (Repl. Pamp. 1993).

113 *Id.*

4.1 RURAL INFRASTRUCTURE ACT

The Rural Infrastructure Act (RIA)[114] was enacted in order to provide financial assistance to local authorities[115] for the construction or modification of water supply facilities[116] to correct demonstrably hazardous or inadequate conditions.[117]

4.1.1 Rural Infrastructure Revolving Loan Fund

The RIA establishes the Rural Infrastructure Revolving Loan Fund (RIRLF), the proceeds of which may be used to make loans and grants to local authorities for water supply facilities. Money appropriated to RIRLF or to the New Mexico Environment Department (NMED) to carry out the provisions of the RIA as well as receipts from the repayment of loans and earnings on the fund balance provide the funding for RIRLF.[118]

4.1.2 Administration of RIRLF

EIB is responsible for adopting regulations to govern the application procedure and requirements for disbursing grants and loans, including requirements for determining the eligibility and priority of local authorities for such grants and loans. NMED is responsible for administering RIRLF and for making grant and loan disbursements in accordance with the RIA.[119]

4.1.3 Terms and Conditions for Grants and Loans

Grants and loans may be made only to local authorities that (1) agree to operate and maintain the water supply facility so that the facility will function properly for not less than 20 years, (2) require the contractor to post a performance and payment bond, (3) provide assurance that there are proper title, easements, and rights-of-way for the facility, (4) meet the requirements of financial capability to assure sufficient revenues to operate and maintain the facility and to repay the loan, (5) pledge sufficient revenues for repayment of the loan, and (6) agree to maintain and audit the project's financial records.[120]

A loan term may not exceed 20 years, nor may the amount of the loan exceed $500,000. The interest rate on the unpaid balance is to be five percent unless the State

---

114 N.M. Stat. Ann. §§ 75-1-1 to -6 (Repl. Pamp. 1991).

115 "Local authority" means any incorporated city, town or village, county, mutual domestic association, public water cooperative association, or sanitation district whose water supply facility serves a population of less than ten thousand. N.M. Stat. Ann. § 75-1-2(D) (Repl. Pamp. 1991).

116 "Water supply facility" includes the source of supply of water, pumping equipment, storage facilities, transmission lines, treatment works, and distribution systems. N.M. Stat. Ann. § 75-1-2(F) (Repl. Pamp. 1991).

117 N.M. Stat. Ann. § 75-1-2.1 (Repl. Pamp. 1991).

118 N.M. Stat. Ann. § 75-1-3(A), (E) (Repl. Pamp. 1991).

119 N.M. Stat. Ann. § 75-1-3(D) (Repl. Pamp. 1991).

120 N.M. Stat. Ann. § 75-1-4(A) (Repl. Pamp. 1991).

Board of Finance specifies a lower rate.[121] Repayment of loans is to be in equal annual installments.[122]

The maximum assistance which a local authority may receive, including both loans and grants, is $500,000.[123] No loan recipient eligible to receive a grant may receive grants in any one year totaling more than $200,000.[124]

Plans and specifications for a water supply facility construction project must be approved by NMED before grant or loan funds may be disbursed to pay for construction costs.[125] However, interim loan disbursements to pay for engineering and other professional services may be made prior to approval of the plans and specifications.[126]

Grants and loans may be made only for eligible items, which include the cost of engineering feasibility reports, contracted engineering design, inspection of construction, special engineering services, archaeological surveys, and contracted construction.[127] The costs of water rights, land, system acquisition, easements and rights-of-way, legal costs, and fiscal agents' fees are alone eligible for loan funds.[128] Local authority administrative costs are not eligible items.[129]

In the event the local authority fails to make the required loan repayment, NMED is authorized to set water user rates in the area of the local authority's jurisdiction in order to provide sufficient money for repayment of the loan as well as proper operation and maintenance of the facility.[130]

4.1.4 Emergency Loans and Grants

Ten percent of the proceeds of each severance tax bond issue or other appropriation for the purpose of carrying out the provisions of the RIA are to be reserved for emergencies and may be allocated by NMED only upon approval of the State Board of Finance. Emergency loans and grants are to be made in accordance with the applicable provisions for loans pursuant to the RIA, provided that a grant may not exceed $200,000. While the ten percent set aside is not to be deposited in RIRLF and is to be allocated only for emergency loans and grants, at the end of the third quarter of each fiscal year the unexpended balance of the

---

121 N.M. Stat. Ann. § 75-1-4(B) (Repl. Pamp. 1991).

122 *Id.*

123 N.M. Stat. Ann. § 75-1-4(D) (Repl. Pamp. 1991).

124 N.M. Stat. Ann. § 75-1-4(C) (Repl. Pamp. 1991).

125 N.M. Stat. Ann. § 75-1-4(E) (Repl. Pamp. 1991).

126 *Id.*

127 N.M. Stat. Ann. § 75-1-4(G) (Repl. Pamp. 1991).

128 *Id.*

129 *Id.*

130 N.M. Stat. Ann. § 75-1-4(H) (Repl. Pamp. 1991).

reserved amount may be transferred by NMED to RIRLF for use thereafter in accordance with the RIA.[131]

4.1.5 Cost Reduction Grants and Zero Percent Loans

No more than 25 percent of the proceeds of each severance tax bond issue or other appropriation for the purpose of carrying out the provisions of the RIA may be reserved for average residential user cost reduction grants or zero percent loans to reduce average residential user cost to a reasonable level for eligible financially needy loan recipients whose water supply facilities serve less than 3,000 persons.[132]

Average residential user cost reduction grants and zero percent loans are allocated by NMED in accordance with the provisions for grants and loans pursuant to the RIA, provided that an average residential user cost reduction grant or loan may not exceed $200,000.[133] Such grants and loans may reduce only the principal and interest portion of the average residential user cost to a reasonable cost as determined by NMED.[134]

A zero percent loan or average residential user cost reduction grant must be approved when, subsequent to the receipt of construction bids, the following conditions have been met: (1) the project is designed using the most cost effective and dependable option, (2) the system is designed with adequate built-in expansion capacity, (3) other sources of grant funds have been sought and are not available in a timely manner, (4) the project cannot feasibly be reduced in scope or phased, and (5) the local authority's average residential user cost is at least $18 per month.[135]

4.2 WASTEWATER FACILITY CONSTRUCTION LOAN ACT

The purpose of the Wastewater Facility Construction Loan Act (WFCLA)[136] is to provide local authorities[137] with low cost financial assistance in the construction of necessary

---

131 N.M. Stat. Ann. § 75-1-5 (Repl. Pamp. 1991).

132 N.M. Stat. Ann. § 75-1-6(A) (Repl. Pamp. 1991).

133 N.M. Stat. Ann. § 75-1-6(B) (Repl. Pamp. 1991).

134 *Id.*

135 N.M. Stat. Ann. § 75-1-6(C) (Repl. Pamp. 1991).

136 N.M. Stat. Ann. §§ 74-6A-1 to -15 (Repl. Pamp. 1993).

137 "Local authority" means any municipality, county, incorporated county, sanitation district, water and sanitation district or any similar district, recognized Indian tribe or other issuing agency created pursuant to a joint powers agreement acting on behalf of any entity listed in this subsection. N.M. Stat. Ann. § 74-6A-3(E) (Repl. Pamp. 1993).

wastewater facilities[138] in order to improve and protect water quality and public health.[139]

4.2.1 Water Quality Control Commission and NMED

The Water Quality Control Commission (WQCC) is authorized to establish procedures and adopt regulations to administer the Wastewater Facility Construction Loan Fund (WFCLF) in accordance with the CWA and state law.[140] NMED administers the WFCLF on behalf of WQCC.[141] However, WQCC is required to adopt a system for the ranking of wastewater facility construction projects for financial assistance.[142]

NMED is responsible for establishing a program to provide financial assistance to local authorities, individually or jointly, for acquisition, construction, or modification of wastewater facilities.[143] NMED is authorized to enter into contracts and other agreements to carry out the provisions of the WFCLA.[144]

4.2.2 Funding of The WFCLF

The following are deposited directly into the WFCLF: (1) grants from the federal government or its agencies allotted to the state for the capitalization of the fund, (2) funds appropriated by the legislature to implement the WFCLA or to provide state matching funds that are required by the terms of any federal grant under the CWA, (3) loan principal, interest, and penalty payments if required by the terms of any federal grant under the CWA, (4) money transferred from the wastewater suspense account as needed to fulfill requirements of the CWA, and (5) any other public or private money dedicated to the fund.[145]

---

138 "Wastewater facility" means a publicly owned system for treating or disposing of sewage or wastes either by surface or underground methods, including any equipment, plant, treatment works, structure, machinery, apparatus, or land, in any combination, that is acquired, used, constructed, or operated for the storage, collection, reduction, recycling, reclamation, disposal, separation, or treatment of water or wastes, or for the final disposal of residues resulting from the treatment of water or wastes, such as pumping and ventilating stations, facilities, plants and works, outfall sewers, interceptor sewers and collector sewers, and other real or personal property and appurtenances incident to their use or operation. Wastewater facility also includes a non-point source water pollution control project as eligible under the federal Clean Water Act of 1977. N.M. Stat. Ann. § 74-6A-3(G) (Repl. Pamp. 1993).

139 N.M. Stat. Ann. § 74-6A-2 (Repl. Pamp. 1993).

140 N.M. Stat. Ann. § 74-6A-4A (Repl. Pamp. 1993).

141 *Id.*

142 N.M. Stat. Ann. 74-6A-7(B) (Repl. Pamp. 1993).

143 N.M. Stat. Ann. § 74-6A-7(A) (Repl. Pamp. 1993).

144 *Id.*

145 N.M. Stat. Ann. § 74-6A-4(B) (Repl. Pamp. 1993).

There is also a provision for the issuance of bonds or the refunding of bonds by the State Board of Finance on recommendation of WQCC in order to implement the provisions of the WFCLA.[146]

4.2.3 Permitted Uses of Funds

The money in the fund is available to (1) provide loans, (2) purchase, refund or refinance obligations incurred after March 7, 1985, (3) guarantee, or purchase insurance for, obligations to improve credit market access or reduce interest rates, (4) provide a source of revenue or security for the payment of principal and interest on bonds, (5) provide loan guarantees for similar revolving funds established by local authorities, (6) fund the administrative expenses of the state board of finance, WQCC, and NMED, and (7) fund other programs for which the federal government authorizes use of wastewater grants or provide for any other expenditure consistent with the CWA grant program and state law.[147]

NMED is responsible for establishing fiscal contracts and accounting procedures and for providing an annual report and independent audit to the Governor and the EPA.[148]

4.2.4 Eligibility for Financial Assistance

Financial assistance is provided only to local authorities that (1) meet the NMED requirements for financial capability to assure sufficient revenue to operate and maintain the wastewater facility for its useful life and to repay the financial assistance, (2) agree to properly operate and maintain the wastewater facility, (3) agree to maintain separate project accounts in accordance with government accounting standards and to audit the records, (4) provide written assurance, signed by an attorney, that proper title, easements, and rights-of-way have been or will be acquired, (5) require the contractor to post a performance and payment bond, (6) provide written notice of completion and start of operation, (7) appear on the priority list of the WFCLA and (8) provide such information to NMED as required by WQCC in order to comply with the CWA and state law.[149]

4.2.5 Conditions and Terms of Loans

Loans are made only to local authorities that establish one or more dedicated sources of revenue to repay WQCC and provide for operation, maintenance, and equipment replacement expenses.[150]

---

146 N.M. Stat. Ann. § 74-6A-10(A) (Repl. Pamp. 1993).

147 N.M. Stat. Ann. § 74-6A-4(C) (Repl. Pamp. 1993).

148 N.M. Stat. Ann. § 74-6A-4(G) (Repl. Pamp. 1993).

149 N.M. Stat. Ann. § 74-6A-8(A) (Repl. Pamp. 1993).

150 N.M. Stat. Ann. § 74-6A-8(B) (Repl. Pamp. 1993).

Repayment of the loan must begin not later than one year after completion of construction of the wastewater facility project for which the loan was made.[151] It must be repaid in full no later than 20 years after completion of construction.[152]

The applicable interest rate is ordinarily an annual rate of five percent or less as determined by WQCC.[153] A zero percent interest rate may be approved by NMED when the following conditions exist within the jurisdiction of the local authority: (1) average user cost is at least $15 per month or a higher amount is determined by WQCC and (2) median household income is less than three-fourths of the statewide non-metropolitan median household income.[154]

Financial assistance received may not be used on any wastewater facility project in full or partial fulfillment of requirements which a subdivider must satisfy under the Land Subdivision Act or the New Mexico Subdivision Act.[155] However, the proceeds may be used to provide a local match or any other nonfederal share of a wastewater facility construction project as allowed by the CWA.[156]

In order to obtain funding, the local authority must employ or contract with a registered professional engineer to provide and be responsible for engineering services on the project including an engineering report, construction contract documents, supervision of construction, and start-up services.[157]

Financial assistance is available only for eligible items. If only state funds are involved, eligible items include engineering feasibility reports, contracted engineering design, inspection of construction, special engineering services, start-up services, contracted construction, materials purchased or equipment leased for force account construction, and land or acquisition of existing facilities.[158] However, the costs of water rights and local authority administrative costs are not eligible items.[159] For financial assistance made from federal funds, eligible items are those identified in the CWA.[160]

---

151 N.M. Stat. Ann. § 74-6A-8(C) (Repl. Pamp. 1993).

152 *Id.*

153 N.M. Stat. Ann. § 74-6A-8(D) (Repl. Pamp. 1993).

154 N.M. Stat. Ann. § 74-6A-8(E) (Repl. Pamp. 1993).

155 N.M. Stat. Ann. § 74-6A-8(G) (Repl. Pamp. 1993).

156 N.M. Stat. Ann. § 74-6A-8(F) (Repl. Pamp. 1993).

157 N.M. Stat. Ann. § 74-6A-8(H) (Repl. Pamp. 1993).

158 N.M. Stat. Ann. § 74-6A-8(I) (Repl. Pamp. 1993).

159 *Id.*

160 *Id.*

4.3 NEW MEXICO COMMUNITY ASSISTANCE ACT

The New Mexico Community Assistance Act (NMCAA)[161] was enacted to aid local communities in providing adequate, safe, and sanitary water, sewage treatment, power, transportation, and communication services.[162]

Funding sources for the program include (1) severance tax bonds, (2) community development block grants from the federal government, and (3) such other sources of funding as specified by the Legislature.[163]

4.3.1 New Mexico Community Development Council

The NMCAA creates the New Mexico Community Development Council (NMCDC) which consists of (1) the Secretary of Finance and Administration or a staff member designated by the Secretary, (2) the Governor or a staff member designated by the Governor, (3) the Secretary of Health and Environment[164] or a staff member designated by the Secretary, (4) the Lieutenant Governor or a staff member designated by the Lieutenant Governor, and (5) seven members appointed by the Governor, each of whom shall represent a separate geographical district within the state.[165]

NMCDC has the authority to carry out the purposes of the NMCAA, including the authority to (1) develop and oversee the administration of community assistance programs,[166] (2) adopt, amend, and repeal all regulations necessary to administer and enforce the provisions of the NMCAA, (3) apply to any appropriate federal agency for aid from any program designed to assist local community infrastructure development, and (4) oversee the administration of all funds received, controlled, or disbursed for the purposes of carrying out the provisions of the community assistance program.[167]

---

161 N.M. Stat. Ann. §§ 11-6-1 to -9 (Repl. Pamp. 1983 & Supp. 1993).

162 N.M. Stat. Ann. § 11-6-2(A), (B) (Supp. 1993).

163 N.M. Stat. Ann. § 11-6-2(B) (Supp. 1993).

164 The Health and Environment Department was split into two separate departments during the 1991 legislative session. N.M. Stat. Ann. §§ 9-7-1 to -12 and 9-7A-1 to -12 (Repl. Pamp. 1991). The Secretary of the Environment Department and the Secretary of the Health Department, or their designees, are members of the NMCDC.

165 N.M. Stat. Ann. § 11-6-4(B) (Supp. 1993).

166 "Community assistance program" means a program to assist political subdivisions with infrastructure development, which may include but is not limited to: (1) a grant or loan of funds to the political subdivisions; (2) gathering data about the political subdivisions; (3) providing technical assistance to analyze the needs and seek solutions to problems related to infrastructure development and political subdivisions; and (4) providing technical assistance in seeking funds from sources other than the council. N.M. Stat. Ann. § 11-6-3(C) (Supp. 1993).

167 N.M. Stat. Ann. § 11-6-5 (Supp. 1993).

4.3.2 Regulations

NMCDC is responsible for adopting regulations to provide for (1) procedures and forms for making grants under the NMCAA, (2) documentation to justify the need for the community assistance program, (3) procedures for review, evaluation, and approval of grants, (4) procedures for reporting of information necessary to the review, evaluation, and approval of a grant, (5) a guide for the evaluation of the ability and competence of a grantee to provide for the completion of the project, (6) development and phase-in of a common application form and funding cycle for all grant or loan programs for local community infrastructure development administered or coordinated by the Local Government Division (LGD) of the Department of Finance and Administration,[168] (7) procedures for the coordination and handling of applications for all grant or loan programs administered and coordinated by the LGD, (8) procedures to control the number of applications from each political subdivision,[169] and (9) such other requirements as are deemed necessary by NMCDC to ensure that the state receives the services for which the Legislature appropriated money.[170]

Regulations adopted by NMCDC become effective when filed according to the provisions of the State Rules Act.[171]

4.3.3 Responsibility and Authority of LGD

LGD, in accordance with applicable regulations, has the responsibility and authority, among other things, to (1) act as a clearinghouse, provide coordination, and handle applications for all state and federal grant or loan programs for local community infrastructure development, (2) develop and adopt a common application form and funding cycle for all state and federal grant or loan programs for local community infrastructure development, including but not limited to programs under (a) the NMCAA, (b) the Water Supply Construction Act, (c) the development fund, (d) any state or federal solid waste management program, (e) the federal wastewater treatment construction grants program, (f) any state wastewater treatment construction grant or loan programs, and (g) federal community development block grant funds, (3) with certain exceptions, forward all applications for federal wastewater treatment construction grants to WQCC or its designated constituent agency, and (4) administer federal community development block grant funds and all other federal and state grant

---

168 The staff of the LGD is the staff of the NMCDC and provides technical assistance, compiles data, evaluates the effectiveness of the program, and reports its findings to the Legislature. N.M. Stat. Ann. § 11-6-8 (Supp. 1993).

169 "Political subdivision" means any county; incorporated city; town or village; drainage, conservancy, irrigation, water and sanitation or other district; mutual domestic association; public water cooperative association; or community ditch association. N.M. Stat. Ann. § 11-6-3(E) (Supp. 1993).

170 N.M. Stat. Ann. § 11-6-4.1(A) (Supp. 1993).

171 N.M. Stat. Ann. § 11-6-4.1(B) (Supp. 1993).

or loan programs for local community infrastructure development for which NMCDC has oversight responsibility or where administration is not otherwise provided for by law.[172]

4.3.4 Community Assistance Applications

A political subdivision seeking a grant of funds is required to file an application which contains at least (1) a general description of the project[173] and related existing facilities, (2) a general description of all real estate necessary for the project, (3) preliminary plans and other documents indicating the type, structure, and general character of the project, (4) estimated cost of the project, (5) a general description and statement of value of any property, real or personal, of the political subdivision applied or to be applied to the project, (6) a statement of cash funds previously applied or available for the project, (7) evidence of the arrangements for the financing of all costs of the project in excess of the requested assistance, (8) evidence that the political subdivision has the organizational and technical competence to utilize the requested funds efficiently, and (9) evidence that the political subdivision can properly operate and maintain the facility to be constructed for its useful life.[174]

After receipt of an application, LGD seeks input from appropriate state agencies and communicates their comments to NMCDC together with LGD's recommendations.[175] In determining whether or not to approve assistance funds, NMCDC must, at a minimum, consider (1) the health and safety of the residents to be served by the project, (2) the needs of other political subdivisions for infrastructure development funding, and (3) other sources of funds available to the political subdivision to fund the project.[176]

All action must be taken by a vote of a majority of the members of NMCDC.[177] Following a decision by NMCDC to approve assistance funds, LGD notifies all appropriate

---

172 N.M. Stat. Ann. § 11-6-5.1 (Supp. 1993).

173 "Project" means, except as limited by the state constitution, the purchase, construction, lease, gift, grant, reconstruction, improvement, option to purchase, or other acquisition of educational, cultural, recreational, community, municipal, social service, or other facilities by a political subdivision, including but not limited to publicly owned water systems, sewer systems, municipal utilities, roads, streets, highways, curbs, gutters, sidewalks, storm sewers, street lighting, traffic control devices, parking facilities, vocational training and rehabilitation facilities, airports, hospitals, nursing homes, publicly owned mental health, alcohol, and drug abuse, child abuse, and family counseling facilities, juvenile detention homes, swimming pools, parks, auditoriums, public buildings, libraries, fire and police stations, jails, waste disposal systems and sites, special assessment district improvements, and all necessary real and personal property therefor, but does not include facilities for the public schools. N.M. Stat. Ann. § 11-6-3(B) (Supp. 1993).

174 N.M. Stat. Ann. § 11-6-6(A) (Supp. 1993).

175 N.M. Stat. Ann. § 11-6-6(B) (Supp. 1993).

176 *Id.*

177 N.M. Stat. Ann. § 11-6-6(C) (Supp. 1993).

state agencies of the project and requests that they monitor it to assure that all statutes, rules, and regulations are complied with and that standards are maintained.[178]

4.3.5 Limitations and Special Requirements

No project which will result in increased demand for water may be recommended for approval until the NMCDC is satisfied that the political subdivision either holds or can acquire water rights sufficient to meet the increase in demand.[179] Further, NMCDC may not approve a grant of funds unless the political subdivision has taken all reasonable steps to use other sources of funding.[180] Of the grants made in any one fiscal year, at least 15 percent of the dollar amount must be made to counties with populations of less then 15,000 and other political subdivisions with populations of less than 3,000 or on behalf of areas with populations of less than 3,000.[181] For such grants, NMCDC may waive any requirements to use other sources of funding.[182]

No grant in excess of $500,000 for any one project may be made to a political subdivision in any one fiscal year, provided this maximum does not apply to state funds for matching federal wastewater treatment facility construction grants.[183] In making grants from state funds that are not limited to a particular type of project, NMCDC must give priority to the needs of political subdivisions impacted either by rapid growth or loss of tax base.[184] The political subdivision will own the project upon completion.[185]

4.4 POLLUTION CONTROL REVENUE BOND ACT

The purpose of the Pollution Control Revenue Bond Act (PCRBA)[186] is to protect and promote the health, welfare, and safety of the citizens of New Mexico and its habitat and wildlife by authorizing municipalities to acquire, own, lease, or sell projects[187] for the pur-

---

178 N.M. Stat. Ann. § 11-6-6(D) (Supp. 1993).

179 N.M. Stat. Ann. § 11-6-6.1(A) (Supp. 1993).

180 N.M. Stat. Ann. § 11-6-6.1(B) (Supp. 1993).

181 N.M. Stat. Ann. § 11-6-6.1(C) (Supp. 1993).

182 *Id.*

183 N.M. Stat. Ann. § 11-6-6.1(D) (Supp. 1993).

184 N.M. Stat. Ann. § 11-6-6.1(E) (Supp. 1993).

185 N.M. Stat. Ann. § 11-6-7 (Repl. Pamp. 1983).

186 N.M. Stat. Ann. §§ 3-59-1 to -14 (Repl. Pamp. 1984).

187 "Project" means any land, interest in land, building, structure, facility, system, fixture, improvement, appurtenance, machinery, equipment, or any combination thereof, or any interest in any one or more of the foregoing, whether or not presently in existence or under construction, used by any individual, partnership, firm, company, corporation (including a public utility), association, trust, estate, political subdivision, state agency, or any other legal entity, or its legal representative, agent, or assigns, substantially for the reduction, abatement, or prevention of pollution, including but not

pose of reducing, abating or preventing pollution,[188] including, but not limited to, removing pollutants, contaminants or foreign substances from land, air or water or removing or treating any substance in a processed material which otherwise would cause pollution when such material is used.[189] It is not the intention of the PCRBA to authorize any municipality itself to operate any manufacturing, industrial or commercial enterprise.[190]

4.4.1 Powers Conferred on Municipalities

In addition to other municipal powers, the PCRBA grants to each municipality the following powers: (1) to acquire one or more projects located within New Mexico, not more than 15 miles outside the corporate limits of the municipality, unless there is no municipality within 15 miles of the project, in which case any municipality in the county in which the project(s) is or may be located will have these powers, (2) to dispose of any or all of its projects upon such terms and conditions as the local governing body deems advisable which do not conflict with the PCRBA, and (3) to issue revenue bonds for the purpose of acquiring, constructing, reconstructing, improving, maintaining, equipping, or furnishing any project(s) and to secure the payment of the bonds.[191]

4.4.2 Bonds Issued to Finance Projects

Bonds issued by a municipality under the PCRBA are not the general obligation of the municipality. The bonds are payable solely out of the revenue derived from the project or from the sale or lease of the project.[192]

4.4.3 Security for Bonds

The principal and interest on any bonds are paid from and secured by a pledge of the project revenues and may be secured by a mortgage covering all or any part of the project(s) and/or by a pledge of the lease or the agreement of sale of such project(s). The ordinance and proceedings under which such bonds are authorized to be issued or any mortgage may

---

limited to the removal of pollutants, contaminants or foreign substances from land, air, or water, or for the removal or treatment of any substance in a processed material which otherwise would cause pollution when such material is used. N.M. Stat. Ann. § 3-59-2(B) (Repl. Pamp. 1984).

188 "Pollution" means any form of environmental pollution including but not limited to water pollution, air pollution, pollution caused by solid waste disposal, thermal pollution, radiation contamination, or noise pollution. N.M. Stat. Ann. § 3-59-2(F) (Repl. Pamp. 1984).

189 N.M. Stat. Ann. § 3-59-3 (Repl. Pamp. 1984).

190 *Id.*

191 N.M. Stat. Ann. § 3-59-4 (Repl. Pamp. 1984).

192 N.M. Stat. Ann. § 3-59-5 (Repl. Pamp. 1984).

contain other relevant agreements and provisions, examples of which are set forth in the PCRBA.[193]

4.4.4 Project Lease or Sale Requirements

Prior to the leasing, selling or other disposition of any project(s), the local governing body must determine (1) the amount necessary each year to pay the principal and interest on the bonds and (2) the amount necessary to be paid each year into any reserve fund which the governing body may deem advisable.[194]

Prior to the issuance of the bonds, the municipality must lease or sell the project(s) to a lessee or purchaser under an agreement conditioned upon completion of the project(s) and providing for payment of such rentals or payments as will be sufficient (1) to pay the principal and interest on the bonds, (2) to build up and maintain any reserve deemed to be advisable, and (3) to pay the costs of maintaining the project(s) and keeping the project(s) properly insured.[195]

4.4.5 Refunding Bonds and Proceeds from Sale of Bonds

Any bonds issued may be refunded by a municipality by the issuance of its refunding bonds in such amounts as the governing body deems necessary.[196] The proceeds from the sale of any bonds may be applied only for the purpose for which the bonds were issued, subject to certain exceptions set forth in the PCRBA.[197] The cost of acquiring any project(s) is deemed to include (1) the cost of construction, including architects', attorneys' and engineers' fees, (2) the purchase price, (3) the cost of the extension of any utility to the project site(s), (4) the expenses in connection with the authorization, sale and issuance of the bonds, and (5) the interest on any bonds issued for the same or any other project(s) for a reasonable time prior to construction, during construction and for a period not exceeding six months after completion of construction.[198]

4.4.6 No Contribution by Municipality

No municipality may pay out of its general funds or otherwise contribute any part of the costs of acquiring a project, nor does it have the power to use land already owned by the municipality, or in which the municipality has an equity, for construction of a project, unless the municipality is fully reimbursed for the value of the land as may be determined by a current appraisal, or unless the municipality leases the land at an annual rental fee of not less

---

193 N.M. Stat. Ann. § 3-59-6 (Repl. Pamp. 1984).

194 N.M. Stat. Ann. § 3-59-7 (Repl. Pamp. 1984).

195 N.M. Stat. Ann. § 3-59-7(B) (Repl. Pamp. 1984).

196 N.M. Stat. Ann. § 3-59-8 (Repl. Pamp. 1984).

197 N.M. Stat. Ann. § 3-59-9 (Repl. Pamp. 1984).

198 *Id.*

than five percent of the appraised value.[199] The entire cost of acquiring any project must be paid out of the proceeds from the sale of bonds; provided, however, that a municipality may accept donations of property to be used as a part of any project or money to be used for defraying any part of the cost of any project.[200]

4.4.7 Legal Status of Bonds

Bonds issued under the PCRBA are legal investments for savings banks and insurance companies organized under the laws of New Mexico and are eligible for pledging as collateral for public deposits.[201] The bonds authorized by the PCRBA and the income from these bonds, all mortgages or other security instruments executed as security for these bonds, all lease agreements made pursuant to the provisions of the PCRBA and revenue derived from any lease or sale by the municipality of any project are exempt from all taxation by the State of New Mexico or any subdivision of New Mexico.[202]

4.4.8 Construction of the PCRBA

Neither the PCRBA nor anything contained in the PCRBA should be construed as a limitation upon any powers which a municipality might otherwise have, but should be construed as cumulative. The PCRBA does not require an election by the voters of a municipality prior to the issuance of bonds, and all other laws of the state relative to public contracts and properties have no application to projects or bonds issued under the PCRBA.[203]

4.4.9 Issuance and Sale of Bonds

The issuance and sale of bonds pursuant to the PCRBA is authorized by ordinance adopted by the governing body of the municipality issuing the bonds.[204]

No notice, consent, or approval by any governmental body or public officer is required as a prerequisite to the sale or issuance of any bonds or the making of a mortgage under the authority of the PCRBA except as provided in the PCRBA.[205]

4.5 COUNTY POLLUTION CONTROL REVENUE BOND ACT

The purpose of the County Pollution Control Revenue Bond Act (CPCRBA)[206] is to protect and promote the health, welfare, and safety of the citizens of New Mexico and its

---

199 N.M. Stat. Ann. § 3-59-10 (Repl. Pamp. 1984).

200 *Id.*

201 N.M. Stat. Ann. § 3-59-11 (Repl. Pamp. 1984).

202 N.M. Stat. Ann. § 3-59-12 (Repl. Pamp. 1984).

203 N.M. Stat. Ann. § 3-59-13 (Repl. Pamp. 1984).

204 N.M. Stat. Ann. § 3-59-14 (Repl. Pamp. 1984).

205 *Id.*

206 N.M. Stat. Ann. §§ 4-60-1 to -15 (Repl. Pamp. 1992).

habitat and wildlife by authorizing counties to acquire, own, lease, or sell projects[207] for the purpose of reducing, abating, or preventing pollution,[208] including but not limited to removing pollutants, contaminants, or foreign substances from land, air, or water or removing or treating any substance in a processed material which otherwise would cause pollution when such material is used.[209] It is not the intention of the CPCRBA to authorize any county itself to operate any manufacturing, industrial, or commercial enterprise.[210]

4.5.1 Powers Conferred on Counties

In addition to any other powers, the CPCRBA grants to each county the following powers: (1) to acquire one or more projects located within New Mexico and outside a municipality in the county, (2) to dispose of any or all of its projects upon such terms and conditions as the governing body deems advisable which do not conflict with the CPCRBA, and (3) to issue revenue bonds for the purpose of acquiring, constructing, reconstructing, improving, maintaining, equipping, or furnishing any project(s) and to secure the payment of the bonds.[211]

4.5.2 Bonds Issued to Finance Projects

Bonds issued by a county under the CPCRBA are not the general obligation of the county.[212] The bonds are payable solely out of the revenue derived from the project or from the sale or lease of the project.[213]

---

207 "Project" means any land, interest in land, building, structure, facility, system, fixture, improvement, appurtenance, machinery, equipment, or any combination thereof or any interest in any one or more of the foregoing located outside a municipality in the county, or in the county and an adjoining county if part of the project is located in the county and the balance of the project is located in an adjoining county at a location contiguous thereto, whether or not presently in existence or under construction, used by any individual, partnership, firm, company, corporation (including the public utility), association, trust, estate, political subdivision, state agency, or any other legal entity, or its legal representative, agent, or assigns, substantially for the reduction, abatement, or prevention of pollution, including but not limited to the removal of pollutants, contaminants, or foreign substances from land, air, or water or for treatment of any substance in a processed material which otherwise would cause pollution when such material is used. N.M. Stat. Ann. § 4-60-2(C) (Repl. Pamp. 1992).

208 "Pollution" means any form of environmental pollution including, but not limited to, water pollution, air pollution, pollution caused by solid waste disposal, thermal pollution, radiation contamination or noise pollution. N.M. Stat. Ann. § 4-60-2(G) (Repl. Pamp. 1984).

209 N.M. Stat. Ann. § 4-60-3 (Repl. Pamp. 1992).

210 *Id.*

211 N.M. Stat. Ann. § 4-60-4 (Repl. Pamp. 1992).

212 N.M. Stat. Ann. § 4-60-5 (Repl. Pamp. 1992).

213 *Id.*

4.5.3 Security for Bonds

The principal and interest on any bonds are paid from and secured by a pledge of the project revenues and may be secured by a mortgage covering all or any part of the project(s) and/or by a pledge of the lease or the agreement of sale of such project(s).[214] The resolution and proceedings under which such bonds are authorized to be issued or any mortgage may contain other relevant agreements and provisions, examples of which are set forth in the CPCRBA.[215]

4.5.4 Project Lease or Sale Requirements

Prior to the leasing, selling, or other disposition of any project(s), the governing body must determine (1) the amount necessary each year to pay the principal and interest on the bonds and (2) the amount necessary to be paid each year into any reserve fund which the governing body may deem advisable.[216]

Prior to the issuance of bonds, the county must lease or sell the project(s) to a lessee or purchaser under an agreement conditioned upon completion of the project(s) and providing for payment of such rentals or payments as will be sufficient (1) to pay the principal and interest on the bonds, (2) to build up and maintain any reserve deemed to be advisable, and (3) to pay the costs of maintaining the project(s) and keeping the project(s) properly insured.[217]

4.5.5 Refunding Bonds

Any bonds issued may be refunded by a county by the issuance of its refunding bonds in such amounts as the governing body deems necessary.[218]

4.5.6 Use of Proceeds from Sale of Bonds

The proceeds from the sale of any bonds may be applied only for the purpose for which the bonds were issued, subject to certain exceptions set forth in the CPCRBA.[219] The cost of acquiring any project(s) is deemed to include (1) the cost of construction, including architects', attorneys' and engineers' fees, (2) the purchase price, (3) the cost of the extension of any utility to the project site(s), (4) the expenses in connection with the authorization, sale, and issuance of the bonds, and (5) the interest on any bonds issued for the same or any other project(s) for a reasonable time prior to construction, during construction, and not exceeding six months after completion of construction.[220]

---

214 N.M. Stat. Ann. § 4-60-6 (Repl. Pamp. 1992).

215 *Id.*

216 N.M. Stat. Ann. § 4-60-7 (Repl. Pamp. 1992).

217 *Id.*

218 N.M. Stat. Ann. § 4-60-8 (Repl. Pamp. 1992).

219 N.M. Stat. Ann. § 4-60-9 (Repl. Pamp. 1992).

220 *Id.*

4.5.7 No Contribution by County

No county may pay out of its general funds or otherwise contribute any part of the costs of acquiring a project, nor does it have the power to use land already owned by the county, or in which the county has an equity, for construction of a project, unless the county is fully reimbursed for the value of the land as may be determined by a current appraisal, or unless the county leases the land at an annual rental fee of not less than five percent of the appraised value.[221] The entire cost of acquiring any project must be paid out of the proceeds from the sale of bonds, provided a county may accept donations of property to be used as a part of any project or money to be used for defraying any part of the cost of any project.[222]

4.5.8 Bonds Made Legal Investments

Bonds issued under the CPCRBA are legal investments for savings banks and insurance companies organized under the laws of New Mexico and are eligible for pledging as collateral for public deposits.[223]

4.5.9 Exemption from Taxation

The bonds authorized by the CPCRBA and the income from these bonds, all mortgages or other security instruments executed as security for these bonds, all lease agreements made pursuant to the provisions of the CPCRBA and revenue derived from any lease or sale by the county of any project are exempt from all taxation by New Mexico or any subdivision of New Mexico.[224]

4.5.10 Construction of Act

Neither the CPCRBA nor anything contained in the CPCRBA should be construed as a limitation upon any powers which a county might otherwise have, but should be construed as cumulative. The CPCRBA does not require an election by the voters of a county prior to the issuance of bonds, and all other laws of the state relative to public contracts and properties have no application to projects or bonds issued under the CPCRBA.[225]

4.5.11 Issuance and Sale of Bonds

The issuance and sale of bonds pursuant to the CPCRBA is authorized by resolution adopted by the governing body of the county issuing the bonds.[226]

---

221 N.M. Stat. Ann. § 4-60-10 (Repl. Pamp. 1992).

222 *Id.*

223 N.M. Stat. Ann. § 4-60-11 (Repl. Pamp. 1992).

224 N.M. Stat. Ann. § 4-60-12 (Repl. Pamp. 1992).

225 N.M. Stat. Ann. § 4-60-14 (Repl. Pamp. 1992).

226 N.M. Stat. Ann. § 4-60-13 (Repl. Pamp. 1992).

No notice, consent, or approval by any governmental body or public officer is required as a prerequisite to the sale or issuance of any bonds or the making of a mortgage under the authority of the CPCRBA except as provided in the CPCRBA.[227]

5.0 NATURAL RESOURCES TRUSTEE ACT

The Natural Resources Trustee Act (NRTA) was recently enacted to protect natural resources within the state and natural resources belonging to or managed by the state.[228] The NRTA establishes the position of the Natural Resources Trustee (Trustee), who is appointed by and serves at the pleasure of the Governor and who acts on behalf of the public as trustee of natural resources within the state or belonging to, managed by, controlled by, or appertaining to the state.[229] The Trustee also protects and represents the state's interest under applicable federal laws regarding injury to, destruction of, or loss of natural resources in the state.[230] The office of the Trustee is administratively attached to the New Mexico Department of the Environment (NMED) and is headed by the Trustee.[231]

5.1 POWERS AND DUTIES

The Trustee is empowered to take all action necessary to carry out the responsibilities provided by applicable federal law.[232] These responsibilities include investigation of any injury to natural resources and recovery of damages for the same, determination of the cause of any injury to natural resources, determination of liability for any injury to natural resources, and assessment and collection of damages for any injury to natural resources.[233] The Trustee may hire staff and expert consultants and accept gifts and grants in order to carry out these provisions.[234]

5.2 AWARDS FOR DAMAGES

Awards for damage to natural resources are calculated in accord with federal law and include the cost of restoration, replacement, or acquisition of equivalent resources plus compensation for the loss of use or enjoyment of the natural resources, as well as compensa-

---

227 *Id.*

228 N.M. Stat. Ann. § 75-7-1 to -5 (Supp. 1993).

229 N.M. Stat. Ann. § 75-7-2(A) (Supp. 1993). The position of Trustee is established to function in accordance with CERCLA, 42 U.S.C. §§ 9601 to 9675 (1980), as amended by the Superfund Amendments and Reauthorization Act of 1986, the Federal Water Pollution Control Act, 33 U.S.C. §§1151 to 1165 and any other applicable federal law.

230 *Id.*

231 N.M. Stat. Ann. § 75-7-2(B) (Supp. 1993).

232 N.M. Stat. Ann. § 75-7-3(A) (Supp. 1993).

233 *Id.*

234 N.M. Stat. Ann. § 75-7-3(B) (Supp. 1993).

tion for the state's expenses in investigating, assessing, and collecting damages and enforcing the state's rights.[235]

5.3 NATURAL RESOURCES TRUST FUND

The Natural Resources Trust Fund (NRTF) is created as part of the state treasury and administered by the Trustee and is the repository for money appropriated or accrued to it through gifts, grants, fees, penalties, bequests, or any other source, including money recovered for the state by or on behalf of the Trustee.[236] Funds are disbursed upon warrants drawn by the Secretary of Finance and Administration pursuant to vouchers signed by the Trustee or designated representative.[237]

The Legislature appropriates money annually to carry out the NRTA's provisions for restoring, replacing, or acquiring resources in damaged areas and for costs associated with personnel, investigation, enforcement, assessment, and collection.[238]

6.0 WILDLIFE CONSERVATION ACT

The Wildlife Conservation Act (WCA)[239] was enacted by the Legislature to protect endangered species within the state and the country. The Legislature has recognized that species and subspecies of wildlife[240] indigenous to the state which are endangered[241] must be managed[242] to maintain or enhance their numbers within the carrying capacity of the habitat.[243] The Legislature has also empowered the state to assist in management of species endangered outside of the state by prohibiting actions within the state aimed at

---

235 N.M. Stat. Ann. § 75-7-4 (Supp. 1993).

236 N.M. Stat. Ann. § 75-7-5(A) (Supp. 1993).

237 *Id.*

238 N.M. Stat. Ann. § 75-7-5(B) (Supp. 1993).

239 N.M. Stat. Ann. §§ 17-2-37 to -46 (Repl. Pamp. 1988).

240 "Wildlife" means any nondomestic mammal, bird, reptile, amphibian, fish, mollusk, or crustacean or any part, egg, or offspring, or the dead body or parts thereof. N.M. Stat. Ann. § 17-2-38(G) (Repl. Pamp. 1988).

241 "Endangered species" means any species of fish or wildlife whose prospects of survival or recruitment within the state are in jeopardy or may be in the foreseeable future due to threatened habitat, overutilization of the species for scientific, commercial, or sporting purposes, disease, predation, or any other natural or man-made factors. N.M. Stat. Ann. § 17-2-38(D) (Repl. Pamp. 1988).

242 "Management" means collection and application of biological information for the purposes of establishing and maintaining a congruous relationship between individuals within species and populations of wildlife and the carrying capacity of their habitat. N.M. Stat. Ann. § 17-2-38(E) (Repl. Pamp. 1988).

243 N.M. Stat. Ann. § 17-2-39(A) (Repl. Pamp. 1988).

procurement of or trade in species listed on the United States lists of endangered fish and wildlife.[244]

6.1 ENDANGERED SPECIES LIST

The State Game Commission (Commission) must develop a list of those species and subspecies determined to be endangered.[245] The Director of the Department of Game and Fish (Director) reviews the list biennially and presents to the Commission recommended additions or deletions.[246]

It is unlawful for any person to take[247], possess, transport, export, process, sell or offer for sale, or ship any species or subspecies listed by the state or by the United States as endangered.[248] Species may be transported across the state to a point beyond the state pursuant to a federal or state permit.[249]

6.2 MANAGEMENT PROGRAMS

The Director must establish programs as authorized and deemed necessary by the Commission for management of endangered species.[250] The Director may authorize by permit the taking, possession, transportation, exportation, or shipment of endangered species or subspecies if the use is for scientific, zoological, or educational purposes, for propagation in captivity, or for protection of private property.[251] Endangered species and subspecies may be removed, captured, or destroyed when they are a threat to property or human health pursuant to a permit or, in emergencies, without a permit.[252] Any person who fails to procure a permit as required by the WCA is guilty of a misdemeanor and upon conviction faces a fine or imprisonment.[253]

6.3 ENFORCEMENT

The Director, conservation officers, sheriffs, and state police must enforce the WCA and, when probable cause exists, seize any endangered species or subspecies held in violation

---

244 N.M. Stat. Ann. § 17-2-39(B) (Repl. Pamp. 1988).

245 N.M. Stat. Ann. § 17-2-41(A) (Repl. Pamp. 1988).

246 N.M. Stat. Ann. § 17-2-41(B) (Repl. Pamp. 1988).

247 "Take" means to harass, hunt, capture, or kill any wildlife or attempt to do so. N.M. Stat. Ann. § 17-2-38(F) (Repl. Pamp. 1988).

248 N.M. Stat. Ann. § 17-2-41(C) (Repl. Pamp. 1988).

249 *Id.*

250 N.M. Stat. Ann. § 17-2-42(A) (Repl. Pamp. 1988).

251 N.M. Stat. Ann. § 17-2-42(C) (Repl. Pamp. 1988).

252 N.M. Stat. Ann. § 17-2-42(D) (Repl. Pamp. 1988).

253 N.M. Stat. Ann. § 17-2-45 (Repl. Pamp. 1988).

of the WCA and arrest any person believed to be guilty of a violation.[254] Enforcement officials may open, enter and examine all camps, vehicles, tents, and containers if the contents are believed to be in violation of the WCA.[255] Arrest warrants and search warrants are issued as in criminal cases.[256] The Director may establish checking stations along established roads as necessary.[257]

7.0 ENDANGERED PLANTS

The Legislature enacted N.M. Stat. Ann. § 75-6-1 (Repl. Pamp. 1991) (Endangered Plants) to protect endangered plants[258] within the state.

7.1 ENDANGERED PLANTS LIST

Under Endangered Plants, the Natural Resources Department (NRD) is empowered to investigate all plant species in the state and develop biological and ecological data in order to determine conservation requirements.[259] On the basis of these investigations NRD must establish a list of endangered species.[260] The list must include those species listed under the federal Endangered Species Act.[261]

7.2 MANAGEMENT OF PROGRAMS

NRD must establish a program for the conservation of listed endangered plant species.[262] The program must include research, census, law enforcement, habitat maintenance, propagation, and transportation.[263]

7.3 ENFORCEMENT

NRD has authority to protect endangered plant species by prohibiting the taking, possession,[264] transportation, exportation from this state of such species. Violators will be

---

254 N.M. Stat. Ann. § 17-2-46(A) (Repl. Pamp. 1988).

255 *Id.*

256 N.M. Stat. Ann. § 17-2-46(B) (Repl. Pamp. 1988).

257 N.M. Stat. Ann. § 17-2-46(C) (Repl. Pamp. 1988).

258 "Endangered plant species" means any plant species whose prospects of survival within the state are in jeopardy or are likely, within the foreseeable future, to become jeopardized. N.M. Stat. Ann § 75-6-1(A) (Repl. Pamp. 1991).

259 N.M. Stat. Ann. § 75-6-1(B) (Repl. Pamp. 1991).

260 *Id.*

261 N.M. Stat. Ann. § 75-6-1(A) (Repl. Pamp. 1991); 16 U.S.C. §§ 1531 to 1536, 1538 to 1540, & 1542.

262 N.M. Stat. Ann. § 75-6-1(C) (Repl. Pamp. 1991).

263 *Id.*

264 "Possession" means possession of listed plants or plant materials for purposes of taking, transportation, exportation from this state, processing, sale or offer for sale, or shipment within this state. N.M. Stat. Ann. § 75-6-1(D) (Repl. Pamp. 1991).

fined a minimum of $300, and up to $1,000, and/or will be imprisoned for up to 120 days.[265] The NRD may, by permit, allow collection of endangered plants for scientific purposes or to enhance the propagation or survival of the species by transporting or other means, but such permit must not authorize any action which would violate federal laws or regulations.[266]

265 *Id.*

266 N.M. Stat. Ann. § 75-6-1(E) (Repl. Pamp. 1991).

CHAPTER XI
ENVIRONMENTAL MANAGEMENT BY INDIAN TRIBES AND PUEBLOS

1.0 NEW MEXICO TRIBES AND PUEBLOS

In New Mexico four Indian tribes and nineteen Pueblos[1] occupy lands, shown on the map on the facing page, which encompass over 8 million acres of land (about 12,720 square miles or 10.5% of the land area in New Mexico). The 1990 Census reports a Native American population of 134,355 in New Mexico, about 9% of the state's population. A list of telephone numbers and addresses for each tribe, Navajo community, and Pueblo is provided in this chapter.

1.1 TRIBES

1.1.1 Navajo Nation

The largest area of Indian land in New Mexico is part of the Navajo Nation in the northwest corner of the state. The Navajo Nation is the largest Native American group in the United States; its lands are in Arizona, Utah, and New Mexico. The Navajo Reservation was created by treaty in 1868[2] and encompasses 16 million acres. Almost one-third of the Nation's land (4,468,000 acres) and about 50,000 of its members are in New Mexico. The seat of Navajo tribal government is Window Rock, Arizona. The Navajo Nation's legislative body is the Navajo Nation Council, and its judicial branch has both trial and appellate courts. A discussion of the Navajo Nation's environmental programs is provided in Section 3.1 of this Chapter.

1.1.2 Separate Navajo Communities

The Navajo Nation contains 110 Chapters, whose representatives comprise the Navajo Nation Council. The Chapters function as local governments similar to counties. Three of the first Chapters to be established, based on historical settlement patterns, are the Alamo, Cañoncito, and Ramah Chapters. The Alamo Chapter encompasses over 75,400 acres about 90 miles southwest of Albuquerque and has a population over 1,200. The Cañoncito Chapter is located about 30 miles west of Albuquerque on over 76,700 acres of reservation land, and has a population of almost 1,200. The Ramah Chapter encompasses almost 147,000 acres and is located about 35 miles southeast of Gallup, New Mexico.

---

1 The terms "tribe" and "tribal" are generally used to refer to both Pueblos and tribes.

2 Treaty of June 1, 1868, 15 Stat. 667, and subsequent executive orders.

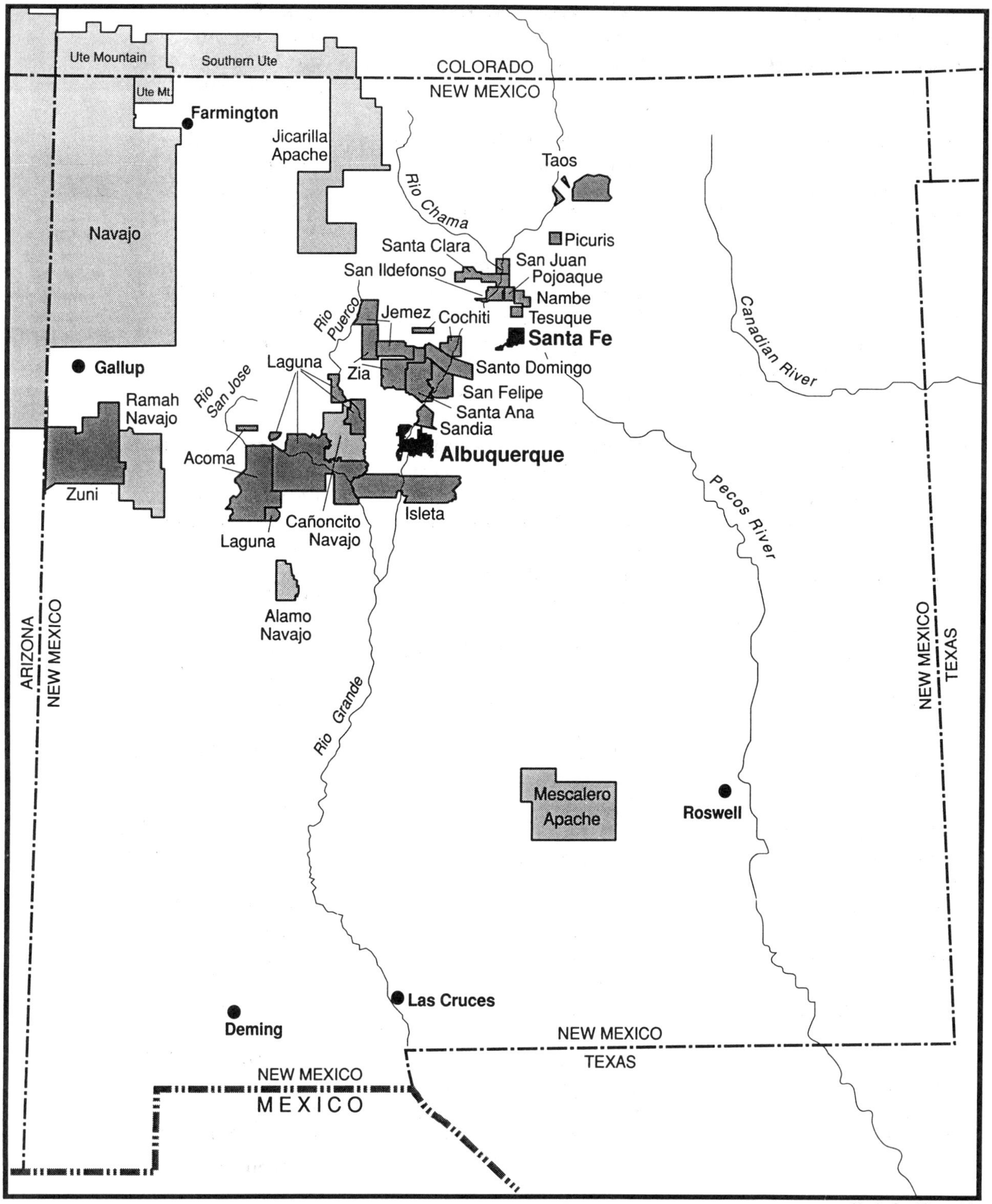

Map by Carol Cooperrider

NEW MEXICO PUEBLOS AND TRIBES

ACOMA PUEBLO
P. O. Box 309
Pueblo of Acoma, NM 87034
(505) 552-6604/6605/6606/6607

COCHITI PUEBLO
P. O. Box 70
Cochiti Pueblo, NM 87041
(505) 465-2244/2245

ISLETA PUEBLO
P. O. Box 1270
Isleta Pueblo, NM 87022
(505) 869-3111/6333/3994

JEMEZ PUEBLO
P. O. Box 100
Jemez Pueblo, NM 87024
(505) 834-7359/7525

LAGUNA PUEBLO
P. O. Box 194
Laguna Pueblo, NM 87026
(505) 552-6654/6655

NAMBE PUEBLO
Route 1, Box 117-BB
Santa Fe, NM 87501
(505) 455-2036

PICURIS PUEBLO
P. O. Box 127
Penasco, NM 87553
(505) 587-2519/2043

POJOAQUE PUEBLO
Route 11, Box 71
Santa Fe, NM 87501
(505) 455-2278/2279

SANDIA PUEBLO
Box 6008
Bernalillo, NM 87004
(505) 867-3317

SAN FELIPE PUEBLO
P. O. Box A
San Felipe Pueblo, NM 87001
(505) 867-3381/3382/3383

SAN ILDEFONSO PUEBLO
Route 5, Box 315-A
Santa Fe, NM 87501
(505) 455-2273/2274

SAN JUAN PUEBLO
P. O. Box 1099
San Juan Pueblo, NM 87566
(505) 852-4400/4210

SANTA ANA PUEBLO
Star Route Box 37
Bernalillo, NM 87004
(505) 867-3301/3302/3303

SANTA CLARA PUEBLO
P. O. Box 580
Espanola, NM 87532
(505) 753-7330/7326

SANTO DOMINGO PUEBLO
P. O. Box 99
Santo Domingo Pueblo, NM 87052
(505) 465-2214/2215

TAOS PUEBLO
P. O. Box 1846
Taos, NM 87571
(505) 758-9593

TESUQUE PUEBLO
Route 11, Box 1
Santa Fe, NM 87501
(505) 983-2667

ZIA PUEBLO
135 Capitol Square Drive
Zia Pueblo, N.M. 87053-6013
(505) 867-3304/3305/3306

ZUNI PUEBLO
P. O. Box 339
Zuni, NM 87327
(505) 782-4481

JICARILLA APACHE TRIBE
P. O. Box 507
Dulce, NM 87528
(505) 759-3242

MESCALERO APACHE TRIBE
P. O. Box 176
Mescalero, NM 88340
(505) 671-4494/4495/4496

NAVAJO NATION
P. O. Box 308
Window Rock, AZ 86515
(602) 871-6352 through 6357

ALAMO NAVAJO CHAPTER
Box 383
Magdalena, NM 87825
(505) 854-2686

CAÑONCITO NAVAJO CHAPTER
P. O. Box 398
Cañoncito, NM 87026
(505) 836-4221/831-2843

RAMAH NAVAJO CHAPTER
Route 2, Box 13
Ramah, NM 87321
(505) 775-3310

UTE MOUNTAIN UTE TRIBE
P.O. Box 52
Towaoc, CO 81334
(303) 565-3751

1.1.3 Mescalero Apache Tribe

The 460,000-acre reservation[3] of the Mescalero Apache Tribe located in the southeastern part of the state is home to about 3,200 tribal members; Mescalero is the tribal capital. The Tribe has been working with the U.S. Environmental Protection Agency (EPA) to satisfy the standards of the Safe Drinking Water Act and regulations promulgated pursuant thereto. The Tribe is also developing a solid waste program to comply with EPA requirements for solid waste landfills.

1.1.4 Jicarilla Apache Tribe

Located in northwestern New Mexico, the reservation[4] of the Jicarilla Apache Tribe encompasses over 850,000 acres. The present tribal enrollment is about 3,100; the tribal capital is at Dulce, New Mexico. The Tribe has an Environmental Office (Box 507, Dulce, N.M. 87528) within the Natural Resources Department to administer its environmental laws. In 1984 the Tribe enacted an ordinance (summarized in the Tribal Environmental Codes Section of this Chapter) that mandates broad environmental disclosures for all tribal actions significantly affecting the reservation environment, and in 1991 the Tribe enacted a Weed Control and Pesticide Regulation and Enforcement Ordinance.

1.1.5 Ute Mountain Ute Tribe

The Ute Mountain Ute Reservation of 105,000 acres was established by statute[5] in 1913. Reservation land in northwestern New Mexico is used for grazing and oil and gas production. None of the 1,830 tribal members lives in New Mexico. The constitution of the Ute Mountain Ute Tribe was approved on June 6, 1940. Although the Tribe has not enacted any environmental regulations, it has developed a water quality program in conjunction with EPA and has treatment as a state (TAS) status for purposes of Section 106 of the federal Clean Water Act (CWA).[6]

1.2 PUEBLOS

The nineteen Pueblos in New Mexico have an aggregate population of over 40,000. They are located in the northwest quadrant of the state and for the most part are situated along the Rio Grande and its tributaries. Each Pueblo ("village" in Spanish) is a small town, often built around a central plaza, with outlying irrigated farms and grazing lands. Unlike the territory now owned by tribes in New Mexico that did not live in settled communities, the lands of the Pueblos were granted to them by the King of Spain during the Spanish colonial period and were confirmed by patents from the United States, in most cases in 1864.

---

[3] Created by Executive Order initially in 1873 and finally located by the E.O. of Mar. 24, 1883, *reprinted in* 1 C. Kappler, *Indian Affairs, Laws and Treaties* 872-73 (1904).

[4] Created by Executive Order of Feb. 11, 1887, *reprinted in* 1 C. Kappler at 875.

[5] 38 Stat. 77, 82-83 (1913), *reprinted in* 3 C. Kappler at 566-67.

[6] 36 U.S.C. § 1256. *See* Section 2.3.2 of this Chapter.

An important environmental focus of the Pueblos is water quality. In the early 1960s eight of the Pueblos (Nambe, Picuris, Pojoaque, San Ildefonso, San Juan, Santa Clara, Taos, and Tesuque) formed the Eight Northern Indian Pueblos Council (ENIPC), which is now incorporated, to assist the Pueblo governments in taking over and administering many community services from the Bureau of Indian Affairs (BIA). The ENIPC has established an Office of Environmental Protection Management to assist its tribal members in dealing with water quality and solid waste problems. The eight northern Pueblos have TAS status for purposes of CWA § 106. The ENIPC has received a CWA grant to develop water quality standards for a model ordinance for tribal regulation, which has been referred to the ENIPC's member Pueblos for enactment.

1.2.1 Acoma Pueblo

Built before 900 A.D., Acoma Pueblo is one of the oldest continuously occupied villages in North America. Acoma is located about 40 miles west of Albuquerque. Present tribal membership numbers over 4,070, and Pueblo land encompasses almost 380,000 acres. The Pueblo is currently developing water quality standards under CWA and has received a grant and TAS status for purposes of CWA § 314 from EPA to restore Lake Acomita.

1.2.2 Cochiti Pueblo

Situated on the west bank of the Rio Grande, Cochiti Pueblo is located 45 miles north of Albuquerque and 30 miles southwest of Santa Fe. The Pueblo was established before 1250 A.D. and currently has over 1,000 members. Pueblo land encompasses over 50,000 acres. The Pueblo does not have any environmental regulations at present but is working with the state for natural resource protection and planning in the area.

1.2.3 Isleta Pueblo

Isleta Pueblo is about 15 miles south of Albuquerque and owns land on both sides of the Rio Grande. Occupied since about 1200 A.D., the current Pueblo membership numbers about 3,780. Tribal land encompasses 211,000 acres. The Pueblo received TAS status for purposes of CWA §§ 106 and 303 and is working with the EPA to develop a wastewater treatment facility with a grant under the CWA. Pursuant to Resolution No. 92-14, Isleta Pueblo adopted its own water quality standards under CWA § 303, which EPA approved on December 24, 1992.

1.2.4 Jemez Pueblo

Located in the canyons of the Jemez Mountains at the headwaters of Rio Jemez, the Jemez Pueblo is about 50 miles northwest of Albuquerque. The Pueblo was well established when Coronado arrived in 1540. Current Pueblo land includes over 89,000 acres and has about 3,030 members. The Pueblo has no environmental regulations at present.

1.2.5 Laguna Pueblo

Laguna Pueblo is composed of six villages about 45 miles west of Albuquerque. The newest of the Pueblos, it was established in 1699 for refugees from other Pueblos who fled the Spanish reconquest of New Mexico. Pueblo land encompasses about 480,000 acres and has about 6,840 members. The Pueblo is not presently working on any environmental regulations, but it has participated through tribal enterprises in cleanup work on the former Jackpile uranium mine on tribal land.

1.2.6 Nambe Pueblo

Nambe Pueblo was established before 1300 A.D. at the headwaters of the Rio Nambe, a tributary of the Rio Pojoaque. Pueblo grant and reservation land encompasses about 19,000 acres located about 20 miles north of Santa Fe. The Pueblo membership is now 604. The Pueblo has received TAS status for purposes of CWA § 106 and is working on water quality standards.

1.2.7 Picuris Pueblo

In existence near its present site by the mid-1200's, Picuris Pueblo is located about 30 miles northeast of Santa Fe. The current population of 291 Pueblo members occupies its original grant of about 15,000 acres. The Pueblo has received TAS status for purposes of CWA § 106 and is working on water quality standards.

1.2.8 Pojoaque Pueblo

Pojoaque Pueblo is located in the middle of the Pojoaque Valley about 17 miles north of Santa Fe. Reorganized in 1946, the Pueblo is situated on 11,600 acres of grant land and has 133 members. The Pueblo has TAS status for purposes of CWA § 106 and is considering water quality standards. The Pueblo has received a grant from the New Mexico Environment Department (NMED) for the construction of a wastewater treatment facility. The Pueblo is also working on a wellhead protection program and a solid waste program.

1.2.9 San Felipe Pueblo

South of Santo Domingo, San Felipe Pueblo lands straddle the Rio Grande. The Pueblo was well established when Coronado's expedition arrived in 1540. The present Pueblo has about 2,500 members; Pueblo land encompasses almost 49,000 acres. The Pueblo is not considering any environmental regulations at present.

1.2.10 San Ildefonso Pueblo

San Ildefonso Pueblo is located 25 miles northwest of Santa Fe. The present village was constructed about 1300 A.D. at the confluence of the Rio Pojoaque and the Rio Grande. The current Pueblo membership is over 650. Pueblo grant and reservation land encompasses over 26,000 acres. The Pueblo has TAS status for purposes of CWA § 106 and is working on environmental regulations for future implementation.

1.2.11 San Juan Pueblo

Thirty miles north of Santa Fe, San Juan Pueblo, at least 700 years old, is located on a grant of over 12,000 acres at the confluence of the Rio Chama and the Rio Grande. Pueblo membership numbers over 2,400; the tribal council headquarters is located at the

Pueblo. The Pueblo has received TAS status for purposes of the CWA §§ 106 and 303 and has adopted water quality standards, which EPA approved on September 16, 1993.

1.2.12 Sandia Pueblo

Sandia Pueblo adjoins the northern boundary of Albuquerque. The Pueblo was constructed around 1300 A.D. Current tribal membership numbers 379, and Pueblo land encompasses almost 23,000 acres. The Pueblo has received TAS status for purposes of CWA §§ 106 and 303 and has adopted water quality standards under CWA § 303, which EPA approved on August 10, 1993. The Pueblo is also working with EPA to comply with the federal Clean Air Act.

1.2.13 Santa Ana Pueblo

Santa Ana Pueblo is located about 23 miles north of Albuquerque on the Rio Jemez and the Rio Grande. Pueblo land includes almost 62,000 acres, and Pueblo membership numbers 617. The Pueblo is not working on environmental regulations at present.

1.2.14 Santa Clara Pueblo

Located 26 miles north of Santa Fe, Santa Clara Pueblo was established on the west side of the Rio Grande at least 700 years ago. Pueblo land includes almost 46,000 acres of grant and reservation lands, with a population of about 1,600 members. Santa Clara Pueblo is in the process of developing a comprehensive environmental program. Santa Clara Pueblo has received three grants from EPA, has TAS status for purposes of CWA § 106, and has developed draft water quality standards, a draft solid waste ordinance, and a draft wetlands management plan. The water quality standards and the solid waste ordinance will become part of the tribal code after adoption by the tribal council. Santa Clara is beginning a water quality monitoring program for all tribal waters.

1.2.15 Santo Domingo Pueblo

Reconstructed in the late 1800's, Santo Domingo Pueblo of about 4,000 members is located between Albuquerque and Santa Fe. Pueblo land includes over 70,000 acres. The Pueblo is working with EPA to meet the standards of a number of federal environmental regulations including those under CWA. The Pueblo has established an Environment Department which has been evaluating water quality and solid waste issues.

1.2.16 Taos Pueblo

The present Pueblo, famous for its multistory structures divided by the Rio Pueblo into North and South Houses, has existed at its present site since at least 900 A.D. The Pueblo is located 74 miles north of Santa Fe and encompasses over 95,000 acres. Pueblo membership numbers over 2,200. The Pueblo has no environmental regulations at present but has received TAS status for purposes of CWA § 106.

1.2.17 Tesuque Pueblo

Tesuque Pueblo was established before 1250 A.D. on the Rio Tesuque, a tributary of the Rio Pojoaque, about 10 miles north of Santa Fe. The Pueblo's grant covers about

16,800 acres. There are 489 present Pueblo members. The Pueblo is planning to establish an environmental office, has received TAS status for purposes of the CWA § 106, and is considering proposed water quality standards.

1.2.18 Zia Pueblo

Established around 1250 A.D., Zia Pueblo is situated along the Rio Jemez about 35 miles northwest of Albuquerque. Pueblo land encompasses almost 122,000 acres and has a membership of 815. Zia Pueblo is not working on any environmental regulations at present.

1.2.19 Zuni Pueblo

Zuni Pueblo is located about 30 miles south of Gallup, abutting the western boundary of the state. The Pueblo was established long before 1540 when Coronado first encountered the aboriginal population of New Mexico at one of its villages. The current Pueblo membership is about 8,080; its lands include about 407,000 acres. The Pueblo has received an Indian Set-Aside Grant from EPA to construct a wastewater treatment facility under the CWA and has also been awarded an EPA grant under the Resource Conservation and Recovery Act (RCRA)[7] for solid waste education and outreach programs.

2.0 JURISDICTION

2.1 BACKGROUND

Ordinarily, EPA relies on the states to regulate and enforce federally sanctioned environmental standards upon activities with environmental effects. When the activity occurs on tribal land (or within the broader Indian country jurisdiction of the tribe, as explained below), state law has limited effect and Congress has (under some environmental statutes) directed EPA to treat the tribal government in the same manner as a state. Thus, EPA could rely on the tribal government for direct regulation and enforcement within the limits of tribal jurisdiction. Beyond those limits EPA would have to enforce the requirements of federal law directly. Each Indian tribe or Pueblo has the power (as an aspect of its inherent sovereignty, under agreements with nonmembers for the use of tribal lands and resources, and as an attribute of its power to exclude nonmembers from lands under its control) to regulate environmentally significant activity on its lands by nonmembers.[8] Unless the tribe in a lease or contract conditions a nonmember's use of tribal land on its acceptance of criminal penalties for violation of tribal regulations, such penalties may not be imposed, and federal criminal sanctions would be imposed by EPA. State regulation is generally inapplicable.[9]

---

7 42 U.S.C. §§ 9601-9675.

8 EPA has ruled that Congress has not delegated to Indian tribes treated as states under the CWA, federal powers of regulation and enforcement. Such tribes must rely on their tribal governmental authority to enforce federal or tribal environmental regulations within their geographical jurisdiction. 58 Fed. Reg. 8172 (1993).

9 *See New Mexico v. Mescalero Apache Tribe,* 462 U.S. 324, 336 (1983).

An Indian tribe or Pueblo lacks governmental authority directly to regulate non-members' activities outside its Indian country jurisdiction unless federal law gives effect to such tribal regulations.

2.2 TRIBAL JURISDICTION, GENERALLY

Each of the 19 New Mexico Indian Pueblos existed as a settled community with a traditional government before the first Spanish *entrada* in 1540 and the first settlement of Spanish immigrants in 1598. Their tribal lands were granted, and their governments were recognized, by Spain and after 1821 by Mexico, and after the American conquest in 1846, the United States has continued to recognize their tribal authority as "dependent sovereigns."[10] The Navajo, Ute, and Apache Tribes remained largely unsettled before their reservations were established[11]. The Indian Reorganization Act (IRA)[12] authorized Indian tribes and Pueblos to adopt a written constitution and bylaws[13] and to obtain a federal charter of incorporation.[14] Both Apache tribes and the Ute Mountain Utes adopted constitutions, and the Apache tribes also received charters under the IRA,[15] but the only Pueblo to adopt an IRA constitution was Santa Clara.[16] Laguna Pueblo adopted a written constitution on January 1, 1908. The Navajo Nation, the largest Indian tribe, has not adopted an IRA constitution, but it nevertheless has developed an extensive Navajo Tribal Code of laws adopted as resolutions of the Navajo Nation Council.

---

10 *Santa Clara Pueblo v. Martinez*, 436 U.S. 49 (1978). According to Felix Cohen's famous dictum, "those powers which are lawfully vested in an Indian tribe are not, in general, delegated powers granted by express acts of Congress, but rather inherent powers of a limited sovereignty which has never been extinguished." F. Cohen, *Handbook of Federal Indian Law* 122 (1942). The Supreme Court has stated: "Indian tribes still possess those aspects of sovereignty not withdrawn by treaty or statute, or by implication as a necessary result of their dependent status." *United States v. Wheeler, 435 U.S. 313, 323 (1978).*

11 *See* description of these Tribes above, in this Chapter.

12 The Act is sometimes called the Wheeler-Howard Act, or Act of June 18, 1934, 48 Stat. 984 (codified as amended at 25 U.S.C. §§ 461 - 479).

13 25 U.S.C. § 476.

14 25 U.S.C. § 477.

15 Jicarilla Apache Tribe Const., Aug. 4, 1937 & Charter Sept. 4, 1937; Mescalero Apache Tribe Const., Mar. 25, 1936 & Charter Aug. 1, 1936; Ute Mountain Ute Const., May 8, 1940.

16 Pueblo of Santa Clara Const., Dec. 14, 1935.

2.3 CIVIL JURISDICTION

2.3.1 Tribal

Tribes and Pueblos exercise sovereign power over their members and their lands.[17] The Supreme Court has limited the geographic range of tribal jurisdiction to "Indian country."[18] Under the Supreme Court's decisions in *Oklahoma Tax Commission v. Sac & Fox Nation*[19] and *Oklahoma Tax Commission v. Citizen Band of Potawatomi Indian Tribe*,[20] Indian country includes, for a tribe, its reservation or for a Pueblo, its original grant lands, and in both cases subsequent federal reservations (by executive order, proclamation, or statute) and land held in trust or otherwise "validly set apart for the use of the Indians as such, under the superintendence of the Government."[21]

The Supreme Court has upheld tribal jurisdiction to tax nonmembers as well as members residing within the geographic boundaries of tribal Indian country. In *Sac & Fox*, the tribe imposed a tribal earnings tax on the earnings of any employee (both members and nonmembers) employed within tribal jurisdiction. The Supreme Court merely noted Oklahoma's contention that residents within Sac and Fox jurisdiction "are subject to both state and tribal taxes," leaving the implication that the tribal tax is valid as an exercise of the tribe's "right to self-governance."[22] The same principles are applicable to tribal regulations.

In *Montana v. United States*[23] the Supreme Court defined the inherent power of a tribe or Pueblo to regulate non-Indians within its Indian country jurisdiction and the limits of that power:

> A tribe may regulate, through taxation, licensing, or other means, the activities of nonmembers who enter consensual relationships with the tribe or its members, through commercial dealing, contracts, leases, or other arrangements.... A tribe may also retain inherent power to exercise civil authority over the conduct of non-Indians on fee lands [owned by nonmembers] within

---

17 *United States v. Wheeler*, 435 U.S. 313, 323 (1978); *Santa Clara Pueblo v. Martinez*, 436 U.S. 49, 55-66 (1978).

18 "Indian country" is defined for purposes of the federal Major Crimes Act at 18 U.S.C. § 1151. The Tenth Circuit recently held that the statutory definition also applies to questions of civil jurisdiction, *Texaco, Inc. v. Zah*, No. 92-2141, 1993 WL 379514 (10th Cir. Sept. 29, 1993).

19 113 S.Ct. 1985 (1993).

20 498 U.S. 505, 111 S. Ct. 905, 910 (1991) (quoting *United States v. John*, 437 U.S. 634, 648.49 (1978)).

21 Arguably, lands within a Pueblo's original grant that were confirmed to non-members by proceedings under the Pueblo Lands Act of 1924, 43 Stat. 636, remain Indian country "for tribal immunity purposes" under those cases.

22 113 S. Ct. at 1988.

23 450 U.S. 544, 564-65 (1981).

> its reservation when that conduct threatens or has some direct effect on the political integrity, the economic security, or the health or welfare of the tribe....

The Ninth Circuit Court of Appeals succinctly summarized tribal power over non-members:[24]

> The power to exercise tribal civil authority over non-Indians derives not only from the tribe's inherent powers necessary to self-government and territorial management, but also from the power to exclude nonmembers from tribal land. *See Merrion v. Jicarilla Apache Tribe*, 455 U.S. 130, 141-44 (1982). This "limited authority" over nonmembers "does not arise until the nonmember enters the tribal jurisdiction ... [by entering] tribal lands or [conducting] business with the tribe." *Id.* at 142. Nonmembers lawfully entering tribal lands -- for example, pursuant to contract with the tribe -- nonetheless remain "subject to the tribe's *power* to exclude them." *Id.* at 144 (emphasis in original). A tribe has the power "to place conditions on entry, on continued presence, or on reservation conduct ..., [and] nonmember[s] who [enter] the jurisdiction of the tribe [remain] subject to the risk that the tribe will later exercise [this] sovereign power." *Id.* at 144-45 (footnote omitted).
>
> ...
>
> Recent decisions ... have upheld the enforcement of tribal economic and health and welfare regulations against nonmembers present on the reservation or transacting business with the tribe. *See, e.g., Cardin v. De La Cruz*, 671 F.2d 363 (9th Cir.) (tribe retains inherent sovereign power to impose its health, building, and safety regulations on non-Indian's business, which is located on land that non-Indian owns in fee, but also is within reservation boundaries), *cert. denied,* 459 U.S. 967 (1982); *Confederated Salish and Kootenai Tribes v. Namen*, 665 F.2d 951 (9th Cir.) (court upheld tribe's right to regulate federal common-law riparian rights of non-Indians who owned reservation land to which the tribe had beneficial title), *cert. denied,* 459 U.S. 977 (1982); *Knight v. Shoshone & Arapahoe Indian Tribes*, 670 F.2d 900 (10th Cir. 1981) (court held as valid exercise of tribal power zoning regulation that affected fee lands owned by non-Indians located within reservation).
>
> Congress has acknowledged that such regulation is a necessary tool of self-government and control. *See, e.g., White Mountain Apache Tribe v. Bracker*, 448 U.S. 136, 149 (1980) (There is a "general federal policy of encouraging tribes 'to revitalize their self-government' and to assume control over their 'business and economic affairs'") (quoting *Mescalero Apache Tribe v. Jones*, 411 U.S. 145, 151 (1973)). As the Supreme Court noted, the Senate Judiciary Committee "as early as 1879" stated:
>
> > We have considered [Indian tribes] as invested with the right of self-government and jurisdiction over the persons and property within the limits of the territory they occupy, except so far

24 *Babbitt Ford, Inc. v. Navajo Indian Tribe*, 710 F.2d 587, 592-93 (9th Cir. 1983).

> as that jurisdiction has been restrained and abridged by treaty or act of Congress. Subject to the supervisory control of the Federal Government, *they may enact the requisite legislation to maintain peace and good order, improve their condition,* establish school systems, and aid their people in their efforts to acquire the arts of civilized life.

S. Rep. No. 698, 45th Cong., 3d Sess. 1-2 (1879) (emphasis added), *quoted in Merrion v. Jicarilla Apache Tribe*, 455 U.S. 130, 140 (1982).

2.3.1.1 Power To Control Nonmember Land Use

Tribal zoning regulation of nonmember-owned land within an Indian reservation was sustained by a divided Supreme Court[25] in a decision under the General Allotment Act,[26] which was held to terminate the power of the tribe to exclude nonmembers who owned lands allotted from the reservation.[27] The Court held that the inherent sovereignty of the tribe was divested by its dependent status with respect to such nonmembers unless their activities imperiled the tribe's "protectable interests" of political integrity, economic security, or health or welfare.[28] Among New Mexico tribes and Pueblos, only the Navajo Nation was affected

---

[25] *Brendale v. Confederated Tribes & Bands of Yakima Indian Nation*, 492 U.S. 408, 109 S. Ct. 2994 (1989). Six Justices rejected tribal zoning of nonmember-owned allotments in an "open" portion of the Reservation; five Justices sustained tribal zoning of similar land in the "closed" area of the Reservation. *California Coastal Comm'n v. Granite Rock Co.*, 480 U.S. 572, 587-89 (1987), noted that environmental regulation, which does not mandate particular uses of land, may be authorized even where land use regulation would be prohibited.

[26] 24 Stat. 388 (1887).

[27] Most Pueblos lost lands to non-Indians under the Pueblo Lands Act of 1924, 43 Stat. 636, but Congress has never acted to terminate or limit the governmental powers of the Pueblos, which was the "avowed purpose" of the Allotment Act. *Montana v. United States,* 450 U.S. at 559 n.9. Nevertheless, the power of a Pueblo government within its Indian country jurisdiction to control the activities of nonmember owners of "private claims" that were confirmed under the 1924 Act probably rests solely on its "inherent sovereignty" to protect its political integrity, economic security, or community health and welfare against nonmember activities that imperil those protectible interests and upon consensual agreements such as leases and contracts; the Pueblos' power to exclude non-Indian owners of confirmed private claims within their original grant boundaries was no doubt extinguished by the 1924 Act.

[28] *Brendale*, 109 S. Ct. at 3008. Justice White indicated that a "protectable interest" in an activity should be based on a showing that the activity's effect on the tribe is "demonstrably serious." *Id.* The EPA ruled that tribes seeking to administer the dredge and fill permit program under CWA § 404 should prove their regulatory jurisdiction over nonmembers by showing that the potential impacts of regulated activities on the tribe are serious and substantial. 58 Fed. Reg. 8172, 8174 (1993).

by the General Allotment Act;[29] nevertheless, the power of a New Mexico tribe or Pueblo to regulate environmentally significant activities by nonmembers is probably defined and limited by that decision and by the *Montana* case.[30]

2.3.1.2 Jurisdiction of Tribal Courts

The Supreme Court has long supported the civil jurisdiction of tribal courts as an essential power of tribal self-government.[31] The traditional jurisdiction of tribal courts is limited to tribal members. With respect to jurisdiction over nonmembers, a tribal court has authority to determine its jurisdiction.[32] If the tribal court exercises jurisdiction, the nonmember may challenge its assertion of jurisdiction in federal court after exhausting tribal remedies.[33]

---

29 The "checkerboard" area of the Eastern Navajo Agency, Crownpoint, N.M., was created by allotments of reservation lands. The Allotment Act did not apply to the Pueblos' "grants" from the Spanish king that were confirmed by Congress in 1858, 11 Stat. 374, and for the most part patented by President Lincoln in 1864. Some Pueblos have reservation lands in addition to grants; such lands were not allotted, nor were lands of the Ute and Apache Reservations.

30 In addition to inherent sovereignty to protect protectible tribal interests, the *Brendale* opinion confirmed tribal power to regulate, through taxation, licensing, or other means, the activities of nonmembers based upon consensual relationships, such as commercial dealings, contracts, leases, or other arrangements, even where tribal regulation arguably extended beyond the zone of protectible tribal interests. *Brendale*, 109 S. Ct. at 3007.

31 *Williams v. Lee*, 358 U.S. 217 (1959); *Fisher v. District Court*, 424 U.S. 382, 388-89 (1976).

32 *National Farmers Union Ins. Cos. v. Crow Tribe*, 471 U.S. 845, 856-57 (1985); *Iowa Mut. Ins. Co. v. LaPlante*, 480 U.S. 9, 15 (1987). In *National Farmers Union*, the Supreme Court characterized the tribal court's jurisdictional inquiry as "a careful examination of tribal sovereignty, the extent to which the sovereignty has been altered, divested, or diminished, as well as a detailed study of relevant statutes, Executive Branch policy as embodied in treaties and elsewhere, and administrative or judicial decisions." 471 U.S. at 855-56. Exhaustion of tribal remedies is not required for cases that do not have an Indian party, arose off the reservation, or do not otherwise concern reservation affairs. *Stock West Corp. v. Taylor*, 942 F.2d 655, 660, 663 n.7 (9th Cir. 1991), *reh'g, en banc, granted*, 956 F.2d 207 (1992). The Tenth Circuit recently ruled that the exhaustion rule applies where the case challenged tribal taxes applicable to non-Indian activities in Navajo Indian county, although beyond reservation boundaries and not on trust lands. *Texaco, Inc. v. Zah*, No. 92-2141, 1993 WL 379514 (10th Cir. Sept. 29, 1993).

33 *National Farmers Union* unanimously held that whether an Indian tribe retains the power to compel a non-Indian to submit to the civil jurisdiction of a tribal court constitutes a federal question under 28 U.S.C. § 1331. 471 U.S. at 857. *Iowa Mutual* held that exhaustion of tribal remedies is a rule of comity between federal and tribal courts, not a question of subject matter jurisdiction. But federal abstention will hold

If the tribal court determines that it lacks jurisdiction, a federal court may have diversity jurisdiction to hear the case, but if the tribe itself is a party, diversity may not exist under the stateless-person cases,[34] and if the suit is against a tribe or a tribal enterprise, the court may reject diversity jurisdiction as an impermissible interference with tribal self-government.[35] Federal question jurisdiction is not created merely because a party is an Indian or the subject matter touches Indian property or contracts.[36] A state court will not have jurisdiction of a suit against an Indian or a tribe because the exercise of state judicial power would interfere with tribal sovereignty and self-government.[37]

2.3.1.3 Tribal Sovereign Immunity

As a limited or dependent sovereign, an Indian tribe or Pueblo cannot be sued without its consent.[38] Congress may in unequivocal terms waive the immunity of a tribe, and the tribe itself may waive its immunity or the immunity of a tribal business enterprise by express and unequivocal language.[39] An effective waiver of immunity cannot be implied,[40] but an

---

until appellate tribal courts have completed their review of the case. 480 U.S. at 19; *Burlington N.R.R. v. Crow Tribal Council*, 940 F.2d 1239, 1245 (9th Cir. 1991).

34 *See Standing Rock Sioux Indian Tribe v. Dorgan*, 505 F.2d 1135, 1140 (8th Cir. 1974) ("An Indian tribe is not a citizen of any state and cannot sue or be sued in federal court under diversity jurisdiction.").

35 *Williams v. Lee*, 358 U.S. 217 (1959); Fisher v. District Court, 424 U.S. 382, 388-89 (1976).

36 *Martinez v. Southern Ute Tribe*, 249 F.2d 915, 917 (10th Cir. 1957), *cert. denied*, 356 U.S. 960 (1958).

37 *Three Affiliated Tribes v. Wold Eng'g, P.C.*, 467 U.S. 138 (1984); *Fisher v. District Court*, 424 U.S. 382, 388-89 (1976); *Williams v. Lee*, 358 U.S. 217 (1959).

38 *Santa Clara Pueblo v. Martinez*, 436 U.S. 49, 58-60 (1978); *United States v. United States Fidelity & Guar. Co.*, 309 U.S. 506 (1940); *Thebo v. Choctaw Tribe*, 66 F. 372 (8th Cir. 1895).

39 *Merrion v. Jicarilla Apache Tribe*, 617 F.2d 537, 540 (10th Cir. 1980) (tribe adopted a constitution pursuant to the IRA and Secretary approved ordinance waiving immunity in suit to test validity of tribal tax), *aff'd*, 455 U.S. 130 (1982); *Weeks Constr., Inc. v. Oglala Sioux Housing Auth.*, 797 F.2d 668, 671-73 (8th Cir. 1986) (suit against tribal housing enterprise dismissed for lack of federal question jurisdiction, despite effective waiver of enterprise's immunity and refusal of diversity jurisdiction, where federal court "would infringe on the tribe's right of self-government"); *Namekagon Dev. Co. v. Bois Forte Reservation Housing Auth.*, 517 F.2d 508 (8th Cir. 1975).

40 *Ramey Constr. Co. v. Apache Tribe*, 673 F.2d 315 (10th Cir. 1982); *American Indian Agricultural Credit Consortium, Inc. v. Standing Rock Sioux Tribe*, 780 F.2d 1374 (8th Cir. 1985) (waiver cannot be implied from resolution authorizing $80,000 tribal loan and promissory note alluding to "rights and remedies provided by law" in the event of default).

agreement to submit disputes under a tribal agreement to a federal district court[41] or to arbitration[42] may constitute an effective waiver. The scope of a waiver will be strictly construed.[43]

2.3.2 Federal

Federal statutes that by their terms are applicable to Indian tribes and Pueblos, or to their lands, are effective within the jurisdiction of the tribe or Pueblo, and tribal sovereign immunity is not available as a defense to the tribal government.[44] The following federal environmental laws are applicable to Indian lands, and the first four expressly permit EPA to treat tribal governments in the same fashion as states: (1) Clean Air Act (CAA),[45] (2) Clean Water Act (CWA),[46] (3) Safe Drinking Water Act (SDWA),[47] (4) Comprehensive Environmental Response, Compensation and Liability Act (CERCLA),[48] (5) Resource Conservation and Recovery Act (RCRA),[49] (6) Toxic Substances Control Act (TSCA),[50] (7) Federal Insecticide, Fungicide, and Rodenticide Act (FIFRA),[51] and (8) Surface Mining Control and Reclamation Act (SMCRA).[52] TAS status was intended to cover the absence of state regulatory jurisdiction over tribal lands.

EPA's designation of Indian tribes as states has been spelled out in greatest detail in CWA Section 518 of the CWA. In Section 518 of the CWA, Congress provided that Indian

---

41 *United States v. Oregon*, 657 F.2d 1009, 1014-16 (9th Cir. 1981).

42 *Native Village of Eyak v. GC Contractors*, 658 P.2d 756, 760-61 (Alaska 1983); *Val/Del, Inc. v. Superior Court*, 703 P.2d 502, 508-09 (Ariz. Ct. App.), *cert. denied*, 474 U.S. 920 (1985).

43 *Twin Cities Chippewa Tribal Council v. Minnesota Chippewa Tribe*, 370 F.2d 529 (8th Cir. 1967).

44 *Santa Clara Pueblo v. Martinez*, 436 U.S. 49, 55-57 (1978); *United States v. United States Fidelity & Guar. Co.*, 309 U.S. 506, 512-13 (1940); *Blue Legs v. BIA*, 867 F.2d 1094 (8th Cir. 1989); *Iron Crow v. Oglala Sioux Tribe*, 231 F.2d 89, 94 (8th Cir. 1956).

45 42 U.S.C. §§ 7401-7642; *See Id.* § 7601(d).

46 33 U.S.C. §§ 1251-1387; *See Id.* § 1377(e).

47 42 U.S.C. §§ 201, 300f to 300j-26; See Id. § 300j-11.

48 42 U.S.C. §§ 9601-9675; *See Id.* § 9626 (a).

49 42 U.S.C. §§ 6901-6992k. Under the RCRA, tribes are currently defined as municipalities. 42 U.S.C. § 6903(13).

50 15 U.S.C. §§ 2601-2692.

51 7 U.S.C. §§ 136-136y.

52 30 U.S.C. §§ 1201-1328; *See Id.* § 1291(9). *Valencia Energy Co.*, 109 I.B.L.A. 40, 16 Indian L. Rep. (Am. Indian Law. Training Program) 7062 (1989); *Montana v. Clark*, 749 F.2d 740 (D.C. Cir. 1984), *cert. denied*, 474 U.S. 919 (1985); *In re Surface Mining Regulation Litig.*, 627 F.2d 1346, 1363-65 (D.C. Cir. 1980);

tribes meeting minimum criteria of governmental competence shall be treated as states for purposes of specific sections of the CWA and directed EPA to issue regulations specifying how that mandate will be carried out.[53] In a long preamble to its 1993 amendments to the regulations under Section 404 of the CWA, EPA determined that Section 518 did not delegate federal regulatory power to qualified tribes and that a tribe could exercise Section 404 regulatory authority only under its inherent powers to safeguard its protectible interests in water resources within the borders of its reservation or broader Indian country jurisdiction.[54] None of the tribes and pueblos in New Mexico has been accorded TAS status for purposes of Sections 309 (enforcement), 319 (nonpoint source management), 401 (state certification), 402 (NPDES discharge permits), or 404 (dredge and fill permits).

A tribe or pueblo treated as a state for purposes of adopting water quality standards under Section 303 cannot enforce them under its inherent governmental powers against point sources of pollution outside its Indian country jurisdiction.[55] However, if the tribe is treated as a state for purposes of state certification of NPDES permits under § 401, its water quality standards approved by EPA must be included as an additional condition of the permit.[56] Where conflicting tribal and state water quality standards are applicable to common waters, it remains unclear how EPA will achieve § 518's direction to provide a mechanism for the resolution or avoidance of any unreasonable consequences of such conflict.[57]

---

53 33 U.S.C. § 1377(e). Treatment as a state ("TAS") pursuant to CWA § 518 typically makes the tribe eligible for grants, e.g., § 106 (pollution control studies), § 314 (clean lakes), § 319 (source pollution studies), and § 303 (water quality standards). Isleta, Sandia, and San Juan Pueblos have received TAS status for purposes of CWA §§ 106 and 303; Acoma Pueblo has TAS status for § 314; and Tesuque, Pojoaque, Nambe, San Ildefonso, Santa Clara, Picuris, and Taos Pueblos have TAS status for § 106. Isleta and Sandia Pueblos have adopted water quality standards; Taos and other Pueblos have prepared such standards for adoption by their tribal councils.

54 58 Fed. Reg. 8172-84, (1993), amending 40 C.F.R. Parts 232-233.

55 The Pueblos of Isleta, Sandia, and San Juan have received § 303 TAS, but their water quality standards have no enforcement provisions. They have not received TAS status for purposes of § 401.

56 40 C.F.R. § 122.44(d)(1).

57 The City of Albuquerque has sued in federal court seeking judicial review of EPA's approval of Isleta Pueblo's water quality standards that (following an EPA model) applied drinking water criteria to the silt-laden Rio Grande into which the City's waste water system is discharged. *City of Albuquerque v. Reilly*, No. CV-93-82 (D.N.M. filed Jan. 25, 1993). The suit asks the court to protect the City from the "unreasonable consequences" of the Pueblo's stringent water quality standards. The District Court initially rejected the City's challenge. *See* C. McCutcheon, *Judge Backs EPA on Isleta Water*, Albuquerque Journal, Oct. 22, 1993, at 1.

2.3.3 State

New Mexico may not regulate tribal land[58] or the activities of tribal members thereon.[59] New Mexico did not, before 1968, acquire jurisdiction over Indian lands under Pub. L. 280,[60] and its governmental power with respect to nonmembers' activities on Indian land is limited by two principles:[61] (1) a state may not act in a manner that "infringes on the right of reservation Indians to make their own laws and be ruled by them,"[62] and (2) state authority may be asserted only if not preempted by the operation of federal law.[63] Pre-

---

58 *Your Food Stores, Inc. v. Village of Espanola*, 68 N.M. 327, 361 P.2d 950 (1961) (village could not annex portion of Santa Clara Grant leased by Pueblo to non-Indian corporation and could not collect municipal gross receipts tax from such corporation), *cert. denied*, 368 U.S. 915 (1961). The Court cited Section 2 of the New Mexico Enabling Act, 36 Stat. 557, Ch. 310 (1910), requiring the state Constitution to disclaim jurisdiction over all tribal and Pueblo lands, N.M. Const. art. XXI, § 2, and the "broad principles" of *Worcester v. Georgia*, 31 U.S. (6 Pet.) 515, 561 (1832), but the Court recognized that later decisions of the United States Supreme Court might affect the scope of federal preemption. Under *Oklahoma Tax Commission v. Sac & Fox Nation*, 113 S.Ct. 1985 (1993), the state's gross receipts tax could be collected from the Pueblo's non-Indian lessee. *Rice v. Rehner*, 463 U.S. 713 (1983), recognized that 18 U.S.C. § 1161 conferred concurrent state and tribal jurisdiction over the regulation and licensing of liquor sales on Indian lands. *See Citizen Band of Potawatomi Indian Tribe v. Oklahoma Tax Comm'n*, 975 F.2d 1459 (10th Cir. 1992). The concurrent jurisdiction rule is limited to alcoholic beverages.

59 *Toledo v. Pueblo de Jemez*, 119 F. Supp. 429 (D.N.M. 1954); *State v. Begay*, 320 P.2d 1017 (N.M. 1956), *cert. denied*, 357 U.S. 918 (1958). *Moe v. Confederated Salish & Kootenai Tribes*, 425 U.S. 463 (1976), required Indian vendors of cigarettes on the reservation to collect and pay over the state excise tax on purchases by non-Indians, stressing that the collection duty was not a tax on the reservation sale.

60 Act of Aug. 15, 1953, 67 Stat. 589 (1953), 28 U.S.C. § 1360. Section 6 of the Act consented to amendment of state constitutions to delete the disclaimer of state jurisdiction over Indian land. 12 U.S.C. § 1360 note. *See Washington v. Confederated Bands & Tribes of Yakima Indian Nation*, 439 U.S. 463 (1979); *Bryan v. Itasca County*, 426 U.S. 373 (1976). Section 7 of the Act, which allowed states to acquire jurisdiction over Indians and Indian lands, was repealed by the Indian Civil Rights Act of 1968, 25 U.S.C. § 1324(b); present law requires tribal consent to any extension of state jurisdiction, *id.* §§ 1322(a), 1326. *See Kennerly v. District Court*, 400 U.S. 423 (1971).

61 *New Mexico v. Mescalero Apache Tribe*, 462 U.S. 324, 330-36 (1983).

62 *McClanahan v. Arizona State Tax Comm'n*, 411 U.S. 164, 171-72 (1973) (quoting *Williams v. Lee*, 338 U.S. at 219-20). *White Mountain Apache Tribe v. Bracker*, 448 U.S. 136, 142 (1980), recognized that this principle prohibits concurrent state and tribal jurisdiction on any matter within the inherent sovereignty of the tribe or Pueblo. *See* Sections 2.3.1 and 2.3.1.1 of this Chapter.

63 *New Mexico v. Mescalero Apache Tribe*, 462 U.S. at 333. The Court noted that the broad pre-emption analysis would bar any state interest that would interfere or be incompatible with federal or tribal interests "reflected in federal law," at 334, and that

emption typically relies on the status of the land involved in the activity.[64] In *Oklahoma Tax Commission v. Sac & Fox Nation*,[65] the Supreme Court followed the "per se" pre-emption rule for state (and local) taxation of tribes, their members, and their enterprises: "Absent explicit congressional direction to the contrary, we presume against a State's having jurisdiction to tax within Indian country...." If Congress has not expressly granted permission to tax, state or local taxation in Indian country is forbidden.[66] Accordingly, the Oklahoma income tax could not be imposed on tribal members who work or reside within the Indian country jurisdiction of the tribe; nor could Oklahoma impose its motor vehicle excise tax and registration fees on tribal members who live and garage their cars on tribal land and register their cars with the tribe.

The per se pre-emption rule is applicable only to taxes on tribes, tribal members, and tribal enterprises. The *Sac & Fox* decision implicitly approved the Tenth Circuit's opinion[67] that income of non-members who reside or work in Indian country is not immune from state and local taxation.[68] Under those decisions only tribal members (members of the tribe for which the land was reserved or held in trust) who reside in Indian country as defined in the *Potawatomi* decision, are exempt from state and local taxes. But *Sac & Fox* left undecided the question whether "the Tribe's right to self-governance could operate independently of its

---

a state's regulatory interest should focus on "off-reservation effects," *id.* at 336.

64 *Wauneka v. Campbell*, 526 P.2d 1085 (Ariz. Ct. App. 1974) (Arizona auto licensing laws); *Bryan v. Itasca County*, 426 U.S. 373 (1976) (personal property tax on property on trust land); *Chase v. McMasters*, 573 F.2d 1011 (8th Cir. 1978) (municipal utility fees), *cert. denied*, 439 U.S. 965 (1978); *White Mountain Apache Tribe v. Bracker*, 448 U.S. 136 (1980) (Arizona motor carrier license and fuel taxes inapplicable to non-Indian logging company); *City of Sault Ste. Marie v. Andrus*, 532 F.Supp. 157 (D.D.C. 1980) (land use regulations); *New Mexico v. Mescalero Apache Tribe*, 462 U.S. 324 (1983) (New Mexico hunting/fishing laws); *United States v. Harvey*, 701 F.2d 800 (9th Cir. 1983) (Montana traffic safety laws); *Zachary v. Wilk*, 219 Cal. Rptr. 122 (Ct. App. 1985) (municipal rent control ordinance inapplicable to non-Indian lessee of tribal land), *cert. denied*, 479 U.S. 818 (1986); *California v. Cabazon Band of Mission Indians*, 480 U.S. 202 (1987) (California gambling laws inapplicable to tribal bingo).

65 U.S. 113 S. Ct. 1985, 1993 (1993).

66 In two notable cases, the Supreme Court sustained state taxation of tribal natural resources. In *Montana v. Blackfeet Tribe*, 471 U.S. 759 (1985), state taxation of tribal royalties from mineral leases under a 1924 statute was sustained because Congress had specifically authorized the tax; however, tribal royalties under leases not made pursuant to the 1924 statute were not subject to the tax. *Cotton Petroleum Corp. v. New Mexico*, 490 U.S. 163 (1989), sustained the applicability of New Mexico production taxes to oil and gas production on Jicarilla leases; the Jicarilla Apache Tribe was not a party in the litigation and presumably did not object to the state taxes.

67 967 F.2d 1425, 1429-30 (10th Cir. 1992).

68 113 S. Ct. at 1988.

territorial jurisdiction to pre-empt the State's ability to tax income earned from work performed for the Tribe itself when the employee does not reside in Indian country."[69]

2.3.4 Jurisdiction of New Mexico Courts

The extent to which a New Mexico court has jurisdiction to consider suits involving individual Indians or Indian tribes is governed by the principles of tribal authority and non-interference first stated in a case involving suit in an Arizona court by an Indian trader against his customer to collect the balance of the customer's account.[70] Although Justice Rehnquist in a later dissent interpreted the principles of tribal autonomy to preclude state court jurisdiction of suits either by or against Indians in actions arising on Indian lands,[71] the Court held that the non-interference principle applies only in a suit against a tribe or against a tribal member on a cause of action arising on the reservation.[72] Thus, under present rulings, a New Mexico court has subject matter jurisdiction over any cause of action arising outside tribal lands, regardless of the parties, and over causes arising on tribal lands, only where the Indian parties are plaintiff or both parties are non-Indian.

2.4 CRIMINAL

2.4.1 Tribal

An Indian tribe or Pueblo has criminal jurisdiction over its members,[73] but it has no criminal jurisdiction over nonmembers.[74] The Supreme Court has drawn a distinction between a tribe's adjudicatory power and its prosecuting power, which "involves a far more

---

69 113 S. Ct. at 1992. The reserved question implicates the Court's decisions in *Montana v. United States*, 450 U.S. at 564-66, and *Brendale v. Confederated Tribes & Bands Yakima Indian Nation*, 109 S. Ct. at 3005-06 which recognized that an Indian tribe has "inherent power" to regulate activities of non-Indians present on its lands "when [their] conduct threatens or has some direct effect on the political integrity, the economic security, or the health or welfare of the tribe." 450 U.S. at 566. A state may not exercise authority over non-Indians in Indian country if the "protectible interests" of a tribe or Pueblo would be impaired by the state action. However, *County of Yakima v. Confederated Tribes & Bands of Yakima Indian Nation*, 112 S. Ct. 683, 692-93 (1992), held that the "protectible interests" analysis is not applicable in determining whether a state tax on Indian land has been authorized by Congress.

70 *Williams v. Lee*, 358 U.S. 217 (1959).

71 *Three Affiliated Tribes*, 467 U.S. at 164 (Rehnquist, J., dissenting).

72 *Id.* at 148. The Court noted that the tribal court lacked jurisdiction over the tribe's claim at the time the suit was instituted, *id.* at 149, but there was no indication that absence of tribal court jurisdiction was a prerequisite to state jurisdiction.

73 *United States v. Wheeler*, 435 U.S. 313 (1978). The Indian Civil Rights Act, 25 U.S.C. § 1302(7), prohibits any criminal fine on tribal members in excess of $5,000.

74 *Oliphant v. Suquamish Indian Tribe*, 435 U.S. 191 (1978); *Duro v. Reina*, 459 U.S. 676, 110 S. Ct. 2053 (1990).

direct intrusion on personal liberties."[75] A criminal prosecution of a nonmember would be a "manifestation of external relations between the Tribe and outsiders [that is] inconsistent with the tribe's dependent status, and could only have come to the Tribe by delegation from Congress, subject to the constraints of the Constitution."[76] However, the Court left open for later consideration a "formal acquiescence to tribal [criminal] jurisdiction that might be made, for example, in return for a tribe's agreement not to exercise its power to exclude an offender from tribal lands."[77] Where a tribe's jurisdiction over a non-Indian also rests on a consensual relationship, as in a contract or lease of tribal land, acceptance of tribal environmental regulations by the non-Indian party, including acceptance of criminal penalties that might follow a tribal prosecution for a violation in tribal court, would presumably validate the tribe's criminal process, particularly if the stated consideration was tribal forbearance in the exercise of its inherent power to exclude the non-Indian from tribal land.

2.4.2 Federal

The United States as early as 1790 assumed jurisdiction over crimes in "Indian country"[78] by non-Indians against Indians,[79] and that jurisdiction was made exclusive in 1817.[80] Crimes involving only Indians remained exclusively tribal until passage of the Major Crimes Act in 1885,[81] and crimes not included therein remain exclusively tribal.

2.4.3 State

Apart from Pub.L. 280, Congress has not given states any criminal jurisdiction in Indian country.[82] Because tribal criminal jurisdiction is limited to tribal members, there may be a jurisdictional void if nonmember Indians are involved in a violation.[83]

---

75 *Duro*, 110 S. Ct. at 2061.

76 *Id.* at 2060. The EPA has ruled that TAS status under Section 518 of the CWA does not delegate federal powers to the tribe granted such status. 58 Fed. Reg. 8172, 8176 (1993).

77 *Duro* 110 S. Ct. at 2061-62.

78 18 U.S.C. § 1151.

79 Trade and Intercourse Act, 1 Stat. 138, ch. 33 (1790). *Duro*, 110 S. Ct. at 2068.

80 18 U.S.C. § 1152.

81 18 U.S.C. § 1153. Federal jurisdiction attaches only to enumerated crimes involving two Indians, who need not be members of the same tribe. *Duro*, 110 S. Ct. at 2069 (Brennan, J., dissenting).

82 *See Worcester v. Georgia*, 31 U.S. (6 Pet.) 515 (1832).

83 *Duro*, 110 S. Ct. at 2066 (Brennan, J., dissenting). The EPA has recognized that TAS status under 518 can be conferred on a tribe for such regulatory purposes as Section 404 despite the absence of tribal criminal jurisdiction over non-members. Where necessary, the tribe would refer a Section 404 violation to EPA or to the Army Corps of Engineers. 58 Fed. Reg. 8172, 8180 (1993).

3.0 TRIBAL ENVIRONMENTAL CODES

3.1 NAVAJO NATION

The Navajo Nation is working with EPA to develop their own regulatory agencies and to comply with EPA regulations. The Navajo Nation has established an Environmental Protection Administration which includes the following programs: Air Quality, Pollution Prevention, Asbestos, Pesticides Enforcement, Public Water Systems, Ground Water and Nonpoint Source Pollution Control, Hazardous Waste Management pursuant to RCRA, Wetlands Management, Underground Storage Tank Management, Radon Pilot Project, Solid Waste Management and Integrated Waste Management. Many of these Programs have draft environmental codes and regulations including a Trespass Code for illegal dumping of waste, a Land Use Code, a Minerals Code, and a Forestry Code.

In addition, the Navajo Nation has established a Superfund Program pursuant to a Superfund Memorandum of Agreement between the Navajo Nation and EPA. This Superfund Program is a commenting agency for two Superfund sites on Navajo land and is working on developing a Superfund code and regulations.

3.1.1 Pesticide Code

The Navajo Nation enacted its Pesticide Code in 1986.[84] The Navajo Nation will recognize the EPA classification of pesticides for general or restricted use,[85] and the Resources Committee of the Navajo Nation Council may restrict the use of additional pesticides to protect vegetation, animals, or people.[86] The Director of the Division of Natural Resources or his designee is the Administrator[87] of the Code, who issues tribal licenses to "applicators"[88] classed as public, commercial, or private, and to "pesticide dealers,"[89] who distribute restricted pesticides on the Navajo Reservation. Tribal licensing relies upon state licenses in New Mexico, Arizona, or Utah; without a state license, an applicant must meet the competency standards of the Code.[90] The Code prohibits use of pesticides contrary to label instructions, other unauthorized uses, furnishing pesticides to persons not authorized to use them, false statements in a license application, false records, misuse and improper disposition of pesticide containers, and refusal to permit inspection of areas affected by pesticides.[91]

---

84 Navajo Nation Council Resolution CJY-46-86, July 17, 1986, as amended by Council Resolution CMY-28-90, May 3, 1990.

85 Navajo Nation Pesticide Code § III.

86 *Id.*

87 Navajo Nation Pesticide Code § I(A).

88 Navajo Nation Pesticide Code § I(B).

89 Navajo Nation Pesticide Code § I(M) (amendment May 3, 1990).

90 Navajo Nation Pesticide Code §§ VII - VIII.

91 Navajo Nation Pesticide Code § XV.

Penalties are both criminal and civil, and any person not subject to criminal prosecution is subject to exclusion from the reservation.[92] The Administrator may bring a suit in tribal court for damages to tribal land, costs incurred in enforcement of the Code, and expenses of the suit.[93] The power, under federal law, of the tribal court may be challenged, after exhaustion of all tribal remedies, in an independent action in federal district court.[94]

3.1.2 Solid Waste Code

The Navajo Nation enacted its Solid Waste Code in 1990.[95] The Solid Waste Code was adopted in the exercise of the Navajo Nation's "inherent powers of self-government,"[96] perhaps implying that the Code does not also rest upon the Nation's power to exclude offenders from the reservation. However, if a person is not subject to criminal prosecution, he or she is subject to exclusion.[97]

The Code declares use of any land to dispose of solid waste unlawful unless Code requirements have been satisfied.[98] Responsibility for compliance is placed on past as well as present owners and occupiers of land.[99] Operators of solid waste disposal areas must submit a Solid Waste Management Plan for approval[100] and pay a fee.[101] Thereafter, all solid waste must be stored, transported, and disposed of in accordance with the approved plan.[102] The Administrator is the Executive Director of the Division of Natural Resources.[103] A three-member commission is established to hear appeals from decisions of the Administrator.[104] Penalties are both criminal and civil;[105] repeat violations are subject to greater penalties,[106] and the Administrator may impose additional penalties not explicitly

---

92 Navajo Nation Pesticide Code § XVI(C).

93 Navajo Nation Pesticide Code § XVI(D).

94 *See* Section 2.3.1.2. of this Chapter.

95 Navajo Nation Council Resolution CO-58-90, Oct. 18, 1990.

96 Navajo Nation Solid Waste Code § 101.

97 Navajo Nation Solid Waste Code § 1004(b)(i).

98 Navajo Nation Solid Waste Code § 102.

99 Navajo Nation Solid Waste Code §§ 103, 501.

100 Navajo Nation Solid Waste Code §§ 601-602.

101 Navajo Nation Solid Waste Code § 607 imposes a fee of $200 per year.

102 Navajo Nation Solid Waste Code § 701.

103 Navajo Nation Solid Waste Code § 201(A).

104 Navajo Nation Solid Waste Code § 901(a). Before the Commission is in operation, appeals may be taken to the Resources Committee of the Navajo Nation Council. *Id.* § 901(f).

105 Navajo Nation Solid Waste Code § 1004.

106 Navajo Nation Solid Waste Code § 1004(a)(iii).

authorized.[107] The Administrator may bring suit in tribal court for damages to tribal land, costs of enforcement, and the expenses of suit[108] and may seek a tribal court injunction to prevent immediate and irreparable injury.[109]

3.1.3 Water Code

The Navajo Nation also has a Water Code, which is incorporated into the Navajo Nation Code as Title II, Chapter 7. The Water Code, which was last amended in 1984, is in the process of being revised as of October 1993.

3.2 JICARILLA APACHE

3.2.1 Environmental Protection

Title 14, Jicarilla Apache Tribal Code, effective April 13, 1984, entitled "Environmental Protection," is intended to obtain for the benefit of the tribal government, particularly for the Tribal Council, factual information regarding the expected environmental consequences of proposed tribal action. Title 14 incorporates[110] the National Environmental Policy Act (NEPA),[111] regulations of the Council on Environmental Quality (CEQ),[112] the Environmental Quality Handbook,[113] the National Historic Preservation Act (NHPA)[114] and regulations thereunder,[115] and the Archeological and Historic Preservation Act.[116] Copies of all draft environmental assessments (EA) and draft environmental impact statements (EIS) prepared under applicable federal law must be furnished to the tribe,[117] and the responsible federal agency is requested to designate the tribe as a cooperating agency.[118]

---

107 Navajo Nation Solid Waste Code § 1004(b)(v).

108 Navajo Nation Solid Waste Code § 1004(d)(iii).

109 Navajo Nation Solid Waste Code § 1004(d)(iv). An independent action may be filed in the United States District Court under the *National Farmers Union* decision. *See* Section 2.3.1.2. of this Chapter.

110 Jicarilla Apache Tribal Code § 14-6-3 (1987).

111 42 U.S.C. §§ 4321-4370c.

112 40 C.F.R. Part 1508.

113 30 BIAM Supp. 1, Release 1 (2/22/82).

114 16 U.S.C. §§ 470 to 470w-6.

115 36 C.F.R. Parts 60, 63.

116 16 U.S.C. §§ 469 to 469c-1.

117 Jicarilla Apache Tribal Code § 14-6-3 (1987).

118 Jicarilla Apache Tribal Code § 14-6-2 (1987).

Unlike the federal process, the tribal law applies to any "development plan or activity" and is not limited to major tribal action,[119] but the activity must significantly affect the environment of the reservation,[120] and the Tribal Council may decide on the basis of a preliminary outline of the environmental consequences of proposed non-oil/gas action[121] whether to require a full environmental statement.[122] If required, the statement must cover a very broad "inventory" of information, including plants, animals, water, air, radiation, particulates, soils, historic and cultural properties, aesthetics, climate, and present land uses,[123] and must describe probable effects on present and future social, political, economic, and cultural structures, land and water uses, and the resources of the area, indicating long- and short-term depletion, restoration, and regional effects.[124] Possibly detrimental effects must be described, including hazardous materials; airborne emissions, effluents, solid waste, and noise emissions during both construction and operation; and other uncontrolled emissions and discharges.[125] Alternatives must be evaluated, all benefits and detriments considered, and all irretrievable, irreversible, and unavoidable commitments of tribal resources identified.[126]

Any oil and gas proposal must be described in a "plan of development" that shows the location of all wells, roads, pipelines, and excavations involved and proposes coordinated development with adjacent areas to minimize impacts.[127] The approved plan becomes a provision of the tribal lease or contract, and the tribe issues a Tribal Environmental Permit subject to enforcement provisions.[128]

Existing operations must be licensed,[129] and the Business or Operator's Permit may, presumably, include conditions and mitigation measures[130] subject to tribal enforcement.

A violation can be dealt with in several ways. A notice of non-compliance identifying the violation, corrective action required, and time limits for compliance is the first step.[131]

---

119 Jicarilla Apache Tribal Code §§ 14-1-1, 14-5-1 (non-oil/gas operations), 14-6-2 (1987).

120 *Id.*

121 Jicarilla Apache Tribal Code § 14-5-2 (1987).

122 *Id.*

123 Jicarilla Apache Tribal Code § 14-5-3(B) (1987).

124 Jicarilla Apache Tribal Code § 14-5-3(C) (1987).

125 Jicarilla Apache Tribal Code § 14-5-3(D) (1987).

126 Jicarilla Apache Tribal Code § 14-5-3(E) (1987).

127 Jicarilla Apache Tribal Code § 14-6-4(A) (1987).

128 Jicarilla Apache Tribal Code § 14-6-4(D) (1987).

129 Jicarilla Apache Tribal Code § 14-1-5 (1987).

130 *See* Jicarilla Apache Tribal Code § 14-6-4(D) (1987).

131 Jicarilla Apache Tribal Code § 14-2-1 (1987).

If the violation has not ceased after five days, the tribal officer designated by the Council to be responsible for enforcement of the Title may, without further notice, order cessation of the violation, impound vehicles and equipment, and restrict access to the area or site.[132] The order must include a statement of reasons for the order and actions to be taken before the order will be lifted.[133] The order must be furnished to the President of the Jicarilla Apache Tribe and the Superintendent of the Jicarilla Agency of the Bureau of Indian Affairs (BIA) at Dulce, New Mexico.[134] Cooperative enforcement by BIA and Bureau of Land Management (BLM) officials under federal laws or regulations which do not interfere with action being taken by the tribe is authorized and encouraged.[135]

If a violation persists, the tribe may ask the Secretary of the Interior to begin the process of canceling a lease or mineral agreement and to assess penalties authorized by federal regulations, and it may impose civil penalties under the Title and take any other action deemed appropriate.[136] A civil penalty of up to $5,000 per day may be imposed by a notice of assessment, and the penalty is payable within 20 days after such notice.[137] Failure to pay constitutes an additional violation.[138]

An appeal may be taken to the Jicarilla Tribal Council, but an appeal does not stay any orders or penalties unless a stay shall be granted by the Council.[139] The Council may allow such evidence and argument in appeals as it deems appropriate,[140] and it may affirm, reverse, or modify any earlier tribal orders[141] and may rebate penalties paid.[142] The Council's decision is final, but the tribe's power to impose any sanction may be a federal question on which a nonmember could appeal to the United States District Court.[143]

3.2.2 Weed Control and Pesticide Regulation and Enforcement Ordinance

In 1991 the Jicarilla Apache Tribal Council enacted the Weed Control and Pesticide Regulation and Enforcement Ordinance which was incorporated into the Jicarilla Apache

---

132 Jicarilla Apache Tribal Code § 14-2-2 (1987).

133 *Id.*

134 *Id.*

135 Jicarilla Apache Tribal Code § 14-2-3 (1987).

136 Jicarilla Apache Tribal Code § 14-3-1 (1987).

137 Jicarilla Apache Tribal Code § 14-3-2 (1987).

138 *Id.*

139 Jicarilla Apache Tribal Code § 14-7-1 (1987).

140 Jicarilla Apache Tribal Code § 14-7-1(C) (1987).

141 Jicarilla Apache Tribal Code § 14-7-1(B) (1987).

142 Jicarilla Apache Tribal Code § 14-7-1(A) (1987).

143 *National Farmers Union Ins. Co. v. Crow Tribe*, 471 U.S. 845 (1985); *see* Section 2.3.1.2 of this Chapter.

Tribal Code, Title 14 - Environmental Protection.[144] This Ordinance establishes, within the Tribal Environmental Office, a Pesticide Control Office[145] and an Interdisciplinary Review Team.[146] The Tribe has incorporated in the Ordinance[147] any EPA and federal Occupational Safety and Health Administration (OSHA) pesticide regulations, the FIFRA, and the New Mexico Pesticide Control Act (PCA), as amended, and authorized the Pesticide Control Office to promulgate tribal regulations,[148] which may be "stricter" than the comparable federal and state provisions.[149]

All pesticide applicators are required to hold an applicator's license from EPA or NMED[150] and to register with the Pesticide Control Office.[151] Before using a pesticide on Jicarilla Reservation land, a pesticide use proposal must be submitted to the Pesticide Control Office and the Interdisciplinary Review Team.[152] The proposal must include information regarding the pesticide, the target pests and weeds, the place of application, descriptions of pesticides previously used at such location, identification of sensitive areas near the site, an "environmental assessment or environmental impact statement" identifying people, plants, and animals that may have contact with the pesticide, the possible movement of the pesticide, and whether the pesticide will break down in any "water system."[153]

The Pesticide Control Office will issue a notice of violation that is punishable by civil fine and penalty plus treble damages.[154] The violator may within 10 days after receiving the notice request a hearing in Tribal Court, which is authorized to impose a civil penalty, fine, or damages.[155] An appeal may be requested within 10 days after the civil penalty is imposed.[156]

---

144 The Jicarilla Apache Tribe Weed Control & Pesticide Regulation and Enforcement Ordinance, No. 92-0-282-2 (1991), as amended by Council Resolution No. 93-R-445-4 (Apr. 2, 1993). The ordinance is not codified.

145 Ordinance Section 1.5.3.

146 Ordinance Section 2.1.

147 Ordinance Section 4.1.

148 Ordinance Section 2.2.1.

149 Ordinance Section 4.1.

150 Ordinance Section 4.3.1.

151 Ordinance Section 4.3.2.

152 Ordinance Section 4.4.

153 *Id.*

154 Ordinance Section 5.2.

155 Ordinance Section 5.3.

156 Ordinance Section 5.4.

CHAPTER XII
NEW MEXICO ENVIRONMENTAL COMMON LAW

Common law is that body of law, originally adopted from centuries of English judicial practice, which has continued to guide American courts in determining legal rights and remedies. This Chapter addresses the claims available under the common law to a person or entity seeking judicial relief, in the form of an injunction or money damages, as a result of the actions of another.

1.0 NUISANCE

A nuisance claim arises out of non-trespassory invasion or substantial interference with the private use and enjoyment of land.[1] A "private nuisance" action may be brought by a person seeking to enjoin or obtain damages resulting from any activity that significantly and unreasonably interferes with his or her use and enjoyment of property.[2] A "public nuisance" action may be brought by the government to abate an activity which adversely affects public health, welfare, or safety.[3] Pursuant to common law, an individual could seek damages under a claim of public nuisance if he or she suffered a harm different in kind from that suffered by the general public.[4]

1.1 PRIVATE NUISANCE

The central theory of private nuisance is an unreasonable interference with the use and enjoyment of property.[5] Liability is not dependent on proof of the defendant's fault.[6] An interference with the use of property is unreasonable if the gravity of the resulting harm outweighs the utility of the challenged conduct[7] or if the harm caused by that conduct is serious and the financial burden of compensating for the harm would not make continuing the conduct infeasible.[8] New Mexico has recognized the rule that damages may be

---

1 *Scott v. Jordan*, 99 N.M. 567, 570, 661 P.2d 59, 62 (Ct. App. 1983) (operation of livestock feedlot which emitted foul odors and attracted flies enjoined as nuisance).

2 *Padilla v. Lawrence*, 101 N.M. 556, 685 P.2d 964 (Ct. App. 1984).

3 *Town of Clayton v. Mayfield*, 82 N.M. 596, 485 P.2d 352 (1971) (operation of unfenced junk yard held to constitute public nuisance and injunctive relief granted).

4 Restatement (Second) of Torts § 821C (1977).

5 *Padilla v. Lawrence*, 101 N.M. 556, 685 P.2d 964 (Ct. App. 1984).

6 *Wofford v. Rudick*, 63 N.M. 307, 311, 318 P.2d 605, 608 (1957).

7 *See Scott v. Jordan*, 99 N.M. 567, 661 P.2d 59 (Ct. App. 1983).

8 *Padilla*, 101 N.M. at 560, 685 P.2d at 968. *See State ex rel. Baxter v. Egolf*, 107 N.M. 315, 757 P.2d 371 (Ct. App. 1988) (violation of laws or regulations is probative but not dispositive as to whether conduct constitutes nuisance).

appropriate even if the utility of the activity outweighs the harm caused.[9] The determination of what constitutes an unreasonable invasion is a problem of relative values to be determined by the trier of fact in each case in the light of all the circumstances.[10] Factors to be considered include the severity of the harm, the type of use or enjoyment invaded, the suitability of the particular use or enjoyment to the character of the locality, the burden on the person harmed of avoiding the harm, the social value of the conduct causing the harm,[11] the suitability of that conduct to the character of the locality, the impracticality of preventing or avoiding the harm, and the priority of occupation.[12]

The traditional equitable remedy for common-law nuisance is abatement: the defendant is ordered to cease the offensive conduct. Abatement is generally granted in the form of an injunction, and damages may be recovered for injuries suffered up to the time the injunction issues.[13] In some circumstances, a nuisance will be allowed to continue and the defendant ordered to pay compensatory damages.[14]

Abatement is considered a drastic remedy to be used only in cases of pressing necessity where there is a showing of irreparable injury for which there is no adequate remedy through the award of money damages.[15] Damages are inadequate where the harm is continuous in nature and its constant reoccurrence would generate a multiplicity of lawsuits.[16]

Normally, damages in a nuisance claim are based on the depreciation in value of the plaintiff's property, either permanently or during the period in which a temporary nuisance exists.[17] However, a plaintiff in a nuisance action may seek compensation for interference with personal comfort and need not demonstrate a diminution in value to recover for annoyance and inconvenience.[18] New Mexico courts have stated no precise rule for quantifying such damages and leave that determination to the trier of fact.[19] Plaintiff has the burden

---

9 *Padilla*, 101 N.M. at 560, 685 P.2d at 968.

10 *Id.*

11 *See, e.g.,* N.M. Stat. Ann. §§ 47-9-1 to -7 (Repl. Pamp. 1982 & Supp. 1993) (Agricultural activities cannot be deemed a nuisance due to a change in the surrounding locale which has occurred since the inception of the agricultural activity).

12 *Padilla*, 101 N.M. at 560 n.1, 685 P.2d at 968 n.1.

13 *Hines Corp. v. City of Albuquerque*, 95 N.M. 311, 612 P.2d 1116 (1980).

14 *See Padilla*, 101 N.M. 556, 685 P.2d 964.

15 *Scott v. Jordan*, 99 N.M. 567, 572, 661 P.2d 59, 64 (Ct. App. 1983).

16 *Winrock Enters. v. House of Fabrics*, 91 N.M. 661, 664, 579 P.2d 787, 790 (1978).

17 W. Keeton et al., *Prosser and Keeton on the Law of Torts* § 89 (5th ed. 1984).

18 *Aguayo v. Village of Chama*, 79 N.M. 729, 731, 449 P.2d 331, 333 (1969); *see Wofford v. Rudick*, 63 N.M. 307, 318 P.2d 605 (1957).

19 *Aguayo*, 79 N.M. at 731, 449 P.2d at 333.

of proving damages[20] and must do so with reasonable certainty.[21] Punitive damages are recoverable if the nuisance was the result of wrongful intent or reckless disregard.[22]

1.2 PUBLIC NUISANCE

New Mexico has a public nuisance statute which defines a public nuisance as knowingly creating, performing, or maintaining anything affecting any number of citizens, without lawful authority,[23] which either is injurious to public health, safety, morals, or welfare or interferes with the exercise and enjoyment of public rights, including the right to use public property.[24] In order to constitute a public nuisance, the activity must affect a considerable number of people or an entire community or neighborhood.[25] Polluting water is also specifically defined as a public nuisance.[26]

Commission of a public nuisance constitutes a petty misdemeanor.[27] Civil actions to abate public nuisances may be brought by private citizens in the name of the state, and a private complainant is entitled to receive attorney's fees when judgment is issued against a defendant.[28]

2.0 TRESPASS

A claim for trespass arises out of the invasion of an interest in the rightful exclusive possession of property.[29] The invasion need not be in person but may be made by causing or permitting something to cross the boundary of the plaintiff's property. There must be a

---

20 *Hase v. Summers*, 35 N.M. 274, 295 P.293 (1930).

21 *Jemez Properties, Inc. v. Lucero*, 94 N.M. 181, 608 P.2d 157 (Ct. App. 1979), *cert. denied*, 94 N.M. 628, 614 P.2d 545 (1980).

22 *Samedan Oil Corp. v. Neeld*, 91 N.M. 599, 601, 577 P.2d 1245, 1246 (1978).

23 *City of Albuquerque v. State ex rel. Village of Los Ranchos de Albuquerque*, 111 N.M. 608, 808 P.2d 58 (Ct. App. 1991) (lawful activities of government authorized by legislative authority cannot be deemed public nuisance per se).

24 N.M. Stat. Ann. § 30-8-1 (Repl. Pamp. 1984).

25 *Padilla v. Lawrence*, 101 N.M. 556, 562, 685 P.2d 964, 970 (Ct. App. 1984); *but see* Final Judgment in *Paine v. Basin Disposal, Inc.*, No. CIV-87-569-3 (Eleventh Judicial District of N.M. June 6, 1989) (a district court decision in which a small group of plaintiffs successfully pursued a public nuisance action arising out of the defendants' operation of a waste disposal site on land adjacent to land owned and inhabited by plaintiffs. The court's decision rested partially on the determination that the plaintiffs, although small in number, constituted a community.).

26 N.M. Stat. Ann. § 30-8-2 (Supp. 1993).

27 N.M. Stat. Ann. § 30-8-1 (Repl. Pamp. 1984). Polluting water, however, constitutes a misdemeanor. N.M. Stat. Ann. § 30-8-2.

28 N.M. Stat. Ann. § 30-8-8 (Repl. Pamp. 1984).

29 *Pacheco v. Martinez*, 97 N.M. 37, 41, 636 P.2d 308, 312 (Ct. App. 1981).

physical invasion, however, rather than an intangible intrusion such as noise or odor which may serve as the basis for a nuisance claim.[30] For pollution to constitute a trespass, therefore, the pollutant must actually enter or settle upon and damage property.[31]

Upon a finding of trespass the plaintiff is automatically entitled to an award of nominal damages,[32] whether or not actual damages can be shown. In order to recover actual damages, however, the evidence of damage must be reasonably certain.[33] The trespass need not be intentional for the damaged party to recover. A person who engages in an activity authorized by governmental license is not immunized from liability if the activity results in a trespass.[34] Punitive damages may be awarded where the trespass was accomplished intentionally and in known violation of the plaintiff's right in the land.[35]

3.0 NEGLIGENCE

A negligence claim arises out of a failure to exercise ordinary care[36] for the welfare or protection of others. Along with nuisance and trespass, negligence is one of the traditional claims used by those seeking recourse for environmental damage to property.[37] In addition, negligence is the primary basis for claims seeking damages for personal injury arising from exposure to toxic substances or environmentally hazardous or dangerous conditions.

Under New Mexico law, a plaintiff alleging negligence must prove that the alleged wrongdoer had a duty of care to the plaintiff which he breached and that the breach proximately caused the plaintiff's injury.[38] In addition, the plaintiff must establish that a reasonably prudent person, acting under the same circumstances, would have foreseen the risk

---

30 *Padilla*, 101 N.M. at 563, 685 P.2d at 971.

31 *Id.*

32 *Pueblo of Sandia ex rel. Chaves v. Smith*, 497 F.2d 1043 (10th Cir. 1974).

33 *Jemez Properties Inc. v. Lucero*, 94 N.M. 181, 608 P.2d 157 (Ct. App. 1979), *cert. denied*, 94 N.M. 628, 614 P.2d 545 (1980).

34 *Snyder Ranches, Inc. v. Oil Conservation Comm'n*, 110 N.M. 637, 640, 798 P.2d 587, 590 (1990).

35 *North v. Public Serv. Co.*, 94 N.M. 246, 608 P.2d 1128 (Ct. App). *cert. denied*, 94 N.M. 629, 614 P.2d 546 (1980).

36 "Ordinary care" is the degree of care that a reasonably prudent person would use in the circumstances. As the risk of danger that should reasonably be foreseen increases, the amount of care required also increases. *See* N.M. U.J.I. Civ. 13-1603 (Repl. Pamp. 1991).

37 *See, e.g., State ex rel. New Mexico Water Quality Control Comm'n v. City of Hobbs,* 86 N.M. 444, 525 P.2d 371 (1974) (allegations of negligence and nuisance in connection with city sewage treatment plant which contaminated water table).

38 *See Cotter v. Novak*, 57 N.M. 639, 261 P.2d 827 (1953) (adopting Restatement of Torts § 284 (1934)).

of injury.[39] Finally, there must be substantial evidence of specific rather than speculative damages suffered by the plaintiff as a result of the breach.[40]

In the environmental context, a claim of negligence could be used to seek damages from manufacturers or users of hazardous substances for personal injury resulting from a lack of due care in the manufacturing, use, storage, or disposal of such substances or a failure to provide an adequate warning about the dangers of such substances.[41] A negligence action could also be used to pursue damages for injuries resulting from emotional distress suffered by an individual who must live with the potential long-term consequences of exposure to a toxic substance. A negligence claim might exist for damage to foliage or water supply due to the improper use of pesticides or other toxins,[42] damage to water supply or soil as a result of leakage from an underground storage tank, or environmental contamination resulting from the migration of toxic substances or polluted water from adjoining property.[43]

Punitive damages may be recovered in a negligence case for conduct that was grossly negligent, reckless, malicious, willful, or wanton.[44] Malicious, willful, or wanton conduct is conduct which shows a deliberate intention to harm or an utter indifference to or conscious disregard for the consequences.[45]

3.1 NEGLIGENCE PER SE

Negligence per se is established by showing that the defendant violated a statute, ordinance, or regulation which prohibits certain action or defines a standard of care either explicitly or implicitly, if (1) the plaintiff is one of the class of persons sought to be protected by the statute, ordinance, or regulation and (2) the injury to the plaintiff is generally of the type that the provision which was violated was intended to prevent.[46] If these factors are established, the defendant is held to have been negligent as a matter of law.

The concept of negligence per se is particularly applicable in the environmental field in light of the proliferation of environmental legislation and regulations. Courts have often rejected assertions of negligence per se, however, by finding that the statute or regulation

---

39 *See Ramirez v. Armstrong*, 100 N.M. 538, 541, 673 P.2d 822, 825 (1983).

40 *See Sanchez v. Martinez*, 99 N.M. 66, 71, 653 P.2d 897, 902 (Ct. App. 1982).

41 *See, e.g., First Nat'l Bank in Albuquerque v. Nor-Am Agricultural Prods., Inc.*, 88 N.M. 74, 537 P.2d 682 (Ct. App.), *cert. denied*, 88 N.M. 29, 536 P.2d 1085 (1975).

42 *See, e.g., Jesko v. Stauffer Chem. Co.*, 89 N.M. 786, 558 P.2d 55 (Ct. App. 1976).

43 In light of a recent case, *City of Santa Fe v. Komis*, 114 N.M. 659, 845 P.2d 753 (1992), a plaintiff also may be able to recover for the diminution in property value due to the public's perception of the effect on the property of a nearby source of contamination.

44 *See* N.M. U.J.I. Civ. 13-1827 (Repl. Pamp. 1991).

45 *See* N. M. U.J.I. Civ. 13-1619. (Repl. Pamp. 1991).

46 *See Archibeque v. Homrich*, 88 N.M. 527, 532, 543 P.2d 820, 825 (1975).

allegedly violated was not intended to protect the class of persons of which the plaintiff was a member or to prevent the type of harm being alleged.[47] Additionally, although a plaintiff need not prove negligence if negligence per se can be established, the plaintiff must still prove that the conduct in question proximately caused the injury.[48]

4.0 STRICT LIABILITY

Strict liability means liability without regard to fault. The doctrine of strict liability discards the notion that damages may be recovered only if the person causing an injury acted negligently. Under the modern theory of strict liability, if the plaintiff establishes that the defendant was engaged in an abnormally dangerous or ultrahazardous activity then the defendant will be held liable for any damages resulting from the activity even in the absence of fault.[49] New Mexico courts have recognized this theory of strict liability for damage resulting from the use of explosives[50] but have not yet extended this theory to other activities. New Mexico courts have also imposed strict liability on the employer of an independent contractor where the contractor has failed to take reasonable precautions in performing work involving a peculiar risk of physical harm to others.[51]

Courts in some states have expanded the doctrine of strict liability in the past few decades to allow the recovery of damages from manufacturers and suppliers of products that are found to be unreasonably dangerous because of defects in design or manufacture or because of a failure to warn of the dangers inherent in their use. In order to prevail on a strict products liability claim, the plaintiff must prove that (1) a defect existed in the product, (2) the injury suffered was proximately caused by the defect, and (3) there were no substantial changes in the condition of the product after it was sold.[52]

In the environmental context, strict products liability could provide a basis for claiming compensation for personal injuries resulting from the storage or use of toxic substances.[53] The doctrine might also support claims for other types of injuries.[54]

---

47 *Id.*

48 *Id.*

49 *Gutierrez v. Rio Rancho Estates, Inc.,* 94 N.M. 84, 88, 607 P.2d 622, 624 (Ct. App. 1979), *aff'd*, 93 N.M. 755, 605 P.2d 1154 (1980).

50 *Thigpen v. Skousen & Hise*, 64 N.M. 290, 327 P.2d 802 (1958).

51 *Saiz v. Belen School Dist.*, 113 N.M. 327, 827 P.2d 102 (1992).

52 *Fabian v. E. W. Bliss Co.*, 582 F.2d 1257, 1260 (10th Cir. 1978).

53 *See, e.g., First Nat'l Bank in Albuquerque v. Nor-Am Agricultural Prods., Inc.*, 88 N.M. 74, 537 P.2d 682 (Ct. App.), *cert. denied*, 88 N.M. 29, 536 P.2d 1085 (1975).

54 The New Mexico Supreme Court has not yet resolved the question whether a strict products liability claim is available to seek compensation for a purely economic loss. *But see Utah Int'l, Inc. v. Caterpillar Tractor Co.*108 N.M. 539, 775 P.2d 741 (Ct.

5.0 TOXIC TORTS

A toxic tort has been defined as "alleged personal injury and related harm resulting from exposure to a toxic substance -- usually chemical, but perhaps a biological or radiological agent. Generally in toxic torts: (1) the injury is neither traumatic nor an acute toxic response but results in genetic or biochemical disruption; (2) exposure is typically, although not necessarily, chronic and repeated; and (3) injury manifests itself after a latency period."[55]

A toxic tort suit, in which an individual seeks compensation for damages arising out of personal injuries sustained as a result of exposure to some toxic substance, may be pursued through either negligence or strict products liability claims. Regardless of which theory of liability is relied upon, a plaintiff may face difficulties in establishing a case. The plaintiff may be hampered by the potential involvement of multiple suppliers or manufacturers of the toxic substance in question. For example, in an asbestos case the plaintiff may have difficulty proving that his exposure was to a particular asbestos product manufactured or supplied by a particular company or individual. The plaintiff also may encounter obstacles resulting from the long latency period often associated with injuries caused by exposure to toxic substances.

In most states, courts have allowed plaintiffs to meet these difficulties in various ways. One approach has been to adopt a "market share" theory of apportioning causation.[56] Under this theory, the plaintiff need only prove that the companies against which he seeks to recover were actively involved in marketing the offending product at the time of his exposure. The plaintiff may then recover against those defendants on a pro rata basis relative to their share of the market at the time the exposure occurred.

Another approach to apportioning liability in toxic exposure cases might involve shifting some of the burden of proof from the plaintiff to the defendants.[57] For example, in a case involving toxic exposure from a dump site in which the identities of three companies that had dumped toxins at the site are known and all three companies are named as defendants, the court could shift the burden of proof to each defendant to prove that the toxins that it dumped were not responsible for the plaintiff's injuries. Any defendant failing to do so might be held jointly and severally liable[58] for the plaintiff's injuries.

App.), *cert. denied*, 108 N.M. 354, 772 P.2d 884 (1989) (in commercial context, economic losses are recoverable only under a contract claim).

55 Gold, *Causation and Toxic Torts: Burdens of Proof, Standards of Persuasion, and Statistical Evidence*, 96 Yale L. J. 376, 376 n. 1 (1986).

56 *See Sindell v. Abbott Laboratories*, 607 P.2d 924, 936-38 (Cal. 1980).

57 *See Summers v. Tice*, 199 P.2d 1 (Cal. 1948) (where either of two defendants acting independently could have been sole cause of plaintiff's injuries, each defendant had burden of proving non-liability).

58 Joint and several liability exists where any one of several persons whose concurrent negligence contributed to cause plaintiff's injury may be held liable for the entire amount of the resulting damages. *Bartlett v. New Mexico Welding Supply, Inc.*, 98

In addition to the difficult matter of proving which of several companies produced the toxic substance that actually caused the injury, a toxic tort plaintiff may also face the problem of demonstrating that the injuries resulted from exposure to a specific toxic agent many years earlier. This problem may arise because scientific research has not yet reached the point at which scientists are willing to state as a matter of scientific probability that a particular agent or exposure was the proximate cause of a particular disease or illness. One commentator, in discussing this problem, foresees that causation will become less difficult for plaintiffs to prove in the not too distant future as a result of the information gathering and monitoring mandated by statutes such as the federal Comprehensive Environmental Response, Compensation and Liability Act (CERCLA).[59] The commentator suggests that CERCLA and similar statutes will have the additional effect of lessening the occurrence of toxic tort injuries because the periodic medical testing and production and dissemination of information required will help prevent toxic exposures.

The long latency period for toxic injuries may create a problem of claim preclusion by operation of the statute of limitations. In New Mexico, the three-year statute of limitations for personal injuries[60] and the four-year statute of limitations for injuries to property[61] have barred claims filed more than three or four years after the injury was or should have been discovered. This has traditionally been interpreted to mean that the statute runs from the time of incident or exposure ultimately leading to the injury or illness. For example, a federal court applying New Mexico law held that a victim of asbestosis could not assert claims based on exposure to asbestos that occurred more than three years before the suit was filed.[62] In more recent cases, however, New Mexico courts have held that the limitations period for personal injury suits begins to run when the claim "accrues," which occurs at the time of the injury rather than the time of the negligent act.[63] Most recently, the New Mexico Supreme Court has held in the medical malpractice context that a personal injury claim does not accrue for statute of limitations purposes until the plaintiff knows or reasonably should have known of both the injury and its cause.[64] The New Mexico statute of limitations for

N.M. 152, 646 P.2d 579 (Ct. App.), *cert. denied,* 98 N.M. 336, 648 P.2d 794 (1982).

59 Kanner, *Future Trends in Toxic Tort Litigation*, 20 Rutgers L.J. 667 (1989).

60 N.M. Stat. Ann. § 37-1-8 (Repl. Pamp. 1990).

61 N.M. Stat. Ann. § 37-1-4 (Repl. Pamp. 1990).

62 *Bassham v. Owens-Corning Fiber Glass Corp.*, 327 F. Supp. 1007 (D.N.M. 1971).

63 *New Mexico Elec. Serv. Co. v. Montanez*, 89 N.M. 278, 551 P.2d 634 (1976) (citing *Spurlin v. Paul Brown Agency, Inc.*, 80 N.M. 306, 454 P.2d 963 (1969)).

64 *Roberts v. Southwest Community Health Servs.*, 114 N.M. 248, 837 P.2d 442 (1992) (adopting what is known as the "discovery rule" for accrual of a cause of action).

property damage claims states that the limitations period for such claims does not begin to run until the claim accrues.[65]

A provision of CERCLA overrides state statutes of limitations in certain circumstances and may allow the assertion of a toxic tort claim that otherwise would be barred by New Mexico law. CERCLA creates a special statute of limitations for claims which are "caused or contributed to by exposure to any hazardous substance, or pollutant or contaminant, released into the environment from a facility."[66] For such claims, the limitations period does not begin to run until "the date the plaintiff knew (or reasonably should have known) that the personal injury or property damages ... were caused or contributed to by the hazardous substance or pollutant or contaminant concerned."[67]

6.0 BREACH OF WARRANTY

In environmental litigation, it is not uncommon for a plaintiff to assert claims under any legal theory that might be available. Where allegedly defective products are involved, for example, the plaintiff may seek to hold the manufacturer or supplier liable under common-law theories of negligence and strict liability. In some circumstances, such as where the plaintiff was a direct purchaser of the product, claims based on the contract of sale of the product may also exist. While these contract claims developed historically under the common law, to a large extent they now arise under a statute, the Uniform Commercial Code.[68]

Contract-based claims include claims for breach of warranty. The contract may contain an express warranty that the product will conform to a certain standard of quality.[69] In many instances an implied warranty that the product is "merchantable" exists.[70] To be merchantable a product must be fit for the ordinary purposes for which it is used, adequately contained, packaged, and labeled, and in conformity with any statements of fact made on the container or label.[71] The contract may also include an implied warranty that the product is fit for the particular purpose for which it is to be used.[72] A plaintiff who suffers personal

---

65 N.M. Stat. Ann. § 37-1-7 (Repl. Pamp. 1990).

66 42 U.S.C. § 9658(a)(1).

67 42 U.S.C. § 9658(b)(4)(A); *but see Knox v. AC & S, Inc.*, 690 F. Supp. 752 (S.D. Ind. 1988) (CERCLA limitations provision inapplicable to claim for long-term exposure to asbestos in construction work).

68 *See* N.M. Stat. Ann. §§ 55-2-101 to -725 (Repl. Pamp. 1993).

69 *See* N.M. Stat. Ann. § 55-2-313 (Repl. Pamp. 1993).

70 *See* N.M. Stat. Ann. § 55-2-314(1) (Repl. Pamp. 1993).

71 *See* N.M. Stat. Ann. § 55-2-314(2) (Repl. Pamp. 1993).

72 *See* N.M. Stat. Ann. § 55-2-315 (Repl. Pamp. 1993).

injury or economic loss resulting from a breach of one of these warranties may pursue a claim for damages.[73]

[73] *See Ligocky v. Wilcox*, 95 N.M. 275, 620 P.2d 1300 (Ct. App. 1980). Similar warranty claims may arise under the common law in situations involving a contract for services rather than for the sale of a product.

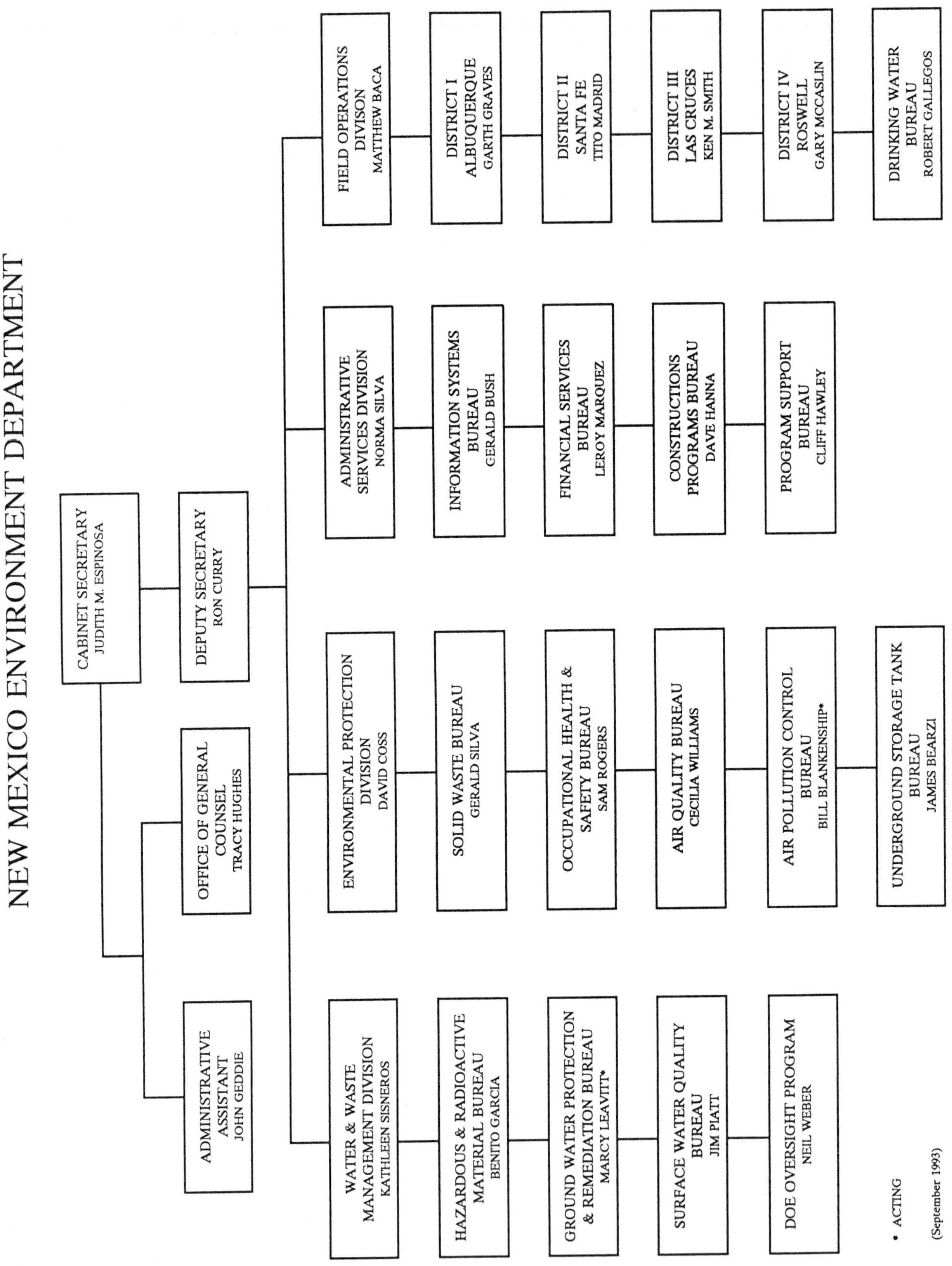
NEW MEXICO ENVIRONMENT DEPARTMENT
CABINET SECRETARY JUDITH M. ESPINOSA
DEPUTY SECRETARY RON CURRY
OFFICE OF GENERAL COUNSEL TRACY HUGHES
ADMINISTRATIVE ASSISTANT JOHN GEDDIE
FIELD OPERATIONS DIVISON MATTHEW BACA
DISTRICT I ALBUQUERQUE GARTH GRAVES
DISTRICT II SANTA FE TITO MADRID
DISTRICT III LAS CRUCES KEN M. SMITH
DISTRICT IV ROSWELL GARY MCCASLIN
DRINKING WATER BUREAU ROBERT GALLEGOS
ADMINISTRATIVE SERVICES DIVISION NORMA SILVA
INFORMATION SYSTEMS BUREAU GERALD BUSH
FINANCIAL SERVICES BUREAU LEROY MARQUEZ
CONSTRUCTIONS PROGRAMS BUREAU DAVE HANNA
PROGRAM SUPPORT BUREAU CLIFF HAWLEY
ENVIRONMENTAL PROTECTION DIVISION DAVID COSS
SOLID WASTE BUREAU GERALD SILVA
OCCUPATIONAL HEALTH & SAFETY BUREAU SAM ROGERS
AIR QUALITY BUREAU CECILIA WILLIAMS
AIR POLLUTION CONTROL BUREAU BILL BLANKENSHIP*
UNDERGROUND STORAGE TANK BUREAU JAMES BEARZI
WATER & WASTE MANAGEMENT DIVISION KATHLEEN SISNEROS
HAZARDOUS & RADIOACTIVE MATERIAL BUREAU BENITO GARCIA
GROUND WATER PROTECTION & REMEDIATION BUREAU MARCY LEAVITT*
SURFACE WATER QUALITY BUREAU JIM PIATT
DOE OVERSIGHT PROGRAM NEIL WEBER
* ACTING
(September 1993)

LIST OF ACRONYMS, TERMS AND ABBREVIATIONS

Federal agencies, departments, acts and publications are designated with an asterisk (*).

New Mexico agencies, departments, acts and regulations are in bold.

AD	**Agriculture Department**
AEHD	Albuquerque Environmental Health Department
ALARA	As Low As Reasonably Achievable
AMRA	**Abandoned Mine Reclamation Act**
AQCA	**Air Quality Control Act**
AQCB	**Air Quality Control Board**
AQCRs	**Air Quality Control Regulations**
ARARS	Applicable or Relevant and Appropriate Standards
BACT	Best Available Control Technology
BIA	Bureau of Indian Affairs*
BLM	Bureau of Land Management*
BTU	British Thermal Unit
CAA	Clean Air Act of 1970 and 1990 Amendments*
CAF	**Corrective Action Fund**
CEPA	**Civil Emergency Preparedness Act**
CEQ	Council on Environmental Quality*
CERCLA	Comprehensive Environmental Response, Compensation, and Liability Act of 1980*
C.F.R.	Code of Federal Regulations*
CID	**Construction Industries Division**
CO	Carbon Monoxide
Court of Appeals	**New Mexico Court of Appeals**
CPCA	**Core Program Cooperative Agreement**
CPCRBA	**County Pollution Control Revenue Bond Act**
CRCPD	Conference of Radiation Control Program Directors
CSMC	**Coal Surface Mining Commission**
CVSA	Commercial Vehicle Safety Alliance
CWA	Clean Water Act of 1972*

DEA	**Department of Environment Act**
DOE	Department of Energy*
DOT	Department of Transportation*
DPSA	**Department of Public Safety Act**
EA	Environmental Assessment
ECA	**Environmental Compliance Act**
EEG	**Environmental Evaluation Group**
EIA	**Environmental Improvement Act**
EIB	**Environmental Improvement Board**
EIS	Environmental Impact Statement
EMA	**Emergency Management Act**
EMNRD	**Energy, Minerals and Natural Resources Department**
EMTF	**Emergency Management Task Force**
ENIPC	Eight Northern Indian Pueblos Council
EP Toxicity	Extraction Procedure Toxicity
EPA	Environmental Protection Agency*
EPCB	**Emergency Planning and Coordination Bureau of PSDept.**
EPCRA	Emergency Planning and Community Right-to-Know Act*
FIFRA	Federal Insecticide, Fungicide and Rodenticide Act of 1972*
Fed. Reg.	Federal Register*
FOIA	Freedom of Information Act*
GWPA	**Ground Water Protection Act**
HCIA	**Hazardous Chemicals Information Act**
HCL	Hydrochloric Acid
HEDA	**Health and Environment Department Act**
HMERA	**Hazardous Materials Emergency Response Administrator**
HMSB	**Hazardous Materials Safety Board**
HOC	Halogenated Organic Compounds
HRCQ	Highway Route Controlled Quality
HSWA	Hazardous and Solid Waste Amendments of 1984*
HWA	**Hazardous Waste Act**
HWF	**Hazardous Waste Fund**

HWEF	**Hazardous Waste Emergency Fund**
HWFR	**Hazardous Waste Fee Regulations**
HWFSA	**Hazardous Waste Feasibility Study Act**
HWMR	**Hazardous Waste Management Regulations**
IRA	Indian Reorganization Act of 1934*
kg(s)	Kilogram(s)
LAER	Lowest Achievable Emission Rate
lbs.	Pounds
Legislature	New Mexico Legislature
LEPC	Local Emergency Planning Committee
LGD	**Local Government Division of the Department of Finance and Administration**
LWDR	**Liquid Waste Disposal Regulations**
MCL	Maximum Contaminant Levels
MMD	**Mining and Minerals Division**
MRHSA	**Medical Radiation Health and Safety Act**
MSCA	**Multi-Site Cooperative Agreement**
MSHA	**Mine Safety and Health Administration**
MSDS	Material Safety Data Sheets
NAAQS	National Ambient Air Quality Standards*
NCP	National Contingency Plan*
NEPA	National Environmental Policy Act*
NESHAPs	National Emission Standard for Hazardous Air Pollutants*
NHPA	National Historic Preservation Act*
NMCAA	**New Mexico Community Assistance Act**
NMMA	**New Mexico Mining Act**
NMCDC	**New Mexico Community Development Counsel**
NMED	**New Mexico Environment Department**
N.M.	New Mexico
N.M. Stat. Ann.	**New Mexico Statutes Annotated**
NO_x	Nitrogen Oxide
NORM	Naturally Occurring Radioactive Materials

NPDES	National Pollutant Discharge Elimination System*
NPL	National Priorities List*
NRC	Nuclear Regulatory Commission*
NRTA	**Natural Resources Trustee Act**
NSPS	New Source Performance Standards
NUPAC 72B	Container Designed to Transport Remote-Handled WIPP Waste
OCC	**Oil Conservation Commission**
OCD	**Oil Conservation Division**
OELs	Occupational Exposure Limits
OGA	**Oil and Gas Act**
OHSA	**Occupational Health and Safety Act**
OHSRC	**Occupational Health and Safety Review Commission**
OSHA	Occupational Safety and Health Administration*
OSWER	Office of Solid Waste and Emergency Response*
Pb	Lead
pH	Acid Concentration of a Liquid
PCA	**Pesticide Control Act**
PCBs	Polychlorinated Biphenyls
PCRBA	**Pollution Control Revenue Bond Act**
PM10	Fine Particulate Matter
ppm	Parts Per Million
PSCA	**Petroleum Storage Cleanup Act**
PSD	Prevention of Significant Deterioration
PSDept.	**Public Safety Department**
Plan	Solid Waste Management Plan
Program	Solid Waste Management Program
RCRA	Resource Conservation and Recovery Act of 1976*
Regents	**Board of Regents of New Mexico State University**
Repl. Pamp.	**Replacement Pamphlet**
RHMA	**Radioactive and Hazardous Materials Act**
RHMC	**Radioactive and Hazardous Materials Committee**
RIA	**Rural Infrastructure Act**
RIRLF	**Rural Infrastructure Revolving Loan Fund**
RPA	**Radiation Protection Act**
RTAC	**Radiation Technical Advisory Council**
RWCTF	**Radioactive Waste Consultation Task Force**

SARA	Superfund Amendments and Reauthorization Act of 1986*
Secretary	Secretary of New Mexico Environment Department
SDWA	Safe Drinking Water Act of 1974*
SERC	**State Emergency Response Commission**
SIC	Standard Industrial Classification
SIP	State Implementation Plan*
Supp.	**Supplement**
SMA	**Surface Mining Act**
SMCRA	Surface Mining Control and Reclamation Act*
SO_2	Sulfur Dioxide
Superfund	Vernacular for CERCLA*
SWA	**Solid Waste Act**
SWFGF	**Solid Waste Facility Grant Fund**
SWMU	Solid Waste Management Unit
TAS	Treatment as a State
TDS	Total Dissolved Solids
TESD	**Technical and Emergency Support Division of PSDept.**
Title III	Emergency Planning and Community Right-to-Know Act of 1986*
TRANSCOMM	System for Monitoring Transport of WIPP Waste
Transporter	Transporter of Hazardous Waste
TRU	Transuranic
TRUPACT-II	Container Designed to Transport Contact-Handled WIPP Waste
TSCA	Toxic Substances Control Act*
TSD	Treatment, Storage or Disposal
TSDF	Treatment, Storage or Disposal Facility
UIC	Underground Injection Control
UOCA	**Utility Operators Certification Act**
U.S.C.	United States Code*
UST	Underground Storage Tank
USTC	**Underground Storage Tank Committee**
USTF	**Underground Storage Tank Fund**
VOC	Volatile Organic Compound
WCA	**Wildlife Conservation Act**

WFCA	**Wastewater Facility Construction Act**
WFCLA	**Wastewater Facility Construction Loan Act**
WFCLF	**Wastewater Facility Construction Loan Fund**
WIPP	Waste Isolation Pilot Plant*
WQA	**Water Quality Act**
WQCC	**Water Quality Control Commission**

INDEX

J, K

L

M

N

O

P